THE FACTS ON FILE

STUDENT'S THESAURUS

THE FACTS ON FILE

STUDENT'S THESAURUS

Edited by

Paul Hellweg

Contributors

Norman Schur
Robyn Battle
Marvin Vernon

Facts On File
New York • Oxford • Sydney

THE FACTS ON FILE STUDENT'S THESAURUS

Copyright © 1991 by Paul Hellweg

Facts On File, Inc.   Facts On File Limited
460 Park Avenue South   Collins Street
New York NY 10016   Oxford OX4 1XJ
USA   United Kingdom

Library of Congress Cataloging-in-Publication Data

Hellweg, Paul.
   The Facts on File student's thesaurus / Paul Hellweg.
     p.   cm.
   Summary: Provides synonyms and antonyms for over 5000 words listed in alphabetical order.
   ISBN 0-8160-1634-8
   1. English language— Synonyms and antonyms.   [1. English language— Synonyms and antonyms.]   I. Title. II. Title: Student's thesaurus.
PE1591.H45   1990
423′.1— dc20   90-3185

A British CIP catalogue record for this book is available from the British Library.

Facts On File books are available at special discounts when purchased in bulk quantities for businesses, associations, institutions or sales promotions. Please call our Special Sales Department in New York at 212/683-2244 (dial 800/322-8755 except in NY, AK or HI) or in Oxford at 865/728399.

Text design by Catherine Hyman
Jacket design by Catherine Hyman
Composition by Facts On File, Inc.
Manufactured by the Maple-Vail Manufacturing Group
Printed in the United States of America

10 9 8 7 6 5 4 3 2 1

This book is printed on acid-free paper.

Introduction

What Is a Thesaurus?

A thesaurus is a book that lists *synonyms* and *antonyms*. *Synonyms* are words that have the same or similar meanings, and they can generally be substituted for each other. *Antonyms*, on the other hand, are words that have opposite meanings. By way of example, *shy* and *bashful* are synonyms for *timid*, and *bold* and *assertive* are its antonyms.

Why Use a Thesaurus?

A thesaurus is a valuable reference tool for improving your writing. But how can it be valuable to you? For starters, it can help you avoid overusing any particular word, thus making your writing more lively and interesting. As a case in point, the word *valuable* has already appeared twice in this paragraph. If it were to be seen again, it might prove to be a little tiresome. For its next use, a synonym such as *important* would probably be more appealing (*appealing*, by the way, is used here as a synonym for *interesting*).

There is another important way in which a thesaurus can be of value to you. If you know a word that isn't quite right for your needs, then a thesaurus should be able to provide the perfect alternative. Let's say you want to find the right word to describe a *skinny* friend, but you don't want to use *skinny* because it sounds too harsh. You can look in this thesaurus and find other possibilities, such as *thin* or *lean*.

How Do You Use This Thesaurus?

This thesaurus has been organized to be simple and easy-to-use. The word you're looking for is known as a primary entry, and you can find it in alphabetical order. A primary entry is presented in **bold** type, and its part of speech follows immediately. Next comes a list of synonyms and then a sample sentence to show how the primary entry can be used. If it can be used in more than one way, additional synonym lists will follow. Finally, if there are any antonyms, they'll appear at the end of the synonym lists.

A variety of abbreviations are utilized in this thesaurus (they're mainly used for parts of speech). Since it's important to know them, here's a guide to the abbreviations:

Ant.	=	Antonym
Adj.	=	Adjective
Adv.	=	Adverb
Conj.	=	Conjunction
N.	=	Noun
Prep.	=	Preposition
Vb.	=	Verb

This thesaurus lists more than 5,000 of the most commonly used words; however, there may be occasions when the word you're looking for can't be found. This means that it was either judged to be too obscure or else there weren't any good synonyms. For example, *alphabetize* means "to arrange in the order of the letters of the alphabet." But there just aren't any synonyms that mean the same thing, so *alphabetize* isn't included.

Finally, a word of caution is in order. In some of the synonym lists, you will find words that look like they can't be substituted for the primary entry, or at least not in the accompanying sentence. This happens because there are very few words in the English language that are truly interchangeable. The synonyms that won't work in the sample sentence are included because there are other situations and other sentences for which they might be just right. As a general rule of thumb, synonyms that most closely resemble the primary entry are listed first.

Now you know how to use this thesaurus. Keep it on your bookshelf right next to your dictionary, for it should prove to be just as valuable.

The Facts On File

Student's Thesaurus

abandon *vb.* **1.** desert, reject, forsake, drop, renounce. *Uncaring people abandon their friends in a crisis.* **2.** discontinue, abort, cease, stop, forgo. *A major avalanche forced the climbers to abandon their attempt on Mt. McKinley.* –*n.* **3.** gusto, dash, animation, verve. *Break-dancers perform with abandon.* **Ant. 1.** keep, claim. **2.** continue, maintain. **3.** self-control, restraint, caution, moderation.

abandoned *adj.* **1.** shameless, wild, loose, immoral. *The playboy led an abandoned way of life.* **2.** vacant, deserted, unoccupied, neglected. *An abandoned building typically becomes a ruin.* **Ant. 1.** upright, moral, virtuous, chaste. **2.** occupied, maintained.

abandonment *n.* discontinuance, cessation, halt, stoppage. *The abandonment of the mission was caused by a defect in the rocket.* **Ant.** continuation, prolongation, extension.

abbey *n.* monastery, convent, friary, priory. *The abbey is a refuge for those monks and nuns who seek to live an uncomplicated life.*

abbreviate *vb.* condense, shorten, contract, compress, reduce. *"Mister" is usually abbreviated as "Mr."* **Ant.** lengthen, extend, increase, expand, protract, prolong.

abbreviation *n.* condensation, shortening, abridgment, compression, reduction. *Virtually everyone knows the abbreviation for "Doctor."* **Ant.** expansion, enlargement, extension, increase.

abdicate *vb.* resign, renounce, relinquish, abandon, vacate, surrender. *The rebels forced their king to abdicate his throne.*

abduct *vb.* kidnap, shanghai, steal, grab, seize. *Terrorists abducted the ambassador.* **Ant.** free, release, return.

abhor *vb.* loathe, detest, despise, hate, disdain, reject. *Vampires abhor garlic, crosses, sun-light, and—most of all—wooden stakes.* **Ant.** adore, love, admire, prize, cherish, treasure.

abhorrence *n.* loathing, repugnance, aversion, detestation, disgust, hatred. *Most people react with abhorrence to the thought of increased taxation.* **Ant.** approval, admiration, acceptance, endorsement.

abhorrent *adj.* revolting, nauseating, abominable, detestable, repugnant. *Cruelty to children is the worst kind of abhorrent conduct.* **Ant.** admirable, commendable, laudable, praiseworthy.

abide *vb.* **1.** remain, linger, stay, tarry. *Please don't hurry off, but abide here with me.* **2.** endure, tolerate, bear, suffer. *Many people can't abide the smell of cheap cigars.* **Ant. 1.** leave, depart, quit. **2.** reject, decline, spurn, oppose.

abiding *adj.* unshakable, firm, constant, lasting, enduring. *Honest people have abiding trust in others.* **Ant.** passing, momentary, temporary.

ability *n.* capability, competence, capacity, aptitude, skill, talent, qualification. *She has the ability to excel in graduate school.* **Ant.** inability, incapability, incompetence, inadequacy.

abject *adj.* **1.** wretched, hopeless, miserable, terrible, piteous. *His abject condition is the result of losing his job.* **2.** servile, cringing, groveling, subservient, spiritless. *The student's abject apology made little impression on her teacher.* **Ant. 1.** dignified, hopeful. **2.** assured, spirited, admirable.

ablaze *adj.* **1.** burning, blazing, flaming, flaring, aflame, afire. *The building was totally ablaze before anyone knew what was happening.* **2.** bright, shiny, aglow, luminous, radiant. *The boy was ablaze with love for the girl next door.* **Ant. 1.** extinguished. **2.** gloomy, somber, depressed, dispirited.

able *adj.* capable, qualified, competent, effective, proficient. *The personnel director was looking for able employees.* **Ant.** inept, unable, incapable, unqualified.

abnormal *adj.* odd, unusual, unnatural, irregular, extraordinary, uncommon. *The boy's abnormal behavior was a source of concern for his parents.* **Ant.** normal, common, ordinary, natural, usual, typical.

abnormality *n.* oddity, exception, irregularity, peculiarity, aberration. *Her only abnormality was putting ketchup on her ice cream.*

abode *n.* home, house, residence, dwelling, habitation, quarters. *If I were rich, my abode would be a truly grand old castle.*

abolish *vb.* eliminate, negate, disallow, end, cancel, nullify, rescind, revoke. *The Emancipation Proclamation abolished slavery.* **Ant.** conserve, retain, establish, create, institute.

abort *vb.* cancel, terminate, abandon, halt, stop, cease. *A computer malfunction forced flight controllers to abort the shuttle launch.* **Ant.** conclude, complete, finish, achieve.

about *prep.* **1.** almost, approximately, around, nearly. *It's about 93 million miles from the Earth to the Sun.* **2.** concerning, regarding, involving. *The movie was about ghosts and goblins.* *-adv.* **3.** around, throughout, everywhere. *As the man walked through the dark cemetery, he kept looking carefully about.*

above *prep.* **1.** over, beyond, past. *This book is not intended for people above the age of eighteen.* **2.** over, higher than. *Her name was above his on the list.* *-adv.* **3.** over, overhead. *His bedroom is on the floor above.* **Ant.** 1–3. under, below, beneath.

abrasive *adj.* harsh, annoying, irritating, unpleasant, grating, disagreeable, caustic. *Chalk makes an abrasive sound when it is scraped across a blackboard.* **Ant.** soothing, comforting, pleasant, agreeable.

abridged *adj.* condensed, shortened, reduced, compressed, abbreviated. *In order to save time, the student read an abridged version of the assigned book.* **Ant.** expanded, extended, increased, augmented.

abroad *adv.* **1.** overseas. *She spent a delightful summer vacation abroad.* **2.** astir, active, afoot, restless. *Ghosts are typically abroad after midnight.* **Ant.** 1. stateside. 2. asleep, quiet, still.

abrupt *adj.* **1.** curt, blunt, rude, rough, gruff. *Abrupt responses often cause hurt feelings.* **2.** sudden, hasty, instantaneous, precipitous. *Careful drivers rarely have to make abrupt stops.* **3.** steep, sheer, vertical, perpendicular. *The cliff's face has an abrupt drop.* **Ant.** 1. polite, courteous, civil. 2. gradual, unhurried, deliberate. 3. gradual, slow, easy.

absence *n.* **1.** want, need, lack, deficiency, inadequacy, shortcoming. *Absence of effort will get you nowhere.* **2.** nonattendance, nonappearance. *Unexcused absences from work can result in dismissal.* **Ant.** 1. supply, abundance. 2. presence, attendance, appearance.

absent *adj.* **1.** away, missing, truant, elsewhere. *My best friend was absent from school today.* **2.** absentminded, bemused, preoccupied, inattentive, distracted, oblivious, dreamy. *His absent look betrayed his lack of attention.* **Ant.** 1. present, available. 2. attentive, alert, aware.

absolute *adj.* complete, conclusive, perfect, whole, total, full, unqualified, unlimited. *The United States no longer has absolute domination of Olympic basketball.* **Ant.** restricted, partial, limited, incomplete, conditional.

absolutely *adv.* definitely, doubtlessly, completely, entirely, wholly, thoroughly. *I am absolutely certain he was the man I saw.* **Ant.** possibly, probably, somewhat.

absorb *vb.* **1.** assimilate, incorporate, digest, retain. *People with photographic memories absorb everything they read.* **2.** engross, preoccupy, captivate, enthrall, hold, engage, fascinate. *She was so absorbed in the computer game that she lost track of time.* **Ant.** 1. lose, eliminate. 2. bore, distract.

absorbing *adj.* engrossing, interesting, fascinating, exciting, captivating, intriguing, thrilling. *Network television has a noticeable lack of absorbing shows.* **Ant.** boring, dull, tiresome, unexciting, uninteresting.

abstain *vb.* avoid, forgo, refrain, spurn, resist. *Many people abstain from drinking hard liquors.* **Ant.** indulge, revel, overdo.

abstract *adj.* **1.** hypothetical, theoretical, speculative, conceptual, ideal. *Scientists frequently deal with abstract questions.* –*n.* **2.** abridgment, condensation, synopsis, summary, extraction. *The conference speaker presented an abstract of his latest article.* **Ant. 1.** concrete, specific, practical. **2.** enlargement, expansion.

absurd *adj.* foolish, ridiculous, preposterous, laughable, irrational. *Parents frequently think their children's behavior is absurd.* **Ant.** reasonable, sensible, rational, logical.

absurdity *n.* foolishness, nonsense, craziness, silliness, idiocy, ridiculousness. *The audience enjoyed the comedian's absurdities.* **Ant.** sense, wisdom, reality.

abundance *n.* **1.** profusion, sufficiency, ampleness, excess, surplus. *The local library has an abundance of excellent books.* **2.** wealth, riches, prosperity. *Who wouldn't like to live in abundance?* **Ant. 1.** scarcity, lack, deficiency. **2.** poverty, destitution.

abundant *adj.* plentiful, ample, copious, rich, bountiful, bounteous. *Farmers are always hoping for abundant rainfall.* **Ant.** scarce, rare, meager, scant, insufficient.

abuse *vb.* **1.** insult, malign, slander, scold, berate, reproach. *A considerate employer will not verbally abuse his or her employees.* **2.** misuse, exploit, mishandle, misapply. *A good leader does not abuse her power.* **3.** hurt, harm, injure, mistreat. *To abuse an animal is unforgivable.* –*n.* **4.** misuse, mistreatment, cruelty, injury, harm, hurt. *Child abuse can never be condoned.* **5.** insults, scolding, berating, tirade. *An old-fashioned tongue-lashing is a kind of abuse that makes many people angry.* **Ant. 1.** praise, compliment. **2.** respect, honor, protect. **5.** praise.

abusive *adj.* insulting, offensive, offending, rude, contemptuous. *Considerate people try not to use abusive language.* **Ant.** respectful, complimentary, courteous, polite.

abyss *n.* chasm, pit, emptiness, nothingness, void. *On the brink of an abyss is not a good place to get sweaty hands.*

academic *adj.* **1.** scholarly, studious, scholastic, educational, pedantic. *He has no practical experience— his background is entirely academic.* **2.** hypothetical, conjectural, theoretical, speculative, moot, impractical. *Since she's now deceased, any discussion of how she should have spent her life is purely academic.* **Ant. 1.** uneducated, unschooled, unlearned. **2.** practical, realistic.

accelerate *vb.* hasten, hurry, quicken, speed, expedite, rush. *The runner suddenly accelerated as she neared the finish line.* **Ant.** decelerate, slow, delay, retard, brake.

accent *n.* **1.** emphasis, stress, accentuation. *In the word "wonderful," the accent is on the first syllable.* **2.** inflection, tone, intonation, pronunciation, enunciation. *He speaks with a foreign accent.* –*vb.* **3.** enhance, emphasize, stress, accentuate, highlight. *Fresh flowers accented the room's decor.* **Ant. 3.** underplay, minimize, underemphasize.

accept *vb.* **1.** receive, acquire, gain, obtain, take. *He was more than happy to accept the gift.* **2.** acknowledge, affirm, concur, approve, agree. *The hostess accepted her guest's explanation for his late arrival.* **3.** assume, acknowledge, endure, tolerate, submit. *He finally learned to accept his defeat.* **Ant. 1–2.** reject, refuse, resist. **3.** deny, repudiate, disavow.

acceptable *adj.* **1.** adequate, sufficient, tolerable, average, passable, fair. *A report card full of Cs may be acceptable, but it's definitely not outstanding.* **2.** satisfactory, suitable, worthy, fit, proper. *The editor thought the manuscript was acceptable.* **Ant. 1–2.** unacceptable, substandard, poor, unsatisfactory.

acceptance *n.* approval, recognition, endorsement, sanction, confirmation. *The appointed official has yet to gain public acceptance.* **Ant.** rejection, repudiation, scorning, spurning.

accepted *adj.* proper, approved, suitable, conventional, standard, customary, established. *Blue jeans are not the accepted mode of dress at formal weddings.* **Ant.** unsuitable, improper, unconventional.

access *n.* admittance, approach, entrance, entry, passage, route. *The president has access to the nation's top secrets.*

accessory *n.* **1.** addition, accompaniment, appendage, supplement, attachment, extension. *Most cars come with optional accessories.* **2.** accomplice, confederate, partner, coconspirator, assistant. *The bank teller was an unwitting accessory to the robbery.*

accident *n.* **1.** misfortune, mishap, calamity, misadventure, crash, collision. *Automobile accidents claim thousands of lives every year.* **2.** chance, luck, fortune, happenstance, fluke. *She made the discovery by accident.* **Ant. 2.** intent, intention, plan, design.

accidental *adj.* undesigned, unintended, unintentional, unplanned, unexpected, unforeseen. *Some of our most significant scientific discoveries have been accidental.* **Ant.** intended, planned, designed, expected, foreseen.

acclaim *n.* **1.** applause, honor, homage, praise, enthusiasm. *The best-selling author's new book was greeted with great acclaim.* *–vb.* **2.** commend, applaud, compliment, praise. *All the leading critics acclaimed her latest movie.* **Ant. 1.** condemnation, criticism. **2.** berate, denounce, criticize.

accommodate *vb.* contain, hold, house, admit, include, lodge, shelter, quarter. *This classroom can accommodate 25 students.*

accompany *vb.* attend, escort, join, follow. *Mary's little lamb accompanied her everywhere.* **Ant.** desert, leave, abandon, forsake.

accomplice *n.* confederate, collaborator, cohort, helper, partner, associate. *The man's wife was his accomplice in crime.* **Ant.** opponent, adversary, rival, competitor.

accomplish *vb.* achieve, attain, reach, realize, fulfill, complete, finish, perform. *Charles Lindbergh accomplished his goal when he flew across the Atlantic.* **Ant.** fail, forsake, abort, attempt, neglect.

accomplished *adj.* **1.** skilled, masterly, expert, gifted, brilliant, talented, polished, experienced. *Laurence Olivier was an accomplished actor.* **2.** completed, established, proven, realized, accepted. *The control of polio is an accomplished fact.* **Ant. 1.** incompetent, amateurish. **2.** unproven, unestablished.

accomplishment *n.* **1.** achievement, attainment, triumph, victory, success. *Hillary's 1953 climb of Mt. Everest was a notable accomplishment.* **2.** skill, gift, talent, expertness, proficiency. *Learning to dance beautifully is just one* of her many accomplishments. **Ant. 1.** failure, mishap, disappointment. **2.** lack, deficiency.

accord *n.* **1.** agreement, harmony, concurrence, concord, tune, uniformity, conformity. *His views on disarmament are in accord with mine.* *–vb.* **2.** agree, conform, correspond, coincide, concur, match. *Her views on the environment accord with his.* **Ant. 1.** discord, conflict, difference. **2.** differ, disagree.

accordingly *adv.* therefore, consequently, hence, thus, then, ergo. *He spends all his time at a computer; accordingly, he doesn't have much of a social life.*

account *n.* **1.** story, report, description, explanation, narrative, tale. *The victim gave police a full account of the robbery.* **2.** importance, worth, significance, value, regard. *Since he has been known to lie, his explanation is of very little account.* **3.** record, register, invoice, bill, statement. *She owes almost $1,000 on her credit-card account.* *–vb.* **4.** explain, justify, rationalize, interpret, clarify. *Please account for your activities last night.* **Ant. 2.** insignificance, unimportance, worthlessness.

accountable *adj.* responsible, liable, answerable, guilty, blameworthy. *The girl's parents held her accountable for damages to the family car.* **Ant.** unaccountable, unanswerable, blameless, innocent.

accumulate *vb.* collect, gather, amass, assemble, stockpile, hoard. *The collector accumulated an impressive quantity of rare coins.* **Ant.** decrease, diminish, lessen, disperse, scatter.

accuracy *n.* precision, correctness, exactness, preciseness, authenticity. *Teachers have to evaluate term papers for accuracy.* **Ant.** error, mistake, faultiness, inaccuracy.

accurate *adj.* correct, right, perfect, faultless, precise, true, reliable. *At the county fair, the weight-guesser's estimates were mostly accurate.* **Ant.** inaccurate, incorrect, wrong, mistaken, imperfect.

accusation *n.* allegation, charge, claim, complaint, assertion. *Your accusation is totally unfounded.*

accuse *vb.* blame, charge, implicate, incriminate, indict, reproach. *Don't be hasty and accuse* someone before you have all the facts. **Ant.** clear, acquit, absolve, exonerate.

accustomed *adj.* **1.** habitual, ordinary, everyday, usual, common, regular, customary, conventional, routine. *For many people, fresh coffee in the morning is part of their accustomed behavior.* **2.** adapted, used to, familiar with. *After twenty years of marriage, the woman was accustomed to her husband's little quirks.* **Ant. 1.** unfamiliar, strange, unusual. **2.** unfamiliar, unaccustomed.

ache *vb.* **1.** hurt, throb, smart, pain, suffer. *Even after all these weeks, my back still aches.* **2.** crave, yearn, desire, covet, want, need, suffer, agonize. *The young man's heart aches for love.* –*n.* **3.** pain, hurt, discomfort, soreness. *Some people see a doctor for every little ache.* **Ant. 3.** relief, comfort.

achieve *vb.* attain, reach, complete, accomplish, realize, fulfill, conclude. *The newspaper achieved its circulation goal.* **Ant.** fail, miss.

achievement *n.* attainment, accomplishment, fulfillment, realization, feat, deed. *Graduating from college is quite an achievement.* **Ant.** failure, disappointment, defeat.

acid *adj.* **1.** sour, tart, citrus, vinegarish, sharp, bitter. *Lemons and limes are known for their acid taste.* **2.** sarcastic, caustic, satirical, sardonic, biting, acerbic. *The comedienne was known for her acid wit.* **Ant. 1.** sweet, sugary, saccharine. **2.** gentle, kind, mild, soft.

acknowledge *vb.* **1.** admit, allow, concede, accept, concur, recognize. *He was finally forced to acknowledge that he wasn't suited for college.* **2.** consider, deem, hold, agree, recognize. *Einstein is generally acknowledged to be one of the greatest scientists of all time.* **3.** accept, receive, respond, answer, recognize. *The young woman was unwilling to acknowledge the boy's interest in her.* **Ant. 1.** refuse, refute, deny. **2–3.** ignore, neglect, overlook.

acknowledgment *n.* **1.** admission, confession, concession, disclosure. *His acknowledgment of guilt made an investigation unnecessary.* **2.** credit, recognition, attention, notice. *Most people like to receive acknowledgment for their efforts.* **Ant. 1.** denial, refusal, rejection, disavowal.

acquaint *vb.* **1.** introduce, meet, present. *Are the two of you acquainted?* **2.** inform, advise, notify, familiarize, divulge, reveal. *Are you acquainted with the facts of the case?* **Ant. 2.** withhold, conceal, hide, retain.

acquaintance *n.* **1.** familiarity, experience, awareness, knowledge, appreciation. *She has a considerable acquaintance with contemporary theater.* **2.** colleague, associate, companion, comrade. *Most people have lots of acquaintances but only a few close friends.* **Ant. 1.** ignorance, inexperience, unawareness. **2.** stranger, outsider.

acquire *vb.* obtain, attain, get, gain, procure, secure, achieve, receive, realize. *After spending several months in Japan, he acquired a taste for Oriental cooking.* **Ant.** lose, forfeit, forgo, relinquish.

acquisition *n.* **1.** acquirement, attainment, obtainment, gain. *Acquisition of knowledge is a desirable goal.* **2.** possession, purchase, property, belongings. *The book collector's latest acquisition is a rare first edition.*

acquit *vb.* **1.** excuse, forgive, exonerate, absolve, clear, exempt. *The defendant was acquitted of all charges after new evidence proved his innocence.* **2.** behave, comport, conduct, deport. *The new police officer acquitted herself well on her first dangerous assignment.* **Ant. 1.** condemn, sentence, convict. **2.** misbehave, misconduct.

act *n.* **1.** action, deed, accomplishment, achievement, feat, exploit. *The young woman received a medal for her act of heroism.* **2.** law, decree, statute, edict, bill, resolution. *War was declared by act of Congress.* **3.** pretense, pretension, show, fake, insincerity, deceit, affectation. *The young boy's tantrum was just an act to get attention.* –*vb.* **4.** perform, operate, function, behave, work, serve. *When the president was incapacitated, the vice-president acted in his place.* **5.** portray, impersonate, pretend, simulate, play. *She acted so well that she got the lead in her next film.* **Ant. 1.** inaction, inactivity. **3.** sincerity, candor, forthrightness.

action *n.* **1.** activity, work, effort, achievement, accomplishment, act, deed, feat, exploit. *The firefighter was praised for his actions.* **2.** combat, fighting, conflict, hostilities, warfare. *Did you see any action when you were in Vietnam?* **3.** activity, excitement, adventure, stimulation.

She likes movies with lots of action. **Ant. 1.** inaction, inactivity. **2–3.** peace, quiet, serenity.

activate *vb.* turn on, start, mobilize, energize, animate, stimulate. *Dialing 911 activates your community's emergency-response program.* **Ant.** deactivate, turn off, halt, stop, arrest.

active *adj.* **1.** lively, energetic, dynamic, animated, spirited, vibrant, industrious. *Despite his stroke, he's still a very active person.* **2.** functioning, working, operating. *Our club has more than 100 active members.* **Ant. 1.** inactive, idle, lethargic. **2.** inactive, nonfunctioning.

activity *n.* **1.** action, work, effort, function, movement, commotion, tumult. *The laundromat is full of activity on Monday mornings.* **2.** project, pursuit, endeavor, undertaking, avocation, occupation. *She is busy with numerous after- school activities.* **Ant. 1.** inactivity, quiet, calm.

actor *n.* performer, entertainer, player, participant. *This movie features one of my favorite actors.*

actual *adj.* true, real, genuine, certain, verifiable, concrete, tangible. *Though he claimed illness, the actual reason he didn't go is that he can't stand parties.* **Ant.** false, unreal, fake, imaginary, fictional.

actuality *n.* reality, essence, fact, truth, substance. *Despite what she told her editor, in actuality she hadn't even started the book.*

actually *adv.* genuinely, really, truly, literally, indeed. *It did not actually happen like she said.*

acute *adj.* **1.** severe, intense, piercing, strong, sharp, keen. *He's in acute pain.* **2.** perceptive, discerning, discriminating, sensitive, intuitive, precise. *She has an acute understanding of what's going on.* **3.** critical, crucial, grave, serious, perilous, urgent. *This country has an acute shortage of low-income housing.* **Ant. 1.** mild, moderate, weak, dull. **2.** imperceptive, imprecise, inaccurate. **3.** noncritical, unimportant.

adage *n.* proverb, saying, maxim, epigram, cliche. *"An apple a day keeps the doctor away" is an example of an old adage.*

adapt *vb.* modify, alter, adjust, accommodate, conform, reconcile, fit, change. *The small company is having trouble adapting to the latest changes in technology.*

adaptable *adj.* versatile, flexible, adjustable, accommodating, tractable. *This electric drill is adaptable for use as a screwdriver.* **Ant.** rigid, fixed, inflexible.

adaptation *n.* version, alteration, modification, revision, conversion. *His new novel is merely an adaptation of the same plot he's used before.*

add *vb.* **1.** join, affix, include, attach, append. *Before you ring up my purchases, please add this item.* **2.** total, sum up, calculate, compute. *He asked the waitress to add up his bill.* **3.** increase, augment, supplement, swell, enlarge. *The new project added significantly to her workload.* **Ant. 1.** remove, withdraw, eliminate. **2.** subtract, deduct. **3.** reduce, diminish, lessen.

addict *n.* fan, devotee, adherent, fanatic, enthusiast, lover. *She's a movie addict.*

addiction *n.* obsession, fixation, preoccupation, mania. *He's been struggling to overcome his addiction to cigarettes.*

addition *n.* increase, raise, supplement, extension, expansion. *The new baby was a welcome addition to their family.* **Ant.** deduction, reduction, lessening.

additional *adj.* supplemental, extra, added, more, increased, further. *She will need additional income to afford the house she'd like.*

address *n.* **1.** location, place, residence, abode, dwelling, street number. *Please include your phone number and address.* **2.** speech, lecture, talk, presentation, oration. *The president's address will be carried on all major networks.* –*vb.* **3.** focus on, concentrate on, apply, direct, devote. *You're wasting your time by not addressing the real issue.* **4.** speak, talk, lecture, orate. *The principal will address the entire student body at tomorrow's assembly.*

adequate *adj.* sufficient, enough, suitable, satisfactory, fitting, acceptable. *The student's work was not outstanding, but it was adequate for a passing grade.* **Ant.** inadequate, insufficient, unsuitable.

adhere *vb.* **1.** cling, stick, hold, attach, fasten. *This sticker won't adhere to my chrome bumper.* **2.** follow, keep, be faithful, be loyal, be devoted. *Despite the injustices she's suffered, she still adheres to her principles.* **Ant. 1.** disjoin, loosen, separate. **2.** be disloyal, be untrue.

adjacent *adj.* next to, adjoining, touching, near, bordering, neighboring. *My property is adjacent to hers.* **Ant.** remote, distant, separate, removed.

adjourn *vb.* defer, delay, postpone, suspend, interrupt, discontinue. *The chairman adjourned the committee meeting till next week.* **Ant.** convene, assemble, gather.

adjust *vb.* **1.** set, regulate, change, order, repair, fix. *He had to adjust his VCR's tracking control to play the new movie.* **2.** adapt, reconcile, accommodate, attune, conform. *She's having difficulty adjusting to the demands of her new job.*

adjustment *n.* **1.** alignment, modification, ordering, fixing, regulating. *Your television's color control is out of adjustment.* **2.** accommodation, settlement, compromise, adapting. *The returning astronauts had trouble making the adjustment to Earth's gravity.*

administer *vb.* **1.** manage, direct, supervise, run, govern, control. *Who will administer the new research project?* **2.** provide, dispense, apply, give, distribute. *Paramedics administered first aid at the accident site.*

admirable *adj.* excellent, praiseworthy, commendable, superb, wonderful. *Her kindness is admirable.* **Ant.** bad, contemptible, despicable, worthless.

admiration *n.* esteem, high regard, reverence, approval, respect, awe. *She has great admiration for Hemingway's writing ability.* **Ant.** contempt, disdain, scorn, disapproval.

admire *vb.* respect, esteem, value, revere, venerate, honor. *I admire anyone who acts unselfishly for the benefit of others.* **Ant.** dislike, detest, scorn, hate.

admit *vb.* **1.** confess, acknowledge, concede, confide, reveal. *George Washington admitted to chopping down a cherry tree.* **2.** let in, let enter, induct, initiate, install. *Three new members were admitted to the exclusive club.* **Ant. 1.** deny, conceal, withhold. **2.** obstruct, reject.

adopt *vb.* embrace, assume, appropriate, take, use, employ. *The city council voted to adopt new methods for raising revenues.* **Ant.** reject, spurn, discard, repudiate.

adorable *adj.* lovable, attractive, enchanting, captivating, lovely. *She got an adorable little bunny for her birthday.* **Ant.** unlovable, unlikable, offensive.

adoration *n.* worship, veneration, reverence, devotion, love, honor. *It's rare to find a slave who has much adoration for his master.* **Ant.** antipathy, dislike, aversion, detestation.

adore *vb.* love, cherish, revere, venerate, worship, idolize. *She adores her grandfather.* **Ant.** abhor, hate, despise, dislike.

adorn *vb.* decorate, embellish, ornament, beautify, furbish, trim. *She wore a blouse adorned with lace.* **Ant.** divest, strip, mar, deface.

adult *n.* **1.** grownup, mature person, man, woman. *This movie is rated for adults only.* –*adj.* **2.** mature, grown-up, grown, aged, developed, experienced. *He was attacked by an adult bear.* **Ant. 1.** infant, child, adolescent. **2.** immature, inexperienced.

advance *vb.* **1.** move forward, go forward, proceed, progress, march. *The army advanced toward the enemy's castle.* **2.** improve, further, promote, upgrade, strengthen, assist, benefit. *The scientist's discovery advanced our knowledge of medicine.* **3.** propose, suggest, submit, offer, propound. *He advanced a controversial new theory on the origin of disease.* **4.** prepay, lend, loan. *His parents advanced him his next week's allowance.* –*n.* **5.** progress, progression, headway, advancement, improvement. *The computer industry has benefited from advances in technology.* **6.** promotion, upgrade, rise, elevation. *Her advance to personnel manager was the result of many years of hard work.* **7.** prepayment, down payment. *The writer received a large advance for her latest book.* **Ant. 1.** recede, retreat, withdraw. **2.** hinder, impede, decrease. **3.** withhold, suppress. **5.** setback, reversal. **6.** demotion, reduction.

advantage *n.* asset, edge, favor, help, benefit, aid, service. *The boxer favored to win has the* *advantage of a longer reach.* **Ant.** disadvantage, drawback, hindrance.

advantageous *adj.* helpful, favorable, beneficial, valuable, fortunate. *He was in an advantageous position for a promotion.* **Ant.** disadvantageous, unfavorable, unhelpful.

adventure *n.* escapade, venture, exploit, feat, hazard, peril, risk. *She dreams of leading a life full of adventure.*

adventurous *adj.* **1.** bold, daring, rash, intrepid, brave. *The adventurous boys snuck into a cemetery at midnight.* **2.** challenging, perilous, hazardous, risky, dangerous. *Their climb of Mt. Everest promised to be adventurous.* **Ant. 1.** cautious, timid, cowardly. **2.** safe, boring, routine.

adversary *n.* opponent, foe, rival, competitor, enemy. *Her former instructor was her main adversary in the golf tournament.* **Ant.** ally, partner, colleague, friend.

adverse *adj.* unfavorable, bad, detrimental, hostile, destructive. *Adverse weather forced us to postpone our camping trip.* **Ant.** beneficial, good, favorable.

adversity *n.* misfortune, suffering, difficulty, trouble, calamity, hardship. *Try to show courage when faced with adversities.* **Ant.** success, fortune, good luck.

advertise *vb.* publicize, promote, proclaim, announce, feature, display. *The company advertised its latest product on television.*

advice *n.* counsel, guidance, recommendation, suggestion, opinion, warning, information. *She doesn't seem to want my advice.*

advise *vb.* **1.** counsel, recommend, suggest, urge, warn, caution. *His doctor advised him to lower his intake of cholesterol.* **2.** inform, notify, apprise, acquaint, tell. *We have been advised that there will be a big storm tomorrow.*

advocate *vb.* **1.** recommend, support, promote, endorse, encourage, defend, uphold. *He advocates stricter laws against drunk drivers.* –*n.* **2.** supporter, upholder, backer, champion, proponent, promoter. *She is an advocate of tougher environmental laws.* **Ant. 1.** oppose, discourage. **2.** opponent, adversary, critic.

affair *n.* **1.** business, matter, concern, undertaking, activity, occasion, episode. *Starting your own company can be a complex affair.* **2.** celebration, festival, party, event, ceremony, function. *The senior prom will be quite an affair this year.* **3.** liaison, romance, relationship. *The actress is having an affair with her director.*

affect *vb.* **1.** influence, alter, change, transform, modify. *Our vacation plans were affected by the airline strike.* **2.** touch, move, stir, impress, upset, trouble. *He was deeply affected by reports of famine in Africa.*

affection *n.* love, warmth, tenderness, fondness, liking, concern. *He has deep affection for his wife and children.* **Ant.** hate, loathing, dislike.

affectionate *adj.* loving, tender, warm, fond, devoted, caring. *She adores her kitten because it's so affectionate.* **Ant.** cold, distant, unfeeling, uncaring.

affirm *vb.* **1.** swear, declare, assert, claim, insist, maintain. *She affirmed that he was the one who stole her purse.* **2.** ratify, confirm, approve, endorse, uphold. *Congress failed to affirm the president's nominee for the Supreme Court.* **Ant. 1.** deny, refute, renounce. **2.** reject, veto, nullify.

afflict *vb.* plague, trouble, distress, burden, torment, beset. *She was afflicted with a bad cold.*

affliction *n.* misfortune, trouble, distress, hardship, adversity, pain, misery. *Chronic headaches are but one of his afflictions.* **Ant.** benefit, blessing, comfort.

affluent *adj.* wealthy, rich, prosperous, privileged. *She lives in an affluent neighborhood.* **Ant.** poor, impoverished, underprivileged.

afford *vb.* **1.** pay for, bear, manage, support. *I can't afford to take a vacation this summer.* **2.** provide, supply, furnish, offer, give. *This vista affords a panoramic view of the Grand Canyon.*

afraid *adj.* **1.** fearful, frightened, terrified, scared, anxious, nervous, alarmed. *He's afraid of heights.* **2.** sorry, remorseful, unhappy, hesitant, reluctant. *I'm afraid I won't be able to lend you the money for a new car.* **Ant. 1.** bold, courageous, fearless. **2.** happy, pleased.

age *n.* **1.** era, epoch, period, time, generation, season. *We live in the computer age.* **2.** years, eon, millennium, eternity. *I haven't been to a movie in* *ages.* –*vb.* **3.** mature, ripen, season, develop, grow old. *This cheese has aged nine months.*

aged *adj.* **1.** old, elderly, mature, advanced, ancient. *She takes care of her aged parents.* **2.** mellow, mature, ripe, ripened, developed. *He's a connoisseur of aged wines.* **Ant. 1.** young, youthful, juvenile. **2.** immature, green.

agency *n.* organization, bureau, bureaucracy, office, department. *He got a job working for a government agency.*

agent *n.* **1.** delegate, representative, advocate, negotiator. *The writer had her agent negotiate the book contract.* **2.** power, force, means, medium, mechanism, instrument. *Scouring powder is an effective cleansing agent.*

aggravate *vb.* **1.** intensify, worsen, exacerbate, increase, exaggerate. *Scratching only aggravated his case of poison ivy.* **2.** irritate, annoy, exasperate, provoke, irk, bother. *She was aggravated by her neighbor's barking dogs.* **Ant. 1.** lessen, diminish, relieve. **2.** calm, soothe.

aggravation *n.* annoyance, bother, exasperation, vexation, irritation. *His noisy neighbors were a constant source of aggravation.*

aggression *n.* hostility, belligerence, combativeness, assault, attack. *A naval blockade is considered an act of aggression.* **Ant.** friendliness, peacefulness, peace.

aggressive *adj.* **1.** hostile, belligerent, combative, warlike, militant, offensive. *The nation's aggressive actions led to a war.* **2.** bold, forceful, assertive, competitive, vigorous, energetic. *We need an aggressive mayor to solve our city's problems.* **Ant. 1.** peaceful, friendly, defensive. **2.** timid, shy, retiring.

agile *adj.* **1.** athletic, nimble, spry, supple, lithe, limber. *The cat made an agile leap to the bookshelf.* **2.** quick, sharp, clever, keen, bright, perceptive. *Algebra isn't hard if you have an agile mind.* **Ant. 1.** clumsy, awkward, inept. **2.** slow, dull, sluggish.

agitate *vb.* **1.** stir, mix, shake, churn, beat, toss. *A washing machine agitates clothes to clean them.* **2.** upset, excite, incite, arouse, provoke. *The revolutionary's speech agitated the mob.* **Ant. 2.** calm, soothe, pacify.

agitated *adj.* upset, disturbed, excited, worried, nervous, jittery. *Everyone was agitated when a major earthquake was predicted.* **Ant.** serene, tranquil, calm.

agony *n.* pain, suffering, torment, anguish, distress, torture. *He was in agony with two broken legs.* **Ant.** comfort, pleasure, bliss, joy.

agree *vb.* **1.** consent, assent, concede, accept, allow. *She agreed to lend me ten dollars.* **2.** concur, coincide, correspond, harmonize, fit, match. *His account of the accident does not agree with mine.* **Ant. 1.** deny, oppose, dissent. **2.** disagree, differ, contradict.

agreement *n.* **1.** understanding, harmony, accord, conformity. *It looks as if the two sides will never be in agreement with each other.* **2.** deal, pact, compact, treaty, arrangement, settlement. *Management and union officials reached an agreement that ended the strike.* **Ant. 1.** disagreement, discord, dissension.

aid *vb.* **1.** help, assist, support, serve, back. *Unless you aid me, I won't be able to finish the project in time.* –*n.* **2.** assistance, help, support, service, backing. *I wouldn't have been able to fix my car without your aid.* **Ant. 1.** obstruct, hinder, oppose. **2.** hindrance, obstacle.

ail *vb.* trouble, disturb, bother, distress, afflict. *She looks as if something ails her.*

ailment *n.* disorder, discomfort, sickness, illness, affliction, disease. *He constantly complains about his minor ailments.*

aim *vb.* **1.** point, direct, level, sight, focus. *He aimed his arrow at a makeshift target.* **2.** try, strive, plan, endeavor, seek, intend, attempt. *She aims for perfection in her writing.* –*n.* **3.** goal, target, intention, intent, objective, ambition. *His aim is to make the honor roll.*

aimless *adj.* directionless, unorganized, purposeless, pointless, erratic, unguided. *Some people lead aimless lives.* **Ant.** purposeful, intentional, systematic.

air *n.* **1.** atmosphere, sky, wind, breeze. *The kite floated through the air.* **2.** aura, quality, flavor, mood, appearance, character. *He's secretive because he likes to maintain an air of mystery.* –*vb.* **3.** ventilate, aerate. *This room needs to be aired out.* **4.** voice, express, declare, reveal, disclose, expose, communicate. *The personnel manager made herself available for employees who wanted to air their complaints.* **Ant. 4.** conceal, hide, suppress.

aisle *n.* corridor, passage, passageway, walkway, path, lane. *Fire regulations prohibit sitting in the aisles of a movie theater.*

alarm *n.* **1.** warning, alert, signal, bell, buzzer, siren. *Many people have burglar alarms in their homes.* **2.** fear, fright, apprehension, dismay, distress, dread. *The smell of smoke filled her with alarm.* *–vb.* **3.** scare, frighten, startle, shock, disturb, dismay. *The sound of screeching brakes alarmed him.* **Ant. 2.** serenity, tranquillity. **3.** calm, reassure, relieve, comfort.

alarming *adj.* frightening, startling, disturbing, shocking, appalling. *She has an alarming lack of responsibility.* **Ant.** reassuring, soothing, comforting.

alert *adj.* **1.** attentive, awake, aware, watchful, vigilant, observant. *An alert employee spotted the shoplifter.* **2.** quick, nimble, lively, sharp, brisk, agile. *The alert child learned to read at an early age.* *–n.* **3.** warning, alarm, signal, siren. *There will be a practice air-raid alert at noon today.* *–vb.* **4.** warn, caution, advise, signal, notify. *Police alerted the bank's employees to expect a robbery.* **Ant. 1.** inattentive, unaware, unconcerned. **2.** slow, dull, listless.

alibi *n.* excuse, story, explanation, plea, defense. *The defendant could find no one to confirm his alibi.*

alien *adj.* **1.** strange, foreign, different, unfamiliar, exotic. *She's fascinated by the alien customs of primitive tribes.* **2.** opposed, incompatible, contradictory, inconsistent, unlike. *Lying is alien to her character.* *–n.* **3.** foreigner, stranger, outsider, immigrant. *Because he is a citizen of a different country, he is classified as an alien here.* **Ant. 1.** familiar, common, commonplace. **2.** compatible, consistent, like. **3.** native, citizen.

alike *adj.* **1.** like, identical, similar, equal, even, matched. *No two snowflakes are exactly alike.* *–adv.* **2.** similarly, identically, equally, evenly, likewise. *The twins are hard to tell apart since they dress alike.* **Ant. 1.** different, unlike, opposite. **2.** differently, distinctly.

alive *adj.* **1.** live, living, existing, animate. *You need to water your lawn if you want to keep the grass alive.* **2.** lively, animated, active, alert, vivacious, vital, vigorous. *She seems to be more alive with the coming of spring.* **Ant. 1.** lifeless, dead, deceased. **2.** slow, lethargic, inactive.

allegiance *n.* loyalty, faithfulness, devotion, fidelity, obedience. *He pledged allegiance to the fraternity and its members.* **Ant.** disloyalty, treachery, treason.

alliance *n.* agreement, pact, bargain, understanding, treaty, union. *The two countries formed an alliance against their mutual enemy.*

allied *adj.* joined, combined, united, joint, connected, affiliated. *The peasants were allied with the middle class in the civil war.* **Ant.** disunited, unconnected, uncombined.

allot *vb.* assign, allocate, distribute, allow, share, divide. *The president allotted each person fifteen minutes for an interview.* **Ant.** withhold, deny, refuse.

allow *vb.* **1.** permit, let, authorize, grant, approve, sanction. *Smoking is not allowed at school.* **2.** allot, allocate, give, assign, provide. *Allow yourself enough time to get your homework done.* **Ant. 1.** forbid, prohibit, refuse. **2.** withhold, deny.

allude *vb.* mention, suggest, hint, refer, imply, speak of. *He's sensitive about his size, so let's not allude to it.*

allure *vb.* **1.** fascinate, attract, captivate, enchant, draw, charm. *She was allured by his intelligence.* *–n.* **2.** attraction, lure, fascination, temptation, enticement, charm. *Dragons can't resist the allure of gold.* **Ant. 1.** repel, alienate, estrange.

ally *n.* **1.** colleague, friend, helper, partner, associate, assistant. *The criminal needed to find an ally to help with the robbery.* *–vb.* **2.** combine, join, unite, unify, connect. *The citizens allied together in their fight against crime.* **Ant. 1.** enemy, foe, opponent. **2.** separate, divide.

almost *adv.* nearly, practically, about, mostly, largely, somewhat. *She's almost finished the book she's reading.* **Ant.** definitely.

alone *adv.* **1.** solitarily, singly, individually, separately. *He went to the movie alone.* *–adj.* **2.**

secluded, isolated, unaccompanied, unattended, unescorted. *She was alone in the woods.* **Ant.** **1–2.** accompanied, escorted, attended.

aloof *adj.* cold, cool, detached, distant, withdrawn, uninterested. *An aloof person has difficulty finding friends.* **Ant.** warm, friendly, involved.

aloud *adv.* audibly, out loud, openly, loudly, distinctly, clearly. *He enjoys reading aloud to himself.* **Ant.** silently, inaudibly.

alter *vb.* change, modify, vary, transform, revise, remake. *His new beard completely alters his appearance.* **Ant.** maintain, continue, keep.

alternate *vb.* **1.** switch, interchange, rotate, intersperse, change. *Blue stripes alternate with yellow stripes on his shirt.* *–adj.* **2.** alternating, reciprocal, successive. *The American flag has alternate red and white stripes.* **3.** substitute, another, different, additional. *Since she missed her plane, she had to take an alternate flight.* *–n.* **4.** substitute, replacement, second, backup. *Since our elected delegate could not go to the meeting, we had to send an alternate.*

alternative *n.* choice, selection, possibility, option, preference. *She had difficulty choosing an ice cream flavor because there were so many alternatives.*

altogether *adv.* completely, entirely, wholly, totally, thoroughly, absolutely. *He missed the target altogether.* **Ant.** partially, partly, incompletely.

always *adv.* eternally, perpetually, forever, ever, unceasingly, continually. *I'll love you always.* **Ant.** never, rarely.

amateur *n.* **1.** nonprofessional, novice, beginner, apprentice, hobbyist. *The pro tennis player didn't want to compete against amateurs.* *–adj.* **2.** amateurish, nonprofessional, inexperienced, unskilled. *She joined an amateur theater group.* **Ant.** **1.** professional, expert. **2.** professional, experienced.

amaze *vb.* astonish, surprise, astound, bewilder, stun, impress. *Her command of the English language never ceases to amaze me.* **Ant.** bore, tire, anticipate, expect.

amazement *n.* astonishment, wonder, surprise, bewilderment, awe. *I was filled with amazement as I watched the magician perform.* **Ant.** boredom, apathy, indifference.

ambition *n.* **1.** desire, will, determination, drive, energy, resolve. *To succeed as a writer, you must have lots of ambition.* **2.** goal, end, aspiration, objective, purpose, dream. *Her ambition is to become a doctor.* **Ant. 1.** indifference, apathy, laziness.

ambitious *adj.* **1.** determined, dynamic, energetic, eager, intent. *He will probably succeed because he's so ambitious.* **2.** audacious, bold, daring, grandiose, difficult, challenging. *Humanity's desire to conquer space is an ambitious dream.* **Ant. 1.** purposeless, apathetic, lazy. **2.** modest, simple, easy.

amble *vb.* walk, stroll, ramble, saunter, wander, drift. *The old man ambled through the park.* **Ant.** rush, run, sprint, dash.

amend *vb.* improve, better, correct, perfect, reform, revise, change, alter, modify. *To make that proposal legal, the constitution will have to be amended.* **Ant.** worsen, weaken, keep.

amiable *adj.* friendly, agreeable, pleasant, congenial, gracious, sociable, cordial. *Small towns typically have an amiable atmosphere.* **Ant.** unfriendly, disagreeable, unpleasant.

amicable *adj.* peaceful, peaceable, friendly, cooperative, harmonious, civil. *The mediator hoped to find an amicable settlement to the international dispute.* **Ant.** hostile, belligerent, unfriendly.

among *prep.* amid, amidst, amongst, between, in with. *The pirates divided the treasure among themselves.*

amount *vb.* **1.** total, comprise, add up, come to. *His debts amount to several thousand dollars.* **2.** equal, approach, correspond, imply, suggest. *Her remark amounts to a rebuke.* *–n.* **3.** sum, total, extent, measure, quantity. *We have only a small amount of money left.*

ample *adj.* plentiful, abundant, sufficient, adequate, enough. *We have ample time for a leisurely dinner before the movie starts.* **Ant.** meager, scarce, insufficient, inadequate.

amplify *vb.* expand, enlarge, increase, extend, intensify, strengthen. *The cheerleaders* used hand-held megaphones to amplify their voices. **Ant.** reduce, decrease, diminish, lower.

amuse vb. entertain, please, occupy, interest, divert, charm. *The kitten's antics amused us all.* **Ant.** bore, weary, tire.

amusement n. **1.** pleasure, relaxation, entertainment, pastime, diversion. *What are your favorite amusements?* **2.** laughter, mirth, enjoyment, merriment, pleasure. *Watching the children play filled him with amusement.* **Ant. 2.** sadness, displeasure.

amusing adj. entertaining, pleasurable, pleasing, pleasant, delightful, charming. *Her stories are always amusing.* **Ant.** boring, dull, uninteresting.

analyze vb. examine, investigate, study, evaluate, scrutinize. *If you analyze your motives, you'll know the right thing to do.* **Ant.** ignore, disregard, neglect.

ancestor n. **1.** forebear, forefather, foremother. *His ancestors came to America in the 19th century.* **2.** predecessor, forerunner, precursor, antecedent, prototype. *The ancestor of the automobile was the horse-drawn carriage.* **Ant. 1.** descendant, offspring, heir. **2.** successor, follower.

anchor vb. **1.** fasten, attach, fix, affix, secure. *She anchored her bookshelves to the wall.* –n. **2.** mainstay, support, foundation, bulwark. *His religion is the anchor of his life.* **Ant.** detach, disconnect, loosen.

ancient adj. old, antique, aged, archaic, old-fashioned, primitive. *Grandfather still drives his ancient Model-T Ford.* **Ant.** recent, new, modern.

anecdote n. story, narrative, tale, yarn, account, reminiscence. *I love Grandmother's amusing anecdotes about her childhood.*

anger n. **1.** rage, wrath, ire, fury, vexation, annoyance, irritation, displeasure. *She insulted him in a fit of anger.* –vb. **2.** enrage, outrage, infuriate, incense, irritate, annoy, upset. *His cruel remark angered me.* **Ant. 1.** calm, peacefulness, forbearance. **2.** soothe, pacify, mollify, calm.

angry adj. mad, furious, irate, wrathful, enraged, infuriated, irritated, annoyed, upset. *Please don't be angry with me.* **Ant.** happy, content, pleased.

anguish n. distress, agony, torment, misery, anxiety, despair, pain, suffering. *He was in anguish after breaking up with his girlfriend.* **Ant.** comfort, solace, pleasure.

animal n. **1.** fauna, creature, beast, game. *She doesn't like to see wild animals imprisoned in zoos.* **2.** beast, brute, barbarian, savage. *The football player was flattered when he was called an animal.*

animated adj. lively, spirited, energetic, vigorous, dynamic, exciting. *She was the most animated person at the party.* **Ant.** boring, dull, lifeless.

animosity n. antagonism, hate, enmity, hostility, antipathy, malice, dislike, bitterness. *He felt unjust animosity towards the person who got the job he had wanted.* **Ant.** friendship, kindness, love, sympathy.

annex vb. **1.** add, attach, append, acquire, appropriate, connect, join. *The imperialist country annexed some of its neighbor's territory.* –n. **2.** addition, extension, supplement, wing, branch. *A new annex for the library is under construction.* **Ant. 1.** detach, separate, disconnect.

annihilate vb. demolish, destroy, exterminate, kill, eradicate, obliterate. *The army's offensive annihilated all opposition.*

announce vb. proclaim, declare, report, disclose, reveal, publish. *She announced her candidacy for the U.S. Senate.* **Ant.** hide, conceal, withhold.

annoy vb. irk, irritate, bother, vex, pester, disturb, harass, distract. *Don't annoy your brother while he's using the computer.* **Ant.** comfort, soothe, please.

answer n. **1.** reply, response, acknowledgment, reaction, return. *She eagerly awaited an answer to her letter.* **2.** result, solution, resolution. *It is often difficult to find the right answers for a crossword puzzle.* –vb. **3.** respond, reply, acknowledge, rejoin, return. *He answered her letter.* **4.** be accountable, be responsible, pay, atone. *The law says that we must answer for our crimes.* **Ant. 3.** ask, question, inquire.

antagonist *n.* opponent, adversary, rival, competitor, foe, enemy. *He bravely faced his antagonist in the boxing ring.* **Ant.** friend, ally, partner.

antagonize *vb.* irritate, alienate, insult, offend, annoy. *The child's rude behavior antagonized everyone.* **Ant.** please, charm, appease.

anticipate *vb.* expect, foresee, foretell, predict, forecast. *She anticipates a good turnout for her lecture.*

antique *adj.* **1.** old, aged, ancient, antiquated, old-fashioned. *He collects antique cars.* –*n.* **2.** relic, curio, rarity, memorabilia, souvenir. *This store has an impressive assortment of antiques.* **Ant. 1.** new, recent, modern.

anxiety *n.* apprehension, uneasiness, distress, worry, concern, foreboding, suspense. *She was filled with anxiety when she heard about her friend's accident.* **Ant.** relief, peacefulness, calmness.

anxious *adj.* **1.** worried, uneasy, concerned, apprehensive, restless, fearful. *He felt anxious the night before he was to undergo surgery.* **2.** eager, desirous, keen, impatient, intent. *She was anxious to get tickets for the hit musical.* **Ant. 1.** confident, collected, relieved. **2.** reluctant, hesitant.

apart *adv.* **1.** distant, removed, away, aside. *I don't see how both bookstores can succeed, since they're less than a block apart.* **2.** alone, separately, individually, aside, isolated. *Our house sits apart from the others on the block.* **3.** asunder, into parts, into pieces. *He took the engine apart, but he couldn't get it back together.* **Ant. 1.** near, together.

apathetic *adj.* indifferent, unconcerned, unfeeling, uninterested, unmoved, uncommitted, cold. *Too many people are apathetic about environmental issues.* **Ant.** concerned, interested, committed.

apathy *n.* indifference, unconcern, disinterest, passiveness, lethargy, coldness. *If people had less apathy, we'd be able to solve more of our problems.* **Ant.** enthusiasm, fervor, interest, concern.

apex *n.* highest point, peak, zenith, top, pinnacle, summit, climax. *Winning an Oscar was the apex of her acting career.* **Ant.** lowest point, bottom, nadir.

apologetic *adj.* sorry, contrite, repentant, regretful, remorseful. *I couldn't be mad at her because she was so apologetic.* **Ant.** unrepentant, unremorseful.

apology *n.* explanation, excuse, acknowledgment, confession, regret. *He offered an apology for his lateness.*

appall *vb.* horrify, shock, alarm, dismay, outrage, stun, offend, revolt. *Investors were appalled by news of the stock-market crash.* **Ant.** reassure, please, comfort.

appalling *adj.* fearful, frightening, alarming, dreadful, horrible, awful. *There was an appalling loss of life during World War II.* **Ant.** reassuring, comforting, pleasing.

apparatus *n.* machinery, equipment, implements, tools, gear. *The local gym has installed a new set of weightlifting apparatus.*

apparel *n.* clothing, clothes, garments, attire, wear, outfit. *I'm looking for a store that sells men's apparel.*

apparent *adj.* plain, obvious, evident, clear, manifest, unmistakable. *Her love of teaching is apparent to her students.* **Ant.** doubtful, uncertain, obscure.

apparently *adv.* evidently, seemingly, plainly, clearly, obviously. *He apparently won't be coming to the party.*

appeal *n.* **1.** request, plea, entreaty, application, petition. *The court turned down her appeal for a new trial.* **2.** attraction, allure, charm, draw, fascination. *Diamonds have an appeal that's hard for some people to resist.* –*vb.* **3.** beg, beseech, plead, pray, implore. *Farmers victimized by the drought appealed for federal assistance.* **4.** attract, excite, interest, fascinate, tempt. *Chinese food does not appeal to me.* **Ant. 1.** refusal, rejection, objection. **2.** repulsiveness, unpleasantness. **3.** reject, refuse, deny. **4.** repulse, revolt.

appealing *adj.* attractive, inviting, alluring, tempting, desirable. *That pizza certainly looks appealing.* **Ant.** unappealing, repugnant, disagreeable.

appear *vb.* **1.** seem, look, act, sound. *Though he appears to like school, he really can't stand it.* **2.** arise, rise, arrive, emerge, show up, turn up. *The sun appeared from behind a mountain.* **Ant. 2.** disappear, vanish.

appearance *n.* **1.** arrival, emergence, coming, advent, appearing. *Though it was a cloudy day, the sun made a brief appearance.* **2.** look, image, demeanor, visage, aspect. *Appearances can be deceiving.* **Ant. 1.** disappearance, withdrawal, vanishing.

appease *vb.* placate, pacify, calm, soothe, ease, allay, quench. *The sandwich appeased her hunger.* **Ant.** irritate, aggravate, provoke.

appendix *n.* supplement, addition, postscript, attachment. *This dictionary has an appendix which lists computer terms.*

appetite *n.* hunger, craving, desire, taste, want, need. *He hasn't been able to control his appetite for sweets.* **Ant.** aversion, revulsion, repugnance.

appetizing *adj.* appealing, inviting, tempting, tantalizing, attractive. *Boiled fish and cabbage soup is not very appetizing.* **Ant.** unappetizing, unattractive, repugnant.

applaud *vb.* praise, acclaim, compliment, commend, approve. *We all applauded her decision to look for a better job.* **Ant.** criticize, condemn, ridicule.

applause *n.* clapping, ovation, praise, acclaim, accolades. *After the opera was over, the audience's applause lasted for quite some time.* **Ant.** booing, hissing, denunciation.

appliance *n.* apparatus, implement, equipment, device, fixture. *Stoves and refrigerators are examples of kitchen appliances.*

applicable *adj.* relevant, pertinent, suitable, appropriate, fitting. *Though her idea has merit, it isn't really applicable to our problem.* **Ant.** inapplicable, inappropriate.

application *n.* **1.** use, purpose, function, relevance, pertinence. *Her new invention doesn't have any practical applications.* **2.** request, requisition, petition, form. *He has submitted his application for a driver's license.*

apply *vb.* **1.** use, utilize, employ, exercise, administer. *The accident was her first chance to apply her knowledge of first aid.* **2.** put, lay, spread, rub, deposit, smear. *He applied two coats of varnish to his snowshoes.* **3.** refer, pertain, relate, involve, concern. *This law applies to everyone.* **4.** devote, dedicate, give, assign, commit. *She applied herself wholeheartedly to her new job.*

appoint *vb.* designate, select, assign, place, name, nominate. *He has been appointed to temporarily fill the vacant congressional seat.* **Ant.** dismiss, discharge.

appointment *n.* **1.** assignment, designation, placement, selection, nomination. *She received an appointment to the Supreme Court.* **2.** engagement, meeting, booking, date. *He has a doctor's appointment this afternoon.*

appreciate *vb.* **1.** realize, understand, comprehend, recognize, perceive. *He doesn't appreciate how much trouble he's caused.* **2.** value, esteem, prize, admire, honor, cherish. *It's difficult to work for someone who doesn't appreciate your efforts.* **Ant. 1.** misunderstand, misjudge. **2.** dislike, disdain, scorn.

appreciation *n.* **1.** gratitude, thankfulness, thanks, gratefulness. *She expressed her appreciation for all the help she'd received..* **2.** awareness, understanding, comprehension, realization, sensitivity. *That uneducated man has no appreciation of the finer things in life.* **Ant. 1.** ingratitude, ungratefulness. **2.** disregard, ignorance.

approach *vb.* **1.** approximate, equal, resemble, parallel, border. *His writing talent approaches that of Hemingway.* **2.** near, reach, gain, achieve, make. *The car slowed down as it approached town.* **3.** begin, start, commence, undertake, enter. *She approached her new job with a strong desire to succeed.* *–n.* **4.** method, procedure, system, manner, style. *He pioneered a new approach for the treatment of disease.* **5.** access, entry, route, entrance, passage. *Heavy snowfall blocked all approaches to the remote village.* **Ant. 1.** differ, diverge. **2.** recede, retreat, withdraw. **3.** finish, conclude, end. **5.** exit, outlet.

appropriate *adj.* **1.** suitable, proper, fitting, applicable, correct. *The invitation stated that appropriate attire was required.* *–vb.* **2.** confiscate, seize, commandeer, steal, take. *The ruthless dictator appropriated the private holdings of his enemies.* **3.** allocate, assign, allot, disburse, authorize. *The town council appropriated funds for construction of a new library.* **Ant. 1.** inappropriate, unfitting, unsuitable. **2.** return, relinquish, surrender. **3.** withhold, misappropriate.

approval *n.* **1.** admiration, acceptance, respect, favor, praise. *She worked hard to win her employer's approval.* **2.** permission, consent, authorization, sanction, validation. *She needs her father's approval before she can use the family car.* **Ant. 1.** disapproval, dissatisfaction. **2.** disapproval, prohibition.

approve *vb.* **1.** appreciate, like, respect, praise, commend, value. *I approve your choice of music.* **2.** permit, allow, condone, support, uphold, sanction. *His parents don't approve of his working during the school year.* **Ant. 1.** disapprove, dislike, criticize. **2.** disapprove, disallow.

approximate *adj.* **1.** estimated, rough, comparable, near, inexact. *The approximate time is two o'clock.* –*vb.* **2.** estimate, judge, gauge, reckon, compute. *She asked the mechanic to approximate the cost of repairs.* **Ant. 1.** exact, precise, accurate.

approximately *adv.* about, roughly, almost, nearly, around. *This test will take approximately one hour to complete.* **Ant.** exactly, precisely.

aptitude *n.* gift, talent, ability, capability, flair, capacity. *This test will measure your scholastic aptitude.*

arbitrary *adj.* subjective, whimsical, capricious, unreasonable, irrational, inconsistent. *His business failed because he was prone to making arbitrary decisions.* **Ant.** objective, prudent, consistent.

archaic *adj.* old-fashioned, obsolete, outdated, ancient, antiquated. *Now that we're in the computer age, typewriters seem almost archaic.* **Ant.** new, modern, current.

arduous *adj.* difficult, trying, exhausting, fatiguing, rigorous. *Her proposed climb of Mt. Everest will be an arduous undertaking.* **Ant.** easy, effortless, simple.

area *n.* **1.** expanse, extent, stretch, space, scope. *Our town covers an area of five square miles.* **2.** region, territory, terrain, district, zone. *Bears live in wilderness areas.* **3.** field, sphere, realm, domain. *That does not fall within my area of expertise.*

argue *vb.* **1.** quarrel, dispute, feud, disagree, haggle, bicker. *The children argued over whose turn it was to do the dishes.* **2.** assert, maintain, plead, discuss, debate. *She argued that the city should build a shelter for homeless people.* **Ant. 1.** agree, concur, concede.

argument *n.* **1.** quarrel, altercation, feud, dispute, disagreement. *When the referee called a foul, one of the players got into an argument with him.* **2.** case, grounds, reason, evidence, justification. *He doesn't have a valid argument to support his claim that the city should adopt a mass-transit system.* **Ant. 1.** agreement, harmony, unanimity.

arid *adj.* dry, parched, waterless, withered, barren, sterile. *Without irrigation, you can't grow crops on arid land.* **Ant.** moist, wet, damp, fertile.

arise *vb.* rise, emerge, appear, originate, begin, start. *Misunderstandings can arise when people don't communicate properly.* **Ant.** sink, cease, end, disappear.

arm *n.* **1.** limb, branch, projection, extension, appendage. *Please don't sit on that chair's arm.* **2.** weapon, armament, ordnance, firearm, gun, ammunition. *Some people would like to see military arms turned into plowshares.* –*vb.* **3.** prepare, protect, strengthen, fortify, equip, outfit. *She armed herself with an umbrella before venturing out into the storm.*

army *n.* force, troop, legion, host, horde, swarm, throng. *An army of locusts descended on the unlucky farmer's field.*

aroma *n.* fragrance, scent, smell, odor. *The aroma of a pie baking in the oven made my mouth water.* **Ant.** stink, stench, reek.

around *prep.* about, approximately, roughly, near. *I will be there around nine o'clock.*

arouse *vb.* awaken, waken, rouse, stir, excite, stimulate. *Her strange story aroused my curiosity.* **Ant.** settle, stifle, repress.

arrange *vb.* **1.** place, order, group, position, organize. *He arranges his books according to subject matter.* **2.** plan, prepare, schedule, design, devise. *She arranged a picnic for all her employees.* **Ant. 1.** disorder, disorganize, disarrange.

arrangement *n.* **1.** order, array, pattern, layout, setup, system. *She devised an unusual arrangement for her coin collection.* **2.** plan, preparation, provision, reservation. *Father made all the arrangements for our vacation.*

arrest *vb.* **1.** apprehend, capture, catch, seize, detain. *Police arrested two suspects in the recent robbery.* **2.** stop, stay, check, halt, obstruct, delay. *Radiation therapy should arrest the growth of your tumor.* –*n.* **3.** capture, apprehension, detention, seizure, restraint. *Police announced the arrest of a major drug dealer.* **Ant. 1.** release, free, liberate. **2.** encourage, continue.

arrival *n.* coming, appearance, entrance, advent, approach. *We eagerly awaited the arrival of my sister's plane.* **Ant.** departure, leaving, withdrawal.

arrive *vb.* reach, attain, enter, come, approach, near. *She arrived at work ten minutes late.*

arrogant *adj.* haughty, presumptuous, pretentious, conceited, proud, egotistical. *His arrogant attitude made him quite unpopular.* **Ant.** modest, humble, unassuming.

art *n.* **1.** artwork, painting, drawing, engraving, etching. *He invited us over to view his collection of wilderness art.* **2.** skill, talent, craft, technique, knowledge. *She has mastered the art of making people feel welcome.*

article *n.* **1.** object, item, piece, thing, element. *This store carries a variety of religious articles.* **2.** composition, essay, story, feature, theme. *He makes his living writing magazine articles.*

artificial *adj.* fake, phony, false, unreal, unnatural. *This ring is made with artificial diamonds.* **Ant.** real, genuine, authentic.

artisan *n.* craftsman, technician, handicraftsman, artificer, artist. *The local crafts fair displayed the works of numerous artisans.*

artist *n.* **1.** painter, sculptor, photographer, writer, singer, composer. *Our museum will be displaying the work of a local artist.* **2.** master, professional, pro, expert, genius. *He's a real artist when it comes to making up excuses.* **Ant. 2.** amateur, novice, beginner.

ascend *vb.* climb, mount, scale, rise, advance. *A priest ascended the steps to the altar.* **Ant.** descend, fall, drop.

ascent *n.* climb, climbing, scaling, mounting, surmounting. *Their ascent of Mt. McKinley took three weeks.* **Ant.** descent.

ashamed *adj.* embarrassed, humiliated, chagrined, mortified, uneasy. *You should be ashamed to wear such sloppy attire to work.* **Ant.** unashamed, proud, honored.

ask *vb.* **1.** question, query, quiz, inquire, interrogate. *The new student had to ask for directions to her classroom.* **2.** request, seek, beg, plead, implore. *She asked him to stop smoking in her presence.* **3.** invite, summon, bid, beckon. *He asked her to dinner.* **Ant. 1.** answer, respond, reply.

asleep *adj.* sleeping, dozing, napping, slumbering, dormant. *The house was quiet because everyone was asleep.* **Ant.** awake, up, active.

aspect *n.* **1.** look, appearance, manner, bearing, demeanor. *She does not like to hike in that forest because of its gloomy aspect.* **2.** facet, side, angle, phase, feature, point. *Have you analyzed all aspects of the problem?*

aspire *vb.* desire, want, wish, crave, yearn, seek. *He aspires to be a famous actor.*

assassin *n.* killer, murderer, slayer, executioner, triggerman. *An assassin was responsible for the death of Martin Luther King, Jr.*

assassinate *vb.* kill, murder, slay, execute, liquidate. *Terrorists assassinated our ambassador.*

assault *n.* **1.** attack, onslaught, offensive, rush, storming. *The goblin army was routed when the elves made their assault.* –*vb.* **2.** attack, rush, storm, raid, strike, charge. *An army of dwarves assaulted the goblins' last stronghold.*

Ant. 1. retreat, withdrawal. **2.** retreat, retire, withdraw.

assemble *vb.* **1.** gather, collect, accumulate, congregate, meet. *A crowd began to assemble at the accident site.* **2.** put together, fabricate, make, construct, manufacture. *It took him all day to assemble the model airplane.* **Ant. 1.** scatter, disperse, disband. **2.** disassemble, dismantle.

assembly *n.* gathering, meeting, grouping, rally, convention. *Our principal will speak at tomorrow's assembly.* **Ant.** separation, dispersion.

assert *vb.* affirm, declare, announce, proclaim, swear. *Despite his team's recent loss, he still asserts that they're the best.* **Ant.** deny, refute, disavow.

assertion *n.* claim, avowal, declaration, statement, proclamation. *It's foolish to make assertions that you can't support.* **Ant.** denial, contradiction.

assertive *adj.* forceful, aggressive, insistent, forward, overbearing. *She's so assertive she won't take "no" for an answer.* **Ant.** timid, hesitant, shy.

asset *n.* **1.** advantage, benefit, strength, blessing, resource. *Her strong arm is a great asset when it comes to playing tennis.* **2.** property, holdings, possessions, belongings, wealth, riches. *His savings account is just one of his numerous assets.* **Ant. 1.** disadvantage, liability, drawback.

assign *vb.* **1.** distribute, dispense, give, allocate, allot. *Her students think she assigns too much homework.* **2.** appoint, designate, name, nominate, delegate. *He was assigned to serve on the personnel committee.*

assignment *n.* responsibility, duty, task, chore, job. *I can't go out because I have homework assignments from three different classes.*

assist *vb.* help, aid, support, further, advance. *She assisted him with his homework.* **Ant.** hinder, impede, hamper.

assistance *n.* help, aid, support, cooperation, backing. *He wouldn't have been able to finish the book without her assistance.* **Ant.** hindrance, opposition, resistance.

assistant *n.* **1.** aide, helper, attendant, subordinate, associate. *The manager hired an assistant because his store was getting very busy.* –*adj.* **2.** helping, aiding, assisting, accessory, attendant. *She was excited to get a job as an assistant editor.*

associate *vb.* **1.** relate, connect, identify, attach, combine. *Most people associate Thanksgiving with turkey dinners.* **2.** socialize, mingle, mix, accompany. *I don't like the people you associate with.* –*n.* **3.** partner, colleague, confederate, peer, co-worker. *She took her business associates out to lunch yesterday.* **Ant. 1.** separate, divide, divorce.

association *n.* **1.** organization, alliance, syndicate, society, party. *He's a member of an association for screenwriters.* **2.** companionship, friendship, acquaintance, fellowship, intimacy. *My parents don't approve of my association with you.*

assorted *adj.* various, varied, mixed, miscellaneous, diverse. *This sofa is available in assorted color combinations.* **Ant.** identical, uniform, similar.

assortment *n.* variety, mixture, collection, selection, array. *This hardware store carries a large assortment of tools.*

assume *vb.* **1.** presume, suppose, postulate, suspect, infer. *His boss assumed he'd be at work on time.* **2.** adopt, embrace, acquire, take, undertake. *She assumed his responsibilities after he was fired.* **Ant. 1.** know, prove. **2.** renounce, abandon, relinquish.

assumption *n.* presumption, belief, supposition, conjecture, surmise. *He bought the used television on the assumption that it worked.*

assurance *n.* pledge, vow, oath, promise, guarantee. *She gave me her assurance that she would repay the loan.*

assure *vb.* reassure, promise, pledge, affirm, guarantee. *The mechanic assured us that our car would be ready by noon.* **Ant.** deny, refute, question.

astonish *vb.* amaze, surprise, astound, startle, stun, dazzle. *She was astonished to learn she had just won the lottery.*

astonishing *adj.* amazing, surprising, astounding, startling, impressive. *He has the astonishing ability to recall everything he reads.* **Ant.** ordinary, routine, expected.

astonishment *n.* amazement, surprise, wonder, shock, bewilderment. *We were filled with astonishment as we watched the daredevil perform.* **Ant.** apathy, indifference, boredom.

astound *vb.* astonish, amaze, surprise, startle, stun. *The Wright brothers astounded the whole world with their first airplane flight.*

astute *adj.* sharp, shrewd, keen, clever, canny. *She got her wealth by making some very astute investments.* **Ant.** dumb, naive, stupid, unintelligent.

athletic *adj.* robust, vigorous, strong, muscular, sturdy. *His athletic body is the result of daily exercise.* **Ant.** frail, feeble, weak.

atmosphere *n.* **1.** air, sky, heavens. *Scientists hope to establish a space station well beyond Earth's atmosphere.* **2.** feeling, mood, tone, character, spirit. *This restaurant has a cozy atmosphere.*

atrocious *adj.* horrible, terrible, dreadful, evil, cruel, brutal. *The Nazis were guilty of committing atrocious crimes.* **Ant.** good, kind, benevolent.

atrocity *n.* outrage, horror, brutality, cruelty, crime. *The world was stunned by the news of the terrorist's atrocity.*

attach *vb.* **1.** join, connect, secure, fasten, add. *Please attach this donor's certificate to your driver's license.* **2.** bind, tie, attract, captivate, enamor. *The boy is very attached to his puppy.* **Ant. 1.** detach, unfasten, disconnect.

attachment *n.* **1.** accessory, addition, supplement, extension, extra. *Her new computer has space for a hard disk and other attachments.* **2.** bond, tie, devotion, love, fondness, affection. *He has a strong attachment to his grandfather.* **Ant. 2.** hatred, dislike, indifference.

attack *vb.* **1.** assault, charge, storm, rush, raid. *A band of Indians attacked the wagon train.* **2.** criticize, denounce, censure, revile, berate. *Congress attacked the president's stand on foreign policy.* *–n.* **3.** assault, offensive, onslaught, charge, invasion. *The soldiers were nervous be-* cause they were expecting an enemy attack. **4.** spasm, fit, seizure, stroke, disease. *Exercise and proper diet are the best ways to prevent heart attacks.* **Ant. 1.** retreat, retire, withdraw. **2.** defend, uphold, support. **3.** retreat, withdrawal, defense.

attain *vb.* achieve, reach, acquire, gain, win, accomplish. *Van Gogh did not attain great fame as an artist until after his death.* **Ant.** lose, forfeit, miss.

attainment *n.* achievement, accomplishment, acquirement, realization, success, skill, talent. *Proficiency in foreign languages is just one of her numerous attainments.*

attempt *vb.* **1.** strive, endeavor, try, seek, venture, struggle. *She will attempt to swim the English Channel next week.* *–n.* **2.** try, effort, trial, attack, endeavor, undertaking. *His attempt to climb Mt. Everest was unsuccessful.*

attend *vb.* **1.** go to, be present at, visit, frequent. *She can't go on vacation because she has to attend summer school.* **2.** serve, tend, care for, wait on, minister to. *The paramedics attended to the most critical patients first.* **Ant. 1.** miss, be absent. **2.** ignore, neglect, disregard.

attendant *n.* servant, aide, assistant, helper. *He has a part-time job as a gas-station attendant.*

attention *n.* heed, notice, observance, regard, concentration. *This lecture will require everyone's full attention.* **Ant.** inattention, disregard, neglect.

attentive *adj.* observant, heedful, mindful, alert, watchful. *Please try to be more attentive when I speak to you.* **Ant.** inattentive, unobservant, heedless.

attire *vb.* **1.** dress, clothe, array, bedeck, outfit. *The queen was attired in a luxurious gown.* **2.** clothing, garments, apparel, outfit, costume. *The soldiers wore standard military attire.*

attitude *n.* mood, disposition, temperament, outlook, perspective. *His failing grades can be attributed to his poor attitude.*

attract *vb.* draw, pull, lure, catch, invite, entice. *Her odd behavior attracted everyone's attention.* **Ant.** repel, repulse, rebuff.

attraction *n.* appeal, allure, lure, bait, draw, fascination, charm. *The Grand Canyon is Arizona's biggest tourist attraction.* **Ant.** repulsion, revulsion.

attractive *adj.* appealing, alluring, enticing, inviting, pleasing, pretty, handsome. *He certainly looks attractive in his new suit.* **Ant.** unattractive, unappealing, plain, ugly.

audience *n.* **1.** spectators, onlookers, listeners, gallery, house. *The audience was restless before the concert began.* **2.** interview, reception, consultation, meeting, hearing. *Sir Lancelot could meet with King Arthur without having to formally request an audience.*

augment *vb.* increase, enlarge, extend, raise, expand, swell. *She augmented her income by taking on an additional job.* **Ant.** decrease, lessen, diminish.

austere *adj.* severe, rigid, strict, stern, harsh, stiff, formal. *Her austere look means we're in trouble.* **Ant.** cheerful, friendly, lenient.

authentic *adj.* genuine, real, true, actual, legitimate, pure. *An authentic first edition of any Dickens novel is incredibly valuable.* **Ant.** fake, imitation, unreal, false.

author *n.* writer, novelist, poet, creator, originator. *His dream is to become a best-selling author.*

authority *n.* **1.** command, power, influence, rule, domination. *I have to bow to my father's authority.* **2.** expert, master, genius, wizard, specialist. *She's an authority when it comes to discussing politics.* **3.** right, privilege, permission, approval, authorization. *Who gave you authority to use my computer?* **4.** police, sheriff, lawmakers. *She notified the authorities when she discovered her car was missing.* **Ant. 3.** refusal, denial, prohibition.

authorize *vb.* approve, permit, allow, entitle, enable. *The bank's manager is the only one authorized to grant loans.* **Ant.** prevent, disallow, disapprove.

authorization *n.* authority, approval, permission, privilege, right. *The lawyer requested authorization to study certain police files.* **Ant.** refusal, denial, ban, prohibition.

autograph *n.* **1.** signature, inscription, endorsement. *He collects the autographs of famous ballplayers.* –*vb.* **2.** sign, inscribe, endorse, dedicate. *Would you mind autographing your book for me?*

automatic *adj.* **1.** self-operating, self-acting, self-moving. *Her new camera is completely automatic.* **2.** involuntary, unplanned, instinctive, spontaneous, uncontrolled. *His reaction was automatic when the dog ran in front of his car.* **Ant. 1.** manual. **2.** deliberate, planned, intentional.

available *adj.* obtainable, accessible, reachable, attainable, handy. *Since the restaurant had no available tables, we had to wait.* **Ant.** unavailable, unobtainable, inaccessible.

avenge *vb.* revenge, vindicate, retaliate, repay, punish. *Rather than seeking to avenge injustices, try a little forgiveness.* **Ant.** forgive, pardon, excuse.

avenue *n.* **1.** street, road, boulevard, thoroughfare. *The village's avenues are paved with brick.* **2.** route, means, path, course, road. *Hard work is the best avenue to success.*

average *adj.* **1.** standard, normal, typical, ordinary, usual. *The average temperature of the human body is 98.6 degrees.* **2.** mean, middle, median, medium. *She ran the marathon at an average speed of six miles per hour.* –*n.* **3.** mean, median, par, norm, standard. *His score on the test was close to the national average.* **Ant. 1.** exceptional, extraordinary, unusual.

aversion *n.* repugnance, antipathy, hatred, revulsion, dislike. *She has an aversion to horror movies.* **Ant.** liking, attraction, fondness.

avoid *vb.* evade, elude, dodge, escape, duck, shun. *Let's go to an afternoon matinee in order to avoid the evening crowds.* **Ant.** face, confront, meet.

awaken *vb.* wake, awake, rouse, arouse, stir. *We were awakened by someone pounding on the front door.*

award *vb.* **1.** bestow, give, grant, accord, render. *The court awarded the woman custody of her children.* –*n.* **2.** reward, prize, trophy, decoration, citation. *The firefighter received an award for bravery.* **Ant. 1.** withhold, deny, refuse.

aware *adj.* mindful, conscious, informed, apprised, knowing. *Are you aware of the dangers of drug addiction?* **Ant.** unaware, unfamiliar, uninformed.

awful *adj.* dreadful, terrible, horrible, appalling, bad, poor. *That was an awful thing to say to your friend.* **Ant.** delightful, wonderful, pleasant.

awfully *adv.* very, exceedingly, extremely, greatly, terribly. *I'm awfully glad to see you.*

awkward *adj.* **1.** clumsy, inept, ungraceful, uncoordinated, bungling, ungainly. *He made an awkward attempt to catch the ball.* **2.** embarrassing, disconcerting, difficult, ticklish, delicate. *We both felt uncomfortable during the awkward pause in our conversation.* **3.** unwieldy, unmanageable, cumbersome, unhandy. *The heavy hammer felt awkward to the small boy.* **Ant. 1.** graceful, coordinated. **2–3.** pleasant, comfortable, easy.

baby *n.* **1.** infant, newborn, toddler, tot, babe. *The baby slept soundly in its crib.* *–vb.* **2.** pamper, spoil, coddle, overprotect, indulge. *Everyone babied the youngest member of our family.* **Ant. 1.** adult, grownup. **2.** deny, neglect.

back *n.* **1.** backside, reverse, rear, posterior, tail, spine. *What's on the back of your T-shirt?* *–adj.* **2.** behind, rearmost, hind, end, posterior. *You may exit through the back door.* *–vb.* **3.** reverse, withdraw, recede, retreat. *She backed the car out of the driveway.* **4.** support, favor, promote, encourage, endorse. *Who will you back in next month's election?* **Ant. 1.** front, anterior. **2.** front, near, fore. **3.** forward, advance, progress. **4.** oppose, fight, undermine.

background *n.* **1.** setting, environment, landscape, backdrop. *He helped build the background for the school play.* **2.** experience, preparation, upbringing, rearing. *The personnel manager questioned applicants about their educational background.* **Ant. 1.** foreground, forefront. **2.** prospects, future.

bad *adj.* **1.** wicked, immoral, naughty, sinful, corrupt, evil. *The bad guys in movies often wear black clothes.* **2.** defective, faulty, incorrect, poor. *The mechanic fixed the car's bad brakes.* **3.** foul, decayed, rotten, spoiled, polluted. *I bit into a bad apple.* **4.** harmful, destructive, hurtful, deadly. *Large cities are often criticized for their bad air.* **5.** severe, dangerous, serious, critical, extreme. *The plane was delayed by a bad storm.* **6.** sorry, regretful, upset, apologetic. *She felt bad about having lied to him.* **7.** sick, unwell, weak, ill, indisposed, poor, miserable. *He stayed home because he was feeling bad.* **Ant. 1.** good, moral, virtuous. **2.** good, perfect. **3.** good, fresh, edible. **4.** helpful, healthy. **5.** trivial, minor, insignificant. **6.** pleased, unashamed. **7.** well, healthy.

badger *vb.* harass, pester, bother, torment, tease, annoy, irritate. *He badgered me to return his book.* **Ant.** comfort, calm, soothe.

bait *n.* **1.** lure, inducement, enticement, attraction, temptation. *Cheese makes a good bait for catching mice.* *–vb.* **2.** provoke, tease, goad, annoy, harass, tempt, lure. *Reporters baited the actor with personal questions.* **Ant. 2.** soothe, calm, humor, flatter.

balance *vb.* **1.** stabilize, equalize, steady, match. *The president tried to balance the nation's budget.* *–n.* **2.** equilibrium, poise, stability. *The gymnast lost her balance and fell to the ground.* **3.** remainder, residue, excess, difference, remains. *She will pay five dollars today and the balance tomorrow.* **Ant. 1.** topple, upset. **2.** imbalance, shakiness.

bald *adj.* bare, hairless, barren, smooth, exposed. *The Buddhist monk kept his head bald by shaving off his hair.* **Ant.** covered, hairy, unshorn, bristly.

ballot *n.* **1.** vote, election, poll, polling, referendum. *The class president was elected by secret ballot.* **2.** ticket, slate, candidate list. *Three people had their names on the ballot for treasurer.*

ban *n.* **1.** prohibition, restriction, injunction, embargo, taboo. *Most countries have a ban on hunting whales.* *–vb.* **2.** forbid, disallow, prohibit, outlaw, censor. *Many dangerous chemicals are banned from being used on food crops.* **Ant. 1.** permission, sanction, approval. **2.** allow, endorse.

bandit *n.* robber, outlaw, brigand, thief, hoodlum, gangster, pirate. *Bandits robbed the stagecoach.*

banish *vb.* exile, outlaw, deport, eject, expel. *The queen banished the evil sorcerer from her realm.* **Ant.** welcome, embrace, receive.

banquet *n.* feast, dinner, meal, regale, spread. *The king held a banquet for his knights.* **Ant.** snack, fasting.

bar *n.* **1.** rod, rail, spar, grating, pole. *The prison had bars on its windows.* **2.** tavern, pub, saloon, alehouse. *The bar sold whiskey and beer.* **3.** ingot, slab, block. *Bars of gold were stored in the bank's vault.* **4.** barrier, hindrance, obstacle, obstruction, barricade. *The ship hit a sand bar.* –*vb.* **5.** block, stop, curb, restrict, lock. *The school barred its students from leaving campus.* **Ant. 4.** aid, assistance, opening. **5.** admit, allow, unlock.

barbarian *n.* outlander, savage, vandal, brute, primitive. *Rome claimed to have civilized the barbarians of faraway lands.*

barbaric *adj.* uncivilized, uncultured, coarse, brutish, savage, cruel. *The pirates acted in the most barbaric manner.* **Ant.** civilized, cultured, refined, enlightened.

bare *adj.* **1.** naked, stripped, nude, uncovered, undressed. *The nurse gave him a shot in his bare behind.* **2.** empty, blank, barren, vacant, void. *She found nothing to eat in the bare cupboard.* **3.** simple, plain, undisguised, pure, basic. *Sherlock Holmes was interested in only the bare facts of a case.* –*vb.* **4.** uncover, expose, show, reveal. *Taking off his cap, he bared his head to the rain.* **Ant. 1.** clothed, covered. **2.** filled, stocked. **3.** disguised, embellished. **4.** cover, conceal.

barely *adv.* just, scarcely, hardly, only. *She was barely tall enough to reach the cookie jar.* **Ant.** amply, profusely, sufficiently.

bargain *n.* **1.** agreement, understanding, pact, contract, treaty. *The suspect made a bargain in which he pleaded guilty to a lesser crime.* **2.** discount, reduction, deal, buy, steal. *There were many good bargains at the swap meet.* –*vb.* **3.** barter, negotiate, haggle, deal, dicker. *The president bargained for release of the hostages.*

barren *adj.* bare, dead, empty, depleted, desolate, sterile, unfruitful. *The farmer was unable to grow crops on the barren land.* **Ant.** lush, fertile, fruitful.

barrier *n.* blockade, obstruction, obstacle, barricade, impediment, stop, bar. *The Great Wall of China was built as a barrier against nomadic barbarians.* **Ant.** passage, opening, entrance.

barter *vb.* trade, swap, bargain, exchange, negotiate. *I bartered my sandwich for her apple.*

base *n.* **1.** foundation, foot, stand, bottom, substructure. *I had my picture taken at the base of the Statue of Liberty.* **2.** station, post, headquarters, garrison, camp. *Scientists hope to establish a base on the moon.* –*vb.* **3.** establish, ground, root, form, rest. *The writer based her tale of King Arthur on historical facts.* –*adj.* **4.** coarse, vile, low, immoral, vulgar, obscene. *People were offended by his base jokes.* **Ant. 1.** top, pinnacle, summit. **3.** invalidate, uproot. **4.** noble, honorable, exalted.

baseless *adj.* unsupported, groundless, unjustified, unfounded, unreasonable. *The judge refused to accept the baseless accusations against the defendant.* **Ant.** supported, justified, reasonable.

bashful *adj.* reserved, shy, sheepish, timid, demure. *The bashful child peeked at us from behind a couch.* **Ant.** forward, outgoing, brazen.

basic *adj.* fundamental, rudimentary, elementary, essential. *We will cover basic vocabulary in our first-year Spanish class.* **Ant.** advanced, additional, supplementary.

battery *n.* **1.** electric cell, storage cell. *Did you buy batteries for the toy?* **2.** series, cluster, set, group, batch. *The applicant had to take a battery of tests.* **3.** beating, attack, maiming, onslaught, mayhem. *He was arrested for assault and battery.* **Ant. 2.** scattering, individual. **3.** kindness, gentleness.

battle *n.* **1.** fight, conflict, war, skirmish, confrontation. *The Germans fought the Americans in a battle for control of the Rhine River.* –*vb.* **2.** fight, clash, skirmish, feud, argue. *Two students battled for the lead in the school play.* **Ant. 1.** peace, armistice, truce. **2.** agree, concur.

beach *n.* seacoast, coast, shore, bank, seashore, sand. *Waves washed driftwood up onto the beach.*

beacon *n.* signal, light, beam, guide, lighthouse, radar. *The beacon warned ships to avoid the shallow reef.*

beam *n.* **1.** rafter, timber, brace, girder, support. *The ceiling of our cabin is constructed with open beams.* **2.** ray, shaft, streak, flash, stream. *A beam of sunlight broke through the clouds.* –*vb.* **3.** radiate, broadcast, transmit, gleam, shine. *The television program was beamed to us via satellite.* **Ant. 3.** retain, withhold, absorb.

bear *vb.* **1.** tolerate, endure, suffer, stand, withstand. *He couldn't bear hearing such terrible sounds.* **2.** carry, haul, transport, bring, convey. *The hotel porter bore the luggage to our room.* **3.** produce, deliver, generate, make, form. *The apple trees bore fruit.* **4.** display, exhibit, show, possess. *My school diploma bears the principal's signature.* **5.** push, thrust, strain, drive, press. *You'll have to bear down on the saw to cut through that thick board.*

bearing *n.* **1.** carriage, posture, conduct, demeanor, poise. *The princess had a regal bearing.* **2.** relevance, significance, reference, connection. *The judge claimed that the defendant's wealth had no bearing on the outcome of the trial.* **Ant. 2.** insignificance, irrelevance.

beast *n.* **1.** animal, mammal, creature. *The donkey is sometimes called a beast of burden.* **2.** monster, brute, savage, ogre. *"Beauty and the Beast" is a famous fairy tale.*

beastly *adj.* brutish, loathsome, cruel, repulsive, horrid, nasty. *We've had some beastly weather.* **Ant.** appealing, humane, cultured.

beat *vb.* **1.** hit, pound, batter, thrash, pummel. *He was robbed and beaten by a mugger.* **2.** whip, whisk, stir, mix. *Please beat the cookie dough.* **3.** defeat, win, overcome, conquer, vanquish. *Our team beat the opposing team by three points.* **4.** vibrate, pulse, pulsate, throb, tremble. *I could hear her heart beat.* *-n.* **5.** rhythm, cadence, meter, pulse, measure. *The audience clapped their hands to the beat of the music.* **Ant. 1.** fail, succumb, lose.

beautiful *adj.* gorgeous, enchanting, attractive, lovely, pretty, appealing. *These roses are beautiful.* **Ant.** ugly, hideous, unsightly, repulsive.

beckon *vb.* motion, summon, signal, hail, call, gesture. *The teacher beckoned me to come to her desk.*

become *vb.* turn into, emerge as, develop into, convert. *He became a werewolf when the moon was full.*

becoming *adj.* seemly, befitting, proper, appropriate, right. *That hairstyle is very becoming on you.* **Ant.** unbecoming, unsuitable, unflattering.

bedlam *n.* uproar, pandemonium, clamor, riot, turmoil, upheaval. *Bedlam erupted in the stadium when the home team lost.* **Ant.** peacefulness, order.

before *prep.* **1.** in advance of, prior to, previous to, ahead of. *Please take out the trash before dark.* *-adv.* **2.** previously, earlier, formerly, already. *He didn't want to go to the movie because he had seen it before.* **Ant. 1.** after, later than. **2.** after, behind.

beg *vb.* plead, implore, ask, entreat, beseech. *She begged her parents for a larger allowance.* **Ant.** insist, demand, order.

begin *vb.* start, commence, initiate, found, introduce, establish, launch. *She plans to begin a rock band.* **Ant.** stop, finish, end, terminate, abandon.

behavior *n.* conduct, attitude, actions, performance, manners. *She received a demerit for bad classroom behavior.*

behind *prep.* **1.** in back of, beyond, after, following. *The parking lot is behind the store.* *-adv.* **2.** after, following, in back of, in the rear of. *The students walked behind the museum guide.* **3.** late, slow, tardily, behindhand. *My watch is behind by one hour.* **Ant. 1–2.** before, in front of. **3.** early, ahead.

behold *vb.* see, observe, witness, view, notice. *Behold, the rabbit has disappeared.*

believe *vb.* accept, trust, affirm, hold, maintain. *She believes that life exists on other planets.* **Ant.** disbelieve, reject, doubt, question.

belligerent *adj.* unfriendly, hostile, argumentative, quarrelsome, warlike. *The United States considered Germany a belligerent nation during World War II.* **Ant.** friendly, peaceful, easygoing.

belongings *n.* property, possessions, effects, goods. *Students keep their belongings in lockers.*

below *adv.* beneath, underneath, under, lower, down. *We drove below the freeway overpass.* **Ant.** above, over, atop.

beneath *adv.* **1.** below, under, underneath, lower. *His car was buried beneath several feet of snow.* -*prep.* **2.** below, under, underneath, unbefitting. *The school's seniors felt cleaning the auditorium was beneath them.* **Ant. 1–2.** above, over.

beneficial *adj.* good, helpful, advantageous, useful, healthy. *Exercise is a beneficial activity.* **Ant.** harmful, bad, detrimental.

best *adj.* **1.** greatest, finest, unrivaled, top, superior. *My friend and I have the best treehouse in the neighborhood.* -*n.* **2.** finest, first, foremost, champion. *She is among the best in that field of medical research.* -*vb.* **3.** beat, defeat, conquer, surpass. *He thinks he can best me at a game of table tennis.* **Ant. 1–2.** worst, poorest.

bet *n.* **1.** wager, gamble, chance, stake, venture. *They made a bet on tomorrow's game.* -*vb.* **2.** gamble, wager, dare, challenge, risk. *She bet ten dollars that the spotted horse would win.*

betray *vb.* **1.** deceive, trick, forsake, desert, abandon. *The traitor betrayed her country by selling secret documents.* **2.** disclose, reveal, expose, divulge, show. *My father accidentally betrayed where he hid the candy.* **Ant. 1.** support, protect, guard. **2.** safeguard, guard.

better *adj.* **1.** preferable, improved, superior, finer. *She hopes to get a better grade on the next test.* **2.** greater, larger, bigger, longer. *He spent the better part of his vacation painting the house.* **3.** improving, recovering, healthier, stronger. *She's feeling better today.* -*vb.* **4.** enrich, advance, improve, strengthen, enhance. *He went to school to better himself.* **Ant. 1.** poorer, inferior, second-rate. **2.** lesser, smaller. **3.** weaker, sicker. **4.** downgrade, lessen.

between *prep.* among, within, amidst, amongst, betwixt. *The number five is between four and six.*

beware *vb.* mind, avoid, shun, heed, notice, watch. *Please beware the vicious dog next door.* **Ant.** disregard, ignore, overlook.

bewilder *vb.* daze, confuse, obscure, disorient, puzzle. *The foreign city bewildered him.* **Ant.** explain, inform, enlighten.

beyond *prep.* past, after, above, behind, farther on, yonder. *The store is just beyond the next intersection.*

bias *n.* **1.** preference, favoritism, prejudice, partiality, bent. *I have a bias for small pets like cats.* -*vb.* **2.** prejudice, predispose, influence, sway. *His fancy clothes biased the judges in his favor.* **Ant. 1.** fairness, impartiality.

bid *vb.* **1.** propose, offer, submit, venture. *She bid one million dollars for the famous painting.* **2.** instruct, charge, command, order, direct. *The teacher bid us to do our homework.* -*n.* **3.** proposal, proposition, offer, submittal. *That company made a bid on the new construction project.* **Ant. 2.** prohibit, withhold, forbid. **3.** retraction, withdrawal.

big *adj.* **1.** large, huge, immense, enormous, giant, massive, gigantic. *Alaska is a big state.* **2.** significant, important, serious, vital, momentous. *Tomorrow's game is a big one for our team.* **Ant. 1.** small, tiny, little. **2.** small, insignificant, unimportant.

bind *vb.* **1.** fasten, lash, constrict, tie, tether, secure. *He bound her sprained ankle with a bandage.* -*n.* **2.** dilemma, quandary, predicament, impasse, difficulty. *He found himself in a bind when his car broke down.* **Ant. 1.** loosen, untie, unfasten, free.

birth *n.* **1.** childbirth, delivery, breeding, reproduction. *The zoo announced the birth of a baby panda bear.* **2.** ancestry, heritage, descent, lineage, background. *The man claimed to be of aristocratic birth.* **3.** beginning, debut, start, genesis, origin. *The year 1776 marked the birth of the United States of America.* **Ant. 1.** death. **3.** end, finish, termination.

bite *vb.* **1.** chew, crunch, gnaw, snap, nibble. *Vampires are reputed to bite people's necks.* -*n.* **2.** sting, edge, punch, prickle, nip. *He commented on the weather's cold bite.* **3.** puncture, prick, injury, wound. *I bandaged the dog bite on her leg.* **4.** snack, mouthful, morsel, nibble. *I haven't had a bite to eat all day.*

bitter *adj.* **1.** stinging, harsh, tart, acid, biting. *He finds black coffee too bitter to drink.* **2.** resentful, hostile, angry, spiteful, sore. *The team members were bitter over their loss.* **Ant. 1.** mild, bland, sugary, sweet. **2.** forgiving, pleasant, joyful.

blade *n.* knife, razor, edged tool, cutter, point. *Early humans used stone blades for cutting.*

blame *n.* **1.** accusation, implication, reproach, fault, guilt. *She always receives the blame when things go wrong.* –*vb.* **2.** accuse, charge, fault, reprimand, reproach. *My brother blamed me for breaking the stereo.* **Ant. 1.** acquittal, exoneration, vindication. **2.** acquit, absolve.

blameless *adj.* guiltless, faultless, innocent, clean, clear, irreproachable. *The jury found the defendant blameless on all counts.* **Ant.** guilty, faulty.

bland *adj.* tasteless, dull, boring, uninteresting, flavorless, flat. *Many people think oatmeal is bland.* **Ant.** stimulating, exciting, zestful.

blank *adj.* **1.** bare, unfilled, clear, unmarked, barren. *Please get out a blank piece of paper for your essay.* **2.** empty, dull, vacant, expressionless. *She gave me a blank look when I asked for directions.* –*n.* **3.** void, emptiness, space, gap, hollowness. *We had to fill in the blanks with the correct answers.* **Ant. 1.** marked. **2.** sharp, attentive.

blast *vb.* **1.** explode, detonate, burst, erupt, demolish. *The bomb blasted a hole in the building.* –*n.* **2.** surge, gust, flurry, gale, blow. *A blast of cold air entered through the open window.* **3.** burst, explosion, eruption, detonation, discharge. *The bomb's blast could be heard for miles.*

blaze *vb.* **1.** flare up, flame, burn. *Rebellion blazed throughout the poverty-stricken country.* –*n.* **2.** shimmer, shine, glow, glare, flash. *A blaze of light drew our attention to the flying saucer.* **3.** burning, flames, fire, conflagration. *When the forest burned, the blaze could be seen miles away.*

bleak *adj.* grim, dismal, disheartening, barren, desolate. *My chances for doing well on tomorrow's test seem bleak.* **Ant.** promising, bright.

blemish *n.* **1.** flaw, imperfection, defect, blotch, discoloration, impurity. *Pimples left blemishes on my face.* –*vb.* **2.** mar, flaw, spoil, mark, spot. *The painting was blemished with water stains.* **Ant. 1.** purity, perfection, flawlessness. **2.** improve, perfect.

blend *vb.* **1.** combine, mingle, merge, mix, unite. *Blue and yellow blended together produce green.* –*n.* **2.** combination, mixture, compound, merger, mingling. *The punch was a blend of orange and pineapple juices.* **Ant. 1.** split, separate, divide. **2.** division, separation.

bless *vb.* anoint, sanctify, consecrate, dedicate, honor. *The priest blessed the temple after its construction.* **Ant.** curse, damn, blaspheme.

blight *n.* **1.** disease, affliction, decay, withering, scourge. *Blight ruined the farmer's crops.* –*vb.* **2.** ruin, spoil, contaminate, shrivel, wither. *The one mistake blighted the politician's career.* **Ant. 1.** bounty, blessing. **2.** foster, favor, benefit.

blind *adj.* **1.** unseeing, sightless, visionless, unsighted. *The blind man used a cane to cross the street.* **2.** unaware, ignorant, dense, naive, unknowing. *He was blind to her faults.* –*n.* **3.** cover, shade, screen, shield, concealment. *The deer hunter built a blind to conceal himself.* –*vb.* **4.** make sightless, daze, dazzle, stun. *She was blinded by his good looks and didn't notice his shortcomings.* **Ant. 1.** seeing, sighted. **2.** observant, aware.

bliss *n.* delight, ecstasy, happiness, joy, rapture, enchantment. *Our vacation in Hawaii was pure bliss.* **Ant.** grief, anguish, misery, depression.

blissful *adj.* pleasurable, enraptured, joyous, exhilarated, delighted, happy. *She spent a blissful day at the beach.* **Ant.** miserable, unhappy, distressful.

blizzard *n.* snowstorm, tempest, gale, storm, squall. *A blizzard trapped the Donner Party in the High Sierra.*

bloat *vb.* swell, enlarge, expand, stretch, inflate, distend. *Eating those three pizzas caused my stomach to bloat.* **Ant.** contract, wither, shrink, deflate.

block *vb.* **1.** interfere, impede, obstruct, prevent, stop. *A tall man sitting in the front blocked our view.* –*n.* **2.** square, bar, slab, chunk, brick. *They built the wall with cement blocks.* **3.** obstacle, barrier, barricade, hindrance, constraint. *Hair and dirt formed a block in our drainpipe.* **Ant.**

1. advance, unblock, open. **3.** passageway, entrance, opening.

blockade   *n.* barrier, obstacle, obstruction, hurdle, stoppage. *A naval blockade kept enemy ships from leaving the harbor.* **Ant.** access, opening, entry.

bloom   *vb.* **1.** blossom, flourish, flower, sprout, prosper. *Their friendship bloomed into love.* *-n.* **2.** flower, blossom, bud. *The gardener tended her blooms with care.* **Ant. 1.** shrivel, fade, wither.

blossom   *vb.* **1.** bloom, thrive, grow, flower, flourish. *The beginning violinist eventually blossomed into a virtuoso.* *-n.* **2.** flower, bud, bloom. *She stuck a lily blossom in her hair.* **Ant. 1.** wither, wilt, fade.

blow   *n.* **1.** smack, hit, punch, cuff, whack. *I received a strong blow to my leg when the bike ran into me.* **2.** shock, surprise, jolt, jar. *It came as quite a blow to learn I failed the test.* *-vb.* **3.** puff, exhale, expel, huff, breathe. *She blew air into the balloons.* **4.** sail, drift, flutter, fly, waft. *Several pieces of paper blew past us in the parking lot.* **5.** erupt, explode, detonate, burst. *People hurriedly left when they learned the volcano was about to blow.* **Ant. 2.** comfort, relief, pleasure. **3.** inhale.

bluff   *n.* **1.** fake, deception, lie, bragging, boast. *We discovered his threats were just a bluff.* **2.** crag, cliff, precipice, scarp. *The eagle built its nest high up on the bluff.* *-vb.* **3.** fool, deceive, trick, delude, mislead. *The robber bluffed the police into thinking she had a bomb.* **Ant. 1.** fact, truth, candor.

blunder   *n.* **1.** error, mistake, indiscretion, lapse, slip. *Buying the wrong kind of milk was a blunder on his part.* *-vb.* **2.** bungle, slip, stumble, stagger, flounder. *She blundered into a beehive.* **Ant. 1.** accomplishment, success, achievement.

blunt   *adj.* **1.** unsharpened, dull, edgeless, unpointed. *Her knife was too blunt to cut the rope.* **2.** frank, candid, tactless, abrupt, short, direct. *He was quite blunt in telling me he disliked my shirt.* *-vb.* **3.** dull, deaden, numb, stifle, impair, lessen. *Lack of sleep blunted our senses.* **Ant. 1.** sharp, pointed, edged. **2.** subtle, indirect, tactful. **3.** sharpen, excite, stimulate.

blur   *n.* **1.** smear, haze, blot, cloud, smudge. *The hummingbird flew by in a blur of color.* *-vb.* **2.** obscure, shroud, confuse, smear, cloud. *Wearing someone else's glasses can blur your vision.* **Ant. 1.** clarity. **2.** clarify, focus, define.

board   *n.* **1.** beam, plank, timber, slat. *Let's jump off the pool's diving board.* **2.** council, panel, committee, cabinet, directors. *The company's board voted to buy out their competitors.* **3.** meals, food, dinners, suppers, breakfasts. *Hotel prices in Europe usually include room and board.* *-vb.* **4.** enter, mount, embark. *Passengers were instructed to board the airplane.* **5.** quarter, house, lodge, accommodate, feed. *Host families boarded the foreign-exchange students for a month.* **Ant. 4.** depart, disembark, leave, vacate.

boast   *vb.* **1.** brag, gloat, swagger, flaunt, crow. *She boasted that she could run the mile in less than four minutes.* *-n.* **2.** brag, bragging, bravado, bluster. *We disbelieved his boast that he knew the famous rock star.* **Ant. 1.** disavow. **2.** disavowal.

boastful   *adj.* vain, conceited, pretentious, arrogant, cocky. *The boastful student said he was very rich.* **Ant.** humble, modest.

body   *n.* **1.** figure, frame, form, physique, build. *The model spent long hours trying to get his body in top condition.* **2.** corpse, carcass, cadaver, remains. *The body of the dead king was carried through the city.* **3.** group, assembly, society, council, organization. *The town council is our local governing body.* **Ant. 1.** spirit, soul, psyche, intellect.

boisterous   *adj.* noisy, rowdy, uproarious, loud, tumultuous, unrestrained, unruly. *It was a very boisterous party.* **Ant.** calm, quiet, restrained, tranquil.

bold   *adj.* **1.** fearless, brave, adventuresome, reckless, courageous. *The two bold girls spent the night in a haunted house.* **2.** vivid, bright, striking, strong, powerful. *One should never wash bold colors in bleach.* **Ant. 1.** fearful, cowardly, timid. **2.** dull, pale, colorless.

bolt   *n.* **1.** fastening, spike, rivet, pin, peg. *The shelf fell down when its restraining bolt broke.* **2.** flash, brand, missile, arrow, dart. *A bolt of lightning hit the tree.* *-vb.* **3.** run, rush, dash, sprint, flee. *Students bolted from class when the bell* *rang.* **4.** fasten, lock, latch, bar, secure. *She bolts the front door before going to sleep.* **Ant. 3.** stroll, ramble, saunter. **4.** unlock, unlatch, open.

bonus *n.* addition, reward, extra, benefit, gratuity. *The employees received bonuses for their excellent work.*

boom *n.* **1.** blast, bang, explosion, roar, report. *We heard the space shuttle's sonic boom.* **2.** improvement, upswing, growth, expansion, rise. *California experienced an economic boom during the Gold Rush.* *-vb.* **3.** resound, thunder, rumble, roar, reverberate. *A cannon shot boomed over the valley.* **4.** prosper, thrive, flourish, swell, advance. *Business boomed during the tourist season.* **Ant. 2.** slump, decline, recession. **4.** dwindle, fail, collapse.

boost *vb.* **1.** lift, raise, elevate, hoist, heft. *He boosted himself over the wall.* **2.** expand, increase, build up, develop, promote. *Hosting the Olympics helped to boost the local economy.* *-n.* **3.** raise, lift, hoist, heave, shove. *Will you give me a boost up?* **Ant. 1.** drop, lower. **2.** decrease, diminish, curtail, reduce.

booty *n.* pillage, spoils, loot, takings, plunder. *The raiders hid their booty on a desert island.*

bore *vb.* **1.** exhaust, tire, weary, fatigue. *The lecture bored me.* **2.** burrow, tunnel, gouge, mine, drill. *The termite bored its way into the tree trunk.* *-n.* **3.** nuisance, pest, bother, annoyance, irritation. *She found the self-centered actor to be a real bore.* **Ant. 1.** interest, intrigue, excite. **2.** fill, cap, plug.

boring *adj.* unexciting, tedious, wearisome, dull, monotonous, tiring. *He fell asleep during the boring movie.* **Ant.** exciting, amusing, arousing, delightful, thrilling.

borrow *vb.* obtain, get, appropriate, adopt, assume. *May I borrow your book?* **Ant.** lend, return.

boss *n.* **1.** manager, supervisor, director, executive, employer, administrator. *My boss scheduled me to work on Christmas Eve.* *-vb.* **2.** command, direct, order, control. *My older brother bosses me around when my parents leave.* **Ant. 1.** worker, employee, subordinate, helper. **2.** follow, obey.

bother *vb.* **1.** pester, aggravate, irritate, annoy, harass, disturb. *Noisy crickets bothered me all night.* *-n.* **2.** irritation, annoyance, problem, worry, vexation, nuisance. *It's too much of a bother to clean my room.* **Ant. 1.** please, placate, comfort. **2.** enjoyment, pleasure, ease.

bottom *n.* **1.** foot, underside, ground, base, foundation, underpart, lowest part. *Her friend waited for her at the bottom of the water slide.* **2.** rump, buttocks, posterior, behind. *He tripped and fell on his bottom.* *-adj.* **3.** ground, lowest, deepest, undermost. *The gift shop is on the bottom floor.* **Ant. 1.** summit, top, peak, pinnacle. **3.** upper, highest.

bound *adj.* **1.** secured, wrapped, tied, roped, shackled. *The captive was found bound and gagged.* **2.** sure, fated, destined, certain. *Your lie is bound to create more problems.* **3.** committed, obligated, beholden, compelled, obliged. *The renegade felt bound to no laws.* *-vb.* **4.** spring, jump, bounce, leap, skip. *She bounded over the mud puddle.* **5.** enclose, restrict, encircle, limit, delimit. *A fence bounds the baseball field.* *-n.* **6.** boundary, perimeter, border, extremity. *The river marks the bounds of our property.* **7.** leap, hop, spring, jump, bounce. *Superman can leap over tall buildings in a single bound.* **Ant. 1.** unfastened, loose, untied. **3.** free, released. **4.** hobble, shuffle, crawl.

boundary *n.* rim, border, edge, frontier, perimeter, fringe, frame, extent. *The fence marks the boundary of our property.*

boundless *adj.* infinite, limitless, endless, immense, perpetual, immeasurable. *Some astronomers believe the universe is boundless.* **Ant.** limited, bounded, restricted, narrow.

bow *n.* **1.** curtsy, greeting, salaam, obeisance. *The magician gave a bow at the end of his act.* **2.** prow, fore, head, front. *A lookout was posted at the ship's bow.* *-vb.* **3.** bend, concede, yield, submit, capitulate. *The private refused to bow to the sergeant's foolish orders.* **4.** curtsy, kneel, salaam, stoop. *All the citizens bowed as their queen passed by.* **Ant. 2.** stern, rear. **3.** contest, oppose, resist.

box *n.* **1.** crate, container, trunk, carton, receptacle. *She packed her things in several boxes.* *-vb.* **2.** spar, cuff, fight, belt, hit, strike. *The two men boxed for the championship title.* **3.** enclose, package, confine, cage. *Traffic boxed us in on all sides.* **Ant. 3.** release, liberate.

boycott *n.* **1.** rejection, ban, exclusion, spurning, repudiation. *Students organized a boycott of the school cafeteria because its food was so bad.* –*vb.* **2.** refuse, reject, ostracize, ban, bar. *Upset consumers boycotted the company's products.* **Ant. 1.** support, patronage, usage. **2.** accept, use, purchase.

brace *n.* **1.** prop, reinforcement, backing, support, band, crutch, splint. *The runner wore a brace around his knee.* –*vb.* **2.** bolster, strengthen, hold, reinforce, fortify, prepare. *The astronauts braced themselves for the takeoff.* **Ant. 2.** weaken, cripple, undermine.

brag *vb.* **1.** boast, exaggerate, exult, gloat. *The warrior bragged that she could kill the dragon with one sword blow.* –*n.* **2.** boast, bragging, exaggeration, pretension, self-praise. *Unfortunately, no one believed her brags that she could slay the dragon so easily.* **Ant. 1.** disavow, disclaim. **2.** disavowal.

brake *n.* **1.** restraint, curb, reign, check, constraint. *The president put the brakes on the economy in an attempt to avoid inflation.* –*vb.* **2.** slow, decelerate, slacken, halt, stop. *The trolley braked to avoid hitting the pedestrian.* **Ant. 1.** accelerator, starter. **2.** accelerate, quicken, speed.

branch *n.* **1.** stem, limb, bough, fork, arm, extension. *Our treehouse is supported by four thick branches.* **2.** division, bureau, department, member, section. *He works at the West Valley library branch.* –*vb.* **3.** fork, separate, divide, spread, diverge. *The river branches into two smaller streams.* **Ant. 1.** trunk, main part. **2.** headquarters, main office.

brand *n.* **1.** label, trademark, seal, stamp, mark. *The ranchers placed a brand on all their livestock.* **2.** kind, make, type, variety, nature. *What cereal brand do you normally eat?* –*vb.* **3.** mark, stamp, label, stain, stigmatize. *His past behavior has branded him an unreliable person.*

brave *adj.* **1.** fearless, courageous, gallant, heroic, daring, bold. *The brave woman rescued a drowning child from icy waters.* –*vb.* **2.** dare, face, challenge, confront, defy. *He left his cabin and braved the blizzard outside.* **Ant. 1.** cowardly, timid, fainthearted. **2.** retreat, withdraw.

brawl *n.* **1.** scuffle, ruckus, fight, riot, uproar, dispute. *Police broke up the barroom brawl.* –*vb.* **2.** fight, quarrel, battle, scuffle. *Players brawled on the football field.*

brazen *adj.* insolent, forward, outspoken, defiant, rash. *The brazen student told the principal he was doing a lousy job.* **Ant.** shy, timid, reserved.

break *vb.* **1.** wreck, smash, fragment, shatter, snap, crack, splinter. *The plate broke when I dropped it.* **2.** beat, exceed, surpass, pass, top. *The swimmer broke the world record in the 100-meter freestyle.* **3.** disclose, inform, reveal, communicate. *He broke the news of the girl's death to her parents.* **4.** burst, erupt, initiate, begin. *The crowd broke into singing.* –*n.* **5.** rupture, fault, crack, opening, gap, rift, split. *The earthquake left a break in the concrete of our patio.* **6.** rest, interlude, intermission, pause, lull. *Employees get a 45-minute lunch break.* **7.** chance, stroke of luck, opportunity. *Being chosen to co-star in the film was the actor's big break.* **Ant. 1.** fix, heal, repair. **2.** fail, miss. **3.** conceal, withhold, hide. **4.** cease, halt. **5.** mending, repair. **6.** continuation.

breed *vb.* **1.** reproduce, procreate, create, generate, produce, cultivate. *Many animals breed during the spring months.* –*n.* **2.** type, kind, species, variety, stock, race. *What breed of dog do you have?*

brevity *n.* shortness, quickness, briefness, conciseness, terseness. *The students appreciated the brevity of their principal's speech.* **Ant.** lengthiness, longwindedness, verbosity.

brief *adj.* **1.** momentary, abrupt, swift, temporary, quick, fleeting. *A butterfly's life span seems brief compared to that of a human.* –*vb.* **2.** instruct, advise, inform, explain. *The president's advisors briefed him on the overnight development.* **Ant. 1.** prolonged, extended, lengthy, long. **2.** conceal.

bright *adj.* **1.** dazzling, illuminated, shining, radiant, glowing. *The road sign was painted bright yellow.* **2.** smart, clever, intelligent, alert, quick. *The bright child was moved a grade ahead.* **3.** promising, favorable, hopeful, cheerful, joyful. *The outlook on the patient's condition is bright.* **Ant. 1.** dim, dark, faded. **2.** stupid, dumb, slow. **3.** grim, hopeless.

brilliance n. **1.** glow, radiance, splendor, shine, brightness. *The moonlight's brilliance made it possible to take a midnight walk.* **2.** intelligence, genius, cleverness, wisdom. *The brilliance of his poetry impressed all of us.* **Ant. 1.** darkness, dimness, gloom. **2.** stupidity, mediocrity.

brilliant adj. **1.** gleaming, afire, shining, sparkling, intense. *Sunlight reflected off her brilliant diamond.* **2.** profound, ingenious, clever, intelligent, splendid, glorious. *The lawyer's defense of her client was simply brilliant.* **Ant. 1.** dull, drab, dark. **2.** unimpressive, awful, stupid, dumb.

bring vb. **1.** bear, fetch, tote, get, convey. *Will you bring me a glass of water?* **2.** invoke, produce, cause, create, start. *Sad movies bring tears to my eyes.* **3.** make, motivate, persuade, induce, force. *I couldn't bring myself to eat the green beans.* **Ant. 1.** send, leave, take away. **2.** prevent, stop, quench, suppress.

brisk adj. **1.** lively, swift, quick, busy, energetic. *You should brush your teeth in a brisk manner.* **2.** sharp, exhilarating, nipping, crisp, keen, bracing. *We stood shivering in the brisk wind.* **Ant. 1.** slow, sluggish. **2.** dead, stagnant, mellow.

brittle adj. weak, breakable, fragile, crumbly, delicate. *The dead leaves were quite brittle.* **Ant.** strong, unbreakable, sturdy, solid, durable.

broad adj. **1.** spacious, extensive, outstretched, wide, sweeping, large. *Books about gorillas will be listed under the broad category of African animals.* **2.** bare, plain, visible, direct, glaring. *The crime was committed in broad daylight.* **Ant. 1.** confining, meager, limited. **2.** obscured, unclear, hidden.

broadcast n. **1.** program, show, telecast, transmission, newscast. *The station's news broadcast comes on at six o'clock.* –vb. **2.** announce, televise, transmit, send, air, beam. *The Olympics were broadcast to almost all countries around the world.*

broken adj. **1.** fractured, damaged, shattered, destroyed, mangled, smashed, crushed, injured. *The doctor put a cast on my broken arm.* **2.** discontinued, interrupted, unconnected, intermittent. *Earth received a broken and garbled message from the distant space probe.* **Ant. 1.** mended, repaired, fixed. **2.** continuous, unbroken, connected.

browse vb. **1.** look over, scan, peruse, flip, skim, survey, windowshop. *He browsed through the store's sports equipment.* **2.** graze, feed, nibble, pasture. *Sheep browsed on the clover.*

bruise n. **1.** blemish, discoloration, abrasion, mark. *The apple had a bruise where it hit the ground.* –vb. **2.** injure, hurt, scrape, bump, wound. *Your unkind words bruised his feelings.*

brush n. **1.** shrubs, undergrowth, wood, bushes, thicket. *The jackrabbit hid from the coyote in the desert brush.* **2.** meeting, encounter, clash, engagement. *He had a brush with death when his car turned over.* –vb. **3.** sweep, whisk, groom, clean, polish. *She brushed the snarls out of her sister's hair.* **4.** graze, skim, touch, scrape. *The waiter brushed our table as he passed by.*

brutal adj. barbaric, unmerciful, savage, cruel, mean, vicious, harsh, ruthless. *The critics wrote brutal reviews of that movie.* **Ant.** kind, gentle, merciful, humane, tender.

buckle n. **1.** catch, fastener, clasp, hook. *After losing weight, I could tighten my belt buckle one more notch.* –vb. **2.** hook, attach, clasp, fasten, join, strap. *The motorcyclist buckled on her helmet.* **3.** crumple, collapse, warp, bend, distort. *The submarine's prow buckled when it hit a reef.* **Ant. 2.** unbuckle, loosen, undo, release. **3.** straighten, unbend.

budge vb. move, stir, go, slide, shift, yield. *Though we pushed and pulled, the mule refused to budge.* **Ant.** stay, remain.

budget n. **1.** financial plan, expenses, costs, allowance, program. *The governor set aside a portion of the state budget for health care.* –vb. **2.** plan, program, forecast, allocate, ration. *You must budget your time for both fun and work.*

build vb. **1.** create, make, manufacture, construct, fashion, assemble, erect, forge, develop. *Let's build a snowman.* –n. **2.** figure, shape, physique, body, frame. *That athlete has a great build.* **Ant. 1.** wreck, demolish, destroy, dismantle.

bulky adj. hulking, cumbersome, unwieldy, lumpish, ponderous, portly, ungainly, big. *My ski* *jacket is too bulky to pack in a suitcase.* **Ant.** compact, manageable, small.

bully *n.* **1.** tormentor, oppressor, ruffian, persecutor. *No one liked the school bully.* *–vb.* **2.** terrorize, scare, harass, threaten, abuse. *She bullied her younger brother into washing the dishes.* **Ant. 2.** charm, persuade, entice.

bump *n.* **1.** bulge, lump, protuberance, swelling, nodule. *It's best to slow down when driving over speed bumps.* **2.** whack, knock, jolt, thump, crash. *We felt a bump as our boat touched the dock.* *–vb.* **3.** whack, slam, collide, jar, knock, bounce. *I bumped my knee against the table.* **Ant. 1.** hole, depression.

bunch *n.* **1.** group, clump, cluster, crowd, assemblage, heap, stack, pile. *A bunch of us went up to the park yesterday.* *–vb.* **2.** amass, collect, cluster, huddle. *People bunched around the snack bar.* **Ant. 2.** scatter, disband, disperse.

bundle *n.* **1.** stack, package, sack, pack, collection, bunch. *He bought a bundle of logs for his fireplace.* *–vb.* **2.** wrap, swaddle, package, group, bunch. *We bundled the newspapers for recycling.* **Ant. 2.** disperse, scatter.

burden *n.* **1.** weight, cargo, load, baggage, payload. *The camel collapsed under its heavy burden.* **2.** trouble, hardship, grief, misfortune, duty, responsibility. *Managing two stores was a burden she could have done without.* *–vb.* **3.** weight, load, overload, encumber, tax. *Please don't burden me with more responsibilities.*

burglar *n.* robber, thief, ransacker, prowler, criminal. *The burglar crept from the house with his bag of loot.*

burn *vb.* **1.** blaze, scorch, ignite, singe, sear, overcook. *Her father burned the hamburgers on the barbecue.* **2.** hurt, sting, smart, throb, ache. *My eyes burned from the chlorinated water.* **Ant. 1.** extinguish, douse, quench. **2.** relieve, soothe.

burning *adj.* **1.** blazing, fiery, scorching, flaming, smoldering. *Firefighters sprayed water on the burning house.* **2.** biting, stinging, smarting, sharp, cutting. *Hot peppers can leave a burning sensation in your mouth.* **3.** excited, raging, passionate, urgent, impatient. *I have a burning desire to be with you.* **Ant. 2.** soothing, dulling, numbing. **3.** indifferent, uncaring.

burst *vb.* **1.** explode, break, rupture, erupt, gush. *The water balloon burst when it hit the wall.* *–n.* **2.** outpouring, flow, rush, eruption. *The musician's popular song was received with a burst of applause.*

bury *vb.* **1.** entomb, enclose, inter, enshrine. *The dead man was buried in our local cemetery.* **2.** cover, hide, conceal, screen, cloak, veil. *He buried the sensitive information in a secret file.* **Ant. 1.** unearth, exhume. **2.** expose, disclose, reveal.

business *n.* **1.** enterprise, company, store, corporation, firm. *My uncle owns a business which rents videos.* **2.** work, occupation, job, trade, pursuit, career. *My mother is in the hotel business.* **3.** selling, commerce, marketing, dealings. *The store opens for business at nine o'clock.* **4.** concern, interest, affair, problem. *It's none of your business.*

busy *adj.* **1.** industrious, engaged, occupied, active, working. *She was too busy to speak with me.* **2.** moving, crowded, bustling, hectic. *Stores are often very busy during the holidays.* **Ant. 1.** idle, unoccupied, inactive. **2.** motionless, empty, relaxed.

button *n.* **1.** knob, disk, dial, switch, control. *Please push the elevator button for the fifth floor.* **2.** fastener, link, buckle, stud. *We used pieces of coal for the snowman's buttons.* *–vb.* **3.** fasten, clasp, buckle, close. *He doesn't like shirts that button up the front.*

buy *vb.* purchase, acquire, obtain, get, procure, order. *Where did you buy your jacket?* **Ant.** steal, rent, sell, lease.

by *prep.* **1.** next to, close to, beside, alongside, near. *Our school is by the courthouse.* *–adv.* **2.** near, close to, through. *We watched the parade pass by.*

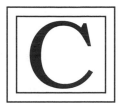

cabin *n.* **1.** cottage, lodge, chalet, bungalow, shack. *She went to her mountain cabin for the weekend.* **2.** room, quarters, chamber, compartment, stateroom. *The ship's captain asked all passengers to return to their cabins.*

cable *n.* **1.** cord, rope, line, strand, wire. *The aerial tramway runs on a thick cable.* **2.** telegram, cablegram, wire, message. *She received a cable informing her of the package's arrival.* *-vb.* **3.** wire, telegraph. *The student cabled his parents for more money.*

cache *n.* hoard, store, stockpile, supply, savings. *Pioneers often kept caches of meat for the hard winter months.*

cafeteria *n.* lunchroom, coffee shop, restaurant, cafe, snack bar, diner. *Many students dislike our cafeteria's food.*

cage *n.* **1.** pen, enclosure, dungeon, prison, coop, pound, box. *She keeps her canary in a bird cage.* *-vb.* **2.** confine, jail, imprison, impound, enclose, restrain. *The evil sorceress caged the prince in her dungeon.* **Ant. 2.** release, free.

calculate *vb.* **1.** compute, determine, figure, estimate, work out. *This problem asks us to calculate the square root of 256.* **2.** plan, expect, intend, mean. *I didn't calculate on the delay and thus missed my bus.*

call *vb.* **1.** shout, yell, exclaim, cry, hail, say. *Did you hear someone call my name?* **2.** telephone, phone, dial, ring. *I called the hotel for reservations.* **3.** command, order, summon, ask, invite. *The judge called the witness to the stand.* **4.** label, name, title, designate. *Our softball team is called the Matadors.* *-n.* **5.** scream, shout, cry, yell, holler. *Give a call if you need anything.* **6.** summons, appeal, bidding, invitation, declaration, order, command. *The president issued a call to arms.*

callous *adj.* hard, tough, unsympathetic, uncaring, indifferent, insensitive, cold. *Some peo-ple criticized the mayor for being callous towards the poor.* **Ant.** tender, sympathetic, caring, soft.

calm *adj.* **1.** relaxed, tranquil, untroubled, still, peaceful, composed. *Few public speakers feel truly calm when giving a speech.* *-vb.* **2.** quiet, soothe, pacify, assuage, lull. *The teacher attempted to calm his rowdy students.* **Ant. 1.** excited, agitated, upset. **2.** disturb, excite, agitate.

camouflage *n.* **1.** cloak, disguise, mask, screen, concealment. *The hunters used some small branches for camouflage.* *-vb.* **2.** conceal, disguise, cover, mask, cloak. *Butterflies have colors that camouflage them from predators.* **Ant. 2.** expose, reveal, show.

campaign *n.* **1.** plan, operation, drive, effort, offensive, maneuvers. *Napoleon's military campaign bogged down in Russia.* *-vb.* **2.** run, canvass, crusade, stump, push. *She is campaigning for the office of class treasurer.*

cancel *vb.* stop, drop, delete, repeal, revoke, nullify, void. *The network canceled the low-rated television series.* **Ant.** maintain, keep, confirm, uphold.

cancellation *n.* deletion, discontinuance, recall, withdrawal, annulment. *Fans were upset by the show's cancellation.* **Ant.** continuation, reintroduction.

candid *adj.* **1.** truthful, direct, frank, honest, forthright, open, sincere. *Please be candid about your feelings.* **2.** informal, spontaneous, unrehearsed, unplanned. *He likes taking candid photographs of people.* **Ant. 1.** fake, untruthful, insincere. **2.** formal, rehearsed, planned.

candidate *n.* office seeker, nominee, runner, contender, hopeful, applicant. *She was running as a candidate for governor.*

canoe *n.* outrigger, kayak, dugout, longboat, boat. *Indians traveled in canoes.*

capable *adj.* able, skillful, competent, efficient, talented, experienced, qualified. *Our company is looking for a capable programmer.* **Ant.** incapable, unskilled, incompetent.

capacity *n.* **1.** size, dimensions, content, volume, range, measure, space. *This bottle has a capacity of two liters.* **2.** ability, competence, potential, aptitude, intelligence. *The child is unschooled but has a large capacity for learning.* **3.** position, role, job, function. *The student talked to a reporter in his capacity as student-body president.* **Ant. 2.** inability, incapacity, incompetence.

capital *n.* money, assets, funds, principal, savings. *My capital is all tied up in stocks and bonds.* **Ant.** deficit, debts.

captain *n.* **1.** commander, skipper, master, chief, leader, head. *The team captains chose five players each.* –*vb.* **2.** lead, skipper, pilot, head, command, direct. *She has captained the starship for the last ten years.*

captivate *vb.* enchant, charm, dazzle, fascinate, tantalize, delight. *The sight of Saturn's rings captivated the spaceship's passengers.* **Ant.** repel, disgust, offend.

capture *vb.* **1.** catch, hold, trap, seize, apprehend. *In chess, you lose when the other player captures your king.* –*n.* **2.** seizure, arrest, ensnaring, trapping, taking. *The prince was held for ransom following his capture by pirates.* **Ant. 1.** liberate, release. **2.** release, freeing, liberation.

car *n.* automobile, vehicle, sedan, motorcar, auto. *His car got a flat tire on the way to school.*

caravan *n.* convoy, file, column, train, procession, company, troop. *A caravan of nomads straggled over the sand dunes.*

care *vb.* **1.** protect, attend, watch, mind, tend. *A baby-sitter cared for the young children until their parents returned.* **2.** like, wish, crave, want, desire. *Would you care for another slice of pizza?* –*n.* **3.** worry, concern, burden, sorrow, responsibility. *Our lazy cat doesn't have a care in the world.* **4.** caution, wariness, attention, concentration, thought. *One should take care when using a power saw.* **5.** safekeeping, custody, protection, guardianship, keep, charge. *I left my dog in my neighbor's care.* **Ant. 1.** neglect, ignore.

2. hate, dislike, reject. **3.** relaxation, enjoyment, pleasure. **4.** disregard, recklessness. **5.** neglect.

career *n.* job, occupation, business, employment, work, living, trade, vocation. *Teaching is my career.*

carefree *adj.* untroubled, unworried, cheerful, happy, easygoing, joyful, merry. *The princess had a carefree life as a child.* **Ant.** troubled, burdened, worried, difficult.

careful *adj.* thoughtful, cautious, concerned, wary, guarded, mindful, accurate. *Be careful that you don't miss any problems on the test.* **Ant.** careless, unthinking, mindless, negligent.

careless *adj.* forgetful, thoughtless, unthinking, uncaring, unwary, negligent. *It was careless of him to leave the door unlocked.* **Ant.** careful, exact, cautious.

caress *n.* **1.** stroke, touch, cuddle, embrace, hug, kiss. *The child gave her puppy a caress.* –*vb.* **2.** touch, brush, graze, stroke, massage. *A gentle breeze caressed his face.*

carriage *n.* coach, buggy, cart, trap, gig, stagecoach. *The queen and king were brought to the palace in a carriage.*

carry *vb.* **1.** bear, move, lug, bring, cart, transport, convey. *He carries his schoolbooks in a backpack.* **2.** support, shoulder, bear, maintain, undertake. *Do you think this bridge can carry the weight of a two-ton truck?* **3.** offer, supply, provide, furnish. *The local market carries three types of onions.* **Ant. 1.** drop, let fall. **3.** remove, omit, withhold.

carve *vb.* **1.** sculpt, whittle, fashion, shape, form, chisel. *She likes to carve animals out of pieces of wood.* **2.** partition, slice, divide, quarter, split, chop. *Politicians carved the large district into three smaller ones.*

cascade *n.* **1.** waterfall, fall, rapids, cataract. *She hiked up to the stream's cascade.* –*vb.* **2.** plunge, fall, rush, surge, avalanche. *His marbles cascaded to the ground when their bag broke.* **Ant. 2.** trickle, drip, leak.

case *n.* **1.** example, sample, situation, event, happening, occasion. *In this case, I think you are correct.* . **2.** lawsuit, argument, plea, presentation, explanation. *The lawyer presented his case* to the jury. **3.** holder, container, canister, box, carton, package. *She keeps her glasses in a leather case.* **4.** patient, invalid, subject. *The doctor has several difficult cases.*

cast *n.* **1.** casing, support, splint, brace. *Doctors put a cast on his broken arm.* **2.** mold, copy, replica, pattern, impression. *This museum makes casts of famous actors, then fills them with wax.* **3.** look, appearance, demeanor, suggestion, shade, trace. *In "Dr. Jekyll and Mr. Hyde," Mr. Hyde has an evil cast to his face.* **4.** launch, throw, fling, toss, heave. *In a game of horseshoes, each player is allowed three casts.* –*vb.* **5.** toss, hurl, send, throw, emit, project. *A fisherman cast his line into the lake.* **6.** award, allot, bestow, give, select. *Who did you cast your ballot for?* **7.** set, sculpt, shape, mold, arrange. *The artist cast her sculpture in bronze.*

castle *n.* fortress, citadel, hold, keep, palace, manor, mansion, tower. *Ireland is famous for its impressive castles.*

casual *adj.* informal, relaxed, offhand, loose, nonchalant, carefree. *There's no need to dress up for a casual dinner party.* **Ant.** formal, stiff, reserved.

casualty *n.* injury, fatality, victim, loss, sufferer. *It is sad when civilians become casualties of war.*

catalog *n.* **1.** directory, list, inventory, index, schedule, program. *We looked through the store's clothes catalog.* –*vb.* **2.** classify, record, list, arrange, categorize, rank. *Library personnel have cataloged all the books on their shelves.*

catastrophe *n.* tragedy, misfortune, disaster, devastation, calamity, ruin. *The catastrophe would have been avoided if the stoplight had been working.* **Ant.** good fortune, blessing.

catch *vb.* **1.** seize, snatch, grasp, grab, capture, trap. *He caught several fish.* **2.** discover, detect, surprise, find, startle. *My mother caught me taking the cookies she was saving.* **3.** overtake, reach, attain, intercept. *She caught and passed the two leading runners on the final lap.* **4.** understand, comprehend, perceive, discern, hear. *I didn't catch what you were saying.* –*n.* **5.** grab, snatch, capture, seizure, snare. *The baseball player made a spectacular catch.* **6.** hook, fastener, clasp, lock, latch. *The catch on the door is stuck.* **7.** snag, trick, trap, snare. *The catch in*

this contract is that you must pay by tomorrow. **Ant. 1.** miss, free, release. **5.** miss, drop, fumble. **7.** boon, advantage, blessing.

category *n.* type, brand, class, classification, grouping. *How many categories of music can you name?*

cause *vb.* **1.** create, provoke, generate, kindle, incite, motivate. *What caused the fire?* –*n.* **2.** origin, source, creator, reason, motive, root. *The cause of the plane crash was a faulty engine.* **3.** belief, goal, ideal, object, principle. *The activist fought for environmental causes.* **Ant. 1.** prevent, block, halt. **2.** outcome, result.

caution *n.* **1.** care, discretion, wariness, alertness, vigilance. *We proceeded with caution on the icy road.* –*vb.* **2.** warn, alert, advise, counsel, admonish. *A sign cautioned us to slow down because there was a curve ahead.* **Ant. 1.** carelessness, rashness.

cautious *adj.* careful, watchful, attentive, alert, wary, vigilant, aware, guarded. *One should be cautious when crossing a busy street.* **Ant.** rash, daring, careless, foolhardy.

cavity *n.* hole, pit, crevasse, gap, hollow, cavern, crater, opening. *The explosion made a large cavity in the ground.*

cease *vb.* stop, discontinue, suspend, quit, terminate, halt, desist, conclude. *Will this rain never cease?* **Ant.** continue, start, begin.

cede *vb.* surrender, yield, relinquish, give, release, grant. *The team was forced to cede the title to their challengers.* **Ant.** keep, retain, hold.

celebrate *vb.* observe, honor, commemorate, keep, glorify. *Some friends and I celebrated my birthday at an amusement park.* **Ant.** ignore, forget, dishonor, desecrate.

celebrity *n.* **1.** star, notable, heroine, hero, dignitary, personage. *Many celebrities showed up for the Academy Awards ceremony.* **2.** popularity, fame, renown, note, stardom. *The triumphant space explorers welcomed their new-found celebrity.* **Ant. 2.** nonrecognition, obscurity, oblivion.

cell *n.* enclosure, cubicle, lockup, stall, cage, pen. *The bank robber was put in the prison's holding cell.*

cement *n.* **1.** plaster, concrete, mortar, glue, stucco, asphalt. *She wrote her name in the wet cement of the new sidewalk.* *–vb.* **2.** bind, glue, seal, fix, stick, join, connect. *He cemented the broken wing on his model airplane.*

cemetery *n.* graveyard, burial ground, resting place, mortuary. *My uncle is buried in that cemetery.*

censor *vb.* **1.** ban, forbid, edit, suppress, purge, delete. *Many countries censor political books and magazines.* *–n.* **2.** examiner, inspector, abridger, reviewer, editor. *The station's censor deleted bad language with loud "bleeps."* **Ant. 1.** allow, accept, approve.

censure *n.* **1.** condemnation, rebuke, criticism, scolding, disapproval. *He received his parent's censure for staying out all night.* *–vb.* **2.** blame, criticize, reprimand, scold, reproach, judge. *The school board censured the teacher for her nontraditional teaching style.* **Ant. 1.** praise, approval, endorsement. **2.** praise, encourage.

center *n.* **1.** middle, midway, focus, heart, core, hub, pivot, crux. *The center of the earth is thought to be made up of nickel and iron.* *–vb.* **2.** converge, focus, concentrate, centralize, consolidate. *Their conversation often centers around sports.* **Ant. 1.** side, surface, exterior. **2.** spread, scatter, disperse.

central *adj.* **1.** middle, midmost, midway, inmost, inside. *Colorado is a central state.* **2.** prime, principal, dominant, pivotal, key, essential, main. *Tom Sawyer is the central character in Mark Twain's famous book.* **Ant. 1.** outside, exterior, rim. **2.** minor, secondary.

ceremony *n.* **1.** celebration, rite, ritual, observance, services. *The graduation ceremony will take place on the football field.* **2.** etiquette, formality, protocol, solemnity, politeness. *The royal wedding was performed with a great deal of ceremony.* **Ant. 2.** informality, casualness.

certain *adj.* **1.** convinced, definite, sure, positive, undoubting. *Are you certain you want to buy this car?* **2.** undeniable, evident, conclusive, guaranteed, reliable, foolproof. *I will only bet on a certain winner.* **3.** specific, particular, precise, express. *There are certain rules that I must discuss with you.* **Ant. 1.** uncertain, unsure. **2.**

uncertain, unreliable, questionable. **3.** uncertain, vague, indefinite.

certainly *adv.* surely, unquestionably, positively, definitely, clearly, undoubtedly. *It's certainly cold out today.*

certify *vb.* guarantee, verify, establish, validate, promise. *You'll need a witness to certify your signature on this document.* **Ant.** invalidate, question.

chain *n.* **1.** metal links, cable, irons, shackles, manacles. *The dog had a chain around its neck.* **2.** train, line, series, string, procession. *His request went up the chain of command to the commanding general.* *–vb.* **3.** connect, secure, fasten, manacle, handcuff, restrain. *She chained her bike to the metal rack.* **Ant. 3.** unchain, release, free.

chair *n.* **1.** seat, stool, bench, rocker, couch. *Pull up a chair and join us.* **2.** chairwoman, chairman, leader, director, moderator, facilitator. *She was voted in as chair of the math department.* *–vb.* **3.** oversee, facilitate, direct, moderate, lead. *He chaired the committee meeting.*

challenge *n.* **1.** dare, threat, provocation, summons, ultimatum. *Sir Lancelot received a challenge at the jousting tournament.* **2.** trial, venture, test, puzzle, difficulty. *The obstacle course proved to be a difficult challenge.* *–vb.* **3.** dare, summon, bid, defy, confront. *She challenged him to a game of chess.* **4.** test, strain, try, tax, stimulate. *The computer malfunction challenged her problem-solving abilities.* **5.** contradict, question, dispute, contest, object. *The lawyer challenged the defendant's statement.* **Ant. 5.** accept, believe, support.

champion *n.* **1.** winner, victor, hero, conqueror, leader, title holder. *After winning the final game, he was crowned the champion.* **2.** defender, supporter, backer, protector, guardian. *The humane society considers itself the champion of abused animals.* *–vb.* **3.** promote, defend, support, protect, uphold, back, guard. *He championed the group's right to march.* **Ant. 1.** loser, fallen. **2.** enemy, antagonist. **3.** oppose, obstruct.

chance *n.* **1.** opportunity, prospect, opening, occasion. *Don't blow it; this may be your big chance.* **2.** fate, accident, happenstance, luck, coincidence. *It was only by chance that we found* *the hotel.* **3.** possibility, probability, likelihood, odds, tendency. *There is a good chance that the game will be canceled.* **4.** danger, gamble, risk, peril, venture. *When you cheat, there is always the chance that you will be caught.* *-adj.* **5.** accidental, unforeseen, random, unexpected, uncertain. *My meeting him last Sunday was a chance occurrence.* *-vb.* **6.** occur, happen, befall, transpire, result. *It chanced that my birthday fell on a holiday this year.* **7.** risk, attempt, hazard, gamble, try. *The two hikers decided not to chance crossing the raging river.* **Ant. 2.** plan, proposal, intent. **3.** impossibility, improbability. **5.** expected, foreseen, planned.

change *vb.* **1.** alter, vary, modify, transform, fluctuate, turn, shift. *The ship's captain changed course when she saw the iceberg.* **2.** replace, exchange, swap, trade, substitute. *I went inside to change my dirty shirt.* *-n.* **3.** transformation, difference, switch, variation, reversal. *A remarkable change came over her when she began exercising and eating right.* **Ant. 1.** maintain, remain, hold. **2.** keep, maintain. **3.** stability, sameness, permanence.

channel *n.* **1.** canal, watercourse, passage, duct, strait, artery, route. *The tugboat guided the large ship into the main channel.* *-vb.* **2.** route, direct, convey, conduct, guide, steer. *The teacher said we should channel our energy into our homework.*

chaos *n.* disorder, confusion, disarray, mess, disorganization, jumble. *His Hawaiian-print shirt is a chaos of colors.* **Ant.** organization, harmony, order, calm.

chapter *n.* **1.** section, episode, part, subdivision, portion. *He is writing the book's final chapter.* **2.** group, branch, gathering, unit, assembly. *She joined the local chapter of the Sierra Club.*

character *n.* **1.** individual, person, role, part, portrayal. *Frodo is the main character in J.R.R. Tolkien's "The Hobbit."* **2.** honesty, morality, courage, integrity, respectability, sincerity. *Eleanor Roosevelt was a woman of renowned character.* **3.** attitude, personality, temperament, quality, nature. *The dark and gloomy castle had a rather forbidding character.* **4.** letter, figure, symbol, insignia, sign. *You can choose different characters for a computer printout.* **5.** eccentric, oddball, nonconformist, maverick. *The old hermit*

was quite a character. **Ant. 2.** dishonesty, corruption, immorality.

characteristic *adj.* **1.** typical, distinctive, marked, representative, particular, specific. *I heard my friend's characteristic laugh.* *-n.* **2.** feature, mannerism, trait, attribute, distinction, peculiarity, quirk. *His most noticeable characteristic is his kindness.* **Ant. 1.** uncharacteristic, atypical.

charge *vb.* **1.** rush, surge, storm, attack, thrust, push. *The soldiers charged up the hill.* **2.** bill, assess, ask, tax, fine. *The store charged forty dollars for this shirt.* **3.** blame, accuse, indict, arraign, incriminate. *The city attorney's office charged her with one count of fraud.* **4.** load, pack, instill, infuse, stack. *The singer's entrance charged the auditorium with excitement.* **5.** order, urge, direct, bid, demand. *My father charged me to take out the trash.* *-n.* **6.** price, bill, cost, expense, fare, fee. *The charge for a one-night stay in our hotel is sixty dollars.* **7.** custody, care, guardianship, protection, keeping. *The young boy was left in his grandparents' charge.* **8.** attack, offensive, drive, onslaught, thrust, push. *The cavalry charge overran the defenders' position.* **9.** accusation, implication, complaint, allegation, citation. *The charge you are accused of is burglary.* **10.** dependent, ward, responsibility, minor. *She became a charge of the state when her parents died.* **Ant. 1.** retreat, withdraw. **3.** absolve, acquit. **4.** empty, discharge. **8.** withdrawal, retreat. **9.** absolution, acquittal.

charitable *adj.* **1.** giving, unselfish, generous, unsparing, humanitarian, nonprofit. *The charitable organization gave food and housing to the needy.* **2.** lenient, tolerant, forgiving, kind, sympathetic. *This time I will be charitable and not punish you.* **Ant. 1.** selfish, ungenerous, stingy. **2.** rigid, unforgiving.

charm *n.* **1.** allure, appeal, captivation, pull, enchantment, attractiveness, magnetism. *The charm of the quaint old house convinced the couple to buy it.* **2.** amulet, spell, chant, lucky piece. *The sorceress gave him a charm that scares away evil goblins.* *-vb.* **3.** delight, captivate, enthrall, mesmerize, attract, bewitch, hypnotize. *A fakir charmed the king cobra with a flute.* **Ant. 1.** aversion, repulsion, revulsion. **3.** disgust, revolt, repel.

charming *adj.* enchanting, captivating, delightful, pleasing, enjoyable, fascinating. *He has a charming smile.* **Ant.** repulsive, disagreeable, nauseating, unpleasing.

charter *n.* **1.** license, contract, permit, lease, agreement, compact, franchise. *The national board for our fraternity said it would revoke our charter if we didn't pay our dues.* –*vb.* **2.** license, grant, sanction, allot, authorize. *The state chartered the bank to do business.* **3.** rent, lease, hire, engage, employ. *We chartered a boat for the afternoon.*

chase *vb.* **1.** pursue, follow, trail, tail, track. *The dog chased a car down the street.* **2.** drive out, evict, repulse, dispel, disperse. *We chased the dog off our lawn.* –*n.* **3.** hunt, pursuit, tracking, race, quest. *The rider was thrown off his horse during the chase.*

chaste *adj.* wholesome, virginal, innocent, celibate, righteous, uncorrupted. *The monks led a chaste life.* **Ant.** unchaste, wanton, corrupt.

chat *vb.* **1.** talk, chatter, converse, gossip, discuss. *My hairdresser often chats with me about her friends and family.* –*n.* **2.** talk, discussion, conversation, visit. *He dropped by for a chat.*

chatter *vb.* **1.** babble, talk, jabber, gossip, prattle. *My younger brother chattered on about his soccer game.* –*n.* **2.** babble, talking, blather, gossip, jabbering, chatting. *The teacher quieted the students' chatter.*

cheap *adj.* **1.** inexpensive, low-priced, thrifty, reduced, lowered, reasonable. *An imitation diamond is relatively cheap compared to a real one.* **2.** shoddy, trashy, poor, mean, low. *We stayed at a cheap motel.* **3.** miserly, stingy, ungenerous, grudging, tight. *He was too cheap to buy his mother a gift.* **Ant. 1.** expensive, unreasonable, high-priced. **2.** excellent, superior. **3.** generous, unselfish, unsparing.

cheat *vb.* **1.** defraud, swindle, deceive, bilk, trick, mislead. *He cheated me by charging $120 for a $15 watch.* –*n.* **2.** swindler, trickster, crook, con artist, fraud. *I refuse to play cards with that cheat.*

check *vb.* **1.** explore, review, inspect, examine, investigate. *Security guards checked for a prowler after they heard the alarm.* **2.** stop, pre-vent, brake, halt, inhibit, curb, slow, restrain. *A severe storm checked the ship's progress.* **3.** agree, correspond, concur, tally, harmonize. *The detective said the suspect's story checks with the facts.* **4.** mark, tally, note, register, score. *The teacher checked wrong answers with a red pen.* –*n.* **5.** inspection, examination, study, investigation. *All new cars are subject to a factory check before being shipped.* **6.** obstacle, barrier, restriction, block, rejection, stoppage. *His habitual tardiness is a check against his chances for promotion.* **7.** slash, mark, notation, impression. *When completing this form, please put a check next to those items you wish to order.* **8.** bill, tab, ticket, receipt. *We were shocked at the price of dinner when we received the check.* **Ant. 1.** overlook, neglect. **2.** encourage, start, release. **3.** contradict, disagree. **6.** start, promotion, advance.

cheer *vb.* **1.** shout, applaud, yell, encourage, acclaim. *We cheered for our team.* **2.** console, comfort, reassure, brighten, enliven. *He cheered his sad friend with funny stories.* –*n.* **3.** shout, yell, hooray, roar, cry. *She gave a cheer when she won the award.* **4.** sparkle, animation, merriment, joy; happiness. *The sunny wallpaper added a note of cheer to the hospital rooms.* **Ant. 1.** boo, hiss. **2.** discourage, demoralize. **3.** boo, hiss. **4.** discouragement, gloom, dejection.

cheerful *adj.* merry, joyous, happy, bright, carefree, jolly, playful, delighted. *The students were cheerful when they learned they had the day off from school.* **Ant.** depressed, sad, cheerless.

cheerless *adj.* bleak, gloomy, dismal, miserable, joyless. *The overcast winter day was totally cheerless.* **Ant.** cheerful, bright, joyous.

cherish *vb.* love, honor, revere, respect, nurture, adore, value. *I cherish the time I've had with my daughter.* **Ant.** hate, detest, dislike.

chest *n.* **1.** box, container, trunk, dresser, case, locker. *My parents keep their family mementos in a wooden chest.* **2.** breast, bosom, pectorals, front. *Bodybuilders lift weights to expand their chests.* **Ant. 2.** back.

chew *vb.* crunch, munch, grind, gnaw, bite, eat, nibble. *I often chew gum when I watch movies.*

chief *n.* **1.** leader, captain, head, ruler, director, boss, manager. *The police chief had a hun-*

dred officers under his command. –adj. **2.** main, principal, first, primary, major, greatest. *Beef is the chief export of Argentina.* **Ant. 1.** follower, subject. **2.** minor, least, secondary.

chiefly adv. first, primarily, mainly, particularly, especially. *Expensive running shoes are bought chiefly by serious athletes.*

child n. young adult, youth, teenager, boy, girl, kid, adolescent, juvenile. *If you are a child, you can get in free with an adult.* **Ant.** adult, senior citizen, grownup.

chill n. **1.** coolness, bite, frostiness, nip, crispness, coldness, briskness. *The chill of the mountain air surprised us.* –vb. **2.** cool, refrigerate, freeze, frost. *Please chill the soda before serving it.* –adj. **3.** cold, frosty, cool, icy, frigid, harsh. *He wore a hat in the chill wind.* **Ant. 1.** heat, warmth. **2.** warm, heat. **3.** warm, balmy, hot.

chilly adj. cold, frigid, cool, icy, frozen, harsh. *No one wanted to swim in the chilly water.* **Ant.** warm, hot, balmy.

chisel vb. **1.** sculpt, carve, shape, engrave, form. *The artist chiseled a totem from the large tree.* –n. **2.** blade, gouge, knife, edge. *The sculptor used a chisel and mallet.*

chivalrous adj. polite, courtly, mannerly, noble, virtuous. *Giving up your bus seat to an elderly rider is a chivalrous thing to do.* **Ant.** obnoxious, loutish, discourteous.

choice n. **1.** selection, option, alternative, possibility, pick. *The theater gave us a choice between five different movies.* **2.** decision, wish, preference, judgment. *It's your choice whether or not you study for the test.* –adj. **3.** fine, superior, supreme, prime, first-rate. *He only buys the choice cuts of meat.* **Ant. 2.** force, coercion. **3.** inferior, poor.

choke vb. **1.** strangle, smother, suffocate, gasp, drown. *The man died after choking on a piece of meat.* **2.** block, stop, plug, obstruct, impede, clog. *Thick jungle choked the trail.* **Ant. 2.** unclog, unplug.

choose vb. decide, determine, select, prefer, like, pick, elect. *The players will choose a team captain on Saturday.* **Ant.** discard, reject, refuse.

chore n. **1.** job, duty, task, errand, assignment. *Taking the trash out is one of my chores.* **2.** burden, trouble, nuisance, bother, annoyance, problem. *It's such a chore to walk to school every day.* **Ant. 2.** pleasure, enjoyment, delight.

chronic adj. continual, endless, persistent, habitual, recurrent, established. *He suffers from chronic asthma.* **Ant.** infrequent, occasional, unusual.

chronicle n. **1.** record, history, story, biography, account, diary, narrative. *The medicine man recited a chronicle of the tribe.* –vb. **2.** report, record, document, log, register. *The reporter chronicled the events that led up to the catastrophe.*

church n. cathedral, chapel, sanctuary, temple, tabernacle. *They went to church on Easter Sunday.*

cinch vb. belt, bind, girdle, clasp, fasten, latch. *She cinched her belt tighter.*

circle n. **1.** hoop, ring, disk, wheel, orbit, circuit. *Covered wagons used to form circles for protection against attack.* –vb. **2.** loop, ring, enclose, surround, revolve. *Please circle those answers which you got wrong.* **Ant. 1.** square, rectangle, triangle.

circulate vb. **1.** distribute, spread, disperse, pass, flow. *Turn on a fan to circulate the air.* **2.** visit, wander, travel, tour, journey. *The hostess circulated among her guests.* **Ant. 1.** keep, hold, retain. **2.** stop, stay.

circumstance n. happening, event, episode, fact, incident, occurrence, case. *The man died under suspicious circumstances.*

citation n. **1.** charge, penalty, ticket, writ, warrant. *The police gave her a citation for jaywalking.* **2.** honor, award, decoration, medal, recognition. *He received a citation for his outstanding work.* **3.** quotation, quote, reference, documentation, passage, mention. *Be sure to list the sources for all citations in your paper.*

citizen n. native, national, resident, member, subject. *Only citizens are allowed to vote.* **Ant.** alien, foreigner, nonresident.

civil adj. **1.** nonmilitary, civilian, public, secular, citizen. *The soldier was tried before a civil rather than military judge.* **2.** kind, mannerly, courteous, polite, pleasant, nice. *He told the two students to stop fighting and be civil to one another.* **Ant. 1.** military, religious. **3.** uncivil, insulting, impolite.

civilian *n.* **1.** nonmilitary person, private citizen, noncombatant. *After leaving the army, he had to get used to being a civilian again.* *–adj.* **2.** nonmilitary, civil, secular, public, lay. *The soldier put on his civilian clothes when he went into town.* **Ant. 1.** soldier, military person. **2.** military.

civility *n.* politeness, courtesy, respect, consideration, tact, respectfulness. *Despite disliking your cousin you should treat him with civility.* **Ant.** disrespect, impoliteness, rudeness.

civilization *n.* sophistication, progress, development, socialization, refinement, cultivation. *The Babylonians were an ancient culture with a high degree of civilization.* **Ant.** barbarism, savagery.

claim *vb.* **1.** state, declare, insist, maintain, profess. *She claims to be descended from royalty.* **2.** take, demand, seize, appropriate, request. *Colonists often claimed land belonging to the Indians.* *–n.* **3.** ownership, grant, deed, title, rights. *My claim to the money I found was denied.* **4.** declaration, assertion, statement, pronouncement, proclamation, avowal. *I don't believe his claim that he climbed Mt. Everest.* **Ant. 1.** deny, repudiate, disavow. **2.** relinquish, renounce, reject. **4.** disavowal, denial, repudiation.

clamor *n.* **1.** commotion, shouting, noise, uproar, disturbance, loudness. *She went outside to see what the clamor was all about.* *–vb.* **2.** shout, yell, howl, argue, quarrel. *The small children clamored for attention.* **Ant. 1.** quiet, silence, peacefulness.

clarify *vb.* explain, define, show, interpret, describe, illustrate. *We asked the teacher to clarify the example in our textbook.* **Ant.** confuse, obscure.

class *n.* **1.** section, session, lecture, seminar, subject. *Her calculus class starts at noon.* **2.** rank, category, species, group, classification, division, set. *Monkeys belong to a class of animals known as primates.* **3.** position, rank, status, caste, clique, standing, grade. *Most Americans consider themselves part of the middle economic class.* *–vb.* **4.** classify, group, rank, label, cate-

gorize. *The company classes its new car as a luxury model.*

classify *vb.* arrange, rank, class, group, categorize, index, type, organize. *They classified their students by scholastic ability.*

clean *vb.* **1.** wash, bathe, wipe, scrub, disinfect, neaten. *Will you please clean your hands before dinner?* *–adj.* **2.** washed, wiped, spotless, stainless, bathed, sanitized. *I set the table with four clean plates.* **3.** unpolluted, healthy, pure, uncontaminated, unspoiled. *One should drink only clean water.* **4.** honorable, wholesome, virtuous, moral, upright. *She runs a clean business.* **Ant. 1.** soil, dirty. **2.** messy, dirty, soiled. **3.** polluted, contaminated, unhealthy. **4.** dirty, immoral, unwholesome.

clear *adj.* **1.** transparent, colorless, unclouded, translucent. *The ceramic pots were covered with a clear glaze.* **2.** apparent, plain, distinct, evident, conclusive. *It's quite clear he did not know the answer.* **3.** open, empty, free, unblocked, unhindered. *He made sure the area was clear before firing the rifle.* *–vb.* **4.** clarify, explain, enlighten, simplify, unravel. *Has my explanation cleared up the problem?* **5.** empty, remove, free, unblock, open, unclog. *The plumber cleared the pipes.* **6.** skip, pass, leap, fly over, make. *The high jumper cleared the pole at eight feet.* **7.** free, acquit, absolve, exonerate, excuse. *The jury cleared him of all charges.* *–adv.* **8.** fully, completely, totally, wholly, altogether. *She threw the ball clear across the field.* **Ant. 1.** muddy, clouded, murky. **2.** unclear, perplexing, unapparent. **3.** blocked, closed, clogged. **4.** confuse, muddle. **5.** block, clog, close. **7.** accuse, blame.

clemency *n.* forgiveness, pardon, mercy, kindness, charity. *Roy Bean did not earn the nickname "the hanging judge" by showing clemency.*

clever *adj.* intelligent, sharp, witty, bright, shrewd, skillful. *She is clever enough to think her way out of difficult situations.* **Ant.** unintelligent, dumb, slow.

client *n.* customer, buyer, patron, shopper, protégé. *The stockbroker has several clients whose accounts he oversees.* **Ant.** seller, dealer, vender.

climate *n.* **1.** weather, clime, temperature, atmosphere. *Southern California has a sunny* *climate.* **2.** tone, attitude, feel, spirit, character. *The climate of the meeting was friendly.*

climax *n.* **1.** crisis, culmination, peak, summit, top. *The story's climax came when the giant trapped Jack.* *-vb.* **2.** culminate, top, intensify, peak, complete, terminate. *The argument climaxed in a fistfight.* **Ant. 1.** anticlimax, bottom. **2.** diminish, lessen, continue.

climb *vb.* **1.** scale, rise, ascend, lift, top, march, plod. *My friend and I climbed to the top of the hill.* *-n.* **2.** ascent, scaling, incline, elevation, march, plod. *The climb to the top was difficult.* **Ant. 1.** descent, sink. **2.** descent, dip.

clinch *vb.* **1.** establish, settle, complete, fix, secure. *Our volleyball team clinched the championship with its final win.* **2.** fasten, attach, bind, secure, grip, seize. *He clinched the buckle on his backpack.*

clique *n.* gang, club, circle, sorority, fraternity, set, crowd, faction. *He wanted to be part of the popular clique.*

cloak *n.* **1.** cape, overcoat, shawl, jacket, coat. *The Phantom of the Opera wore a thick black cloak.* **2.** screen, veil, mask, cover, disguise, shroud. *She used the bushes as a cloak behind which she changed her clothes.* *-vb.* **3.** cover, hide, conceal, veil, screen, disguise. *The spy cloaked her identity.* **Ant. 3.** reveal, uncover, expose.

close *vb.* **1.** shut, secure, lock, block, bar, seal. *They close the store at nine o'clock.* **2.** complete, finish, end, conclude, cease. *The festival closes with a big parade.* **3.** join, attach, merge, connect, unite. *The doctor closed the wound with stitches.* **4.** approach, near, surround, envelop, box. *The police closed in on the thief.* *-adj.* **5.** near, nearby, imminent, impending, forthcoming. *When the snow begins to melt, spring is close.* **6.** friendly, familiar, special, loyal, faithful. *I have two really close friends.* **7.** similar, alike, resembling, comparable, parallel. *His hair color is close to the color of mine.* **8.** tight, firm, secure, solid, careful. *The mother kept a close watch on her children.* *-n.* **9.** end, ending, conclusion, termination, finish. *The environmentalist looked forward to the close of hunting season.* *-adv.* **10.** near, nearby, closely, nigh, nearly. *Stand close to me.* **Ant. 1.** open, unlock, unbar. **2.** open, begin, start. **3.** open, separate. **5.** far,

distant. **6.** cold, unfriendly, distant. **7.** dissimilar, uneven, unequal. **8.** loose, weak, careless. **9.** start, beginning, opening. **10.** far.

cloudy *adj.* **1.** overcast, gloomy, dark, foggy, gray. *The sky is so cloudy that it looks like it may rain.* **2.** vague, unclear, confused, uncertain, foggy. *My understanding of the problem is rather cloudy.* **Ant. 1.** clear, light. **2.** clear, understandable, certain.

clown *vb.* **1.** joke, jest, play, fool, ridicule. *When she gets bored she often clowns in class.* *-n.* **2.** buffoon, joker, jester, fool, comic. *He's such a clown in front of groups of people.*

club *n.* **1.** group, gang, organization, league, team, society. *She likes skiing, so she joined the ski club.* **2.** lodge, center, facility, haunt, hall, joint. *My friend and I play tennis at the sports club.* **3.** bat, stick, hammer, cudgel, baton, mallet. *She used a club to drive off the vicious dog.* *-vb.* **4.** whack, batter, bash, bat, hit, beat. *Chimpanzees tried to club the cheetah with sticks.*

clue *n.* **1.** evidence, trace, hint, sign, suggestion, idea. *I haven't a clue as to where they went.* *-vb.* **2.** suggest, intimate, hint, reveal, advise. *Clue me in as to what you want for your birthday.*

clumsy *adj.* bungling, awkward, ungainly, bumbling, uncoordinated. *Colts are clumsy because of their long legs.* **Ant.** graceful, agile.

cluster *n.* **1.** group, clump, collection, band, gathering, pack, mass. *Our galaxy is part of a large cluster that includes many other galaxies.* *-vb.* **2.** gather, mass, group, collect, assemble. *We seem to have a lot of exams clustered around our vacation week.* **Ant. 2.** scatter, disperse.

coach *n.* **1.** manager, leader, director, trainer, teacher, instructor. *The basketball coach made his players run ten laps.* *-vb.* **2.** train, instruct, tutor, teach, guide, drill. *She coached him on what to say in court.* **Ant. 1.** student, player. **2.** learn, study.

coarse *adj.* **1.** rough, bristly, uneven, scraggly, gnarled, rugged. *My grandfather has a coarse beard.* **2.** rude, uncivilized, impolite, crude, ill-mannered. *The arrogant prince considered the peasants a coarse lot.* **Ant. 1.** soft, smooth, even. **2.** polite, mannered, refined.

coast *n.* **1.** seashore, shore, beach, shoreline, seaside. *A pirate ship was sighted off the coast.* –*vb.* **2.** glide, skim, drift, slide, flow. *The bicyclist stopped pedaling and simply coasted along.*

coax *vb.* persuade, urge, influence, charm, steer. *Do you think you can coax your mother into letting me stay the night?* **Ant.** force, intimidate, pressure.

code *n.* system, law, regulation, statute, principle, ethic. *She lives her life by a strong code of honor.*

coerce *vb.* pressure, force, intimidate, compel, frighten, harass. *The soldier coerced the prisoner into revealing his identity.* **Ant.** ask, request, coax.

coil *n.* **1.** ring, spiral, loop, roll, reel, circle. *He carries a coil of wire in his tool kit.* –*vb.* **2.** wind, twist, loop, roll, reel. *Please coil the rope when you're through using it.*

coin *vb.* create, originate, devise, invent, mint, issue. *She coined a new word to describe her computer's unusual malfunction.*

coincide *vb.* agree, concur, correspond, fit, accord, match. *My version of the accident doesn't coincide with the other driver's story.* **Ant.** disagree, differ, conflict.

coincidence *n.* accident, chance, fate, happening, fluke. *It was pure coincidence that we named our sons the same thing.* **Ant.** plan, intent.

cold *n.* **1.** chill, chilliness, frost, iciness, coolness, frigidity. *The cold of the night air made our breath fog up.* **2.** illness, sickness, virus, fever, bronchitis. *He went to the doctor about his bad cold.* –*adj.* **3.** chilly, chilled, cool, cooled, shivering, wintry, icy. *Put on a sweatshirt if you're cold.* **4.** unresponsive, indifferent, uncaring, unfriendly, chilly. *He gave me a cold greeting.* –*adv.* **5.** absolutely, completely, thoroughly, perfectly, precisely. *She had the material down cold.* **Ant.** **1.** warmth, heat. **3.** hot, scorching, sweltering. **4.** warm, feeling, friendly. **5.** incompletely, imperfectly.

collapse *vb.* **1.** sink, deflate, crumble, disintegrate, fall, fail. *The hot-air balloon collapsed when a tree gashed a hole in it.* –*n.* **2.** breakdown, downfall, failure, exhaustion, disintegra-

tion. *The building was so old that no one was surprised by its collapse.*

colleague *n.* peer, associate, co-worker, teammate, ally, companion, partner. *Her colleagues threw her a going-away party at work.* **Ant.** enemy, rival, competitor.

collect *vb.* **1.** gather, assemble, amass, accumulate, compile. *She collects postage stamps.* **2.** raise, acquire, obtain, receive, solicit. *You may collect $200 when you pass "Go."* **3.** compose, calm, control, recover, prepare. *I was so upset that I had to collect myself before I could speak.* **Ant.** **1–2.** scatter, disperse, distribute.

collection *n.* assemblage, assembly, gathering, group, hoard. *Have you seen my coin collection?*

collective *adj.* joint, shared, common, united, unified, mutual. *It will take everyone's collective efforts to end pollution.* **Ant.** individual, separate, divided.

collide *vb.* crash, hit, smash, strike, bump. *The two skiers were not injured when they collided on the slopes.*

collision *n.* crash, impact, accident, contact, encounter, meeting. *The large asteroid broke apart in its collision with the moon.*

color *n.* **1.** tint, shade, hue, tone, coloration, tinge. *What color do you plan to paint your bike?* –*vb.* **2.** tint, tinge, dye, stain, paint. *He colored his hair so the gray wouldn't show.*

colorful *adj.* **1.** brilliant, multicolored, gaudy, vivid, bright. *The circus performers wore colorful costumes.* **2.** eccentric, odd, unique, quaint, lively. *The old woman who sleeps on the park bench is a rather colorful character.* **Ant.** **1.** pale, faded, dull. **2.** boring, uninteresting, colorless.

colossal *adj.* huge, large, gigantic, massive, mammoth, immense, enormous, mighty. *King Kong was a colossal ape.* **Ant.** small, tiny, little.

combat *n.* **1.** battle, fight, war, confrontation, conflict, dispute. *He was wounded in combat.* –*vb.* **2.** fight, battle, confront, attack, oppose, resist. *Some members of the community tried to combat drug use in their neighborhood.* **Ant.** **1.** peace, truce, harmony.

combine *vb.* mix, scramble, join, blend, fuse, merge, unite, mingle. *To make chocolate milk, one must combine milk with cocoa.* **Ant.** scatter, separate, divide.

come *vb.* **1.** move, approach, go toward, near, advance. *Come over here so I can show you how it's done.* **2.** show up, arrive, appear, turn up, materialize. *Do you think the package will come today?* **3.** occur, happen, chance, befall, transpire. *Halloween comes on October 31.* **4.** issue, arise, spring, emanate, originate. *She comes from France.* **5.** cover, reach, attain, go, extend. *These socks come all the way up to my knees.* **Ant. 1.** go, leave, depart.

comfort *vb.* **1.** cheer, ease, relieve, console, reassure. *She comforted the crying child.* *–n.* **2.** relief, reassurance, cheer, sympathy, satisfaction, consolation. *It was a comfort to know I could depend on my friends.* **3.** luxury, plenty, contentment, happiness, pleasure, enjoyment. *The queen and king lived in great comfort.* **Ant. 1.** irritate, annoy, upset. **2.** displeasure, trouble, worry. **3.** poverty, sorrow, discomfort.

comfortable *adj.* **1.** relaxed, restful, contented, untroubled, calm. *I felt comfortable talking to him, although I had only known him for a short time.* **2.** luxurious, pleasant, cozy, soft, pleasing, snug. *The chairs at school are not very comfortable.* **Ant. 1.** uncomfortable, anxious. **2.** uncomfortable, unpleasant.

comical *adj.* humorous, funny, amusing, witty, entertaining. *It was a comical moment when the cat fell into the trash can.* **Ant.** sad, tragic, somber.

command *vb.* **1.** order, tell, demand, instruct, direct, charge. *She commanded her dog to sit.* **2.** control, head, direct, supervise, manage, rule. *She commands the city's police department.* *–n.* **3.** order, instruction, request, rule, directive, charge. *The knights obeyed the queen's commands.* **4.** control, authority, leadership, domination, power, regulation. *The general has one thousand soldiers under his command.* **Ant. 1.** beg, ask, plead.

commence *vb.* begin, start, initiate, launch, embark, undertake. *The meeting will commence at noon.* **Ant.** end, finish, terminate, conclude.

commend *vb.* praise, applaud, honor, compliment, celebrate, approve. *I must commend you on your beautiful speech.* **Ant.** criticize, condemn, disapprove.

comment *vb.* **1.** remark, state, discuss, mention, express. *My grandfather always comments on how tall I have grown.* *–n.* **2.** remark, statement, mention, observation, explanation. *I was offended by her comment about the weight I have gained.*

commerce *n.* business, trade, traffic, industry, exchange. *That truck line is engaged in interstate commerce.*

commit *vb.* **1.** perform, do, execute, produce, enact, effect, pursue. *He was accused of having committed a serious crime.* **2.** promise, pledge, obligate, swear, bind. *Everyone must commit to bringing something for the party.*

common *adj.* **1.** typical, normal, usual, frequent, customary, habitual. *It's quite common for football players to get hurt.* **2.** mutual, communal, public, collective, joint. *A common wall separates the two properties.* **3.** plain, simple, average, unknown, ordinary, obscure. *No one listened to him because he was just a common foot soldier.* **4.** cheap, mean, low, vulgar, coarse, rude. *Her language was filled with common expressions she had heard on the streets.* *–n.* **5.** square, green, park, quad, mall. *Students gathered on the university common to hear the speeches.* **Ant. 1.** unusual, unique, uncommon. **2.** individual, personal. **3.** uncommon, special, extraordinary. **4.** cultured, refined.

commonly *adv.* usually, ordinarily, generally, normally, regularly. *She commonly goes to the beach on sunny weekends.* **Ant.** rarely, infrequently, never.

commotion *n.* uproar, frenzy, turmoil, disturbance, upheaval. *There was a commotion in the chicken coop when the fox got in.* **Ant.** calm, peacefulness, quiet.

communicate *vb.* **1.** speak, talk, converse, confer, correspond. *My pen pal and I communicate through letters.* **2.** impart, share, inform, show, announce, teach. *The old sage communicated her wisdom to the young novice.*

communication *n.* **1.** conversation, speaking, talking, writing, rapport. *The problem* *stemmed from a lack of communication within the office.* **2.** message, dispatch, communique, notification, bulletin. *There has been no communication from the city since the earthquake.*

community *n.* society, city, neighborhood, town, state, population, group. *The farmer lived in a rural community.*

commute *vb.* **1.** travel, journey, drive, bus, shuttle. *Most of our students commute to school.* **2.** reverse, reduce, change, diminish, decrease. *A governor has the power to commute a criminal's sentence.*

compact *adj.* **1.** small, compressed, packed, dense, crowded. *She drives a compact car.* *–vb.* **2.** pack, condense, press, stuff, cram, compress. *A machine in our kitchen compacts the trash.* *–n.* **3.** agreement, contract, deal, treaty, pledge. *Management and labor signed a compact giving the workers a raise.* **Ant. 1.** large, loose. **2.** loosen, unpack, scatter.

companion *n.* **1.** friend, comrade, protector, attendant, partner, mate. *A dog makes a good companion.* **2.** accessory, complement, accompaniment, supplement, appendage. *This thin volume is the companion to the required text.* **Ant. 1.** enemy, stranger.

company *n.* **1.** corporation, business, firm, partnership, establishment. *My sister works for a large engineering company.* **2.** group, assembly, gathering, party, team, unit, circle. *These actors are from a local theater company.* **3.** visitors, friends, guests, relatives, callers. *He's having company over for dinner tonight.* **4.** companionship, fellowship, friendship, association, intimacy. *I don't feel comfortable in the company of strangers.* **Ant. 3.** host, hostess. **4.** loneliness, solitude, isolation.

compare *vb.* **1.** relate, contrast, balance, review, consider. *It's best to compare prices before buying a car.* **2.** match, equal, rival, resemble, equate. *A frozen pizza cannot compare to a homemade one.*

comparison *n.* analogy, match, parallel, resemblance, similarity. *There's no comparison between reading about spaceflight and actually voyaging through outer space.* **Ant.** difference, dissimilarity, discrepancy.

compassion *n.* sympathy, tenderness, kindliness, mercy, feeling, love, concern, caring, warmth. *Mother Teresa was a woman of great compassion who devoted her life to helping the poor and sick.* **Ant.** indifference, coldness, unconcern.

compassionate *adj.* sympathetic, tender, kind, merciful, loving. *A compassionate person never turns away anyone truly in need.* **Ant.** uncompassionate, unfeeling, heartless.

compatible *adj.* agreeable, agreeing, cooperative, harmonious, compliant. *Fortunately, my roommate and I are quite compatible.* **Ant.** incompatible, clashing, disagreeing.

compel *vb.* force, oblige, pressure, coerce, drive, urge, impel. *Losing my job compelled me to make some changes in my lifestyle.* **Ant.** stop, deter, prevent, block.

compensation *n.* **1.** payment, settlement, damages, coverage, satisfaction. *He was awarded $1,000 in compensation for his work-related injury.* **2.** pay, salary, wages, earnings, remuneration. *She doesn't receive adequate compensation for the work she performs.*

compete *vb.* contest, contend, strive, fight, vie, challenge, combat. *Two actors are competing for the starring role.* **Ant.** quit, surrender, yield.

competent *adj.* able, trained, skillful, dependable, capable, experienced, qualified. *Make sure you go to a competent dentist.* **Ant.** incompetent, unskilled, unqualified.

competition *n.* **1.** contest, tournament, meet, game, match, bout. *The Olympics are a competition for athletes from all over the world.* **2.** competitor, rival, challenger, opponent, adversary. *My competition in the wrestling tournament is said to be quite good.* **3.** rivalry, opposition, struggle, contention, conflict. *There is a fierce competition between the top two students in our class.* **Ant. 2.** ally, comrade, teammate. **3.** teamwork, cooperation.

compile *vb.* assemble, gather, collect, accumulate, amass. *The coach compiled a list of his players' phone numbers.*

complain *vb.* criticize, protest, object, gripe, lament, whine. *The diner complained that his* *meat was undercooked.* **Ant.** approve, compliment, praise.

complaint *n.* **1.** criticism, objection, condemnation, reprimand, rebuke. *She lodged a complaint with the hotel manager about the lack of towels.* **2.** illness, sickness, disorder, infirmity, ailment. *The man suffered from several serious complaints.* **Ant. 1.** praise, approval, compliment. **2.** remedy, cure.

complement *n.* **1.** addition, companion, counterpart, accessory, supplement. *Your choice of wine was a fine complement to the dinner.* **2.** quota, limit, totality, entirety, maximum. *The ship left, although its full complement of crew members was not on board.* –*vb.* **3.** supplement, complete, perfect, fulfill, satisfy. *The illustrations really complement this book.* **Ant. 3.** ruin, lessen, diminish.

complete *vb.* **1.** finish, conclude, end, perform, accomplish, fulfill. *She completed her homework five minutes before class started.* –*adj.* **2.** entire, total, whole, full, absolute, uncut. *We bought the complete set of thirty volumes.* **3.** thorough, in-depth, perfect, extensive, exhaustive, widespread. *The mechanic gave my car a complete tune-up.* **Ant. 1.** start, begin, initiate. **2.** incomplete, partial, deficient. **3.** spotty, partial, superficial.

complex *adj.* **1.** complicated, difficult, involved, perplexing, intricate. *Mathematicians often use complex equations.* –*n.* **2.** maze, network, system, labyrinth, structure. *We wandered around the mall complex.*

complicate *vb.* confuse, muddle, involve, entangle, mix up. *Getting a second job will complicate your life.* **Ant.** simplify, clarify, disentangle.

complicated *adj.* complex, involved, difficult, intricate, hard, elaborate. *The musician played a very complicated piece of music.* **Ant.** easy, simple, uninvolved.

compliment *n.* **1.** praise, acclaim, approval, commendation, congratulation, flattery. *She received several compliments on her excellent performance in the play.* –*vb.* **2.** praise, acclaim, commend, congratulate, applaud. *He complimented her on her win in the track meet.* **Ant. 1.** disapproval, insult, complaint. **2.** insult, condemn.

complimentary *adj.* **1.** praising, approving, flattering, admiring, favorable. *His new book received complimentary reviews.* **2.** free, gratis, gratuitous, donated. *I have two complimentary tickets for tonight's movie.* **Ant. 1.** uncomplimentary, unflattering, disapproving.

comply *vb.* follow, conform, observe, obey, satisfy, fulfill, consent. *My brother did not comply with my parents' rules.* **Ant.** disobey, evade, disregard, oppose.

compose *vb.* **1.** create, conceive, produce, write, devise. *She composed a new play for her theater group.* **2.** comprise, constitute, embody, form, fashion. *Copper and tin are the elements that compose bronze.* **3.** settle, calm, quiet, soothe, arrange. *Try to compose yourself before you tell him the tragic news.* **Ant. 1.** destroy, demolish, take apart. **3.** excite, upset, agitate.

composure *n.* self-control, calm, quiet, assurance, poise, dignity. *The angry man regained his composure and quietly sat down.* **Ant.** passion, agitation, excitement.

compound *vb.* **1.** increase, augment, intensify, worsen, complicate. *You'll only compound the problem if you put it off any longer.* **2.** mix, blend, mingle, combine, devise, make. *A pharmacist is a person who compounds medicinal drugs.* –*adj.* **3.** multiple, complex, composite, complicated, mixed. *She has sustained a compound fracture of the left arm.* –*n.* **4.** combination, composite, blend, mixture, fusion. *Brass is a compound made of copper and zinc.* **Ant. 1.** lessen, decrease, reduce. **2.** separate, divide, isolate. **3.** simple, elemental, unmixed.

comprehend *vb.* understand, grasp, perceive, appreciate, discern, follow. *I cannot comprehend why you like green beans.* **Ant.** misunderstand.

comprehensive *adj.* complete, thorough, sweeping, broad, extensive, inclusive. *The final exam will be a comprehensive test covering the entire year's work.* **Ant.** partial, incomplete, specialized.

comprise *vb.* include, embrace, contain, cover, involve, enclose. *Eggs, toast and orange juice comprise my typical breakfast.*

compromise *n.* **1.** bargain, arrangement, agreement, understanding, accommodation, settlement. *We made a compromise wherein each of us would pay for half.* –vb. **2.** agree, accommodate, settle, negotiate, exchange, yield. *Why don't we compromise by staying at your house the first night and mine the second?* **3.** risk, endanger, jeopardize, embarrass, discredit, expose. *By blurting out my identity, you have compromised my safety.* **Ant. 1.** argument, quarrel, disagreement. **2.** argue, dispute, disagree. **3.** support, strengthen, guard.

compulsory *adj.* enforced, required, necessary, mandatory, unavoidable, binding. *School is compulsory until the age of sixteen.* **Ant.** optional, elective, voluntary.

compute *vb.* calculate, determine, figure, add, ascertain. *Astronomers have computed the distance from the Earth to the Sun to be 93 million miles.*

comrade *n.* friend, partner, associate, teammate, companion, colleague. *The lost explorer's comrades searched the jungle for him.* **Ant.** enemy, stranger, outsider.

conceal *vb.* hide, camouflage, cover, mask, disguise, bury, cloak, veil. *He concealed the Easter eggs in different parts of the room.* **Ant.** reveal, expose, show.

concealment *n.* covering, masking, disguising, hiding, concealing. *The newspaper exposed the government's concealment of its dealings with terrorists.* **Ant.** showing, disclosure, presentation.

concede *vb.* **1.** accept, agree, grant, acknowledge, recognize, allow. *Because of the article you showed me, I must concede that you were correct.* **2.** surrender, relinquish, resign, yield, transfer, deliver. *The champion conceded her title to this year's winner.* **Ant. 1.** reject, disagree, deny. **2.** win, defeat.

conceited *adj.* arrogant, vain, snobbish, smug, egotistical. *The conceited athlete thought he was the best in the state.* **Ant.** humble, modest, unassuming.

conceive *vb.* **1.** create, form, generate, initiate, produce, originate. *She conceived a plan to expand her company's business.* **2.** imagine, think, suppose, dream, consider, comprehend. *I can't conceive of a place I would rather be than in the mountains.*

concentrate *vb.* **1.** study, ponder, think, contemplate, analyze. *I must concentrate hard to memorize all these dates.* **2.** center, converge, focus, gather, collect, localize. *They concentrated their search in the local neighborhood.* **3.** condense, compress, reduce, consolidate, thicken. *Please concentrate the soup by adding less water than the directions call for.* **Ant. 1.** ignore, neglect. **2.** scatter, spread. **3.** dilute, weaken.

concentration *n.* **1.** thought, attention, regard, study, application. *This problem requires my total concentration.* **2.** collection, mass, gathering, centralization, convergence. *There's a concentration of motels on the edge of town.* **Ant. 1.** inattention, disregard. **2.** scattering, dispersion.

concept *n.* idea, theory, thought, notion, belief, conjecture. *My concept of your house is different now that I've seen it.*

concern *n.* **1.** matter, affair, interest, business, consideration. *My brother's whereabouts is not my concern.* **2.** care, attention, regard, worry, anxiety. *Local citizens listened with concern to news of the approaching tornado.* –vb. **3.** disturb, distress, worry, perturb, bother, pain. *His continual sickness concerned his father.* **4.** affect, interest, involve, influence. *This talk does not concern you.* **Ant. 2.** coldness, indifference, disregard.

concert *n.* **1.** performance, show, symphony, festival, recital. *Fans jumped onto the stage at the rock concert.* **2.** agreement, harmony, closeness, unity, accord. *The troop of soldiers marched in concert.* **Ant. 2.** discord, disagreement, separation.

concise *adj.* short, brief, condensed, compact, abridged, consolidated. *The newscaster gave a concise review of the day's news.* **Ant.** lengthy, long, wordy, rambling.

conclude *vb.* **1.** finish, complete, end, terminate, halt, stop. *The performer concluded her show with her most popular song.* **2.** reason, decide, determine, deduce, assume, suppose. *When he didn't show up, we concluded that he didn't want to come.* **Ant. 1.** begin, start, continue.

conclusion *n.* **1.** finish, close, completion, termination, end. *At the movie's conclusion, the audience applauded.* **2.** decision, judgment, determination, understanding, observation. *Have you reached a conclusion about what college you're going to attend?* **Ant. 1.** beginning, start, opening. **2.** uncertainty, indecision.

concrete *n.* **1.** cement, pavement, asphalt, mortar. *Outside Mann's Chinese Theater, the concrete contains the handprints of movie stars.* –*adj.* **2.** direct, actual, real, physical, solid, conclusive. *She said she needed concrete proof before she would believe that ghosts exist.* **Ant. 2.**vague, theoretical, obscure.

concur *vb.* agree, assent, consent, approve, ratify. *I must concur with your mother's decision not to let you attend the party.* **Ant.**disagree, disapprove, reject.

condemn *vb.* **1.** denounce, reproach, criticize, rebuke, accuse. *The media condemned the police officer for his cruel treatment of the suspect.* **2.** sentence, convict, doom, judge, ban. *The tribal council condemned the thief to twelve years as an outcast.* **Ant. 1.** applaud, admire, praise. **2.**acquit, free, excuse.

condemnation *n.* denunciation, reproach, criticism, rebuke, disapproval. *The Soviet Union received worldwide condemnation for its shooting down of an airliner.* **Ant.** praise, approval, acclaim.

condense *vb.* compress, reduce, shorten, compact, consolidate, trim. *He condensed his ten-page report down to five pages.* **Ant.** expand, increase, enlarge.

condition *n.* **1.** state, shape, form, situation, status. *Our school's dirt racetrack was in poor condition after the heavy rains.* **2.** problem, illness, ailment, complaint, sickness. *The elderly woman suffers from an arthritic condition of the bones.* **3.** term, provision, restriction, demand, requirement, limitation. *I told her a secret, on the condition she tell it to no one else.* –*vb.* **4.** train, shape, practice, prepare, coach, equip. *The athletes conditioned themselves for the upcoming competition.*

condolence *n.* sympathy, support, compassion, comfort, pity, understanding. *We sent our condolences to the bereaved family.* **Ant.** congratulations, rejoicing.

condone *vb.* pardon, forgive, excuse, disregard, justify, approve. *Her parents refused to condone to her late-night partying.* **Ant.** criticize, condemn, disapprove.

conduct *n.* **1.** behavior, manner, actions, habits, performance. *His wild conduct at the formal dinner annoyed the host.* **2.** operation, management, administration, direction, supervision. *The manager's job is to oversee the conduct of all operations.* –*vb.* **3.** behave, carry, direct, handle, manage, supervise. *We were pleased that you conducted yourself in a mature manner.* **4.** lead, guide, convoy, escort, usher. *An usher conducted us to our seats.*

confederate *n.* ally, partner, associate, accomplice, colleague. *The criminal's confederates were also arrested.* **Ant.** opponent, enemy, rival.

confer *vb.* **1.** discuss, converse, consult, deliberate, talk. *I conferred with my dentist about getting braces for my teeth.* **2.** award, present, give, grant, bestow. *The queen conferred the highest honor of her realm on the brave warrior.* **Ant. 2.** revoke, withhold, deny.

conference *n.* meeting, discussion, talk, session, deliberation, interchange. *Our teachers have conferences with their students' parents each semester.*

confess *vb.* admit, concede, acknowledge, own, disclose, reveal. *He confessed to his roommate that he broke the stereo.* **Ant.** hide, deny, withhold.

confession *n.* admission, acknowledgment, telling, disclosure, assertion, revelation. *The prisoner made a written confession.* **Ant.** denial, disclaimer, repudiation.

confide *vb.* tell, disclose, reveal, divulge, entrust, trust, impart. *I confide my secrets to my best friend.*

confidence *n.* **1.** self-reliance, sureness, certainty, assurance, conviction. *It takes confidence to run for political office.* **2.** faith, reliance, trust, belief, dependence, conviction. *I have confidence in your ability to pass the test.* **Ant. 1.** uncertainty, self-doubt. **2.** distrust, doubt, suspicion.

confident *adj.* **1.** certain, assured, convinced, sure, optimistic, positive. *I'm confident I can do the job.* **2.** self-assured, bold, daring, fearless, assertive. *My confident friend has no* *trouble asking people out on a date.* **Ant. 1.** doubtful, uncertain. **2.** hesitant, anxious, insecure.

confidential *adj.* private, secret, classified, restricted, undisclosed. *Only highly trusted employees could look at the confidential report.* **Ant.** open, circulated, public.

confine *vb.* **1.** restrict, limit, hold, imprison, cage, constrain, enclose. *The sheep were confined in a pen.* *–n.* **2.** limit, margin, boundary, edge, border. *Inmates were not allowed beyond the confines of the prison yard.* **Ant. 1.** free, loose, liberate.

confirm *vb.* uphold, verify, prove, affirm, establish. *The letter confirmed my worst suspicions.* **Ant.** oppose, contradict, refute.

confiscate *vb.* take, seize, impound, claim, secure, possess. *A teacher confiscated the student's squirt gun.* **Ant.** return, release, deliver.

conflict *n.* **1.** fight, battle, struggle, clash, warfare, hostilities, combat. *The conflicts in the Middle East have been going on for years.* *–vb.* **2.** clash, disagree, struggle, contradict, differ. *My views on the environment conflict with his.* **Ant. 1.** peace, settlement, agreement. **2.** agree, concur.

conform *vb.* obey, follow, comply, observe, adapt, accommodate. *In the corporate world, one must conform to a formal dress code.* **Ant.** differ, disobey, oppose.

confront *vb.* meet, encounter, face, challenge, oppose, tackle, resist. *She confronted her fears by entering the haunted house.* **Ant.** avoid, flee, evade.

confrontation *n.* clash, showdown, challenge, defiance, conflict. *She had a confrontation with her boss involving her request for a raise.*

confuse *vb.* bewilder, puzzle, baffle, perplex, mystify. *The problems in my physics class often just confuse me.* **Ant.** clarify, enlighten, explain.

confusing *adj.* puzzling, obscure, baffling, perplexing, disturbing, disconcerting. *Finding an address in a big city can be confusing.* **Ant.** orderly, clear, simple.

confusion *n.* **1.** bewilderment, puzzlement, mystification, perplexity, disorientation. *His look of confusion told me he didn't understand my explanation.* **2.** turmoil, agitation, disorder, upheaval, disarray, disorganization. *There was a great deal of confusion at the airport due to the construction going on.* **Ant. 1.** clarification, enlightenment, explanation. **2.** orderliness, order, organization.

congested *adj.* plugged, filled, jammed, choked, blocked, crowded, stuffed. *The freeways were congested with traffic.* **Ant.** empty, clear, uncrowded.

congratulate *vb.* compliment, praise, salute, applaud, cheer. *I congratulated him on his recent marriage.* **Ant.** criticize, rebuke, condemn.

congratulation *n.* best wishes, compliments, blessings, praise. *I sent her my congratulations when she graduated from college.* **Ant.** criticism, condemnation, reproach.

congregate *vb.* gather, assemble, mass, meet, collect, group, swarm, cluster. *Several dogs congregated about the fire hydrant.* **Ant.** separate, scatter, disband.

connect *vb.* **1.** join, unite, attach, bind, couple, link, tie. *A small road connects the two towns.* **2.** equate, relate, identify, associate, correlate. *It took me a while to connect the voice I was hearing to my old friend from elementary school.* **Ant. 1.** disconnect, separate, split. **2.** dissociate, separate.

connection *n.* **1.** junction, union, conjunction, bond, coupling. *The television repairman said the problem was a faulty connection.* **2.** association, relationship, attachment, alliance, relation. *I no longer have any connections with that company.* **Ant. 2.** alienation, separation, detachment.

conquer *vb.* overcome, defeat, subdue, master, crush, vanquish, overpower. *Attila the Hun tried to conquer Europe in the fifth century.* **Ant.** lose, fall, surrender.

conqueror *n.* victor, winner, champion, vanquisher, defeater. *Citizens of the defeated city-state were forced to pay tribute to their conquerors.* **Ant.** vanquished, defeated, loser.

conscience *n.* principles, standards, morals, ethics, scruples. *Doesn't it bother your conscience to lie?*

conscientious *adj.* responsible, reliable, trustworthy, sincere, dependable, dedicated. *She was a conscientious employee who never left before her work was done.* **Ant.**unreliable, irresponsible, undependable.

conscious *adj.* **1.** awake, aware, sensible, thinking, alert. *The doctors said we could visit him when he becomes conscious.* **2.** aware, knowledgeable, knowing, informed, mindful. *Are you conscious of the amount of pollution in our environment?* **3.** deliberate, willful, intentional, planned, purposeful. *We made a conscious effort to notice the shy girl..* **Ant. 1.** unaware, unconscious, asleep. **2.** unaware, unknowing, uninformed. **3.** unintentional, unconscious, accidental.

consecutive *adj.* successive, uninterrupted, continuous, unbroken, sequential. *He hit three consecutive home runs.* **Ant.** interrupted, broken, discontinuous.

consensus *n.* agreement, consent, accord, unanimity, concord. *The council reached a consensus on the date of the election.* **Ant.** disagreement, discord, dissension.

consent *vb.* **1.** agree, allow, accept, grant, approve, permit, sanction. *The actor consented to having his picture taken with me.* *–n.* **2.** agreement, permission, approval, endorsement, assent, leave, sanction. *You need the principal's consent to leave campus.* **Ant. 1.** disagree, disapprove, refuse. **2.** disagreement, disapproval.

consequence *n.* **1.** aftermath, outcome, result, upshot, development. *All those cavities are the consequence of not brushing properly.* **2.** importance, significance, moment, note, seriousness. *What you do with your life is of no consequence to me.* **Ant. 1.** source, cause, origin. **2.** unimportance, insignificance.

conservative *adj.* **1.** right-wing, traditional, nonliberal, conventional, reactionary. *The Republicans are known for their conservative policies.* **2.** cautious, safe, prudent, careful, sparing, wary. *I try to be conservative with my spending.* *–n.* **3.** right-winger, rightist, traditionalist, conventionalist, reactionary. *The city's conservatives did not like the new dance club.* **Ant. 1.** liberal, progressive, radical. **2.** risky, careless, daring. **3.** radical, liberal, progressive.

conserve *vb.* save, preserve, guard, maintain, protect, safeguard. *The marathon runner conserved her energy for the final mile.* **Ant.** waste, exhaust, consume.

consider *vb.* **1.** study, review, deliberate, contemplate, examine, evaluate. *Why don't you consider my offer and tell me your decision tomorrow?* **2.** judge, view, think, believe, regard, feel. *I consider smoking cigarettes an unhealthy habit.* **Ant. 1.** disregard, ignore, overlook.

considerable *adj.* **1.** significant, important, noteworthy, great, major, impressive. *Winning the Nobel Peace Prize is a considerable honor.* **2.** large, substantial, abundant, sizable, extensive, massive. *It looked like he had gained a considerable amount of weight.* **Ant. 1.** unimportant, trivial, minor. **2.** small, scant, meager.

considerate *adj.* thoughtful, kind, sensitive, concerned, tactful. *A considerate woman held the door open for me.* **Ant.** inconsiderate, thoughtless, unkind.

consideration *n.* **1.** thought, attention, study, reflection, regard, examination, deliberation. *I have agreed to your proposal after giving it much consideration.* **2.** thoughtfulness, concern, kindliness, respect, courtesy, regard. *Out of consideration for your neighbors, don't play your music too loud.* **3.** factor, concern, point, aspect, detail, item. *The distance one must drive is an important consideration in deciding which job to take.* **Ant. 1.** inattention, oversight, omission. **2.** discourtesy, rudeness.

consist *vb.* contain, comprise, involve, include, embody. *My family consists of my mother, my two brothers, and myself.*

consistency, *n.* **1.** firmness, thickness, texture, composition, density, nature. *The soup had a thin consistency.* **2.** agreement, conformity, harmony, accord, compatibility, unity. *Her taste in movies has no consistency.* **Ant. 2.** inconsistency, disagreement, incompatibility.

consolation *n.* relief, sympathy, comfort, condolence, support. *As a consolation to the losers, each was given a ribbon.* **Ant.** discouragement, dismay, discomfort.

console *vb.* comfort, aid, help, support, hearten, cheer. *We took him out for pizza to* *console him after he didn't get the job he wanted.* **Ant.** hurt, upset, bother, disturb.

consolidate *vb.* join, combine, unite, merge, pool, concentrate. *If we consolidate our efforts, we'll get the job done much faster.* **Ant.** separate, divide, part.

conspicuous *adj.* obvious, plain, visible, apparent, evident, noticeable, prominent. *I was upset because my pimple was so conspicuous.* **Ant.** invisible, concealed, unnoticeable.

conspiracy *n.* plot, scheme, intrigue, treason, deception, trick. *The two generals were involved in a conspiracy to topple the government.*

constant *adj.* **1.** unchanging, fixed, even, regular, uniform, steady. *The rower maintained a constant pace.* **2.** continual, nonstop, unbroken, uninterrupted, endless, persistent. *There has been a constant downpour all day.* **3.** devoted, faithful, loyal, dedicated, trustworthy. *The dog has been her constant companion for years.* **Ant. 1.** changing, irregular, uneven. **2.** infrequent, occasional, erratic. **3.** unfaithful, disloyal, undependable.

constantly *adv.* regularly, continually, frequently, habitually, continuously. *He's constantly losing his car keys.* **Ant.** occasionally, seldom, rarely.

constrain *vb.* restrain, restrict, confine, bind, detain, contain. *We constrained the dog to the pole with a chain.* **Ant.** free, release, loose.

constrict *vb.* **1.** pinch, cramp, bind, squeeze, strangle. *The tight shirt collar constricted my throat.* **2.** obstruct, block, clog, close, congest, choke. *Dead trees constricted the stream.* **Ant. 1.** loosen, unbind, swell. **2.** unclog, clear, open.

construct *vb.* build, make, create, erect, assemble, form, produce. *She spent all day constructing a treehouse in her backyard.* **Ant.** destroy, demolish, dismantle.

constructive *adj.* useful, helpful, valuable, beneficial, practical, usable. *I hate it when someone tells me they're giving me constructive criticism.* **Ant.** destructive, harmful, worthless.

consult *vb.* talk, confer, discuss, deliberate, counsel. *She and I consulted on the best time for a party.*

consultation *n.* council, conference, meeting, discussion, deliberation, analysis. *I was having computer troubles, so I called in an expert for a consultation.*

consume *vb.* **1.** absorb, eat, devour, drink, drain, use. *I was so thirsty, that I consumed three cans of soda.* **2.** destroy, devastate, demolish, waste, ravage. *Fire consumed the old building.* **Ant. 1.** produce, supply, save. **2.** save, restore.

consumption *n.* use, expenditure, depletion, usage, draining. *Americans drive so much that our national gasoline consumption is huge.* **Ant.** conservation, production, saving.

contact *n.* **1.** touch, connection, meeting, encounter, joining, impact. *The whole world burst into applause when the Apollo landing craft made contact with the Moon's surface.* –*vb.* **2.** communicate with, approach, reach, meet, touch, seek. *Scientists are trying to contact extraterrestrial life.*

contagious *adj.* catching, transmittable, infectious, spreadable, transmissible. *You should not be around someone with the measles, because it is a very contagious disease.* **Ant.** noncontagious, noninfectious.

contain *vb.* **1.** include, hold, carry, bear, retain, embrace. *This bottle contains apple juice.* **2.** restrain, control, check, limit, bind, suppress. *A large cage was used to contain the gorilla.* **Ant. 2.** free, release, loosen.

contaminate *vb.* pollute, poison, foul, soil, taint, defile, corrupt. *Toxic waste from the factory contaminated our drinking water.* **Ant.** clean, cleanse, purify.

contemplate *vb.* ponder, consider, meditate, study, deliberate. *Please contemplate my request before answering.*

contemplation *n.* thought, thinking, reflection, deliberation, study. *She reached her decision after much contemplation of the problem.*

contempt *n.* scorn, hatred, disrespect, revulsion, disgust, distaste, detestation. *I have great contempt for people who hurt others.* **Ant.** respect, admiration, affection.

contemptible *adj.* shameful, low, mean, revolting, dishonorable, offensive. *The way in which he treats his children is contemptible.* **Ant.**

admirable, honorable, respectable, praiseworthy.

contend *vb.* **1.** battle, fight, struggle, compete, wrestle, contest. *Two chimpanzees contended for one banana.* **2.** claim, hold, maintain, assert, state, declare. *I still contend there's no way you can hike up there in a single day.* **Ant. 1.** surrender, quit, yield. **2.** reject, deny, disclaim.

content *n.* **1.** insides, ingredients, substance, matter, subject. *The contents of the sealed box remain a mystery.* **2.** size, capacity, volume, area, scope, extent. *The container has a three-gallon content.* **3.** satisfaction, happiness, comfort, gladness, pleasure, delight. *She got some content out of knowing her rival had failed.* *-adj.* **4.** satisfied, pleased, delighted, happy, unworried, untroubled. *Are you content with your new apartment?* *-vb.* **5.** please, satisfy, delight, comfort, gladden, pacify. *I tried to content the baby with a lollipop.* **Ant. 3.** discontent, annoyance, displeasure. **4.** dissatisfied, displeased, troubled. **5.** upset, irritate, annoy.

contented *adj.* pleased, happy, satisfied, content, comfortable. *My teacher was not contented with my paper and asked me to rewrite it.* **Ant.** unhappy, discontented, concerned, irritated.

contest *n.* **1.** competition, meet, tournament, trial, match, game. *I entered a drawing contest.* **2.** fight, battle, encounter, struggle, conflict, clash. *The couple is often engaged in a contest of wills.* *-vb.* **3.** fight, battle, struggle, contend, strive, compete. *Two top executives contested over control of the company.* **4.** challenge, oppose, dispute, argue, counter. *The millionaire's disinherited daughter contested his will.* **Ant. 2.** truce, peace, agreement. **3.** surrender, yield, quit. **4.** acknowledge, accept, adopt.

contestant *n.* competitor, entrant, participant, contender, rival. *There were more than fifty contestants in the chess tournament.*

context *n.* framework, setting, situation, circumstance, surroundings. *The problem arose from her hearing my statement out of context.*

continual *adj.* **1.** unending, unbroken, nonstop, uninterrupted, ceaseless. *A continual stream of toxic waste entered the ocean from the factory.* **2.** constant, frequent, habitual, regular, repeated. *Their fighting is a continual thing.* **Ant.**

1. broken, erratic, fitful. **2.** infrequent, occasional.

continue *vb.* **1.** extend, proceed, progress, project, resume. *This road continues for fifty more miles before reaching the ocean.* **2.** remain, endure, stay, last, abide. *How long will you continue at your current job?* **Ant. 1.** discontinue, stop, pause. **2.** resign, quit, leave.

continuous *adj.* unbroken, unending, uninterrupted, constant, endless. *This spring provides us with a continuous water supply.* **Ant.** broken, disconnected, infrequent.

contort *vb.* twist, bend, distort, knot, deform. *The basketball player had to contort himself to get into the compact car.* **Ant.** straighten, smooth, unbend.

contract *n.* **1.** agreement, arrangement, deal, understanding, compact, bargain. *The baseball player signed a contract to play for two years.* *-vb.* **2.** engage, agree, pledge, promise, undertake, vow. *A carpenter contracted to rebuild our kitchen cabinets for $500.* **3.** assume, acquire, develop, incur, catch. *She contracted malaria in the jungle.* **4.** compress, shorten, reduce, tighten, decrease, constrict. *I could feel my heart contract in fear.* **Ant. 2.** refuse, withdraw. **3.** evade, dodge, avoid. **4.** lengthen, expand, increase.

contradict *vb.* refute, deny, differ, counter, challenge, oppose, dispute. *I must contradict you when you say the world is flat.* **Ant.** confirm, verify, support.

contradictory *adj.* contrary, opposing, disagreeing, conflicting, different. *We have contradictory views on the topic of disarmament.* **Ant.** similar, comparable, equivalent.

contrary *adj.* **1.** against, opposed, opposite, different, other. *Contrary to the advertisement, this cleanser does not remove tough stains.* **2.** disagreeable, stubborn, obstinate, unpredictable, unaccommodating, unfriendly. *Mules are known to be contrary animals.* **Ant. 1.** consistent, similar. **2.** agreeable, friendly, accommodating.

contrast *vb.* **1.** differentiate, deviate, differ, diverge, depart, vary. *Make the lettering light so it will contrast with the dark background.* *-n.* **2.** difference, variation, distinction, divergence, unlikeness. *There was quite a contrast between the* *owner's mansion and the worker's shack.* **Ant. 1.** compare, relate, resemble. **2.** similarity, resemblance.

contribute *vb.* **1.** give, donate, volunteer, bestow, grant, supply. *Will you contribute money to help save the whales?* **2.** influence, advance, promote, aid, supplement. *The prime minister's death contributed to the nation's downfall.* **Ant. 1.** take, keep, receive. **2.** avert, detract, curb.

contribution *n.* donation, gift, grant, offering, endowment, bestowal. *Would you like to make a contribution to the United Way?*

contrite *adj.* sorry, remorseful, repentant, ashamed, regretful, apologetic. *The man who hit my car had a contrite look.* **Ant.** unapologetic, unremorseful, unashamed.

contrive *vb.* invent, imagine, design, create, plan, improvise. *He contrived an illness to miss a day of school.*

control *vb.* **1.** rule, direct, manage, run, supervise, administer, govern, oversee. *Who really controls the government?* **2.** check, curb, restrain, contain, suppress, leash. *Try to control your anger.* –*n.* **3.** direction, management, supervision, command, regulation, rule. *It's out of my control.* **4.** check, curb, restraint, constraint, damper, block. *Congress must put stronger controls on the spending of government money.* **Ant. 2.** express, release, lose.

controversial *adj.* sensitive, delicate, questionable, debatable, arguable, doubtful. *The new law requiring dogs to wear diapers is highly controversial.* **Ant.** safe, certain, noncontroversial.

controversy *n.* debate, disagreement, dispute, argument, quarrel, strife, contention. *There's controversy surrounding the question of life on other planets.* **Ant.** agreement, harmony, accord.

convene *vb.* assemble, gather, collect, meet, congregate, rally. *Our Boy Scout troop will convene on Saturday for an awards ceremony.* **Ant.** disperse, disband, scatter.

convenience *n.* handiness, usefulness, advantage, comfort, benefit. *His cabin lacks the convenience of indoor plumbing.* **Ant.** inconvenience, disadvantage, hardship.

convenient *adj.* **1.** fitted, suitable, advantageous, useful, beneficial. *Let's make the appointment at a time that is convenient for you.* **2.** handy, near, nearby, accessible, available. *The neighborhood park is a convenient place for walking my dog.* **Ant. 1.** inconvenient, inappropriate. **2.** remote, inaccessible.

conventional *adj.* normal, usual, traditional, customary, common, proper. *He would like a conventional wedding.* **Ant.** unusual, unconventional, uncommon.

converge *vb.* join, meet, unite, merge, approach, link. *Any two sides of a triangle converge at a single point.* **Ant.** diverge, separate, disperse, part.

conversation *n.* discussion, talk, chat, dialogue, conference. *I had a long conversation with my parents about my failing grades.*

converse *vb.* talk, discuss, chat, speak, communicate, confer. *I wish to converse with you in private.*

convert *vb.* **1.** turn, change, alter, transform, modify, reshape. *We had to convert our dollars to British pounds when we visited England.* –*n.* **2.** disciple, follower, recruit, believer, proselyte. *The converts were instructed in the teachings of their new religion.*

convey *vb.* **1.** carry, move, transport, transfer, bear, haul, deliver. *Trucks were used to convey the soldiers to their new base.* **2.** communicate, impart, send, tell, reveal, relate. *I spent a lot of time choosing a card that would convey just the right message.*

convict *vb.* **1.** condemn, sentence, blame, judge, doom. *The jury convicted the defendant on one count of murder.* –*n.* **2.** felon, criminal, violator, offender, lawbreaker, prisoner. *The convicts spent their work time making license plates.* **Ant. 1.** acquit.

convince *vb.* persuade, influence, impress, sway, satisfy, assure. *I tried to convince her that I was telling the truth.*

convoy *vb.* **1.** escort, accompany, lead, conduct, usher, pilot, guide. *Two tugboats convoyed the damaged ship to safety.* –*n.* **2.** escort, guard, cover, protection, group, fleet. *During World War*

II, ships traveled with convoys to protect themselves from enemy submarines.

cook *vb.* prepare, make, concoct, bake, roast, grill, fry. *Whose turn is it to cook dinner tonight?*

cool *adj.* **1.** chilly, cold, icy, freezing, nippy. *I love cool summer evenings.* **2.** composed, calm, controlled, collected, serene. *It's a rare person who can remain cool during an earthquake.* **3.** unfriendly, distant, indifferent, detached, apathetic. *He's rather cool towards his little sister.* –*vb.* **4.** lose heat, chill, refrigerate, ice, freeze. *My coffee needs to cool before I can drink it.* **5.** calm, moderate, control, dampen, quiet. *It would be best to let your temper cool before you speak to him.* **Ant. 1.** warm, hot, sweltering. **2.** excited, agitated, disturbed. **3.** friendly, attached, warm. **4.** heat, warm. **5.** aggravate, intensify.

cooperate *vb.* collaborate, coordinate, unite, combine, join. *The groups that cooperated the most were the first to finish.* **Ant.** fight, oppose, disagree.

cooperation *n.* participation, collaboration, teamwork, association, help. *I need your cooperation to finish this project on time.* **Ant.** opposition, hindrance, dissension.

coordinate *vb.* harmonize, match, balance, organize, adjust, order, arrange. *I try to buy clothes that coordinate well.* **Ant.** disorganize, jumble, disrupt.

cope *vb.* manage, control, survive, endure, handle. *She coped really well with the tragedy.*

copy *n.* **1.** reproduction, duplicate, imitation, replica, likeness, representation. *That painting is just a copy of the original.* –*vb.* **2.** imitate, mirror, repeat, mimic, echo, follow. *My little brother copies every movement I make.* **3.** duplicate, reproduce, replicate. *Please copy this report for me.* **Ant. 1.** original, prototype. **2.** invent, originate, develop.

cord *n.* string, rope, thread, twine, line. *I need a piece of cord to tie this package.*

cordial *adj.* friendly, warm, gracious, sociable, kindly, pleasant, cheerful. *He was not very cordial to his girlfriend's old boyfriend.* **Ant.** unfriendly, cold, reserved.

core *n.* center, middle, heart, nucleus, kernel. *How many seeds does the average apple have in its core?*

corporation *n.* company, enterprise, business, association, firm, partnership. *They both work for the same corporation.*

correct *vb.* **1.** fix, repair, remedy, amend, rectify, right. *Can you correct the malfunction in my computer?* **2.** reprimand, reprove, rebuke, discipline, punish. *He corrected the small child for biting the dog.* –*adj.* **3.** right, exact, accurate, precise, proper, suitable. *You must have the correct change for this vending machine.* **Ant. 1.** ruin, spoil, damage. **2.** praise, compliment, excuse. **3.** wrong, bad, incorrect.

correction *n.* remedy, improvement, alteration, repair, modification, revision. *He typed my name wrong and had to make a correction.*

correspond *vb.* **1.** communicate, write, report, signal. *Although I'm moving away, we can still correspond.* **2.** agree, coincide, match, parallel, equate. *The red dots correspond to our team, the blue dots to the opposing team.* **Ant. 2.** disagree, differ, contrast.

corridor *n.* passageway, hall, hallway, walkway, avenue, lane, route. *The elevators are at the end of this corridor.*

corroborate *vb.* verify, validate, substantiate, confirm, document. *My new employer telephoned my old employer to corroborate the information on my job application.* **Ant.** invalidate, disprove, contradict.

corrode *vb.* erode, consume, deteriorate, disintegrate, rust. *Acid will corrode certain types of metal.*

corrupt *adj.* **1.** dishonest, immoral, crooked, dishonorable, wicked. *The corrupt police officer took bribes.* –*vb.* **2.** degrade, debase, taint, pollute, poison, blight. *The conservative minister believed rock music corrupts teenagers.* **Ant. 1.** honest, moral, honorable. **2.** improve, redeem, save.

corruption *n.* immorality, dishonesty, fraud, graft, vice, wickedness. *There's too much corruption in our local government.* **Ant.** morality, goodness, honesty, integrity.

cost *n.* **1.** price, charge, expense, value, worth, bill. *The cost of the skis is one thousand dollars.* –*vb.* **2.** damage, harm, injure, hurt, burden. *Dropping out of college has really cost me.*

costume *n.* outfit, ensemble, attire, uniform, habit, clothing. *She wore a pirate costume to the Halloween party.*

cottage *n.* cabin, bungalow, lodge, hut, shack, hovel. *His parents own a cottage in the country.* **Ant.** mansion, palace, manor.

council *n.* committee, board, assembly, panel, directorate, cabinet. *The city council voted to extend the library's hours.*

counsel *n.* **1.** advice, opinion, guidance, recommendation, instruction. *She sought her best friend's counsel on dating.* **2.** attorney, lawyer, advisor, counselor. *Counsel for the defense presented the first witness.* –*vb.* **3.** advise, guide, instruct, recommend, suggest. *I counseled my brother to take easy classes his first year of college.*

count *vb.* **1.** number, tally, score, total, enumerate. *I counted fifteen people at the dinner party.* **2.** rely, depend, trust, reckon, bank. *You can count on my being there.* **3.** matter, regard, consider, weigh, tell. *Your opinion doesn't count, since you didn't see what happened.* –*n.* **4.** sum, tally, total, numbering, calculation. *Do you have a count of the number of cassettes you own?*

counter *adv.* **1.** opposite, contrary, contrarily, against. *One normally walks counter to the direction of traffic.* –*adj.* **2.** opposing, rival, different, opposite, conflicting. *She made him a counter offer.* –*vb.* **3.** return, retaliate, answer, combat, offset. *The boxer countered the punch with a right hook.* –*n.* **5.** tabletop, table, bar, stand, booth. *Please take your purchases to the check-out counter.*

counterfeit *adj.* **1.** fake, forged, imitation, false, bogus. *The bank refused to take the counterfeit money.* –*vb.* **2.** forge, copy, falsify, imitate, duplicate. *He makes his living counterfeiting passports and other legal documents.* –*n.* **3.** copy, reproduction, imitation, forgery, fake. *The dealer refused to buy the painting because she believed it to be a counterfeit.* **Ant. 1.** genuine, original, authentic.

country *n.* **1.** nation, state, realm, domain, commonwealth. *He visited seven countries when he toured Europe.* **2.** countryside, terrain, territory, land, district. *They hiked for days through forested country.* –*adj.* **3.** rural, rustic, provincial, pastoral, secluded. *My friend just bought a country house.* **Ant. 3.** city, urban, cosmopolitan.

courage *n.* bravery, valor, daring, spirit, fearlessness, heroism. *It takes courage to say no to drugs.* **Ant.** cowardice, timidity, fear.

courageous *adj.* daring, brave, bold, gallant, fearless, heroic, unafraid. *The courageous woman was the only one willing to enter the cave to look for the lost dog.* **Ant.** cowardly, timid, fearful.

course *n.* **1.** route, path, passage, track, direction, way, approach. *He took the easiest course to success.* **2.** class, lecture, program, seminar, subject. *I signed up for a women's studies course.* **3.** development, progress, advance, flow, progression. *The course of history was changed by the discovery of electricity.* –*vb.* **4.** flow, rush, run, surge, race. *Sweat coursed down her face.*

courteous *adj.* polite, gracious, kindly, mannerly, thoughtful, considerate. *The courteous host introduced me to all his guests.* **Ant.**discourteous, impolite, inconsiderate, rude.

cover *vb.* **1.** coat, mantle, envelop, spread, overlay. *During cold winter nights, we cover ourselves with thick quilts.* **2.** shield, shelter, protect, house, defend, guard. *The canopy covered us from the sun.* **3.** disguise, conceal, hide, screen, cloak. *He tried to cover his embarrassment.* **4.** describe, investigate, study, report, recount. *My freshman geology class covers just the basics.* **5.** replace, substitute, double, alternate, relieve. *The back-up pitcher covered for her until she got over the flu.* **6.** journey, travel, traverse, cross, pass. *I can normally cover five hundred miles in a single day's driving.* –*n.* **7.** top, lid, wrapper, roof, blanket, layer, jacket. *The trash can was so full I couldn't get the cover on.* **8.** disguise, camouflage, pretense, screen, cloak. *Superman used his Clark Kent identity as a cover.* **9.** shelter, concealment, protection, refuge, hiding. *The tree gave us cover from the sun.* **Ant. 1.** expose, uncover, remove. **2.** expose, reveal. **3.** expose, reveal, unmask. **4.** omit, delete, pass over.

covert *adj.* hidden, masked, disguised, secret, stealthy. *She made covert glances at the boy sitting beside her.* **Ant.** overt, apparent, obvious.

covet *vb.* desire, wish, long for, hunger for, crave, envy. *He coveted a fast sports car.* **Ant.** reject, decline, spurn.

cowardice *n.* fearfulness, faintheartedness, spinelessness, fear, fright. *Cowardice is a bad trait for a soldier to have.* **Ant.** bravery, courage, fearlessness.

cowardly *adj.* timid, uncourageous, fearful, fainthearted, scared. *In "The Wizard of Oz," the cowardly Lion searches for courage.* **Ant.** brave, fearless, courageous, bold.

cower *vb.* tremble, cringe, quail, quake, shrink, grovel. *The young boy cowered behind a rock when he saw the bear approaching.*

cozy *adj.* snug, warm, comfortable, relaxing, sheltered, pleasant, homey. *We stayed at a cozy little inn on the beach.* **Ant.** cold, uncomfortable, unpleasant.

crack *vb.* **1.** break, split, burst, snap, fracture, splinter. *My glasses cracked when I stepped on them.* **2.** snap, clap, pop, crackle, beat, slap. *The cowboy cracked his whip at the wild mustang.* –*n.* **3.** burst, snap, bang, shot, pop, explosion. *We heard the crack of a hunter's rifle.* **4.** fissure, crevice, split, break, fracture. *We noticed there was a crack in the building's foundation.* **5.** joke, jest, wisecrack, quip, insult. *He made a crack about my new haircut.*

craft *n.* **1.** ability, proficiency, skill, artistry, talent. *His model airplane was built with great craft.* **2.** trade, occupation, work, job, profession. *Cabinetmaking is a difficult craft to learn.* **3.** deception, cunning, trickery, deceit, guile. *She used craft in trying to get the elderly man to sell his house.* **4.** vessel, boat, ship, plane, spaceship. *His yacht is a beautiful craft.* **Ant. 1.** inability, unskillfulness, incompetency. **3.** frankness, openness, honesty.

crafty *adj.* shifty, sly, deceitful, scheming, tricky, cunning, crooked. *The Joker in "Batman" is a crafty villain.* **Ant.** honest, straightforward, direct.

cram *vb.* stuff, pack, jam, crowd, ram, squeeze. *She crammed all her clothes into one suitcase.* **Ant.** unpack, empty, remove.

cramp *n.* **1.** spasm, contraction, convulsion, twitch, seizure. *He experienced abdominal cramps after eating the garlic and anchovy pizza.* **2.** restraint, obstruction, hindrance, damper, control. *Lack of money has put a cramp in her formerly extravagant lifestyle.*

crash *vb.* **1.** smash, bump, collide, hit, plow. *The skier crashed into a tree.* **2.** wreck, demolish, batter, destroy, break, shatter. *I crashed my car.* –*n.* **3.** bang, blast, crack, clatter, explosion. *We heard a distant crash of thunder.* **4.** collision, accident, pileup, wreck, smash. *He got hurt in the car crash.*

crave *vb.* desire, want, long for, hunger for, covet, need. *When I've been by myself for awhile, I often crave companionship.* **Ant.** dislike, reject, detest.

craving *n.* desire, need, longing, hunger, thirst, yearning. *Right now I have a craving for some junk food.* **Ant.** dislike, abhorrence, hate.

crawl *vb.* **1.** creep, drag, squirm, wiggle, wriggle. *The caterpillar slowly crawled across a leaf.* **2.** teem, swarm, abound, flow, bristle. *In the summertime, our kitchen crawls with ants.* –*n.* **3.** creep, walk, plod, trudge, shuffle. *Heavy rain slowed traffic to a crawl.* **Ant. 1.** walk, run, dash. **3.** run, sprint, dash.

crazy *adj.* **1.** stupid, foolish, insane, mad, insensible, reckless, irrational. *Walking alone in a big city is a crazy thing to do.* **2.** wild, infatuated, raving, excited, passionate, mad. *I'm crazy about chocolate-chip ice cream.* **3.** strange, peculiar, bizarre, unusual, outrageous. *We've had some crazy weather lately.* **Ant. 1.** sane, sensible, smart. **2.** indifferent, uninterested, unexcited. **3.** usual, normal, average.

crease *n.* **1.** fold, ridge, crinkle, wrinkle, furrow, pleat. *There are creases in my new pants.* –*vb.* **2.** pleat, wrinkle, fold, crinkle, furrow. *Years of exposure to the weather has creased the old fisherman's face.*

create *vb.* make, produce, invent, devise, design, generate, build. *She can create fantastic graphics with her new computer software.* **Ant.** destroy, demolish, eliminate.

creation *n.* **1.** masterpiece, masterwork, artwork, production, invention. *The artist stood back and let people admire his creation.* **2.** formation, development, making, birth, nativity. *Scientists are exploring the mysteries behind the creation of the universe.* **Ant. 2.** extinction, destruction, death.

creative *adj.* inventive, imaginative, ingenious, artistic, visionary, productive. *I admire his creative nature.* **Ant.** unimaginative, unoriginal, uninspired.

creature *n.* being, animal, beast, mortal, soul. *She loves all the Earth's creatures.*

credit *n.* **1.** recognition, commendation, acknowledgment, approval, acclaim. *Don't take all the credit for yourself.* **2.** deferred payment, charge, installment, time. *He bought a new car on credit.* **3.** asset, honor, boon, benefit, plus. *You're a credit to your profession.* *–vb.* **4.** recognize, acknowledge, attribute, assign, honor. *Who is credited with the discovery of electricity?* **5.** accept, trust, believe, hold, deem. *I credit what she says as the truth.* **Ant. 1.** discredit, disapproval, blame. **2.** cash, check. **3.** liability, handicap, hindrance. **5.** question, distrust, disbelieve.

creed *n.* belief, doctrine, dogma, tenet, faith. *Though he considers himself religious, he doesn't hold to a specific creed.*

creek *n.* stream, brook, rivulet, branch, run. *You won't catch any fish in that little creek.*

creep *vb.* crawl, drag, squirm, wiggle, wriggle, sneak, steal. *The spider crept across its web.* **Ant.** walk, run, dash.

crest *n.* top, peak, summit, ridge, tip, crown. *I'll race you to the crest of that hill.* **Ant.** bottom, base, foot.

crew *n.* hands, team, squad, band, company, group. *The crew of the starship were eager for shore leave.*

crime *n.* misdeed, violation, offense, transgression, wrongdoing, felony, misdemeanor. *It is a crime to steal.* **Ant.** virtue, legality.

criminal *adj.* **1.** illegal, unlawful, immoral, wrong, dishonest. *The selling of drugs is a criminal act.* *–n.* **2.** offender, culprit, crook, felon, outlaw. *The police are looking for the criminals who robbed our local bank.* **Ant. 1.** legal, lawful, honest.

cripple *vb.* disable, weaken, damage, paralyze, stop, incapacitate. *The loss of our two star players crippled our team.* **Ant.** assist, encourage, strengthen.

crisis *n.* emergency, disaster, predicament, plight, climax, crux. *The big crisis last weekend was our house catching on fire.*

critical *adj.* **1.** urgent, important, crucial, grave, decisive, momentous. *It is critical that a snakebite victim get help as soon as possible.* **2.** disapproving, discriminating, condemning, derogatory, severe. *My boss is too critical about the job I do.* **Ant. 1.** irrelevant, insignificant. **2.** uncritical, indiscriminating.

criticize *vb.* censure, denounce, fault, ridicule, condemn, judge. *My parents criticize almost everything I do.* **Ant.** praise, commend, acclaim.

critique *n.* review, examination, commentary, analysis, assessment. *Our class project is to attend an opera and write a critique on it.*

crop *n.* **1.** harvest, yield, reaping, product, production. *The farmer hurried to harvest his crop before it rained.* *–vb.* **2.** trim, clip, cut, mow, shear. *My task is to crop our overgrown hedges.*

cross *n.* **1.** blend, hybrid, combination, crossbreed, mixture. *A tangelo is a cross between a tangerine and a pomelo.* *–vb.* **2.** traverse, ply, transit, span, pass. *It'll take us all day to cross the lake in this old rowboat.* **3.** mingle, mix, interbreed, combine, crossbreed. *If you cross a goat and a sheep, you end up with a geep.* **4.** crisscross, intertwine, interlock, twist, weave. *When she crosses her arms like that, it means she's angry.* *–adj.* **5.** opposed, opposing, contrary, opposite, counter. *We've been working to cross purposes.* **6.** angry, mad, sullen, moody, touchy. *Why are you so cross today?* **Ant. 6.** agreeable, pleasant, amiable.

crouch *vb.* squat, stoop, bend, kneel, dip, bow. *The catcher crouched behind home plate.*

crowd *n.* **1.** horde, throng, mob, mass, assemblage, group. *I don't go to the beach on weekends because I can't stand crowds.* **2.** clique, gang, circle, set, party. *Parents often warn their children not to hang around with the wrong* crowd. **3.** spectators, viewers, audience, listeners. *The crowd clapped at the end of the performance.* –vb. **4.** assemble, congregate, cluster, collect, huddle. *Everyone crowded around the snack table.* **5.** jam, shove, push, squeeze, compress, cram. *People crowded into the elevator.* **Ant. 4.** disperse, disband, scatter.

crucial *adj.* critical, essential, important, urgent, grave, vital. *It is crucial that you don't become dehydrated in the desert.* **Ant.** unessential, trivial, unimportant.

crude *adj.* **1.** coarse, primitive, unfinished, unrefined, unpolished. *She made a crude telescope out of a tube and magnifying glass.* **2.** rude, vulgar, uncivilized, tasteless, offensive, revolting, gross. *He made a crude remark at the party.* **Ant. 1.** refined, processed, finished. **2.** courteous, polite, elegant.

cruel *adj.* savage, vicious, ruthless, barbaric, merciless, heartless. *It was very cruel of you to tease him about his lost puppy.* **Ant.** kind, considerate, compassionate.

cruise *vb.* **1.** navigate, sail, coast, float, travel, journey. *Her dream is to cruise the seven seas.* –n. **2.** voyage, sail, journey, trip, tour. *Let's go on a cruise next summer.*

crumble *vb.* collapse, fragment, disintegrate, powder, decay. *The cake crumbled in my hand.*

crumple *vb.* crinkle, squash, rumple, crush, smash. *I crumpled up the newspaper to fit it in the trash can.*

crusade *n.* **1.** campaign, drive, movement, action, struggle. *He's waging a personal crusade to save our neighborhood.* –vb. **2.** march, drive, fight, battle, struggle. *A group called M.A.D.D. crusades for tougher laws against drunk drivers.*

crush *vb.* **1.** smash, squash, pulverize, stomp, grind, squeeze, mash. *We crushed the aluminum cans for recycling.* **2.** destroy, overcome, quash, overwhelm, topple, demolish. *His rejection crushed her.*

cry *vb.* **1.** weep, sob, bawl, wail, lament. *She cried at her friend's wedding.* **2.** shout, yell, call, scream, clamor. *The stranded climber cried for help.* –n. **3.** shout, yell, call, scream, bellow. *He gave a cry of warning when he saw the forest fire.*

cryptic *adj.* secret, mysterious, hidden, perplexing, obscure. *There was a cryptic message in the bottle I found on the beach.* **Ant.** obvious, clear, apparent.

cuddle *vb.* snuggle, embrace, hug, nuzzle, caress. *She likes to cuddle soft furry animals.*

culminate *vb.* climax, end, conclude, finish, terminate, complete. *The wedding culminated with a big dance.* **Ant.** begin, start, commence.

culprit *n.* criminal, offender, lawbreaker, wrongdoer, transgressor. *Who is the culprit who ran off with my backpack?*

cultivate *vb.* **1.** farm, till, plow, garden, plant. *Farmers cultivate many kinds of crops.* **2.** promote, encourage, support, foster, develop, improve. *It is important to cultivate a sense of self-worth in children.* **Ant. 2.** hinder, obstruct, discourage.

cultivation *n.* **1.** planting, farming, agriculture, gardening. *The farmer explained the steps necessary for successful rice cultivation.* **2.** promotion, advancement, encouragement, fosterage, development. *I really work on the cultivation of my friendships.* **Ant. 2.** hindrance, obstruction, discouragement.

culture *n.* civilization, society, attainments, accomplishments, refinement. *We are studying the culture of medieval Europe in our history class.*

cultured *adj.* civilized, sophisticated, enlightened, educated, knowledgeable. *She felt quite cultured after spending four years at a European university.* **Ant.** uncultured, crude, uneducated.

cumbersome *adj.* awkward, unwieldy, burdensome, weighty, clumsy, bulky. *A long run-on sentence can be quite cumbersome to read.* **Ant.** manageable, easy, compact.

cunning *adj.* **1.** crafty, sly, calculating, deceptive, scheming, shrewd. *The cunning businesswoman sold the house for two times what it was worth.* –n. **2.** craftiness, trickery, slyness, guile, deception. *Watch out for the cunning behind his charm.* **3.** skill, genius, talent, mastery, cleverness. *The shipwrecked man had to use his cunning to survive in the wilderness.* **Ant. 1.** clumsy, artless, naive. **2.** sincerity, openness, frankness. **3.** clumsiness, awkwardness.

cure *n.* **1.** remedy, treatment, medicine, antidote, corrective. *Do you think any cure exists for the problem of poverty? -vb.* **2.** heal, remedy, correct, alleviate, relieve, lessen. *The doctor prescribed medicine to cure my illness.* **Ant. 1.** sickness, illness, ailment. **2.** sicken, worsen, weaken.

curiosity *n.* **1.** inquisitiveness, questioning, interestedness, interest. *Please relieve my curiosity by telling me how this works.* **2.** eccentricity, novelty, wonder, peculiarity, oddity. *The exotic stranger was a curiosity to the local residents.* **Ant. 1.** indifference, disregard, unconcern.

curious *adj.* **1.** inquisitive, questioning, searching, investigative, nosy, snooping. *I am curious about the meaning of your name.* **2.** peculiar, unusual, weird, strange, odd, exotic, rare. *That's a curious object you found on the beach.* **Ant. 1.** indifferent, uninterested. **2.** normal, usual, conventional.

currency *n.* money, coin, cash, bills, legal tender. *When traveling abroad, you need to exchange your dollars for the local currency.*

current *adj.* **1.** present, latest, prevailing, popular, voguish. *She wore only current fashions.* *-n.* **2.** flow, course, stream, tide, flood. *The swimmer got caught in a current and was pulled away from shore.* **Ant. 1.** past, antique, outmoded, unpopular.

curse *n.* **1.** oath, profanity, swearing, blasphemy, obscenity. *I would rather he didn't voice so many curses.* **2.** spell, invocation, charm, hex, jinx. *The wizard's curse changed her into a tree.* **3.** torment, burden, misfortune, plague, affliction. *Buying cars that break down seems to be my curse in life.* *-vb.* **4.** swear, blaspheme, cuss, fulminate. *People sometimes curse when they're angry.* **5.** burden, plague, afflict, torment, harass, trouble. *She says she is cursed by bad luck.* **Ant. 3.** blessing, joy, relief. **4.** bless, commend, praise. **5.** assist, relieve, help.

curtail *vb.* shorten, reduce, trim, cut, lessen, decrease, restrict. *To lose weight, one must curtail one's eating.* **Ant.** increase, extend, expand.

curve *n.* **1.** arc, bend, bow, turn, crook, crescent. *This roller coaster has lots of dips and curves.* *-vb.* **2.** bend, bow, hook, arch, curl, swerve. *The road curves to the left just ahead.*

cushion *n.* **1.** pillow, pad, padding, buffer, mat. *His sofa is comfortable because of its thick cushions.* *-vb.* **2.** pillow, soften, lessen, dampen, cradle. *The helmet cushioned the blow to his head.*

custody *n.* **1.** guardianship, supervision, trusteeship, charge, protection. *If my parents should ever die, my grandparents will get custody of me.* **2.** holding, detention, possession, confinement, imprisonment. *That criminal is now in police custody.*

custom *n.* tradition, convention, practice, fashion, procedure. *It is the custom in Japan to take off your shoes before entering a house.* **Ant.** oddity, abnormality, rarity.

customary *adj.* usual, habitual, common, regular, normal. *She greeted me with her customary smile.* **Ant.** unusual, uncommon, rare.

customer *n.* shopper, purchaser, buyer, patron, client. *The store was full of customers buying gifts for the holidays.* **Ant.** seller, vendor.

cut *vb.* **1.** slash, slice, carve, chop, clip, nip. *I cut the tags off my new clothes.* **2.** cross, traverse, move, pass, ply. *He cut across the lawn to reach the building.* **3.** shorten, reduce, edit, abridge, condense, delete. *The playwright decided to cut her play by several scenes.* **4.** halt, stop, interrupt, thwart, obstruct. *The mechanic yelled for me to cut the engine.* *-adj.* **5.** severed, separated, sliced, pared, sectioned, divided. *I put a cut banana in my oatmeal.* **6.** shortened, reduced, abridged, condensed. *We saw the cut version of the movie.* *-n.* **7.** wound, incision, nick, gash, slash. *I put a bandage on my cut.* **8.** reduction, decrease, lessening, decline, fall. *The city will be faced with a major budget cut next year.* **Ant. 3.** expand, add, increase. **4.** begin, start, activate. **6.** expanded, extended, lengthened. **8.** increase, raise, boost.

cycle *n.* revolution, rotation, period, series, succession, sequence. *The rinse cycle on this washing machine lasts ten minutes.*

cynical *adj.* doubting, unbelieving, disbelieving, skeptical, suspicious. *I'm too cynical to believe in psychic phenomena.* **Ant.** believing, accepting, unsuspicious.

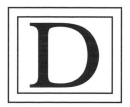

D

dab *n.* **1.** pat, touch, morsel, bit, speck. *She put another dab of butter on her pancakes.* –*vb.* **2.** swab, daub, smear, touch, wipe. *He dabbed a little cologne on his neck.*

dabble *vb.* fool, tinker, fiddle, putter, dally. *I'm not an artist, but I do dabble around with paints.*

dagger *vb.* knife, dirk, stiletto, blade, pocket-knife. *Brutus killed Caesar with a dagger.*

dainty *adj.* **1.** delicate, fine, petite, exquisite, graceful, refined. *She prepared dainty sandwiches for her tea party.* **2.** finicky, fussy, discriminating, particular, scrupulous. *His cat is a dainty eater.* **Ant. 1.** unappealing, gross, vulgar. **2.** hearty, robust.

damage *vb.* **1.** hurt, injure, harm, wound, break, cripple, wreck. *High winds damaged our barn.* –*n.* **2.** hurt, injury, harm, destruction, devastation, blow. *Her car received minor damage in the accident.* **Ant. 1.** repair, fix, heal.

damp *adj.* **1.** moist, wet, soggy, dank, clammy, sodden. *The grass is still damp from yesterday's rain.* **2.** indifferent, uncaring, lukewarm, spiritless, unenthusiastic. *I received a damp response to my proposal.* –*n.* **3.** moisture, wetness, dankness, sogginess, clamminess. *The damp seemed to penetrate to his bones.* **Ant. 1.** dry, arid. **2.** enthusiastic, warm. **3.** heat, dryness.

dance *vb.* **1.** prance, frolic, cavort, leap, skip. *We danced with joy when our team won the championship.* –*n.* **2.** ball, prom, party, hop, social. *There's a big dance at school this weekend.*

danger *n.* risk, threat, hazard, peril, jeopardy, menace. *Smokey the Bear warns about the dangers of unwatched campfires.* **Ant.** safety, security, safeness.

dangerous *adj.* unsafe, threatening, risky, hazardous, menacing, perilous. *Rattlesnakes are dangerous if provoked.* **Ant.** safe, harmless, innocuous.

dangle *vb.* hang, drag, trail, droop, swing, sag. *She dangled a fishing line in the lake.*

dare *vb.* **1.** defy, challenge, taunt, goad, provoke. *I admit I broke the window, but my brother dared me to do it.* **2.** venture, risk, challenge, face, brave, confront. *She dared to run the rapids in a fragile kayak.* –*n.* **3.** bet, provocation, challenge, taunt. *He swallowed the goldfish on a dare.*

daring *adj.* adventurous, bold, courageous, brave, fearless, gallant. *She made a daring leap across the chasm.* **Ant.** timid, cowardly, fearful.

dark *n.* **1.** night, nightfall, nighttime, darkness, blackness. *He wants to get back before dark.* –*adj.* **2.** lightless, unlit, black, sunless. *It gets dark here about nine o'clock.* **3.** deep, dim, dusky, swarthy, murky. *His hair is a dark brown.* **4.** glum, brooding, gloomy, sullen, dreary, cheerless. *She's in a dark mood.* **Ant. 1.** dawn, daytime. **2.** light, bright, lit. **3.** pale, pastel, fair. **4.** happy, joyful, cheerful.

darling *n.* **1.** love, beloved, sweetheart, jewel, favorite. *Her youngest grandson is her darling.* –*adj.* **2.** loved, treasured, valued, dear, favorite. *This is my darling nephew.*

dart *vb.* **1.** leap, sprint, rush, spring, bolt, fly, dash. *I thought I was going to be first in line until he darted in front of me.* –*n.* **2.** dash, rush, spring, leap, bolt, sprint, bound. *The runner made a dart for the finish line on the final lap.* **3.** bolt, shaft, arrow, quarrel, projectile. *Can you throw the dart into the bull's-eye?*

dash *vb.* **1.** hurry, rush, sprint, race, hasten. *She had to dash to the station to catch her bus.* **2.** ruin, spoil, thwart, frustrate, foil. *Our dream of victory was dashed in the semifinals.* **3.** hurl, fling, slam, thrust, smash. *Heavy surf dashed* *against the pier.* —n. **4.** race, rush, run, sprint, dart. *We all made a dash for the exit when class was over.* **5.** touch, bit, hint, suggestion, trace. *This soup needs a dash more salt.*

data *n.* information, facts, statistics, figures, details. *My driver's license contains data on my height, weight, and address.*

date *n.* **1.** time, day, month, year, season, period. *I've forgotten the date of your birthday.* **2.** appointment, engagement, rendezvous, meeting. *Let's make a date to meet here tomorrow at five o'clock.* **3.** escort, companion, boyfriend, girlfriend, friend. *Do you have a date for the prom?*

daunt *vb.* thwart, deter, dishearten, intimidate, frighten. *The great importance of her assignment did not daunt her.* **Ant.** encourage, rouse, stir.

dawdle *vb.* idle, dally, fiddle, poke, daydream, loaf. *She dawdled all day and had no time left to finish her homework.* **Ant.** hurry, rush, hustle.

dawn *n.* **1.** sunrise, daybreak, sunup, morning, daylight. *He gets up at dawn to go jogging.* **2.** birth, emergence, beginning, awakening, start, appearance. *It was the dawn of a new age.* —vb. **3.** begin, start, arise, originate, emerge. *A new day dawned for the settlers.* **4.** register, strike, appear, occur, hit. *It finally dawned on me what he was trying to say.* **Ant. 1.** sunset, evening, dusk. **2.** ending, finish, termination. **3.** end, finish, terminate.

day *n.* **1.** daytime, daylight, sunlight, sunshine. *He works during the day and parties at night.* **2.** age, epoch, period, time, generation. *The old woman liked to talk about how things were during her day.*

daze *vb.* **1.** stun, confuse, bewilder, muddle, dazzle, blind. *The strong sunlight momentarily dazed me when I stepped outside.* —n. **2.** muddle, confusion, bewilderment, trance, stupor. *The man was in a daze after he ran into a tree.*

dazzling *adj.* brilliant, stunning, blinding, vivid, overpowering, exciting. *The skaters gave a dazzling performance.* **Ant.** dull, ordinary, routine.

dead *adj.* **1.** lifeless, deceased, perished, extinguished, expired. *She buried the dead sparrow in her backyard.* **2.** uninterested, bored, unresponsive, emotionless, cool. *The audience seems rather dead tonight.* **3.** obsolete, extinct, discontinued, defunct, passé. *At one time, Hebrew was considered a dead language.* **4.** spiritless, dull, listless, boring, uneventful. *Dance clubs are usually dead on week nights.* **5.** motionless, stationary, still, standing, quiet. *After losing power, the boat was dead in the water for two hours.* **6.** absolute, complete, total, outright, utter. *The train came to a dead stop to avoid the moose.* —n. **7.** silence, hush, stillness, quiet, calm. *The dead of the night was broken by a loud crash.* —adj. **8.** directly, exactly, straight, right. *The beach is dead ahead.* **9.** totally, entirely, completely, thoroughly, absolutely, utterly. *You're dead wrong about this.* **Ant. 1.** alive, living, live. **2.** alive, wild, responsive. **3.** existing, modern, current. **4.** lively, active, spirited. **5.** alive, moving, operative. **6.** partial, incomplete.

deaden *vb.* numb, extinguish, quench, diminish, dampen, blunt, lessen. *Novocaine will deaden the pain of a toothache.* **Ant.** stimulate, rouse, excite.

deadly *adj.* poisonous, fatal, lethal, toxic, harmful, dangerous, hazardous. *Arsenic is a deadly substance.* **Ant.** safe, harmless, innocuous.

deal *vb.* **1.** distribute, bestow, dispense, assign, give. *Deal each person five cards.* **2.** trade, bargain, transact, sale, retail. *The store says it only deals in one type of computer.* **3.** consider, concern, treat, handle, manage. *This article deals with pollution issues.* —n. **4.** contract, agreement, arrangement, pact, negotiation. *I made a deal with my sister in which she agreed to do my chores for ten dollars.* **5.** amount, quantity, allotment, extent, degree. *I don't have a great deal of time for recreation.* **Ant. 1.** receive, take, collect. **3.** ignore, overlook.

death *n.* passing, dying, demise, departure, termination, extinction. *He missed school because of a death in his family.* **Ant.** life, existence, birth.

debate *vb.* **1.** ponder, deliberate, contemplate, consider, think. *He debated which college to attend.* **2.** discuss, argue, dispute, question, contest. *The existence of a supreme being has* *been debated throughout much of human history.* –n. **3.** discussion, argument, dispute, disagreement, wrangle. *We got into a debate over whether or not it was a good movie .*

debris *n.* trash, wreckage, junk, waste, rubble, flotsam, garbage. *Space debris orbits the earth.*

debt *n.* indebtedness, obligation, bill, arrears, liability. *She is in debt to her parents for $100.*

decay *vb.* **1.** deteriorate, rot, decompose, disintegrate, decline. *Vegetables were starting to decay in the untended garden.* –n. **2.** deterioration, decomposition, disintegration, rot, rotting. *That old abandoned house is in a bad state of decay.* **Ant. 1.** flourish, thrive, grow. **2.** health, vigor, development.

deceit *n.* deception, dishonesty, trickery, cheating, cunning, fraud. *He used deceit to cheat us out of our rightful inheritance.* **Ant.** honesty, truthfulness, sincerity.

deceive *vb.* fool, mislead, trick, delude, dupe, misinform. *She deceived me into believing she had completed all her work.*

decelerate *vb.* brake, check, slow down, halt, stop, cease. *The space shuttle decelerated as it entered the atmosphere .* **Ant.** accelerate, speed up, start.

decency *n.* modesty, dignity, propriety, suitability, seemliness. *Pornography offends my sense of decency.*

decent *adj.* **1.** modest, proper, respectable, dignified, tasteful. *My pants are so torn they are no longer decent to wear.* **2.** sufficient, reasonable, adequate, passable. *That was the first decent meal he's had all week.* **3.** mannerly, kind, generous, thoughtful, courteous, considerate. *It was decent of you to offer to pay for dinner.* **Ant. 1.** indecent, immodest, improper. **2.** insufficient, inadequate. **3.** unmannerly, unthoughtful, inconsiderate.

decide *vb.* choose, select, elect, pick, resolve, judge. *He couldn't decide which jacket to wear.*

decision *n.* verdict, conclusion, determination, resolution, judgment, opinion. *Have you reached a decision as to where you want to go?*

decisive *adj.* determined, firm, resolute, fixed, conclusive, deciding, final. *She made a decisive move that won the game.* **Ant.** indecisive, undetermined, inconclusive.

declare *vb.* announce, proclaim, express, pronounce, claim, assert. *The United States declared its independence from Britain in 1776.*

decline *vb.* **1.** reject, refuse, shun, veto, deny, rebuff. *She declined her friend's offer to stay the night.* **2.** decrease, wane, ebb, subside, lessen, lower. *Deaths due to pneumonia have declined since the introduction of penicillin.* –n. **3.** wane, ebb, downswing, decrease, lessening, lowering. *Smoking is on the decline.* **4.** slope, descent, dip, slant, angle. *The astronauts drove their moon buggy down the decline.* **Ant. 1.** accept, consent, adopt. **2.** rise, increase. **3.** rise, upswing, upturn. **4.** ascent, incline.

decorate *vb.* adorn, ornament, garnish, festoon, bedeck, trim, embellish. *He decorated his room with posters.*

decrease *vb.* **1.** reduce, lower, lessen, diminish, cut, shrink. *The state decreased the speed limit to 55 mph.* –n. **2.** reduction, lowering, lessening, cutback, diminishing, slackening. *I asked my boss for a decrease in my workload.* **Ant. 1.** increase, lift, raise. **2.** increase, lift, extension.

decree *n.* **1.** edict, ruling, proclamation, law, command, ordinance, regulation. *The king's decree says no one may hunt in the royal forest.* –vb. **2.** rule, command, proclaim, instruct, order, dictate, demand. *Our leader has decreed that all members of the commune must shave their heads.*

decrepit *adj.* old, dilapidated, ancient, deteriorated, rickety, run-down. *We were terrified to go flying in that decrepit plane.*

dedicate *vb.* devote, inscribe, address, offer, give, consecrate. *The book was dedicated to the author's husband.*

deduce *vb.* infer, conclude, reason, interpret, assume, analyze. *Even though there were very few clues, Sherlock Holmes deduced the identity of the criminal.*

deduct *vb.* subtract, remove, withdraw, take, eliminate. *Please deduct the price of the broken* *lamp from my allowance.* **Ant.** add, increase, extend.

deed *n.* act, action, work, feat, performance, task, enterprise, turn. *Robin Hood is known for the good deeds he did for the poor.*

deep *adj.* **1.** extensive, vast, immeasurable, cavernous, fathomless. *I was unable to see to the bottom of the deep hole.* **2.** profound, critical, important, vital, intense. *Her words almost always have an underlying deep meaning.* **3.** absorbed, immersed, engrossed, preoccupied, engaged. *I was deep in thought.* **4.** powerful, sincere, earnest, impassioned, intense. *He has a deep love for his country.* **Ant. 1.** shallow. **2.** shallow, trivial, superficial. **4.** shallow, light, weak.

defeat *vb.* **1.** conquer, vanquish, master, overcome, overthrow. *The Allies defeated the Axis powers in W.W. II.* –*n.* **2.** loss, downfall, failure, ruin, setback. *She took her team's defeat very hard.* **Ant. 1.** lose, surrender, yield. **2.** victory, triumph, success.

defect *n.* **1.** fault, flaw, error, mistake, failing, snag. *The cars were recalled due to a defect in their brakes.* –*vb.* **2.** desert, bolt, mutiny, secede, leave. *The foreign diplomat defected to the U.S.*

defection *n.* desertion, changeover, switchover, conversion, withdrawal. *News of the diplomat's defection was on the front page.*

defective *adj.* flawed, faulty, broken, marred, warped, imperfect. *He returned the defective merchandise to the manufacturer.* **Ant.** perfect, faultless, unmarred.

defend *vb.* protect, safeguard, guard, shield, shelter, save. *She hired a lawyer to defend her in court.* **Ant.** attack, assail, endanger.

defense *n.* protection, preservation, guard, security, support. *A moat was the castle's first line of defense.*

defer *vb.* **1.** delay, postpone, suspend, table, shelve. *She asked her apartment manager if she could defer payment to the end of the month.* **2.** yield, submit, accede, listen, assent, obey. *He defers to her because she's his boss.*

defiant *adj.* disobedient, rebellious, recalcitrant, insubordinate, unruly, stubborn. *The de-fiant student refused to do his homework.* **Ant.** obedient, submissive, agreeable.

deficient *adj.* lacking, incomplete, wanting, insufficient, short. *The accident was attributed to the driver's deficient judgment.* **Ant.** complete, sufficient, adequate.

deficit *n.* shortage, shortfall, insufficiency, deficiency. *Look's like we're going to have another budget deficit this year.*

define *vb.* describe, explain, specify, depict, characterize, label. *If you can't define that word, consult a dictionary.*

definite *adj.* **1.** specific, fixed, determined, particular, clear. *Let's establish a definite time and place for the game.* **2.** certain, positive, sure, settled, conclusive, decided. *It's not definite that I'll be able to attend.* **Ant. 1.** indefinite, unspecific, vague. **2.** uncertain, unsure.

definitely *adv.* certainly, obviously, decidedly, conclusively, positively. *It was definitely a raccoon I saw.* **Ant.** possibly, perhaps, maybe.

definition *n.* **1.** description, explanation, specification, depiction. *Instead of giving the definition of a word, a thesaurus lists synonyms.* **2.** sharpness, distinctness, clarity, clearness, visibility. *This television is known for its high definition.*

deform *vb.* mar, disfigure, mutilate, distort, maim. *The Phantom of the Opera wore a mask because a fire had deformed his face.*

defy *vb.* disobey, disregard, resist, spurn, withstand, challenge, dare. *The child defied his baby-sitter by refusing to go to bed.* **Ant.** obey, follow, observe, respect.

degrade *vb.* humiliate, shame, dishonor, debase, reduce, demean, lower. *She refused to degrade herself by supporting his lie.*

degree *n.* level, order, measure, amount, extent, magnitude. *The dive he just made has a high degree of difficulty.*

dejected *adj.* depressed, unhappy, sorrowful, disheartened, downcast, despondent. *He was dejected because he couldn't find his lost dog.* **Ant.** happy, joyous, cheerful.

delay *vb.* **1.** interrupt, postpone, detain, suspend, prolong, hinder, impede. *Rain delayed the game.* –*n.* **2.** wait, lag, postponement, stay, suspension, interruption, break. *The pilot said there would be a ten-minute delay before takeoff.*

delegate *vb.* **1.** assign, relegate, name, designate, charge. *My manager delegated to me the job of sweeping out the store.* –*n.* **2.** representative, spokesperson, diplomat, envoy, ambassador. *Most countries send delegates to the United Nations.*

delete *vb.* erase, eradicate, cancel, remove, cut, omit. *She accidentally deleted an important computer file.* **Ant.** insert, add, include.

deliberate *vb.* **1.** examine, consider, weigh, ponder, study. *The jury deliberated for two weeks before reaching a verdict.* –*adj.* **2.** intentional, planned, thoughtful, calculated, prearranged. *His remark was a deliberate attempt to insult me.* **Ant. 2.** spontaneous, hasty, rash.

deliberately *adv.* intentionally, purposefully, willfully, thoughtfully, wittingly. *Did you deliberately slam the door in my face?* **Ant.** unintentionally, unwittingly.

delicacy *n.* **1.** fineness, fragility, flimsiness, slightness, frailness. *The delicacy of the spider web delighted us.* **2.** tact, finesse, sensitivity, consideration, gentleness. *Use delicacy when telling someone they have bad breath.* **3.** tidbit, morsel, treat, luxury. *Frogs' legs are considered a delicacy in France.* **Ant. 1.** coarseness, roughness. **2.** bluntness, insensitivity.

delicate *adj.* **1.** fragile, frail, flimsy, fine, slight, small. *Be careful—this is very delicate china.* **2.** difficult, touchy, ticklish, dangerous, critical. *The surgeon performed a delicate operation.* **3.** tactful, sensitive, considerate, careful, diplomatic. *She tried to be delicate when she told him she no longer loved him.* **Ant. 1.** rough, coarse, sturdy. **2.** easy, safe. **3.** inconsiderate, insensitive, careless.

delicious *adj.* appetizing, rich, luscious, tasty, savory, pleasing, delightful. *That cream pastry was delicious.* **Ant.** sickening, unpleasant, terrible.

delight *vb.* **1.** thrill, excite, please, cheer, amuse, gladden. *Winning the award delighted him.* –*n.* **2.** excitement, pleasure, joy, happiness, rapture, exhilaration. *It was such a delight to see you after all these years.* **Ant. 1.** displease, sadden, depress. **2.** displeasure, unhappiness.

delightful *adj.* pleasurable, pleasant, enjoyable, agreeable, happy. *We had a delightful time on our vacation.* **Ant.** unpleasant, depressing, unhappy.

deliver *vb.* **1.** transfer, transmit, send, convey, bear, present. *Mail is delivered every day except holidays and Sundays.* **2.** speak, voice, utter, give, impart, communicate. *The woman delivered a moving speech.* **3.** rescue, save, free, release, protect, liberate. *The aliens said they came to deliver Earth from its impending doom.* **Ant. 1.** keep, hold, retain.

delivery *n.* transfer, conveyance, transmittal, transmission, distribution. *The messenger had several deliveries to make.*

delude *vb.* deceive, mislead, fool, dupe, trick, misguide. *I deluded myself into believing she liked me.*

deluge *n.* **1.** avalanche, flood, downpour, overflow, inundation, barrage. *The newspaper received a deluge of letters protesting the article.* –*vb.* **2.** flood, swamp, drown, engulf, inundate, overrun, submerge. *The school was deluged by calls from angry parents.*

delusion *n.* illusion, misbelief, misconception, fantasy, hallucination. *He has delusions of grandeur.* **Ant.** fact, reality, actuality.

deluxe *adj.* choice, select, prime, splendid, luxurious. *Let's order a deluxe pizza.* **Ant.** common, ordinary, average.

demand *vb.* **1.** require, claim, ask, need, want, invoke. *I demand my rights.* –*n.* **2.** order, bidding, command, ultimatum, direction, requirement. *Will our government meet the terrorist's demands?*

demolish *vb.* wreck, ruin, destroy, break, devastate, pulverize, annihilate. *The meteorite demolished the house on which it fell.* **Ant.** build, restore, create.

demon *n.* devil, fiend, ghoul, ogre, hobgoblin, spook, evil spirit. *The sorcerer called a demon from the pool of darkness.*

demonstrate *vb.* **1.** protest, march, rally, picket, strike. *Protestors demonstrated outside the White House.* **2.** show, display, exhibit, illustrate, describe. *This model demonstrates how a nuclear-power plant works.*

demonstration *n.* **1.** march, protest, rally, parade, picketing. *She plans to attend tomorrow's antiwar demonstration.* **2.** show, exhibit, exhibition, display, presentation. *The inventor plans to conduct a public demonstration of his antigravity device.*

demote *vb.* lower, downgrade, reduce, degrade, displace. *The lieutenant was demoted to private for his refusal to follow orders.* **Ant.** elevate, raise.

den *n.* lair, shelter, retreat, sanctuary, hideaway, nest. *The coyote pups were not yet old enough to leave their den.*

denial *n.* refusal, veto, disapproval, disavowal, disclaimer. *Her denial of the charges against her caused an uproar in the courtroom.* **Ant.** acceptance, affirmation, approval.

denomination *n.* sect, faith, order, group, body, school. *What church denomination did she say she belongs to?*

denote *vb.* indicate, symbolize, designate, signify, represent, mark. *Red circles denote danger zones on this map.*

denounce *vb.* condemn, attack, assail, criticize, rebuke, upbraid. *Students gathered in the administration building to denounce the school's discriminatory practices.*

dense *adj.* compact, compressed, thick, congested, massed. *The fog was so dense I couldn't see anything.* **Ant.** sparse, thin, scattered.

deny *vb.* **1.** contradict, disaffirm, dispute, protest, disavow. *She denied any knowledge of the theft.* **2.** withhold, refuse, veto, forbid, prohibit. *My parents denied my request to use the car.* **Ant. 1.** affirm, concede, admit. **2.** grant, allow, permit.

depart *vb.* leave, exit, withdraw, go, embark. *What time will the train depart?* **Ant.** arrive, enter, appear.

department *n.* division, section, bureau, branch, unit. *She heads the personnel department.*

departure *n.* **1.** leaving, exit, withdrawal, embarking, takeoff, parting. *The time of our departure is nine o'clock.* **2.** shift, change, deviation, divergence, swerving. *Allowing employees to wear blue jeans was a departure from the usual rules.* **Ant. 1.** arrival, coming, entrance. **2.** conformity, adherence.

depend *vb.* **1.** rely, bank, count, trust, believe. *You can depend on her to have the work done in time.* **2.** hinge, rest, turn, hang, stand. *Whether or not we go depends upon the weather.*

dependable *adj.* trustworthy, trusty, reliable, responsible, faithful, conscientious. *She needs a dependable person to take care of her house while she's away.* **Ant.** undependable, unreliable, untrustworthy.

depict *vb.* describe, portray, picture, characterize, represent. *Antarctica is often depicted as a cold and forbidding place.*

deplete *vb.* drain, exhaust, empty, consume, weaken, reduce, diminish. *Running your radio all night will deplete the batteries.* **Ant.** restore, replenish, increase.

deplorable *adj.* wretched, miserable, pathetic, regrettable, contemptible, shameful. *She left her room in a deplorable condition.* **Ant.** acceptable, good, agreeable.

deport *vb.* expel, eject, evict, remove, banish, dislodge. *Foreign citizens crossing U.S. borders without proper papers are deported.*

deposit *vb.* **1.** place, set, put, insert, lay, bank. *I just deposited $100 in my checking account.* –*n.* **2.** precipitation, sediment, silt, dregs, alluvium. *The chemist boiled the solution until only a blue deposit remained.* **3.** money, assets, savings, payment, installment. *His deposits total over $10,000.* **Ant. 1.** withdraw, remove.

depraved *adj.* evil, wicked, immoral, corrupt, vile, base, foul. *The depraved count murdered several hundred villagers.* **Ant.** good, moral, virtuous.

depreciate *vb.* lower, reduce, devalue, deflate, cut, decrease, diminish. *Inflation depreci-*

ates the value of money. **Ant.** increase, raise, boost.

depress *vb.* **1.** sadden, dishearten, discourage, deject, dispirit. *Losing his job depressed him.* **2.** lower, reduce, flatten, level, sink. *The dollar's loss of value depressed the stock market.* **Ant. 1.** gladden, encourage, cheer. **2.** raise, lift, boost.

depressed *adj.* unhappy, miserable, downcast, sorrowful, dejected. *The astronaut was very depressed when her spaceship left without her.* **Ant.** happy, joyous, delighted.

depression *n.* **1.** melancholy, sadness, despair, despondency, hopelessness. *He went through a period of depression after breaking up with his girlfriend.* **2.** crater, cavity, hole, hollow, pit. *There was a big depression in the ground where the meteorite hit.* **3.** recession, decline, slump, stagnation, crash. *The economy is headed toward a depression.* **Ant. 1.** cheerfulness, optimism, happiness. **3.** boom, progress.

deprive *vb.* strip, divest, rob, deny, withhold, remove, seize. *Loud music next door deprived him of a good night's sleep.*

derelict *adj.* **1.** abandoned, deserted, discarded, forsaken, forlorn. *The derelict ship rusted away.* **2.** negligent, slack, lax, delinquent, loose, lazy. *He's been derelict in doing his chores.*

deride *vb.* belittle, scorn, knock, ridicule, mock, tease, taunt. *Please don't deride my belief in UFOs.*

derive *vb.* obtain, reap, extract, come, arise, gather, get. *This potion is derived from bat wings.*

descend *vb.* **1.** drop, fall, plunge, sink, dive, subside, submerge. *The submarine descended to the bottom of the sea.* **2.** come, spring, issue, derive. *He is descended from native American Indians.* **3.** pounce, swoop, attack, assault, invade. *Barbarian hordes descended on the unprotected village.* **Ant. 1.** ascend, rise, climb.

descendant *n.* offspring, issue, family, progeny, brood, daughter, son. *She is a descendant of 18th-century immigrants.* **Ant.** ancestor, parent.

descent *n.* **1.** fall, plunge, drop, dip, droop, settling, decline. *The gull made a quick descent and plucked a fish from the water.* **2.** ancestry, heritage, lineage, parentage, origin, roots, stock.

He is of Arabic descent. **Ant. 1.** ascent, climb, rise.

describe *vb.* depict, define, portray, illustrate, picture, relate, recount. *The police asked her to describe what she saw last night.*

description *n.* account, report, depiction, portrayal, sketch. *Can you give a description of the thief?*

desert *vb.* abandon, forsake, leave, quit, renounce. *My friends deserted me when things got bad.*

deserve *vb.* merit, earn, warrant, qualify, rate. *After working so many extra hours, he deserves the promotion.*

design *vb.* **1.** plan, fashion, arrange, draft, develop, imagine, visualize. *Engineers have designed the car so that it is both comfortable and fast.* –*n.* **2.** plan, pattern, scheme, arrangement, outline, diagram. *She oversaw the design and building of her new house.* **3.** intent, objective, intention, purpose, aim, goal, desire. *It was not my design to get your position on the team.*

designate *vb.* name, nominate, appoint, select, assign, choose. *The teacher has designated me as group leader.*

desirable *adj.* attractive, inviting, agreeable, valuable, worthy, excellent. *This is a desirable job because of the high salary and pleasant environment.* **Ant.** undesirable, unattractive, repulsive.

desire *vb.* **1.** want, wish for, fancy, covet, crave. *She's desired a new car for some time.* –*n.* **2.** wanting, wishing, yearning, longing, attraction, craving. *He felt a strong desire to see his family again after so many years.* **Ant. 2.** aversion, distaste, dislike.

despair *n.* hopelessness, dismay, distress, depression, dejection. *They felt despair when they realized there was no way to save him.* **Ant.** hopefulness, hope, optimism.

desperate *adj.* **1.** frantic, hasty, wild, risky, reckless. *He made a desperate grab for his hat as it flew out the window.* **2.** hopeless, despairing, wretched, despondent, depressed. *She felt desperate because she had no date and the dance was only one day away .* **Ant. 1.** cautious, careful. **2.** happy, hopeful, optimistic.

despise *vb.* detest, hate, loathe, scorn, dislike, abhor, disdain. *I've always despised a person who says nasty things about others.* **Ant.** like, admire, respect.

destination *n.* goal, objective, stop, end, target, aim. *The plane's destination is Beijing.*

destiny *n.* fortune, luck, lot, fate, providence. *She felt that it was her destiny to become president.*

destitute *adj.* impoverished, poor, penniless, broke, needy. *The massive earthquake left thousands of people homeless and destitute.* **Ant.** rich, affluent, wealthy.

destroy *vb.* wreck, ruin, demolish, level, raze, devastate, crush. *A mudslide destroyed several houses in our neighborhood.* **Ant.** restore, save, preserve.

destruction *n.* ruination, devastation, wrecking, razing, demolition, leveling. *Rabbits are responsible for the destruction of our garden.* **Ant.** preservation, conservation.

detach *vb.* disconnect, unfasten, separate, free, loosen. *She had trouble detaching the gum from her shoe.* **Ant.** attach, fix, secure.

detail *n.* **1.** part, item, particular, specific, feature, aspect. *His paintings are known for their fine attention to detail.* -*vb.* **2.** itemize, specify, depict, recount, relate. *He detailed all his expenses.*

detain *vb.* **1.** delay, slow, hinder, retard, check, impede. *She was detained by an important phone call.* **2.** arrest, hold, stop, restrain, imprison, confine. *Security personnel detained the woman after finding a gun in her baggage.*

detect *vb.* see, discover, uncover, notice, spot, observe, find. *The doctor could detect no signs of infection.*

deter *vb.* discourage, prevent, stop, thwart, block, hinder. *Hopefully, our new alarm system will deter burglars.* **Ant.** encourage, reassure, stimulate.

determine *vb.* settle, decide, ascertain, resolve, discover. *Have you determined which movie you're going to see?*

determined *adj.* decided, fixed, settled, purposeful, firm, resolute. *His determined look made me realize I couldn't talk him out of going.* **Ant.** undetermined, indecisive, undecided.

detest *vb.* hate, dislike, despise, loathe, abhor, disdain. *I really detest worms.* **Ant.** love, like, adore.

detour *vb.* **1.** route, direct, skirt, bypass. *Due to construction work, we were detoured onto a side street.* -*n.* **2.** bypath, byroad, byway, diversion, digression. *I know we're late, but I need to make a quick detour to the rest room.*

devastate *vb.* ravage, waste, ruin, destroy, despoil, raze, level. *Locusts devastated the farmer's crops.*

develop *vb.* **1.** enlarge, expand, improve, broaden, increase. *Lifting weights developed my biceps.* **2.** generate, invent, form, fashion, establish, organize. *Scientists spent years developing a spacecraft that could surpass the speed of light.* **3.** acquire, get, contract, obtain, gain. *He developed a serious case of pneumonia.*

development *n.* **1.** evolution, growth, rise, progress, history. *The development of the laser promises to benefit medical science.* **2.** event, incident, happening, occurrence, episode. *Stay tuned to this station for the latest developments.*

deviate *vb.* stray, diverge, wander, turn, depart. *His account of the accident seems to deviate from the facts.*

device *n.* **1.** gadget, instrument, equipment, apparatus, implement, tool. *The aliens had devices that allowed them to read our minds.* **2.** scheme, strategy, plot, design, intrigue. *My parents used several devices to try to get me to choose the college they preferred.*

devious *adj.* underhand, sneaky, tricky, scheming, calculating, deceitful. *That was a devious way of getting your needs met.* **Ant.** honest, straightforward.

devise *vb.* invent, conceive, formulate, forge, construct, arrange. *She devised a way to turn lead into gold.*

devote *vb.* give, commit, surrender, pledge, dedicate, offer, apply. *She devoted many hours to the project.*

devoted *adj.* loyal, faithful, dedicated, committed, true. *Her dog is her devoted companion.* **Ant.** unfaithful, disloyal, untrue.

devotion *n.* dedication, attachment, loyalty, faithfulness, love, regard. *She appreciates her husband's devotion.* **Ant.** indifference, disinterest, disregard.

devour *vb.* gobble, swallow, gulp, consume, eat, finish. *He devoured two hamburgers in less than three minutes.*

devout *adj.* faithful, pious, earnest, sincere, heartfelt, reverent. *He is a devout Catholic.*

dexterity *n.* skill, agility, facility, proficiency, adroitness. *The basketball player was known for her dexterity on the court.* **Ant.** clumsiness, awkwardness, ineptitude.

diagram *n.* sketch, drawing, outline, blueprint, picture, illustration. *Please draw a diagram of the building.*

dialogue *n.* conversation, talk, exchange, chat, discourse. *I couldn't follow the play's dialogue .*

diary *n.* journal, log, logbook, chronicle, record. *The ship's captain kept a diary of his journeys.*

dictate *vb.* **1.** communicate, speak, say, utter, transmit. *The lawyer dictated a letter to her secretary.* **2.** direct, ordain, command, order, decree, determine. *I won't let you dictate where I go.* **Ant. 2.** follow, obey.

die *vb.* **1.** perish, expire, decease, end, succumb, fail. *When the plane began shaking, he thought he was going to die.* **2.** thirst, hunger, desire, want, crave, yearn, long. *She's dying for a tall glass of lemonade.* **Ant. 1.** live, survive, exist.

differ *vb.* **1.** vary, deviate, contrast, disagree, conflict. *Estimates to fix his car differed by as much as $500.* **2.** disagree, dispute, squabble, quarrel, argue, wrangle. *We differed on where to go for our vacation.* **Ant. 1.** match, correspond, coincide. **2.** agree, concur.

difference *n.* **1.** dissimilarity, contrast, divergence, variation, deviation. *Do you think there is a big difference between people in New York and those in Los Angeles?* **2.** argument, dispute, squabble, quarrel, feud, clash. *I quit after my boss and I had some major differences.* **Ant. 1.** similarity, likeness. **2.** agreement, harmony, accord.

different *adj.* **1.** separate, distinct, assorted, varied, unrelated. *She painted her car several different colors.* **2.** unusual, strange, odd, unique, extraordinary. *He has a different way of doing things.* **3.** dissimilar, unlike, contrasting, opposed, divergent. *My taste in movies is quite different from hers.* **Ant. 2.** ordinary, common, usual. **3.** identical, alike, same.

difficult *adj.* hard, troublesome, tough, laborious, strenuous, exhausting, tedious. *It's difficult writing a twenty-page paper the night before it's due.* **Ant.** easy, simple, pleasant.

difficulty *n.* strain, trouble, labor, problem, bother, ordeal, trial. *After gaining twenty pounds, he had difficulty getting into his jeans.*

dig *vb.* **1.** scoop, burrow, excavate, tunnel, shovel, mine. *She dug for clams.* *–n.* **2.** jab, poke, prod, thrust, push. *Give the mule a light dig in the ribs to get it going.*

digest *vb.* **1.** absorb, assimilate, grasp, understand, comprehend. *Give me a minute to digest what you said.* *–n.* **3.** summary, abstract, condensation, abridgment, brief. *I just finished reading a digest of his latest book.*

dignity *n.* formality, respectability, reserve, solemnity, loftiness. *His sense of dignity would not allow him to act so foolishly.*

digress *vb.* deviate, wander, stray, drift, depart, veer, straggle. *Sorry, but I seem to have digressed from my topic.*

dilate *vb.* expand, enlarge, widen, swell, broaden, inflate. *The optometrist's solution dilated the pupils of my eyes.* **Ant.** shrink, contract, constrict.

dilemma *n.* quandary, bind, predicament, question, stalemate, perplexity. *Two parties are going on tonight, and it's a dilemma trying to decide which one to attend.*

diligence *n.* persistence, perseverance, earnestness, exertion, application. *It takes diligence to successfully pan for gold.* **Ant.** laziness, sloth, lethargy.

diligent *adj.* industrious, persevering, hardworking, painstaking, persistent, zealous. *She gets good grades because she's diligent in her studying.* **Ant.** lazy, indifferent, careless.

dilute *vb.* **1.** thin, mix, weaken, cut, adulterate. *She dilutes her orange juice with water.* *–adj.* **2.** diluted, thin, watery, weak, adulterated. *The cook's vegetable soup is usually very dilute.* **Ant. 1.** thicken, concentrate. **2.** thick, concentrated, strong.

dim *adj.* **1.** low, soft, weak, dark, murky, indistinct. *This light is too dim for reading.* **2.** discouraging, somber, unpromising, depressing, ominous. *The surrounded troops thought their prospects were pretty dim.* **Ant. 1.** bright, brilliant, strong. **2.** hopeful, promising.

dimension *n.* measure, size, magnitude, extent, expanse, spread, range, volume. *Do you understand the full dimensions of the problem?*

diminish *vb.* lessen, reduce, decrease, recede, shrink, lower, dwindle, subside. *The sound diminished as we got farther away.* **Ant.** increase, magnify, enlarge.

din *n.* noise, clamor, uproar, racket, commotion. *The din of my neighbor's stereo is getting on my nerves.* **Ant.** silence, stillness, quiet.

dine *vb.* eat, feed, feast, sup, banquet. *Let's dine out tonight.*

dingy *adj.* shabby, dirty, seedy, run-down, grimy, drab, gloomy. *The cheap motel had small and dingy rooms.* **Ant.** luxurious, shiny, clean.

dip *vb.* **1.** immerse, submerge, soak, plunge, dunk. *She dipped her feet in the pool's cool water.* **2.** sink, set, settle, descend, drop. *The sun dipped below the horizon.* **Ant. 2.** rise, climb, ascend.

diplomat *n.* envoy, ambassador, emissary, mediator, negotiator, consul. *Diplomats from two nations met to sign the treaty.*

dire *adj.* **1.** grievous, awful, alarming, terrible, horrible, fearsome. *She was suffering from a dire illness.* **2.** critical, urgent, vital, desperate, crucial. *The accident victims were in dire need of care.*

direct *vb.* **1.** run, manage, lead, supervise, administer, control. *She is responsible for directing the play.* **2.** point, guide, aim, steer, lead, send. *Will you direct me to the post office?* **3.** command, instruct, tell, charge, bid, order. *My instructions directed me to meet him at the train station.* *–adj.* **4.** straight, short, true, unwinding, unswerving. *Is this path the most direct route to the top?* **5.** frank, honest, candid, blunt, truthful, sincere. *Please be direct with me.* **Ant. 4.** indirect, roundabout, winding. **5.** indirect, subtle, devious.

direction *n.* **1.** path, course, heading, way, route, bearing. *In which direction did they go?* **2.** administration, management, control, supervision, handling, leadership. *The business has profited under his direction.* **3.** instruction, command, order, guidelines, teaching. *My boss told me to follow his directions carefully.*

directly *adv.* straight, right, immediately, quickly, promptly, instantly. *If you land on this space, you go directly to jail.* **Ant.** later, eventually, indirectly.

dirty *adj.* **1.** soiled, filthy, unwashed, grimy, unclean, stained. *I took my dirty clothes to the laundry.* **2.** indecent, obscene, smutty, vulgar, pornographic. *He has a dirty mind.* **3.** illegal, crooked, dishonorable, deceitful, villainous, corrupt. *The politician made some dirty deals.* **4.** angry, annoyed, offended, resentful, bitter. *She gave me a dirty look.* *–vb.* **5.** soil, smear, tarnish, smudge, stain, blacken. *The scandal has dirtied her name.* **Ant. 1.** clean, spotless, washed. **2.** clean, decent, virtuous. **3.** clean, legal. **5.** clean, sanitize, wash.

disadvantage *n.* handicap, detriment, drawback, minus, liability, burden. *Your lack of education is a real disadvantage.* **Ant.** advantage, strength, plus.

disagree *vb.* differ, conflict, clash, argue, quarrel, debate. *They disagreed over which team had the better quarterback.* **Ant.** agree, concur, reconcile.

disagreeable *adj.* **1.** unpleasant, disgusting, repulsive, distasteful, repellent. *She finds the thought of eating cooked snails rather disagreeable.* **2.** unfriendly, surly, irritable, grouchy, sullen. *He doesn't get along with anyone because of his disagreeable nature.* **Ant. 1.** agreeable, pleasant, appealing. **2.** agreeable, friendly.

disagreement *n.* quarrel, dispute, fight, clash, rift, split. *We had a disagreement over who* could use the car. **Ant.** agreement, concurrence, accord.

disappear vb. vanish, dematerialize, dissolve, vaporize, depart, fade. *The ship disappeared in the Bermuda Triangle.* **Ant.** appear, emerge, materialize.

disappoint vb. disillusion, dissatisfy, sadden, dishearten, discourage, frustrate. *The producers disappointed me by making a bad movie.* **Ant.** please, satisfy, delight.

disappointment n. dissatisfaction, frustration, regret, letdown, disillusionment. *The children made their disappointment obvious when their trip to the circus was postponed.* **Ant.** satisfaction, contentment, happiness.

disapprove vb. criticize, dislike, condemn, reject, deplore, denounce. *His parents disapprove of the way he dresses.* **Ant.** approve, praise, commend.

disaster n. catastrophe, tragedy, misfortune, calamity, accident, mishap. *At least 1,500 people died in the Titanic disaster.*

disbelief n. doubt, distrust, skepticism, scorn, rejection, incredulity. *His story of the purple aliens was met with disbelief.* **Ant.** belief, acceptance, trust.

discard vb. **1.** eliminate, dispose, dump, drop, shed, scrap, abandon. *Please discard your litter in the trash can.* –n. **2.** reject, castaway, scraps, throwaway, garbage. *Put your discards in this pile.* **Ant. 1.** retain, keep, save.

discern vb. ascertain, decipher, discover, distinguish, see, notice. *I think I've discerned the purpose of her visit.*

discharge vb. **1.** explode, detonate, shoot, burst, activate. *Pulling this pin will discharge the bomb.* **2.** gush, ooze, emit, eject, leak, empty. *Sewer pipes discharged polluted wastes into the ocean.* **3.** release, free, dismiss, fire, relieve. *The soldier was honorably discharged after serving four years.* –n. **4.** blast, explosion, shooting, firing, detonation. *The rifle's discharge shattered the peacefulness of the forest.* **5.** emission, ejection, flow, seepage, issue, secretion. *Automobile discharge is a major source of pollution.* **6.** release, dismissal, expulsion, removal. *She was*

informed of her discharge from the company. **Ant. 3.** hold, keep, hire.

disciple n. follower, devotee, adherent, convert, supporter, student. *The guru's disciples followed him wherever he went.* **Ant.** master, leader, teacher.

discipline n. **1.** practice, drilling, preparation, instruction, training. *It takes years of discipline to learn how to rock-climb.* **2.** regulation, restriction, direction, control, punishment, correction. *My parents are strict when it comes to discipline.* **3.** subject, specialty, major, curriculum. *The instructor is very knowledgeable in his discipline.* –vb. **4.** train, drill, school, prepare, instruct, toughen. *She disciplined herself to feel no pain.* **5.** punish, correct, chastise, reprimand, criticize. *I disciplined my dog for tearing up the neighbor's flower garden.*

disclose vb. reveal, tell, divulge, expose, unmask, show, release. *I can't disclose the source of my information.* **Ant.** hide, conceal, mask.

discomfort n. uneasiness, distress, suffering, misery, ache, pain. *Is your sprained knee giving you much discomfort?* **Ant.** comfort, ease, pleasure.

discontented adj. dissatisfied, displeased, unhappy, impatient, frustrated. *She is discontented with her job.* **Ant.** satisfied, pleased, happy.

discontinue vb. stop, cease, end, terminate, suspend, interrupt. *My parents threatened to discontinue my allowance if I didn't behave.* **Ant.** continue, maintain, start.

discord n. conflict, hostility, friction, strife, disharmony. *The mounting discord between the two nations was cause for concern.* **Ant.** harmony, peace, accord.

discount n. **1.** reduction, deduction, decrease, lessening, rebate. *You can get a discount if you buy two of the same items.* –vb. **2.** reduce, lessen, decrease, subtract, deduct. *This store discounts everything by 25%.* **3.** disregard, ignore, overlook, omit, slight. *The jury discounted my testimony, since I hadn't seen the crime.* **Ant. 2.** hike, raise, boost.

discourage vb. **1.** deject, dismay, unnerve, dishearten, depress, disenchant. *I was discour-*

aged by the fact that no publisher seemed interested in my book. **2.** dissuade, warn, caution, deter, restrain. *The ranger strongly discouraged those who lacked training from attempting the climb.* **Ant. 1.** encourage, hearten, excite. **2.** encourage.

discouragement *n.* despair, setback, frustration, worry, dismay. *Her failure to win the lead part was a major discouragement to her.* **Ant.** encouragement, uplift, boost.

discover *vb.* find, unearth, uncover, locate, detect, recognize, spot, see. *The California Gold Rush occurred in 1848, after gold was discovered at Sutter's Mill.* **Ant.** miss, overlook.

discovery *n.* detection, unearthing, uncovering, finding, find, locating. *William Herschel is credited with the discovery of the planet Uranus in 1781.*

discreet *adj.* guarded, cautious, diplomatic, tactful, careful. *Please be discreet when telling them the nature of my problem.* **Ant.** indiscreet, incautious, careless.

discretion *n.* judgment, preference, inclination, thoughtfulness, wisdom. *Television viewers should use their own discretion in deciding what to watch.*

discrimination *vb.* **1.** bigotry, prejudice, bias, intolerance, racism, sexism. *It is unlawful for employers to practice discrimination based on sex, creed, or color.* **2.** judgment, insight, discernment, discretion, forethought. *Use some discrimination in choosing a car.*

discuss *vb.* talk about, debate, review, examine, consider, study. *Let's discuss this before we go ahead and do it.*

discussion *n.* debate, conversation, talk, discourse, conference, meeting. *He fell asleep during the class discussion.*

disease *n.* illness, sickness, ailment, malady, affliction. *Leprosy is one of the least contagious diseases.*

disfigure *vb.* deface, deform, damage, scar, blemish, flaw. *The fire disfigured a valuable painting.*

disgrace *n.* **1.** dishonor, shame, embarrassment, humiliation, stain, taint. *We viewed our loss to the worst team in the league as a major disgrace.* –*vb.* **2.** dishonor, shame, discredit, tarnish, embarrass, humiliate. *The warrior's dishonorable actions disgraced his tribe.* **Ant. 1.** honor, glory. **2.** honor, credit, distinguish.

disgraceful *adj.* shameful, embarrassing, degrading, shocking, scandalous, humiliating. *It's disgraceful that many hardworking people earn so little.* **Ant.** worthy, becoming, honorable.

disguise *vb.* **1.** camouflage, mask, conceal, veil, cloak, cover. *Batman disguises himself by wearing a mask.* –*n.* **2.** camouflage, mask, costume, veil, guise, covering. *Everyone must wear a disguise to the costume party.* **Ant. 1.** uncover, reveal, disclose.

disgust *vb.* **1.** sicken, revolt, shock, nauseate, repel, appall. *The movie's gore and blood disgusted me.* –*n.* **2.** revulsion, repulsion, distaste, repugnance, loathing. *I could not hide the disgust I felt at the slovenly way in which he ate.* **Ant. 1.** please, delight. **2.** pleasure, satisfaction, liking.

disheveled *adj.* messy, sloppy, ruffled, unkempt, tousled, disorderly. *She looked rather disheveled after her twelve-hour flight.* **Ant.** neat, tidy, trim.

dishonest *adj.* crooked, deceitful, untrustworthy, dishonorable, false, corrupt. *Never buy a car from a dishonest dealer.* **Ant.** honest, honorable, trustworthy.

disintegrate *vb.* shatter, crumble, decompose, fragment, decay. *The ancient bones disintegrated as soon as the tomb was opened.*

dislike *vb.* **1.** hate, detest, despise, loathe, abhor. *She dislikes tests.* –*n.* **2.** hatred, loathing, revulsion, disgust, abhorrence, aversion. *He has a strong dislike of war.* **Ant. 1.** like, love, admire. **2.** like, love, admiration.

disloyal *adj.* unfaithful, traitorous, treasonable, false, untrue, treacherous. *I think it's rather disloyal of him to root for the other school's team.* **Ant.** loyal, faithful, true.

dismal *adj.* bleak, gloomy, cheerless, dreary, somber, depressing, drab. *This has been a rather dismal winter.* **Ant.** cheerful, sunny, bright.

dismantle *vb.* disassemble, tear down, remove, raze, strip, fell. *Stagehands dismantled the* *backdrop when the play was over.* **Ant.** build, assemble, construct.

dismay *vb.* **1.** dishearten, distress, alarm, discourage, frighten, appall. *She was dismayed by all the homework she had to do.* *–n.* **2.** distress, discouragement, dread, alarm, agitation, concern. *I felt enormous dismay upon realizing how much farther I had to walk.* **Ant. 1.** encourage, hearten, relieve. **2.** encouragement, assurance.

dismiss *vb.* **1.** excuse, release, free, discharge, expel, fire. *The teacher dismissed him from class after he became ill.* **2.** disregard, reject, rebuff, scorn, discredit. *Don't dismiss what she has to say.* **Ant. 1.** accept, admit, hire. **2.** accept, receive, consider.

dismissal *n.* release, discharge, removal, suspension, expulsion. *His poor attitude at the office was the reason for his dismissal.*

disobedient *adj.* rebellious, defiant, unruly, insubordinate, ungovernable. *She took her disobedient dog to training school.* **Ant.** obedient, submissive.

disobey *vb.* defy, disregard, ignore, flout, resist, oppose. *The soldier was court-martialed for disobeying orders.* **Ant.** obey, heed, follow.

disorderly *adj.* **1.** messy, untidy, disorganized, chaotic, confused. *His room is always disorderly.* **2.** unruly, disruptive, unlawful, lawless, improper. *She was arrested for disorderly conduct.* **Ant. 1.** tidy, neat, clean. **2.** civil, lawful, proper.

dispel *vb.* scatter, disperse, banish, repel, dismiss, remove, expel. *His lantern dispelled the gloom of the cave.*

dispense *vb.* **1.** distribute, give, furnish, supply, allot, administer. *Nurses dispense medicines to their patients.* **2.** forgo, abstain, cancel, waive, relinquish, release. *Since we all know each other, let's dispense with the introductions.*

disperse *vb.* scatter, disband, dissolve, separate, spread. *Police dispersed the unruly crowd.* **Ant.** assemble, gather, collect.

display *vb.* **1.** exhibit, show, expose, reveal, demonstrate, array. *Where are they displaying your artwork?* *–n.* **2.** show, exhibition, exhibit, presentation, demonstration. *That was a fine display of skateboard riding.*

dispose *vb.* **1.** incline, motivate, induce, move, tempt. *I'm disposed toward being charitable today.* **2.** discard, unload, dump, throw out, distribute. *Where should he dispose of his trash?*

dispute *vb.* **1.** question, challenge, oppose, doubt, argue, contradict. *She disputed his claim to royalty.* *–n.* **2.** argument, disagreement, quarrel, feud, conflict, debate. *The two countries are in a dispute over which owns the land.* **Ant. 1.** support, affirm, confirm. **2.** agreement, accord.

disregard *vb.* **1.** ignore, forget, overlook, skip, reject, neglect. *Disregard the last note I sent, since I've changed my mind.* *–n.* **2.** indifference, neglect, inattention, oversight, disdain. *I'm angry with my friend because of her disregard for my feelings.* **Ant. 1.** heed, regard, notice. **2.** regard, attention, interest.

disrespectful *adj.* rude, impolite, discourteous, irreverent, brash. *He was cautioned against being disrespectful in court.* **Ant.** respectful, polite, courteous.

disrupt *vb.* interrupt, upset, halt, disturb, disorganize, agitate. *A dog entered the church and disrupted the wedding ceremony.*

dissatisfied *adj.* disappointed, discontented, displeased, unhappy. *My parents seem dissatisfied with everything I do.* **Ant.** pleased, happy, satisfied.

dissent *vb.* **1.** disagree, oppose, object, differ, protest. *Several people dissented with the coach's decision to forfeit the game.* *–n.* **2.** opposition, protest, objection, discord, disagreement. *There was dissent among the students when told school hours would be extended.* **Ant. 1.** agree, consent, concur. **2.** agreement, consent, accord.

dissolve *vb.* **1.** melt, liquefy, disappear, vanish, fade, disintegrate. *This powder dissolves when added to water.* **2.** end, terminate, conclude, cancel, dismiss, disband. *Since no one attended the meetings, we decided to dissolve our club.* **Ant. 1.** solidify, thicken, congeal. **2.** continue, begin, start.

distance *n.* length, span, stretch, expanse, space, gap, interval. *The distance between school and the arcade is about five blocks.*

distant *adj.* **1.** remote, faraway, far, outlying, yonder. *We set sail for the distant island.* **2.** withdrawn, uncommunicative, cool, unfriendly, reserved. *He seems so distant since our argument.* **Ant. 1.** near, close. **2.** close, friendly, communicative.

distend *vb.* bloat, expand, swell, enlarge, spread, inflate, fatten, balloon. *The dog's stomach distended from eating too much food.* **Ant.** shrink, contract, constrict.

distinct *adj.* **1.** individual, separate, different, discrete, dissimilar. *Scottish clans each have a distinct plaid from which their kilts are made.* **2.** clear, obvious, plain, apparent, evident, certain, unmistakable. *Skunks give off a distinct odor.* **Ant. 1.** similar, identical, like. **2.** indistinct, vague, unclear.

distinction *n.* **1.** separation, differentiation, division, discernment, discrimination. *Only an expert can discern the distinction between these two bird species.* **2.** importance, prominence, rank, consequence, significance. *The vineyard advertised its product as a wine bought by people of distinction.*

distinctive *adj.* particular, special, unique, unusual, different. *That artist has a very distinctive painting style.* **Ant.** typical, average, usual.

distinguish *vb.* **1.** differentiate, determine, decide, identify, detect, recognize. *How can I distinguish between the twins?* **2.** honor, memorialize, dignify, glorify, ennoble. *The knight distinguished himself by his bravery.*

distinguished *adj.* famous, renowned, celebrated, prominent, illustrious, eminent. *The distinguished scientist is known for her brilliant research.* **Ant.** undistinguished, unknown.

distort *vb.* warp, deform, twist, contort, knot, misshape. *Anger distorted his features.*

distract *vb.* divert, interrupt, sidetrack, disturb, annoy, trouble. *I was distracted by my neighbor's barking dog.*

distress *vb.* **1.** upset, disturb, worry, trouble, sadden, depress. *The queen was distressed when her knights failed to return.* –*n.* **2.** agony, sorrow, anguish, misery, sadness, depression. *I felt great distress over not being accepted at the* university. **Ant. 1.** comfort, console, relieve. **2.** relief, solace, comfort.

distribute *vb.* give, dispense, deliver, allocate, spread, scatter. *A group on the corner distributed religious pamphlets.* **Ant.** take, collect, gather.

distribution *n.* **1.** dispersion, dispensation, spreading, scattering, circulation. *His job is to oversee distribution of the company's products.* **2.** placement, location, arrangement, order, disposition. *This map shows the distribution of our defense forces.*

district *n.* area, territory, region, section, zone, community. *She lives in the Richmond district.*

disturb *vb.* **1.** bother, annoy, interrupt, pester, harass. *Loud construction work outside disturbed him as he studied.* **2.** trouble, upset, confuse, distress, worry. *I am disturbed by my friend's odd behavior.*

disturbance *n.* **1.** commotion, tumult, turmoil, uproar, racket. *The principal investigated the disturbance in the school cafeteria.* **2.** interruption, distraction, annoyance, vexation, bother. *Where can I work without disturbance?* **Ant. 1–2.** peace, quiet, calm.

dive *vb.* **1.** plunge, plummet, jump, leap, fall, pitch. *I dove for cover when I heard the explosion.* –*n.* **2.** lunge, plunge, descent, drop, jump, leap. *The swimmer executed a graceful dive.*

diverge *vb.* separate, divide, split, fork, swerve, part. *This corridor diverges into two passageways.* **Ant.** merge, join, unite.

diverse *adj.* varied, assorted, diversified, unlike, mixed. *Her favorite restaurant has a diverse selection of international foods.* **Ant.** identical, similar, same.

diversity *n.* difference, variance, variety, distinctiveness, dissimilarity. *The diversity of our population is one of this country's strengths.* **Ant.** similarity, uniformity, likeness.

divert *vb.* deflect, shift, sidetrack, swerve, shunt. *Engineers diverted the runaway train onto a secondary track.*

divide *vb.* **1.** separate, part, split, cut, partition. *The teacher divided the class into two* groups. **2.** distribute, dispense, share, allot, dole. *The pirates divided the booty amongst themselves.* **Ant. 1.** join, unite, combine.

divine *adj.* **1.** holy, sainted, sacred, heavenly, blessed, godly. *It was once thought in Japan that the emperor ruled by divine right.* *–vb.* **2.** prophesy, predict, foresee, foretell, anticipate, portend. *The fortune teller claimed she could divine the future.*

division *n.* branch, part, section, portion, component. *My favorite team won the championship in the western division.*

divorce *n.* **1.** disunion, separation, split, dissolution, severance. *My parents are going to get a divorce.* *–vb.* **2.** separate, disunite, split, detach, part, divide. *I divorced myself from their argument.* **Ant. 1.** union, unity, harmony. **2.** join, unite, merge.

divulge *vb.* tell, reveal, confide, bare, expose, disclose, release. *She refused to divulge her secret to us.* **Ant.** hide, conceal, cloak.

do *vb.* **1.** perform, execute, administer, undertake, fulfill. *Please do what I tell you.* **2.** finish, conclude, end, complete, accomplish. *Have you done your homework?* **3.** suffice, serve, satisfy, answer, work. *Will this room do, or would you like to see another?* **4.** render, give, pay, afford, bear. *Do me a favor and quit talking so much.* **5.** cover, traverse, manage, fare, proceed. *She can do a mile in under five minutes.*

docile *adj.* gentle, passive, subdued, agreeable, tame, obedient, manageable. *Tranquilizers made the tiger docile.* **Ant.** unruly, rebellious, wild.

doctrine *n.* creed, principle, dogma, belief, teaching, theory, maxim. *The cult members obeyed their leader's doctrines.*

document *n.* **1.** paper, record, certificate, credential, voucher, deed. *You need the right documents to get into certain countries.* *–vb.* **2.** record, verify, certify, authenticate, chronicle. *Scholars have documented the existence of the ancient civilization.*

dodge *vb.* **1.** duck, sidestep, dart, swerve, shift, bolt. *The matador dodged out of the way of the charging bull.* *–n.* **2.** dart, duck, sidestep, swerve, shift. *The rabbit escaped the hawk by making a dodge into the brush.*

domain *n.* territory, area, region, zone, realm, empire. *This valley is the domain of our people.*

domestic *adj.* **1.** family, home, household, residential. *They prefer the domestic life.* **2.** tame, tamed, domesticated, trained, broken. *Sheep, cows and goats are all domestic animals.* **3.** native, internal, homemade, endemic, indigenous. *Are these computers of domestic make?* **Ant. 2.** wild, feral, untamed. **3.** foreign, non-native, exotic.

dominant *adj.* strongest, prominent, prime, controlling, principal. *Usually, the dominant wolf in the pack becomes the leader.* **Ant.** weakest, subordinate, inferior.

dominate *vb.* **1.** control, rule, command, overpower, direct. *The talkative man dominated the conversation.* **2.** pervade, overspread, overrun, characterize, permeate. *Rose bushes dominate our garden.*

donate *vb.* give, present, bestow, offer, impart, confer, grant. *My parents donated some old furniture for the school rummage sale.*

done *adj.* finished, completed, concluded, ended, through. *Is the turkey done yet?* **Ant.** incomplete, undone, unfinished.

donor *n.* contributor, donator, giver, benefactor, supporter. *We need more donors for the blood drive.*

doom *n.* **1.** destiny, lot, fate, death, extinction, ruin. *The soldiers faced their impending doom with bravery.* *–vb.* **2.** fate, destine, predetermine, ordain, condemn. *His efforts are doomed to fail.*

door *n.* entrance, portal, gate, hatch, entranceway, exit. *Please close the door.*

dormant *adj.* inactive, sleeping, lethargic, sluggish, passive, quiet. *Bears remain dormant during the winter months.* **Ant.** active, wakeful, alert.

dose *n.* measure, portion, quantity, quota, allowance. *Make sure you take the correct dose of medicine.*

doubt *vb.* **1.** suspect, distrust, mistrust, question, disbelieve. *Do you doubt my word?* –*n.* **2.** misgiving, disbelief, uncertainty, suspicion, skepticism. *I have doubts about whether she'll really show up.* **Ant. 1.** trust, believe, accept. **2.** trust, belief, certainty.

doubtful *adj.* unlikely, questionable, uncertain, debatable, dubious. *It's doubtful that she'll get off work in time to join us.* **Ant.** probable, likely, certain.

down *adj.* **1.** dejected, discouraged, depressed, despondent, melancholy. *He's been feeling down ever since he lost his job.* –*adv.* **2.** downward, downhill, below, beneath, underneath. *She fell down.* –*vb.* **3.** swallow, gulp, take, drop, fell. *He downed a soda.* **Ant. 1.** up, elated, happy. **2.** up, upward.

downfall *n.* **1.** fall, crash, ruin, collapse, overthrow, breakdown, destruction. *Who can say when the downfall of civilization will occur?* **2.** rainstorm, shower, cloudburst, thunderstorm, deluge. *There's a heavy downfall outside.*

doze *vb.* **1.** nap, sleep, slumber, snooze, drowse. *He dozed off in class today.* –*n.* **2.** nap, slumber, snooze, siesta. *She fell into a doze beside the stream.*

drab *adj.* dull, dreary, lusterless, dingy, dismal, somber, gloomy. *We need some new furniture to liven up this drab room.* **Ant.** vivid, colorful, bright.

draft *n.* **1.** outline, sketch, overview, synopsis, plan. *Have you finished the first draft of your novel?* **2.** breeze, flow, stream, current, wind. *There's a cold draft coming through the window.* **3.** induction, conscription, impressment, call, summons. *During the Vietnam War, some men avoided the draft by going to Canada.* –*vb.* **4.** draw, sketch, diagram, outline, design, plan. *Engineers drafted plans for the new spaceship.* **5.** induct, conscript, impress, summon, call. *The U.S. drafts men into the armed forces during times of war.*

drag *vb.* **1.** tug, haul, draw, lug, tow, pull, trail. *The lion dragged its kill to its den.* **2.** plod, creep, crawl, straggle, limp. *The boring lecture seemed to drag on for hours.* **Ant. 1.** push, shove, thrust. **2.** rush, race, speed.

drain *vb.* **1.** sap, empty, extract, tax, deplete, withdraw. *The hot sun drained me of my energy.* **2.** leak, drip, ooze, seep, flow, discharge. *The infected wound was lanced so the pus would drain.*

dramatic *adj.* intense, striking, sensational, emotional, theatrical. *Shaving off his beard created a dramatic change in his appearance.*

drastic *adj.* extreme, radical, forceful, severe, intensive, harsh. *Don't you think starving yourself is a drastic way to lose weight?*

draw *vb.* **1.** sketch, diagram, picture, outline, trace, depict. *The pirates drew a map of where they had buried the treasure.* **2.** charm, attract, lure, tempt, invite, allure. *Tales of wondrous beauty drew people to the islands.* **3.** extract, pull, remove, take, acquire, obtain. *The doctor drew a blood sample.* **4.** lengthen, extend, prolong, continue, elongate. *He drew out his story until everyone was quite bored.* **5.** drag, tug, tow, haul, lead, pull. *We'll need two horses to draw this wagon.* –*n.* **6.** tie, stalemate, checkmate, deadlock, truce. *The judge finally declared the game a draw.* **Ant. 2.** repulse, repel. **4.** shorten, reduce. **5.** push, shove.

drawback *n.* problem, flaw, defect, weakness, handicap, block, hurdle. *Your plan has several serious drawbacks.*

dread *vb.* **1.** fear, cower, cringe, worry, tremble, quail. *I dread giving my speech in front of the entire class.* –*n.* **2.** fear, terror, dismay, alarm, fright, anxiety. *They beheld the werewolf with dread.* **Ant. 2.** bravery, courage, confidence.

dreadful *adj.* fearful, frightful, ghastly, horrible, awful, offensive. *The roach-infested hotel we stayed in was simply dreadful.*

dream *n.* **1.** reverie, fantasy, vision, desire, wish, hope. *Her dream is to write a best-seller.* –*vb.* **2.** conceive, daydream, think, wish, desire. *I dream about making a million dollars.*

dreary *adj.* uninteresting, tedious, wearisome, dismal, cheerless, bleak. *Washing a sink full of dishes can be a dreary task.* **Ant.** interesting, exciting, cheerful.

drench *vb.* soak, drown, saturate, douse, flood, splash, immerse. *We were drenched by a sudden thunderstorm.*

dress *n.* **1.** clothing, apparel, attire, garb, wardrobe, covering. *We found the dress of the alien visitors rather odd.* *-vb.* **2.** clothe, outfit, garb, attire, adorn, deck. *Dress yourself for cold weather.* **3.** treat, bandage, splint, bind, remedy. *The doctor dressed her patient's wound.*

drift *vb.* **1.** wander, tramp, ramble, amble, meander. *She drifted from job to job.* *-n.* **2.** course, flow, trend, tendency, bearing. *The country is experiencing a drift toward conservatism.* **3.** meaning, direction, sense, object, implication. *He didn't quite get the drift of the conversation.* **4.** heap, pile, bank, mass, mound. *A deer was caught in the snowdrift.*

drill *n.* **1.** training, workout, exercise, instruction, routine. *Her soccer coach makes the players perform numerous drills.* *-vb.* **2.** bore, pierce, ream, penetrate. *A carpenter drilled several holes in the board.* **3.** train, instruct, coach, teach, school, tutor. *Paramedics are drilled in proper lifesaving techniques.*

drink *vb.* **1.** imbibe, quaff, swallow, sip, gulp. *She drinks two cups of coffee every morning.* *-n.* **2.** beverage, liquid, water, alcohol. *Would you like a drink?*

drive *vb.* **1.** steer, guide, operate, ride, control. *He just learned how to drive a car.* **2.** push, propel, thrust, move, shove, hurl. *This spray will drive the insects away.* **3.** press, overwork, tax, spur, motivate, urge. *The coach drove his players hard.* *-n.* **4.** ride, trip, journey, excursion, run. *It was a long drive up to the ski lodge.* **5.** push, thrust, movement, advance, surge. *The team's final drive resulted in a touchdown.* **6.** ambition, initiative, energy, hustle, aggressiveness. *I admire her drive to better herself.* **7.** road, driveway, path, route. *There is a winding drive up to the mansion.*

droop *vb.* drop, sag, slump, sink, wilt, dip, bend, bow. *His long mustache droops at the ends.* **Ant.** rise, stand, stiffen.

drop *n.* **1.** bead, tear, speck, dab, particle, splotch. *The leaves sparkled with drops of dew.* **2.** fall, descent, plunge, abyss, chasm, precipice. *It's a long drop from where we stand on this ledge.* **3.** decline, decrease, reduction, downslide, lessening. *Her drop in weight concerns us.* *-vb.* **4.** fall, plunge, descend, sink, plummet, dive. *Strong winds caused pine cones to drop from the trees.*

5. abandon, leave, dismiss, omit, discontinue, forgo. *The band dropped the last song from its act.* **7.** reduce, cut, decrease, diminish, lessen, lower. *The store has recently dropped its prices.* **Ant. 2.** rise, climb, ascent. **3.** increase, rise, gain. **4.** rise, soar, ascend. **7.** increase, augment.

drown *vb.* submerge, immerse, flood, deluge, inundate. *She drowned her pancakes in syrup.*

drowsy *adj.* sleepy, tired, listless, dozy, groggy. *If you feel drowsy, go to bed.* **Ant.** alert, wakeful, rested.

drunk *adj.* **1.** intoxicated, inebriated, tipsy, sodden, stupefied. *Drunk drivers are the cause of many fatal accidents.* *-n.* **2.** drunkard, inebriate, sot, lush, alcoholic. *The drunk stumbled from the bar and fell into a gutter.* **Ant. 1.** sober, abstinent.

dry *adj.* **1.** arid, rainless, parched, waterless, dehydrated. *We followed the dry river bed for several miles.* **2.** deadpan, droll, subdued, subtle, sarcastic. *She has a dry sense of humor.* *-vb.* **3.** dehydrate, parch, wither, shrivel, wilt. *The sun dried my skin.* **Ant. 1.** wet, damp, soggy. **3.** wet, soak, dampen.

dubious *adj.* questionable, debatable, doubtful, uncertain, unclear. *Receiving the award for most talkative student is a dubious honor.* **Ant.** certain, sure, definite.

duck *vb.* squat, bend, drop, dodge, swerve, veer. *She ducked to avoid the ball heading straight for her.*

due *adj.* **1.** expected, awaited, scheduled, payable, anticipated. *When is the term paper due?* **2.** justified, fitting, adequate, sufficient, appropriate, proper. *Her behavior has given me due cause for alarm.* **Ant. 2.** inappropriate, insufficient, inadequate.

dull *adj.* **1.** boring, uninteresting, dreary, wearisome, tedious, monotonous. *It's hard not to fall asleep reading this dull textbook.* **2.** blunt, pointless, unsharpened, edgeless. *This knife is too dull to carve the turkey.* **3.** colorless, pale, faded, lusterless, softened, muted. *I think a dull color would look better than this bright yellow.* *-vb.* **4.** lessen, fade, dim, reduce, soften, deaden. *Age has dulled her vision.* **Ant. 1.** interesting, lively, exciting. **2.** sharp, pointed. **3.** sharp, vivid, bright. **4.** sharpen, increase, improve.

dunk *vb.* submerge, immerse, dip, plunge, drop. *Her friends tried to dunk her into the swimming pool.*

duplicate *vb.* **1.** reproduce, repeat, copy, replicate, clone. *Several labs have tried to duplicate the scientist's findings.* –*n.* **2.** copy, reproduction, likeness, double, facsimile. *Make a duplicate of your term paper in case the teacher loses the original.*

durable *adj.* strong, sound, enduring, reliable, dependable, stout. *That company makes durable clothing.* **Ant.** weak, flimsy, fragile.

duration *n.* space, span, stretch, course, extent, term, sentence. *Please do not smoke for the duration of the flight.*

dusk *n.* twilight, sunset, evening, darkness, night. *The park closes at dusk.*

duty *n.* **1.** chore, job, assignment, task, responsibility, function. *My duty at summer camp was to wash the dishes.* **2.** tax, tariff, fee, toll, dues, levy. *The foreign ship had to pay a duty to enter port.*

dwell *vb.* live, reside, stay, abide, inhabit, populate. *No one dwells in this bleak and forbidding land.*

dwindle *vb.* fade, wither, ebb, shrink, diminish, disappear. *The stream dwindles into nothing about five miles from here.* **Ant.** increase, grow, thrive.

dye *vb.* **1.** color, stain, tint, shade, paint. *She dyed her hair green.* –*n.* **2.** color, stain, tint, paint, pigment. *Do you think the dye will wash out?*

dynamic *adj.* vigorous, active, energetic, electrifying, spirited, lively. *Berkeley was a dynamic place in which to live during the sixties.* **Ant.** inactive, dull, listless.

eager *adj.* avid, keen, enthusiastic, excited, intent, willing. *We were eager to start the canoe trip.* **Ant.** adverse, reluctant, unconcerned.

earn *vb.* **1.** make, collect, receive, gain, acquire, draw, realize. *She earns enough money to live comfortably.* **2.** deserve, merit, warrant, reap, achieve. *I feel that I've earned my vacation.* **Ant. 1.** spend, forfeit, lose.

earnest *adj.* serious, sincere, eager, intent, determined, heartfelt. *They made an earnest attempt to clear up the misunderstanding.* **Ant.** insincere, halfhearted, frivolous.

earth *n.* **1.** planet, world, globe, sphere, orb. *Ozone depletion is an environmental problem that threatens the entire Earth.* **2.** soil, ground, dirt, sod, land, turf. *The farmer surveyed the parched earth of his fields.*

ease *n.* **1.** comfort, naturalness, readiness, leisure, easiness, facility. *He swims with ease.* –*vb.* **2.** relieve, comfort, soothe, lessen, diminish, decrease. *Her kind words eased his grief.* **Ant. 1.** difficulty, discomfort, effort. **2.** worsen, aggravate.

easy *adj.* **1.** simple, effortless, painless, light, undemanding. *The first part of the obstacle course is easy.* **2.** comfortable, relaxed, carefree, untroubled, satisfying. *Her summer on the French Riviera was full of easy living.* **3.** lenient, permissive, pleasant, easygoing, friendly. *He's an easy person to work for.* **Ant. 1.** hard, difficult, strenuous. **2.** awkward, uncomfortable, miserable. **3.** unfriendly, harsh, strict.

eat *vb.* **1.** devour, consume, ingest, swallow, chew. *I feel like I could eat a horse.* **2.** rust, wear, corrode, erode, dissolve. *Rust has slowly eaten away at the iron gate.*

ebb *vb.* **1.** recede, decrease, decline, reduce, lessen, diminish. *The storm began to ebb in the evening.* –*n.* **2.** withdrawal, retreat, lowering, decrease, decline. *Some beautiful shells were uncovered when the tide was at low ebb.* **Ant. 1.** increase, heighten, intensify. **2.** rising, advancement.

eccentric *adj.* **1.** odd, peculiar, weird, queer, strange, bizarre. *Her eccentric habits made her friends feel uncomfortable.* –*n.* **2.** crank, misfit, character, nonconformist, screwball, crackpot. *Eccentrics may be a little strange, but they can make life interesting.* **Ant. 1.** normal, ordinary, regular. **2.** conformist, conventionalist.

echo *vb.* **1.** reverberate, resound, ring, reply, resonate. *A shotgun blast echoed throughout the canyon.* **2.** imitate, mimic, impersonate, copy, parrot, repeat. *The macaw echoed everything I said.* –*n.* **3.** answer, reflection, response, repetition, reaction. *He shouted a greeting in the large hall and listened for an echo.*

eclipse *n.* **1.** masking, shadowing, veiling, covering, darkening. *There will be a lunar eclipse tonight.* –*vb.* **2.** obscure, darken, shadow, dim, conceal, hide. *Our view was partially eclipsed by the trees.* **3.** overshadow, surpass, outdo, exceed, outshine, transcend. *His effort at the high jump eclipsed all other attempts.* **Ant. 2.** uncover, expose, clear.

economical *adj.* frugal, thrifty, economic, prudent, saving, sparing. *It is more economical to buy the large box of cereal.* **Ant.** generous, wasteful, extravagant.

economize *vb.* save, conserve, skimp, scrimp, pinch. *Inflation has forced us to economize.* **Ant.** spend, waste, squander.

economy *n.* **1.** income, earnings, production, enterprise. *The national economy is threatened by a recession.* **2.** frugality, thrift, thriftiness, prudence, restraint. *We need to practice economy now that Father has retired.* **Ant. 2.** extravagance, squandering, waste.

75

ecstasy *n.* pleasure, delight, rapture, joy, bliss, elation. *The double fudge cake was pure ecstasy.* **Ant.** misery, suffering, torment.

ecstatic *adj.* delighted, overjoyed, happy, elated, joyful. *She was ecstatic when she got the part in the movie.* **Ant.** gloomy, despondent, unhappy.

edge *n.* **1.** rim, border, margin, boundary, brim, verge. *The old man lived in a little shack on the edge of town.* **2.** advantage, lead, superiority, jump, start. *Her quickness gave her an edge over the competition.* –*vb.* **3.** border, outline, trim, rim, hem. *We edged the herb garden with chives.* **4.** inch, slide, creep, stalk, sneak. *The cat slowly edged closer to the unsuspecting mouse.* **Ant. 1.** center, middle, interior. **2.** disadvantage, hindrance. **3.** rush, run, race.

edict *n.* order, command, decree, law, rule, statute, proclamation. *A herald announced the king's edict in the town square.*

edit *vb.* correct, revise, amend, check, alter, arrange. *The book will be finished as soon as it has been edited.*

educate *vb.* teach, tutor, train, instruct, school, inform, coach. *The job of a teacher is to educate.*

education *n.* schooling, learning, instruction, training, study. *He attended a prestigious school in order to get a good education.*

eerie *adj.* spooky, ghostly, weird, creepy, strange, unearthly. *I have an eerie feeling that someone is watching us.*

effect *n.* **1.** result, outcome, upshot, consequence, aftermath. *The full effect of today's election will not be known for years.* **2.** impact, influence, impression, bearing, effectiveness. *The rain came too late to have an effect on this year's harvest.* **3.** operation, action, execution, force, power. *The new law will go into effect on the first of next year.* –*vb.* **4.** make, produce, accomplish, cause, create, realize. *The airline strike has effected a change in our vacation plans.* **Ant. 1.** origin, source, beginning. **4.** prevent, stop, block.

effective *adj.* **1.** useful, helpful, efficient, practical, competent. *I need to find a more effective studying method.* **2.** active, current, operational, operative. *Do you know when the new*
store hours become effective? **3.** powerful, forceful, impressive, striking, successful. *The ending of the horror movie was so effective that I couldn't sleep all night.* **Ant. 1.** useless, worthless, ineffective. **2.** inoperative, inactive, inert. **3.** weak, pointless, unimpressive.

efficient *adj.* effective, competent, productive, capable, practical. *Alphabetical filing is an efficient method of organization.* **Ant.** ineffective, inefficient, unworkable.

effort *n.* **1.** attempt, endeavor, venture, try, struggle. *Try to make an effort to be on time.* **2.** energy, force, exertion, work, labor, toil. *The effort needed to build Hoover Dam was immense.*

effortless *adj.* easy, painless, simple, smooth, light, natural. *The gazelle made an effortless leap over the fence.* **Ant.** hard, difficult, strenuous.

eject *vb.* **1.** project, emit, expel, erupt, spew, discharge. *Foul fumes ejected from the exhaust pipe.* **2.** banish, dismiss, exclude, remove, evict. *He was ejected from the club for unruly behavior.* **Ant. 1.** retain, keep, hold. **2.** admit, receive, introduce.

elaborate *adj.* **1.** ornate, detailed, fancy, complex, complicated. *We were impressed by his elaborate needlepoint designs.* –*vb.* **2.** explain, clarify, specify, expand, embellish, expound. *Would you elaborate on your plans to run for office?* **Ant. 1.** simple, plain, basic. **2.** condense, summarize, simplify.

elastic *adj.* flexible, pliable, stretchable, adaptable, bendable. *This elastic belt is suitable for all waist sizes.* **Ant.** stiff, inflexible, rigid.

elated *adj.* delighted, excited, happy, overjoyed, joyful, cheerful. *She was elated to find a gold coin on the sidewalk.* **Ant.** sad, unhappy, gloomy, morose.

elder *adj.* **1.** older, senior, ranking, superior, earlier. *He is the elder brother of a family of five.* –*n.* **2.** senior, veteran, ancestor, patriarch, matriarch. *All important decisions were made by the tribal elders.* **Ant. 1.** younger, newer, later. **2.** junior, youth, novice.

elderly *adj.* old, ancient, aged, olden, mature. *The elderly woman lives with her grandson.* **Ant.** young, youthful, juvenile.

elect *vb.* select, pick, vote, choose, decide, opt, determine. *We elected to have our annual picnic at the beach .*

election *n.* vote, voting, balloting, referendum, selection. *Who do you plan to vote for in next week's election?*

elegance *n.* richness, grandeur, opulence, grace, dignity, refinement. *The coronation ceremony was conducted with great elegance.* **Ant.** tastelessness, plainness, crudeness.

elegant *adj.* grand, majestic, stylish, refined, dignified, tasteful, opulent. *She looked elegant in her new evening gown.* **Ant.** plain, common, tasteless.

element *n.* part, piece, component, ingredient, substance, factor. *Vegetables and fruits are important elements of a proper diet.* **Ant.** mass, sum, whole.

elementary *adj.* **1.** basic, fundamental, principal, primary, elemental. *Food, water, and shelter are elementary human needs.* **2.** simple, plain, clear, easy, uncomplicated. *Surely you can do an elementary thing like combing your own hair.* **Ant. 1.** secondary, unimportant, lesser. **2.** complex, complicated.

elevate *vb.* lift, raise, hoist, boost, uplift, erect. *The stage was elevated to allow a clear view for the spectators.* **Ant.** lower, drop, depress.

elevation *n.* height, altitude, lift, rise, prominence, loftiness. *My mountain cabin is at an elevation of 5,000 feet.*

eligible *adj.* qualified, suitable, suited, fitting, acceptable. *You are eligible for our grand prize of one million dollars.* **Ant.** ineligible, unqualified, unsuitable.

eliminate *vb.* remove, omit, exclude, expel, erase, drop, cancel. *She eliminated sugar from her diet.* **Ant.** include, admit, obtain.

eloquent *adj.* persuasive, expressive, articulate, fluent, poetic, impassioned. *The writer's eloquent prose made me cry.* **Ant.** dull, ordinary, weak.

elude *vb.* avoid, dodge, escape, evade, shun, duck. *The rabbit eluded the hunter by running into a brush thicket.* **Ant.** encounter, face, chase.

elusive *adj.* **1.** evasive, illusory, fleeting, slippery, tricky. *We are searching for the elusive unicorn.* **2.** baffling, puzzling, mysterious, confusing, deceptive. *She gave us an elusive theory when we wanted hard facts.*

emancipate *vb.* liberate, free, release, deliver, redeem, unchain. *The rebels wished to emancipate their country from foreign invaders.* **Ant.** enslave, subjugate, dominate.

embark *vb.* **1.** start, begin, undertake, commence, enter. *The movie actor embarked on a stage career.* **2.** board, go aboard, sail, leave, depart. *All passengers must embark in ten minutes.* **Ant. 1.** finish, end, terminate. **2.** disembark, land.

embarrass *vb.* shame, humiliate, upset, discomfort, humble. *Why did you embarrass me in front of our friends?*

embarrassment *n.* chagrin, shame, uneasiness, discomfort, bewilderment. *His racist remark was an embarrassment to us all.*

embellish *vb.* adorn, decorate, garnish, enhance, enrich, elaborate. *The country singer embellished his suit with rhinestones.*

embezzle *vb.* steal, defraud, swindle, cheat, pilfer, rob, misuse. *How much money did she embezzle from her employer?*

emblem *n.* sign, symbol, badge, insignia, trademark, label. *The lumber company has a drawing of a tree on their emblem.*

embrace *vb.* **1.** hug, hold, clasp, caress, enfold, grasp. *They embraced their long-lost son.* **2.** include, cover, enclose, contain, involve, encompass. *A successful treaty must embrace the concerns of all involved parties.* **Ant. 2.** exclude, omit, ignore, neglect.

emerge *vb.* appear, rise, arise, surface, issue, show, spring. *A sea serpent emerged from the depths of the ocean.* **Ant.** sink, disappear, recede, retreat.

emergency *n.* crisis, extremity, predicament, difficulty, accident. *Call an ambulance and tell them it's an emergency.*

emigrate *vb.* move, migrate, resettle, relocate, depart, leave. *My father's job will force us to emigrate to Canada.*

eminent *adj.* important, famous, renowned, celebrated, prominent, notable. *Arthur C. Clarke is an eminent science-fiction writer.* **Ant.** unimportant, unknown, unremarkable.

emit *vb.* discharge, expel, release, issue, shed, eject. *My car is emitting some rather noxious fumes.* **Ant.** retain, keep, hold.

emotion *n.* feeling, passion, sentiment, reaction, excitement. *You can hear the deep emotion in her voice.*

emotional *adj.* **1.** sensitive, feeling, moving, stirring, touching, heartwarming. *The family reunion was an emotional moment.* **2.** excited, excitable, hysterical, passionate, temperamental. *An emotional person makes a terrible poker player.* **Ant. 1.** cold, unfeeling, unemotional. **2.** calm, placid, reserved.

emperor *n.* sovereign, monarch, czar, ruler, empress, czarina. *Charlemagne was crowned emperor by Pope Leo III.*

emphasis *n.* stress, weight, accent, force, importance, attention. *I enjoy games that put more emphasis on fun than on winning.*

emphasize *vb.* stress, accent, highlight, spotlight, press. *She emphasized the need for donations to keep the day-care center open.* **Ant.** minimize, underplay, understate.

emphatic *adj.* strong, definite, powerful, forceful, decisive, assertive. *She made an emphatic denial of any knowledge of the theft.* **Ant.** weak, hesitant, indecisive.

employ *vb.* **1.** hire, retain, engage, enlist, contract. *Businesses should employ more handicapped people.* **2.** use, apply, utilize, operate, handle. *He employed a crowbar to open the crate.* **Ant. 1.** fire, discharge, dismiss.

employee *n.* worker, laborer, hand, servant, helper, assistant. *The employees are demanding a higher wage.* **Ant.** employer, boss, manager.

employer *n.* boss, manager, proprietor, hirer, contractor. *My new employer is an easy person to work for.* **Ant.** employee, servant, worker.

employment *n.* **1.** job, placement, work, position, profession, occupation. *I hope you enjoy your employment with our firm.* **2.** use, usage, using, operation, service, application. *The employment of smoke alarms is an excellent safety measure.*

empty *vb.* **1.** clear, drain, void, deplete, exhaust. *She emptied the glass of its contents.* –*adj.* **2.** vacant, void, unfilled, unoccupied, blank. *He opened the barrel and discovered that it was empty.* **3.** meaningless, worthless, senseless, purposeless, futile. *All we received was a bunch of empty promises.* **Ant. 1.** fill, pack, stock. **2.** full, complete, packed. **3.** meaningful, worthwhile, valuable.

enable *vb.* allow, permit, empower, qualify, authorize, license. *A college degree will enable you to get a better job.* **Ant.** disallow, disqualify, stop, prevent.

enchant *vb.* **1.** bewitch, charm, hex, conjure. *The evil witch enchanted the prince by turning him into a frog.* **2.** delight, please, fascinate, enthrall, captivate. *The children were enchanted by the puppet show.* **Ant. 1.** release, exorcise, free. **2.** bore, tire, repel.

enchanting *adj.* charming, fascinating, captivating, intriguing, alluring. *It was an enchanting evening.*

enclose *vb.* **1.** encircle, surround, confine, envelope, contain. *The lions in the zoo were enclosed by a deep moat.* **2.** include, insert, place, append, add. *He enclosed his receipt when he mailed the letter of complaint.*

encounter *vb.* **1.** meet, face, confront, engage, experience. *The king's soldiers encountered heavy resistance from the Cyclops.* –*n.* **2.** meeting, confrontation, collision, conflict, clash, brush. *He had an encounter with a grizzly bear on the narrow mountain trail.* **Ant. 1.** avoid, escape, elude. **2.** avoidance, evasion.

encourage *vb.* **1.** persuade, inspire, support, spur, hearten, urge. *She was encouraged to run for class president.* **2.** foster, promote, boost, heighten, increase, advance. *Brushing after meals encourages the development of healthy teeth and gums.* **Ant. 1.** dissuade, discourage, deter. **2.** retard, prevent, hinder.

encouragement *n.* reassurance, support, encouraging, help, aid, assistance. *He needed a little encouragement to complete the marathon.* **Ant.** discouragement, hindrance, constraint.

end n. **1.** limit, border, boundary, extremity, edge, tip. *There's a good restaurant on the west end of town.* **2.** conclusion, close, finish, finale, completion, termination. *The cowboy rode off into the sunset at the end of the movie.* **3.** aim, goal, objective, intent, intention, purpose. *She's going to need plenty of time and money to achieve her end.* –vb. **4.** finish, stop, halt, close, terminate, conclude, cease. *Let's end this meeting at a reasonable time.* **Ant. 1.** center, middle, heart. **2.** start, beginning, opening. **4.** start, initiate, open, begin.

endanger vb. threaten, risk, imperil, jeopardize, expose. *Mountain climbing sounds like just another way to endanger your life.* **Ant.** protect, safeguard, preserve.

endeavor vb. **1.** attempt, try, undertake, strive, aim, venture, seek. *We endeavored to save the old theater from being demolished.* –n. **2.** effort, attempt, try, undertaking, struggle, exertion. *Scott's endeavor to be the first man to reach the South Pole ended in failure.*

endless adj. eternal, infinite, limitless, everlasting, unending, ceaseless. *The line for concert tickets seemed to be endless.* **Ant.** finite, limited, definite.

endorse vb. support, back, approve, confirm, recommend, certify. *The actress was asked to endorse a new line of cosmetics.* **Ant.** condemn, criticize, disapprove.

endurance n. stamina, durability, persistence, fortitude, hardiness, tolerance. *Triathlon athletes must have incredible endurance.* **Ant.** weakness, weariness, frailty.

endure vb. **1.** last, continue, remain, persist, hold, stay, prevail. *I need a house paint that will endure for many years.* **2.** suffer, experience, bear, tolerate, withstand, sustain. *The lost desert patrol endured thirst and heat exhaustion before they were rescued.* **Ant. 1.** fail, decay, perish. **2.** escape, avoid, succumb.

enemy n. foe, opponent, adversary, rival, antagonist, nemesis. *I wouldn't want to make a dragon my enemy.* **Ant.** friend, ally, partner.

energetic adj. active, vigorous, lively, tireless, animated, dynamic. *The energetic puppy tired us out.* **Ant.** tired, weary, lazy.

energy n. **1.** power, strength, force, might, muscle, effort. *You are wasting energy trying to push that boulder off the road.* **2.** vigor, vitality, drive, zip, zest, punch, pep. *The school wants cheerleaders who have lots of energy.* **Ant. 2.** sluggishness, laziness, lethargy.

enforce vb. compel, force, require, impose, execute, invoke. *The speed limit is strongly enforced in this state.*

engage vb. **1.** occupy, involve, engross, concern, absorb, preoccupy. *I was so engaged in the conversation that I lost track of time.* **2.** hire, retain, employ, contract, commission. *The club engaged a caterer for their annual banquet.* **3.** pledge, commit, promise, betroth. *They are engaged to be married in June.*

engaging adj. charming, captivating, enchanting, pleasing, likable, delightful. *The comedian had a very engaging personality.* **Ant.** unlikable, unpleasant, dull.

engrave vb. carve, etch, cut, inscribe, chisel, scratch. *Her initials were engraved on the bracelet.*

engross vb. involve, immerse, absorb, occupy, preoccupy, engage. *She was engrossed in trying to complete the jigsaw puzzle.* **Ant.** bore, tire, weary.

enhance vb. enrich, improve, better, magnify, heighten, intensify. *A good polishing will enhance the appearance of your shoes.* **Ant.** lessen, reduce, diminish, decrease.

enigma n. puzzle, riddle, mystery, secret, problem, question. *The Loch Ness Monster will remain an enigma until there is documented proof of its existence.*

enjoy vb. like, appreciate, delight, love, relish, fancy, savor. *She enjoyed her day at the beach.* **Ant.** dislike, hate, despise.

enjoyment n. pleasure, delight, satisfaction, happiness, amusement, joy, fun. *He experienced many hours of enjoyment at the zoo.* **Ant.** misery, suffering, displeasure.

enlarge vb. increase, extend, expand, augment, lengthen, broaden, widen. *The playground will be enlarged to include a tennis court.* **Ant.** decrease, reduce, shrink.

enlighten *vb.* educate, inform, instruct, explain, clarify, teach. *Would you please enlighten me on your country's customs?* **Ant.** confuse, mislead, perplex.

enlist *vb.* **1.** enroll, register, enter, volunteer, sign up. *He enlisted in the army for two years.* **2.** recruit, engage, secure, procure, obtain. *Will you help us enlist donors for the blood drive?*

enliven *vb.* brighten, cheer, vitalize, excite, animate, stimulate, rouse. *A good rock band would enliven this party.* **Ant.** dampen, deaden, subdue.

enormous *adj.* huge, giant, immense, gigantic, colossal, tremendous, mammoth. *Some dinosaurs were enormous creatures.* **Ant.** tiny, small, slight.

enough *adj.* **1.** adequate, ample, sufficient, plenty, abundant. *Do you have enough chairs for your classroom?* *–adv.* **2.** adequately, sufficiently, satisfactorily, passably, amply. *I'm tired enough to sleep through an earthquake.* **Ant. 1.** scant, meager, inadequate.

enrage *vb.* anger, madden, infuriate, inflame, provoke, incense. *His rude manners enraged her.* **Ant.** please, delight, calm.

enrich *vb.* improve, better, enhance, upgrade, develop, embellish. *The farmer enriched his field with fertilizers.* **Ant.** downgrade, degenerate, impoverish.

enroll *vb.* register, enlist, join, engage, enter, serve. *We must enroll in school by Friday.* **Ant.** withdraw, drop, leave, quit.

enrollment *n.* roster, register, record, roll, registration. *My history class has an enrollment of thirty students.*

enslave *vb.* indenture, subjugate, subdue, dominate, master, control. *The captured Athenians were enslaved by the Spartans.* **Ant.** free, liberate, release.

ensure *vb.* insure, assure, confirm, guarantee, secure, certify, warrant. *Your term paper is good enough to ensure a passing grade.*

entangle *vb.* snare, catch, trap, involve, ravel, ensnarl. *The fly found itself entangled in a spider's web.* **Ant.** disentangle, free, extricate.

enter *vb.* **1.** arrive, go in, come in, penetrate, intrude. *She entered the room with a flourish.* **2.** begin, start, join, commence, enroll. *He is going to enter a ballet class in the fall.* **3.** register, list, catalog, record, write. *Please enter your answers in the appropriate space.* **Ant. 1.** leave, exit, escape. **2.** end, finish, conclude.

enterprise *n.* **1.** project, undertaking, operation, program, venture, business. *Her lemonade stand proved to be a profitable enterprise.* **2.** drive, energy, ambition, zeal, courage, boldness. *The boxer lacked the enterprise to become a champion.*

entertain *vb.* **1.** amuse, divert, delight, please, engross, interest. *We hired a comedian to entertain our guests.* **2.** heed, consider, imagine, harbor, foster, contemplate. *The workers would not entertain the thought of a salary decrease.* **Ant. 1.** bore, weary, tire. **2.** reject, neglect, ignore.

entertainment *n.* amusement, diversion, pastime, performance, play. *We were all looking forward to the evening's entertainments.*

enthusiasm *n.* zeal, eagerness, fervor, passion, ardor, excitement. *We cheered our team with enthusiasm.* **Ant.** apathy, coldness, unconcern.

enthusiastic *adj.* eager, passionate, zealous, avid, fervent, ardent. *The school band has many enthusiastic musicians.* **Ant.** indifferent, halfhearted, reluctant.

entice *vb.* coax, tempt, lure, induce, attract, persuade. *A neighbor enticed her into buying a ticket for the church raffle.* **Ant.** discourage, dissuade, frighten.

entire *adj.* complete, whole, intact, total, full, undivided, unbroken. *He sold his entire collection of science-fiction books.* **Ant.** partial, incomplete, divided.

entirely *adv.* wholly, altogether, fully, completely, perfectly. *Your solution to the puzzle is entirely right.* **Ant.** partially, partly, somewhat.

entitle *vb.* **1.** allow, authorize, permit, enable, sanction, license. *This coupon entitles you to one free snow cone.* **2.** name, title, dub, call, designate. *Benny Goodman was entitled the King of Swing.*

entrance *n.* **1.** entry, portal, doorway, door, gate, access. *The entrance to the museum is located on the other side.* **2.** admission, entry, admittance, approach, arrival, coming. *The queen's entrance was accompanied by much fanfare.* *–vb.* **3.** fascinate, enchant, wonder, delight, charm, enrapture. *I was entranced by the dancing fairies.* **Ant. 1.** exit, outlet, egress. **2.** exit, departure, leaving. **3.** bore, disinterest, disappoint.

entrust *vb.* commit, assign, trust, delegate, consign, charge. *The dying pirate entrusted his treasure map to the cabin boy.*

entry *n.* **1.** entrance, door, doorway, gate, threshold. *There's a stalled car blocking the parking lot's entry.* **2.** admission, admittance, entrance, access, initiation. *Minors are not allowed entry into taverns.* **3.** item, account, statement, note, record. *She has just finished making an entry in her diary.* **Ant. 1.** exit, outlet, egress. **2.** exit, departure, leaving.

envelop *vb.* enfold, wrap, surround, cover, encircle, enclose. *The forest fire enveloped 5,000 acres.*

envelope *n.* cover, wrapper, wrapping, jacket, case, sheath. *The Earth's envelope of air protects us from harmful solar radiation.*

envious *adj.* jealous, covetous, desirous, yearning, resentful. *She was envious of her friend's new sports car.*

environment *n.* surroundings, habitat, setting, element, conditions, neighborhood. *Eskimos live in a cold environment.*

envy *vb.* **1.** covet, desire, want, crave, resent, begrudge. *The farmer envied his neighbor's new team of horses.* *–n.* **2.** jealousy, resentment, spite, grudging, malice. *Envy of her classmates affected her attitude toward them.*

epidemic *n.* **1.** plague, outbreak, pestilence, scourge, contamination. *An epidemic of measles broke out in our summer camp.* *–adj.* **2.** widespread, prevailing, rampant, extensive, prevalent. *Incidents of crime have reached epidemic proportions.*

episode *n.* **1.** incident, event, occurrence, scene, experience, affair. *He frequently has episodes in which he feels like he is another person.* **2.** installment, chapter, scene, act, section, part. *In the last episode, our hero was about to be eaten by giant termites.*

equal *adj.* **1.** even, uniform, identical, similar, same, like. *She divided the pie into four equal slices.* *–vb.* **2.** match, correspond to, amount to, reach, tally. *One plus two equals three.* *–n.* **3.** match, rival, peer, equivalent, parallel. *He has not met his equal on the basketball court.* **Ant. 1.** uneven, unbalanced, different.

equate *vb.* identify, compare, liken, equalize, associate, treat. *It is wrong to equate money with happiness.*

equilibrium *n.* stability, balance, steadiness, poise, evenness, symmetry. *She lost her equilibrium and fell off the log.*

equip *vb.* supply, provide, furnish, outfit, prepare, fit. *Travelers to Alaska should equip themselves with plenty of warm clothes.*

equipment *n.* gear, material, instruments, supplies, outfit, kit. *Let's check our camping equipment before we leave.*

equitable *adj.* fair, even, just, impartial, objective, unbiased, reasonable. *I'm sure that we can reach an equitable settlement for your damaged property.* **Ant.** uneven, unfair, unjust.

equivalent *adj.* equal, alike, similar, comparable, identical. *One gallon is equivalent to four quarts.* **Ant.** unequal, dissimilar, different.

era *n.* age, epoch, period, generation, time. *The industrial era started in the late 18th century.*

eradicate *vb.* erase, eliminate, remove, destroy, exterminate, demolish. *I wish we could eradicate suffering from our lives.* **Ant.** create, establish, generate.

erase *vb.* remove, cancel, delete, scratch, eliminate, clear. *Would you please erase the writing on the blackboard?* **Ant.** add, restore, insert.

erect *adj.* **1.** upright, raised, vertical, straight, stiff, rigid. *The prairie dogs were standing erect outside their burrows.* *–vb.* **2.** build, construct, raise, establish, create. *A monument to the pioneers will be erected in the town square.* **Ant. 1.** stooped, limp, prone. **2.** demolish, destroy, raze.

erode *vb.* waste, wear, deteriorate, decay, eat. *Each spring the hills are slowly eroded by rain.*

errand *n.* chore, task, job, duty, assignment, undertaking, mission. *He will return after he completes his errand.*

erratic *adj.* irregular, unpredictable, unsteady, uneven, odd, eccentric. *My computer has been acting very erratic lately.* **Ant.** regular, normal, constant.

erroneous *adj.* wrong, incorrect, false, mistaken, inaccurate, faulty, untrue. *The reports of pink elephants on Main Street were erroneous.* **Ant.** right, correct, true, accurate.

error *n.* mistake, blunder, slip, oversight, fallacy, inaccuracy. *There are too many errors in your report.* **Ant.** accuracy, correctness.

erupt *vb.* burst, explode, expel, eject, spew, gush, discharge. *Steam erupted from the broken pipe.*

escape *vb.* **1.** flee, fly, run, break out. *The prisoners planned to escape from the evil prince's dungeon.* **2.** avoid, elude, dodge, evade, bypass. *There is no way to escape the final exam.* **3.** leak, erupt, issue, flow, seep. *Gas is escaping from the fuel line.* –*n.* **4.** breakout, getaway, flight, departure, release. *Their only escape from the dragon was through a haunted forest.* **Ant. 1.** capture, apprehend, imprison. **2.** meet, face, confront. **4.** capture, imprisonment, retention.

escort *vb.* **1.** conduct, guide, lead, usher, accompany, attend, chaperon. *I would be pleased to escort you to the dance.* –*n.* **2.** guard, retinue, attendant, companion, guide, chaperon. *The queen's escort walked with her to the carriage.*

especially *adv.* specially, particularly, notably, chiefly, principally. *I bought this gift especially for you.*

essay *n.* article, paper, piece, composition, discourse, theme, study. *Your essay on the Boston Tea Party is due tomorrow.*

essence *n.* **1.** nature, character, basis, substance, meaning, spirit. *The essence of the rock singer's appeal is his boyish looks.* **2.** odor, perfume, scent, fragrance, smell. *An essence of roses lingered in the room.*

essential *adj.* vital, necessary, important, required, fundamental, critical. *It is essential that you show up in class tomorrow.* **Ant.** unimportant, unnecessary, inessential.

establish *vb.* **1.** found, form, create, settle, organize, build. *England established colonies all over the world.* **2.** prove, verify, confirm, substantiate, demonstrate. *New research has established the dangers of consuming too much cholesterol.* **Ant. 1.** abolish, eliminate, discontinue. **2.** disprove, refute, deny.

establishment *n.* **1.** institution, foundation, organization, business, company. *What is the name of the establishment you work for?* **2.** founding, formation, construction, start, installation. *The city council voted funds for the establishment of a new library.* **Ant. 2.** closing, removal, ending.

esteem *n.* **1.** respect, admiration, honor, reverence, regard. *The mayor of this town is held in high esteem.* –*vb.* **2.** value, regard, respect, admire, revere, treasure. *Abraham Lincoln is esteemed as one of America's greatest presidents.* **Ant. 1.** contempt, disdain, ridicule. **2.** belittle, disregard.

estimate *vb.* **1.** guess, reckon, judge, evaluate, calculate, figure. *I estimate that it will be another hour before the plane arrives.* –*n.* **2.** evaluation, assessment, guess, judgment, opinion, appraisal. *The dealer gave him an estimate of the value of his coin collection.*

eternal *adj.* everlasting, endless, unending, ceaseless, perpetual, continual. *Romeo and Juliet pledged eternal love to each other.* **Ant.** temporary, limited, passing.

ethical *adj.* moral, proper, virtuous, upright, honorable. *She lost the election but was admired for running an ethical campaign.* **Ant.** unethical, improper, corrupt.

etiquette *n.* manners, conduct, behavior, customs, decorum, protocol, courtesy. *Please show me the proper etiquette for meeting the queen.*

evacuate *vb.* leave, vacate, withdraw, abandon, depart, clear. *We must evacuate the building before it collapses.* **Ant.** enter, occupy, return.

evade vb. avoid, elude, shun, escape, dodge, neglect. *She's been evading me all evening.* **Ant.** encounter, confront, face, meet.

evaluate vb. assess, rate, appraise, value, judge, estimate. *Would you evaluate the worth of my stamp collection?*

evaporate vb. vaporize, dissipate, vanish, disappear, fade, dissolve. *The sorcerer waved his arms, and the pile of gold evaporated.* **Ant.** solidify, appear, materialize.

even adj. **1.** level, flat, smooth, plane, uniform. *This table's top doesn't appear to be even.* **2.** steady, constant, regular, stable, uniform, unchanging. *Her heart was beating at an even rate.* **3.** equal, balanced, parallel, similar, fair, just. *The two soccer teams seemed to be an even match.* –vb. **4.** equalize, balance, adjust, level, square. *The successful field goal evened the score.* **Ant. 1.** rough, uneven, coarse. **2.** unsteady, irregular, changing. **3.** unfair, unequal, different.

evening n. sunset, sundown, dusk, twilight, nightfall. *The weather tends to be cooler in the evenings.* **Ant.** morning, sunrise, dawn.

event n. **1.** occurrence, episode, happening, occasion, incident, experience. *College graduation was an important event in my life.* **2.** competition, match, game, contest, tournament. *The Olympics feature a wide variety of sporting events.*

eventful adj. momentous, notable, memorable, fateful, exciting, unforgettable. *It was an eventful day at the carnival.* **Ant.** ordinary, usual, dull, unexciting.

eventually adv. ultimately, finally, sometime, someday, hereafter. *Eventually the sun will burn out, but I wouldn't stock up on extra flashlights at this time.* **Ant.** now, immediately, never.

ever adv. always, constantly, continuously, eternally, forever. *In many fairy tales, the people live happily ever after.* **Ant.** never.

every adj. all, each, any, whole, total. *Please pick up every item you dropped.* **Ant.** one, some, none.

everyday adj. common, usual, ordinary, familiar, customary. *Exercise should be part of your everyday routine.* **Ant.** rare, occasional, infrequent.

evict vb. eject, remove, expel, dismiss, oust. *She was evicted because she did not pay her rent.*

evidence n. proof, facts, documentation, confirmation, verification. *Do you have any evidence that you were kidnaped by little green men from outer space?*

evident adj. clear, plain, obvious, apparent, certain, unmistakable, distinct. *It is evident that you are not enjoying the concert.* **Ant.** unclear, uncertain, doubtful.

evil adj. **1.** wicked, sinful, bad, wrong, immoral. *The sorcerer wanted to rule the kingdom for his own evil purpose.* –n. **2.** sin, sinfulness, wickedness, vice, corruption. *The warrior thought his king's command to remove evil from the world was a pretty tall order.* **Ant. 1.** good, moral, virtuous. **2.** good, virtue, righteousness.

evoke vb. summon, awaken, invoke, provoke, arouse, induce. *Sunny days at the beach always evoke memories of my Hawaiian vacation.* **Ant.** suppress, prevent, repress.

evolve vb. develop, grow, progress, emerge, result, unfold. *Her profitable chain of restaurants evolved from a single hot dog stand.*

exact adj. **1.** right, correct, accurate, true, precise, specific. *You need the exact combination to open the lock.* –vb. **2.** demand, take, force, extract, levy, impose. *The law exacts a heavy penalty for reckless driving.* **Ant. 1.** wrong, imprecise, inexact.

exaggerate vb. overstate, amplify, embellish, magnify, inflate, stretch. *He exaggerated when he said he could hold his breath for five minutes.* **Ant.** understate, underrate, minimize.

exalted adj. revered, glorified, honorable, noble, dignified, lordly. *It is customary to bow when the tribe's exalted chief enters.* **Ant.** lowly, common, humble.

examination n. **1.** inspection, observation, study, survey, probe. *My doctor gave me a thorough examination.* **2.** test, quiz, exam, interrogation, midterm, final. *She has to study for tomorrow's history examination.*

examine *vb.* **1.** inspect, study, probe, explore, investigate, search. *The art expert examined the painting carefully.* **2.** question, quiz, test, ask, query, interrogate. *It was the district attorney's turn to examine the witness.*

example *n.* model, sample, specimen, type, instance, illustration. *This museum has many examples of Indian pottery.*

exasperate *vb.* annoy, irritate, aggravate, bother, irk, provoke, anger. *His constant humming exasperates me.* **Ant.** calm, tranquilize, soothe.

excavate *vb.* uncover, unearth, dig, quarry, exhume. *The archaeologists are excavating an Aztec temple.* **Ant.** fill, cover, bury.

exceed *vb.* surpass, excel, outdo, better, beat, pass, transcend. *Her score on the exam exceeded the instructor's expectations.*

excel *vb.* prevail, predominate, surpass, outdo, best, better, exceed. *A man with his height and speed should excel in basketball.*

excellence *n.* quality, perfection, eminence, supremacy, superiority. *Her music is famous for its excellence.* **Ant.** mediocrity, inferiority, shortcoming.

excellent *adj.* superior, fine, choice, outstanding, great, splendid, wonderful. *This is an excellent day to go sailing.* **Ant.** terrible, awful, inferior.

except *prep.* but, excepting, excluding, barring, besides, save. *The room was silent except for the ticking of a clock.* **Ant.** including, counting, adding.

exception *n.* **1.** deviation, anomaly, exclusion, exemption, limitation. *There is an exception to every rule.* **2.** objection, complaint, disagreement, criticism, offense. *The senator took exception to his colleague's speech.* **Ant. 1.** consistency, conformity. **2.** agreement, acceptance, support.

exceptional *adj.* rare, unusual, uncommon, extraordinary, unique, remarkable. *He has exceptional strength for such a small boy.* **Ant.** ordinary, common, average.

excerpt *n.* extract, passage, selection, fragment, piece, section. *Our teacher read us an excerpt from "David Copperfield."*

excess *n.* **1.** surplus, abundance, oversupply, glut, profusion. *I wish I had an excess of money.* –*adj.* **2.** abundant, surplus, excessive, extra, spare. *Save your excess energy for the uphill hike.* **Ant. 1.** shortage, lack, need. **2.** sparse, meager, scanty.

excessive *adj.* extreme, unreasonable, overdone, undue, excess. *His excessive shouting made him hoarse.* **Ant.** deficient, conservative, insufficient.

exchange *vb.* **1.** trade, swap, barter, switch, change, replace. *The boys exchanged baseball trading cards.* –*n.* **2.** interchange, trade, swap, dealing, transfer. *There will be a cultural exchange between the two countries.*

excite *vb.* arouse, stimulate, incite, stir, provoke, awaken. *If you excite the horses, they might stampede.* **Ant.** quiet, calm, soothe.

excitement *n.* stimulation, adventure, thrill, arousal, frenzy, commotion. *I had too much excitement for one day.* **Ant.** boredom, serenity, quiet.

exclaim *vb.* proclaim, declare, yell, shout, blurt. *"You're out!" the umpire exclaimed.* **Ant.** whisper, mumble, murmur.

exclamation *n.* shout, outcry, yell, bellow, scream. *He made an exclamation of dismay when he saw the rattlesnake.* **Ant.** whisper, mumble, murmur.

exclude *vb.* ban, bar, prohibit, preclude, remove, eliminate. *The Galactic Council excludes Martians from its meetings.* **Ant.** include, allow, permit.

excursion *n.* trip, outing, voyage, tour, journey, expedition. *We are going on an excursion to Israel.*

excuse *vb.* **1.** pardon, forgive, tolerate, indulge, overlook. *Please excuse my carelessness.* **2.** free, exempt, release, absolve, dismiss, spare. *The judge excused her from jury duty.* –*n.* **3.** reason, alibi, plea, explanation, defense. *I will accept no excuses for being late.* **Ant. 1.** blame, punish, condemn. **2.** obligate, compel, oblige.

execute *vb.* **1.** kill, murder, assassinate, dispatch, eliminate. *They executed the spy at sunrise.* **2.** perform, accomplish, complete, fulfill, implement. *The figure skater executed his routine with ease.*

executive *adj.* **1.** managerial, supervisory, administrative, directing, official. *We need a person with executive skills to manage this department.* –*n.* **2.** manager, official, officer, administrator, director. *She was the youngest executive in the office.*

exemplify *vb.* embody, depict, represent, typify, epitomize. *Her conduct exemplifies the high standards we should all maintain.*

exempt *adj.* immune, excused, free, released, spared, excepted. *Women are exempt from the draft.* **Ant.** responsible, liable, subject.

exercise *n.* **1.** workout, drill, exertion, activity, training. *He does twenty minutes of aerobic exercise every day.* –*vb.* **2.** train, drill, practice, work out, condition. *A good athlete must exercise daily.* **3.** use, apply, employ, implement, utilize. *Citizens should exercise their right to vote.*

exert *vb.* use, employ, apply, utilize, wield. *She exerted all her energy in planning the charity event.*

exertion *n.* effort, work, energy, strain, strength, action. *I don't like jogging because it requires too much exertion.* **Ant.** rest, leisure, inactivity.

exhaust *vb.* **1.** tire, weaken, fatigue, enfeeble, weary. *The long swim exhausted him.* **2.** deplete, use, spend, expend, drain, finish, consume. *We must not exhaust the earth's natural resources.* **Ant. 1.** refresh, revive, renew. **2.** restore, replenish, conserve.

exhaustion *n.* fatigue, weariness, tiredness, draining, depletion. *The soldiers collapsed in exhaustion after their long march.* **Ant.** strength, energy, replenishment.

exhaustive *adj.* thorough, complete, extensive, full, total, profound. *She made an exhaustive search of all files.* **Ant.** incomplete, partial, superficial.

exhibit *vb.* **1.** show, display, reveal, present, demonstrate, expose. *I wish to exhibit our new line of computer software.* –*n.* **2.** show, showing, display, demonstration, exhibition. *The art museum has a fine exhibit of bronze sculptures.* **Ant. 1.** hide, conceal, suppress.

exhilarate *vb.* stimulate, excite, energize, invigorate, cheer, delight. *The skiers were exhilarated by the fresh snowfall.* **Ant.** sadden, depress, dishearten.

exile *vb.* **1.** banish, remove, eject, expel, deport, oust. *The defeated rebel was exiled for his crimes.* –*n.* **2.** expulsion, banishment, removal, deportation, dislocation. *All convicted criminals will face exile.* **3.** refugee, outcast, deportee, expatriate, alien. *The exiles were seeking a new country.* **Ant. 1.** recall, return, restore.

exist *vb.* **1.** live, survive, endure, subsist, remain, last. *A camel can exist many days without water.* **2.** occur, happen, arise, emerge, prevail. *I don't believe a better opportunity will ever exist.* **Ant. 1.** die, expire, perish. **2.** disappear, vanish, cease.

existence *n.* **1.** reality, presence, actuality, fact, occurrence. *The possibility of the existence of life on other planets is highly debatable.* **2.** being, survival, life, condition, endurance. *The polar research team's existence was threatened by the severe cold.* **Ant. 1.** nonexistence, fantasy, fiction.

exit *n.* **1.** egress, outlet, opening, door, doorway. *All auditorium exits must be kept open.* **2.** departure, leaving, withdrawal, retreat, exodus. *The actress made a hasty exit when she saw the photographers approaching.* –*vb.* **3.** leave, go, depart, withdraw, retreat, retire. *He exited the room quietly.* **Ant. 1.** entrance, entry, inlet. **2.** entrance, arrival, return. **3.** enter, come, arrive.

exodus *n.* flight, exit, departure, withdrawal, migration, emigration. *Moses led the Israelites' exodus from Egypt.* **Ant.** return, influx, immigration.

exorbitant *adj.* unreasonable, excessive, overpriced, extreme, enormous. *The drought has raised the price of vegetables to an exorbitant level.* **Ant.** reasonable, modest, fair, just.

exotic *adj.* foreign, strange, unfamiliar, unusual, unique, different. *I often dream of traveling to exotic lands.* **Ant.** familiar, normal, ordinary.

expand *vb.* increase, enlarge, widen, grow, stretch, spread. *Her dance class expanded from a part-time hobby to a thriving business.* **Ant.** decrease, shrink, contract.

expect *vb.* **1.** hope, await, look, anticipate, foresee. *She expects to get off work early today.* **2.** demand, require, want, insist, wish. *The teacher expects all homework to be completed by tomorrow morning.* **3.** guess, predict, suppose, presume, believe, assume. *I expect it will rain this afternoon.*

expectation *n.* hope, promise, anticipation, confidence, prospect. *She had great expectations when she left for college.*

expedient *adj.* useful, helpful, practical, profitable, beneficial, worthwhile. *Since her boss was in a bad mood, she felt it would not be expedient to ask for a raise.* **Ant.** futile, ineffective, useless.

expedition *n.* journey, trip, voyage, safari, mission, exploration. *In 1856, Sir Richard Burton led an expedition to discover the source of the Nile River.*

expel *vb.* discharge, eject, oust, banish, exile, remove. *The unruly student was expelled from school.* **Ant.** admit, accept, invite.

expend *vb.* spend, exhaust, consume, waste, dispense, disperse. *She expended too much energy for such a small profit.* **Ant.** save, receive, conserve.

expense *n.* cost, price, amount, payment, charge, outlay. *The trip's expense was over their budget.*

expensive *adj.* costly, exorbitant, overpriced, steep, extravagant. *Diamond rings are expensive items.* **Ant.** cheap, reasonable, moderate.

experience *vb.* **1.** feel, know, encounter, undergo, meet, enjoy. *You can't know how much fun a roller coaster is until you experience one.* *–n.* **2.** incident, event, ordeal, encounter, adventure, episode. *The airplane crash was an experience I hope to never have again.* **3.** knowledge, practice, background, skill, training. *The orchestra needs a conductor with experience.* **Ant. 1.** miss, avoid, evade. **3.** inexperience, untried, unskilled.

experienced *adj.* trained, practiced, accomplished, skilled, qualified. *We are hiring only experienced workers.* **Ant.** unskilled, untrained, inexperienced.

experiment *n.* **1.** trial, test, research, analysis, examination, investigation. *We performed some experiments in my science class.* *–vb.* **2.** test, try, study, analyze, examine, investigate. *The football team experimented with some new plays.*

expert *n.* **1.** authority, master, specialist, professional, genius. *The candle maker is an expert at her craft.* *–adj.* **2.** proficient, skilled, experienced, masterful, practiced. *This rug was made by expert weavers.* **Ant. 1.** amateur, novice, beginner. **2.** inept, unskilled, untrained.

expertise *n.* skill, training, experience, proficiency, knowledge. *It takes a lot of expertise to succeed as a stuntman.*

expire *vb.* **1.** end, terminate, discontinue, stop, lapse. *Your club membership has expired.* **2.** die, decease, succumb, perish, pass. *With one last breath the old man expired.* **Ant. 1.** begin, start, continue. **2.** live, thrive.

explain *vb.* **1.** clarify, define, interpret, teach, demonstrate, describe. *The astronomer explained the difference between a lunar eclipse and a solar eclipse.* **2.** account, justify, excuse, rationalize, answer. *Can you explain why you failed your math test?*

explanation *n.* reason, account, answer, cause, motive. *I hope you have a good explanation for your tardiness.*

explode *vb.* burst, erupt, blast, detonate, discharge. *The time bomb might explode at any moment.*

exploit *vb.* **1.** use, utilize, manipulate, apply, work. *She exploited every available opportunity to get a part in the school play.* *–n.* **2.** adventure, achievement, feat, act, deed, accomplishment. *The African explorer's exploits were well documented in his autobiography.*

explore *vb.* **1.** examine, probe, investigate, research, pry. *We must explore new ways to produce energy.* **2.** travel, search, traverse, survey, scout. *Coronado explored much of southwest*

America while searching for the Seven Cities of Cibola.

explosion *n.* blast, detonation, burst, outburst, eruption. *When the bomb went off, the explosion was heard for miles.*

expose *vb.* reveal, uncover, bare, disclose, open, show, exhibit. *An informer exposed the details of the government's secret plot.* **Ant.** cover, hide, conceal.

exposure *n.* disclosure, discovery, revealing, revelation, uncovering. *The politician feared public exposure of his secret trust fund.* **Ant.** hiding, concealment, covering.

express *vb.* **1.** state, speak, say, declare, utter, tell. *You should express your opinions clearly.* **2.** show, reveal, exhibit, represent, symbolize, signify. *Art often expresses the philosophical viewpoints of the artist.* *–adj.* **3.** distinct, specific, exact, precise, particular, explicit. *The express purpose of her trip to Arizona was to see the Grand Canyon.* **4.** speedy, fast, quick, rapid, swift. *The letter will arrive tomorrow if you send it by express mail.* **Ant. 2.** conceal, hide, suppress. **3.** indirect, vague, general. **4.** slow, sluggish, creeping.

expression *n.* **1.** phrase, statement, declaration, saying, cliche. *Have you ever heard the expression "The early bird gets the worm"?* **2.** look, appearance, air, aspect, countenance. *She knew by his expression that he was surprised.* **3.** representation, depiction, show, communication, delivery. *Her stare was an expression of displeasure.*

expulsion *n.* ejection, eviction, dismissal, exile, banishment. *Fighting will result in expulsion from the playground.* **Ant.** inclusion, acceptance.

exquisite *adj.* delicate, elegant, beautiful, precious, perfect, lovely. *My mother does exquisite needlepoint.* **Ant.** ugly, common, plain.

extend *vb.* **1.** expand, lengthen, stretch, broaden, spread, increase. *The contest deadline has been extended to the end of the month.* **2.** offer, grant, give, present, bestow. *The master of ceremonies extended his welcome to the audience.* **Ant. 1.** shorten, reduce, decrease. **2.** withdraw, remove.

extension *n.* addition, expansion, attachment, increase, augmentation. *He has received a six-month extension on the deadline for his book.*

extensive *adj.* vast, large, broad, wide, widespread, spacious, ample. *He owns an extensive ranch in Wyoming.* **Ant.** small, limited, restricted.

extent *n.* size, span, amount, degree, measure, range, reach. *There is no limit to the extent of her magical powers.*

exterior *n.* **1.** outside, surface, shell, face, covering. *The building's exterior was covered with graffiti.* *–adj.* **2.** outer, outside, external, outward, outermost. *The patio is equipped with exterior lighting.* **Ant. 1.** inside, center, interior. **2.** inner, interior, internal.

exterminate *vb.* destroy, kill, murder, eliminate, slaughter. *The mad scientist's new weapon will exterminate every living thing on earth.* **Ant.** save, conserve, create.

external *adj.* outside, outer, outermost, exterior, outward, surface. *He gave no external indications of the anger he was feeling.* **Ant.** inside, internal, inner.

extinct *adj.* vanished, dead, lost, deceased, departed. *Both the dodo and the passenger pigeon are extinct species of birds.* **Ant.** living, thriving, flourishing.

extinguish *vb.* **1.** put out, quench, smother, douse, suffocate. *Please extinguish the campfire before you leave.* **2.** destroy, demolish, eliminate, erase, crush. *The quarterback's injury extinguished our hopes for winning the championship.* **Ant. 1.** light, start, ignite. **2.** heighten, foster, increase.

extort *vb.* blackmail, exact, extract, force, coerce, cheat, fleece. *The bully extorted lunch money from the other students.*

extra *adj.* **1.** additional, more, spare, surplus, excess, further. *Extra guards were hired to protect the gold shipment.* *–n.* **2.** addition, supplement, bonus, plus, accessory. *The boss added a little extra to my check.* *–adv.* **3.** especially, unusually, uncommonly, extremely, particularly. *She prefers her chili extra hot.* **Ant. 1.** fewer, less, lesser. **3.** barely, scarcely, less.

extract *vb.* **1.** remove, withdraw, pry, extort, pluck. *The spy extracted the secret plans from a security guard.* –*n.* **2.** essence, concentrate, extraction, juice. *Vanilla extract is a common ingredient in candies.* **3.** excerpt, selection, quotation, passage, fragment. *The magazine printed an extract from the author's latest novel.* **Ant. 1.** install, insert, implant.

extraordinary *adj.* unusual, uncommon, rare, exceptional, unique, amazing. *My teacher has an extraordinary amount of patience.* **Ant.** usual, common, normal, average.

extravagant *adj.* **1.** lavish, wasteful, excessive, exorbitant, spendthrift. *His extravagant buying sprees will have to stop.* **2.** wild, fanciful, fantastic, outrageous, foolish, outlandish. *The prospector told an extravagant tale of a lost gold mine.* **Ant. 1.** thrifty, frugal, economical. **2.** realistic, true, reasonable.

extreme *adj.* **1.** farthest, furthest, outermost, utmost, ultimate. *There's an oasis at the extreme south end of the desert.* **2.** severe, excessive, intense, harsh, drastic, great. *The factory workers wore ear plugs as protection against the extreme noise.* –*n.* **3.** limit, end, boundary, ultimate, height, depth. *Marathon runners must often push their endurance to the extreme.* **Ant. 1.** near, nearest, closest. **2.** moderate, reasonable, average.

extremely *adv.* very, quite, exceedingly, unusually, especially. *She has been extremely kind to us.*

exuberance *n.* enthusiasm, vitality, exhilaration, eagerness, excitement. *He was full of exuberance on the day of his wedding.* **Ant.** despair, dejection, depression.

exuberant *adj.* spirited, exciting, lively, zestful, enthusiastic. *She enjoyed the exuberant style of the rock band.* **Ant.** lethargic, dispirited, solemn.

eye *n.* **1.** sight, eyesight, perception, vision, viewpoint. *She has a great eye for details.* –*vb.* **2.** watch, observe, scan, gaze, stare, view, ogle. *Our cat eyed the fish in the aquarium.*

eyesight *n.* vision, sight, perception, seeing, gaze. *His eyesight was correctable to 20/20 with glasses.*

eyewitness *n.* witness, spectator, observer, viewer, onlooker. *Were there any eyewitnesses to the bank robbery?*

fable *n.* myth, legend, tale, story, parable, allegory. *My favorite fable is the one about the tortoise and the hare.*

fabric *n.* **1.** cloth, textile, material, weave, goods. *Denim is the fabric commonly used to make blue jeans.* **2.** structure, texture, organization, framework, construction. *The fabric of space is distorted by intense gravitational fields.*

fabricate *vb.* make, manufacture, assemble, construct, create, devise. *He fabricates computers from components made by other manufacturers.* **Ant.** disassemble, demolish, destroy.

fabulous *adj.* marvelous, amazing, incredible, remarkable, fantastic. *She had a fabulous time on her summer vacation.* **Ant.** ordinary, routine, common.

face *n.* **1.** features, countenance, visage, expression, look, aspect. *Clowns paint their faces to look funny.* **2.** front, facade, surface, exterior, outside. *He climbed straight up the cliff's main face.* **3.** reputation, honor, prestige, image, repute. *The politician hoped to save face by denying any knowledge of the scandal.* –*vb.* **4.** meet, encounter, confront, brave, challenge. *I can't face the day without my morning coffee.* **5.** front, overlook, look, border, meet. *My bedroom window faces west.* **Ant. 2.** back, reverse.

facetious *adj.* humorous, funny, amusing, comic, witty, clever. *She wrote a facetious story about meeting a goldfish from outer space.* **Ant.** serious, grave, solemn.

facilitate *vb.* simplify, accelerate, expedite, ease, assist. *The payroll department uses a computer to facilitate the processing of checks.* **Ant.** hinder, obstruct, delay.

facility *n.* **1.** complex, system, network, office, building. *The hospital has a modern research facility.* **2.** ease, skill, dexterity, proficiency, ability, talent. *My two-year-old nephew reads with*

surprising facility. **Ant. 2.** difficulty, clumsiness, inability.

fact *n.* truth, reality, certainty, actuality, event, act. *It is a known fact that Mars is an arid planet.* **Ant.** fiction, falsehood, lie.

factor *n.* consideration, element, part, component, influence. *There are many factors to consider when looking for a job.*

factory *n.* plant, shop, workshop, mill, works. *My father works at the local automobile factory.*

factual *adj.* true, real, actual, certain, accurate, correct. *The witness gave a factual account of the crime.* **Ant.** erroneous, untrue, fictional.

fad *n.* whim, craze, rage, fancy, fashion, vogue. *She ignores the latest clothing fads by dressing as she pleases.*

fade *vb.* pale, dim, dull, blanch, weaken, lessen, diminish. *Too many washings have faded the colors of her dress.* **Ant.** brighten, increase, grow.

fail *vb.* **1.** abort, miscarry, flounder, falter, collapse, miss. *The goblin attack failed when the dwarves rallied their forces.* **2.** decline, weaken, dwindle, wane, ebb, sink. *His health is beginning to fail.* **3.** neglect, avoid, evade, ignore, omit. *My friend failed to water my plants while I was on vacation.* **Ant. 1.** succeed, win, triumph. **2.** thrive, prosper, flourish.

failure *n.* **1.** failing, nonsuccess, disappointment, defeat, frustration. *Her last book was a commercial failure.* **2.** bankruptcy, default, collapse, breakdown, crash. *There have been a lot of failures in the savings-and-loan industry.* **3.** delinquency, negligence, neglecting, omission, dereliction. *Failure to make timely payments can result in the repossession of your car.* **Ant. 1.** success, victory, triumph. **2.** prosperity, solvency.

faint *adj.* **1.** weak, feeble, indistinct, dim, slight, low. *Mission Control received a faint signal from the distant space probe.* **2.** dizzy, light-headed, woozy, giddy, fatigued. *She felt faint from working in the hot sun all day.* *–vb.* **3.** swoon, collapse, pass out, black out. *He fainted when he heard about the stock-market crash.* **Ant. 1.** strong, clear, distinct.

fair *adj.* **1.** just, honest, impartial, unprejudiced, legitimate. *The defendant felt the jury had reached a fair verdict.* **2.** average, moderate, adequate, passing, tolerable. *She has a fair chance of winning the election.* **3.** clear, open, cloudless, sunny, bright. *Fair weather is predicted for the day of our picnic.* **4.** lovely, attractive, beautiful, pretty, comely. *In fairy tales, dragons have a tendency to abduct fair maidens.* **5.** light, pale, creamy, light-colored, blond. *He sunburns easily because of his fair complexion.* *–adv.* **6.** justly, fairly, legally, honestly, honorably, rightly. *She may have won, but she didn't play fair.* *–n.* **7.** show, exhibit, exposition, pageant, display. *The county fair opens this weekend.* **Ant. 1.** prejudiced, biased, dishonest. **2.** superior, poor. **3.** cloudy, stormy, inclement. **4.** unattractive, ugly, homely. **5.** dark, dusky, swarthy. **6.** unfairly, dishonestly.

faith *n.* **1.** belief, confidence, dependence, reliance, trust. *I have a lot of faith in her reliability.* **2.** creed, doctrine, sect, teaching, orthodoxy. *There are many different religious faiths in the world.* **Ant. 1.** doubt, uncertainty, mistrust.

faithful *adj.* **1.** reliable, trustworthy, loyal, steadfast, devoted. *My dog is a faithful companion.* **2.** exact, precise, accurate, close, correct. *This painting is a faithful reproduction of the original.* **Ant. 1.** disloyal, faithless, unfaithful. **2.** inexact, imprecise.

fake *n.* **1.** fraud, forgery, imitation, counterfeit, fabrication. *He just paid $100,000 for a painting that turned out to be a fake.* *–adj.* **2.** false, imitation, phony, bogus, unreal, artificial. *Her ring is set with a fake diamond.* *–vb.* **3.** pretend, simulate, feign, assume, counterfeit. *She faked interest in her friend's boring story.* **Ant. 2.** real, genuine, authentic.

fall *vb.* **1.** collapse, drop, plunge, tumble, crash. *During the earthquake, my books fell off their shelves.* **2.** lessen, diminish, reduce, descend, lower, decline. *Their voices fell to a whis-*per when the teacher entered the room. **3.** succumb, submit, yield, surrender, capitulate. *During W.W. II, France fell to the invading German army.* **4.** happen, occur, chance, arrive, come. *Easter always falls on a Sunday.* *–n.* **5.** plunge, drop, descent, tumble, crash. *She took a bad fall on her bike.* **6.** downfall, ruin, collapse, seizure, capture, overthrow. *Historians still debate the reasons for the fall of Rome.* **Ant. 1–2.** rise, climb, ascend. **3.** withstand, resist, repel. **5.** rise, ascent, climb.

false *adj.* **1.** incorrect, untrue, mistaken, erroneous, inaccurate. *The witness perjured himself by making a false statement in court.* **2.** artificial, fake, bogus, counterfeit, spurious. *She's living under a false name.* **Ant. 1.** true, correct, accurate. **2.** real, genuine, authentic.

falter *vb.* hesitate, waver, vacillate, fluctuate, stumble. *The knight's determination faltered when he saw the size of the dragon.*

fame *n.* reputation, repute, renown, celebrity, distinction, honor. *Marie Curie's fame spread when she won her second Nobel Prize.* **Ant.** obscurity, anonymity, dishonor.

familiar *adj.* **1.** known, accustomed, well-known, common, everyday. *It's sure nice to see a familiar face.* **2.** acquainted, versed, aware, apprised, informed, experienced. *She's not familiar with the facts of the case.* **3.** friendly, close, intimate, cordial, informal. *Soldiers are not supposed to get too familiar with their officers.* **Ant. 1.** unfamiliar, unknown, rare. **2.** unaware, ignorant, uninformed. **3.** remote, distant, formal.

family *n.* **1.** clan, brood, tribe, kin, relatives, relations. *His family includes his parents, a brother and two sisters.* **2.** group, class, division, order, category, classification. *Donkeys and zebras are members of the horse family.*

famine *n.* starvation, hunger, privation, scarcity, want, need. *The recent African drought resulted in widespread famine.* **Ant.** abundance, bounty, glut.

famous *adj.* well-known, celebrated, renowned, eminent, distinguished, popular. *Elvis Presley was a famous singer.* **Ant.** unknown, obscure, unpopular.

fan *n.* admirer, follower, devotee, enthusiast, addict. *Some science-fiction fans are so devoted they publish their own magazines.*

fanatic *n.* **1.** zealot, extremist, partisan, fiend, freak. *The religious fanatic started a new cult.* *-adj.* **2.** fanatical, extremist, zealous, fervent, enthusiastic. *She's a fanatic supporter of environmental causes.*

fancy *adj.* **1.** ornate, elegant, elaborate, exceptional, special. *He showed up at the party wearing very fancy clothes.* *-n.* **2.** liking, fondness, inclination, desire, want. *I wish she hadn't developed a fancy for expensive restaurants.* **3.** imagination, fantasy, whim, notion, idea. *It's his fancy to become president some day.* *-vb.* **4.** like, favor, relish, enjoy, crave. *He fancies women with superior intellects.* **5.** imagine, suppose, believe, think, presume. *She fancies herself a better artist than Picasso.* **Ant. 1.** plain, simple, ordinary. **2.** dislike, distaste, aversion.

fantastic *adj.* **1.** great, exceptional, marvelous, terrific, superb. *You look fantastic today.* **2.** unbelievable, odd, weird, bizarre, absurd, crazy. *He told a fantastic story about being abducted by creatures from outer space.* **Ant. 1.** ordinary, average, common. **2.** believable, reasonable.

fantasy *n.* imagination, fancy, illusion, daydream, fiction. *Mermaids are creatures of fantasy.*

far *adv.* **1.** much, considerably, greatly, immeasurably, quite. *Dinner was far better than I expected.* *-adj.* **2.** distant, remote, removed, faraway, inaccessible. *She lives on the far side of town.* **Ant. 1.** less, little, barely. **2.** close, near, adjacent.

fare *vb.* **1.** manage, proceed, prosper, thrive, happen. *She's faring well at her new job.* *-n.* **2.** charge, cost, fee, price, amount. *Airline fares have gone down since deregulation.* **3.** food, provisions, board, menu, diet. *If you think you wouldn't like prison fare, don't commit a crime.*

farm *vb.* **1.** cultivate, grow, till, raise, sow, plant. *The land he farms belongs to his neighbor.* *-n.* **2.** farmstead, plantation, ranch, acreage, spread. *My sister's farm has over 300 acres of soybeans.*

fascinate *vb.* enrapture, charm, enchant, captivate, delight, absorb. *She fascinated the* audience with tales of her adventures. **Ant.** bore, weary, disenchant.

fascinating *adj.* enthralling, captivating, engrossing, absorbing, interesting. *He has a fascinating collection of antique bottles.* **Ant.** boring, uninteresting, dull.

fashion *vb.* **1.** form, make, shape, create, construct. *She fashioned a belt out of soda-can pull tabs.* *-n.* **2.** style, taste, custom, vogue, convention, practice. *Bell-bottom trousers were once in fashion.*

fast *adj.* **1.** speedy, quick, rapid, swift, fleet. *He likes fast cars.* **2.** immovable, fixed, firm, secure, tight. *She kept a fast grip on her daughter's hand.* *-adv.* **3.** swiftly, rapidly, quickly, hastily, speedily. *Please don't drive so fast.* **4.** firmly, securely, soundly, tightly, solidly. *The climber held fast to his safety rope.* **Ant. 1.** slow, sluggish. **2.** insecure, loose, uncertain. **3.** slowly, slow, leisurely. **4.** loosely, insecurely.

fasten *vb.* secure, fix, attach, bind, tie, connect. *She fastened the tent line to a tree.* **Ant.** free, release, loosen.

fat *adj.* **1.** obese, overweight, stout, corpulent, plump, heavy. *If you think you're fat, you should try eating less and exercising more.* **2.** thick, broad, wide, immense, extensive, large. *An unabridged dictionary is a fat book.* *-n.* **3.** grease, lard, tallow, oil, blubber. *He fried the meat in its own fat.* **Ant. 1.** slender, thin, lean. **2.** narrow, thin, small.

fatal *adj.* **1.** lethal, mortal, deadly, terminal, killing. *We were all saddened to hear about the fatal plane crash.* **2.** disastrous, ruinous, catastrophic, critical, crucial. *Telling her boss to go jump in a lake was a fatal mistake.* **Ant. 1–2.** harmless, beneficial, minor.

fate *n.* destiny, fortune, lot, luck, providence, chance. *It seems to be my fate to buy losing lottery tickets.*

fatigue *n.* **1.** weariness, tiredness, exhaustion, feebleness, weakness. *Her fatigue was caused by hiking all day with a heavy pack.* *-vb.* **2.** weary, tire, exhaust, weaken, drain. *Playing softball in the hot sun fatigued him.* **Ant. 1.** strength, vigor, vitality. **2.** refresh, renew, restore.

fault *n.* **1.** responsibility, guilt, lapse, blame, crime, error. *It's not my fault you can't find your car keys.* **2.** defect, blemish, flaw, imperfection, shortcoming. *Her new car had so many faults she had to return it to the dealer.*

faulty *adj.* defective, imperfect, damaged, deficient, unsatisfactory, bad. *His car doesn't run well because it has a faulty valve.* **Ant.** perfect, satisfactory, good.

favor *n.* **1.** service, courtesy, kindness, boon, good deed. *She did me a favor by lending me lunch money.* **2.** approval, admiration, esteem, regard, respect. *The candidate promised to cut taxes in an attempt to win our favor.* –*vb.* **3.** approve, support, prefer, like, advocate. *I favor spending public funds to help the homeless.* **Ant. 2.** disfavor, disapproval, antipathy. **3.** disapprove, dislike.

favorable *adj.* good, promising, auspicious, beneficial, advantageous, satisfactory. *Her new play received favorable reviews.* **Ant.** bad, adverse, unsatisfactory.

favorite *adj.* **1.** preferred, liked, esteemed, special, choice. *What's your favorite movie?* –*n.* **2.** preference, choice, fancy, liking, beloved. *Vanilla ice cream is my favorite.*

fear *n.* **1.** dread, terror, fright, horror, anxiety, phobia. *He has a fear of high places.* –*vb.* **2.** dread, be afraid, apprehend, mistrust. *She fears the dark.*

fearless *adj.* brave, courageous, valiant, valorous, gallant. *The fearless maiden told the dragon to leave her alone.* **Ant.** cowardly, fearful, afraid.

feasible *adj.* possible, practical, achievable, attainable, reasonable. *It's not yet feasible to send colonists to other planets.* **Ant.** impractical, impossible, unfeasible.

feast *n.* **1.** banquet, meal, dinner, occasion, celebration. *The queen held a feast in honor of her son's marriage.* –*vb.* **2.** dine, banquet, feed, gorge, glut, indulge. *On Thanksgiving Day, we usually feast on turkey.*

feat *n.* deed, act, achievement, accomplishment, maneuver, trick. *Balancing three pails of water on your head is quite a feat.*

feature *n.* **1.** highlight, attribute, quality, trait, characteristic. *She knew exactly what features she wanted in a new computer.* –*vb.* **2.** star, highlight, headline, emphasize, promote. *This movie features my favorite actress.*

fee *n.* charge, payment, price, cost, compensation, stipend. *My agent's fee is 10% of everything I make.*

feeble *adj.* weak, frail, fragile, infirm, delicate, ineffective. *The old man's voice was so feeble we could barely understand him.* **Ant.** strong, vigorous, effective.

feed *vb.* **1.** sustain, nurture, nourish, maintain, support. *My parents have a large family to feed.* **2.** eat, consume, devour, ingest, take. *Birds feed on worms.* **3.** give, deliver, dispense, provide, supply. *I need to feed more paper into my computer's printer.* –*n.* **4.** food, edibles, provisions, fodder, nourishment. *What do cows use for feed?* **Ant. 1.** starve, famish. **3.** withhold, deny, deprive.

feel *vb.* **1.** touch, handle, finger, stroke, manipulate, grope. *I had no idea what the fabric was like until I felt it.* **2.** know, experience, understand, perceive, sense. *A kitten feels pleasure when you pet it.* **3.** think, believe, consider, hold, assume. *She feels we should pay more attention to her.* –*n.* **4.** touch, sensation, feeling, texture, finish. *I like the feel of satin.*

feeling *n.* **1.** sensation, perception, reaction, response, awareness. *He had a bad feeling in his stomach when he saw the vampire.* **2.** view, belief, thought, opinion, conviction. *She had a feeling I would be late again.* **3.** emotion, sentiment, attitude, mood, temper. *Winning the award gave him a feeling of happiness.* –*adj.* **4.** warm, emotional, sensitive, caring, sympathetic, compassionate. *She's a very feeling person.* **Ant. 4.** unfeeling, insensitive, cold.

fell *vb.* raze, level, hew, cut down, destroy. *Every hour of every day, 500,000 rain forest trees are felled.* **Ant.** raise, grow.

felon *n.* criminal, convict, lawbreaker, culprit, offender. *Three felons escaped from the state prison.*

fence *n.* **1.** barrier, railing, wall, enclosure, barricade. *This fence is here to keep the cows in* *the right pasture.* –*vb.* **2.** enclose, encircle, surround, encase, wall. *She fenced her backyard.*

ferocious *adj.* fierce, savage, brutal, violent, cruel, wild. *That ferocious dog should be sent to the pound.* **Ant.** tame, docile, submissive.

fertile *adj.* productive, fruitful, rich, prolific, fecund. *The farmer felt himself lucky to have such fertile fields.* **Ant.** sterile, barren, unproductive.

fervent *adj.* ardent, zealous, passionate, enthusiastic, intense, heated. *The charity worker made a fervent appeal for donations.* **Ant.** dispassionate, apathetic, cool.

festival *n.* celebration, jubilee, gala, holiday, fete. *The town is having a festival to celebrate its 100th anniversary.*

festive *adj.* gay, joyful, happy, merry, jubilant, joyous. *Everyone at the wedding was in a festive mood.* **Ant.** unhappy, sad, somber.

feud *n.* **1.** fight, conflict, strife, quarrel, vendetta, dispute. *Romeo and Juliet's love affair was tragic because their families were engaged in a feud.* –*vb.* **2.** quarrel, fight, bicker, clash, squabble. *He's always feuding with his parents.*

fever *n.* **1.** temperature, inflammation, flush, illness, sickness. *She stayed home from school because she had a fever.* **2.** turmoil, heat, ferment, panic, fluster, agitation. *We felt the fever of excitement as the big game drew near.* **Ant. 2.** calm, serenity, tranquillity.

few *adj.* limited, scarce, scanty, meager, infrequent, occasional. *There are still a few apples left on the tree.* **Ant.** many, numerous, plentiful.

fiasco *n.* mess, disaster, ruin, defeat, failure. *The football game between the elephants and the mice was a fiasco for the mice.* **Ant.** victory, success, triumph.

fib *n.* **1.** lie, falsehood, untruth, fabrication, deception. *I told a fib when I said I liked his new shirt.* –*vb.* **2.** lie, falsify, misrepresent, misstate, fabricate. *She fibbed when she said she had been studying all day.* **Ant. 1.** truth, fact.

fiction *n.* story, tale, yarn, fantasy, falsehood, lie. *His account of seeing a UFO was pure fiction.* **Ant.** nonfiction, reality, fact.

field *n.* **1.** ground, plot, meadow, pasture, area, region. *We need to find an open field for our*

softball game. **2.** occupation, profession, vocation, line, business, activity. *What field do you plan to go into after you graduate?*

fierce *adj.* violent, savage, ferocious, furious, wild, powerful. *A fierce storm knocked down all the town's power lines.* **Ant.** gentle, moderate, tame.

fight *n.* **1.** struggle, conflict, battle, combat, quarrel, brawl. *The school bully picked a fight with a smaller boy.* –*vb.* **2.** battle, combat, struggle, contend, clash, quarrel. *The villagers fought bravely to defend their homes against Viking raiders.*

figure *n.* **1.** diagram, drawing, picture, illustration, sketch. *She drew a figure of a dragon.* **2.** number, numeral, digit, cipher, integer. *The accountant was busy jotting down figures in his notebook.* **3.** form, shape, silhouette, outline, pattern. *We could barely make out the figure of someone walking in the distance.* **4.** personage, personality, person, character, notable. *The president is an important public figure.* –*vb.* **5.** calculate, reckon, compute, tally, assess. *She figured out the total of her purchases.*

file *n.* **1.** record, archive, dossier, folder, portfolio. *The company's personnel files need reorganizing.* **2.** line, column, queue, row, rank. *The soldiers marched by in a long file.* –*vb.* **3.** organize, classify, arrange, sort, store. *Please file these documents.* **4.** apply, petition, seek, solicit, submit. *The couple filed for a divorce.* **5.** march, hike, walk, parade, troop. *The audience filed out of the theater when the movie was over.*

fill *vb.* **1.** stuff, pack, load, stock, crowd, jam. *The mall was filled with shoppers.* **2.** occupy, pervade, suffuse, permeate, saturate. *Smoke filled the air.* **3.** replenish, refill, resupply, supply, provide, charge. *Please fill the gas tank.* **Ant. 3.** empty, drain, deplete.

filter *n.* **1.** strainer, sieve, screen, sifter, net. *Please use a fresh filter each time you make a pot of coffee.* –*vb.* **2.** strain, filtrate, purify, cleanse, drain. *The backpackers filtered the stream water before drinking it.* **3.** trickle, seep, ooze, leak, flow. *Sunlight filtered through the clouds.*

filthy *adj.* dirty, foul, grimy, soiled, muddy, unclean. *It's time to wash these filthy clothes.* **Ant.** clean, washed, cleansed.

final *adj.* last, concluding, ultimate, terminating, decisive, ending. *The prince and the princess were married in the movie's final scene.* **Ant.** first, beginning, opening.

find *vb.* discover, detect, locate, perceive, gain, attain, recover. *Where did you find your missing car keys?* **Ant.** lose, misplace, mislay.

fine *adj.* **1.** excellent, superior, admirable, outstanding, exceptional. *You did a fine job on that report.* **2.** thin, small, little, minute, delicate, sheer. *Be sure to read the fine print at the bottom of a contract.* –*n.* **3.** penalty, charge, payment, assessment, settlement. *She had to pay a fine on the library books she returned late.* –*vb.* **4.** assess, charge, levy, tax, penalize. *He was fined fifty dollars for speeding.* **Ant. 1.** poor, inferior, mediocre. **2.** coarse, thick, large.

finish *vb.* **1.** complete, conclude, end, cease, stop, terminate. *You can watch TV after you finish your chores.* **2.** consume, devour, deplete, exhaust, empty, kill. *Finish your supper or you'll be sent straight to bed.* –*n.* **3.** conclusion, end, close, completion, finale. *If you start something, you should see it through to the finish.* **4.** surface, texture, coating, polish, exterior. *She sanded the table until it had a perfectly smooth finish.* **Ant. 1.** start, begin, commence. **3.** beginning, opening, start.

fire *n.* **1.** blaze, combustion, burning, conflagration, inferno. *It took three engine companies to put out the fire.* **2.** passion, ardor, heat, fever, spirit. *His voice was full of fire when he spoke about his adventures in Afghanistan.* **3.** shooting, bombardment, shelling, firing. *The soldiers were pinned down by heavy fire.* –*vb.* **4.** light, ignite, kindle, burn, inflame. *An arsonist fired two buildings last night.* **5.** dismiss, discharge, release, depose, terminate. *The manager was forced to fire one of her employees.* **6.** arouse, stir, excite, stimulate, inspire. *Her stories about spaceflight fired my imagination.* **7.** shoot, discharge, detonate, shell, snipe. *The sheriff fired his revolver at the desperado.* **Ant. 2.** apathy, indifference, cool. **4.** extinguish, douse, quench. **5.** hire, employ, engage. **6.** cool, calm, quiet.

firm *adj.* **1.** stiff, hard, rigid, solid, compact. *After hiking through the bog, it was nice to be on firm ground again.* **2.** steady, fixed, settled, definite, immovable, unwavering. *It's my firm opinion that animals should be treated humanely.* –*n.* **3.** company, business, organization, corporation, establishment. *He works for a law firm.* –*vb.* **4.** strengthen, harden, toughen, improve, tone. *She exercises regularly to firm her muscles.* **Ant. 1.** resilient, soft, limp. **2.** unsteady, movable, wavering. **4.** soften, weaken.

first *adj.* **1.** initial, opening, beginning, original, earliest. *The first chapter is good, but the rest of the book is mediocre.* **2.** highest, preeminent, chief, main, foremost. *The president's wife is known as the first lady.* **Ant. 1.** last, concluding, ending. **2.** secondary, subordinate.

fit *adj.* **1.** suitable, proper, right, appropriate, fitting. *This food isn't fit for a dog.* **2.** healthy, sturdy, robust, well, hale, hardy. *She's looking fit as a result of all the exercise she's been getting.* –*vb.* **3.** conform, suit, correspond, harmonize, agree. *The punishment should fit the crime.* **4.** equip, outfit, prepare, ready, furnish. *The ship was fitted out for a long voyage.* –*n.* **5.** seizure, spasm, spell, outburst, tantrum. *The spoiled child always had a fit when he couldn't get what he wanted.* **Ant. 1.** improper, unsuitable, inappropriate. **2.** weak, unfit, sick.

fitting *adj.* suitable, proper, appropriate, seemly, becoming. *Boisterous chatter isn't fitting in church.* **Ant.** unbecoming, improper, wrong.

fix *vb.* **1.** repair, mend, remedy, restore, patch. *We need to get someone to fix the washing machine.* **2.** attach, secure, fasten, tie, connect, anchor. *The soldiers were ordered to fix bayonets.* **3.** set, settle, decide, determine, establish. *They fixed a time for their next meeting.* –*n.* **4.** predicament, quandary, mess, jam, dilemma. *That's quite a fix you've gotten yourself into.* **Ant. 1.** break, damage. **2.** loosen, unfasten, remove.

flag *n.* pendant, emblem, banner, standard, colors. *The flag was positioned at half-mast in honor of the deceased president.*

flagrant *adj.* bold, obvious, brazen, glaring, conspicuous, shocking. *Knocking someone down on the basketball court is a flagrant foul.* **Ant.** inobvious, hidden, concealed.

flame *n.* **1.** fire, blaze, flare, light, glow, flash. *When the oil tank burned, the flames towered hundreds of feet high.* –*vb.* **2.** flare, burn, blaze, flash, fire. *She burned herself when the whole book of matches flamed up in her hand.*

flap vb. flutter, vibrate, wave, beat, flail, swish. *The caged bird flapped its wings in a vain attempt to fly away.*

flash n. **1.** flare, blaze, sparkle, glitter, streak, burst. *We could see lightning flashes in the distance.* **2.** second, instant, moment, minute, wink, jiffy. *I'll be back in a flash.* –vb. **3.** flare, flame, blaze, gleam, glare. *I lost my night vision when he flashed a light in my eyes.* **4.** streak, race, rush, dash, speed, dart. *The car flashed by so quickly we couldn't see the driver.*

flat adj. **1.** level, horizontal, even, smooth, plane. *He prefers hiking across flat ground.* **2.** absolute, definite, unqualified, positive, unconditional. *She gave me a flat refusal when I asked her to do my homework.* **3.** dull, lifeless, tasteless, dead, weak, stale. *This root beer has gone flat.* –adv. **4.** exactly, precisely, evenly, specifically, just, dead. *He ran the mile in four minutes flat.* **Ant. 1.** round, curved, rough. **2.** qualified, conditional, vague. **3.** tasty, savory, interesting.

flatter vb. overpraise, praise, compliment, extol, exalt, please. *He flattered her by saying she looked like a movie star.* **Ant.** insult, belittle, displease.

flaunt vb. display, show off, vaunt, advertise, strut. *He flaunts his good looks.* **Ant.** conceal, hide, cloak.

flavor n. **1.** taste, flavoring, seasoning, relish, tang. *A little salt will enhance the flavor of this stew.* –vb. **2.** season, spice, tinge, color, lace. *She flavors her spaghetti sauce with oregano.*

flaw n. fault, defect, blemish, shortcoming, imperfection. *This shirt is inexpensive because it has a minor flaw.*

flee vb. escape, run, fly, bolt, evade, elude. *Bambi and his friends fled from a terrible forest fire.*

fleet adj. **1.** rapid, swift, quick, fast, speedy, hurried. *The robber made a fleet getaway.* –n. **2.** flotilla, squadron, armada, navy, convoy. *The fleet returned to harbor after a training exercise at sea.* **Ant. 1.** slow, sluggish, unhurried.

flexible adj. bendable, pliable, elastic, versatile, adaptable. *She repaired the leaking pipe with a flexible piece of plastic.* **Ant.** stiff, rigid, hard.

flicker vb. flutter, flash, blink, twinkle, waver. *We could see the light of a jack-o'-lantern flickering on their porch.*

flight n. **1.** soaring, flying, sailing, trip, crossing. *She's suffering from jet lag after her transatlantic flight.* **2.** swarm, wing, flock, formation, squadron. *A flight of geese passed overhead.* **3.** escape, getaway, retreat, exodus, withdrawal. *Moses led the Israelites during their flight from Egypt.*

flimsy adj. frail, fragile, delicate, feeble, weak, unsubstantial. *Not wanting to miss your favorite soap opera is a pretty flimsy excuse for being late to work.* **Ant.** solid, strong, substantial.

flinch vb. wince, shrink, start, cower, cringe, withdraw. *The boy flinched when the dentist began drilling.*

fling vb. **1.** toss, throw, cast, hurl, pitch, heave. *After missing the easy catch, the outfielder stomped away and flung his glove down.* –n. **2.** chance, try, attempt, venture, trial, go. *Anyone willing to give snipe hunting a fling?*

float vb. skim, drift, glide, ride, slip, swim. *As we watched the stream, a piece of wood floated past.* **Ant.** sink, submerge, drown.

flock n. **1.** herd, pack, company, group, swarm, band, crowd. *The shepherd tended his flock.* –vb. **2.** rush, run, go, converge, throng, swarm. *People flocked to the store that was giving away free pizza.*

flood n. **1.** deluge, inundation, torrent, overflow, surge. *Relief workers helped victims of the flood.* –vb. **2.** deluge, inundate, submerge, overflow, overwhelm. *During the Christmas season, the post office is flooded with mail.*

floor n. **1.** story, level, tier, stage, deck. *She lives on the third floor of her apartment building.* **2.** flooring, base, planking, linoleum, tile, parquet. *This floor needs to be waxed.*

flounder vb. wallow, struggle, tumble, lurch, falter, waver. *A small boat floundered helplessly in the heavy waves.*

flourish vb. **1.** grow, succeed, prosper, thrive, develop, bloom. *Her bookstore flourished because she picked a good location.* **2.** brandish, wave, wield, swing, flaunt, display. *The knight flourished his broadsword in the dragon's face.*

-n. **3.** show, exhibition, display, fanfare, embellishment. *The magician pulled a rabbit from her hat with a great deal of flourish.* **Ant. 1.** decline, fail, wither.

flow *vb.* **1.** stream, pour, gush, run, cascade, surge. *Water flowed from the broken fire hydrant.* –n. **2.** stream, course, sweep, current, progression. *An accident interrupted the flow of traffic.*

flower *n.* **1.** blossom, bloom, bud, bouquet, posy. *She sent him flowers as a token of her affection.* **2.** prime, zenith, acme, height, vigor. *Philosophy was in its flower during Greece's Golden Age.* **3.** best, choice, pick, select, elite. *These students are the flower of our class.* –vb. **4.** blossom, bloom, bud, flourish, prosper, thrive. *Her talent flowered when she began taking music lessons.* **Ant. 2.** nadir, low point. **3.** worst, least, poorest.

fluctuate *vb.* waver, vacillate, vary, sway, oscillate, wobble. *The price of wheat fluctuates from year to year.* **Ant.** stabilize, settle, persist.

fluid *n.* **1.** liquid, solution, juice, drink, beverage. *The triathlete was dehydrated because he didn't consume enough fluids during the race.* –adj. **2.** liquid, watery, flowing, liquefied, moist, wet. *This mixture becomes fluid when heated.* **Ant. 2.** solid, hard, firm.

flush *vb.* **1.** redden, blush, color, burn, flame. *He flushed with anger when I insulted him.* **2.** flood, wash, rinse, hose, douse. *She flushed food scraps down the garbage disposal.* –n. **3.** blush, redness, rosiness, ruddiness, glow. *Her face had a healthy flush after her vigorous hike.* –adj. **4.** even, level, flat, straight, true. *He wanted his new countertop to be flush with the stove.*

fly *vb.* **1.** soar, float, glide, wing, sail, coast. *Canadian geese fly south for the winter.* **2.** rush, hasten, hurry, dash, bolt, tear. *She flew out of the room to answer the phone.*

focus *n.* **1.** center, heart, middle, hub, core, point. *The movie star enjoyed being the focus of attention.* –vb. **2.** focalize, concentrate, center, aim, direct. *This course will focus on 20th-century writers.* **Ant. 1.** edge, fringe, margin.

foe *n.* enemy, adversary, rival, opponent, antagonist, competitor. *They are friends at work but foes on the tennis court.* **Ant.** friend, ally, associate.

fog *n.* **1.** mist, haze, steam, vapor, cloud. *The airport was closed due to heavy fog.* –vb. **2.** mist, cloud, obscure, conceal, screen. *Our breath fogged the windshield.* **Ant. 2.** clear, reveal, brighten.

foil *vb.* thwart, frustrate, hinder, prevent, baffle. *An alert guard foiled the robbery attempt.* **Ant.** aid, abet, support.

fold *vb.* **1.** crease, pleat, double, bend, plait. *I always have trouble folding a map properly.* **2.** fail, close, collapse, crash, bomb. *The new play folded after only three performances.* **3.** clasp, embrace, wrap, enfold, envelop. *He folded his arms in anticipation of a long wait at the doctor's office.* –n. **4.** pleat, crease, wrinkle, crimp, bend. *A cat played with the curtain's folds.* **Ant. 1.** straighten, smooth, flatten. **2.** succeed, thrive, prosper, **3.** unfold, unwrap, open.

follow *vb.* **1.** result, ensue, succeed, arise, issue. *From her line of reasoning, it follows that she believes in extraterrestrial life.* **2.** trail, tail, track, shadow, accompany, attend. *Mary's little lamb followed her everywhere.* **3.** comprehend, understand, fathom, grasp, perceive. *I wasn't able to follow the movie's intricate plot.* **4.** heed, obey, mind, regard, observe. *Our cake was a disaster because we didn't follow the directions.* **Ant. 1.** precede, forerun. **2.** elude, evade, avoid. **3.** misunderstand, misinterpret. **4.** ignore, disobey, forsake.

folly *n.* foolishness, nonsense, idiocy, stupidity, absurdity, inanity. *Since Alaska was considered worthless, its purchase was thought to be folly.* **Ant.** wisdom, sanity, prudence.

fond *adj.* **1.** liking, loving, affectionate, devoted, tender, warm. *The lovers exchanged fond glances.* **2.** partial to, enamored of, stuck on, addicted to. *Many people are fond of TV.* **Ant. 1.** distant, hostile, cool. **2.** averse, indifferent.

fondle *vb.* caress, pet, stroke, coddle, cuddle, embrace. *She loves to fondle her Teddy bear.*

food *n.* provisions, rations, victuals, fare, nourishment. *We'd better go to the grocery because we're low on food.*

fool *n.* **1.** idiot, moron, dunce, simpleton, dummy, buffoon, clown. *You're a fool if you think you can pass this test without studying.* –vb. **2.** cheat, trick, dupe, deceive, hoax. *Abraham Lin-*

coln said you can't fool all of the people all the time. **Ant. 1.** sage, genius.

foolish *adj.* unwise, stupid, dumb, thoughtless, silly, senseless. *It is foolish to spend all your money on lottery tickets.* **Ant.** wise, bright, smart, sensible.

foot *n.* bottom, base, foundation, footing, support. *They camped at the foot of the mountain.* **Ant.** head, top, peak.

forbid *vb.* prohibit, ban, disallow, prevent, bar, outlaw. *She thinks the city council should forbid smoking in all restaurants.* **Ant.** allow, permit, approve.

forbidding *adj.* frightening, scary, menacing, threatening, sinister. *That deserted house looks forbidding on dark and stormy nights.* **Ant.** agreeable, pleasant, inviting.

force *n.* **1.** strength, power, might, vigor, energy. *The wind was blowing with great force.* **2.** army, troop, squadron, legion, corps, unit. *An enemy force besieged the castle.* –*vb.* **3.** oblige, compel, coerce, require, persuade. *Sickness forced him to postpone his vacation.* **4.** push, drive, pull, wrench, break, thrust. *Since the window was stuck, we had to force it open.* **Ant. 1.** weakness, feebleness, ineffectiveness.

forceful *adj.* powerful, strong, dynamic, energetic, vigorous, potent. *The lawyer made a forceful appeal on behalf of her client.* **Ant.** weak, powerless, feeble.

foreboding *n.* premonition, apprehension, dread, intuition, misgiving. *The knight had a foreboding that something bad would happen if he entered the dragon's lair.*

forecast *n.* **1.** prediction, prophecy, prognosis, foretelling. *The forecast is for continued rain.* –*vb.* **2.** predict, foretell, prophesy, conjecture, surmise. *She claims to be able to forecast the future.*

foreign *adj.* alien, exotic, strange, unknown, unfamiliar, distant. *He likes to travel to foreign lands.* **Ant.** known, familiar, native.

foreman *n.* manager, supervisor, overseer, superintendent, boss. *She was designated to be the jury's foreman.*

foremost *adj.* leading, principal, main, first, head, chief. *Getting home safely was the lost hiker's foremost thought.* **Ant.** secondary, last, least.

foresee *vb.* anticipate, expect, envision, predict, foretell. *He should have foreseen the threat posed by the storm.*

forest *n.* woods, woodland, timber, grove, thicket, copse. *Most of North America was once covered with forests.*

foretell *vb.* forecast, predict, divine, foresee, presage. *The palm reader foretold that I would meet an attractive stranger.*

forever *adv.* always, eternally, endlessly, perpetually, everlastingly. *I will love you forever.*

forfeit *vb.* lose, renounce, relinquish, sacrifice, yield. *She had to forfeit her title when it was discovered she had used steroids.* **Ant.** keep, retain.

forge *vb.* **1.** mold, cast, make, shape, create, construct. *They forged a lasting friendship.* **2.** falsify, counterfeit, fake, imitate, simulate. *He forged his mother's signature on a note to his teacher.* **3.** push, plod, struggle, strive, drive. *The dog sledder forged ahead despite the heavy snow.*

forget *vb.* misremember, misrecollect, overlook, miss, disregard. *She forgot my name.* **Ant.** remember, recall, recollect.

forgive *vb.* pardon, excuse, absolve, condone, reprieve. *I forgive you this time, but please don't let it happen again.* **Ant.** blame, accuse, condemn.

forgo *vb.* relinquish, renounce, forfeit, surrender, abandon. *If you expect to lose weight, you'll have to forgo sweets.* **Ant.** keep, retain.

fork *vb.* **1.** divide, branch, split, part, diverge. *When the road forks, bear left to reach my house.* –*n.* **2.** branch, branching, split, division, angle. *There's a fork in the road just ahead.*

forlorn *adj.* desolate, hopeless, wretched, miserable, dejected, pitiful. *The lost puppy had a forlorn look.* **Ant.** cheerful, happy, hopeful.

form *n.* **1.** shape, figure, contour, outline, pattern, build. *The sorceress took on the form of* *a swan.* **2.** species, type, variety, kind, class, aspect. *What form of transportation do you prefer?* **3.** method, system, style, manner, procedure. *The gymnast trained hard to improve her form.* **4.** mold, cast, die, framework, pattern. *Work crews constructed a wooden form before pouring the cement.* **5.** document, paper, application, questionnaire. *You'll have to fill out these forms if you wish to apply for a driver's license.* –*vb.* **6.** shape, create, fashion, make, construct, devise. *The goal of our founding fathers was to form a more perfect union.*

formal *adj.* **1.** official, correct, conventional, orthodox, regular. *If you hope to be considered for this job, you'll have to submit a formal application.* **2.** ceremonial, ritualistic, elaborate, elegant, fancy. *The couple planned to have a formal wedding.* **3.** rigid, stiff, aloof, reserved, proper, cool. *She makes me feel uneasy because her manners are so formal.* **Ant. 1.** unofficial, unconventional. **2.** informal, unceremonious. **3.** friendly, warm, casual.

formation *n.* configuration, pattern, design, layout, arrangement. *That cloud formation looks like a person's head.*

former *adj.* previous, prior, earlier, past, preceding, erstwhile. *He's still on good terms with his former boss.* **Ant.** current, present, later.

formidable *adj.* awesome, impressive, intimidating, forbidding, difficult. *Goliath was a formidable opponent for David.* **Ant.** weak, insignificant, easy.

formula *n.* system, method, plan, prescription, recipe, procedure, guideline. *The alchemist claimed to have a secret formula for changing lead into gold.*

forsake *vb.* renounce, forswear, abandon, desert, leave, quit. *She forsook smoking once she became aware of its dangers.*

fort *n.* fortress, fortification, stronghold, stockade, base. *The soldiers hastily constructed a crude log fort.*

forth *adv.* onward, forward, out, outward, ahead. *The brave knight rode forth to confront his opponent.*

fortitude *n.* courage, bravery, valor, resolution, determination. *For some people, it takes a lot of fortitude to say they're sorry.* **Ant.** cowardice, weakness, timidity.

fortunate *adj.* lucky, blessed, favored, charmed, well-off, happy. *You're fortunate to have such a good friend as her.* **Ant.** unfortunate, unlucky, unhappy.

fortune *n.* **1.** money, wealth, riches, prosperity, affluence. *She made her fortune in real estate.* **2.** fate, chance, luck, destiny, providence, accident. *It was his good fortune to buy a winning lotto ticket.* **Ant. 1.** poverty, destitution. **2.** misfortune, design, intent.

forum *n.* meeting, gathering, assembly, discussion, seminar. *The city council held a public forum to discuss the need for new taxes.*

forward *adj.* **1.** bold, brazen, assertive, aggressive, arrogant. *Her forward behavior alienated her colleagues.* **2.** front, fore, foremost, headmost, anterior. *She found a seat in the forward part of the bus.* –*adv.* **3.** onward, ahead, along, outward, before. *I'm looking forward to Christmas vacation.* –*vb.* **4.** advance, encourage, foster, promote, further. *She's been working to forward the cause of world peace.* **Ant. 1.** timid, retiring, modest. **2.** back, rear, posterior. **3.** backward, behind. **4.** hinder, impede, obstruct.

foul *adj.* **1.** disgusting, offensive, repulsive, indecent, obscene, dirty. *Foul language is inappropriate in the classroom.* **2.** rainy, stormy, wet, blustery, bleak, bad. *We shouldn't take the yacht out in this foul weather.* **Ant. 1.** proper, decent, inoffensive. **2.** good, fair, clear.

found *vb.* establish, create, institute, develop, originate. *Our family business was founded by my grandfather.*

foundation *n.* **1.** base, support, underpinning, foot, bed, bottom. *Our house is built on a concrete block foundation.* **2.** establishment, institution, organization, association, society. *He works for a nonprofit foundation.*

fraction *n.* part, portion, piece, fragment, section. *Only a small fraction of our graduating class went on to college.*

fracture *vb.* **1.** break, split, crack, fragment, shatter, splinter. *She fractured her leg playing basketball.* –*n.* **2.** break, split, crack, rupture, fissure. *Her fracture took six weeks to heal.*

fragile *adj.* brittle, breakable, delicate, frail, feeble, weak. *This crystal vase is very fragile.* **Ant.** strong, sturdy, unbreakable.

fragment *n.* **1.** portion, part, piece, section, segment. *There was nothing but fragments left when he dropped the vase.* *–vb.* **2.** splinter, shatter, burst, crumble, disintegrate. *The ancient bones fragmented in her hands when she picked them up.*

fragrance *n.* aroma, scent, smell, odor, perfume. *He likes the fragrance of roses.* **Ant.** stink, reek, stench.

frail *adj.* fragile, delicate, weak, feeble, brittle, breakable. *This parchment is old and frail.* **Ant.** strong, sturdy, tough.

frame *n.* **1.** mounting, framework, casing, housing, edging, border. *She bought a frame for her new painting.* **2.** physique, body, build, figure, shape. *He has such a small frame he'll never make much of a football player.* *–vb.* **3.** mount, border, enclose, surround, encase. *We should frame this picture before sending it to Grandmother.* **4.** formulate, fashion, construct, devise, design. *The lawyer framed her questions in an easily understandable manner.*

frantic *adj.* frenzied, excited, agitated, frenetic, nervous, distraught. *The groom became frantic when the bride was late getting to the church.* **Ant.** composed, calm, serene.

fraud *n.* **1.** deceit, deception, trickery, duplicity, dishonesty. *He was arrested for fraud when he sold a counterfeit painting.* **2.** cheat, swindler, faker, pretender, impostor. *She claims to be a wealthy princess, but she's actually just a fraud.* **Ant. 1.** honesty, integrity, fairness.

fray *n.* **1.** fight, brawl, scuffle, tussle, row, battle. *The personnel manager and the company accountant got into a fray over employee benefits.* *–vb.* **2.** ravel, tatter, frazzle, shred, wear. *Too many washings have frayed her jeans.*

freak *adj.* **1.** odd, unusual, abnormal, strange, unexpected, weird. *A freak snowstorm hit our town last July.* *–n.* **2.** abnormality, oddity, curiosity, deviation, anomaly, monstrosity. *A snake with two heads is a freak of nature.* **Ant. 1.** normal, ordinary, expected.

free *adj.* **1.** complimentary, gratis, gratuitous, chargeless, costless. *She has two free tickets for today's baseball game.* **2.** independent, liberated, emancipated, autonomous, self-governing. *India became a free nation in 1948.* **3.** available, open, idle, vacant, empty, unclaimed. *Now that Grandfather has left, our guest room is free.* **4.** loose, unconfined, unrestrained, unbridled, untied. *The prisoner was set free.* *–vb.* **5.** release, loose, liberate, emancipate, untie, unleash. *Activists broke into the science building and freed the lab animals.* **Ant. 1.** expensive, costly, paid. **2.** dependent, enslaved, restricted. **3.** taken, occupied, unavailable. **4.** confined, restrained, tied. **5.** restrain, confine, imprison.

freedom *n.* independence, liberty, emancipation, liberation, release. *Abraham Lincoln gave America's slaves their freedom.* **Ant.** slavery, servitude, bondage.

freeze *vb.* **1.** ice, frost, refrigerate, chill, cool. *You should freeze this meat if you aren't going to use it till next week.* **2.** stop, halt, harden, stiffen, immobilize. *She froze in her tracks when she saw the bear.* *–n.* **3.** frost, chill, nip, bite, sting. *Last night's freeze killed my tomato plants.* **4.** halt, stop, restraint, moratorium, suspension. *The president put a freeze on new taxes.* **Ant. 1.** thaw, warm, heat.

frenzy *n.* furor, turmoil, rage, rush, agitation. *There was a frenzy of last-minute activity as the cast prepared for opening night.*

frequent *adj.* **1.** common, usual, habitual, regular, customary. *This airline offers discounts for frequent fliers.* *–vb.* **2.** patronize, haunt, visit, attend, go to. *He frequents that bar.* **Ant. 1.** rare, unusual, uncommon. **2.** avoid, shun, spurn.

fresh *adj.* **1.** unspoiled, unfaded, wholesome, new, recent. *Are these eggs fresh?* **2.** refreshing, invigorating, healthy, clean, pure. *Let's step outside to get some fresh air.* **3.** wise, bold, impudent, forward, rude. *Don't get fresh with me.* **Ant. 1.** stale, spoiled, old. **2.** stale, impure, polluted. **3.** polite, courteous, respectful.

friction *n.* **1.** rubbing, abrasion, grinding, grating, chafing. *If you don't keep oil in the engine, friction will wear it out.* **2.** conflict, antagonism, discord, disagreement, dissension. *There was a lot of friction between the two stepbrothers.* **Ant. 2.** harmony, agreement, compatibility.

friend n. comrade, companion, intimate, pal, acquaintance, ally. *They have been friends since childhood.* **Ant.** stranger, adversary, foe.

friendship n. fellowship, comradeship, companionship, intimacy, amity, closeness. *I truly value your friendship.* **Ant.** coolness, indifference, animosity.

fright n. terror, fear, dread, alarm, panic, scare. *The passengers were filled with fright when the pilot parachuted out of the plane.* **Ant.** bravery, courage, fortitude.

frighten vb. scare, terrify, shock, alarm, terrorize, daunt. *Her pit bull frightens me.* **Ant.** reassure, encourage, comfort.

frightening adj. terrifying, scary, fearful, alarming, intimidating. *Last night's thunderstorm was frightening.* **Ant.** calming, reassuring, encouraging.

frigid adj. icy, freezing, cold, chilly, piercing, biting. *How can she enjoy swimming in the frigid water of a mountain lake?* **Ant.** warm, hot, temperate.

fringe n. border, margin, edge, rim, periphery, limit. *He lives on the fringe of poverty.* **Ant.** center, core, heart.

frivolous adj. silly, foolish, senseless, trivial, petty, unimportant. *His parents thought his comic book collection was a frivolous waste of money.* **Ant.** serious, sensible, important.

frolic vb. **1.** cavort, romp, frisk, play, prance, sport. *She enjoys watching the bear cubs frolic at the zoo.* –n. **2.** merriment, gaiety, fun, romp, revel, caper. *The millionaire's daughter enjoyed a life full of frolic.*

front n. **1.** head, top, fore, beginning, forefront, forepart. *He likes to sit at the front of the bus.* **2.** surface, face, facade, bearing, demeanor. *She tried to maintain a brave front despite her depression.* **3.** coalition, alliance, affiliation, union, merger. *The workers formed a united front against management's demands.* –adj. **4.** first, initial, beginning, headmost, foremost. *The only seats we could find were in the front row.* **Ant.** 1–4. back, rear.

frontier n. **1.** boundary, border, edge, perimeter, rim. *The frontier between the United States and Canada is not fortified.* **2.** hinterland, out-skirts, backwoods, bush, outback, boondocks. *Lewis and Clark led an expedition that explored America's frontier.*

frown vb. **1.** scowl, glower, pout, glare, mope, sulk. *She frowned at me when I told her I didn't like her new dress.* –n. **2.** scowl, glower, grimace, pout, glare. *His frown means he's unhappy with me.* **Ant.** 1–2. smile.

fruit n. yield, harvest, crop, return, reward, result. *He's living a life of ease enjoying the fruits of his labor.*

fruitful adj. fertile, plentiful, abundant, prolific, successful. *The Thanksgiving holiday was started by pilgrims celebrating their first fruitful harvest.* **Ant.** scarce, meager, scanty.

frustrate vb. foil, thwart, balk, defeat, discourage, hinder. *Efforts to help the flood victims are being frustrated by the impassable roads.* **Ant.** encourage, help, support.

fugitive n. refugee, runaway, renegade, deserter, exile. *Police mounted a massive search for the two fugitives.*

fulfill vb. satisfy, meet, accomplish, complete, finish, achieve. *She has to take only one more course to fulfill her graduation requirements.*

full adj. **1.** filled, stuffed, replete, saturated, brimming, loaded. *We won't need to stop for gas since we already have a full tank.* **2.** complete, whole, entire, solid, thorough. *He's feeling tired after putting in a full day at the office.* **Ant.** 1. empty, vacant, void. 2. incomplete, partial.

fumble vb. mishandle, mismanage, muff, bumble, botch. *He lost his job when he fumbled an important assignment.*

fun n. pleasure, amusement, enjoyment, merriment, gaiety, sport, recreation. *Are we having fun yet?*

function n. **1.** purpose, role, operation, job, use, capacity. *The function of this wire is to carry electricity to the starter.* **2.** ceremony, affair, gathering, party, celebration. *The local church held a fund-raising function.* –vb. **3.** work, act, perform, serve, operate. *Her watch also functions as a miniature calculator.*

functional adj. practical, suitable, useful, serviceable, efficient, workable. *A chair is a highly* *functional piece of furniture.* **Ant.** impractical, inefficient, unworkable.

fund *n.* **1.** savings, endowment, investment, account, portfolio. *She makes weekly contributions to her retirement fund.* **2.** wealth, riches, money, capital, assets, cash. *He invests his surplus funds in real estate.* –*vb.* **3.** finance, capitalize, endow, patronize, support. *She hasn't yet found anyone to fund her research project.*

fundamental *adj.* **1.** primary, basic, essential, major, indispensable, necessary. *A fundamental knowledge of English is essential for success.* –*n.* **2.** basic, rudiment, principle, essential, foundation. *She has mastered the fundamentals of computer programming.* **Ant. 1.** superficial, secondary, superfluous.

funny *adj.* humorous, amusing, comic, comical, odd, strange. *She told a funny story about the time she forgot her husband's name.* **Ant.** serious, grave, humorless.

furious *adj.* **1.** angry, irate, mad, incensed, infuriated, wrathful. *My parents were furious when I stayed out past midnight.* **2.** wild, turbulent, violent, raging, fierce, savage. *A furious windstorm knocked down all the local power lines.* **Ant. 1.** pleased, gratified, happy. **2.** mild, tame, calm.

furnish *vb.* equip, supply, provide, outfit, appoint, distribute. *The instructor will furnish everything needed for the class.*

further *adj.* **1.** additional, more, supplementary, extra, spare. *There will be further details on the eleven o'clock news.* **2.** farther, yonder, remoter, yon. *That further mountain is the one we're hoping to climb.* –*vb.* **3.** aid, assist, promote, advance, forward, help. *She hoped that taking night classes would further her career.* **Ant. 2.** nearer, closer. **3.** hinder, impede, obstruct.

furtive *adj.* secret, sly, covert, clandestine, hidden, concealed. *She stole a furtive glance at the boy sitting next to her.* **Ant.** open, direct, unconcealed.

fury *n.* **1.** rage, anger, wrath, ire, furor, frenzy. *She had to face her father's fury when she wrecked his car.* **2.** intensity, severity, might, power, force. *We were astonished by the fury of the storm.* **Ant. 1–2.** calmness, serenity, tranquillity.

fuse *vb.* join, merge, weld, link, blend, combine. *The chemist fused two metals together to create a new alloy.* **Ant.** separate, divide, split.

futile *adj.* useless, vain, unproductive, unavailing, ineffective. *He made a futile attempt to quit smoking.* **Ant.** effective, productive, successful.

future *adj.* coming, pending, imminent, prospective, later. *She agreed to meet him at some unspecified future date.* **Ant.** past, former, previous.

gadget *n.* device, contraption, instrument, appliance, tool. *I can't get this gadget to work.*

gain *vb.* **1.** get, earn, acquire, obtain, attain, win, achieve. *The runner managed to gain the lead after the tenth lap.* *–n.* **2.** increase, improvement, profit, advantage, addition, enrichment. *There was a gain in productivity amongst auto workers this year.* **Ant. 1.** lose, forfeit, worsen. **2.** decrease, decline, loss.

gait *n.* stride, step, tread, pace, walk, carriage. *Her thoroughbred runs with a graceful gait.*

gale *n.* wind, storm, tempest, blow, squall, outburst. *We shouldn't go sailing in this gale.*

gall *n.* **1.** boldness, nerve, cheek, audacity, impudence. *He has a lot of gall to ask me for a loan.* *–vb.* **2.** annoy, anger, irritate, irk, provoke, bother, vex. *Her arrogant attitude galled him.* **Ant. 1.** humility, meekness, politeness. **2.** please, cheer, delight.

gallant *adj.* **1.** brave, courageous, heroic, valiant, fearless, bold. *Sir Lancelot was a gallant knight.* **2.** courteous, polite, noble, civil, thoughtful, kind. *The gallant young woman gave her bus seat to an old man.* **Ant. 1.** cowardly, timid, fearful. **2.** rude, impolite, discourteous.

gallery *n.* **1.** passage, passageway, hallway, corridor, aisle. *A long gallery led to the ballroom.* **2.** museum, salon, studio, showroom, arcade. *She exhibited her sculptures at a local gallery.*

gallop *vb.* **1.** run, race, dash, rush, hurry, scurry, scamper. *The wild horses galloped away from the cowboys.* *–n.* **2.** run, gait, speed, clip, ride, dash. *The pony express rider managed a steady gallop to the next station.* **Ant. 1.** walk, crawl, amble. **2.** walk, crawl.

gamble *vb.* **1.** bet, risk, chance, wager, venture. *Don't gamble what you can't afford to lose.* *–n.* **2.** risk, chance, hazard, wager, bet, venture. *Investing in the stock market can be a gamble.*

game *n.* **1.** contest, competition, match, sport, tournament. *Tonight's basketball game will be for the city championship.* **2.** amusement, entertainment, pastime, recreation, fun. *The children went to the park to play games.* **3.** prey, quarry, victims, animals, fish, fowl. *I'll never understand why she likes to hunt big game.* **Ant. 2.** work, toil, labor.

gang *n.* group, band, crew, team, troop, ring, club, company. *A gang of boys were hanging around the drinking fountain.*

gangster *n.* hood, hoodlum, criminal, crook, thug. *The bank was held up by gangsters.*

gap *n.* opening, break, space, rift, breach, split, hole. *The mouse escaped through a gap in the floor .*

gape *vb.* stare, gaze, glare, gawk, peer, ogle. *She gaped at the enormous amount of food on the table.*

garbage *n.* trash, rubbish, waste, junk, debris, refuse. *Please pick up the garbage on the lawn.*

garbled *adj.* distorted, jumbled, confused, warped, twisted. *She could not understand the garbled loudspeaker announcement.* **Ant.** clear, straight, understandable.

garment *n.* clothing, clothes, attire, garb, apparel, outfit, dress. *She hung her garments in the closet.*

garnish *vb.* **1.** decorate, embellish, adorn, enhance, trim, deck. *She garnished her salad with sprigs of watercress.* *–n.* **2.** decoration, ornament, adornment, trimming, embellishment. *A little garnish on the plate will make the food look more attractive.*

gash *n.* **1.** slash, wound, cut, slit, slice. *The pirate had an ugly gash on his right cheek.* *–vb.* **2.** cut, slice, wound, slash, tear, slit, rip. *She gashed her hand on a piece of broken glass.*

gasp *vb.* **1.** pant, puff, huff, wheeze, gulp, choke. *The hiker gasped for air as she reached the high mountain pass.* *–n.* **2.** gulp, wheeze, huff, heave, pant, puff. *He made one last gasp before dying.*

gate *n.* entrance, entry, portal, door, doorway. *Please close the gate so the dog won't get out.*

gather *vb.* **1.** group, assemble, collect, accumulate, mass, convene. *A small crowd gathered around the street performers.* **2.** harvest, reap, collect, garner, take. *It is time to gather the fruit from the trees.* **3.** understand, assume, conclude, deduce, infer, reckon. *I gather that dinner will be late.* **Ant. 1.** separate, disperse, disassemble.

gathering *n.* assembly, crowd, company, group, grouping, throng. *We are expecting a large gathering for our school reunion.*

gaudy *adj.* loud, flashy, garish, vulgar, tawdry, tasteless. *Our neighbor placed a gaudy pink flamingo in his garden.* **Ant.** tasteful, subtle, quiet.

gauge *n.* **1.** measure, test, standard, yardstick, model, pattern. *Test scores are used as a gauge to determine scholastic success.* **2.** tester, measurer, instrument, meter. *Tire pressure can be checked with a gauge.* *–vb.* **3.** estimate, measure, assess, judge, evaluate, appraise. *It is difficult to gauge distances by mere eyesight.*

gaunt *adj.* lean, thin, scrawny, skinny, lanky, bony. *The gaunt man looked like he hadn't eaten in a week.* **Ant.** plump, fat, obese.

gay *adj.* **1.** happy, cheerful, jolly, merry, joyful, joyous, gleeful. *Everyone at the party was in a gay mood.* **2.** colorful, bright, brilliant, vivid, intense, showy. *The painter used gay colors to brighten up the reception area.* **Ant. 1.** gloomy, sad, solemn. **2.** dull, sedate, drab.

gaze *vb.* **1.** stare, peer, look, gape, watch, scan. *I could gaze at the stars for hours.* *–n.* **2.** look, stare, gape, scrutiny, glare. *The child looked upon the magician with a gaze of wonderment.*

gear *n.* **1.** outfit, equipment, apparatus, effects, belongings. *Have you collected all your camping gear?* **2.** mechanism, cog, cogwheel, cam, wheel. *The machine worked perfectly after we oiled its gears.*

general *adj.* **1.** typical, regular, usual, conventional, customary. *Shaking hands is a general form of greeting.* **2.** basic, comprehensive, overall, vague, inexact, indefinite. *She has a general knowledge of Spanish.* **3.** widespread, prevalent, universal, common, popular. *There will be a general strike tomorrow.* **Ant. 1.** uncommon, unique, unusual. **2.** exact, specific, specialized. **3.** local, limited, individual.

generally *adv.* usually, commonly, ordinarily, chiefly, normally, frequently. *I generally go to bed at ten o'clock.* **Ant.** rarely, seldom, occasionally.

generate *vb.* create, produce, make, cause, devise, develop. *The old battery barely generated enough electricity to start the car.* **Ant.** destroy, eliminate, demolish.

generous *adj.* **1.** charitable, unselfish, kindly, considerate, thoughtful. *Your generous offer of help is appreciated.* **2.** ample, large, liberal, abundant, big. *There is a generous amount of space in our backyard.* **Ant. 1.** mean, selfish, miserly. **2.** tiny, small, meager.

genial *adj.* friendly, agreeable, cordial, pleasant, cheerful, comfortable. *We enjoyed the restaurant's genial atmosphere.* **Ant.** uncomfortable, unfriendly, unpleasant.

genius *n.* **1.** talent, ability, gift, flair, aptitude, brilliance. *Mozart's genius is still appreciated today.* **2.** mastermind, master, prodigy, brain, expert. *You don't have to be a genius to work a computer.* **Ant. 2.** idiot, moron, imbecile.

gentle *adj.* **1.** kind, tender, warmhearted, pleasant, harmless, docile. *He may act tough, but he's actually a very gentle person.* **2.** easy, mild, light, moderate, smooth, soft. *We hiked up a gentle grade to the waterfall.* **Ant. 1.** mean, cruel, tough. **2.** hard, difficult, rough.

genuine *adj.* real, true, actual, factual, authentic. *The merchant assured the magician that his magic ring was the genuine article.* **Ant.** false, phony, fake, counterfeit.

gesture *n.* **1.** sign, movement, signal, motion, indication. *At an art auction, buyers use hand gestures to make bids.* –*vb.* **2.** sign, wave, signal, motion, beckon. *The usher gestured for us to follow him.*

get *vb.* **1.** obtain, acquire, receive, attain, gain, secure. *She got an award for selling the most raffle tickets.* **2.** persuade, cause, induce, convince, influence. *How can I get you to change your mind?* **3.** become, turn, grow, begin, go. *Public speaking gets easier as you practice it.* **4.** prepare, make, fix, do, ready. *He's getting dinner ready.* **5.** understand, realize, learn, comprehend, grasp, catch. *I didn't get the meaning of her story.* **6.** come, arrive, approach, reach, near. *When will we get there?* **Ant. 1.** lose, surrender, forfeit. **2.** dissuade, discourage, deter. **3.** remain, stay, continue. **5.** misunderstand, confuse, misinterpret. **6.** leave, go, depart.

ghastly *adj.* horrible, gruesome, hideous, terrible, dreadful, frightful. *She was frightened by the goblin's ghastly appearance.* **Ant.** beautiful, attractive, lovely.

ghost *n.* **1.** phantom, specter, spirit, spook, shade, wraith. *That house is haunted by a ghost.* **2.** trace, suggestion, hint, shadow. *He doesn't have a ghost of a chance to win the race.*

giant *adj.* **1.** huge, gigantic, enormous, monstrous, colossal, mammoth. *Tokyo is being attacked by a giant lizard.* –*n.* **2.** colossus, titan, behemoth, monster, ogre. *The sorcerer's treasure was guarded by a two-headed giant.* **Ant. 1.** tiny, small, miniature. **2.** dwarf, midget, pygmy.

gift *n.* **1.** present, offering, contribution, donation, grant. *She brought a gift to the birthday party.* **2.** talent, ability, aptitude, genius, flair, knack. *He has a gift for getting into trouble.*

gifted *adj.* talented, skilled, adept, capable, creative, inventive. *The talent contest featured many gifted performers.* **Ant.** untalented, unskilled, mediocre.

gigantic *adj.* giant, huge, enormous, monstrous, immense, colossal, titanic. *A gigantic spaceship hovered over the city.* **Ant.** small, tiny, little.

gimmick *n.* stunt, scheme, trick, angle, ruse, ploy. *Advertisers use various gimmicks to sell their products.*

give *vb.* **1.** provide, supply, present, bestow, grant, donate, furnish. *Her parents gave her a pony for her birthday.* **2.** yield, collapse, buckle, fail, loosen, slacken. *The bridge gave under the truck's weight.* **3.** allow, permit, grant, offer, allot, allocate. *Motor vehicles should always give the right-of-way to pedestrians.* **Ant. 1.** get, receive, take. **3.** deny, disallow, refuse.

glad *adj.* happy, delighted, cheerful, pleased, joyful, elated. *I'm so glad you could come to my party.* **Ant.** sad, unhappy, upset, awful.

glamorous *adj.* attractive, exciting, alluring, enchanting, charming. *She thought becoming a fashion model would be glamorous.* **Ant.** dull, ordinary, tedious.

glance *vb.* **1.** look, scan, browse, peek, glimpse, peer. *He glanced at the calendar to check the time of his next appointment.* **2.** ricochet, reflect, bounce, rebound, skim. *The rock glanced off the wall and landed harmlessly on the ground.* –*n.* **3.** look, glimpse, squint, peek, peep. *She stole a quick glance at the boy sitting next to her.* **Ant. 1.** study, stare, examine. **3.** examination, scrutiny, inspection.

glare *vb.* **1.** stare, scowl, glower, frown, scrutinize. *Why is that rude man glaring at me?* **2.** shine, flare, blaze, flash, dazzle. *Bright sunlight glared off the snow.* –*n.* **3.** light, shine, brightness, glimmer, flash, brilliance. *Sunglasses will eliminate the glare.* **4.** stare, scowl, frown, glower, look. *The ogre's fierce glare told me that I was in trouble.*

glaring *adj.* **1.** flagrant, obvious, conspicuous, blatant, prominent. *The telephone company made a glaring error when they charged me $10,000 for a three-minute call to Idaho.* **2.** bright, brilliant, intense, blazing, strong. *She painted her car a glaring shade of red.* **Ant. 1.** inobvious, inconspicuous, hidden. **2.** soft, subdued.

gleam *n.* **1.** glimmer, shine, radiance, sparkle, reflection, glow. *His new car has a beautiful gleam.* –*vb.* **2.** shine, sparkle, glimmer, glow, glisten, beam, radiate. *A lantern gleamed from the far end of the corridor.*

glee *n.* joy, merriment, joyfulness, gladness, ecstasy. *The children shouted with glee when we told them we were going to the circus.* **Ant.** sadness, sorrow, dejection.

glide *vb.* slide, flow, skim, coast, skate, float, slip, fly. *The sailboat glided gracefully over the water.* **Ant.** stagger, crawl, shuffle.

glimmer *n.* **1.** gleam, twinkling, glimmering, shimmer, flicker, flash. *All she could see of the retreating car was the glimmer of its rear lights.* **2.** hint, suggestion, trace, speck, inkling. *There was only a glimmer of hope that the crash victims survived.* *–vb.* **3.** twinkle, flicker, shine, sparkle, shimmer. *Stars glimmered in the night sky.*

glimpse *vb.* **1.** observe, witness, view, sight, spot, see. *We glimpsed a deer running through the forest.* *–n.* **2.** glance, peep, look, view, squint, peep. *She caught a glimpse of the burglar.* **Ant. 1.** stare, scrutinize.

glisten *vb.* shine, glimmer, sparkle, gleam, glow, flash, twinkle. *Her wet hair glistened in the sunlight.*

glitter *vb.* **1.** sparkle, shine, glisten, glimmer, twinkle. *From the top of the hill we could see city lights glittering below.* *–n.* **2.** glamour, grandeur, splendor, excitement, thrill. *The farm boy left home to seek the glitter of Hollywood.*

gloat *vb.* bask, brag, revel, triumph, delight, wallow. *A good winner does not gloat over her victories.* **Ant.** despair, regret, envy, grudge.

global *adj.* worldwide, universal, international, planetary, widespread. *The border dispute had global significance.* **Ant.** local, regional, limited.

globe *n.* **1.** ball, sphere, orb, spheroid, oval. *The Japanese use small glass globes as floats for their fishing nets.* **2.** Earth, planet, world, geosphere, land. *Ferdinand Magellan was the first person to sail around the globe.*

gloom *n.* **1.** sadness, unhappiness, misery, despair, dejection. *War has brought much gloom upon the Earth.* **2.** dimness, darkness, shade, shadow, murkiness. *The gloom of the cave was broken by the spelunker's lantern.* **Ant. 1.** happiness, cheer, delight. **2.** light, brightness, brilliance.

gloomy *adj.* **1.** sad, unhappy, depressed, miserable, downcast, dismal, cheerless. *She has been in a gloomy mood since she lost the contest.* **2.** dreary, dark, murky, overcast, shadowy, dim, dull. *The poor lighting in the room created a gloomy atmosphere.* **Ant. 1.** happy, cheerful, gay. **2.** bright, brilliant, sunny.

glorious *adj.* wonderful, splendid, marvelous, gorgeous, superb, beautiful. *It's a glorious day to go surfing.* **Ant.** awful, terrible, horrible.

glory *n.* **1.** honor, praise, fame, prestige, recognition. *The young police officer had dreams of glory.* **2.** grandeur, splendor, magnificence, elegance, majesty. *The full moon rose in a blaze of glory.* **Ant. 1.** dishonor, disgrace, obscurity.

glow *vb.* **1.** shine, flicker, sparkle, glimmer, blaze, glare. *His secret decoder ring also glows in the dark.* *–n.* **2.** shine, light, brightness, gleam, shimmer, radiance. *The candle's glow was the only visible light.*

glowing *adj.* **1.** favorable, rave, passionate, enthusiastic, complimentary. *We received glowing reports on the work of our volunteers.* **2.** ruddy, vivid, bright, flushed. *I could tell the child was healthy by her glowing face.* **Ant. 1.** critical, disapproving, condemning. **2.** pale, pallid, white.

glue *n.* **1.** adhesive, paste, cement, mucilage, mortar. *You need to add more glue if you want the picture to stick.* *–vb.* **2.** stick, paste, cement, affix, bind, fasten. *He glued the model airplane parts together.*

glut *n.* **1.** surplus, excess, overload, oversupply, abundance. *A glut of fruit resulted in lower produce prices.* *–vb.* **2.** saturate, flood, fill, overload, stuff. *Holiday traffic glutted the freeways.* **Ant. 1.** scarcity, shortage, want.

gnarled *adj.* knotty, knotted, twisted, contorted, distorted, crooked. *An old gnarled tree stood in the center of the cemetery.* **Ant.** straight, smooth, unblemished.

go *vb.* **1.** leave, depart, exit, withdraw, retire. *We need to be going very soon.* **2.** move, proceed, progress, advance, travel, approach. *Anyone want to go to a movie?* **3.** work, run, function, operate, perform, act. *How do you make this machine go?* **4.** reach, run, stretch, extend, expand. *This trail goes about ten miles to an abandoned mine.* **5.** fit, suit, agree, belong, conform, blend, harmonize. *Pickles and ice cream do not go together.* **Ant. 1.** stay, remain, arrive, return.

goad *vb.* urge, push, prod, incite, spur, provoke, exhort. *Don't let anyone goad you into doing something illegal.*

goal *n.* aim, purpose, object, objective, end, target, ambition. *It will be easier to succeed if you clearly define your goals.*

good *adj.* **1.** fine, excellent, pleasant, enjoyable, agreeable, nice. *Did you have a good time at the fair?* **2.** virtuous, kind, honorable, upright, honest, obedient, moral. *Santa Claus knows if you've been bad or good.* **3.** proper, suitable, fit, right, useful, adequate, capable. *A canoe is good for calm waters, but we'll need a raft for the rapids.* –*n.* **4.** benefit, welfare, advantage, interest, gain, success. *It is patriotic to work for the good of your country.* **5.** virtue, value, worth, merit, kindness. *There is a little good in everyone.* **Ant. 1.** terrible, bad, unpleasant. **2.** bad, disobedient, naughty. **3.** improper, worthless, useless. **4.** loss, harm, disadvantage. **5.** evil, wickedness, corruption.

gorge *n.* **1.** canyon, ravine, crevice, abyss, chasm. *The wagon train could not find a way across the deep gorge.* –*vb.* **2.** stuff, glut, fill, cram, sate. *I have a stomachache because I gorged myself during dinner.*

gorgeous *adj.* beautiful, pretty, lovely, attractive, stunning, glorious, splendid. *The hills are gorgeous when the leaves turn gold in autumn.* **Ant.** ugly, drab, plain.

gossip *n.* **1.** rumor, hearsay, chatter, babble, talk. *Movie stars must get tired of all the gossip about them.* **2.** gossiper, tattler, snoop, meddler, chatterbox, busybody. *Don't believe anything a gossip tells you.* –*vb.* **3.** talk, tattle, prattle, blab, chatter, babble. *I have better things to do than to sit around and gossip.*

govern *vb.* manage, direct, lead, control, run, guide, supervise, regulate. *Our weekly meetings are governed by the club president.* **Ant.** follow, comply, obey.

government *n.* administration, management, control, regulation, rule, guidance. *In a democracy, government is controlled by the people.*

gown *n.* dress, apparel, attire, frock, garment. *She bought a new gown for the formal dinner party.*

grab *vb.* **1.** grasp, seize, grip, clutch, clasp, hold, take. *He grabbed his child's arm and pulled her back to the curb.* –*n.* **2.** grasp, lunge, pass, clutch, seizure. *She made a grab for the frog, but it hopped away.* **Ant. 1.** release, free, loose.

grace *n.* **1.** charm, elegance, gracefulness, culture, refinement, manners. *The hostess handled the uninvited guest with grace.* **2.** mercy, charity, pardon, forgiveness, leniency. *The criminal was freed by the grace of the empress.* –*vb.* **3.** honor, dignify, glorify, exalt, favor. *The club's founder graced the banquet with his presence.* **4.** adorn, embellish, enrich, beautify, ornament, decorate. *We graced the funeral site with flowers.* **Ant. 1.** clumsiness, crudeness, coarseness. **2.** cruelty, harshness, disfavor. **3.** dishonor, shame, insult.

graceful *adj.* elegant, limber, lovely, beautiful, delicate. *Ballet dancers are very graceful.* **Ant.** clumsy, awkward, graceless.

gracious *adj.* kind, courteous, polite, friendly, cordial, genial. *Her gracious manners were appreciated by the guests.* **Ant.** haughty, unkind, cool.

grade *n.* **1.** incline, slope, ramp, slant, tilt. *The cross-country skier found the steep grade to be tough going.* **2.** category, type, class, degree, level, step, group. *Crossword puzzles are often classified into grades of difficulty.* –*vb.* **3.** order, classify, rank, sort, class, evaluate, arrange. *The judges graded the contestants according to their talent and creativity.*

gradual *adj.* slow, moderate, steady, measured, continual, continuous. *The tide's gradual advancement eventually destroyed the sand castle.* **Ant.** sudden, instant, abrupt.

graduate *vb.* **1.** finish, complete, succeed, prevail, promote. *After four years of college, I finally graduate this semester.* **2.** calibrate, mark, score, measure, grade. *This thermometer is graduated in centigrade degrees.* –*n.* **3.** alumnus, alumna, bachelor, fellow. *She is a recent law-school graduate.* **Ant. 1.** fail, flunk, drop out.

graft *vb.* **1.** join, implant, transplant, set, inset, splice. *The botanist grafted two different plants together.* –*n.* **2.** transplant, implant, inset, insert. *His burned arm was treated with a skin graft.* **3.** corruption, bribery, fraud, theft, cheating, extortion. *The new governor's first priority is to eliminate political graft.*

grand *adj.* **1.** royal, majestic, stately, impressive, magnificent. *She lives in a grand mansion in Beverly Hills.* **2.** total, complete, full, comprehensive, final. *The grand total of his prize was twenty thousand dollars.* **3.** fine, good, wonderful, great, superb, marvelous. *They had a grand time at the picnic.* **Ant. 1.** mediocre, inferior, unimpressive. **2.** partial, incomplete, fractional. **3.** bad, awful, terrible.

grandeur *n.* splendor, majesty, glory, magnificence, resplendence. *The backpackers delighted in the grandeur of the wilderness.* **Ant.** plainness, squalor, commonness.

grant *vb.* **1.** allow, permit, give, sanction, award, bestow, present. *A genie granted three wishes to the poor fisherman.* **2** concede, allow, accept, concur, admit, agree. *He finally granted that my conclusions were correct.* *–n.* **3.** allotment, award, allowance, bequest, endowment, gift. *The researcher needs a grant if she is to continue her studies.* **Ant. 1.** disallow, deny, refuse. **2.** reject, dispute, deny.

grapple *vb.* contend, struggle, battle, cope, deal. *I don't feel like grappling with unhappy customers today.*

grasp *vb.* **1.** seize, grab, clutch, grip, catch, hold. *She grasped at her toy boat as it floated down the creek.* **2.** understand, perceive, comprehend, see, follow. *I can't seem to grasp the meaning of your story .* *–n.* **3.** hold, reach, possession, grip, clasp. *The football was almost in my grasp.* **4.** understanding, perception, knowledge, sense. *My grasp of Latin is very poor.* **Ant. 1.** release, free, loose. **2.** misunderstand, confuse, misjudge.

grateful *adj.* thankful, indebted, pleased, gratified, appreciative. *She was grateful for the cool weather.* **Ant.** ungrateful, thankless, unappreciative.

gratify *vb.* please, satisfy, delight, content, charm. *I was gratified with my test results.* **Ant.** disappoint, displease, dissatisfy.

gratitude *n.* thanks, thankfulness, appreciation, gratefulness. *I wish to express my gratitude for your help.* **Ant.** ingratitude, ungratefulness.

grave *n.* **1.** tomb, crypt, plot, vault, mausoleum. *The vampire rose from his grave.* *–adj.* **2.** serious, thoughtful, solemn, somber, earnest. *The librarian gave me a grave look that meant "Be quiet and study."* **3.** urgent, important, critical, crucial, vital, severe. *Pollution of the Earth is of grave concern to all.* **Ant. 2.** playful, merry, gay. **3.** unimportant, trivial, minor.

graze *vb.* **1.** feed, browse, eat, pasture. *Cows were grazing in the meadow.* **2.** brush, glance, rub, scrape, scratch, skim. *Branches grazed his arms as he ran through the forest.*

grease *n.* **1.** oil, fat, lard, lubricant, ointment, salve. *She doesn't like foods that have a lot of grease.* *–vb.* **2.** oil, lubricate, anoint, daub, smear. *You need to grease your bike chain.*

great *adj.* **1.** big, large, huge, enormous, immense, vast, tremendous. *Buffalo used to travel in great herds across the plains.* **2.** important, remarkable, outstanding, famous, notable, prominent. *We should learn about the great leaders of our country.* **3.** chief, primary, leading, important, major, principal. *One of the great concerns of the people is the rising crime rate.* **Ant. 1.** small, tiny, meager. **2.** unimportant, trivial, unremarkable. **3.** minor, lesser, secondary.

greatly *adv.* tremendously, immensely, enormously, vastly, largely. *I greatly appreciate your help.* **Ant.** little, somewhat.

greed *n.* hunger, craving, avarice, greediness, desire. *Greed for gold destroyed the two miners' friendship.* **Ant.** unselfishness, generosity, charity.

greedy *adj.* selfish, grasping, avaricious, miserly, desirous. *Don't be so greedy and give me some of your cake.* **Ant.** unselfish, generous, charitable.

greet *vb.* welcome, receive, meet, address, accept, hail. *Tourists in Hawaii are greeted by girls wearing leis.* **Ant.** ignore, neglect, shun.

grief *n.* sorrow, sadness, distress, misery, agony, anguish, despair. *The beggar's life was one of much grief.* **Ant.** happiness, joy, bliss.

grieve *vb.* **1.** mourn, weep, lament, bemoan, deplore. *He grieved the death of his friend.* **2.** distress, sorrow, sadden, depress, dishearten. *It grieves me that nations cannot live peacefully* *together.* **Ant. 1.** praise, celebrate, rejoice. **2.** delight, comfort, please.

grievous *adj.* dreadful, horrible, shameful, painful, unfortunate, tragic. *The assassination of President Kennedy was a grievous incident in American history.* **Ant.** pleasant, happy, joyous.

grill *vb.* **1.** interrogate, examine, question, quiz. *I wish my parents wouldn't grill me about where I've been.* **2.** barbecue, broil, cook, sear, fry. *She grilled the steak over a charcoal fire.*

grim *adj.* **1.** severe, harsh, stern, cold, hard, forbidding. *The grim-looking border guard asked to see my passport.* **2.** ghastly, sinister, horrible, terrible, grisly, gruesome. *The pile of bones in the werewolf's den left a grim impression on its discoverer.* **Ant. 1.** kind, merciful, gentle. **2.** pleasing, pleasant, cheerful.

grime *n.* dirt, filth, soil, mess, dust. *He hosed the grime off the sidewalk.*

grin *vb.* **1.** smile, beam, smirk, laugh. *She grinned at the chipmunk's antics.* *-n.* **2.** smile, smirk, beam, simper. *Wipe that silly grin off your face.* **Ant. 1.** frown, snarl, scowl. **2.** frown, sneer, grimace.

grind *vb.* **1.** sharpen, whet, smooth, polish, file. *The swashbuckler's sword was ground to a sharp edge.* **2.** crush, crumble, pulverize, crunch, pound. *The giant was grinding rocks into powder with his bare hands.* *-n.* **3.** toil, bore, tedium, drudgery, labor. *This job has become a real grind.* **Ant. 3.** joy, pleasure, amusement.

grip *vb.* **1.** hold, clasp, grasp, clutch, clench, grab. *The softball player gripped her bat tightly.* **2.** hold, attract, retain, enthrall, fascinate. *I'm impressed by a movie that grips the viewer's interest till the end.* *-n.* **3.** hold, grasp, clutch, clinch, clasp, control. *She had a pretty tight grip on the rope.* **Ant. 1.** release, free, loose. **2.** lose, repel, bore.

gripe *n.* **1.** complaint, peeve, grievance, protest, lament. *The chef was tired of the customers' gripes about her cooking.* *-vb.* **2.** complain, grumble, fuss, grouch, whine, protest, mutter. *He was always griping about his problems.* **Ant. 1.** praise, complaint, compliment, flattery. **2.** approve, flatter, praise.

grisly *adj.* gruesome, grim, shocking, hideous, horrid, horrible, frightful. *His grisly zombie costume won first prize at the Halloween party.* **Ant.** pleasant, handsome, pretty.

grit *vb.* **1.** clench, gnash, grind, grate, scrape. *She gritted her teeth and ignored the insults.* *-n.* **2.** dirt, sand, gravel, dust, soot. *The sandstorm left tons of grit all over the house.* **3.** guts, nerve, spunk, courage, pluck, spirit, fortitude. *The early American pioneers had a lot of grit.* **Ant. 3.** cowardice, meekness, timidity.

groan *vb.* **1.** moan, complain, sob, mumble, grumble, whimper. *She groaned when she saw the poor condition of her house.* *-n.* **2.** whine, wail, moan, whimper, cry. *We heard a mysterious groan come from behind the bushes.*

groggy *adj.* dazed, shaky, unsteady, muddled, confused, dizzy, sleepy. *She usually feels a little groggy in the mornings.* **Ant.** alert, awake, sharp.

groom *vb.* **1.** brush, clean, preen, comb, spruce. *He took his dog to the pet shop to be groomed.* **2.** train, prepare, coach, develop, educate. *The new worker is being groomed for a management position.*

groove *n.* **1.** rut, trench, channel, furrow, slot. *A phonograph needle follows the groove on a record.* **2.** habit, routine, rut, custom, pace. *I slowly got into the groove of working on an assembly line.*

grope *vb.* probe, fumble, feel, search, hunt, flounder. *He groped in the grass for his lost contact lens.*

gross *adj.* **1.** total, entire, whole, complete. *What is the gross profit of your business?* **2.** rude, coarse, improper, crude, obscene, vulgar, indecent. *No one is impressed by gross language.* **3.** outrageous, glaring, extreme, complete, flagrant. *Did you really expect to get away with such a gross violation of the rules?* **Ant. 1.** net, partial, limited. **2.** proper, clean, decent. **3.** vague, obscure, minor.

grotesque *adj.* bizarre, queer, weird, strange, freakish, fantastic, unnatural. *A grotesque gargoyle flew into the village.* **Ant.** normal, ordinary, routine.

grouchy *adj.* grumpy, cross, testy, irritable, surly, sulky. *My coach gets grouchy when we lose.* **Ant.** cheerful, agreeable, pleasant.

ground *n.* **1.** land, earth, soil, turf, dirt, terrain. *She was relieved when the plane finally landed on the ground.* **2.** field, area, region, territory, property. *Traveling salesmen have to cover a lot of ground.* **3.** basis, reason, foundation, rationale, motive, cause. *Do you have grounds for your action?*

group *n.* **1.** collection, gathering, assembly, bunch, crowd, band. *A small group of people gathered around the campfire.* **2.** set, category, division, class, batch. *Swedish, Danish and German are all part of the Indo-European language group.* –*vb.* **3.** classify, collect, sort, arrange, organize, gather, assemble. *We grouped the test results according to their final scores.* **Ant. 3.** separate, divide, disperse.

grove *n.* thicket, copse, stand, orchard, woods. *There's a grove of oak trees near our house.*

grovel *vb.* cringe, cower, fawn, stoop, kowtow. *The slave groveled in the presence of his master.*

grow *vb.* **1.** develop, expand, extend, enlarge, increase. *The dragon grew to an enormous size.* **2.** cultivate, breed, raise, tend, produce, nurture. *My mother grows tomatoes in our garden.* **3.** turn, become, wax, develop, get. *My sick friend is growing stronger every day.* **Ant. 1.** shrink, decrease, lessen.

growth *n.* development, increase, growing, progress, expansion, advancement. *The doctor kept a chart of the child's growth.* **Ant.** decline, decrease, regression.

grudge *n.* **1.** resentment, bitterness, spite, malice, ill will. *She's held a grudge against him ever since he beat her in checkers.* –*vb.* **2.** begrudge, resent, envy, refuse, deny. *You shouldn't grudge her small victory.* **Ant. 1.** liking, goodwill, friendliness. **2.** allow, accept, celebrate.

grueling *adj.* difficult, hard, strenuous, tiring, exhausting, taxing, trying. *The last mile of the race was a grueling uphill run.* **Ant.** easy, light, effortless.

gruesome *adj.* ugly, hideous, horrible, horrid, frightening, scary, repulsive. *The Phantom of the Opera removed his mask to reveal a gruesome face.* **Ant.** beautiful, handsome, pleasing.

gruff *adj.* surly, grumpy, rude, crude, abrupt, blunt, coarse, rough. *The waiter's gruff manner ruined our dinner party.* **Ant.** polite, pleasant, civil, friendly.

grumble *vb.* complain, gripe, fuss, protest, growl, mutter, grouch. *He grumbled about the high price of our theater tickets.* **Ant.** praise, compliment, applaud.

grumpy *adj.* grouchy, crabby, cranky, irritable, surly, moody, testy. *Goldilocks met three grumpy bears.* **Ant.** pleasant, cheerful, sweet.

guarantee *n.* **1.** warranty, promise, pledge, assurance, insurance, commitment. *Our flying carpets come with a six-month guarantee.* –*vb.* **2.** promise, pledge, assure, insure, certify, warrant, vouch. *I guarantee there will be no charge for repairs.*

guard *vb.* **1.** protect, defend, watch, shield, patrol, oversee. *The loyal dog guarded his master's property.* –*n.* **2.** sentry, watchman, sentinel, protector, defender, guardian. *A guard was appointed to watch the queen's jewelry.*

guarded *adj.* defensive, cautious, discreet, careful, restrained. *The old prospector was guarded about the location of his gold mine.* **Ant.** open, frank, careless.

guardian *n.* protector, trustee, custodian, caretaker, warden, keeper. *Cinderella's stepmother was a terrible guardian.* **Ant.** foe, enemy, opponent.

guess *vb.* **1.** assume, suppose, think, estimate, believe, imagine. *I guess the meeting will start late.* –*n.* **2.** estimate, opinion, assumption, notion, theory. *Your guess is as good as mine.* **Ant. 1.** know, prove, see. **2.** fact, truth, actuality.

guest *n.* visitor, caller, patron, customer, company. *We will be having some guests for dinner.* **Ant.** host, hostess.

guide *vb.* **1.** lead, direct, conduct, escort, accompany, steer, pilot. *Sacajewa guided the Lewis and Clark expedition.* –*n.* **2.** escort, conductor, director, pilot, leader. *We hired a guide to take us through the caves.* **3.** example, model, pattern, sign, beacon, directory. *She used my dress as a guide for making hers.* **Ant. 1.** follow, misguide, mislead.

guile *n.* trickery, trickiness, cunning, deception, deceit, slyness. *The thief used guile to steal the woman's jewels.* **Ant.** honesty, sincerity, truthfulness.

guilt *n.* **1.** fault, sin, offense, crime, misdeed, misbehavior, misconduct. *The criminal refused to admit her guilt.* **2.** shame, disgrace, dishonor, humiliation, blame, wrong. *He felt guilt over the way he treated his neighbor.* **Ant. 1.** innocence, sinlessness, honesty. **2.** honor, pride, esteem.

guilty *adj.* **1.** criminal, illegal, accountable, responsible, culpable. *The defendant was found guilty.* **2.** ashamed, regretful, sorry, shameful, sheepish. *If you didn't lie, then why do you look so guilty?* **Ant. 1.** innocent, guiltless, blameless. **2.** proud, noble, satisfied.

gulf *n.* **1.** bay, estuary, fjord, cove, lagoon. *Let's go sailing in the gulf.* **2.** gap, abyss, rift, space, distance. *There's a large gulf between developed and undeveloped nations.*

gullible *adj.* naive, innocent, trustful, trusting, unsuspecting, easy. *The little girl was so gullible, she believed that the Moon is really made out of cheese.* **Ant.** skeptical, suspicious, cynical.

gully *n.* ravine, defile, gorge, channel, furrow, trench. *Erosion formed small gullies on the hillside.*

gulp *vb.* **1.** swallow, swill, guzzle, bolt, wolf. *The dog gulped down its dinner.* *–n.* **2.** swallow, swig, mouthful, sip, dose. *She felt better after taking several large gulps of water.*

gust *n.* blast, outburst, burst, flurry, puff, rush, draft. *His hat was blown away by a gust of wind.*

gutter *vb.* sewer, drain, ditch, trough, channel. *She swept the fallen leaves out of the gutter.*

gyp *vb.* **1.** cheat, defraud, swindle, beat, con, trick. *He tried to gyp me out of my money.* *–n.* **2.** cheat, swindle, fraud, hoax, con. *Ten dollars for a candy bar is a real gyp.*

habit *n.* practice, custom, routine, tendency, trait, ritual. *She has a habit of always interrupting me.*

habitation *n.* home, residence, dwelling, house, housing, lodging. *The traditional habitation of the Eskimo is called an igloo.*

habitual *adj.* customary, usual, routine, regular, normal. *He can't get started in the morning without his habitual cup of coffee.* **Ant.** occasional, rare, uncommon.

hack *vb.* chop, cut, axe, split, slash, gash, slice, mangle. *Soldiers hacked their way through the thick jungle.*

haggard *adj.* weary, worn, gaunt, drawn, pale, fatigued, tried. *She looked haggard after her long hike through the desert.* **Ant.** refreshed, energetic, robust.

haggle *vb.* argue, quarrel, bicker, dispute, disagree. *They're constantly, haggling over whose turn it is to use the computer.*

hail *vb.* **1.** call, summon, signal, flag, shout at. *She hailed a taxi.* **2.** greet, welcome, acclaim, cheer, applaud. *Everyone hailed the good news from the peace conference.* **Ant. 2.** ignore, disregard, condemn.

hale *adj.* healthy, robust, hearty, fit, sound, well. *It's a pleasure to see you looking so hale again.* **Ant.** unhealthy, sick, weak.

halfhearted *adj.* lukewarm, cool, indifferent, passive, apathetic, lackluster, unenthusiastic. *His halfhearted attempt at the long jump failed to qualify him for the finals.* **Ant.** wholehearted, enthusiastic, eager.

hallowed *adj.* sacred, holy, consecrated, blessed, sanctified, dedicated. *The evil demon could not enter hallowed grounds.* **Ant.** profane, secular, unholy, unsanctified.

hallucination *n.* delusion, illusion, mirage, vision, fantasy, dream, apparition. *Her hallucinations were caused by illness.*

halt *vb.* **1.** stop, cease, wait, desist, pause, hold, quit. *Traffic halted to let the ducklings cross the road.* –*n.* **2.** stop, end, finish, discontinuance, close, standstill, termination. *Let's put a halt to senseless violence.* **Ant. 1.** continue, proceed, start. **2.** beginning, start, resumption.

hammer *n.* **1.** mallet, gavel, sledge, maul, claw hammer. *Where are the hammer and nails?* –*vb.* **2.** pound, drive, beat, tap, pummel, bang, knock, batter. *The carpenter hammered the pieces of wood together.*

hamper *vb.* hinder, obstruct, impede, prevent, restrain, thwart, inhibit. *The muddy track hampered the horse's performance.* **Ant.** aid, assist, promote, help.

hand *n.* **1.** assistance, aid, help, support, lift. *Do you need a hand with painting the house?* **2.** role, part, share, responsibility. *The principal had a hand in getting an orchestra to play at the school fair.* **3.** laborer, worker, employee, aide, assistant. *We need to hire more hands to work on the farm.* –*vb.* **4.** give, pass, deliver, present, transmit, transfer. *Please hand me the salt.*

handicap *n.* **1.** disadvantage, hindrance, drawback, impediment, burden, disability. *His stuttering was a handicap when meeting new people.* –*vb.* **2.** impede, hamper, hinder, disable, inhibit, frustrate, limit. *Severe heat handicapped their efforts to battle the fire.* **Ant. 1.** advantage, help, benefit. **2.** aid, assist, boost.

handle *vb.* **1.** touch, feel, grasp, finger, hold. *Please handle the glasses with care.* **2.** manage, operate, manipulate, control, direct, run, work. *The farmer handled his tractor expertly.* –*n.* **3.** knob, shaft, grip, hilt, handgrip. *Take hold of the handle and pull.*

handsome *adj.* **1.** attractive, fine, good-looking, comely, pleasing, fair. *She thought the waiter was very handsome.* **2.** generous, liberal, large, ample, big, abundant, plentiful. *He received a handsome reward for finding the lost dog.* **Ant. 1.** ugly, plain, unattractive. **2.** small, stingy, meager.

handy *adj.* **1.** near, close, available, accessible, ready, convenient. *The photographer always kept his camera handy.* **2.** useful, efficient, clever, skillful, proficient, adept, inventive. *Her chauffeur was handy at maneuvering through traffic.* **Ant. 1.** unavailable, far, remote. **2.** useless, clumsy, ineffective.

hang *vb.* **1.** suspend, dangle, droop, drape, sling, attach. *He hung his jacket in the closet.* **2.** depend, rest, stand, wait, hinge. *My promotion hangs on the decision of my boss.* **3.** lynch, execute, kill, string up. *Let's hang the horse thief at sunrise.*

haphazard *adj.* careless, aimless, disorganized, random, purposeless, casual, chaotic. *Her belongings were tossed around the room in a haphazard manner.* **Ant.** organized, careful, neat, orderly.

happen *vb.* occur, take place, arise, befall, result, appear, transpire. *A nice thing happened yesterday.*

happiness *n.* pleasure, joy, delight, cheer, bliss, enjoyment, ecstasy. *Her years in Europe were a time of great happiness.* **Ant.** misery, unhappiness, sadness, sorrow.

happy *adj.* glad, joyful, cheerful, elated, pleased, joyous, delighted, merry. *I'm happy that everything turned out so well.* **Ant.** sad, unhappy, gloomy, depressed.

harass *vb.* bother, annoy, pester, trouble, torment, disturb, harry, plague. *She was always being harassed by salespeople.*

harbor *n.* **1.** port, dock, anchorage, bay, lagoon. *We went to the harbor to watch the boats.* **2.** haven, refuge, shelter, retreat, sanctuary. *The local church served as a temporary harbor for the homeless.* –*vb.* **3.** protect, shelter, house, shield, guard, hide. *The resistance movement harbored refugees from the government.*

hard *adj.* **1.** difficult, tough, exacting, laborious, exhausting, strenuous. *The test was not as hard as I expected.* **2.** severe, harsh, rough, cruel, brutal, vicious, unpleasant. *A drought brought hard times to the village.* **3.** stern, strict, demanding, firm, unrelenting, unfeeling. *The new professor was a hard teacher.* **4.** solid, firm, dense, hardened, rigid, stiff, strong. *The camper found it difficult to sleep on the hard ground.* **Ant. 1.** easy, simple, effortless. **2.** comfortable, pleasant, nice. **3.** lenient, lax, relaxed. **4.** soft, flexible, elastic.

hardly *adv.* barely, rarely, scarcely, narrowly, just. *There was hardly enough time to eat between classes.* **Ant.** easily, usually, certainly.

hardship *n.* misfortune, adversity, burden, difficulty, trouble. *The drought victims endured one hardship after another.*

hardy *adj.* strong, robust, fit, healthy, sturdy, tough, vigorous. *Exercise and a good diet made him hardy.* **Ant.** weak, feeble, unhealthy.

harm *n.* **1.** hurt, injury, pain, damage, abuse. *The one bad movie has done a lot of harm to her acting career.* **2.** evil, mischief, wickedness, wrong, sin, malice. *Don't try to convince me that there's no harm in telling a lie.* –*vb.* **3.** hurt, damage, injure, mistreat, abuse. *My dog won't harm you.* **Ant. 1.** good, assistance, help. **2.** kindness, goodness, benefit. **3.** help, heal, cure.

harmful *adj.* dangerous, injurious, hurtful, damaging, unhealthy, unsafe, bad. *Cigarettes are harmful to your health.* **Ant.** safe, harmless, healthy, beneficial.

harmless *adj.* safe, beneficial, innocent, gentle, inoffensive, benign, good. *Hamsters are harmless creatures.* **Ant.** harmful, dangerous, vicious, unsafe.

harmonious *adj.* **1.** friendly, agreeable, cordial, congenial, pleasing. *The friends settled their argument in a harmonious fashion.* **2.** tuneful, melodious, melodic, harmonic, musical. *The choir was known for its harmonious renditions of classic songs.* **Ant. 1.** disagreeable, unfriendly, quarrelsome. **2.** discordant, harsh.

harmony *n.* agreement, conformity, accord, concord, unity. *Her views on the environment are in harmony with my own.* **Ant.** disagreement, discord, conflict.

harrowing *adj.* alarming, terrifying, scary, upsetting, traumatic. *Being trapped on the cliff ledge was a harrowing experience.*

harsh *adj.* **1.** rough, coarse, grating, jarring, discordant, unpleasant. *His harsh voice really gets on my nerves.* **2.** cruel, severe, mean, tough, unkind, merciless, brutal, heartless. *The prisoners complained of harsh treatment from the guards.* **Ant. 1.** pleasing, pleasant, smooth. **2.** kind, lenient, merciful.

harvest *n.* **1.** crop, yield, produce, outcome, fruit, reward. *The farmers had a good harvest.* –*vb.* **2.** reap, gather, pick, collect. *Our neighbors helped us harvest the corn.*

hassle *n.* **1.** quarrel, dispute, fight, argument, squabble, struggle. *Two people got into a hassle over the one parking space.* –*vb.* **2.** harass, harry, bother, argue, fight, squabble. *My father is always hassling me about getting a haircut.*

haste *n.* hurry, speed, rush, dispatch, rapidity, quickness, swiftness. *She left with haste when my pet rattlesnake got loose.* **Ant.** delay, slowness, sluggishness.

hasten *vb.* race, hurry, rush, speed, quicken, run, dash. *She hastened to catch the bus.* **Ant.** slow, delay, drag, slacken.

hasty *adj.* quick, fast, speedy, swift, rapid, sudden. *It's foolish to make hasty decisions.* **Ant.** slow, deliberate, leisurely.

hatch *vb.* **1.** concoct, devise, plan, create, produce, invent, generate. *He's always hatching schemes to make money.* **2.** breed, incubate, brood, produce. *We hatched the chicken eggs in an incubator.*

hate *n.* **1.** hatred, loathing, hostility, revulsion, malice, scorn. *I can't live in a place where there is so much hate.* –*vb.* **2.** loathe, dislike, detest, despise, abhor, scorn. *The cowboy hated city life.* **Ant. 1.** love, liking, affection. **2.** love, like, adore, cherish.

hateful *adj.* detestable, horrid, vile, despised, odious, offensive. *The travelers avoided the canyon where the hateful goblins lived.* **Ant.** lovable, adorable, likable, decent.

hatred *n.* hate, revulsion, aversion, animosity, hostility. *I have a lot of hatred for people who are cruel to animals.* **Ant.** friendliness, love, affection.

haughty *adj.* proud, arrogant, prideful, conceited, vain, pompous. *Everybody acts so haughty at those high-class charity balls.* **Ant.** humble, modest, simple.

haul *vb.* **1.** heave, pull, draw, drag, tow, tug, carry. *Help me haul the hay bales into the barn.* –*n.* **2.** load, burden, weight, cargo, freight. *There's a huge haul of fish coming into the market today.*

haunt *vb.* **1.** obsess, plague, torment, distress, frighten, terrorize. *Lately she's been haunted by nightmares.* –*n.* **2.** hideaway, hangout, rendezvous, spot, place. *The old haunts aren't what they used to be.*

haunting *adj.* unforgettable, upsetting, disturbing, distressing, hypnotic. *The wolves' haunting howls echoed through the night.*

have *vb.* **1.** own, possess, hold, carry, retain, keep. *Do you have the car keys?* **2.** get, acquire, obtain, take, gain. *I'll have another glass of lemonade.* **3.** experience, undergo, endure, know, enjoy. *Have a good time at the party.*

haven *n.* shelter, retreat, asylum, refuge, sanctuary. *My mountain cabin is my haven from city life.*

havoc *n.* ruin, disaster, destruction, chaos, disorder, devastation. *A motorcycle gang spread havoc through the small town.* **Ant.** peace, calm, order, serenity.

hazard *n.* **1.** danger, risk, peril, threat, chance. *Heat exhaustion is a common hazard of desert hiking.* –*vb.* **2.** venture, risk, guess, gamble, dare, offer, attempt. *I'll hazard a guess that we will be home by Sunday.* **Ant. 1.** protection, security, safeguard.

hazardous *adj.* dangerous, perilous, risky, unsafe, chancy. *It is hazardous to skate on thin ice.* **Ant.** safe, reliable, secure.

hazy *adj.* **1.** foggy, cloudy, misty, murky, bleary, overcast, dim. *The sky is frequently hazy near the ocean.* **2.** unclear, obscure, faint, uncertain, muddled, vague, unsure. *Her thoughts have been a little hazy since she hurt her head.* **Ant. 1.** sunny, clear, bright. **2.** certain, clear, unconfused.

head *n.* **1.** brain, mind, intellect, mentality, aptitude. *Use your head to solve that problem.* **2.** director, supervisor, leader, chief, boss, commander. *They had a meeting with the head of the office.* **3.** start, beginning, front, top, source, peak. *The people at the head of the line have been here for hours.* –*vb.* **4.** lead, direct, command, supervise, manage, control, preside. *The police chief will personally head the investigation.* **5.** go, proceed, start, move, turn, steer. *He headed for the exit.* –*adj.* **6.** leading, chief, main, principal, presiding, commanding. *I will speak only to the head supervisor.* **Ant. 2.** employee, follower, subordinate. **3.** back, bottom, rear. **4.** follow, conclude. **5.** withdraw, retreat. **6.** inferior, lowest.

headstrong *adj.* stubborn, obstinate, willful, bullheaded, pigheaded. *The headstrong woman insisted she was right.* **Ant.** submissive, meek, docile.

headway *n.* progress, improvement, advance, movement, gain, progression. *He made some headway toward getting a job.*

heal *vb.* cure, remedy, restore, repair, mend, treat, ease. *Broken bones take a long time to heal.* **Ant.** hurt, wound, damage, worsen.

health *n.* well-being, fitness, vitality, healthiness, soundness. *It is important to take care of your health.* **Ant.** sickness, illness, disease, weakness.

healthy *adj.* well, fit, strong, robust, hearty, wholesome, hale, sound. *She exercises in order to maintain a healthy body.* **Ant.** sick, ill, unfit, weak, feeble.

heap *vb.* **1.** pile, stack, lump, amass, collect, load, gather. *They heaped the garbage into one big pile.* –*n.* **2.** mass, pile, stack, collection, mound, load, clump, hill. *The dump truck deposited a large heap of dirt.*

hear *vb.* listen, heed, attend, hearken, detect, perceive. *Can you hear the birds singing?*

heart *n.* **1.** kindness, feeling, sympathy, love, mercy, tenderness, compassion. *Have a heart and give the child a cookie.* **2.** spirit, courage, bravery, spunk, desire, valor. *The boxer has no skill but lots of heart.* **3.** center, core, middle, interior, nucleus. *A minotaur lived in the heart of the labyrinth.* **4.** essence, root, source, basis, foundation, focus. *We need to sit down and discuss the heart of the problem..* **Ant. 1.** hatred, indifference, coldness. **2.** cowardice, fear, shyness. **3.** outside, outskirts, exterior.

heartily *adv.* sincerely, fervently, totally, warmly, earnestly, keenly. *I heartily recommend the duck in orange sauce.* **Ant.** coolly, indifferently.

heartless *adj.* cruel, mean, unfeeling, ruthless, merciless, pitiless, callous. *The heartless landlord threw the family out in the streets.* **Ant.** merciful, kind, humane, generous.

heat *n.* **1.** warmth, warmness, hotness, swelter, temperature. *It was difficult to work in the heat of the day.* **2.** excitement, fervor, passion, intensity, fever, frenzy. *The crowd lost control in the heat of the moment.* –*vb.* **3.** warm, cook, reheat, boil, simmer. *He heated water for a cup of tea.* **Ant. 1.** cold, cool. **2.** calmness, peacefulness. **3.** cool, chill.

heave *vb.* hoist, haul, raise, boost, lift, pull, push, fling. *Laborers heaved the crates onto the truck.*

heaven *n.* **1.** paradise, bliss, ecstasy, nirvana, rapture, joy. *It was heaven to float in the swimming pool on a hot day.* **2.** afterlife, paradise, nirvana, eternity, hereafter. *She believes that she will go to Heaven after she dies.* **Ant. 1.** torment, agony, suffering. **2.** hell, nothingness, oblivion.

heavy *adj.* **1.** weighty, bulky, massive, hefty, dense. *The chair was too heavy to lift.* **2.** excessive, abundant, severe, intense, fierce, forceful. *Heavy winds blew down the telephone lines.* **3.** sad, gloomy, depressing, sorrowful, dismal, unendurable. *He's been in a heavy mood since the death of his cat.* **4.** boring, tiresome, tedious, difficult, dreary, dull. *I find my algebra class to be heavy going.* **Ant. 1.** light, weightless, lightweight. **2.** light, minimal, slight. **3.** happy, carefree, cheerful. **4.** light, easy, interesting.

hectic *adj.* frantic, wild, mad, excited, chaotic, feverish. *Shopping is always hectic on Christmas Eve.* **Ant.** quiet, calm, slow, peaceful.

hedge *n.* **1.** boundary, fence, border, barrier. *We couldn't look into the garden due to the high hedges.* **2.** protection, guard, security, insurance. *Health insurance acts as a hedge against unexpected medical expenses.* –*vb.* **3.** evade, avoid, dodge, parry, sidestep. *When I asked about specifics, the senator hedged the question.*

heed *vb.* **1.** follow, regard, obey, notice, mind, observe. *She would not have been arrested had she heeded the officer's warning.* *–n.* **2.** attention, mind, notice, care, regard, consideration. *Pay heed to the instructions.* **Ant. 1.** ignore, disregard, disobey. **2.** disregard, inattention.

height *n.* **1.** tallness, stature, highness, elevation, altitude. *What is the height of that building?* **2.** peak, maximum, crest, climax, pinnacle, apex, zenith. *This is the height of the fishing season.* **Ant. 1.** depth, deepness, lowness. **2.** minimum, depth.

heir *n.* beneficiary, inheritor, recipient, receiver. *I like to dream that I will be the heir to a fortune.*

help *vb.* **1.** aid, assist, benefit, support, sustain, serve. *The boy scout helped a little old man cross the street.* **2.** control, relieve, ease, cure, mend, prevent. *A cup of mint tea should help your stomachache.* *–n.* **3.** assistance, aid, support, backing, service, cooperation. *Can I get some help moving these boxes?* **Ant. 1.** hinder, impede, obstruct. **2.** worsen, aggravate, harm. **3.** opposition, noncooperation, obstruction.

helpful *adj.* useful, beneficial, valuable, supportive, productive, worthwhile. *A list of recommended readings would be helpful.* **Ant.** useless, worthless, harmful.

helpless *adj.* powerless, defenseless, weak, feeble, vulnerable. *The lamb was helpless against the pack of coyotes.* **Ant.** strong, powerful, protected.

herald *n.* **1.** messenger, forerunner, crier, proclaimer, courier. *A herald announced the birth of the princess.* *–vb.* **2.** announce, proclaim, broadcast, declare, trumpet. *"New and approved!" heralded the commercial.*

herd *n.* **1.** pack, crowd, flock, group, drove, swarm, gathering. *The campsite was invaded by a herd of boy scouts.* *–vb.* **2.** drive, guide, lead, group, collect, gather. *Let's herd the horses into the barn.*

heretic *n.* disbeliever, dissenter, nonconformist, renegade, infidel. *Martin Luther was con-*

sidered a heretic. **Ant.** believer, loyalist, traditionalist.

heritage *n.* legacy, inheritance, tradition, birthright. *She is proud of the heritage handed down from her African ancestors.*

hero *n.* heroine, champion, idol, favorite, model, inspiration, ideal. *My childhood hero was the Lone Ranger.* **Ant.** villain, coward.

heroic *adj.* brave, valiant, daring, gallant, bold, courageous, fearless, intrepid. *The heroic princess saved the bungling knight from being eaten by a dragon.* **Ant.** cowardly, scared, timid, fearful.

hesitant *adj.* reluctant, doubtful, undecided, indecisive, uncertain. *She was hesitant to lend money to her irresponsible friend.* **Ant.** decided, decisive, certain.

hesitate *vb.* pause, delay, waver, wait, falter, balk. *The adventurer hesitated briefly before entering the dark and mysterious cavern.* **Ant.** continue, resolve, proceed.

hide *vb.* **1.** conceal, cover, cloak, screen, mask, veil, disguise. *The pirates hid their treasure in a cave.* *–n.* **2.** fur, pelt, skin, leather. *A fox hide looks better on a fox than on a human.* **Ant. 1.** reveal, uncover, expose, display.

hideous *adj.* ugly, repulsive, ghastly, horrible, terrifying, gruesome. *I saw some pretty hideous creatures last Halloween.* **Ant.** beautiful, attractive, pleasing.

high *adj.* **1.** tall, towering, elevated, lofty, soaring. *Redwoods are very high trees.* **2.** extreme, severe, excessive, acute, unreasonable, serious. *With finals approaching, many students are suffering from high stress.* **3.** shrill, raised, sharp, piercing. *The whistle had a very high pitch.* **4.** prominent, important, powerful, superior, great, eminent. *She was promoted to a high position in the office.* **Ant. 1.** low, short, little. **2.** small, limited, reasonable. **3.** deep, lowered. **4.** inferior, secondary, insignificant.

highway *n.* freeway, speedway, expressway, road, route. *The old highway takes longer but is more scenic.*

hike *vb.* **1.** walk, trek, tramp, march, ramble, rove, trudge. *The backpackers hiked to their next campsite.* **2.** raise, boost, lift, increase, upgrade.

The gas stations hiked their prices again. –n. **3.** trek, walk, journey, tramp, jaunt, march. *She enjoys a morning hike in the hills.* **4.** raise, boost, increase, expansion. *The president opposes a tax hike.* **Ant. 2.** reduce, cut, lower. **4.** reduction, cut, decrease.

hilarious *adj.* funny, delirious, hysterical, riotous, laughable, uproarious. *The circus clowns were hilarious.* **Ant.** sad, solemn, depressing.

hill *n.* rise, knoll, mound, hilltop, elevation, prominence. *Her cabin sits on a hill overlooking a wooded valley.* **Ant.** hollow, valley, bottom.

hinder *vb.* delay, obstruct, stop, prevent, stall, detain, interrupt, impede. *Darkness hindered our ability to complete the climb.* **Ant.** support, aid, assist, help.

hindrance *n.* obstacle, obstruction, delay, interference, restriction. *Lack of money need not be a hindrance to having a good time.* **Ant.** help, assistance, aid, support.

hinge *vb.* **1.** revolve, depend, pivot, rely, rest. *The jury's decision hinges on the testimony of one witness.* –n. **2.** joint, pivot, bearing, axis. *Please oil the hinges on the gate.*

hint *vb.* **1.** suggest, imply, tip, mention, insinuate. *The teacher hinted that there would be a surprise test on Tuesday.* –n. **2.** clue, tip, suggestion, implication, allusion. *If you won't tell me the answer, then at least give me a hint.* **3.** taste, trace, tinge, pinch, dash. *Good spaghetti sauce should have just a hint of oregano.* **Ant. 1.** declare, state, announce. **3.** abundance, surplus, excess.

hire *vb.* employ, engage, appoint, retain, contract. *The store hired two more people.* **Ant.** fire, dismiss, release.

history *n.* chronicle, record, account, report, story, annals, saga, narrative. *The history of America is full of great deeds.*

hit *vb.* **1.** strike, knock, punch, beat, slam, slug, pound. *Try to hit the ball on the first pitch.* **2.** touch, affect, overwhelm, move, stir, impress. *The seriousness of the situation finally hit me.* –n. **3.** blow, knock, bump, impact, stroke, slam, punch. *The quarterback took a hard hit when he was tackled.* **4.** triumph, success, winner, sen-

sation, smash. *Her first novel was a surprise hit.* **Ant. 4.** loser, failure, flop.

hitch *vb.* **1.** tie, tether, fasten, harness, join, bind, attach. *The cowboy hitched his horse to a post.* **2.** hike, tug, pull, yank, raise. *She hitched up her pants and waded across the stream.* –n. **3.** snag, obstacle, problem, catch, drawback, difficulty. *His lateness threw a hitch in our plan to see the seven o'clock movie.* **Ant. 1.** untie, release, unfasten. **2.** lower, release, drop.

hoard *vb.* **1.** store, collect, accumulate, stockpile, amass, save. *Pack rats are famous for hoarding objects.* –n. **2.** collection, mass, stock, stockpile, cache, reserve, supply. *A hoard of diamonds was found by the police officer.* **Ant. 1.** waste, spend, surrender.

hoarse *adj.* harsh, rough, raspy, grating, scratchy, cracked, coarse. *All this yelling is making me sound hoarse.* **Ant.** full, clear, smooth.

hoax *n.* **1.** trick, fraud, deception, deceit, sham, joke. *The cockroach festival was a hoax.* –vb. **2.** deceive, trick, fool, dupe, swindle. *I can't believe you were hoaxed into a snipe hunt.* **Ant. 1.** truth, actuality, fact.

hobby *n.* pastime, recreation, diversion, amusement, avocation. *Her hobby is collecting stamps.*

hoist *vb.* pull, yank, raise, lift, heave, elevate. *She hoisted a bucket out of the well.*

hold *vb.* **1.** have, retain, keep, own, possess. *He holds two tickets to the concert.* **2.** grasp, grip, clutch, seize, clench. *Please hold my hand.* **3.** contain, enclose, include, accommodate. *This silo holds a large surplus of wheat.* **4.** remain, stick, adhere, stay, persist, last, endure. *My repairs will hold until you can get the car to a mechanic.* **5.** think, consider, believe, judge, conclude, maintain. *I hold that new research will lead to an improved product.* **6.** conduct, direct, manage, execute. *The tennis finals will be held this weekend.* –n. **7.** grip, grasp, clutch, clamp, embrace. *Get a firm hold on the bat.* **8.** control, possession, sway, power, rule, authority. *Take hold of yourself and don't panic.* **Ant. 2.** release, relinquish, remove. **4.** loosen, yield. **5.** deny, reject, disavow. **6.** cancel, postpone.

hole *n.* **1.** opening, gap, break, leak, crack, slot. *There's a hole in your blue jeans.* **2.** fault, defect, flaw, discrepancy, inconsistency. *There are numerous holes in your line of reasoning.* **3.** depression, pit, concavity, crater, hollow. *You'll need to dig that hole deeper.*

holiday *n.* vacation, leave, break, celebration, festival. *Next Monday is a holiday for all government workers.*

hollow *adj.* **1.** vacant, empty, void, unfilled, depressed, sunken. *The bandits hid their loot in a hollow spot under the floor.* **2.** meaningless, false, vain, pointless, worthless. *A person who cheats will inherit a hollow victory.* –*n.* **3.** cavity, hole, depression, crater, pocket, basin. *The squirrel stored nuts in a hollow of the tree.* –*vb.* **4.** dig, scrape, scoop, excavate, shovel. *Tribesmen hollowed out the log in order to make a canoe.* **Ant. 1.** full, filled, raised. **2.** meaningful, substantial, valuable.

holy *adj.* sacred, saintly, sanctified, hallowed, revered, divine, religious. *Jerusalem is a holy city for three religions.* **Ant.** secular, unsanctified, unholy.

homage *vb.* tribute, praise, honor, respect, reverence, devotion. *Her documentary paid homage to the Apollo astronauts.* **Ant.** criticism, disrespect, dishonor.

home *n.* **1.** house, residence, residency, dwelling, abode, habitation. *He bought a home in the country.* **2.** habitat, haunt, refuge, retreat, homeland, site. *Argentina is the home of the gaucho.*

homicide *n.* murder, manslaughter, killing, assassination, slaughter. *Several gang members were arrested for homicide.*

honest *adj.* **1.** truthful, honorable, reliable, upright, trustworthy, ethical. *We need an honest person to handle the financial arrangements.* **2.** candid, frank, forthright, genuine, real, true. *I'm looking for honest facts, not what the politicians want me to hear.* **Ant. 1.** dishonest, deceitful, unethical. **2.** false, deceiving.

honor *n.* **1.** distinction, regard, respect, esteem, prestige, acclaim, renown. *The Olympic athlete returned to her country with honor.* **2.** honesty, virtue, decency, integrity, character. *The gentleman's honor was at stake.* –*vb.* **3.** respect, revere, regard, dignify, exalt. *We will honor the senator with a parade.* **4.** take, accept,

acknowledge, recognize. *The bank refused to honor my check.* **Ant. 1.** shame, disgrace, humiliation. **2.** dishonesty, shame, dishonor. **3.** dishonor, disgrace, humiliate. **4.** reject, deny, refuse.

honorable *adj.* honest, ethical, virtuous, trustworthy, reliable. *Honorable people do not tell lies.* **Ant.** disreputable, corrupt, dishonest.

hook *n.* **1.** clip, clasp, pin, hanger, fastener. *Hang your jacket on the hook.* –*vb.* **2.** fasten, attach, secure, latch, link, join. *Please hook the door on the bird cage.*

hope *vb.* **1.** wish, desire, trust, expect, anticipate, believe. *We can only hope the trapped miners are still alive.* –*n.* **2.** trust, faith, assurance, reliance, confidence, belief. *Our football team placed all their hopes on the rookie quarterback.* **3.** longing, yearning, expectation, desire, ambition, anticipation. *The college graduate has great hopes for the future.* **Ant. 1.** despair, doubt, fear. **2.** distrust, doubt, disbelief. **3.** hopelessness, despair, pessimism.

hopeful *adj.* optimistic, confident, assuring, expectant, promising, encouraging. *There are hopeful signs of a break in the storm.* **Ant.** hopeless, despairing, depressing.

hopeless *adj.* pessimistic, despairing, depressing, discouraging, helpless, useless, desperate. *Bailing water out of the rapidly sinking boat was a hopeless task.* **Ant.** hopeful, optimistic, favorable.

horde *n.* pack, multitude, swarm, herd, mob, crowd, legion, throng, troop. *Hordes of lemmings jumped into the sea.*

horizontal *adj.* level, even, flat, plane, straight, prone. *Your radio-controlled car will work best on a horizontal surface.* **Ant.** vertical, sloped, uneven, bumpy.

horrible *adj.* terrible, awful, gruesome, dreadful, horrid, frightful, hideous. *We have to report the horrible accident to the police.* **Ant.** delightful, wonderful, good, nice.

horror *n.* **1.** terror, dread, fear, fright, panic, dismay, alarm, repulsion. *He shook with horror when the vampire entered his room.* **2.** cruelty, atrocity, outrage, torment, abomination. *We* *need to put a stop to the horrors committed by terrorists.* **Ant. 2.** good, kindness, happiness.

hospitable *adj.* friendly, gracious, warm, generous, cordial, sociable, open. *Texans are known for being hospitable people.* **Ant.** cold, unfriendly, unwelcome.

host *n.* **1.** hostess, innkeeper, welcomer, entertainer, emcee. *I will be your host for the length of your stay.* **2.** horde, multitude, army, swarm, legion, crowd, mob. *A host of Vandals sacked Rome.*

hostile *adj.* unfriendly, opposing, aggressive, warlike, belligerent, unfavorable. *The hostile guard searched my suitcase thoroughly.* **Ant.** friendly, agreeable, allied, peaceful.

hot *adj.* **1.** heated, scorching, scalding, burning, blazing, boiling. *I moved away from Phoenix because it's too hot there.* **2.** spicy, pungent, biting, sharp, peppery, zesty. *The chicken gumbo was too hot for my taste.* **3.** passionate, violent, intense, fierce, excited, emotional, frenzied. *Congress got into a hot debate today.* **4.** good, excellent, successful, marvelous, popular. *The rock concert was really hot.* **Ant. 1.** cold, cool, freezing. **2.** bland, mild, flat. **3.** quiet, calm, unemotional. **4.** dull, boring, bad.

hotel *n.* inn, lodge, hostel, motel, tavern, lodging. *We stayed at the hotel on the beach.*

house *n.* dwelling, home, residence, shelter, habitation, abode. *My house is on the corner.*

hovel *n.* shack, hut, cabin, shanty, shed, hole. *His home was just a little hovel near the railroad tracks.* **Ant.** castle, mansion, palace.

hover *vb.* **1.** float, drift, hang, flutter, fly. *The helicopter hovered in the air.* **2.** hang, loiter, linger, wait, loom. *The boss hovered over her secretary until the letter was typed.* **3.** vacillate, waver, vary, falter, seesaw. *His final decision has hovered between yes and no for the last hour.*

howl *vb.* **1.** yell, yowl, cry, wail, screech, shriek, bellow, bay. *The coyotes howled at the moon.* **–n. 2.** yelp, scream, cry, clamor, yowl, wail. *She let out a howl when the hammer hit her thumb.*

hub *n.* center, middle, core, focus, midpoint, heart, nucleus. *The bus station is the hub of the city's transportation system.*

huddle *vb.* **1.** bunch, crowd, mass, cram, cluster, snuggle, gather. *The football team huddled together to plan the next play.* **–n. 2.** mass, heap, pile, jumble, mess, clump, bunch. *There was a huddle of unpaid bills on her desk.* **Ant. 1.** separate, divide, scatter, disperse.

hue *n.* color, tint, shade, cast, tinge, tone, complexion. *Please paint the reception room in hues that are relaxing.*

hug *vb.* **1.** embrace, cuddle, hold, grasp, squeeze, enfold, caress. *The little girl hugged her Teddy bear.* **–n. 2.** embrace, squeeze, caress, press, clasp. *Give your dear old grandmother a big hug.*

huge *adj.* enormous, large, giant, massive, immense, gigantic, colossal. *Jack woke up to see a huge beanstalk growing in his yard.* **Ant.** small, tiny, little.

hulking *adj.* bulky, massive, lumbering, heavy, powerful, husky. *The hulking wrestler stepped into the ring.*

humane *adj.* kind, merciful, thoughtful, good, tender, compassionate. *Feeding the starving kittens was a humane act.* **Ant.** cruel, heartless, mean.

humble *adj.* **1.** modest, unassuming, unpretentious, meek, respectful. *The college president was quite humble despite his many accomplishments.* **2.** poor, lowly, low, simple, common, obscure. *She started in a humble job and worked her way to the top.* **–vb. 3.** shame, lower, humiliate, chasten, demean, debase. *The defeated prince was humbled in front of his captors.* **Ant. 1.** vain, proud, arrogant, pompous. **2.** rich, important, prestigious. **3.** praised, exalted, promoted.

humid *adj.* muggy, sticky, damp, steamy, moist, clammy, sultry. *The hot summer days in New York tend to be humid.* **Ant.** dry, arid, parched.

humiliate *vb.* shame, embarrass, disgrace, degrade, dishonor, humble, demean. *She was humiliated when she slipped on the banana peel.* **Ant.** honor, exalt, dignify, elevate.

humiliation *n.* shame, embarrassment, dishonor, degradation, lowering. *It was a great* *humiliation for him to have to ask for help.* **Ant.** honor, prestige, pride, exaltation.

humility *n.* modesty, humbleness, meekness, unpretentiousness, lowliness. *The priest taught that humility is a virtue.* **Ant.** conceit, pride, arrogance.

humor *n.* **1.** ridiculousness, funniness, comedy, amusement, fun, wit. *She didn't see the humor of the situation.* **2.** temperament, mood, disposition, attitude, sentiment, character. *The boss has been in bad humor ever since we lost the contract.* *-vb.* **3.** indulge, pamper, gratify, coddle, oblige, favor. *Let's humor him and maybe he will just go away.* **Ant. 1.** seriousness, gravity, solemnity. **3.** oppose, contradict.

humorous *adj.* funny, hilarious, witty, comical, amusing, laughable. *It wasn't what she said but the way she said it that was so humorous.* **Ant.** sad, serious, grave, sober.

hump *n.* lump, bulge, mound, knob, swelling, ridge, rise. *Would you like your camel with one hump or two?*

hunch *n.* **1.** feeling, thought, intuition, impression, sensation, notion, suspicion. *I have a hunch that you will win first place.* *-vb.* **2.** arch, vault, curve, bend, stoop, tense. *Hunching your back is bad for your posture.*

hunger *n.* **1.** starvation, famine, hungriness, appetite. *There is still hunger in many parts of the world.* **2.** desire, want, craving, longing, yearning, thirst, need. *The library is a good place to satisfy your hunger for knowledge.* *-vb.* **3.** desire, want, crave, yearn, itch, wish, long. *She hungered for the job of chairperson.*

hungry *adj.* **1.** starving, starved, famished, empty, ravenous. *Our church donated food to feed the hungry children.* **2.** eager, greedy, desirous, avid, needful, craving. *The dictator was hungry for power.* **Ant. 1.** full, sated, satiated. **2.** indifferent, satisfied.

hunt *vb.* **1.** track, stalk, chase, pursue, shoot. *We will be hunting for quail during the weekend.* **2.** search, look, probe, seek, quest, scour. *I spent an hour hunting for my keys.* *-n.* **3.** chase, search, pursuit, quest, hunting. *He was offended by the idea of a fox hunt.*

hurdle *n.* **1.** barrier, obstacle, obstruction, barricade, hazard, block. *The oral exam is the last hurdle in completing this class.* *-vb.* **2.** jump, leap, vault, scale, bound, hop, spring. *The mail carrier hurdled over a hedge to escape from a dog.*

hurl *vb.* throw, heave, fling, cast, pitch, toss, sling, launch. *In a fit of rage, she hurled the broken typewriter into the trash.*

hurricane *n.* tropical storm, typhoon, storm, monsoon, tempest, cyclone. *A hurricane is expected to hit the Gulf Coast.*

hurried *adj.* hasty, rushed, pushed, speedy, frantic, abrupt. *His hurried letter had too many mistakes.*

hurry *vb.* **1.** hasten, rush, speed, race, run, scurry. *We hurried through our dinner in order to arrive at the theater on time.* *-n.* **2.** haste, rush, flurry, bustle, dispatch, quickness, speed. *The commuter was in a hurry to get to her train on time.* **Ant. 1.** linger, dawdle, delay. **2.** slowness, delay, sluggishness.

hurt *vb.* **1.** injure, harm, damage, cripple, wound, mar, pain. *You'll hurt your back if you try to lift that crate.* **2.** distress, grieve, upset, insult, offend, abuse. *I didn't mean to hurt his feelings.* **3.** limit, hinder, impede, impair, inhibit, lessen. *The pitcher's injury hurts our team's chances for the championship.* *-n.* **4.** injury, harm, damage, pain, ache, pang. *The hurt in her ankle did not affect her ability to run.* **5.** suffering, torment, discomfort, insult, embarrassment, humiliation. *He was experiencing the hurt of being betrayed by a friend.* *-adj.* **6.** injured, damaged, painful, wounded, impaired. *Androcles pulled a thorn out of the lion's hurt paw.* **Ant. 1.** repair, restore, heal. **2.** praise, compliment, please. **3.** aid, benefit, improve, help. **6.** healed, cured, improved.

hustle *vb.* **1.** hurry, hasten, speed, rush, dash, scurry. *She was always hustling from one meeting to the next.* *-n.* **2.** hurry, fuss, turmoil, stir, flurry, movement, activity. *The play went smoothly, but you should have seen the hustle backstage.* **Ant. 1.** linger, dawdle, loiter. **2.** calmness, peacefulness, rest.

hypnotize *vb.* mesmerize, charm, entrance, enchant, transfix, fascinate. *He was hypnotized by her gorgeous green eyes.*

hypocrite *vb.* deceiver, imposter, pretender, fraud, fake. *A person who preaches simple living and then buys a Cadillac is a hypocrite.*

hypocritical *adj.* false, deceptive, insincere, deceitful, dishonest. *It is hypocritical to insult your friends behind their backs.* **Ant.** sincere, honest, honorable.

hypothesis *n.* theory, assumption, conjecture, speculation, proposition. *The detective's hypothesis was that the butler did it.*

hysterical *adj.* **1.** uncontrollable, frenzied, panicky, emotional, wild, raving. *We could not control the hysterical man.* **2.** funny, hilarious, laughable, comical, absurd. *Her new comedy is hysterical.* **Ant. 1.** controlled, calm, composed. **2.** serious, sad, solemn, somber.

idea *n.* thought, opinion, concept, belief, notion, assumption, conviction. *Your idea is original but impractical.*

ideal *adj.* **1.** perfect, model, fitting, pure, flawless. *This is an ideal place for a campsite.* –n. **2.** model, standard, inspiration, concept, objective. *The Declaration of Independence is based on the ideal that all people are created equal.*

idealist *n.* romantic, visionary, optimist, utopian, dreamer. *Many great people were idealists.* **Ant.** cynic, pessimist, fatalist.

identical *adj.* same, alike, twin, uniform, duplicate. *The two women were wearing identical dresses.* **Ant.** different, distinct, unlike.

identify *vb.* recognize, know, distinguish, place, verify, tell, name. *Can you identify the person who robbed the bank?*

idiot *n.* fool, moron, simpleton, dummy, dunce, imbecile. *Anyone who would drive recklessly is an idiot.*

idle *adj.* **1.** lazy, loafing, sluggish, shiftless, listless, lethargic. *The rich man didn't have to work and thus led an idle life.* **2.** unused, unproductive, futile, fruitless, useless. *Idle factories are a sign of a stagnant economy.* –vb. **3.** laze, loaf, lounge, bum, loiter. *A beach is a great place in which to idle away the day.* **Ant. 1–2.** busy, active, occupied. **3.** work, labor, toil.

idol *n.* **1.** image, statue, god, symbol, icon, effigy. *The explorer was accused of stealing the sacred idol of Chtulu.* **2.** hero, favorite, darling, inspiration, star, superstar. *Elvis Presley was my mother's idol.*

ignite *vb.* **1.** light, burn, fire, kindle. *She ignited the campfire with just one match.* **2.** excite, rile, inflame, rouse, agitate. *The army's actions served only to ignite the crowd's anger.* **Ant. 1.** extinguish, quench, douse. **2.** calm, ease, soothe, quiet.

ignorant *adj.* **1.** unaware, uninformed, innocent, unknowing, unfamiliar. *The defendant was ignorant of the events leading to her arrest.* **2.** illiterate, unlearned, uneducated, unschooled, untaught. *How could he have graduated from high school and still be so ignorant?* **Ant. 1.** informed, knowledgeable, aware. **2.** literate, educated.

ignore *vb.* neglect, overlook, disregard, avoid, omit, snub, skip. *She ignored the shouting from the next apartment.* **Ant.** notice, heed, acknowledge.

ill *adj.* **1.** sick, ailing, sickly, unwell, diseased, unhealthy. *He was too ill to go to school today.* **2.** evil, bad, sinister, harmful, wicked, unfavorable, hostile. *An ill wind is blowing through town.* –n. **3.** harm, evil, abuse, wickedness, misfortune, injury. *They were afraid that the witch would do them ill.* **Ant. 1.** well, healthy, strong. **2.** good, beneficial, helpful.

illegal *adj.* unlawful, illicit, criminal, banned, unauthorized, forbidden, prohibited. *I refuse to do anything that's illegal.* **Ant.** legal, permitted, lawful.

illegible *adj.* unreadable, obscure, unintelligible, unclear, indistinct. *The doctor's prescription is illegible.* **Ant.** readable, clear, legible.

illegitimate *adj.* illegal, unlawful, unauthorized, improper, wrongful. *Blackmail is an illegitimate way of raising money.* **Ant.** legal, lawful, proper.

illiterate *adj.* uneducated, untaught, unschooled, ignorant, untutored. *One who cannot read is considered illiterate.* **Ant.** educated, learned, schooled.

illness *n.* sickness, malady, disease, affliction, ailment, disorder. *He contracted a mysterious illness when he was in the jungle.*

illogical *adj.* irrational, unsound, absurd, unreasonable, inconsistent, preposterous. *It was illogical to try out for the swim team since you don't know how to swim.* **Ant.** logical, sensible, reasonable, sound.

illuminate *vb.* **1.** brighten, lighten, light, emblaze. *Fireworks illuminated the night.* **2.** clarify, clear, explain, enlighten, interpret, reveal. *These recommended readings will help illuminate our class lectures. adj.* **1.** darken, dim, cloud. **2.** confuse, complicate, obscure.

illusion *n.* **1.** vision, mirage, delusion, apparition, phantom. *We thought we saw a ghost on the staircase, but it was just an illusion.* **2.** fallacy, misbelief, fantasy, misconception, dream. *The musician knew that his dream of success was more than an illusion.* **Ant. 1.** reality, actuality, fact. **2.** truth, certainty, probability.

illustrate *vb.* **1.** show, demonstrate, explain, clarify, illuminate. *Could you illustrate your point with examples?* **2.** depict, picture, draw, decorate, embellish. *The artist was asked to illustrate a children's book.*

illustrious *adj.* distinguished, celebrated, famous, noted, prominent, renowned. *She had an illustrious career as an architect.* **Ant.** obscure, undistinguished, lowly.

image *n.* **1.** likeness, resemblance, picture, depiction, form, portrait. *The escaped convict's image was broadcast on the evening news.* **2.** idea, thought, notion, concept, impression, perception. *I have an image of what Heaven should be like.* **3.** idol, statue, effigy, fetish. *He would not bow down to a graven image.*

imaginary *adj.* unreal, nonexistent, fictional, imagined, fantastic, mythical. *Hobbits and elves are imaginary creatures.* **Ant.** real, factual, historical, actual.

imagination *n.* creativity, invention, inventiveness, inspiration, originality. *A science-fiction writer needs a lot of imagination.*

imagine *vb.* **1.** dream, fantasize, picture, envision, conceive, visualize. *She imagined what it would be like to live on Mars.* **2.** suppose, assume, think, believe, gather, suspect, guess. *I imagine it must be cold in Alaska.*

imbecile *n.* fool, moron, dolt, idiot, simpleton, blockhead. *I feel like an imbecile for forgetting your birthday.*

imitate *vb.* copy, duplicate, mimic, simulate, mirror, reproduce. *I hate it when she imitates my actions.*

imitation *n.* **1.** copy, simulation, reproduction, duplication, counterfeit, replica. *This painting is a cheap imitation of the original.* *–adj.* **2.** artificial, phony, simulated, fake, false, copied. *The imitation diamonds looked real to me.* **Ant. 1.** original. **2.** real, authentic, original.

immaculate *adj.* pure, spotless, clean, unstained, unblemished, perfect, flawless. *The restaurant's kitchen was immaculate.* **Ant.** dirty, filthy, imperfect, flawed.

immature *adj.* **1.** young, early, undeveloped, unformed, incomplete, unripe. *The immature fruit is not yet ready to pick.* **2.** juvenile, infantile, childish, irresponsible, inexperienced. *It was immature to lose your temper.* **Ant. 1.** mature, old, grown. **2.** mature, responsible.

immediate *adj.* **1.** direct, adjacent, adjoining, closest, nearest, next. *The bank is on your immediate left.* **2.** instant, prompt, sudden, swift, timely, speedy, direct. *The immediate arrival of the paramedics saved her life.* **Ant. 1.** far, distant, remote. **2.** slow, delayed, pending.

immediately *adv.* directly, instantly, promptly, presently, now. *We will begin the class immediately.* **Ant.** later, shortly, eventually.

immense *adj.* large, enormous, great, vast, huge, gigantic, colossal. *The explorers were astounded by the immense size of the pyramid.* **Ant.** small, little, tiny.

immerse *vb.* **1.** submerge, dunk, dip, plunge, soak, drench. *The hippopotamus immersed itself in the cool river.* **2.** absorb, engross, involve, engage, occupy, preoccupy. *She was totally immersed in the book she was reading.*

immigrate *vb.* migrate, resettle, move, colonize. *My neighbors immigrated from Asia.*

imminent *adj.* near, approaching, immediate, impending, forthcoming, threatening. *The town was in imminent danger from the cyclone.* **Ant.** distant, remote, unlikely.

immoral *adj.* wrongful, unethical, sinful, evil, corrupt, wicked, bad. *Stealing is an immoral act.* **Ant.** moral, good, ethical.

immortal *adj.* eternal, everlasting, undying, deathless, endless. *The Greek gods and goddesses were considered to be immortal.* **Ant.** mortal, temporary, perishable.

immovable *adj.* **1.** unmovable, immobile, set, stationary, fixed, stable. *The trail crew blasted a path through the immovable boulders.* **2.** firm, unchangeable, stubborn, inflexible, unbending, steadfast. *The teacher remained immovable about the date of the exam.* **Ant. 1.** mobile, moveable, portable. **2.** flexible, changeable.

immune *adj.* invulnerable, resistant, safe, unaffected, protected, spared. *She is immune to poison ivy.* **Ant.** susceptible, vulnerable.

impact *n.* **1.** contact, force, crash, collision, strike, blow. *It doesn't take much of an impact to shatter a watermelon.* **2.** influence, effect, impression, force, power. *His experiences in the army have had quite an impact on him.*

impair *vb.* damage, harm, injure, weaken, mar, hurt, ruin. *Reading in dim light can impair your vision.* **Ant.** improve, better, enhance.

impartial *adj.* fair, neutral, objective, unbiased, evenhanded, unprejudiced. *Ideally, your judge will be impartial.* **Ant.** partial, biased, subjective, prejudiced.

impatient *adj.* restless, anxious, fidgety, jumpy, eager, hurried. *After waiting one hour, she started to get impatient.* **Ant.** patient, composed, unhurried.

impeccable *adj.* flawless, faultless, perfect, unblemished, spotless, immaculate. *The gymnast's routine was impeccable.* **Ant.** faulty, imperfect, flawed, defective.

impede *vb.* delay, slow, hinder, inhibit, block, thwart, obstruct. *The senator was indicted for impeding the investigation.* **Ant.** assist, further, support.

impending *adj.* approaching, oncoming, nearing, imminent, threatening, forthcoming, looming. *The wizard spoke of impending doom.*

imperative *adj.* mandatory, compulsive, required, essential, urgent, necessary. *It is impera-* tive that you pay your taxes on time. **Ant.** unimportant, optional, unnecessary.

imperfect *adj.* flawed, faulty, defective, blemished, impaired. *The dishonest jeweler tried to sell an imperfect diamond.* **Ant.** perfect, flawless, ideal.

imperial *adj.* royal, majestic, lordly, regal, grand. *Please refer to the queen as your "imperial majesty."*

imperil *vb.* endanger, risk, jeopardize, hazard, expose. *Careless handling of toxic chemicals imperiled the workers.* **Ant.** protect, preserve, safeguard.

impersonal *adj.* objective, detached, disinterested, indifferent, neutral, impartial. *I was upset because my friend sent me a rather impersonal card.* **Ant.** personal, private, intimate.

implement *n.* **1.** tool, instrument, device, utensil, apparatus, appliance. *Do you have the right implement to do the job?* *–vb.* **2.** start, enact, execute, begin, achieve, accomplish. *We will implement our plan tomorrow.*

implicate *vb.* connect, associate, involve, include, entangle, embroil. *A famous actress was implicated in the scandal.* **Ant.** exclude, eliminate, acquit.

implore *vb.* beg, plead, beseech, entreat, urge. *The peasants implored their king to lower taxes.*

imply *vb.* suggest, hint, indicate, signify, mean, denote. *Her absence implies that she is mad at you.*

impolite *adj.* rude, discourteous, disrespectful, uncivil, inconsiderate. *The children were impolite to their baby-sitter.* **Ant.** polite, mannerly, civil.

important *adj.* **1.** significant, essential, crucial, meaningful, valuable, worthwhile. *I have something important to tell you.* **2.** influential, prominent, distinguished, imposing, powerful. *You have to be an important person to get your name in "Who's Who."* **Ant. 1–2.** unimportant, inconsequential, insignificant.

impose *vb.* **1.** put, institute, levy, introduce, place, order. *The park rangers imposed a fee for campsite use.* **2.** intrude, interfere, inconvenience, bother, trouble. *I don't want to impose on you by staying overnight.*

imposing *adj.* grand, majestic, striking, stately, impressive. *The World Trade Center is one of the most imposing buildings in New York.* **Ant.** ordinary, unimpressive, unimposing.

impossible *adj.* inconceivable, unworkable, unbelievable, unthinkable, ridiculous, absurd. *It's impossible to be in two places at once.* **Ant.** possible, feasible, plausible.

impostor *n.* imitator, impersonator, fraud, deceiver, pretender, phony. *The man in the general's uniform was just an impostor.*

impractical *adj.* unworkable, unrealistic, unfeasible, futile, absurd. *It is impractical to carry the piano up five flights of stairs.* **Ant.** practical, pragmatic, workable.

impress *vb.* **1.** affect, influence, strike, move, touch. *The new teacher impressed me as being very strict .* **2.** imprint, mark, print, indent, stamp. *The postmark was impressed on the envelope.*

impression *n.* **1.** impact, effect, feeling, influence, sensation. *She wanted to make a good impression on the interviewer.* **2.** indentation, imprint, stamp, mark, depression. *The watchband was so tight that it left an impression on his wrist.* **3.** thought, idea, opinion, hunch, notion, sense. *Do you get the impression that he doesn't like me?*

impressive *adj.* imposing, striking, awesome, majestic, stirring, inspiring. *The queen's coronation was an impressive ceremony.* **Ant.** ordinary, routine, unimpressive.

improbable *adj.* unlikely, doubtful, questionable, implausible, dubious. *It is improbable that you will see any robins in the winter.* **Ant.** likely, certain, possible, plausible.

impromptu *adj.* impulsive, unrehearsed, unprepared, spontaneous, improvised. *The host's impromptu dance kept everybody in a light mood.* **Ant.** planned, rehearsed, prepared.

improper *adj.* **1.** incorrect, wrong, faulty, erroneous, unsuitable, inappropriate. *Did you know that's the improper way to hold a tennis racket?* **2.** indecent, naughty, immoral, unbecoming, lewd, offensive. *His obscene remarks were crude and improper.* **Ant. 1.** fitting, proper, correct. **2.** decent, moral, proper.

improve *vb.* better, perfect, enhance, upgrade, amend, refine, correct. *The pianist sought to improve her technique.* **Ant.** impair, worsen, damage.

improvement *n.* betterment, enhancement, correction, progress, development. *The teacher noticed an improvement in his students' grades.* **Ant.** worsening, decline, weakening.

improvise *vb.* invent, make up, devise, create, ad-lib. *I forgot the recipe, so I'm going to improvise.*

imprudent *adj.* unwise, unadvisable, incautious, thoughtless, careless, rash, foolish. *It was imprudent to go camping in the desert without water.* **Ant.** cautious, thoughtful, careful.

impulse *n.* urge, whim, desire, fancy, itch, need. *She had the impulse to jump into the pool with her clothes on.*

impulsive *adj.* impromptu, rash, abrupt, spontaneous, sudden, unplanned. *He went on an impulsive buying spree.* **Ant.** planned, cautious, deliberate.

inaccurate *adj.* wrong, incorrect, false, mistaken, erroneous, imprecise. *The gas-station attendant gave me inaccurate directions.* **Ant.** accurate, correct, right.

inadequate *adj.* insufficient, deficient, meager, short, scanty, incomplete. *The stock clerk ordered an inadequate supply of pencils.* **Ant.** sufficient, adequate, ample.

inane *adj.* silly, senseless, foolish, ridiculous, empty, stupid, absurd. *Not being able to find your sock is an inane reason for waking me up.* **Ant.** sensible, reasonable, intelligent.

inanimate *adj.* lifeless, dead, inert, inorganic. *Someone must have shifted the table, because inanimate objects do not move themselves.* **Ant.** alive, living, animate.

inappropriate *adj.* improper, unfit, unsuitable, wrong, unseemly. *It is inappropriate to talk during the minister's sermon.* **Ant.** appropriate, proper, suitable.

inaugurate *vb.* **1.** begin, start, introduce, commence, open, launch. *The health club inau-*

gurated a morning exercise session. **2.** induct, install, instate, invest, initiate. *The new president was inaugurated with much ceremony.* **Ant. 1.** end, conclude, finish. **2.** remove, impeach, oust.

incapable *adj.* incompetent, ineffective, inefficient, inept, unqualified, powerless, weak. *The business went bankrupt because of its incapable administrators.* **Ant.** competent, effective, strong.

incense *vb.* anger, irritate, enrage, infuriate, inflame, provoke. *The waitress was incensed when her customer refused to tip her.* **Ant.** cheer, calm, soothe.

incentive *n.* motivation, encouragement, motive, spur, inducement, cause, reason. *The theater offered two tickets for the price of one as an incentive to draw customers.* **Ant.** discouragement, deterrent, curb.

incessant *adj.* constant, continual, ceaseless, endless, relentless, unending. *I wish that dog would stop its incessant howling.* **Ant.** occasional, sporadic, irregular.

incident *n.* event, occurrence, experience, happening, episode. *Were you involved in that bizarre incident in the library?*

incidental *adj.* secondary, subordinate, minor, unimportant, trivial, casual. *Any financial reward in the lawsuit is incidental to the principles involved.* **Ant.** major, primary, dominant.

incite *vb.* rouse, arouse, induce, urge, provoke, instigate, encourage. *The speaker was accused of inciting the crowd into rioting.* **Ant.** dissuade, restrain, discourage.

incline *vb.* lean, bend, slope, slant, tilt. *The tree inclines to the left.* –*n.* **2.** hill, slope, grade, bank, rise. *Ivy was planted on the incline to keep it from eroding.*

inclined *adj.* likely, apt, prone, willing, disposed, liable. *I'm inclined to agree with you.* **Ant.** unlikely, unwilling, disinclined.

include *vb.* involve, contain, encompass, embody, comprise, encircle, cover. *The price of dinner includes a free drink.* **Ant.** exclude, omit, preclude.

income *n.* revenue, salary, wage, earning, pay, profit. *She makes a good income from her realty business.*

incomparable *adj.* unequaled, matchless, unrivaled, unique, unparalleled, supreme. *The incomparable beauty of Beethoven's Ninth Symphony has to be heard to be understood.* **Ant.** ordinary, mediocre, fair, average.

incompetent *adj.* incapable, unfit, ineffective, inefficient, inept, unqualified. *The incompetent dishwasher broke most of the dishes.* **Ant.** competent, able, fit, effective.

incomplete *adj.* unfinished, undone, partial, fragmentary, wanting, lacking, deficient. *The jigsaw puzzle was still incomplete at the end of the day.* **Ant.** complete, whole, done, finished.

inconceivable *adj.* unbelievable, unthinkable, incredible, unlikely, unimaginable. *It was inconceivable that the butler would steal the diamonds.* **Ant.** believable, plausible, likely.

inconsiderate *adj.* selfish, thoughtless, unthinking, tactless, negligent. *The inconsiderate neighbor refused to turn down his radio.* **Ant.** considerate, thoughtful, kind.

inconsistent *adj.* **1.** contradictory, illogical, contrary, incompatible, conflicting. *The professor's theory is inconsistent with the scientific facts.* **2.** erratic, fickle, changeable, uncertain, unstable. *The boxer's inconsistent style confused his opponent.* **Ant. 1.** consistent, logical, uniform. **2.** stable, unchanging, steady.

inconspicuous *adj.* indistinct, obscure, unapparent, unnoticeable, muted, dim. *We barely noticed the inconspicuous sparrow in the tree.* **Ant.** obvious, conspicuous, clear.

inconvenient *adj.* annoying, awkward, untimely, bothersome, unhandy, troublesome. *You arrived at an inconvenient time.* **Ant.** convenient, timely, handy.

incorrect *adj.* wrong, false, mistaken, inexact, inaccurate, untrue. *You will fail the test if you have more than ten incorrect answers.* **Ant.** right, true, correct, accurate.

increase *vb.* **1.** enlarge, expand, grow, magnify, inflate, extend, multiply. *Her book collection has increased so much she needs more shelves.* –*n.* **2.** growth, expansion, enlargement, gain, advance, rise, addition. *The increase in his wages was well deserved.* **Ant. 1.** decrease, lessen, diminish. **2.** decrease, drop, reduction.

incredible *adj.* unbelievable, extraordinary, unimaginable, amazing, fantastic. *The explorer told an incredible story about being captured by Amazon warriors.* **Ant.** credible, ordinary, believable.

indecent *adj.* immodest, improper, immoral, offensive, obscene, shameful, tasteless. *The rock singer has been criticized for his indecent behavior on stage.* **Ant.** decent, tasteful, proper.

indecisive *adj.* **1.** unsettled, doubtful, unclear, dubious, arguable, debatable. *She argued that the opinion-poll results were indecisive.* **2.** faltering, hesitant, wavering, uncertain, tentative. *The indecisive shopper couldn't decide what color socks he wanted.* **Ant. 1.** conclusive, certain, decided. **2.** definite, sure, decisive.

indeed *adv.* surely, definitely, certainly, really, honestly, truly. *She is indeed the daughter of the king.*

indefinite *adj.* uncertain, unknown, unsettled, unsure, vague, doubtful, confusing. *The governor will be out of the state for an indefinite period of time.* **Ant.** definite, exact, certain, specific.

independence *n.* freedom, liberty, autonomy, self-government, emancipation. *The rebels fought to win independence for their country.* **Ant.** dependence, subjection, slavery.

independent *adj.* free, uncontrolled, self-reliant, self-governing, separate, unattached. *The millionaire's donation made the art museum financially independent.* **Ant.** dependent, reliant, subject, controlled.

index *n.* catalog, file, register, glossary, directory. *This subject should be mentioned in the book's index.*

indicate *vb.* **1.** suggest, imply, mean, signify, reveal, represent. *The dark clouds indicate a storm is coming.* **2.** point, show, designate, specify, state. *Please indicate where you want me to place the chair.*

indifferent *adj.* **1.** unconcerned, uncaring, unmoved, insensitive, apathetic, neutral. *The doctor seemed indifferent to his patient's medical complaint.* **2.** ordinary, mediocre, average, passable, uninspired. *She was disappointed in the indifferent performance by the string quartet.* **Ant.**

1. concerned, caring, interested. **2.** special, exceptional.

indignant *adj.* angry, irate, incensed, mad, offended, wrathful. *He was indignant when his date didn't show up.* **Ant.** serene, pleased, calm.

indiscreet *adj.* careless, incautious, rash, reckless, foolish, thoughtless. *I would not have told him my secret if I had known he was so indiscreet.* **Ant.** discreet, careful, prudent.

indispensable *adj.* essential, necessary, required, needed, vital, basic. *A paint brush is an indispensable item for an artist.* **Ant.** dispensable, disposable, unnecessary.

indistinct *adj.* vague, unclear, obscure, faint, blurred, hazy, uncertain. *The approaching figures were indistinct in the fog.* **Ant.** clear, distinct, defined.

individual *adj.* **1.** personal, private, separate, special, particular, single, exclusive. *Everyone has their individual likes and dislikes.* –*n.* **2.** person, being, entity, character, somebody, human. *That individual just won a million dollars.* **Ant. 1.** public, general, common, universal.

induce *vb.* cause, prompt, influence, persuade, impel, inspire, urge, convince. *She was induced to move out of the city because of the increase in crime.* **Ant.** dissuade, discourage, hinder, prevent.

indulge *vb.* satisfy, gratify, humor, favor, pamper, spoil, placate. *They indulged their child in her every whim.* **Ant.** deny, forbid, thwart, abstain.

indulgence *n.* **1.** luxury, excess, privilege, allowance, satisfaction. *The trip to Hawaii was a well-deserved indulgence.* **2.** understanding, tolerance, patience, forgiveness, leniency. *I ask for your indulgence if I talk too long.* **Ant. 1.** denial, repression. **2.** intolerance, impatience.

industrious *adj.* hardworking, persistent, diligent, productive, active, tireless. *You must be industrious in order to succeed in your own business.* **Ant.** lazy, sluggish, slothful.

industry *n.* **1.** commerce, business, trade, manufacture, enterprise. *There's been an increase in industry since the trade agreement was signed.* **2.** persistence, diligence, zeal, energy, productiveness. *Good workers are prized for their industry.*

ineffective *adj.* inefficient, useless, worthless, vain, futile, unproductive, fruitless. *Our air conditioner was ineffective during last week's heat wave.* **Ant.** effective, useful, beneficial.

ineffectual *adj.* weak, incompetent, inept, useless, powerless, ineffective. *The townspeople voted against their ineffectual councilman.* **Ant.** competent, powerful, capable.

inefficient *adj.* ineffective, inadequate, incapable, unsuccessful, incompetent, unable. *The new pollution controls were inefficient in reducing smog.* **Ant.** efficient, successful, able.

inert *adj.* unmoving, fixed, motionless, static, inactive, immobile, passive. *You have to lay inert while the X-ray is being taken.* **Ant.** active, moving, mobile.

inevitable *adj.* certain, sure, destined, unavoidable, inescapable, fate. *It is inevitable that Central High will win the football championship this year.* **Ant.** unsure, uncertain, doubtful.

inexpensive *adj.* cheap, reasonable, modest, low-priced, economical. *I'm shopping for an inexpensive watch.* **Ant.** expensive, costly, high-priced.

inexperienced *adj.* untrained, unskilled, new, novice, beginning. *This mountain road is too dangerous for an inexperienced driver.* **Ant.** experienced, expert, trained, skilled.

infallible *adj.* perfect, faultless, flawless, unfailing, unerring, reliable. *She has an infallible ear for music.* **Ant.** faulty, imperfect, unreliable.

infamous *adj.* notorious, scandalous, shameful, villainous, ill-famed. *Al Capone was an infamous gangster.* **Ant.** honorable, respectful, esteemed.

infant *n.* baby, tot, child, newborn, babe. *The infant slept peacefully through the night.*

infect *vb.* **1.** contaminate, taint, poison, sicken, afflict. *Many children at the summer camp were infected with a cold virus.* **2.** influence, affect, touch, stir, move. *His humorous personality infected the entire group.*

infectious *adj.* contagious, catching, infective, transferable, communicable. *Flu is an infec-*

tious disease. **Ant.** noninfectious, incommunicable.

infer *vb.* conclude, reason, guess, reckon, deduce, suppose, presume. *I infer from your statement that you admit your part in the crime.*

inferior *adj.* poor, substandard, secondary, lesser, lower, mediocre. *She regretted using an inferior brand of paint for the house.* **Ant.** superior, better, higher.

infest *vb.* overrun, plague, swarm, beset, invade, ravage, fill. *The old wooden house was infested with termites.*

infinite *adj.* endless, limitless, unlimited, boundless, immense, enormous. *The number of stars in the universe is almost infinite.* **Ant.** limited, finite, restricted.

inflame *vb.* rouse, incite, enrage, provoke, aggravate, ignite. *She was inflamed with anger when her sister tore the dress.*

inflate *vb.* expand, distend, blow up, swell, enlarge. *He inflated the balloon with one huge breath.* **Ant.** deflate, collapse.

inflexible *adj.* **1.** rigid, stiff, unbending, firm, hard. *This inflexible bar will break if you try to bend it.* **2.** stubborn, steadfast, unbending, unyielding, immovable, headstrong. *She is inflexible regarding her decision to move to California.* **Ant. 1–2.** elastic, flexible, yielding.

inflict *vb.* impose, wreak, perpetrate, apply, subject, give. *The bombing inflicted heavy casualties.*

influence *n.* **1.** effect, sway, power, control, importance, weight. *She has a great deal of influence with the school board.* –*vb.* **2.** sway, persuade, move, direct, control, affect, impress. *The contestant was disqualified for trying to influence the judges.* **Ant. 1.** ineffectiveness, unimportance.

inform *vb.* tell, advise, enlighten, notify, acquaint, teach, educate. *Please inform the doctor that I will be late for my appointment.*

informal *adj.* casual, natural, easy, relaxed, simple, unofficial. *The speaker had an informal style that kept everybody at ease.* **Ant.** formal, official, stiff, rigid.

information *n.* facts, news, data, knowledge, intelligence, material. *We need more information in order to make a decision.*

infrequent *adj.* uncommon, occasional, irregular, unusual, sporadic. *Earthquakes are infrequent but frightening events.* **Ant.** common, frequent, usual.

infuriate *vb.* enrage, outrage, inflame, madden, anger, incense, rile. *His arrogant attitude infuriated his supervisor.* **Ant.** please, delight, satisfy.

ingenious *adj.* clever, imaginative, inventive, skillful, resourceful, creative. *The inventor created an ingenious device that irons your clothes while you sleep.* **Ant.** unoriginal, ordinary, unimaginative.

ingredient *n.* element, particle, part, factor, item, piece, aspect, feature. *Blueberries are a primary ingredient in blueberry muffins.*

inhabit *vb.* live, reside, dwell, occupy, abide, lodge. *The hollow tree was inhabited by two squirrels.*

inherent *adj.* essential, natural, inborn, inbred, ingrained, innate, elemental. *The ability to fly is an inherent trait of a bat.* **Ant.** alien, superficial, artificial.

inheritance *n.* legacy, bestowal, endowment, heritage, estate, bequest. *Her late uncle left her a large inheritance.*

initial *adj.* first, beginning, starting, primary, basic, original, opening. *We passed the initial phase of the test.* **Ant.** ending, last, concluding, final.

initiate *vb.* **1.** start, begin, commence, open, introduce, launch. *Our club initiates a membership drive every six months.* **2.** induct, inaugurate, receive, install, enter. *The pledges were initiated into the fraternity.* **Ant. 1.** accomplish, finish, complete. **2.** remove, oust, ban.

injure *vb.* harm, damage, mar, hurt, wound, impair. *He injured his arm while playing baseball.* **Ant.** heal, aid, benefit.

injustice *n.* unfairness, wrong, unjustness, disservice, inequity. *The lawyer felt that her client had suffered an injustice.* **Ant.** justness, fairness, right.

innate *adj.* natural, instinctive, inborn, inbred, inherent. *The figure skater had an innate talent for the sport.* **Ant.** learned, acquired, cultivated.

inner *adj.* interior, inside, inward, internal, central. *The inner core of the sphere was metallic.* **Ant.** outer, outside, exterior, outward.

innocent *adj.* **1.** guiltless, blameless, sinless, faultless, not guilty. *The jury found the defendant innocent.* **2.** harmless, innocuous, inoffensive, simple, safe, unknowing. *How could such an innocent encounter be so tragic?* **Ant. 1.** guilty, sinful, responsible. **2.** offensive, harmful.

innovation *n.* invention, novelty, change, alteration, introduction. *The inventor felt that his self-polishing shoes would be an important innovation in the fashion industry.*

innuendo *n.* allusion, suggestion, hint, implication, insinuation. *The story was nothing but rumor and innuendo.*

innumerable *adj.* countless, many, limitless, unlimited, infinite, numerous. *The mosquitoes at this campsite are innumerable.* **Ant.** limited, few, countable.

inoffensive *adj.* innocent, harmless, innocuous, unoffending. *She tried to make her criticism as inoffensive as possible.* **Ant.** offensive, insulting, harmful.

inquire *vb.* **1.** ask, seek, question, query, quiz. *I'm here to inquire about the room for rent.* **2.** examine, investigate, search, explore, study, research. *This research project will inquire into the mysteries of the atom.*

inquisitive *adj.* inquiring, prying, curious, snooping, nosy, searching. *An inquisitive raccoon investigated every corner of the garage.* **Ant.** indifferent, uninterested, unconcerned.

insane *adj.* **1.** crazy, mad, lunatic, demented, unbalanced, deranged, psychotic. *After spending twenty years alone in the mountains, the hermit was slightly insane.* **2.** senseless, foolish, silly, stupid, dumb, idiotic, moronic, absurd. *It was insane to dive head first into that shallow pond.* **Ant. 1.** sane, sound, rational. **2.** wise, reasonable, sensible.

insatiable *adj.* limitless, unsatisfiable, unquenchable, uncontrolled, demanding. *He has an insatiable appetite for ice cream.* **Ant.** limited, satisfied, controlled.

insecure *adj.* **1.** unstable, unsafe, dangerous, unsteady, hazardous, shaky. *The stack of barrels looked insecure, so we tied them down.* **2.** unsure, uncertain, nervous, anxious, hesitant, uneasy. *I feel insecure about speaking in front of so many people.* **Ant. 1.** stable, safe, secure. **2.** confident, assured, certain.

insensitive *adj.* unconcerned, unfeeling, callous, hard, tough, cold. *You didn't have to be so insensitive about her feelings.* **Ant.** sensitive, warm, caring, feeling.

inseparable *adj.* indivisible, unseparable, undividable, impartible. *The two friends are inseparable.* **Ant.** separable, dividable, partible.

insert *adj.* inject, place, put, implant, enter. *She inserted a dime into the parking meter.* **Ant.** remove, eject, withdraw.

inside *adj.* **1.** inner, interior, inward, internal, indoor. *The inside dining area will be warmer at night.* **2.** private, personal, intimate, confidential, secret. *The director told an inside joke about the film industry.* –*n.* **3.** interior, inner part, inner space. *Please paint the inside of the house too.* **Ant. 1.** outer, outward, external. **2.** public, popular. **3.** exterior.

insight *n.* understanding, perception, knowledge, wisdom, judgment, vision. *New insights can be gained through the exploration of space.*

insignia *n.* badge, emblem, patch, decoration. *The air force cadet wore his insignia proudly.*

insignificant *adj.* trivial, unimportant, trifling, meaningless, inessential, paltry. *An insignificant amount of rain fell on the crops.* **Ant.** significant, important, meaningful.

insincere *adj.* dishonest, false, deceitful, deceptive, untrue, untruthful. *Her feelings for her friend proved to be insincere.* **Ant.** sincere, honest, truthful.

insinuate *vb.* suggest, imply, hint, convey, indicate, state. *Are you insinuating that I didn't study for the test?*

insist *vb.* demand, require, command, request, urge, stress. *The security guard insisted on seeing the intruder's identification.*

insolent *adj.* insulting, disrespectful, rude, surly, arrogant, defiant. *The insolent student had to stay after school as punishment.* **Ant.** polite, courteous, respectful.

inspect *vb.* examine, investigate, observe, study, search, scan, scrutinize. *She inspected the motorcycle before buying it.* **Ant.** overlook, ignore, neglect.

inspiration *n.* **1.** stimulus, incentive, encouragement, motivation, influence. *Her story should be an inspiration to all.* **2.** idea, thought, revelation, enlightenment. *Where did you get the inspiration to create a TV that turns itself off during commercials?*

inspire *vb.* encourage, stimulate, arouse, motivate, stir, prompt, excite. *Reading that novel inspired me to write a book.* **Ant.** discourage, deter, dishearten.

instance *n.* moment, example, case, occasion, occurrence. *The traveler could think of many instances of being lost in a foreign country.*

instant *n.* **1.** moment, minute, second, flash, wink, jiffy. *The meteor could only be seen for an instant.* –*adj.* **2.** immediate, quick, prompt, swift, rapid, hasty. *I hope you don't expect an instant reply to your proposal of marriage.* **Ant. 2.** delayed, slow, lengthy.

instantly *adv.* immediately, instantaneously, suddenly, directly, rapidly, quickly. *A lifeguard instantly jumped into the pool to save the drowning child.* **Ant.** later, eventually, slowly.

instead *adv.* alternatively, rather, alternately, in lieu of. *The baseball game is canceled, so we're going to a movie instead.*

instinct *n.* tendency, aptitude, feeling, intuition, impulse, capacity. *She has a natural instinct for painting.*

institute *vb.* **1.** establish, start, begin, originate, found, initiate. *The library instituted a summer reading program.* –*n.* **2.** school, academy, institution, college, university, organization, establishment. *He is studying painting at the art institute.* **Ant. 1.** finish, conclude, discontinue.

institution *n.* **1.** custom, practice, tradition, convention. *Thanksgiving dinners are a national institution.* **2.** institute, school, university, college, organization, establishment. *There is an institution for almost every field of study.*

instruct *vb.* **1.** teach, educate, inform, train, tutor, enlighten, coach. *Today you will be instructed by a substitute teacher.* **2.** direct, command, order, dictate, told, charge. *He was instructed to leave the application on the desk.*

instrument *n.* tool, device, implement, machine, apparatus, utensil. *The television repairman had many strange instruments in his toolbox.*

instrumental *adj.* useful, helpful, beneficial, handy, effective, valuable. *Radio and television are instrumental in providing information to the public.* **Ant.** useless, worthless, ineffective.

insufficient *adj.* inadequate, incomplete, deficient, skimpy, slim. *There was insufficient evidence to convict the defendant.* **Ant.** adequate, enough, sufficient.

insult *vb.* **1.** offend, humiliate, affront, outrage, ridicule, mock, belittle, scorn. *The waiter was insulted by the small tip.* *–n.* **2.** offense, outrage, slander, scorn, indignity, abuse. *I've had enough of your insults.* **Ant. 1.** flatter, praise, compliment. **2.** respect, flattery, praise.

insure *vb.* protect, safeguard, guarantee, warrant, assure. *The stereo system was insured against any damage for one year.*

insurgent *n.* **1.** rebel, revolutionary, dissident, mutineer, anarchist. *Insurgents stormed the palace.* *–adj.* **2.** rebellious, mutinous, revolutionary, disobedient, lawless. *The dictator jailed everyone found engaging in insurgent activities.* **Ant. 1.** loyalist, patriot. **2.** loyal, obedient, patriotic.

insurrection *n.* revolution, mutiny, rebellion, coup, revolt, uprising. *Peasants planned an insurrection against their king.* **Ant.** submission, obedience.

intact *adj.* whole, complete, unbroken, undamaged, perfect, entire, unharmed. *There was not one dish intact after the earthquake.* **Ant.** broken, incomplete, damaged.

integrate *vb.* blend, mix, combine, unify, fuse, harmonize. *All the suggestions were integrated into one long list.* **Ant.** segregate, separate, part, divide.

integrity *n.* virtue, honesty, honor, goodness, uprightness, morality. *The mayor's integrity was the issue in question.* **Ant.** corruption, dishonesty, immorality.

intellectual *adj.* **1.** learned, academic, thoughtful, intelligent, scholarly, studious. *She is fascinated by philosophy, psychology, and related intellectual subjects.* *–n.* **2.** scholar, academician, thinker, intellect, sage. *It is incorrect to think that only intellectuals like to read.* **Ant. 1.** ignorant, unlearned, thoughtless. **2.** idiot, dummy, moron.

intelligence *n.* **1.** intellect, aptitude, brightness, brains, wisdom. *Stop acting like you have the intelligence of a hamster.* **2.** information, knowledge, news, reports, data, facts. *The president requested to see all the intelligence on the oil crisis.* **Ant. 1.** stupidity, ignorance.

intelligent *adj.* smart, wise, clever, bright, astute, brilliant. *She's too intelligent to wait on tables the rest of her life.* **Ant.** stupid, dumb, ignorant.

intend *vb.* mean, aim, plan, expect, propose, resolve. *Do you intend to mow the lawn today?*

intense *adj.* extreme, severe, great, powerful, strong, acute. *The chess champion played with intense concentration.* **Ant.** weak, mild, moderate.

intensify *vb.* increase, strengthen, magnify, reinforce, concentrate. *We'll have to intensify our efforts if we want to finish on time.* **Ant.** reduce, diminish, lessen.

intensive *adj.* thorough, full, total, exhaustive, concentrated, hard. *An intensive study of the problem will be undertaken.* **Ant.** careless, partial, superficial.

intent *n.* **1.** purpose, intention, aim, goal, plan, object, design. *His intent was to organize a softball team.* *–adj.* **2.** resolute, firm, determined, insistent, intense, fixed. *The pitcher was intent on striking out the batter.* **Ant. 2.** purposeless, uncaring, indifferent.

intentional *adj.* intended, deliberate, purposeful, planned, willful. *The intentional misspell-*

ing of my name was supposed to be a joke. **Ant.** accidental, unplanned, unintended.

intercede *vb.* mediate, moderate, arbitrate, referee, intervene. *The attempt to intercede in the gang war was met with suspicion.*

intercept *vb.* stop, block, obstruct, seize, arrest, grab, interrupt. *A posse intercepted the outlaws at the pass.*

interest *n.* **1.** attention, regard, care, absorption, notice. *It was with great interest that the archaeologist studied the relics.* **2.** benefit, good, advantage, concern, welfare. *Do you ever look out for anybody's interests other than your own?* **3.** percentage, dividend, profit, yield, gain. *He received a good interest on his savings account.* **4.** share, ownership, portion, part, stake, investment. *Her interest in the toy company was inherited from her father.* –*vb.* **5.** intrigue, fascinate, concern, attract, engage, absorb. *He was interested in starting a rock band.* **Ant. 1.** neglect, unconcern, apathy. **2.** loss, disadvantage.

interesting *adj.* fascinating, engaging, entertaining, absorbing, inviting, appealing. *Work is easy when it's interesting.* **Ant.** dull, boring, tedious, monotonous.

interfere *vb.* intrude, intervene, interrupt, meddle, conflict, intercede. *Don't interfere with the decision of the referee.* **Ant.** support, aid, assist.

interior *n.* **1.** inside, middle, center, nucleus, core. *The interior of the cabin needed painting.* –*adj.* **2.** inner, internal, indoor, inside, enclosed. *The interior lighting was inadequate for reading.* **Ant. 1.** exterior, outside. **2.** outer, outdoor, external.

interlude *n.* interval, break, pause, intermission, gap, lull. *There was an interlude between the storms.*

intermediate *adj.* middle, moderate, halfway, intervening, midway. *If you pass this class, you can advance to the intermediate level.*

intermission *n.* break, interlude, rest, stop, pause, recess. *There will be a brief intermission between acts 1 and 2.*

intermittent *adj.* recurrent, spasmodic, occasional, periodic, irregular, alternating. *The*

wind was intermittent throughout the day. **Ant.** steady, continuous.

internal *adj.* inner, inside, inward, interior. *The internal chamber of the tomb revealed many treasures.* **Ant.** outer, external, exterior.

interpret *vb.* **1.** explain, define, construe, clarify, illustrate. *I don't know how to interpret her actions.* **2.** translate, paraphrase, decipher, reword, restate. *Since the traveler could not understand Japanese, he needed someone to interpret for him.*

interrogate *vb.* question, quiz, query, probe, examine, ask. *The suspect was interrogated by the police for hours.*

interrupt *vb.* disturb, interfere, intercept, break, stop, intrude. *His nap was interrupted by a blasting car horn.* **Ant.** resume, continue.

intersect *vb.* cross, crisscross, meet, cut, bisect, traverse, crosscut. *Make a left turn where the highway intersects Main Street.*

interval *n.* period, pause, gap, interlude, interim, break, rest, interruption. *We need a longer interval between classes.*

intervene *vb.* interfere, mediate, intrude, interrupt, intercede. *The police intervened before any serious harm occurred.*

intervention *n.* interference, interruption, intrusion, incursion, intercession. *The president called for military intervention in the Middle East.*

interview *n.* **1.** conference, dialogue, meeting, discussion, conversation, evaluation. *I'm scheduled for an interview with the personnel manager.* –*vb.* **2.** question, converse, query, ask, examine, evaluate. *A reporter interviewed the politician regarding her stand on civil rights.*

intimacy *n.* closeness, caring, fondness, familiarity, friendship. *The family retained their intimacy despite their separation.* **Ant.** indifference, aloofness.

intimate *adj.* **1.** close, familiar, personal, dear, near, loving. *The two friends have an intimate relationship.* **2.** secret, private, personal, confidential, innermost. *The actress revealed her most intimate thoughts in her book.* **3.** thorough, solid, exhaustive, deep, profound, complete. *He has an intimate knowledge of the workings of*

Congress. –vb. **4.** hint, imply, suggest, allude, insinuate, indicate. *She intimated that he was guilty of the crime.* **Ant. 1.** impersonal, unfamiliar, remote. **2.** open, public, known. **3.** shallow, superficial, limited. **4.** declare, state, claim.

intimidate *vb.* scare, frighten, threaten, menace, dismay, alarm, terrify, terrorize. *Don't let that bully intimidate you.*

intolerable *adj.* unbearable, unendurable, insufferable, excessive, unreasonable. *This summer's heat is intolerable.* **Ant.** tolerable, bearable, comfortable, endurable.

intolerant *adj.* biased, prejudiced, bigoted, disdainful, hostile, resentful. *The old man was intolerant of people from foreign lands.* **Ant.** tolerant, fair, accepting.

intoxicated *adj.* **1.** drunk, drunken, tipsy, high, inebriated. *She was arrested for driving while intoxicated.* **2.** enthralled, enchanted, excited, elated, moved. *The dancers were intoxicated by the loud and rhythmic music.* **Ant. 1.** sober, dry, straight. **2.** bored, unmoved.

intrepid *adj.* fearless, bold, brave, heroic, valiant, courageous, daring. *An intrepid knight rode out to slay the dragon.* **Ant.** cowardly, frightened, meek, timid.

intricate *adj.* complex, complicated, elaborate, involved, detailed. *His latest novel has a confusingly intricate plot.* **Ant.** simple, uncomplicated, plain.

intrigue *vb.* **1.** fascinate, interest, captivate, excite, enthrall, charm. *The story of your adventures intrigues me.* –n. **2.** scheme, plot, conspiracy, espionage, ruse. *The rebellious army officers hoped their intrigues would be successful.* **Ant. 1.** bore, tire, weary.

introduce *vb.* **1.** present, announce, acquaint, familiarize. *I would like to introduce you to my husband.* **2.** propose, submit, present, offer, advance, originate. *The Congressman introduced a bill to outlaw slingshots.* **Ant. 2.** withdraw, remove, eliminate.

intrude *vb.* trespass, encroach, infringe, intervene, impose, invade, interfere. *It's impolite to intrude on someone's privacy.*

intuition *n.* instinct, insight, perception, intuitiveness, hunch. *Her intuition told her it was dangerous to drive across the bridge.*

inundate *vb.* flood, overflow, overwhelm, swamp, saturate, engulf. *The graduate was inundated with job offers.*

invade *vb.* attack, assault, raid, penetrate, overrun, swarm. *Wild dogs invaded the chicken coop.*

invalid *adj.* void, null, worthless, useless, unusable, ineffective. *All passes for the movie are invalid on weekends.* **Ant.** useful, valid, effective.

invaluable *adj.* valuable, priceless, precious, expensive, costly, rare. *Rembrandt's paintings are invaluable.* **Ant.** cheap, worthless, common.

invent *vb.* **1.** create, produce, originate, develop, conceive. *The person who invented the alarm clock should be shot.* **2.** imagine, pretend, fabricate, fake, falsify. *She invented a story to explain her absence from school.* **Ant. 1.** copy, imitate, duplicate.

invention *n.* **1.** creation, device, gadget, contraption, innovation. *I hope the professor's newest invention doesn't explode like the last one.* **2.** inventing, creating, creation, development, origination. *The invention of the airplane changed our world.* **3.** inventiveness, creativity, originality, newness, freshness, novelty. *The artistic invention of Picasso is unequaled in the 20th century.* **4.** lie, falsehood, fabrication, fib, fiction, story. *His account of his journey to Atlantis is pure invention.* **Ant. 2.** imitation, copying, reproduction. **3.** conformity, staleness, dullness. **4.** truth, fact, reality.

inventory *n.* **1.** supply, reserve, surplus, goods, stock, merchandise. *The store owner must sell his inventory by April.* **2.** list, catalog, tally, count, index, roster. *She made an inventory of the things she needed for her classroom.*

invest *vb.* **1.** empower, endow, authorize, license, delegate, charge, entrust. *The police are invested with the duty to enforce the law.* **2.** spend, allot, venture, supply, give. *He invested a lot of money in his stamp collection.*

investigate *vb.* probe, examine, explore, study, research, inspect. *A committee was appointed to investigate UFO sightings.*

invigorating *adj.* refreshing, stimulating, bracing, vitalizing, energizing. *A cold shower is invigorating.* **Ant.** weakening, enervating, tiring.

invincible *adj.* invulnerable, unbeatable, unconquerable, untouchable, secure. *The sorceress thought she was invincible.* **Ant.** beatable, vulnerable, weak.

invite *vb.* request, ask, welcome, summon, bid, beckon. *She invited her friends to have dinner at her house.*

invoke *vb.* summon, address, entreat, beseech, call, beg. *The sorcerer invoked the spirits to grant his wish.*

involuntary *adj.* **1.** mandatory, unwilling, forced, coerced, compulsory. *The soldier was on an involuntary assignment.* **2.** automatic, spontaneous, instinctive, unintentional, uncontrolled. *When the doctor hit her knee with a hammer, her leg responded with an involuntary jerk.* **Ant. 1.** voluntary, willing, optional. **2.** intentional, controlled.

involve *vb.* **1.** include, embrace, contain, entail, imply. *A full checkup on your car will involve an oil change.* **2.** absorb, engage, occupy, concern, preoccupy, entangle. *I do not wish to become involved in your problems.* **Ant. 1.** exclude, omit, disregard. **2.** disentangle, disengage.

irate *adj.* angry, enraged, mad, angered, wrathful, infuriated, incensed. *She was irate with the man who stole her idea.* **Ant.** pleased, happy, glad.

irk *vb.* irritate, annoy, vex, bother, trouble, peeve, provoke. *It really irks me when people are late.* **Ant.** cheer, delight, satisfy.

ironic *adj.* **1.** sarcastic, biting, cutting, cynical, caustic, satiric. *Her ironic humor is not always appreciated.* **2.** strange, inconsistent, weird, contradictory, curious, odd. *Isn't it ironic how I always manage to lose something after I organize my room?* **Ant. 1.** tactful, inoffensive. **2.** consistent, understandable.

irrational *adj.* illogical, unreasonable, absurd, ridiculous, crazy. *It's irrational to think you can catch fish in a bathtub.* **Ant.** rational, logical, sane, sensible.

irregular *adj.* **1.** uneven, unequal, unbalanced, rough, rugged. *The irregular surface of this table makes it hard to work on.* **2.** unusual, odd, erratic, abnormal, unconventional, peculiar, strange. *Your request to paint the office purple is highly irregular.* **Ant. 1.** even, level, smooth. **2.** normal, conventional, common.

irrelevant *adj.* unconnected, unrelated, unfitting, immaterial, unimportant. *His comments were irrelevant to the issues.* **Ant.** relevant, related, applicable.

irreverent *adj.* disrespectful, profane, impious, irreligious, uncivil. *The irreverent person was asked to leave the temple.* **Ant.** reverent, respectful, pious.

irritable *adj.* testy, touchy, sensitive, peevish, impatient, cross. *I'm a very irritable person when I get up too early in the morning.* **Ant.** mellow, calm, agreeable.

irritate *vb.* **1.** anger, annoy, bother, provoke, pester, irk. *She was irritated by her roommate's sloppiness.* **2.** pain, chafe, redden, inflame, aggravate. *That brand of soap irritates my skin.* **Ant. 1.** placate, comfort, appease. **2.** relieve, ease, soothe.

island *n.* **1.** isle, islet, atoll, archipelago. *My friend lives on a Caribbean island.* **2.** haven, shelter, refuge, retreat, sanctuary. *The campfire was a little island of warmth surrounded by the cold of the night.*

isolate *vb.* separate, segregate, detach, seclude, disconnect, remove. *Our first step should be to isolate the problem.*

issue *n.* **1.** matter, question, problem, topic, subject, concern. *Housing development is an important issue in our community.* **2.** copy, edition, number, volume, publication. *He collects old issues of science-fiction magazines.* –*vb.* **3.** distribute, circulate, release, dispatch, dispense. *The ice-cream parlor issued coupons for a free sundae.* **4.** flow, emerge, arise, discharge, spring, emit. *Oil issued from the leak in the pipe.* **Ant. 3.** revoke, withdraw, cancel.

item *n.* **1.** thing, article, element, object, unit, particular. *I need one more item from the store.* **2.**

story, feature, account, article, report. *Did you read the item in the paper about the labor strike?*

itemize *vb.* detail, specify, register, list, record, document, count, number. *Every school expense must be itemized.*

jab *vb.* **1.** poke, prod, push, thrust, nudge, elbow, punch. *She jabbed a knife into the watermelon.* –*n.* **2.** poke, prod, blow, punch, hit, dig. *A jab to the stomach knocked the wind out of him.*

jacket *n.* cover, wrapping, wrapper, coat. *Please put the record back in its jacket.*

jagged *adj.* notched, pointed, serrated, toothed, barbed, rough, irregular. *Saws have jagged edges.* **Ant.** smooth, even, straight.

jail *n.* **1.** prison, penitentiary, jailhouse, stockade, brig. *He has spent the past ten years in jail.* –*vb.* **2.** imprison, incarcerate, detain, confine, lock up. *She was jailed for drunk driving.* **Ant. 2.** free, release, liberate.

jam *vb.* **1.** press, pack, crowd, force, squeeze, cram, stuff. *He jammed so many clothes in the drawer that he couldn't close it.* **2.** block, obstruct, clog, stop, cease. *Her gun jammed when she attempted to fire it.* –*n.* **3.** crowd, crush, press, horde, throng, mob. *We were stuck for hours in a traffic jam.*

jar *n.* **1.** bottle, container, vessel, receptacle, jug. *Please pass me that jar of peanut butter.* –*vb.* **2.** annoy, irritate, upset, disturb, perturb. *The sound of squeaking chalk jarred my nerves.* **3.** shake, vibrate, rattle, rock, quake. *A sonic boom jarred our house.* **Ant. 2.** soothe, comfort, calm.

jealous *adj.* **1.** envious, envying, covetous, desirous, resentful. *She was jealous when she saw my new computer.* **2.** suspicious, mistrustful, insecure, anxious, possessive. *He was so jealous of his wife that he didn't like her to go out alone.*

jealousy *n.* envy, suspicion, resentment, mistrust, anxiety, doubt. *Jealousy can destroy friendships.*

jeopardize *vb.* risk, imperil, endanger, menace, threaten. *Smoking jeopardizes your health.* **Ant.** save, protect, defend.

jeopardy *n.* risk, danger, peril, threat, vulnerability. *Her life was in jeopardy when she entered the burning building to save her friend.* **Ant.** safety, security.

jerk *n.* **1.** jolt, shake, twitch, pull, tug, yank. *The car started with a jerk because he had it in the wrong gear.* –*vb.* **2.** pull, tug, yank, snap, pluck. *She jerked on the leash in an effort to control her disobedient dog.*

jest *n.* **1.** joke, quip, witticism, wisecrack. *She must have a strange sense of humor because no one appreciates her jests.* –*vb.* **2.** joke, fool, tease, kid, wisecrack. *We thought he was jesting when he said he didn't want supper.*

jet *vb.* **1.** spurt, spray, squirt, stream, gush, rush. *Water jetted from the broken fire hydrant.* –*n.* **2.** spurt, spray, squirt, geyser, stream. *The drinking fountain sent a jet of water into my eyes.*

jewelry *n.* jewels, gems, stones, ornaments, gold, silver. *She wore lots of expensive jewelry.*

jingle *vb.* **1.** tinkle, clink, clang, ring, chime. *Loose change jingled in her purse.* –*n.* **2.** tinkle, tinkling, ringing, chime, chiming. *We could hear the jingle of the sleigh's bells.* **3.** tune, melody, carol, chorus, chant. *Where did you hear that cute jingle?*

jinx *n.* curse, hex, spell, enchantment, charm. *He had so much bad luck he thought someone had placed a jinx on him.*

job *n.* **1.** employment, work, occupation, position, situation. *He's looking for a summer job.* **2.** task, duty, chore, role, function. *She has some jobs to do around the house before she can go out.*

jockey *n.* **1.** rider, horseman, horsewoman, equestrian. *She wants to be a professional jockey.* –*vb.* **2.** maneuver, deploy, move, steer, turn. *Runners jockeyed for position at the starting line.*

join *vb.* **1.** connect, combine, couple, assemble, fasten, unite, link. *Please join hands.* **2.** enroll, enlist, enter, sign up. *She joined a chess club.* **Ant. 1.** divide, separate, detach. **2.** leave, quit, resign.

joint *n.* **1.** juncture, junction, coupling, connection, link. *He repaired the pipe's leaking joint.* *–adj.* **2.** mutual, combined, shared, common, collective, concerted. *It took our joint efforts to put out the fire.* **Ant. 2.** individual, independent, separate.

joke *n.* **1.** jest, witticism, gag, prank, trick. *Putting a rubber snake in his friend's bed was a foolish joke.* *–vb.* **2.** jest, fool, kid, tease, taunt, ridicule. *She was only joking when she said you should dye your hair pink.*

jolt *n.* **1.** jerk, jump, shake, lurch, surprise, shock. *He got quite a jolt when he touched the frayed electrical wire.* *–vb.* **2.** jar, jerk, shake, shock, disturb, startle. *We were all jolted by the news of our friend's death.*

jostle *vb.* push, bump, shove, joggle, elbow. *Greedy shoppers jostled each other to get at the sale items.*

jot *vb.* scribble, write, record, register, mark. *She jotted down her friend's address and phone number.*

journal *n.* **1.** diary, notebook, log, register, record book. *He kept a daily journal while he was in the army.* **2.** newspaper, magazine, periodical, review, publication. *Her article on ecology was published in a scientific journal.*

journalist *n.* reporter, correspondent, newscaster, newswoman, newsman. *The president granted an interview to several journalists.*

journey *n.* **1.** trip, excursion, tour, expedition, voyage, cruise. *I can't wait to hear about his journey to the North Pole.* *–vb.* **2.** travel, tour, trek, voyage, wander. *She plans to journey through Asia next year.*

jovial *adj.* cheerful, jolly, merry, gay, joyful, joyous. *The circus clown was always jovial.* **Ant. 1.** sad, depressed, melancholy, gloomy.

joy *n.* happiness, delight, ecstasy, glee, rapture, elation. *He was filled with joy when she accepted his marriage proposal.* **Ant.** misery, sadness, sorrow.

joyous *adj.* joyful, happy, glad, jubilant, cheerful, merry. *The family's reunion after years of separation was a joyous occasion.* **Ant.** joyless, sad, unhappy.

jubilant *adj.* ecstatic, elated, exhilarated, thrilled, excited. *She was jubilant when she got the unexpected promotion.* **Ant.** disappointed, dejected, despondent.

judge *n.* **1.** justice, magistrate, jurist. *Our municipal judge has just been appointed to the state supreme court.* **2.** referee, umpire, moderator, evaluator, assessor, critic. *The judges gave the gymnast a perfect 10.* *–vb.* **3.** determine, decree, decide, rule, try. *The suspect's guilt or innocence will be judged in a court of law.* **4.** evaluate, appraise, rate, rank, analyze. *She was asked to judge our local beauty contest.*

judgment *n.* **1.** verdict, decision, ruling, finding, determination. *The jury will deliver its judgment tomorrow.* **2.** discretion, sense, intelligence, wisdom, discernment. *She showed good judgment when she picked me as her friend.*

jug *n.* pitcher, flask, jar, bottle, carafe. *The peasant girl used a jug to carry water from the well.*

juggle *vb.* maneuver, manipulate, fake, alter, tamper, modify. *He juggled his tax receipts to make it look like he had more deductions.*

jumble *vb.* **1.** disorder, disorganize, disarrange, unsettle, mix. *Somehow she managed to jumble her computer files.* *–n.* **2.** muddle, mess, tangle, confusion, mixture. *Your report is just a jumble of unrelated facts.* **Ant. 1.** order, organize, arrange. **2.** arrangement, order.

jumbo *adj.* oversized, huge, immense, colossal, giant, large. *He prefers jumbo shrimp.* **Ant.** small, tiny, average.

jump *vb.* leap, bound, vault, skip, spring, hop. *Fortunately, she had her parachute on when she jumped out of the plane.* *–n.* **2.** bound, leap, vault, spring, hurdle, rise. *His specialty is the high jump.*

junction *n.* joint, link, connection, intersection, interchange. *This road ends at its junction with Highway 5.*

jungle *n.* rain forest, bush, wilds, woods, wilderness. *Tigers live in jungles.*

junior *adj.* lower, lesser, subordinate, secondary, younger. *She's a junior partner in that law firm.* **Ant.** senior, higher, older.

junk *n.* debris, litter, trash, rubbish, garbage, refuse. *Please clean all that old junk out of your closet.*

just *adj.* **1.** fair, impartial, unbiased, reasonable, equitable. *Considering what he had done, his punishment was just.* –*adv.* **2.** exactly, precisely, perfectly, completely, fully. *This present is just what I wanted.* **3.** barely, scarcely, narrowly, hardly, merely. *We had just made it to the theater when the movie started.* **4.** recently, lately, formerly, previously. *I just saw her at the store.* **Ant. 1.** unfair, unreasonable, biased.

justice *n.* fairness, impartiality, justness, equity, rightness. *Slavery is a practice that denies justice to its victims.* **Ant.** injustice, unfairness, inequity.

justify *vb.* **1.** confirm, verify, substantiate, corroborate, vindicate. *She justified my faith in her when she repaid the loan.* **2.** excuse, explain, rationalize, support, defend. *He justified his crime by claiming he needed the money to feed his family.*

jut *vb.* protrude, extend, project, bulge, stick out. *A huge boulder jutted out over the cliff's edge.* –*n.* **2.** protrusion, extension, projection, outthrust. *We beached our boat on a jut of land.*

juvenile *adj.* **1.** young, youthful, immature, childish, adolescent. *Juvenile delinquents vandalized the local park.* –*n.* **2.** child, youngster, youth, minor, kid. *Juveniles are not entitled to vote.* **Ant. 1.** adult, mature, grown-up. **2.** adult, elder.

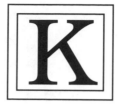

keen *adj.* **1.** sharp, fine, thin, honed. *Be careful; that knife has a keen edge.* **2.** clever, bright, brilliant, shrewd, quick. *She has a keen mind.* **3.** eager, enthusiastic, avid, ardent, zealous. *He was keen on going to the circus.* **Ant. 1.** dull, blunt. **2.** dense, stupid. **3.** apathetic, indifferent.

keep *vb.* **1.** hold, retain, have, possess. *You may keep the record you borrowed.* **2.** restrain, retard, impede, hinder, confine. *The rain kept us from going on a picnic.* **3.** support, sustain, maintain, provision, provide for. *She kept my dog while I was on vacation.* **4.** continue, persist, persevere, endure. *You keep saying you'll try harder, but you don't.* **5.** fulfill, observe, obey, honor. *He kept his promise to be home in time for dinner.* *–n.* **6.** upkeep, sustenance, subsistence, living, livelihood. *It's about time you got a job and paid for your own keep.* **7.** dungeon, cell, stronghold, tower. *The kidnapped prince was locked in the castle's inner keep.* **Ant. 1.** discard, release, abandon. **2.** free, liberate. **4.** stop, halt, cease. **5.** neglect, ignore, disregard.

keg *n.* barrel, cask, drum, tank, container. *They bought a keg of beer for their party.*

key *n.* **1.** solution, explanation, answer, resolution, clue. *The missing piece of evidence was the key to solving the crime.* *–adj.* **2.** main, leading, primary, decisive, crucial. *She's the key member of our band, and we can't perform without her.* *–vb.* **3.** adjust, adapt, suit, fit, harmonize. *He keyed his comments to the audience's level of understanding.* **Ant. 2.** minor, insignificant, inconsequential.

kick *vb.* **1.** boot, hit, strike, push, shove. *Only a cruel person would ever kick a dog.* *–n.* **2.** boot, punt, blow, stroke, hit. *He gave the football a hard kick.*

kid *vb.* **1.** tease, taunt, joke, jest, ridicule. *She was only kidding when she said she saw some Martians in your backyard.* *–n.* **2.** child, young-ster, youth, daughter, son. *He took his kids to a movie.* **Ant. 2.** adult, grownup, elder.

kidnap *vb.* abduct, capture, seize, steal, carry off. *The princess was kidnaped by an evil wizard.* **Ant.** return, release, free.

kill *vb.* **1.** slay, murder, slaughter, assassinate, execute. *The hunter killed a deer.* **2.** ruin, destroy, end, halt, terminate, extinguish. *His mismanagement of the important project killed his chances for a promotion.* **Ant. 2.** revitalize, begin, sustain.

killing *n.* **1.** murder, slaughter, slaying, homicide, bloodshed. *Many people get upset over the killing of laboratory animals.* *–adj.* **2.** lethal, deadly, fatal, deathly, murderous. *The shuttle disaster was almost a killing blow to our space program.*

kin *n.* family, relatives, relations, kinsfolk. *Police would not release the victim's name until his next of kin could be notified.*

kind *adj.* **1.** amiable, friendly, considerate, gentle, benign, loving, caring. *A kind woman held the door open for me.* *–n.* **2.** manner, variety, type, sort, class, make. *What kind of car do you drive?* **Ant. 1.** unkind, unfriendly, inconsiderate.

kindle *vb.* **1.** ignite, light, fire, torch, burn. *She kindled the campfire with only one match.* **2.** arouse, excite, stir, provoke, stimulate. *His warm smile kindled her interest.* **Ant. 1–2.** extinguish, quench, smother.

kindness *n.* charity, humanity, generosity, favor, graciousness. *Acts of kindness are their own reward.*

king *n.* monarch, sovereign, emperor, ruler, lord. *Everyone was required to bow before the king.*

kingdom *n.* realm, domain, dominion, country, nation. *Before the 19th century, Germany was divided into numerous small kingdoms.*

kink *n.* **1.** twist, crimp, crinkle, gnarl, knot. *After swimming all day, her hair was full of kinks.* **2.** pang, spasm, cramp, crick. *He got a kink in his back from trying to lift the heavy weight.*

knack *n.* skill, talent, aptitude, gift, ability. *She has a knack for knowing just the right thing to say.*

kneel *vb.* bow, curtsy, kowtow, salaam. *You must kneel in the presence of the queen.*

knife *n.* **1.** blade, cutlery, dagger, pocket-knife, jackknife. *Knives are useful tools, but they should be handled with caution.* *–vb.* **2.** stab, cut, pierce, slash, lacerate. *The goblin crept forward with the intention of knifing the unsuspecting dwarf in the back.*

knit *vb.* **1.** weave, stitch, braid, crochet, hook. *He likes to knit sweaters in his spare time.* **2.** heal, mend, attach, fasten, join, unite. *The doctor said my broken arm will knit in two months.* **Ant. 2.** separate, split, divide.

knob *n.* **1.** handle, hold, handhold, grip, stud. *She put new knobs on her closet doors.* **2.** lump, bump, knot, knurl, protuberance. *We can't use this piece of wood because it has too many knobs.*

knock *vb.* **1.** rap, tap, beat, strike, pound, hammer. *Let's knock on the door and see if anyone's home.* *–n.* **2.** blow, thump, rap, tap, pounding. *Did you hear a knock at the door?*

knot *n.* **1.** tie, bow, loop, hitch, braid, plait. *The climber secured himself to the rope with a strong knot.* **2.** burl, knurl, knob, bulge. *This is inferior lumber because it has so many knots.* **3.** tangle, snarl, kink, twist, gnarl. *He should brush the knots out of his hair.* **4.** group, cluster, bunch, clump, collection. *A knot of people gathered at the scene of the accident.* *–vb.* **5.** tie, fasten, secure, hitch, fix. *She knotted her hair into a bun.* **Ant. 5.** untie, undo, loosen.

know *vb.* understand, comprehend, perceive, recognize, realize. *Do you know how to drive?*

knowledge *n.* **1.** understanding, experience, familiarity, consciousness, awareness. *His knowledge of computers is very limited.* **2.** scholarship, learning, information, facts, data. *She has assembled a vast body of knowledge about the environment.* **Ant. 1.** ignorance, unfamiliarity.

label *n.* **1.** tag, sticker, mark, stamp, ticket, slip. *The label on a can will tell you what's in it.* –*vb.* **2.** tag, mark, name, stamp, ticket, classify, designate. *Please label all the items on sale.*

labor *n.* **1.** work, toil, effort, drudgery, task, exertion. *Much labor goes into building a house.* **2.** employees, workers, laborers, manpower. *There is a dispute between labor and management about the pay increase.* –*vb.* **3.** work, toil, drudge, slave, strain, strive. *The workers labored from dawn to dusk.* **Ant. 1.** rest, leisure, relaxation. **3.** rest, idle, loaf.

laborious *adj.* strenuous, difficult, burdensome, hard, arduous, tiresome, demanding. *Moving a piano can be a laborious task.* **Ant.** light, easy, simple, effortless.

labyrinth *n.* maze, network, complex, entanglement, tangle, web. *The city was a labyrinth of streets and boulevards.*

lack *n.* **1.** want, shortage, scarcity, need, dearth, absence, deficiency. *She got the job in spite of her lack of experience.* –*vb.* **2.** need, want, require, miss. *He lacks the motivation to succeed in his work.* **Ant. 1.** abundance, plenty, surplus. **2.** have, own, possess, hold.

lag *vb.* **1.** tarry, linger, dawdle, loiter, straggle, falter, delay. *Try not to lag too far behind us.* –*n.* **2.** slowdown, lateness, tardiness, slack, delay, drag. *What is causing the lag in the game?* **Ant. 1.** lead, hurry, go ahead. **2.** advance, acceleration.

lair *n.* **1.** burrow, den, cave, hole, nest. *The coyotes rested peacefully in their lair.* **2.** retreat, hideout, hideaway, sanctuary. *The bandits hid the gold in their lair.*

lame *adj.* **1.** crippled, disabled, limping, deformed, handicapped. *She could not run in the race because of her lame leg.* **2.** poor, weak, unconvincing, feeble, inadequate, sorry, flimsy. *I'm getting tired of your lame excuses.* **Ant. 1.** healthy, agile, functioning. **2.** convincing, plausible.

lament *n.* **1.** cry, moaning, lamentation, wailing, mourning, weeping, sorrow. *The warriors' laments for their fallen leader could be heard throughout the countryside.* –*vb.* **2.** moan, weep, wail, mourn, cry, grieve, deplore. *The children lamented the death of their cat.* **Ant. 1.** celebrating, delight. **2.** celebrate, cheer, enjoy.

lance *vb.* **1.** cut, pierce, puncture, slash, perforate. *A doctor lanced the wound.* –*n.* **2.** spear, javelin, pike, harpoon, weapon. *The knights attacked with their lances.*

land *n.* **1.** ground, soil, turf, field, terra firma. *The sailors have not seen land for six months.* **2.** country, nation, homeland, region, province, realm, territory. *This is the land of his ancestors.* –*vb.* **3.** arrive, disembark, settle, light, debark. *Someday astronauts will land on Mars.* **4.** get, gain, secure, win, obtain, hook. *The sales representative landed three more commissions this week.*

lane *n.* passage, road, way, path, route, alley, byway, track. *The lane was wide enough for only one car.*

language *n.* **1.** speech, tongue, dialect, idiom, vernacular. *The official language of Spain is Spanish.* **2.** jargon, vocabulary, phrasing, expression, lingo. *Programmers use technical language that can't be understood if you aren't familiar with computers.*

languish *vb.* sicken, weaken, fade, wither, decline, deteriorate. *She languished while dieting because she didn't get enough protein.* **Ant.** flourish, revive, recover, thrive.

lanky *adj.* lean, slender, thin, skinny, gaunt, bony, scrawny. *The basketball player was tall and lanky.* **Ant.** plump, chubby, stocky, muscular.

lapse *n.* **1.** error, mistake, slip, blunder, neglect, disregard. *The accident was caused by the driver's lapse of attention.* **2.** descent, decline, drop, regression, deterioration, slump. *Her lapse into a coma was distressing to her doctors.* **3.** interval, intermission, period, interlude, interruption. *There was a lapse of three months in which the Venusians received no contact from Mars.* –*vb.* **4.** decline, slip, fall, worsen, sink, fade, degenerate. *His memory has lapsed as he's grown older.* **5.** stop, expire, terminate, cease, end. *They will look for a new apartment as soon as their lease has lapsed.* **Ant. 2.** advance, improvement, development. **4.** improve, progress, increase. **5.** continue, proceed, start.

larceny *n.* theft, robbery, burglary, stealing, fraud, embezzlement. *Larceny is a serious crime.*

large *adj.* big, huge, massive, immense, enormous, vast, great, extensive, sizable. *The large turnout at the concert was unexpected.* **Ant.** small, little, tiny.

lark *n.* prank, frolic, fling, caper, escapade, romp, spree, whim. *His taking the day off work was just one of his occasional larks.*

lascivious *adj.* indecent, improper, immoral, obscene, vulgar. *He was ejected from the party for rude and lascivious behavior.* **Ant.** moral, decent, proper.

lash *n.* **1.** whip, cane, flail, strap, thong, scourge. *In times now past, students were punished with a lash.* **2.** stroke, blow, whip, hit. *You deserve twenty lashes with a wet noodle.* –*vb.* **3.** whip, beat, flog, thrash, flail. *It is cruel to lash horses.* **4.** scold, berate, criticize, attack, castigate, upbraid. *The teacher lashed out at the students for their unruly behavior.* **5.** tie, rope, bind, fasten, secure, tether. *The sailor lashed the sail to the mast.* **Ant. 4.** praise, commend, compliment. **5.** untie, unbind, release.

last *adj.* **1.** final, ending, conclusive, closing, ultimate, terminal. *This is the last time I'll eat at this restaurant.* –*vb.* **2.** endure, persist, continue, remain, survive, abide. *How long is this rain going to last?* **Ant. 1.** beginning, first, starting. **2.** end, stop, cease, expire.

lasting *adj.* enduring, continuing, permanent, perennial, persistent, lingering. *Doctors have a lasting commitment to save lives.* **Ant.** temporary, brief, passing, momentary.

latch *vb.* **1.** lock, bolt, fasten, secure, catch, close. *The dog escaped because you didn't latch the gate.* –*n.* **2.** bolt, hook, lock, fastening, clamp. *The latch on this suitcase is difficult to open.* **Ant. 1.** open, unlock, unlatch.

late *adj.* **1.** tardy, overdue, behind, slow, delayed, detained. *He was late for his appointment.* **2.** deceased, dead, departed, gone. *The late senator was known for her achievements in civil rights.* **3.** recent, new, fresh, advanced, modern. *This car is the manufacturer's latest model.* **Ant. 1.** early, prompt, punctual. **2.** alive, existing, surviving. **3.** early, old, first.

lately *adv.* recently, currently, presently, of late. *Lately he's been acting a little strange.* **Ant.** formerly, originally, once.

latent *adj.* dormant, hidden, inactive, inert, sleeping, unrealized. *Some people believe that telepathy is a latent power of the mind.* **Ant.** realized, developed, active.

later *adv.* **1.** afterwards, subsequently, next, successively. *We will eat dinner later.* –*adj.* **2.** following, ensuing, subsequent, successive, succeeding. *I will get back to you at a later date.* **Ant. 2.** earlier, prior, first.

latitude *n.* scope, freedom, liberty, range, extent, choice, leeway. *The teacher gave her students a lot of latitude in choosing their science projects.*

latter *adj.* later, final, ending, ensuing, successive, last. *The latter part of the movie was more entertaining.* **Ant.** former, earlier, beginning.

laugh *vb.* **1.** giggle, chuckle, roar, guffaw, snicker, chortle, titter. *The children laughed at the clown.* –*n.* **2.** giggle, chuckle, snicker, roar. *Everybody needs a good laugh now and then.* **Ant. 1.** cry, weep, mourn, frown. **2.** crying, weeping.

laughable *adj.* funny, hilarious, comical, humorous, amusing, ridiculous. *If the incident weren't so embarrassing it would be laughable.* **Ant.** serious, solemn, somber, sad.

launch *vb.* **1.** begin, initiate, start, originate, introduce, establish, inaugurate. *A new sports program will be launched in June.* **2.** propel, fire, thrust, shoot, eject. *Cape Kennedy launched a space shuttle today.* **Ant. 1.** stop, terminate, end.

launder *vb.* wash, clean, scrub, cleanse, scour. *He laundered his clothes.*

lavish *vb.* **1.** squander, waste, shower, bestow, overindulge. *The millionaire lavished her money on her friends.* *-adj.* **2.** liberal, extravagant, abundant, bountiful, generous, plentiful. *I didn't expect such a lavish banquet.* **Ant. 1.** save, retain, withhold. **2.** scanty, economical, stingy.

law *n.* rule, regulation, statute, decree, edict, mandate, code, principle. *Every society has laws that must be observed.*

lawful *adj.* legal, legitimate, authorized, permitted, sanctioned, permissible. *The demonstration was conducted in a lawful manner.* **Ant.** unlawful, illegal, illicit, prohibited.

lawyer *n.* attorney, counsel, counselor, advocate, barrister. *The defendant knew he would need a good lawyer.*

lax *adj.* slack, neglectful, loose, careless, lenient, casual, negligent. *The students were often lax about getting their homework done on time.* **Ant.** precise, careful, strict, rigid.

lay *vb.* **1.** place, deposit, put, set, settle, establish, fix. *Please lay the suitcases on the bed.* **2.** assign, charge, attribute, place, credit, put. *Let's lay the responsibility on someone else.* *-n.* **3.** position, arrangement, alignment, orientation, contour. *She surveyed the lay of the land.*

layer *n.* thickness, stratum, tier, level, fold, coating. *It was so cold that he slept under four layers of blankets.*

lazy *adj.* sluggish, idle, inactive, listless, slow, slothful, lethargic. *She was too lazy to get out of bed.* **Ant.** active, energetic, industrious, busy.

lead *vb.* **1.** guide, direct, show, conduct, escort, steer, pilot. *Would you lead me to the nearest hospital?* **2.** command, head, direct, supervise, manage, govern. *The senior staff member always leads the meetings.* **3.** exceed, surpass, outperform, head, best, better. *Our team was leading by seven points at halftime.* *-n.* **4.** start, advantage, edge, precedence, advance, jump. *The marathon runner took an early lead.* **5.** hint, clue, cue, suggestion, indication. *The detectives needed more leads to solve the murder.* **Ant. 1.** follow,

tail, trail. **2.** follow, obey, heed. **3.** trail, lag, succeed. **4.** disadvantage, handicap. **5.** misdirection, diversion.

leader *n.* director, chief, head, commander, manager, supervisor, superior, boss. *Take me to your leader.* **Ant.** follower, disciple, subordinate.

league *n.* alliance, union, organization, coalition, federation, fellowship, order. *She belongs to the League of Women Voters.*

leak *vb.* **1.** drip, ooze, seep, flow, dribble, trickle, escape. *Water slowly leaked out of the pipe.* **2.** disclose, reveal, divulge, relate, tell. *The president's advisor leaked secrets to a journalist.* *-n.* **3.** hole, opening, break, fissure, puncture, crack. *We need to fix the leak in the pipes.* **Ant. 2.** conceal, hide, suppress.

lean *vb.* **1.** recline, tilt, slant, bend, slope, tip. *This pole leans slightly to the right.* **2.** depend, rely, trust, count. *Sometimes you need someone to lean on.* **3.** tend, incline, aim, favor, verge, trend. *She can't decide which college to attend, but she's leaning toward Harvard.* *-adj.* **4.** skinny, slender, thin, willowy, lithe, lanky. *Movie cowboys are frequently tall and lean.* **5.** meager, scant, spare, sparse, barren, inadequate, poor. *We've had lean times ever since Mother lost her job.* **Ant. 4.** fat, plump, portly. **5.** full, ample, substantial.

leap *vb.* **1.** jump, spring, vault, bound, hop, hurtle, skip. *Look before you leap.* *-n.* **2.** jump, vault, hop, bound, skip, hurtle, spring. *It's a long leap to the other side of the stream.*

learn *vb.* **1.** master, acquire, absorb, assimilate, memorize. *Have you learned the history lesson for today?* **2.** discover, determine, ascertain, detect, comprehend, unearth. *Astronomers want to learn how the universe began.*

learned *adj.* educated, scholarly, literate, knowledgeable, informed. *My teacher is a learned individual.* **Ant.** illiterate, ignorant, uneducated.

lease *vb.* rent, let, engage, secure, sublease, charter. *They leased the house for one year.* *-n.* **2.** agreement, contract, arrangement, pledge, guarantee. *I signed a six-month lease on the apartment.*

leash *vb.* **1.** restrain, control, fasten, rein, check, hold, tie. *All dogs must be leashed while* *in the park.* **–n. 2.** harness, strap, thong, tether, line, rope, restraint. *Hold the leash tight or the dog will get away from you.*

least *adj.* smallest, littlest, slightest, minimal, trivial. *The traffic ticket is the least of your problems.* **Ant.** largest, biggest, major.

leave *vb.* **1.** go, depart, exit, flee, abandon, desert. *The gunfighter was told to leave town by sunset.* **2.** will, bequeath, bequest, commit, entrust, release. *The millionaire left his entire fortune to his cat.* **3.** maintain, retain, keep, sustain. *Leave the books where they are.* **–n. 4.** allowance, permission, consent, freedom, approval, authorization. *The ambassador has leave to address the assembly.* **5.** vacation, absence, furlough, sabbatical, liberty. *She took a one-month leave to go to Europe.* **Ant. 1.** stay, return, arrive. **4.** denial, refusal, rejection.

lecture *vb.* **1.** speak, address, talk, instruct, expound, preach, sermonize. *The doctor lectured us about physical fitness.* **–n. 2.** speech, address, talk, discourse, oration, sermon, lesson. *We heard a lecture on Tasmanian devils.*

ledge *n.* shelf, ridge, edge, projection, shoulder. *The only way to cross the cliff was by a two foot wide ledge.*

leeway *n.* flexibility, latitude, margin, scope, room, range, slack. *She left little leeway in her busy schedule.*

legal *adj.* lawful, legitimate, permissible, sanctioned, permitted. *Is it legal to park here?* **Ant.** illegal, unlawful, illicit.

legend *n.* myth, fable, story, tale, saga, tradition, fiction. *The legend of Paul Bunyan originated in the northern United States.*

legendary *adj.* **1.** mythical, fabled, imaginary, fictitious, fanciful. *Two examples of legendary figures are Robin Hood and Hercules.* **2.** famous, famed, known, celebrated, renown. *The adventures of Annie Oakley are legendary.* **Ant. 1.** historical, factual, authenticated. **2.** unknown, ordinary.

legible *adj.* readable, clear, distinct, understandable, plain, decipherable. *She has very legible handwriting.* **Ant.** illegible, unclear, unreadable.

legion *n.* **1.** army, division, regiment, brigade, corps, troops, battalion. *He left to join the Foreign Legion.* **2.** multitude, mass, crowd, horde, throng, host, mob, army. *A legion of goblins surrounded the unwary travelers.*

legitimate *adj.* legal, lawful, rightful, proper, true, valid, genuine, just. *We feel that our complaints are legitimate.* **Ant.** illegal, unjustified, improper.

leisure *n.* relaxation, ease, comfort, rest, recreation, freedom, liberty, vacation. *After a busy day, she looked forward to a few hours of leisure.*

leisurely *adj.* casual, relaxed, unhurried, restful, comfortable, easy. *We spent a leisurely day at the beach.* **Ant.** hectic, hurried, rushed.

lend *vb.* give, donate, furnish, contribute, grant, loan, bestow, supply. *Can you lend me a hand with my homework?* **Ant.** keep, withdraw, borrow.

length *n.* distance, measure, reach, extent, span, range, stretch. *The carpenter measured the board's length.*

lengthen *vb.* extend, prolong, stretch, expand, elongate, increase. *He lengthened his stay at the hotel to one week.* **Ant.** shorten, decrease, curtail, cut.

lenient *adj.* merciful, kind, tolerant, gentle, lax, forgiving, sparing. *The judge is very lenient with first-time offenders.* **Ant.** strict, harsh, stern, severe.

less *adj.* **1.** fewer, smaller, slighter, lesser, reduced, shorter. *There are less calories in frozen yogurt than in ice cream.* **–adv. 2.** under, little, barely, meagerly, slightly, lesser. *She likes to eat at the less-known restaurants.* **Ant. 1.** more, greater, increased, added.

lessen *vb.* reduce, diminish, dwindle, decline, decrease, shrink, ease. *His kind words lessened her sorrow.* **Ant.** increase, raise, enlarge.

lesson *n.* **1.** instruction, teaching, lecture, exercise, assignment, study. *She has been taking tennis lessons.* **2.** example, message, moral, warning, caution. *Let that be a lesson to you.*

let *vb.* **1.** allow, permit, grant, consent, authorize, sanction. *Please let the person talk.* **2.** rent, lease, hire, sublease, sublet, charter. *The cabin was let for the summer.* **Ant. 1.** forbid, prohibit, refuse. **2.** buy, sell.

lethal *adj.* fatal, deadly, dangerous, destructive, mortal, killing. *My cat had a close encounter of the lethal kind with the neighborhood pit bull.* **Ant.** safe, harmless, beneficial.

letter *n.* **1.** character, symbol, sign, figure, type. *This printer runs at the rate of 120 letters per second.* **2.** note, message, memorandum, document, communication, memo. *She sent a letter to her lawyer.* **3.** exactness, strictness, preciseness, substance, specifics. *The officer observed the letter of the law.*

level *adj.* **1.** even, smooth, flat, horizontal, plane. *Place the bowl on a level surface.* **2.** equal, aligned, flush, proportionate, even. *The top of the porch is level with my bedroom window.* –*n.* **3.** degree, stage, position, layer, plane, station. *The level of workmanship in her sculptures is of the highest quality.* –*vb.* **4.** grade, even, flatten, smooth, plane, equalize. *Let's level the table so our drinks won't slide.* **5.** destroy, raze, demolish, flatten, wreck, devastate. *The Alaskan earthquake leveled the town of Valdez.* **Ant. 1.** uneven, rough, slanted. **2.** unequal, unbalanced, mismatched. **4.** roughen, coarsen. **5.** build, construct, establish.

liable *adj.* **1.** prone, inclined, subject, likely, apt, susceptible. *This hot weather is liable to continue throughout the summer.* **2.** responsible, accountable, answerable, obligated, chargeable. *The truck driver is liable for the damages to your car.* **Ant. 1.** unlikely, improbable, disinclined. **2.** exempt, unaccountable.

liar *n.* fibber, falsifier, fabricator, perjurer, storyteller. *The witness for the prosecution proved to be a liar.*

liberal *adj.* **1.** generous, abundant, lavish, ample, bountiful, unsparing. *Most gardens will flourish with liberal amounts of fertilizer.* **2.** open-minded, broad, tolerant, flexible, unprejudiced, unbiased. *Her liberal attitude allows her to see all sides of an issue.* **3.** progressive, left-wing, leftist. *The senator is considered a liberal Democrat.* **Ant. 1.** stingy, sparse, miserly. **2.** narrow-minded, biased, prejudiced. **3.** conservative, reactionary, right-wing.

liberty *n.* **1.** freedom, independence, liberation, right, privilege. *We often take our liberties for granted.* **2.** permission, allowance, leave, license, sanction, right. *The hospital volunteers have the liberty to use the employee's lounge.* **Ant. 1.** bondage, enslavement, suppression.

license *n.* **1.** permission, liberty, allowance, right, freedom, sanction. *I have my parents' license to use the car.* **2.** permit, certificate, authorization, pass. *May I please see your driver's license?* –*vb.* **3.** allow, permit, sanction, authorize, warrant, approve, commission. *She is licensed to practice physical therapy.* **Ant. 1.** denial, forbiddance, ban. **3.** forbid, prohibit, oppose.

lie *vb.* **1.** recline, rest, sprawl, stretch, lounge. *Lie on the bed until you feel better.* **2.** sit, is situated, is located, is found, belongs, extends. *The Emerald City lies north of the poppy field.* **3.** falsify, fabricate, perjure, fib, misstate, misinform. *The thief lied about where he found the wallet.* –*n.* **4.** falsehood, untruth, fib, perjury, falsification, deceit. *Is it true that George Washington never told a lie?* **Ant. 1.** stand, sit, get up. **4.** truth, fact, veracity.

lift *vb.* **1.** elevate, raise, hoist, boost, heave. *The movers lifted crates onto the truck.* **2.** rescind, cancel, revoke, recall, repeal, reverse. *The government lifted martial law as soon as the riots ceased.* –*n.* **3.** elation, boost, inspiration, encouragement, uplift. *Your get-well card gave me a lift.*

light *n.* **1.** brightness, illumination, brilliance, radiance, shine, glow. *An eerie light glowed throughout the cavern.* **2.** lamp, lantern, torch, candle, match. *Did anyone bring a light?* **3.** understanding, approach, aspect, viewpoint, insight, attitude. *Some writers are important because they shed new light on old matters.* –*adj.* **4.** bright, brilliant, radiant, sunny, shining, gleaming, illuminated. *She prefers a light and airy dining room to a dark and stuffy one.* **5.** whitish, pale, bleached, blond, fair. *People with light complexions get sunburned easily.* **6.** lightweight, airy, buoyant, flimsy, slight. *Why does he always get to carry the light pack?* **7.** mild, weak, slight, faint, gentle, little, minor, trivial. *The rain was too light to be beneficial to the crops.* **8.** cheerful, gleeful, jolly, happy, carefree, gay. *The children are in a light mood because they are* *going to the circus.* –vb. **9.** ignite, fire, kindle, burn, spark. *Whose turn is it to light the campfire?* **10.** brighten, illuminate, shine, lighten, glow. *One candle will light a dark room.* **11.** land, alight, perch, descend, settle, roost. *A sparrow lighted on the branch.* **Ant. 1.** dark, darkness, gloom. **4.** dark, gloomy, shadowy. **5.** dark, shaded. **6.** heavy, hefty, weighty. **7.** strong, substantial, serious. **9.** somber, sad. **10.** douse, extinguish, quench. **11.** leave, ascend.

like *vb.* **1.** favor, admire, love, fancy, enjoy, appreciate. *She likes surfing and beach volleyball.* –adj. **2.** similar, same, identical, equal, comparable, corresponding. *His taste in music is like mine.* **Ant. 1.** dislike, loathe, hate. **2.** unlike, dissimilar, different.

likely *adj.* **1.** reasonable, possible, plausible, credible, probable. *This is a likely spot for our tent.* **2.** probably, presumably, doubtlessly. *It's likely to rain tonight.* **Ant. 1.** unlikely, improbable, doubtful, unreasonable.

likeness *n.* **1.** resemblance, semblance, similarity, comparison. *The likeness between the two sisters is uncanny.* **2.** portrait, picture, image, representation, depiction. *The likeness of Abraham Lincoln appears on a penny.* **Ant. 1.** difference, disparity, dissimilarity.

limber *adj.* **1.** flexible, pliable, agile, elastic, bending, nimble. *Monkeys are very limber animals.* –vb. **2.** loosen, relax, stretch, unwind, slacken. *The quarterback limbered his muscles before the game.* **Ant. 1.** inflexible, stiff, rigid. **2.** stiffen, tighten.

limit *n.* **1.** end, edge, extent, boundary, border, rim, fringe. *The planet Pluto marks the limits of the Venusian empire.* –vb. **2.** confine, restrict, restrain, curb, check, narrow. *Let's limit the number of applicants to ten.*

limited *adj.* restricted, defined, confined, restrained, fixed, finite. *There is a limited supply of pens available.* **Ant.** infinite, unlimited, endless.

limp *vb.* **1.** hobble, stagger, falter, halt, stumble, wobble. *The pirate with the wooden leg limped onto the ship.* –n. **2.** lameness, hobble, falter, shuffle. *The woman was described as having a pronounced limp.* –adj. **3.** flabby, soft, loose, slack, weak, floppy. *He took up weightlifting because he was tired of his limp muscles.* **Ant. 3.** firm, tough, strong, rigid.

line *n.* **1.** row, file, sequence, column, rank, procession. *Please form a line in front of the auditorium.* **2.** stroke, mark, stripe, dash, streak. *Draw a line connecting point A to point B.* **3.** cord, string, rope, thread, strand, cable. *The campers strung up a line to hang their food.* **4.** series, progression, succession, lineage, strain, ancestry. *Our poodle comes from a long line of champions.* **5.** pattern, system, principle, course, procedure, method. *Her solution didn't follow the conventional line of thought.* **6.** business, occupation, work, vocation, calling, trade. *His line is computer maintenance.* **7.** make, brand, kind, type, variety. *She sells several lines of perfume.* **8.** phrase, expression, story, tale. *Don't give me that old line about your dog eating your homework.* –vb. **9.** align, file, arrange, array, rank, range, order. *The recruits were lined up according to height.* **10.** inlay, panel, back, border, rim. *His jacket was lined with silk.* **11.** crease, furrow, wrinkle, score, groove, streak. *Worry has lined his face.* **Ant. 9.** disarray, disorder.

linger *vb.* stay, remain, idle, tarry, persist, loiter, delay, dawdle. *The foul odor lingered long after the room was cleaned.* **Ant.** depart, disappear, hasten.

link *n.* **1.** bond, connection, tie, attachment, association, relationship. *Scientists are investigating the links between pollution and the rise in cancer.* –vb. **2.** connect, tie, associate, bond, attach, join. *The detective tried to link the crimes to her prime suspect.* **Ant. 2.** disconnect, separate, disassociate.

liquid *adj.* **1.** fluid, flowing, molten, liquefied, smooth. *Water is the liquid form of ice.* –n. **2.** fluid, water, drink. *Adding liquid to flour will make a paste.* **Ant. 1–2.** solid.

liquor *n.* alcohol, intoxicant, spirits, drink, booze. *Liquor and driving do not mix.*

list *vb.* **1.** itemize, index, catalog, record, register, file, tabulate. *Please list your qualifications on the application form.* –n. **2.** register, slate, record, roll, inventory, roster. *Santa is making a list and checking it twice.*

listen *vb.* hear, attend, heed, hark, harken. *The soldiers listened carefully to their colonel's orders.* **Ant.** ignore, disregard, neglect.

listless *adj.* sluggish, spiritless, lifeless, dull, inactive, lethargic. *This hot weather makes me feel listless.* **Ant.** lively, energetic, alert, active.

literally *adv.* exactly, precisely, really, actually, indeed. *She didn't expect her criticism to be taken so literally.*

literate *adj.* educated, schooled, learned, informed, cultured, intelligent. *Anyone with a library that large must be quite literate.* **Ant.** illiterate, unschooled, unlearned, ignorant.

lithe *adj.* supple, flexible, limber, pliant, pliable, elastic, bending. *Dancers usually have lithe bodies.*

litter *vb.* **1.** clutter, scatter, strew, disorder. *Thoughtless drivers have littered the roadside with trash.* *–n.* **2.** trash, clutter, waste, refuse, rubbish, mess, debris, junk. *Remember to pick up your litter before you leave.* **Ant. 1.** clean up, tidy, police.

little *adj.* **1.** small, tiny, wee, petite, miniature, minute. *A little dog snapped at the mailman.* **2.** brief, short, limited, momentary, meager, scant, slight. *The track star had little time to rest between events.* *–adv.* **3.** slightly, hardly, somewhat, rather, scarcely. *She was a little tired from the long drive to New York.* **Ant. 1.** big, large, huge. **2.** ample, plentiful. **3.** very, certainly.

live *vb.* **1.** exist, endure, continue, survive, thrive, last. *Some species of tortoises live to be hundreds of years old.* **2.** reside, abide, dwell, stay, settle, inhabit. *She lived in France for two years.* *–adj.* **3.** living, alive, existing, surviving, vital, active. *I'd rather see live animals in a zoo than stuffed ones in a museum.* **Ant. 1.** die, decease, expire. **3.** dead, lifeless, deceased.

lively *adj.* spirited, active, vigorous, brisk, energetic, bouncy. *The folk dancers did a lively rendition of the Mexican Hat Dance.* **Ant.** dull, boring, sluggish.

livid *adj.* **1.** enraged, furious, angry, mad, inflamed, irate. *He was livid over the rude behavior of the salesperson.* **2.** purple, lurid, discolored, bluish. *Whenever she was enraged, her face turned livid.* **Ant. 1.** calm, happy, pleased. **2.** rosy, bright.

living *n.* **1.** livelihood, income, earning, subsistence, career, vocation. *She makes a decent living as a writer.* *–adj.* **2.** alive, existing, live, organic, vital. *The guru advised us to have respect for all living things.* **Ant. 2.** nonexistent, dead, inert.

load *n.* **1.** weight, burden, cargo, freight, haul. *Take the next load to the shipping docks.* **2.** trouble, duty, pressure, worry, charge, responsibility. *Raising a child can be too heavy a load for some people.* *–vb.* **3.** fill, stack, pack, weigh, burden, pile, stuff. *The farmers loaded the wagon with hay.* **Ant. 3.** empty, unload, unpack.

loaf *vb.* idle, lounge, loiter, rest, laze, loll. *It feels nice to just loaf in the sun.* **Ant.** work, toil, labor.

loan *vb.* **1.** lend, advance, allow, credit, finance. *Can you loan me twenty dollars till Monday?* *–n.* **2.** advance, credit, lending, allowance, mortgage. *The loan must be paid off in three years.*

loathe *vb.* hate, detest, despise, abhor, scorn, abominate. *I may dislike beets, but I really loathe lima beans.* **Ant.** love, like, adore, relish.

loathsome *adj.* atrocious, abominable, repulsive, repellent, foul, disgusting. *Ogres are truly loathsome creatures.* **Ant.** lovable, adorable, delightful, charming.

lobby *n.* entrance, hall, foyer, anteroom, entry, waiting room. *I'll meet you in the lobby.*

local *adj.* nearby, close, neighboring, adjoining, surrounding. *Why go into the city when you can get that item in the local store?* **Ant.** faraway, distant.

locate *vb.* **1.** find, discover, detect, uncover, discern, unearth. *The explorer hoped to locate the lost city of Atlantis.* **2.** situate, place, fix, establish, station, put. *He plans to locate the gas station at the town's busiest intersection.*

location *n.* place, site, area, situation, locale, position, spot, point. *This is a great location for a hamburger stand.*

lock *vb.* **1.** latch, bolt, fasten, padlock, secure. *Did you lock the door?* **2.** join, link, grasp, hold, clasp, unite. *He locked his hands around the bar and pulled himself up.* *–n.* **3.** bolt, padlock, latch, clamp, hook. *The lock on the gate is rusty.* **Ant. 1.** unlock, open, unlatch. **2.** release, free, loosen.

lodge *vb.* **1.** stay, room, shelter, reside, board, quarter, accommodate. *The travelers were lodged at the local inn.* **2.** catch, position, settle, fix, place, put. *Her kite was lodged in a tree.* *–n.* **3.** inn, hotel, chalet, cabin, cottage, hut, hostel. *The lodge at the national park has no vacancies.*

lofty *adj.* **1.** haughty, proud, exalted, lordly, arrogant, snobbish. *The count's lofty treatment of his servants was embarrassing to watch.* **2.** towering, high, tall, elevated, soaring. *The climber's goal was to reach the lofty pinnacle.* **Ant. 1.** modest, humble, unassuming. **2.** short, low, stunted.

logical *adj.* rational, reasonable, sound, sensible, valid, clear. *She devised a logical plan to accomplish her project.* **Ant.** irrational, illogical, unsound.

loiter *vb.* linger, dawdle, tarry, delay, idle, loaf, lag. *The shop owner did not like people to loiter in front of his store.* **Ant.** hurry, pass, speed, hasten.

lone *adj.* single, sole, alone, solitary, individual. *A lone coyote howled on the mesa.*

lonely *adj.* **1.** lonesome, alone, friendless, forsaken, companionless, forlorn. *I've been feeling lonely since you moved away.* **2.** isolated, secluded, remote, deserted, unpopulated. *Their house was in a lonely canyon off the main road.* **Ant. 1.** popular, sociable. **2.** populous, crowded, congested.

long *adj.* **1.** extensive, lengthy, extended, prolonged, protracted. *It's going to be a long wait at the dentist's office.* *–vb.* **2.** crave, wish, yearn, desire, covet, hunger, thirst. *She longed for a chocolate shake.* **Ant. 1.** short, brief, small, contracted.

look *vb.* **1.** see, watch, glance, gaze, observe, behold, view. *Look at that cute puppy.* **2.** appear, seem, sound, show, exhibit. *The penguins looked like they were wearing tuxedos.* *–n.* **3.** glance, gaze, peek, glimpse, peep. *Let's take a look at the house on the corner.* **4.** appearance, expression, manner, demeanor, bearing. *Her joyful look tells me that she received good news.*

loom *vb.* tower, rise, reach, appear, threaten, menace. *A hurricane loomed over the Florida coast.*

loop *n.* **1.** circle, coil, noose, ring, spiral, knot. *The cowboy formed a loop at the end of his rope.* *–vb.* **2.** coil, twist, circle, knot, bend, turn. *The sailor looped the line to form a knot.*

loose *adj.* **1.** free, untied, unfastened, unfettered, liberated, unrestricted. *The escaped tiger roamed loose in the city.* **2.** slack, baggy, sagging, drooping. *The loose clothing made him look ten pounds heavier.* **3.** vague, inexact, indefinite, undefined, careless, general. *Her loose work habits caused her to make many mistakes.* **4.** wanton, immoral, sinful, wild, fast, reckless. *His loose lifestyle is responsible for his poverty.* *–vb.* **5.** untie, free, release, liberate, unbind, unfasten. *Every morning they loosed the horses into the meadow.* **Ant. 1.** tied, bound, secured. **2.** tight, confining. **3.** exact, precise, clear. **4.** moral, virtuous, disciplined. **5.** tie, bind, secure.

loot *vb.* **1.** rob, steal, burglarize, plunder, ransack, pilfer. *Outlaws looted the stagecoach.* *–n.* **2.** booty, plunder, spoils, take, prize, haul. *I know where the pirates hid their loot.*

lopsided *adj.* uneven, unbalanced, slanted, distorted, unequal, disproportionate. *The basketball game between the dwarves and the giants was a little lopsided.* **Ant.** even, balanced, equal.

lose *vb.* **1.** misplace, mislay, miss, forget, overlook. *The shopper lost her car in the vast parking lot.* **2.** forfeit, surrender, drop, succumb, yield. *The soccer team lost their third game in a row.* **Ant. 1.** find, retrieve, locate. **2.** win, succeed, triumph.

loss *n.* **1.** deprivation, depletion, decrease, removal, want, need. *When the new roommate moved in, we had trouble adjusting to the loss of privacy.* **2.** ruin, destruction, wrecking, demolition, waste. *The high-speed chase resulted in the loss of three police cars.* **3.** defeat, failure, losing, undoing. *The recent loss ruined our football team's chances for the championship.* **Ant. 1.** return, increase, gain. **2.** saving, preservation. **3.** win, triumph, victory.

lost *adj.* **1.** missing, mislaid, misplaced, stray, absent. *The search-and-rescue team was called out to look for a lost hiker.* **2.** destroyed, demolished, wrecked, ruined, obliterated. *All my possessions were lost in the fire.* **Ant. 1.** found, recovered, returned. **2.** saved, preserved.

lot *n.* **1.** plenty, abundance, quantity, much. *She brought lots of fried chicken to the picnic.* **2.** tract, land, parcel, plot, property, acreage. *We played baseball in a vacant lot across the street.* **3.** portion, share, allotment, part, piece, measure. *The items for auction were divided into lots.* **4.** fate, destiny, fortune, plight, circumstance, chance. *Snow White's lot in life was to bite a poisoned apple.* **Ant. 1.** little, few, scant.

loud *adj.* **1.** noisy, deafening, shrill, blaring, boisterous, booming. *Please don't play your music so loud.* **2.** gaudy, garish, flashy, showy, vulgar. *He dresses so loud that he stands out in a crowd.* **Ant. 1.** quiet, soft, silent. **2.** sedate, tasteful, conservative.

lounge *vb.* **1.** relax, idle, laze, loaf, rest, recline. *The hotel guests lounged by the swimming pool.* *–n.* **2.** waiting room, lobby, anteroom, parlor, salon. *The lounge is a good place to meet people.*

love *n.* **1.** adoration, affection, warmth, devotion, tenderness, attachment. *There is much love between our family members.* *–vb.* **2.** adore, cherish, treasure, like, value. *She loved the sincerity and caring of all her friends.* **Ant. 1.** hatred, loathing, malice. **2.** hate, loathe, detest, abhor.

lovely *adj.* beautiful, attractive, enchanting, adorable, captivating. *The lovely sunset inspired me to write a poem.* **Ant.** ugly, unattractive, plain.

loving *adj.* affectionate, tender, caring, adoring, warm. *His kitten has a very loving nature.* **Ant.** unloving, uncaring, aloof.

low *adj.* **1.** little, small, paltry, slight, trivial, reduced. *The socks were so low in price that she bought a dozen pairs.* **2.** sad, downcast, depressed, unhappy, gloomy, morose. *I'm feeling a little low today.* **3.** degrading, terrible, rude, vulgar, mean, vile, awful. *I have seen some pretty low tricks, but that was the worst.* **4.** humble, modest, lowly, inferior, common. *The peasant boy endured his low status in the village.* **Ant. 1.** high, elevated, substantial. **2.** happy, delighted, elated. **3.** fine, admirable, decent. **4.** high, exalted, important.

loyal *adj.* faithful, true, steadfast, devoted, trustworthy, dependable. *She has been a loyal employee for the last ten years.* **Ant.** unfaithful, disloyal, false, traitorous.

lucid *adj.* **1.** clear, understandable, accurate, sensible, rational, intelligible. *I wish someone could give a lucid explanation for what happened.* **2.** transparent, translucent, clear, light, bright. *The windows were so dirty they were no longer lucid.* **Ant. 1.** vague, confused, unclear. **2.** dim, dark, murky, gloomy.

luck *n.* fortune, chance, fate, fluke, accident. *Winning the lottery is purely a matter of luck.* **Ant.** design, skill, determination.

lucky *adj.* fortunate, fortuitous, favored, successful, blessed. *You were lucky to miss the traffic jam on the freeway.* **Ant.** unfortunate, unlucky, luckless.

ludicrous *adj.* silly, ridiculous, absurd, crazy, laughable, preposterous, bizarre. *The sight of the grown man wearing a hat with moose antlers was ludicrous.* **Ant.** serious, sensible, solemn.

lug *vb.* carry, drag, heave, tug, haul, pull, bear, tote. *Do you really want to lug that sofa up the stairs?*

luggage *n.* baggage, bags, suitcases, trunks, effects, gear. *Please check your luggage at the counter.*

lukewarm *adj.* **1.** warm, tepid, mild, temperate. *She likes her bath water to be lukewarm.* **2.** indifferent, halfhearted, unenthusiastic, cool, aloof. *Congress was lukewarm over the senator's proposal.* **Ant. 1.** cold, hot, freezing, burning. **2.** excited, concerned.

lull *n.* **1.** calmness, pause, stillness, hush, quiet, break, interval. *The sudden lull meant they were in the eye of the hurricane.* *–vb.* **2.** calm, quiet, hush, soothe, pacify, still. *The mother lulled her crying baby with a song.* **Ant. 1.** continuation, turbulence. **2.** excite, rouse, agitate.

luminous *adj.* glowing, radiant, shining, lighted, bright, illuminated. *The sorcerer had a luminous blue glow surrounding him.* **Ant.** dark, dim, dull.

lump *n.* **1.** piece, chunk, clump, clod, block, mass. *She tossed several lumps of coal into the stove.* **2.** bump, swelling, bulge, mass, knot. *He didn't know where the lump on his elbow came from.* *–vb.* **3.** combine, assemble, collect, amass, pool, merge. *They lumped all the camping equip-*

ment together for everyone to use. **Ant. 3.** separate, divide, split.

lunge *vb.* **1.** charge, plunge, thrust, lurch, attack, rush, dive. *The dog lunged at the intruder.* –*n.* **2.** charge, attack, plunge, pounce, jab, stab. *The cat made a lunge at the fleeing mouse.* **Ant. 1.** recoil, parry.

lurch *vb.* pitch, tumble, sway, teeter, toss, swing, reel, roll. *The small boat lurched to the side every time a wave hit.*

lure *vb.* **1.** attract, entice, draw, tempt, allure, coax, bait. *Don't be lured into accepting an easy but ineffective solution.* –*n.* **2.** bait, trap, decoy, enticement, draw, attraction, temptation. *The spy used his charm as a lure to get top-secret information.* **Ant. 1.** repel, repulse, rebuff.

lurid *adj.* shocking, startling, sensational, gruesome, grisly, grim, horrid. *The lurid headline read: "Man Eats His Own Heart."* **Ant.** mild, lighthearted, tame, cheerful.

lurk *vb.* prowl, creep, slink, sneak, skulk. *We knew a tiger was lurking near our campsite.*

luscious *adj.* delicious, succulent, delightful, tasty, delectable, savory. *The apple pie was luscious.* **Ant.** flavorless, nauseating, tasteless.

lust *n.* **1.** craving, passion, desire, longing, thirst, appetite, urge. *King Midas had a lust for riches.* –*vb.* **2.** desire, crave, long, hunger, yearn, covet, want. *The violinist lusted for a chance to lead the orchestra.*

luster *n.* brightness, gloss, shine, sheen, gleam, glow, radiance. *The luster of the antique car greatly increased its value.* **Ant.** dullness, tarnish, drabness.

luxurious *adj.* lavish, opulent, rich, elegant, splendid, magnificent, lush. *The duke lived in a luxurious palace.* **Ant.** poor, spare, shabby, simple.

lyrical *adj.* musical, melodic, songful, tuneful, singing. *Her voice has a lyrical ring.*

machine *n.* **1.** appliance, mechanism, engine, device, apparatus, gadget. *The mechanic said my car was a fine machine.* **2.** structure, organization, party, association, agency, body. *New York City's bureaucracy is a large and complex machine.*

mad *adj.* **1.** angry, furious, infuriated, enraged, irate, irritated. *I was mad at him for breaking my glasses.* **2.** crazy, deranged, insane, demented, unbalanced, lunatic. *The mad dog was put to sleep.* **3.** hysterical, excited, infatuated, passionate, wild. *The fans reacted with mad cheering when their team scored a touchdown.* **Ant. 1.** pleased, glad. **2.** sane. **3.** disinterested, indifferent.

madly *adv.* fiercely, passionately, insanely, wildly, fervently, intensely, deliriously. *I feel madly about you.* **Ant.** calmly, indifferently.

madness *n.* **1.** insanity, insaneness, craziness, lunacy, wackiness, daftness, derangement. *Some people consider war true madness.* **2.** recklessness, folly, silliness, foolishness, absurdity, idiocy. *It is madness for you to attempt to sail around the world by yourself.* **Ant. 1.** sense, sanity. **2.** wisdom, prudence.

magic *n.* **1.** sorcery, voodoo, witchcraft, wizardry, bewitchment, enchantment. *Do you believe in magic?* –*adj.* **2.** alluring, enchanting, charming, bewitching, spellbinding. *It was a magic night.* **Ant. 2.** ordinary, plain.

magician *n.* enchanter, sorcerer, sorceress, conjurer, medium, illusionist, mage. *We had a magician do tricks at the party.*

magnetic *adj.* captivating, appealing, charismatic, alluring, enchanting. *She has a magnetic personality that draws people to her.* **Ant.** repulsive, offensive, disgusting.

magnificent *adj.* fantastic, impressive, superb, extraordinary, wonderful. *On the Fourth of July, we watched a magnificent fireworks display.* **Ant.** poor, ordinary, terrible.

magnify *vb.* enlarge, increase, exaggerate, dramatize, inflate. *Dwelling on the problem will only magnify it.* **Ant.** reduce, diminish, minimize.

mail *n.* **1.** letters, postcards, messages, packages. *Did I receive any mail today?* –*vb.* **2.** send, dispatch, post, express, forward. *Make sure you mail the bills by Monday.*

maim *vb.* mutilate, maul, mangle, cripple, disfigure, disable, injure. *An artillery shell maimed the soldier.*

main *adj.* primary, principal, central, chief, foremost, major, crucial. *Most of the science books are in the main library.* **Ant.** secondary, minor, trivial.

mainly *adv.* primarily, principally, mostly, predominantly, chiefly, especially. *This movie theater is mainly a hangout for teenagers.* **Ant.** slightly, partly, partially.

maintain *vb.* **1.** continue, keep, support, sustain, uphold, preserve. *He maintains his yard quite well.* **2.** assert, claim, insist, contend, swear, declare. *I still maintain that traveling to Asia would be more enjoyable than traveling to Australia.* **Ant. 1.** discontinue, abandon, end. **2.** recant, disclaim.

majestic *adj.* awesome, impressive, grand, elegant, stately, magnificent, imposing. *The eagle is considered a majestic bird.* **Ant.** puny, undistinguished, humble.

major *adj.* **1.** main, primary, principal, greatest, largest. *He's finally playing in the major leagues this year.* **2.** important, great, foremost, leading, significant. *The museum considered the discovery a major find.* **Ant. 1.** minor, lesser, smaller. **2.** insignificant, unimportant.

make *vb.* **1.** create, produce, construct, fashion, build, prepare, develop. *Do you know how to* *make an ice-cream float?* **2.** force, compel, pressure, coerce, drive. *You can't make me go if I don't want to.* **3.** reach, get, attain, gain, acquire. *I hope to make senior salesclerk by this summer.* **4.** deliver, accomplish, cause, start, begin. *The president will make a speech this Sunday.* **5.** total, come to, amount to, equal. *With the jacket, it makes fifty dollars.* **Ant. 1.** destroy, demolish, wreck.

malicious *adj.* vicious, slanderous, hateful, spiteful, nasty, mean. *He told the other kids some really malicious things about me.* **Ant.** nice, kind, friendly.

malignant *adj.* fatal, lethal, deadly, cancerous, harmful. *The doctors must operate, since it is a malignant tumor.* **Ant.** good, healthy, benign.

mammoth *adj.* huge, enormous, gigantic, colossal, monstrous, oversized, immense. *The meteorite left a mammoth hole in the ground.* **Ant.** tiny, little, small, undersized.

manage *vb.* **1.** oversee, supervise, run, direct, administer, guide. *Our boss manages the store quite well.* **2.** cope, function, survive, operate. *Thanks for offering your help, but I think I can manage.* **3.** arrange, manipulate, maneuver, contrive. *How did you manage to get the day off work?*

management *n.* **1.** bosses, executives, managers, supervisors. *The unhappy customer complained to the store's management.* **2.** supervision, running, overseeing, administration, guidance, handling. *The management of this apartment building takes a lot of time and effort.*

manager *n.* boss, supervisor, administrator, chief, superintendent. *My manager scheduled me to work the entire weekend.* **Ant.** employee, underling.

maneuver *n.* **1.** move, movement, tactic, ploy, gambit. *His pawn captured my queen in a maneuver I hadn't anticipated.* *–vb.* **2.** jockey, contrive, plot, scheme, conspire. *She maneuvered to get a better position in the company.* **3.** move, direct, deploy, manipulate, steer. *He maneuvered the television so everyone in the room could see it.*

mangle *vb.* damage, mutilate, twist, ruin, maul, tear. *A vicious gust of wind mangled our kite.*

mania *n.* passion, obsession, craze, fascination, craving, enthusiasm, compulsion. *He has a mania for word games.* **Ant.** dislike, indifference.

manifest *adj.* **1.** evident, obvious, plain, apparent, clear, unmistakable. *Many early pioneers believed it was their manifest destiny to colonize the American West.* *–vb.* **2.** show, display, express, indicate, demonstrate. *Her anger manifests itself as sarcasm.* **Ant. 1.** concealed, masked, hidden. **2.** conceal, veil, hide.

manipulate *vb.* mold, shape, work, steer, maneuver, guide. *He manipulates people into doing things they don't want to do.*

manner *n.* **1.** fashion, way, style, method, pattern. *I was reassured by the friendly manner in which she spoke.* **2.** type, kind, sort, class, category, variety. *What manner of beast is this?*

mannerism *n.* habit, peculiarity, eccentricity, characteristic, quirk. *He likes to crack his knuckles in public, and that's just one of his annoying mannerisms.*

mansion *n.* estate, manor, palace, villa, residence. *The duke and duchess often vacation at their country mansion.*

manual *n.* **1.** handbook, instruction book, guidebook, workbook. *The computer came with an operator's manual.* *–adj.* **2.** physical, arduous, strenuous, heavy. *He spent the summer doing manual labor.*

manufacture *vb.* produce, make, build, create, assemble, fabricate. *The company manufactures airplane parts.*

manuscript *n.* draft, original, typescript, document, script. *She has just completed the manuscript for her latest novel.*

many *adj.* **1.** numerous, countless, innumerable, considerable, abundant. *There were many people at Disneyland.* *–n.* **2.** multitude, masses, majority, scores, crowd. *Do you think the needs of the many should outweigh the needs of the few?* **Ant. 1.** few, limited, scant. **2.** few.

map *n.* **1.** chart, guide, graph, sketch, atlas. *Take the map so you don't get lost.* *–vb.* **2.** plan, outline, arrange, chart, graph, diagram. *She mapped out her strategy for getting a promotion.*

march *vb.* **1.** parade, walk, step, tramp, pace. *Our school band marched in the New Year's Day parade .* –*n.* **2.** walk, hike, trek, tramp, parade. *She took her girl-scout troop on a march to the lake.* **3.** advance, progress, advancement, progression, passage. *No one can stop the march of time.*

margin *n.* **1.** border, boundary, edge, fringe, rim. *When you type your paper, leave a one-inch margin on all sides.* **2.** room, safeguard, allowance, latitude, range, leeway. *Leave some margin in your itinerary for possible delays.*

mark *n.* **1.** streak, spot, blemish, blotch, smudge, stain. *She tried to bleach out the ink mark on her blouse.* **2.** sign, indication, measure, stamp, label, symbol. *The mark of a talented writer is the ability to involve the reader.* **3.** target, goal, objective, standard, norm. *Your work has not been up to the mark.* –*vb.* **4.** spot, streak, stain, mar, blemish, disfigure. *The oil stain permanently marked his jeans.* **5.** identify, tag, indicate, signify, name, specify. *She marked her place in the book by bending a page corner.* **6.** heed, notice, obey, mind, note, respect. *Mark my words: He won't be coming back.* **Ant. 6.** ignore, disregard.

market *n.* **1.** marketplace, supermarket, mart, grocery. *Will you please pick up some milk while you're at the market?* **2.** desire, demand, need, want, call. *Is there a market for your new product?* –*vb.* **3.** sell, retail, vend, merchandise, dispense. *The company tried marketing its cereal in a new package.*

marriage *n.* wedding, nuptials, union, alliance, affiliation. *She was very nervous on the day of her marriage.*

marshal *n.* **1.** sheriff, law officer, police officer. *A marshal broke up the fight in the saloon.* –*vb.* **2.** gather, array, deploy, collect, muster, mobilize, assemble. *We must marshal our forces for an all-out attack.* **Ant. 2.** scatter, disperse.

martial *adj.* military, militant, hostile, aggressive, warlike, combative. *The nomadic tribe was known for its martial tendencies.* **Ant.** peaceful, gentle, friendly.

martyr *n.* sufferer, hero, saint, idol. *He was called a martyr after dying for his beliefs.*

marvel *n.* wonder, spectacle, sight, sensation, phenomenon. *The pyramids are Egypt's most famous marvels.*

marvelous *adj.* terrific, fabulous, great, fantastic, wondrous, exceptional, superb. *We had a marvelous day at the park.* **Ant.** terrible, bad, horrible, awful.

mash *vb.* smash, crush, squash, pound, beat. *She mashed her crackers and added them to her soup.*

mask *n.* **1.** disguise, cover, veil, camouflage. *Everyone must wear a mask to the costume party.* –*vb.* **2.** disguise, cover, veil, hide, shroud, camouflage. *Bruce Wayne masked himself so no one would know he was Batman.* **Ant. 2.** expose, reveal, uncover.

mass *n.* **1.** pile, heap, mount, stack, collection, clump. *He has a huge mass of snow to shovel off the walks.* **2.** gathering, horde, crowd, mob, throng, host, assembly. *There was a mass of people waiting for the store to open.* **3.** matter, material, massiveness. *Your weight will be different on the Moon, but your mass remains the same.* –*vb.* **4.** gather, crowd, clump, cluster, assemble. *Cattle massed around the feed troughs.*

massacre *n.* **1.** slaughter, killing, annihilation, execution, extermination, genocide. *The terrorist attack resulted in the massacre of many innocent people.* –*vb.* **2.** slaughter, kill, annihilate, execute, exterminate. *Renegade soldiers massacred everyone in the village.*

massage *n.* **1.** rub, rubdown, kneading, back rub. *She enjoys a good massage after her workouts.* –*vb.* **2.** rub, knead, stroke, press, caress. *He massaged my forehead to ease my tension.*

massive *adj.* large, huge, enormous, mammoth, gigantic, big, immense. *There was a massive demonstration outside the White House.* **Ant.** tiny, little, small, slight.

master *n.* **1.** controller, manager, administrator, head, ruler. *She is the master of her own fate.* –*adj.* **2.** main, principal, primary, chief, controlling. *The hotel manager has a master key to all the rooms.* **3.** expert, practiced, experienced, proficient, skilled. *She is a master swordswoman.* –*vb.* **4.** learn, grasp, conquer, overcome, vanquish. *It took him five years to master the Russian language.* **Ant. 1.** servant, subject. **2.**

lesser, minor, secondary. **3.** unskilled, amateurish, incompetent.

match *n.* **1.** mate, partner, consort, prospect, wife, husband. *She's a perfect match for you.* **2.** correspondence, parallel, equivalence, replication, complement. *The match between the old and new paint was perfect.* **3.** competitor, contestant, rival, equal, par. *He's no match for you in sports.* **4.** competition, meet, contest, tournament, game. *She won the wrestling match.* **5.** marriage, union, coupling, alliance, affiliation. *It was a match made in Heaven.* *–vb.* **6.** correspond, fit, harmonize, tally, agree, couple. *His socks don't match.* **7.** rival, equal, meet, challenge. *There's no way I can match him in strength..*

material *n.* **1.** cloth, fabric, textile, weave. *He chose a flowered material for the new curtains.* **2.** matter, substance, elements, stuff, components. *A truck brought the building materials to the construction site.*

matter *n.* **1.** material, substance, elements, components, stuff. *The planet Jupiter is made up of a gaseous matter.* **2.** problem, trouble, distress, ailment, sickness, difficulty. *What's the matter with him?* **3.** issue, point, question, topic, subject, concern. *It's a matter of right and wrong.* **4.** importance, significance, consequence, import. *It was of no matter that she came a few minutes late.* **Ant. 4.** insignificance, meaninglessness.

mature *adj.* **1.** grown, adult, developed, wise, sensible. *Apologizing was the mature thing to do.* *–vb.* **2.** develop, evolve, broaden, ripen, season. *Spending four years away at college has matured her.* **Ant. 1.** immature, childlike, juvenile.

maturity *n.* adulthood, development, responsibleness, wiseness, experience. *His maturity showed in the calm way in which he dealt with the problem.* **Ant.** immaturity, youthfulness, childishness.

maul *vb.* mangle, brutalize, batter, rend, injure, strike. *The angry tiger mauled its trainer.*

maximum *adj.* **1.** greatest, largest, extreme, utmost, top, peak. *The maximum speed you can drive on this freeway is 55.* *–n.* **2.** utmost, top, most, extreme, limit, bound. *One hundred dollars is the maximum I am willing to spend.* **Ant. 1.** minimal, lowest, smallest. **2.** minimum, least.

maybe *adv.* perhaps, possibly, conceivably, feasibly, perchance. *Maybe he'll be able to come tomorrow.*

maze *n.* labyrinth, network, tangle, confusion, puzzle, jungle. *We got lost in a maze of narrow streets.*

meager *adj.* skimpy, sparse, inadequate, scarce, slender, insufficient, slight. *We dislike the restaurant because of the meager portions they serve.* **Ant.** large, plentiful, abundant.

mean *vb.* **1.** intend, plan, expect, want, wish. *Did you mean to throw that away, or was it a mistake?* **2.** signify, denote, imply, indicate, symbolize, represent. *The Spanish word "hola" means "hello" in English.* *–adj.* **3.** nasty, rude, unpleasant, disagreeable, grouchy, vicious, cruel. *The mean man screamed at us to get away from his driveway.* **4.** cheap, shoddy, squalid, miserable, shabby, wretched. *The old shack was a mean-looking place.* **5.** average, normal, standard, medium. *The mean temperature of the human body is 98.6 degrees.* *–n.* **6.** median, norm, average, par, center. *The mean for yesterday's test was 75 points.* **Ant. 3.** nice, kind, considerate. **4.** fancy, expensive, superior. **5.** extreme, maximum, minimum.

meaning *n.* sense, significance, idea, implication, intent, purpose. *Philosophers study the meaning of life.*

meaningful *adj.* significant, important, profound, worthwhile, useful. *She's looking for a more meaningful job.* **Ant.** meaningless, senseless, useless.

meaningless *adj.* senseless, purposeless, worthless, valueless, useless. *Watching TV all day is a meaningless waste of time.* **Ant.** meaningful, significant, worthwhile.

measure *vb.* **1.** parcel, ration, portion, gauge, allot. *Please measure out one cup of sugar.* *–n.* **2.** measurement, size, amount, quantity, volume, weight. *I don't think you put in the correct measure.* **3.** sample, example, model, test, pattern, standard, precedent. *His response will give you a measure of his commitment to the relationship.* **4.** procedure, action, course, step. *I put an alarm in my car as a measure against theft.*

medal n. award, honor, medallion, trophy, prize. *The swimmer received two bronze medals at the Olympics.*

meddle vb. interfere, intrude, pry, snoop, intervene. *Don't meddle in my affairs.*

mediate vb. intercede, moderate, negotiate, umpire, referee, intervene. *I tried to mediate between my two arguing friends.*

medicinal adj. curative, therapeutic, remedial, helpful, soothing. *Some people believe herbs have a medicinal effect.* **Ant.** poisonous, harmful, destructive.

medicine n. medication, drug, prescription, antibiotic, potion. *Have you taken any medicine for your headache?*

mediocre adj. inferior, unimpressive, undistinguished, average, ordinary. *We felt the carpenter did a mediocre job on our roof.* **Ant.** fantastic, exceptional, great, superior.

meditate vb. think, ponder, reflect, study, consider, contemplate. *I must meditate on my choices before I decide.*

medium n. **1.** means, agency, instrument, device, way, tool. *She writes poetry as a medium for expressing her feelings.* **2.** environment, atmosphere, surroundings, setting, element. *The high-school student felt out of his medium in the university class.* **3.** psychic, seer, clairvoyant, diviner, fortune teller, soothsayer. *The medium said she could communicate with spirits beyond the grave.* –adj. **4.** middle, intermediate, average, normal, common, ordinary. *She chose a medium shade of brown.* **Ant. 4.** extreme, distinctive, uncommon.

meek adj. unassertive, mild, gentle, docile, submissive, passive, shy, unassuming. *Clark Kent was a meek and mild-mannered reporter.* **Ant.** bold, assertive, aggressive, forward.

meet vb. **1.** contact, greet, encounter. *He would like to meet the president.* **2.** assemble, group, rally, collect, convene. *Let's all meet at the mall.* **3.** reach, equal, satisfy, match, fulfill. *Your work does not meet my expectations.* **4.** reach, adjoin, border, cross, front. *The river meets the sea about twenty miles from here.* –n. **5.** competition, contest, match, tournament, game, race.

The track meet was held last Saturday. **Ant. 1.** avoid, miss, elude.

melancholy adj. **1.** sad, depressed, downcast, dejected, gloomy, unhappy, forlorn. *I was feeling very melancholy after my best friend moved away.* –n. **2.** sadness, depression, despair, despondency, sorrow. *He expressed his melancholy in his poetry.* **Ant. 1.** happy, glad, cheerful. **2.** happiness, joy, exhilaration.

mellow adj. **1.** gentle, mild, light, delicate, moderate. *She likes food that has a mellow rather than spicy flavor.* –vb. **2.** soften, improve, mature, season, develop. *His temper has mellowed over the years.* **Ant. 1.** harsh, sharp. **2.** harden.

melody n. song, tune, theme, strain, ballad. *I recognize that melody from somewhere.*

melt vb. dissolve, liquefy, thaw, defrost, soften. *Her frozen yogurt melted in the sun.* **Ant.** freeze, harden, solidify.

member n. initiate, participant, constituent, component, element. *He's a member of the sailing club.*

memoir n. journal, diary, autobiography, recollections, reflections. *The memoirs of the late actress have just been published.*

memorable adj. unforgettable, important, significant, momentous, eventful, remarkable. *My college graduation was a memorable day.* **Ant.** forgettable, unimportant, insignificant.

memorial n. **1.** monument, shrine, testimonial, statue, monolith, commemoration. *The Vietnam Memorial honors those who died fighting in that war.* –adj. **2.** commemorative, testimonial, eulogizing, honoring. *A memorial service was held for the police officer who was killed in the line of duty.*

memory n. **1.** remembrance, recollection, recall, retention. *I have a good memory for people and places.* **2.** fame, renown, repute, glory, reputation, distinction. *The late Mohandas Gandhi's memory lives on as an inspiration to people everywhere.* **Ant. 1.** forgetfulness.

menace n. **1.** danger, threat, risk, hazard, peril. *Criminals are a menace to society.* –vb. **2.** threaten, endanger, terrorize, frighten, intimidate. *The school bully menaced many of the* students. **Ant. 1.** blessing, friend, boon. **2.** guard, help, aid.

mend *vb.* fix, repair, patch, heal, restore, stitch. *He spent the afternoon mending the holes in his socks.*

menial *adj.* **1.** lowly, humble, degrading, servile, base. *New employees are given the most menial tasks.* –*n.* **2.** servant, domestic, underling, helper, subordinate, slave. *Don't treat me like a menial.* **Ant. 1.** elevated, dignified, stately. **2.** lord, master, superior.

mental *adj.* **1.** cerebral, abstract, intellectual, thinking, cognitive, reasoning. *I like mental games that test my intelligence.* **2.** disturbed, neurotic, psychotic, lunatic, insane. *This hospital treats mental patients.*

mentality *n.* intelligence, intellect, judgment, understanding, temperament. *He acts like he has the mentality of a two-year-old.*

mention *vb.* **1.** remark, state, say, hint, indicate, announce, declare. *Did I mention that I spoke with your sister?* –*n.* **2.** reference, allusion, hint, suggestion, indication, comment, remark. *There was no mention of my accident on the evening news.* **Ant. 1.** neglect, forget, omit. **2.** silence, omission.

mercenary *n.* **1.** hired soldier, hireling, campaigner, legionnaire. *The rebel leader used mercenaries to overthrow the government.* –*adj.* **2.** predatory, greedy, selfish, ravenous, grasping. *We were appalled by the corporation's mercenary tactics.* **Ant. 2.** sharing, unselfish, generous.

merchandise *n.* **1.** stock, wares, goods, commodities, staples. *There was a sale on all merchandise in the store.* –*vb.* **2.** sell, retail, distribute, promote, market. *The company merchandises its products through local distributors.*

merchant *n.* storekeeper, retailer, saleswoman, salesman, vendor. *The city's commercial district has many kinds of merchants.*

mercy *n.* compassion, kindness, pity, tenderness, softness, generosity, charity. *The harsh judge showed no mercy when it came time for sentencing.* **Ant.** cruelty, ruthlessness, harshness.

mere *adj.* simple, plain, sheer, bare, only. *The mere thought of getting in a boat makes me seasick.*

merge *vb.* converge, combine, fuse, join, unite. *A side road merges onto the highway up ahead.* **Ant.** diverge, split, separate.

merger *n.* alliance, union, consolidation, incorporation, fusion. *The two small airlines agreed on a merger into a single larger airline.*

merit *n.* **1.** credit, value, worthiness, worth, justification. *Your idea for saving money has a lot of merit.* –*vb.* **2.** deserve, warrant, justify, rate, earn. *His acting performance merits an award.* **Ant. 1.** discredit, worthlessness.

merry *adj.* happy, jolly, jovial, joyous, gay. *The whole school is quite merry when summer vacation comes around.* **Ant.** sad, unhappy, gloomy.

message *n.* **1.** note, communication, notice, notification. *Are there any telephone messages for me?* **2.** idea, content, meaning, point, theme, moral. *The movie's message was that everyone needs friends.*

messenger *n.* courier, carrier, runner, bearer, deliverer. *In big cities, bicycle messengers deliver packages between office buildings.*

messy *adj.* untidy, disorderly, disorganized, unkempt, jumbled, dirty. *She could never find anything in her messy room.* **Ant.** orderly, tidy, clean, organized.

method *n.* manner, design, technique, program, system, fashion, mode. *What method of transportation did you use?*

microscopic *adj.* infinitesimal, tiny, minute, indiscernible, imperceptible. *The water was unhealthy because it contained microscopic parasites.* **Ant.** huge, immense, gigantic, large.

middle *adj.* **1.** central, midmost, midway, halfway, intermediate. *I'm the middle child in the family.* –*n.* **2.** center, midpoint, heart, midst, focus, core. *Can I sit in the middle?* **Ant. 1.** final, end, initial, beginning. **2.** outskirts, fringe, edge.

mighty *adj.* powerful, forceful, vigorous, gigantic, huge, massive. *She gave a mighty heave and pushed the rock out of the way.* **Ant.** week, feeble, small.

migrate vb. move, journey, travel, relocate, resettle, immigrate. *When did your family migrate to California?*

mild adj. **1.** gentle, easygoing, calm, soft, tender, tranquil, serene. *His mild nature made him easy to work with.* **2.** moderate, light, trivial, average, weak. *She received a mild burn after spending the day on the beach.* **Ant. 1.** harsh, angry, rough. **2.** severe, serious, strong.

militant adj. warlike, aggressive, combative, fierce, activist, belligerent. *The militant environmental group bombed a whaling boat.* **Ant.** peaceful, passive, nonaggressive.

military n. **1.** service, armed forces, militia, troops, army, navy, air force, marines. *During the Vietnam War, men were drafted into the military.* –adj. **2.** soldierly, militaristic, martial, combative, warlike. *He liked the military lifestyle.*

mimic vb. **1.** impersonate, copy, echo, reproduce, imitate, mirror. *The hunter mimicked the call of the bird.* –n. **2.** mime, pantomimist, impersonator, imitator, copyist. *The street mimic repeated everything I did.*

mind n. **1.** intellect, brain, reasoning, intelligence, rationality. *You can solve the problem if you just use your mind.* **2.** memory, remembrance, recall, awareness. *The smell brings apricots and honey to mind.* –vb. **3.** care, resent, dislike, object to, deplore. *Do you mind if I borrow your jacket?* **4.** watch, tend, attend, heed, notice. *Will you mind the children until I return?* **Ant. 4.** ignore, neglect.

mindful adj. attentive, thoughtful, observant, considerate, heedful, aware. *Smokers need to be mindful of the rights of nonsmokers.* **Ant.** thoughtless, inconsiderate.

mingle vb. mix, socialize, circulate, merge, blend. *To meet people at parties, one must mingle.* **Ant.** separate, scatter, disperse.

miniature adj. midget, mini, pygmy, tiny, small, diminutive. *The miniature horse was so small I thought it was a dog.* **Ant.** giant, oversized, large.

minimize vb. reduce, lessen, diminish, limit, curtail. *The businesswoman tried to minimize her losses when the stock market collapsed.* **Ant.** maximize, increase, expand.

minimum adj. least, smallest, tiniest, lowest, slightest. *Two hundred is the minimum crew needed to run this starship.* **Ant.** maximum, greatest, largest.

minister n. **1.** preacher, pastor, reverend, priest, evangelist. *The minister gave an interesting sermon.* –vb. **2.** care, attend, serve, tend, assist. *Nurses minister to the sick.*

minor adj. **1.** slight, light, small, insignificant, unimportant. *There's nothing to worry about; it's only a minor cut.* –n. **2.** child, juvenile, teen, adolescent, youth, youngster. *In many states, you are a minor until you reach the age of 21.* **Ant. 1.** major, serious, severe. **2.** adult, grownup.

minute adj. microscopic, small, tiny, little, infinitesimal, slight. *The bug was so minute I had trouble seeing it.* **Ant.** large, huge, gigantic, enormous.

miracle n. wonder, marvel, blessing, phenomenon, rarity. *It was a miracle that anyone survived the horrible plane crash.*

miraculous adj. wondrous, magical, extraordinary, unbelievable, amazing. *The deathly ill man made a miraculous recovery.* **Ant.** ordinary, natural, common.

mirth n. happiness, cheerfulness, joyfulness, amusement, merriment, gaiety. *Her funny jokes and kind humor filled me with mirth.* **Ant.** sadness, melancholy, depression.

miscellaneous adj. varied, various, mixed, assorted, diverse. *His garage is full of miscellaneous junk.* **Ant.** uniform, identical, similar.

mischievous adj. playful, prankish, impish, teasing, exasperating. *The mischievous child hid in the closet when we tried to find him.*

miser n. scrooge, penny pincher, tightwad, skinflint, hoarder. *The miser died a rich but unhappy man.*

miserable adj. **1.** unhappy, depressed, sad, heartsick, dejected, despondent, forlorn. *I am miserable when all my friends leave town.* **2.** unpleasant, joyless, troublesome, wretched, pitiful. *He said it was miserable camping in the rain.* **Ant. 1.** happy, joyous, cheerful. **2.** comfortable, untroubled.

miserly *adj.* stingy, ungenerous, greedy, selfish, mean, cheap. *My boss is so miserly that it's no use asking him for a raise.* **Ant.** generous, unselfish, charitable.

misery *n.* pain, torment, suffering, sorrow, distress, agony, anguish. *I was in great misery when I broke my leg.* **Ant.** relief, pleasure, comfort.

misfortune *n.* tragedy, calamity, disaster, trouble, catastrophe. *It was a misfortune that you lost your money so early in the trip.* **Ant.** blessing, advantage.

misgiving *n.* doubt, fear, reservation, worry, uncertainty, anxiety. *She had misgivings about scuba diving in the shark-infested waters.* **Ant.** confidence, assurance, reliance.

mishap *n.* accident, misfortune, snag, difficulty, disaster, calamity. *We arrived late due to a mishap on the way.*

mislead *vb.* deceive, delude, dupe, misguide, misdirect, misinform. *The salesman tried to mislead me into believing his car was the better buy.*

misplace *vb.* mislay, lose, forget, displace. *He seems to have misplaced his car keys again.*

miss *vb.* **1.** overlook, neglect, bypass, skip, disregard. *I missed the freeway off-ramp.* **2.** long for, yearn for, desire, want. *We missed him the entire time he was away.* **3.** avoid, escape, avert, dodge, elude. *The dog just missed being hit by the car.* –*n.* **4.** failure, error, mistake, blunder, fumble. *Three misses and you're out.*

missile *n.* projectile, rocket, shell, shot, weapon. *The jet was brought down by a surface-to-air missile.*

mission *n.* **1.** assignment, appointment, task, commission, quest, enterprise. *The scientist is being sent on a mission to Antarctica.* **2.** purpose, objective, calling, job, vocation. *I often wonder about my mission in life.*

mist *n.* **1.** fog, cloud, haze, vapor, drizzle. *We were barely able to see the castle through the mist.* –*vb.* **2.** fog, cloud, blur, film. *My glasses misted over in the sauna.*

mistake *n.* **1.** error, fault, blunder, miscalculation, flaw, oversight. *It's my mistake that we got lost.* –*vb.* **2.** confuse, mix up, misjudge, misidentify, miscalculate, misunderstand. *I mistook the stranger for my brother.*

mistaken *adj.* incorrect, flawed, erroneous, false, faulty, inexact, misunderstood. *It was a case of mistaken identity.* **Ant.** correct, accurate, true.

mistreat *vb.* abuse, maltreat, torment, harass, brutalize, batter, strike. *We got angry at her for mistreating her dog.*

mistrust *vb.* **1.** distrust, disbelieve, doubt, suspect, question. *I mistrusted you after you told me that lie.* –*n.* **2.** distrust, doubt, suspicion, question, skepticism, wariness. *I hold all salespersons in some mistrust.* **Ant. 1.** trust, believe, accept. **2.** trust, belief, confidence.

misunderstand *vb.* misconstrue, misinterpret, misjudge, mistake, confuse. *Because he misunderstood your directions, he put two cups of salt in the cake batter.*

misunderstanding *n.* **1.** disagreement, difference, dispute, discord, squabble, quarrel. *Even small misunderstandings can turn into major arguments.* **2.** misreading, misinterpretation, misconception, mistake, error. *She took the wrong road due to her misunderstanding of the directions.* **Ant. 1.** harmony, accord, agreement. **2.** understanding, comprehension.

mix *vb.* **1.** blend, mingle, merge, scramble, stir, fuse. *The recipe called for all ingredients to be mixed thoroughly.* –*n.* **2.** mixture, combination, compound, mingling, jumble, scramble. *Our dog is a retriever and collie mix.* **Ant. 1.** separate, isolate, divide.

moan *n.* **1.** groan, wail, sob, keen, whimper. *I could hear the moans of the patient in the next room.* –*vb.* **2.** groan, wail, sob, keen, whimper, cry. *They moaned about all the homework they were assigned.*

mob *n.* **1.** crowd, gathering, horde, throng, swarm, group, pack, host. *An angry mob surrounded the bank, demanding their money back.* –*vb.* **2.** surround, crowd, swarm, deluge, inundate, attack. *The famous actress was mobbed by fans seeking her autograph.*

mobile *adj.* movable, moving, portable, flowing, migratory, roving, nomadic. *The retired cou-*

ple went camping in their mobile home. **Ant.** immobile, stationary, fixed, immovable.

mobility *n.* movement, advancement, promotion, betterment, progress. *She's looking for a job that has potential for upward mobility.* **Ant.** immobility, rigidness, fixity.

mobilize *vb.* assemble, organize, summon, muster, marshal. *The senator mobilized all her supporters for her reelection campaign.* **Ant.** disband, demobilize, release.

mock *vb.* **1.** ridicule, insult, abuse, jeer, taunt, tease, deride. *Don't mock my taste in music, even if it is old-fashioned.* *–adj.* **2.** fake, false, imitation, artificial, sham, pretend. *The stage crew built a mock spaceship.* **Ant. 1.** praise, compliment, admire. **2.** real, authentic, genuine.

mockery *n.* **1.** ridicule, insulting, jeering, taunting, teasing, scorn. *The winning team's mockery of the losing team was in bad taste.* **2.** sham, joke, laughingstock, absurdity, farce. *Through your cruel jokes and laughter, you have made a mockery of me.* **Ant. 1.** praise, respect, approval.

mode *n.* **1.** manner, way, technique, method, system. *Horse-drawn carriages are an old-fashioned mode of transportation.* **2.** fad, vogue, fashion, trend, style. *Skinny ties have been out of mode for years.*

model *n.* **1.** prototype, representation, replica, example, duplicate. *Engineers designed a model of the space shuttle before it was actually built.* **2.** subject, source, pattern, mold, archetype. *Her life story served as a model for the television show.* *–vb.* **3.** show, display, wear, demonstrate, parade. *He modeled the designer's clothes in Paris.*

moderate *adj.* **1.** reasonable, average, medium, fair, mild, passable. *Our business has had moderate success.* *–vb.* **2.** check, curb, tame, subdue, reduce, lessen, diminish. *He must moderate his spending.* **3.** lead, manage, direct, chair, oversee, facilitate. *The club president moderated the meeting.* **Ant. 1.** immoderate, extreme, excessive. **2.** increase, intensify.

moderately *adv.* reasonably, fairly, mildly, passably, somewhat. *The Japanese rock band is moderately popular in the United States.* **Ant.** unreasonably, extremely, excessively.

moderation *n.* restraint, self-control, temperance, discipline, frugality. *In all things, one should practice moderation.* **Ant.** immoderation, excess.

modern *adj.* current, contemporary, up-to-date, present, recent, latest, new. *We want our dining room furnished in a modern decor.* **Ant.** old, old-fashioned, outdated.

modernize *vb.* update, renovate, rejuvenate, refurbish, reform. *The new computer allowed us to modernize our bookkeeping procedures.*

modest *adj.* **1.** shy, humble, unassuming, bashful, blushing, unpretentious. *He has a lot to be proud about but is quite modest when people praise him.* **2.** limited, moderate, adequate, small, passable. *The couple retired on a modest income.* **Ant. 1.** immodest, proud, arrogant. **2.** grand, generous, impressive.

modesty *n.* **1.** humbleness, humility, diffidence, bashfulness, shyness. *The famous singer's modesty was surprising.* **2.** decency, reserve, propriety, decorum, discretion. *His sense of modesty is so strong that he refuses to take off his shirt in the pool.* **Ant. 1.** boastfulness, arrogance, vanity. **2.** immodesty, showiness.

modify *vb.* change, adjust, remodel, revise, transform, reshape, alter. *The shop modified the racing bike to fit my needs.*

moist *adj.* damp, wet, clammy, dank, dewy, muggy, watery. *Please use a moist rag to wipe the table.* **Ant.** dry, arid, parched.

moisten *vb.* moisturize, dampen, wet, water, spray. *Since he doesn't like to lick stamps, he moistens them with a sponge.* **Ant.** dehydrate, dry, parch.

moisture *n.* dew, moistness, dampness, wetness, vapor, water, damp. *The lost and dehydrated hiker tried to lick moisture from leaves.* **Ant.** dryness.

mold *n.* **1.** fungus, mildew, blight, rot, lichen. *I threw out the bread because of the mold spotting its surface.* **2.** cast, die, frame, model, pattern, shape, form. *She makes candles by pouring wax into copper molds.* *–vb.* **3.** form, shape, fashion, sculpt, knead, pattern. *The potter molded the clay into a beautiful vase.*

molest *vb.* abuse, harass, assault, torment, annoy, plague. *Please stop molesting that poor dog.*

moment *n.* minute, second, instant, jiffy, twinkling. *Can you wait here a moment while I run back and get my sunglasses?*

momentous *adj.* important, major, significant, memorable, eventful. *The baby's birth was a momentous occasion for the new parents.* **Ant.** insignificant, unimportant, trivial.

momentum *n.* drive, energy, impulse, speed, thrust, velocity. *The car gained so much momentum that it crashed through the brick wall.*

monarch *n.* king, queen, ruler, sovereign, emperor, empress, czar, shah, pharaoh, majesty. *Queen Victoria was Great Britain's monarch from 1837 to 1901.*

money *n.* cash, currency, funds, revenue, capital, wealth. *How much money did you spend for your car?*

monitor *n.* **1.** overseer, director, supervisor, mentor, examiner. *Everyone in class gets to be lunchroom monitor for a week.* *–vb.* **2.** oversee, supervise, observe, check, examine. *Nurses monitored the patient's condition 24 hours a day.*

monotonous *adj.* unchanging, unvarying, dull, boring, tedious, dreary, routine. *The dairy's newest employee got the monotonous job of counting the holes in the Swiss cheese.* **Ant.** exciting, invigorating, changing.

monster *n.* ogre, brute, fiend, beast, demon, ghoul. *Mary Shelley is the creator of the monster known as Frankenstein.*

monstrous *adj.* **1.** horrible, terrifying, frightful, gruesome, evil, foul, vile, diabolical. *The museum displayed the monstrous devices from a medieval torture chamber.* **2.** huge, enormous, gigantic, colossal, immense, mammoth. *He has a monstrous appetite.* **Ant. 1.** pleasing, kindly, gentle. **2.** small, tiny, minute.

monument *n.* remembrance, memorial, shrine, reminder, commemorative. *We went to the Washington Monument while visiting the capital.*

monumental *adj.* **1.** huge, enormous, mammoth, gigantic, massive, immense. *The building of the pyramids was a monumental effort.* **2.** historic, immortal, impressive, striking, memorable, enduring. *The monumental Apollo XI lunar landing took place in 1969.* **Ant. 1.** tiny, small, insignificant. **2.** forgettable, unimportant.

mood *n.* temperament, temper, spirit, humor, attitude, disposition. *Our argument left me in a bad mood.*

moody *adj.* changeable, variable, temperamental, melancholy. *My friend's so moody he can go from happy to sad in a moment's time.*

moor *n.* **1.** heath, marsh, swamp, bog, quagmire, wasteland, grassland. *She crossed the moors to get to the old Celtic ruins.* *–vb.* **2.** anchor, fasten, bind, rope, secure, hitch. *The sailors moored their ship to the dock.* **Ant. 2.** untie, unfasten, release.

mop *n.* **1.** swab, swabber, scrubber, sponge. *The mop was quite dirty after being used to clean the floor.* *–vb.* **2.** swab, wash, wipe, sponge, scrub. *She mopped the sweat from her forehead.*

mope *vb.* droop, sulk, grouch, pout, brood, pine, languish. *She moped about the house all summer because she had nothing to do.*

moral *n.* **1.** lesson, teaching, proverb, meaning, significance, dictum. *The story's moral was that one should never trust a stranger.* *–adj.* **2.** good, upright, ethical, decent, honorable, honest, righteous. *They wanted a moral man as their rabbi.* **Ant. 2.** immoral, unethical, dishonest.

morale *n.* mood, spirit, heart, resolve, attitude, temper, will. *The survivors' morale dipped after the rescue plane failed to see them.*

morality *n.* righteousness, goodness, justice, fairness, correctness, fitness, integrity. *She questioned the morality of taking the kittens to the pound.* **Ant.** immorality, badness, injustice.

morass *n.* swamp, marsh, bog, wallow, quagmire, ooze. *Our car got stuck in a morass of mud.*

morbid *adj.* unwholesome, sickly, unsound, unhealthy, grim, gruesome, macabre. *The writer has a morbid interest in death.* **Ant.** wholesome, sound, healthy.

more *adj.* **1.** additional, supplemental, supplementary, added, extra. *May I have some more soda?* *–adv.* **2.** further, longer, above, beyond.

The movie runs more than two hours. **Ant. 1–2.** less.

morose *adj.* sullen, sulky, grim, gloomy, somber, depressed. *She seemed rather morose at the family reunion.* **Ant.** cheerful, joyful, happy.

morsel *n.* bite, mouthful, scrap, crumb, shred, pinch, bit. *I haven't had a morsel to eat all day.*

mortal *adj.* **1.** transitory, passing, temporary, impermanent, short-lived. *Humans are mortal beings with short life spans.* **2.** fatal, lethal, deadly, killing, critical. *The soldier received a mortal wound in battle.* **Ant. 1.** immortal, permanent, eternal.

mortality *n.* vulnerability, impermanence, humanity, humanness, weakness. *Her brush with death made her aware of her own mortality.* **Ant.** immortality, invulnerability.

most *adj.* **1.** greatest, maximum, utmost, foremost, largest, extreme. *This is the most fun I've had in weeks.* –*n.* **2.** utmost, peak, maximum, optimum. *I want the most you can give.* –*adv.* **3.** extremely, very, quite, unusually, exceptionally. *He was most charming.* **Ant. 1–2.** least, minimum.

mostly *adv.* mainly, primarily, chiefly, principally, largely. *The soup was mostly water.*

motion *n.* **1.** movement, action, change, mobility, activity. *Her hyperactive child is constantly in motion.* **2.** gesture, sign, signal, nod, wave. *My father made a motion for me to join him .* **3.** suggestion, recommendation, proposal, submission. *Someone at the meeting made a motion that fees be reduced.* –*vb.* **4.** gesture, wave, signal, sign, indicate. *The teacher motioned for us to be quiet.*

motivate *vb.* encourage, move, spur, prompt, influence, persuade. *Watching the Olympics motivated the athlete to continue his training.* **Ant.** discourage, deter, hinder.

motive *n.* cause, incentive, reason, purpose, goal, objective, intention, basis. *Have the police determined the motive for the murder?*

motto *n.* slogan, saying, canon, maxim, precept, proverb, dictum. *Alaska's state motto is "North to the future."*

mound *n.* hill, hump, rise, pile, heap, knoll, dome. *Termites build large nesting mounds out of saliva and soil.* **Ant.** hole, depression, hollow.

mount *n.* **1.** mountain, peak, summit, promontory, pinnacle. *Mount McKinley is the highest point in North America.* **2.** horse, steed, mare, stallion, bronco, mustang. *Cavalrymen were concerned with the welfare of their mounts.* –*vb.* **3.** rise, climb, surge, increase, grow, soar, ascend. *Tension mounted in the arena.* **4.** install, position, locate, fix, set, put, place. *He mounted his trophy on the wall.* **Ant. 3.** descend, lower, lessen.

mountain *n.* mount, hill, peak, summit, pinnacle, point, promontory. *It was faster going down the mountain than climbing up it.* **Ant.** bottomland, dale, valley.

mourn *vb.* grieve, lament, sorrow, suffer, regret, weep, despair. *We mourned the loss of our loved one.*

mournful *adj.* sorrowful, joyless, sad, cheerless, painful, unhappy, distressing, grim. *The funeral was a mournful occasion.* **Ant.** happy, joyous, merry, cheerful.

move *vb.* **1.** carry, bear, cart, lug, convey, shift, budge. *It will take two people to move this dresser.* **2.** go, proceed, advance, transfer, depart. *Our family recently moved to Illinois.* **3.** touch, disturb, affect, impress, shock, disquiet. *The sorrowful movie moved me.* **4.** persuade, force, oblige, impel, require. *Complaints from the community finally moved the government to take action.* **5.** suggest, submit, recommend, propose. *I move that we quit for the day.* –*n.* **6.** shift, step, measure, undertaking, deed, feat. *Changing careers was a big move in her life.* **7.** maneuver, tactic, ploy, device, stratagem. *His last chess move was quite clever.* **Ant. 2.** stay, remain.

movement *n.* **1.** motion, action, activity, stir, displacement. *He noticed the deer when he saw movement in the bushes.* **2.** drive, trend, inclination, tendency, drift. *There's been a recent movement in the city council to increase parking fines.*

movie *n.* motion picture, film, cinema, picture, feature. *My favorite movie is "Star Wars."*

mow *vb.* cut, shear, trim, shave, clip, crop. *I mowed the lawn.*

much *adj.* **1.** considerable, abundant, ample, substantial, plentiful. *He never seems to have much money.* –*adv.* **2.** greatly, abundantly, highly, largely, considerably, overly. *I love you very much.* **3.** frequently, often, repeatedly, regularly, habitually. *She goes to the movies too much.* **Ant. 1.** inadequate, insufficient, little.

mud *n.* ooze, muck, mire, slime, slop, swamp, quagmire, morass. *We trudged through the rain and mud.*

muffle *vb.* dampen, mute, quiet, hush, silence, cloak, shroud. *Thick walls muffled the sound of the neighbor's shouting.* **Ant.** heighten, intensify, increase, amplify.

muggy *adj.* humid, sticky, damp, clammy, moist, steaming. *The weather was hot and muggy.* **Ant.** dry, arid.

multiply *vb.* increase, double, mushroom, reproduce, breed, generate. *The roaches seemed to multiply at an incredible speed.*

multitude *n.* crowd, gathering, swarm, mass, pack, assembly, throng, horde. *A multitude of people showed up to hear the president speak.*

mumble *vb.* mutter, murmur, whisper, stammer. *Sometimes it's difficult to understand him because he mumbles.*

murder *n.* **1.** killing, slaying, slaughter, assassination, homicide, extermination. *Lee Harvey Oswald was the man responsible for the murder of President John F. Kennedy.* –*vb.* **2.** kill, slay, slaughter, assassinate, massacre, exterminate. *Terrorists murdered several passengers on the airplane.*

music *n.* songs, singing, instrumentation, rhythm, melody, tune. *Does he like rock music?*

musical *adj.* lyrical, instrumental, orchestral, operatic, symphonic, tuneful, melodic. *Mozart was a musical genius.* **Ant.** unmusical, discordant.

must *vb.* should, ought to, have to, need to. *I must get to the post office today.*

mutilate *vb.* disfigure, mangle, maul, maim, butcher, deform. *The power saw mutilated his fingers.*

mutiny *n.* **1.** rebellion, revolt, insurgency, uprising, takeover, overthrow, coup. *The sailor was tried and executed for his part in the mutiny.* –*vb.* **2.** rebel, revolt, riot, strike, disobey. *My sister and I mutinied against my parents' overly strict rules.*

mutual *adj.* shared, joint, common, interchangeable, reciprocal. *A married couple must have mutual respect for one another.* **Ant.** distinct, unshared, uncommon.

myriad *n.* **1.** assortment, array, host, crowd, swarm, abundance, torrent. *The rainbow was a myriad of colors.* –*adj.* **2.** countless, numerous, immeasurable, innumerable, incalculable, limitless. *Myriad stars filled the night sky.* **Ant. 2.** few, limited.

mystery *n.* **1.** puzzle, riddle, bewilderment, enigma, secret, question. *To this day, the disappearance of planes in the Devil's Triangle remains a mystery.* **2.** secrecy, concealment, obscurity, vagueness, ambiguity. *His past is shrouded in mystery.*

mystify *vb.* puzzle, bewilder, confuse, perplex, baffle, confound, elude. *It mystifies me how he got the ship model into that jar.*

myth *n.* fable, fantasy, yarn, fairy tale, legend, tall tale. *Are the stories of Big Foot myth or reality?* **Ant.** historical fact, reality, truth.

mythological *adj.* mythical, legendary, fabled, imaginary, fictitious, fantasized, fabricated. *Medusa is a mythological creature.* **Ant.** real-life, actual, historical.

mythology *n.* folklore, myths, lore, tradition, legends. *Thor is a figure in Norse mythology.*

nab *vb.* grab, catch, seize, capture, trap, snare, arrest. *The shoplifter was nabbed as he left the store.* **Ant.** free, release, liberate.

nag *vb.* **1.** pester, harass, annoy, bother, irritate, torment, badger. *My parents are always nagging me about getting a job.* –*n.* **2.** nuisance, pest, complainer, whiner, grouch. *I wish my brother would stop being a nag.* **Ant. 1.** appease, soothe.

nail *vb.* hammer, strike, pound, tap, drive, hit. *A carpenter nailed the bookshelves to the wall.*

naive *adj.* innocent, simple, unworldly, unsophisticated, unaffected. *How can a person with her experience be so naive?* **Ant.** sophisticated, experienced, worldly.

naked *adj.* **1.** nude, bare, unclothed, undressed, stripped, uncovered, exposed. *It's against the law to go naked on a public beach.* **2.** plain, simple, unconcealed, open, evident, obvious. *He was afraid that the witness would tell the naked truth.* **Ant. 1.** clothed, dressed, covered. **2.** guarded, shielded, concealed.

name *n.* **1.** title, label, term, designation, appellation. *What is the name of that red flower?* **2.** reputation, repute, character, fame, distinction. *The attorney hopes to make a name for herself by winning this case.* –*vb.* **3.** title, call, label, term, designate, dub. *He named the puppy Patches.* **4.** appoint, designate, elect, assign, choose, nominate. *Last week the club named a new president.*

nap *n.* **1.** sleep, snooze, slumber, doze, siesta, rest. *I think I'll take a little nap before dinner.* –*vb.* **2.** drowse, sleep, doze, rest, snooze. *The director was caught napping during the board meeting.*

narrate *vb.* tell, recite, relate, recount, describe, report. *The speaker presented slides and narrated the story behind them.*

narrow *adj.* **1.** slender, thin, tight, slim, close, restricted. *The bridge was too narrow for the truck to cross.* **2.** bigoted, biased, intolerant, shallow, limited. *People with narrow minds shut themselves off from much of life's pleasures.* **Ant. 1.** wide, broad, spacious. **2.** receptive, unbiased, tolerant.

nasty *adj.* **1.** unpleasant, disagreeable, disgusting, distasteful, terrible, awful. *Washing dishes is a nasty job.* **2.** mean, cruel, vicious, hateful, vile, beastly. *Scrooge was a nasty person.* **Ant. 1.** enjoyable, pleasant, nice. **2.** sweet, kind.

nation *n.* country, kingdom, commonwealth, republic, domain, dominion, realm. *Monaco is an extremely small nation.*

native *n.* **1.** citizen, resident, inhabitant, dweller. *She is a native of California.* –*adj.* **2.** local, original, natural, domestic, native-born. *The platypus is native to Australia.* **Ant. 1.** alien, foreigner, immigrant. **2.** foreign, imported.

natural *adj.* **1.** instinctive, basic, fundamental, inborn, inbred, inherent. *Raccoons have a natural tendency to wash their food before eating it.* **2.** normal, regular, customary, typical, spontaneous. *If you just act natural, you will do well in your interview.* **Ant. 1.** learned, unnatural, alien. **2.** contrived, artificial.

naturally *adv.* **1.** certainly, surely, plainly, normally, usually. *Naturally, the queen will lead the procession.* **2.** freely, simply, normally, sincerely, honestly, candidly. *The children were behaving naturally until they spotted the photographer.* **Ant. 2.** artificially, strangely, pretentiously.

nature *n.* **1.** world, universe, cosmos, creation. *Not even scientists understand all the laws of nature.* **2.** characteristic, disposition, trait, attribute, instinct, personality. *It is her nature to examine every aspect of a question.* **3.** essence, type, sort, character, kind, style, brand. *What is the nature of your visit?*

naughty *adj.* bad, disobedient, mischievous, misbehaving, troublesome. *Putting the goldfish in our soup was a naughty thing to do.* **Ant.** nice, behaved, obedient, good.

nausea *n.* sickness, queasiness, squeamishness, vomiting. *My nausea was caused by eating spoiled meat.*

nauseated *adj.* **1.** disgusted, revolted, offended, repulsed, upset. *She was nauseated by the violent movie.* **2.** ill, sick, queasy, squeamish, unwell. *Mountain driving tends to make me nauseated.*

nautical *adj.* marine, naval, maritime, oceanic, boating. *The sailor was an expert in the nautical arts.*

navigate *vb.* pilot, steer, guide, direct, sail. *It is unsafe to navigate this channel by night.*

near *adj.* **1.** close, nearby, adjacent, neighboring, adjoining, bordering. *The nearest country to the south of the United States is Mexico.* *–vb.* **2.** approach, advance, draw near, move toward. *The train neared the station.*

nearly *adv.* about, almost, near, practically, approximately, roughly. *It's nearly six o'clock.*

neat *adj.* **1.** clean, tidy, orderly, straight, immaculate. *His task is to keep the kitchen neat.* **2.** clever, skillful, effective, competent, great, wonderful. *That was a neat slam dunk.* **Ant. 1.** dirty, sloppy, messy. **2.** incompetent, inept, awful.

necessary *adj.* needed, essential, required, indispensable, important. *Pack only what is necessary for the trip.* **Ant.** unnecessary, nonessential, optional.

need *vb.* **1.** require, want, lack, miss, yearn, covet, crave. *What the coach needs is a quarterback who can throw the ball.* *–n.* **2.** requirement, want, lack, necessity, demand. *The hospital is in need of more nurses.* **3.** poverty, distress, want, neediness, destitution. *This homeless shelter helps those who are in need.* **Ant. 1.** have, possess. **2.** abundance, excess. **3.** wealth, affluence.

needless *adj.* unnecessary, nonessential, useless, pointless, purposeless. *It is needless for you to accompany me to the market.* **Ant.** essential, useful, necessary, required.

needy *adj.* poor, penniless, destitute, broke, impoverished, bankrupt. *Will you donate food for a needy family?* **Ant.** rich, wealthy, affluent.

negative *adj.* opposed, denying, contrary, pessimistic, skeptical, rejecting. *The negative attitude of the jury worried his attorney.* **Ant.** positive, approving, optimistic.

neglect *n.* **1.** disregard, negligence, inattention, neglectfulness, omission. *The poor condition of his car is due to neglect.* *–vb.* **2.** disregard, ignore, overlook, forget, slight. *She neglected her garden and now it's nothing but weeds.* **Ant. 1.** attention, concern, care. **2.** regard, notice.

negligent *adj.* forgetful, careless, indifferent, neglectful, heedless. *The cracks in the wall are evidence of negligent workmanship.* **Ant.** careful, vigilant, attentive.

negotiate *vb.* **1.** arrange, settle, bargain, discuss, arbitrate, transact. *The leaders met secretly to negotiate peace terms.* **2.** handle, manage, clear, make, surmount. *The driver was going too fast to negotiate the turn.*

neighborhood *n.* **1.** community, environs, locality, surroundings, area. *This is a real friendly neighborhood.* **2.** range, order, area, vicinity, extent. *That car's value is in the neighborhood of $20,000.*

nerve *n.* **1.** courage, bravery, fearlessness, boldness, fortitude. *Do you have the nerve to dive off that cliff?* **2.** gall, arrogance, rudeness, cheek, insolence, brashness. *He had the nerve to go to the party uninvited.* **Ant. 1.** cowardice, fearfulness. **2.** reserve, shyness, politeness.

nervous *adj.* edgy, excitable, shaky, agitated, jumpy, uneasy, anxious. *Public speaking makes me nervous.* **Ant.** steady, calm, confident, relaxed.

nestle *vb.* snuggle, settle, cuddle, nuzzle, burrow. *The piglets nestled close to their mother.*

net *n.* **1.** netting, mesh, web, trap, snare. *The fishing boats pulled in their nets.* *–vb.* **2.** catch, snare, trap, capture, snag, bag. *The rangers plan to net the bear and release him in a less populated area.* **3.** make, earn, gain, clear, realize, collect. *We netted a $300 profit.*

neutral *adj.* **1.** uninvolved, indifferent, impartial, unaligned, uncommitted. *The governor preferred to remain neutral on controversial issues.* **2.** ordinary, average, intermediate, indefinite. *A dress in a neutral color would be your safest choice.* **Ant. 1.** biased, partial, partisan.

nevertheless *adv.* nonetheless, yet, however, regardless, anyway. *She's sick; nevertheless, she is going on a date.*

new *adj.* **1.** recent, latest, current, modern. *His new cassette recorder sounds excellent.* **2.** unknown, unfamiliar, unexplored, uncharted, remote. *The explorer realized that she was in new territory.* **3.** original, fresh, creative, novel, unique, unusual. *We seem to have run out of new ideas.* **Ant. 1.** old, used, ancient. **2.** familiar, explored, traveled. **3.** unoriginal, stale, common.

newly *adv.* recently, lately, freshly, anew, of late. *This newly revised almanac has lots of updated material.*

news *n.* information, data, report, knowledge, word, account. *We are expecting news about the hurricane.*

next *adj.* **1.** following, coming, ensuing, subsequent. *Would you call the next applicant?* **2.** adjacent, nearest, closest, bordering, adjoining. *The Johnsons live in the next house.* *–adv.* **3.** after, thereafter, successively, later. *Whose turn is it next?* **Ant. 1.** preceding, previous, first. **2.** farthest, distant, remote.

nibble *vb.* **1.** nip, chew, munch, bite, peck, gnaw. *The mice nibbled at the cheese.* *–n.* **2.** taste, bite, crumb, morsel, tidbit, snack, bit. *I'll have just a nibble of that cake.*

nice *adj.* pleasant, agreeable, pleasurable, delightful, enjoyable, good. *They had a nice day at the zoo.* **Ant.** terrible, unpleasant, awful, miserable.

niche *n.* **1.** corner, nook, alcove, recess, hollow, cavity, hole. *The hiker set her pack in a niche behind the tree.* **2.** calling, position, place, trade, purpose, slot. *He has not yet found his niche in life.*

night *n.* evening, dark, nighttime, nightfall, darkness. *Vampires and werewolves come out at night.* **Ant.** day, daytime, daylight.

nimble *adj.* agile, spry, speedy, active, lively, quick, swift. *Jack was so nimble he could jump over the candlestick.* **Ant.** slow, awkward, clumsy, plodding.

noble *adj.* **1.** exalted, lordly, aristocratic, titled, high-ranking. *The prince could only marry a woman of noble birth.* **2.** honorable, generous, virtuous, moral, superior, heroic. *The rescue failed, but it was a noble attempt.* **3.** stately, grand, majestic, splendid, glorious, awesome. *Colorado is blessed with noble mountains.* *–n.* **4.** lord, lady, aristocrat, noblewoman, nobleman. *The nobles were stunned by the peasant's rebellion.* **Ant. 1.** common, lowborn. **2.** cowardly, despicable. **3.** unimpressive, modest, forgettable. **4.** serf, peasant, commoner.

noise *n.* sound, clamor, clatter, racket, uproar, din, disturbance, commotion. *Do you have to make all that noise in the morning?* **Ant.** quiet, silence, peace, hush.

noisy *adj.* loud, deafening, blaring, clamorous, resounding, boisterous, thunderous. *The fireworks show was a noisy event.* **Ant.** quiet, peaceful, still, noiseless.

nomad *n.* wanderer, migrant, rover, pilgrim, vagabond, drifter, gypsy. *She was a nomad roaming from town to town.*

nominal *adj.* **1.** pretended, theoretical, supposed, surface, token. *Her leadership of the group is purely nominal.* **2.** trivial, trifling, small, slight, minimum, insignificant. *The nominal effects of the boycott will not hurt our business.* **Ant. 1.** real, true, genuine. **2.** considerable, large, substantial.

nominate *vb.* propose, choose, appoint, designate, select, name. *Who did you nominate for secretary?*

nonchalant *adj.* casual, indifferent, unconcerned, cool, easygoing, composed. *He had a nonchalant attitude about the final exam.* **Ant.** anxious, concerned, disturbed.

nonconformist *n.* individualist, eccentric, freethinker, dissenter, rebel, original. *She was considered a nonconformist because she liked to do things her own way.* **Ant.** conformist, follower.

nonsense *n.* silliness, stupidity, folly, foolishness, senselessness. *How much more of this nonsense do we have to take?* **Ant.** sense, reason.

normal *adj.* usual, standard, average, typical, routine, ordinary. *It was a pretty normal day until the flying saucer arrived.* **Ant.** unusual, abnormal, odd.

nostalgia *n.* longing, wistfulness, pining, remembrance. *Sixties music gives my mother a sense of nostalgia.*

nosy *adj.* curious, prying, snooping, meddlesome, inquisitive. *The nosy guest peered in our closets.*

notable *adj.* noteworthy, distinguished, important, prominent. *She has made notable contributions to the field of biology.* **Ant.** unimportant, inconsequential.

note *vb.* **1.** notice, regard, observe, watch, perceive. *Please note the differences between the two species of moths.* *–n.* **2.** message, record, memo, memorandum, letter. *Leave a note on the bulletin board.* **3.** notice, heed, regard, attention, mark. *Did you take note of the deadline for term papers?* **4.** bills, currency, banknote, legal tender. *The ransom was to be paid in ten- and twenty-dollar notes.* **Ant. 1.** ignore, disregard, neglect. **3.** unconcern, indifference.

notice *vb.* **1.** see, observe, heed, note, recognize. *Did you notice the size of that wrestler?* *–n.* **2.** attention, regard, interest, concern, note. *She took notice of the unsafe conditions at the factory.* **3.** announcement, bulletin, sign, statement, notification. *He received a notice regarding his overdue bills.* **Ant. 1.** miss, overlook, disregard. **2.** unawareness, inattention.

notify *vb.* inform, advise, tell, mention, reveal, apprise. *Please notify me when the king arrives.*

notion *n.* idea, belief, thought, view, opinion, concept. *Where did you get such a weird notion?*

notoriety *n.* infamy, scandal, disrepute, disgrace, dishonor, shame. *Billy the Kid achieved much notoriety.* **Ant.** honor, esteem, standing.

notorious *adj.* infamous, renowned, celebrated, scandalous. *Los Angeles is notorious for its smog.*

nourish *vb.* nurture, feed, support, supply, sustain, strengthen. *You need some fertilizer to nourish your plants.* **Ant.** starve, deprive.

nourishment *n.* food, sustenance, support, nutrition. *The starving kitten was in need of nourishment.*

novel *adj.* original, new, unusual, unique, different, imaginative, odd, strange. *The movie had a novel conclusion.* **Ant.** unoriginal, usual, common, typical.

novelty *n.* **1.** change, innovation, originality, variation, surprise. *Ethiopian food was a novelty to her.* **2.** knickknack, curio, trinket, bauble. *The Indian trading post offered many novelties.*

novice *n.* beginner, starter, learner, apprentice, trainee, newcomer, rookie. *All experts start out as novices.* **Ant.** master, expert, veteran.

now *adv.* presently, immediately, at once, instantly, directly. *Take out the trash now.* **Ant.** later, eventually, sometime.

noxious *adj.* toxic, harmful, poisonous, injurious, damaging, foul, lethal. *It is dangerous to work with noxious chemicals.* **Ant.** safe, harmless, healthful.

nucleus *n.* center, core, heart, focus, crux, basis. *We have three veteran players to form the nucleus of this year's team.*

nudge *vb.* **1.** push, shove, poke, jostle, touch, elbow. *He nudged her to get her attention.* *–n.* **2.** push, prod, poke, elbowing, punch, touch. *It will take more than a nudge to get the elephant to move.*

nuisance *n.* bother, annoyance, pest, pain, irritation, trouble, inconvenience. *Little sisters can be a nuisance.* **Ant.** delight, blessing, pleasure, joy.

null *adj.* invalid, void, nonexistent, useless, ineffective, inoperative. *The election was declared null because of cheating.* **Ant.** valid, binding, useful.

numb *adj.* unfeeling, deadened, insensitive, paralyzed, frozen. *I've been sitting cross-legged so long my legs are numb.* **Ant.** alive, responsive, sensitive.

number *n.* **1.** digit, figure, numeral, unit, integer. *What is the number of your hotel room?* **2.** amount, quantity, sum, total, volume, mass. *A large number of people are expected at the fair.* –*vb.* **3.** count, figure, total, calculate, add, estimate, reckon, tally. *She numbered the deer population at about five hundred.*

numerous *adj.* many, abundant, numberless, countless, plentiful. *It was only one of numerous ways he could have played that chess move.* **Ant.** few, scarce, limited.

nurse *n.* **1.** attendant, orderly, aide. *The nurse made sure his patient took her pills.* –*vb.* **2.** nurture, doctor, attend, care for, nourish. *His family nursed him until he was well enough to take care of himself.*

nurture *vb.* **1.** nourish, feed, nurse, strengthen, sustain. *She nurtured the baby squirrel back to health.* **2.** raise, rear, develop, foster, support. *Imagination is a trait that must be nurtured.*

nutrition *n.* nourishment, food, sustenance, foodstuffs, nutrients. *The right nutrition is important to your health.*

nutritious *adj.* healthful, nourishing, wholesome, beneficial. *She starts each day with a nutritious breakfast.* **Ant.** unhealthful, unwholesome.

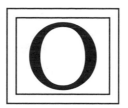

oath *n.* **1.** vow, avowal, pledge, bond, promise. *Every elected official must take an oath of office.* **2.** swearword, swearing, curse, profanity, blasphemy. *He yelled an oath at the reckless driver.* **Ant. 2.** blessing, benediction.

obedient *adj.* dutiful, obliging, respectful, obeying, submissive, compliant. *The soldiers were obedient to their commanding officer.* **Ant.** disloyal, disobedient, rebellious.

obese *adj.* fat, overweight, heavy, plump, portly, fleshy, stout. *The obese woman had trouble climbing the stairs.* **Ant.** underweight, skinny, thin, lean.

obey *vb.* follow, comply, submit, observe, respect, heed, conform. *Always obey the law.* **Ant.** disobey, defy, resist, refuse.

object *n.* **1.** thing, article, form, device, entity. *What is that object over there?* **2.** goal, aim, purpose, objective, target, end, point. *The object of this game is to put the ball in the basket.* *–vb.* **3.** oppose, protest, disapprove, complain, refuse, challenge. *He objected to the unfairness of the test.* **Ant. 3.** approve, agree, praise, assent.

objection *n.* disapproval, opposition, disagreement, protest, complaint. *Do you have any objections to the change in plans?* **Ant.** agreement, approval, acceptance.

objective *adj.* **1.** impartial, impersonal, unprejudiced, unbiased, detached, fair. *We want a judge who will be objective about our case.* *–n.* **2.** goal, purpose, aim, object, intention, mission, target. *The secret agent's objective was to destroy the missile site.* **Ant. 1.** biased, prejudiced, subjective.

obligation *n.* **1.** agreement, contract, stipulation, commitment, pledge, promise. *We met our legal obligations by giving part of our profits to the building fund.* **2.** duty, responsibility, requirement, liability, debt. *Doctors have an obligation to cure the sick.* **Ant. 2.** choice, freedom, decision.

oblige *vb.* **1.** require, obligate, compel, force, coerce, make, constrain, bind. *Since you broke the glass, you are obliged to buy it.* **2.** favor, please, serve, accommodate, help, assist. *The waiter obliged her with a complimentary dessert.* **Ant. 1.** free, release, option. **2.** displease, disfavor.

obliterate *vb.* **1.** destroy, annihilate, raze, level, ruin, crush. *The bombers obliterated an entire town.* **2.** erase, remove, delete, blot, cancel. *A coffee spill obliterated several names and numbers in her address book.* **Ant. 1.** build, restore, create. **2.** add, keep, preserve.

oblivious *adj.* unaware, unobservant, unmindful, heedless, neglectful. *The driver was oblivious to the honking cars.* **Ant.** aware, mindful, conscious, heedful.

obnoxious *adj.* annoying, offensive, objectionable, unpleasant, disagreeable. *He's been obnoxious ever since he won the argument.* **Ant.** pleasant, agreeable, congenial.

obscene *adj.* vulgar, indecent, offensive, pornographic, foul, dirty. *There was too much obscene language in the play.* **Ant.** clean, decent, proper, acceptable.

obscure *adj.* **1.** unclear, vague, indistinct, uncertain, puzzling. *The meaning of his writings remains obscure.* **2.** unknown, unnoticed, undiscovered, nameless, insignificant, minor. *The painting was by an obscure French artist.* *–vb.* **3.** confuse, confound, muddle, cloud, mask, bewilder. *Don't obscure the issue.* **4.** cover, hide, screen, shade, veil, block, conceal. *Dense forest obscured our view.* **Ant. 1.** clear, distinct, obvious. **2.** famous, renown, celebrated. **3.** clarify, clear, simplify. **4.** reveal, expose, uncover.

observant *adj.* watchful, vigilant, alert, attentive, perceptive. *An observant person will be able to spot the owl in the tree.* **Ant.** inattentive, careless, unobservant.

observation *n.* **1.** watching, viewing, seeing, examination, observance, notice. *The police continued their observation of the suspect's house.* **2.** comment, opinion, remark, view, assertion, declaration. *Your observation that the professor was angry is unnecessary.* **Ant. 1.** inattention, neglect, ignoring.

observe *vb.* **1.** watch, see, notice, witness, view, behold. *Please observe how the tennis player swings her racket.* **2.** celebrate, keep, honor, commemorate, remember. *My family observes the religious holidays.* **3.** obey, follow, heed, respect, comply, conform. *A tourist must observe the laws of the country that he or she is visiting.* **Ant. 1.** ignore, disregard, overlook. **2.** dishonor, violate, profane. **3.** disobey, break, infringe.

obsession *n.* passion, compulsion, mania, fixation, preoccupation. *He has an obsession for antique cars.*

obsolete *adj.* old-fashioned, outdated, outmoded, dated, extinct, antiquated. *Calculators have made the slide rule obsolete.* **Ant.** current, fashionable, new, modern.

obstacle *n.* barrier, obstruction, hurdle, hindrance, impediment. *Heat and exhaustion were the marathon runner's primary obstacles.* **Ant.** aid, help, advantage.

obstinate *adj.* stubborn, headstrong, inflexible, unyielding, determined. *The obstinate salesperson would not lower her price.* **Ant.** flexible, pliable, yielding.

obstruction *n.* obstacle, barrier, block, impediment, interference, barricade, bar. *The fallen tree was an obstruction to traffic.* **Ant.** freeing, clearing, aid, opening.

obtain *vb.* get, gain, acquire, achieve, secure, procure, attain. *The warrior's task was to obtain the ring of power.* **Ant.** lose, relinquish, surrender, give.

obtrusive *adj.* **1.** interfering, intruding, pushy, meddlesome, bold, forward. *I would be finished with my work if my boss were not so obtrusive.* **2.** prominent, outstanding, protruding, glaring, conspicuous, obvious. *A giraffe would be obtrusive in a herd of horses.* **Ant. 1.** reserved, patient, unassuming. **2.** concealed, inconspicuous.

obvious *adj.* plain, clear, unmistakable, evident, visible, apparent, distinct. *There was an obvious tone of distress in her voice.* **Ant.** indistinct, obscure, subtle, hidden.

occasion *n.* **1.** time, event, occurrence, incident, juncture, moment. *The wedding was a special occasion for all.* **2.** opportunity, chance, excuse, break, opening. *You might not get another occasion to speak.*

occasional *adj.* irregular, random, infrequent, sporadic, rare. *Except for an occasional hiker, this wilderness is unpopulated.* **Ant.** regular, frequent, constant.

occasionally *adv.* sometimes, irregularly, sporadically, periodically. *I occasionally get an overwhelming desire for a banana split.* **Ant.** continuously, regularly, usually, often.

occupant *n.* resident, tenant, inhabitant, lodger, dweller, occupier. *The last occupants left the apartment in a mess.*

occupation *n.* **1.** profession, trade, calling, business, vocation, work, employment, job, pursuit. *Electronics has been his occupation for ten years.* **2.** conquest, control, ownership, rule, possession. *The British occupation of India ended in 1947.*

occupy *vb.* **1.** dwell, live, reside, inhabit, use, hold, utilize. *She occupied this apartment till last summer.* **2.** employ, engage, use, fill, busy, engross, entertain. *During the slow hours, the security guard occupied himself by reading.* **3.** seize, capture, conquer, obtain, control. *The soldiers were ordered to occupy the seaport.* **Ant. 1.** vacate, depart, leave. **3.** surrender, evacuate, liberate.

occur *vb.* happen, arise, befall, transpire, take place, develop, appear. *When will the next eclipse occur?*

occurrence *n.* event, incident, occasion, happening, episode, affair, experience. *The moon landing was an unforgettable occurrence.*

odd *adj.* **1.** unusual, strange, weird, extraordinary, peculiar, bizarre, curious. *There are some pretty odd characters in "Alice in Wonderland."* **2.** rare, irregular, chance, infrequent, sporadic. *On odd occasions Grandfather would pick up his guitar and sing folk songs.* **3.** single, uneven, unmatched, leftover, surplus, remaining. *Why do I always end up with an odd sock when I do laundry?* **Ant. 1.** normal, usual, ordinary, typical. **2.** regular, frequent, common. **3.** matched, even, mated.

odor *n.* scent, smell, aroma, essence, stench, stink. *She could not remove the unpleasant odor from her kitchen.*

offend *vb.* displease, annoy, irritate, anger, provoke, upset, disturb. *His bad manners offended everyone.* **Ant.** please, delight, charm.

offense *n.* **1.** violation, crime, felony, misdemeanor, infraction, transgression. *The defendant was charged with several offenses.* **2.** insult, disrespect, affront, outrage. *He meant no offense by his comment about her appearance.* **3.** attack, assault, offensive, charge, siege, aggression. *The chess master started his offense early.* **Ant. 2.** honor, delight, praise, compliment. **3.** defense, retreat.

offer *vb.* **1.** propose, submit, suggest, advance, volunteer. *She offered a suggestion on how to cut expenses.* **2.** give, present, bestow, provide, show. *If you offer the dog a bone, he won't bite you.* *–n.* **3.** proposal, proposition, bid, suggestion, invitation. *He made me an offer that I could not refuse.*

office *n.* **1.** position, post, role, capacity, function, duty, task, job. *The office of treasurer is open for nominations.* **2.** working space, room, suite, headquarters. *Come into my office, and we'll discuss the matter.*

official *adj.* **1.** authorized, approved, formal, authentic, real, sanctioned. *The order is not official until the judge signs it.* *–n.* **2.** officer, executive, administrator, commissioner, agent. *An official from the government investigated the accident.* **Ant. 1.** unofficial, informal, unauthorized.

often *adv.* frequently, regularly, repeatedly, constantly, usually, generally. *The stores are often crowded on weekends.* **Ant.** never, rarely, seldom.

old *adj.* **1.** aged, elderly, aging, mature, ancient. *You're only as old as you feel.* **2.** worn-out, shabby, used, decaying, ragged, faded. *This old sweater is ready to fall apart.* **3.** past, bygone, olden, former. *My parents are always talking about the "good old days."* **Ant. 1.** young, imma-

ture, youthful. **2.** unused, new, fresh. **3.** recent, ongoing, current.

omen *n.* sign, warning, portent, indication, foreboding. *The Navajos believe that owls are an omen of death.*

ominous *adj.* sinister, threatening, menacing, disquieting, fateful, dire. *That ominous-looking castle is owned by the local vampire.* **Ant.** promising, favorable, encouraging.

omit *vb.* **1.** delete, remove, exclude, skip, drop. *We omitted the offensive part of the story.* **2.** neglect, ignore, overlook, fail, avoid, forget. *The guide omitted telling the hikers about the swamp.* **Ant. 1.** add, return, include. **2.** remember, recall, recollect.

once *adv.* previously, formerly, earlier, before. *Once upon a time there was a beautiful princess.*

only *adj.* **1.** sole, single, solitary, alone, exclusive, unique. *This is the only gas station within a hundred miles.* *–adv.* **2.** just, merely, simply, solely, singly. *I only wanted to talk to you.* **Ant. 1.** many, several, numerous. **2.** also, furthermore, additionally.

ooze *vb.* seep, drip, trickle, leak, flow, drain, dribble. *Sap oozed from the tree.*

open *adj.* **1.** unclosed, uncovered, ajar, unshut, gaping. *He walked through the open door.* **2.** accessible, available, reachable, unrestricted, public. *The library is open on weekdays.* **3.** wide, expansive, exposed, clear. *Wild horses grazed on the open plains.* **4.** candid, free, honest, frank, fair, sincere, plain. *It is best to be open about your feelings.* **5.** unbiased, unprejudiced, impartial, objective, fair. *The professor has an open mind to any opposing theories.* *–vb.* **6.** unclose, unlock, unfasten, clear, unblock. *Please open the door.* **7.** begin, start, initiate, commence, launch, embark. *We will open our business in July.* **8.** expand, spread, extend, unfold, unfurl. *The bud opened to unveil a beautiful flower.* **Ant. 1–2.** closed, shut. **3.** narrow, cramped. **4.** closed, quiet, reserved. **5.** biased, prejudiced, intolerant. **6.** close, lock, seal. **7.** end, stop, terminate. **8.** shut, fold, close.

operate *vb.* work, run, use, perform, handle, manage. *I'm learning how to operate a sewing machine.*

operation *n.* **1.** performance, functioning, working, action, operating, running. *The mechanics checked the operation of the racing car.* **2.** force, effect, action, use, application, play. *Plan B will go into operation at midnight.*

opinion *n.* viewpoint, belief, conviction, view, idea, judgment, feeling. *Everyone is entitled to his or her own opinion.*

opponent *n.* competitor, enemy, foe, adversary, rival, contestant, challenger. *The tennis player was well matched with his opponent.* **Ant.** colleague, ally, partner, teammate.

opportunity *n.* chance, occasion, time, turn, moment, advantage, opening. *The actress had an opportunity to star in a major film.*

oppose *vb.* defy, resist, protest, battle, contest, withstand, confront. *Pacifists oppose the use of violence.* **Ant.** support, endorse, advocate, defend.

opposite *adj.* **1.** conflicting, opposing, different, diverse, contrary, unlike. *The band broke up because of their opposite views on music.* **2.** facing, other, reverse, converse. *The football teams lined up on opposite sides of the field.* **Ant. 1.** parallel, similar, consistent. **2.** same, identical, exact.

opposition *n.* **1.** resistance, rejection, disagreement, hostility, defiance, disapproval. *The opposition to her new tax proposal was overwhelming.* **2.** opponent, competitor, contender, rival, adversary, foe. *The score is tied, but the opposition has the ball.* **Ant. 1.** approval, support, backing. **2.** ally, colleague, supporter.

oppressive *adj.* **1.** tyrannical, cruel, brutal, harsh, repressive. *The people rebelled against their oppressive dictator.* **2.** burdensome, trying, depressing, overpowering, discouraging, difficult, exacting. *It can be oppressive to accept too many duties at one time.* **Ant. 1.** liberating, humane, just. **2.** heartening, encouraging.

optimistic *adj.* **1.** hopeful, hoping, confident, expectant, upbeat, assured. *The writer was optimistic about selling his book.* **2.** promising, encouraging, favorable, hopeful. *The optimistic weather forecast convinced them to go ahead with their picnic.* **Ant. 1.** pessimistic, despairing. **2.** unpromising, unfavorable.

option *n.* choice, selection, election, alternative, preference, possibility. *They had the option of traveling in the storm or stopping at a hotel.* **Ant.** requirement, compulsion, necessity.

optional *adj.* voluntary, elective, unforced, discretional. *We are conducting an optional course in self-defense.* **Ant.** mandatory, required, compulsory.

opulent *adj.* rich, wealthy, lavish, affluent, well-off, plush, swank. *She lives in an opulent neighborhood.* **Ant.** poor, modest, indigent.

oral *adj.* verbal, spoken, said, uttered, vocal, voiced, vocalized, verbalized. *Had I known this was an oral exam, I would not have brought pen and paper.*

orbit *n.* **1.** course, revolution, path, cycle, route, circuit. *Pluto's orbit around the sun takes 247.7 years.* –*vb.* **2.** circle, revolve, rotate, encircle, compass. *Scientists tried to contact the alien ship as it orbited Earth.*

ordeal *n.* trial, test, hardship, torment, suffering, affliction, misery, pain. *The old prospector told us about his ordeal of being trapped in a mine.* **Ant.** delight, joy, relief.

order *n.* **1.** command, instruction, demand, direction, rule, mandate, decree. *Who gave the order to move the tables?* **2.** arrangement, system, method, sequence, organization, pattern. *The clerk files all certificates in numerical order.* **3.** peace, harmony, calm, control, discipline. *Let's have some order around here.* **4.** shipment, placement, merchandise, consignment. *My order arrived early.* **5.** condition, shape, commission, state, form. *The repairman checked the appliances to see if they were in working order.* –*vb.* **6.** command, instruct, dictate, direct, decree, require, compel. *A police officer ordered him to drop his gun.* **7.** arrange, classify, organize, file, align, array. *She ordered the agenda by placing the most important item on top.* **8.** purchase, request, obtain, reserve, buy. *He likes to order merchandise by mail.* **Ant. 1.** request, plea, suggestion. **2.** mess, disarray. **3.** anarchy, chaos, disorder. **6.** ask, request, plead. **7.** scramble, confuse.

orderly *adj.* **1.** well-behaved, quiet, civil, controlled, disciplined, peaceful. *The crowd remained orderly throughout the day.* **2.** methodical, systematic, neat, ordered, organized, regulated, uniform. *The books were aligned on the shelves in an orderly fashion.* **Ant. 1.** disorderly, undisciplined. **2.** disorganized, unsystematic.

ordinarily *adv.* normally, usually, generally, regularly, primarily. *Ordinarily I wouldn't do this sort of work.* **Ant.** rarely, occasionally, sporadically.

ordinary *adj.* **1.** common, usual, normal, customary, conventional, regular, standard. *The instructor taught the class in her ordinary manner.* **2.** plain, simple, unimpressive, unexceptional, commonplace. *I was surprised to see the millionaire dressed in ordinary clothes.* **Ant. 1.** unique, rare, unusual. **2.** exceptional, extraordinary.

organization *n.* **1.** group, association, alliance, society, league, club. *Our organization was formed with the purpose of preserving our local landmarks.* **2.** arrangement, structure, plan, form, formulation, order. *The lack of organization in the meeting was obvious.* **Ant. 2.** confusion, chaos, disorder.

organize *vb.* **1.** arrange, order, classify, sort, group, catalog, categorize. *Please organize the applications in alphabetical order.* **2.** found, start, form, establish, create, develop. *We organized a coin-collector's club.* **Ant. 1.** disorganize, disarrange, scramble. **2.** dissolve, disband.

origin *n.* beginning, source, start, basis, foundation, root, birth, cause. *The origins of our nation should be taught to all citizens.* **Ant.** end, finish, termination.

original *adj.* **1.** first, primary, initial, beginning, earliest. *The original owners of the house moved out years ago.* **2.** creative, new, novel, unique, inventive, imaginative, fresh, different. *Her drama was one of the most original plays I've ever seen.* **Ant. 1.** next, secondary, final, last. **2.** imitative, ordinary, old.

originate *vb.* **1.** begin, start, arise, commence, derive, spring. *The use of paper money originated in China.* **2.** invent, create, devise, produce, discover, introduce, conceive. *He is known for originating the potion that makes people invisible.* **Ant. 1.** end, terminate, conclude. **2.** imitate, copy, reproduce.

ornament *n.* **1.** decoration, adornment, embellishment, trimming, ornamentation. *We hung party ornaments from the ceiling.* –*vb.* **2.** decorate, beautify, adorn, embellish, trim, garnish. *Her evening gown was ornamented with diamonds.*

ornate *adj.* decorated, ornamental, elaborate, fancy, embellished, florid. *The necklace was very ornate.* **Ant.** plain, unadorned, undecorated.

orthodox *adj.* traditional, accepted, conventional, established, standard. *His religious paintings are done in an orthodox style.* **Ant.** radical, unorthodox, unconventional.

ostentatious *adj.* vain, flaunting, pretentious, pompous, boastful, flashy, showy, conspicuous. *The country singer looked ostentatious in his rhinestone suit.* **Ant.** modest, simple, reserved.

other *adj.* **1.** additional, added, more, extra, further. *I have one other photograph to show you.* **2.** different, contrasting, alternate, separate, opposite. *The other version of the story has a bad ending.* **Ant. 1.** less, fewer. **2.** alike, similar, identical.

oust *vb.* eject, expel, remove, dismiss, evict, banish. *An unruly spectator was ousted from the audience.* **Ant.** install, admit, invite, receive.

outbreak *n.* outburst, eruption, explosion, epidemic, upheaval. *Doctors are warning us about a possible outbreak of the flu.* **Ant.** decrease, waning, reduction.

outburst *n.* outbreak, explosion, eruption, outpouring, flood, rush, torrent. *His outburst of anger was sudden and unexpected.* **Ant.** control, restraint, repression.

outcast *n.* exile, outsider, derelict, outlaw, vagabond, castaway. *The scholar felt like an outcast among the athletes.*

outclass *vb.* exceed, surpass, outdo, outdistance, overshadow, transcend. *The boxer totally outclassed his opponent.*

outcome *n.* result, end, conclusion, consequence, effect, aftermath. *We are awaiting the outcome of the election.*

outcry *n.* cry, uproar, scream, clamor, tumult, shout, outburst. *There was an outcry of* *disagreement to the court's decision.* **Ant.** murmur, whispering, calm.

outdo *vb.* surpass, exceed, beat, excel, best, better, overcome, outshine, outclass. *She was determined to outdo her competition.* **Ant.** equal, match.

outer *adj.* outside, outward, external, exterior, remote, outlying. *The spaceship was headed for the outer edge of the galaxy.* **Ant.** inner, interior, inside, nearer.

outfit *n.* **1.** costume, clothing, ensemble, dress, garb. *The model was wearing a cute outfit.* **2.** group, company, troop, band, gang, team, crew. *His outfit from the army got together for a reunion.* –*vb.* **3.** equip, rig, furnish, supply, provide, provision. *Scuba divers must be outfitted with special equipment.*

outgoing *adj.* **1.** leaving, departing, outbound, exiting. *The outgoing traffic is especially heavy on Fridays.* **2.** sociable, friendly, warm, extroverted, unreserved. *He was chosen as the game show's host because he was so outgoing.* **Ant. 1.** entering, returning, approaching. **2.** reserved, shy, timid.

outgrowth *n.* result, consequence, effect, outcome, product, development. *Lower food prices were the outgrowth of a bountiful harvest.*

outing *n.* trip, excursion, expedition, jaunt, junket. *We went on an outing to the zoo.*

outlaw *n.* **1.** criminal, bandit, fugitive, lawbreaker, desperado, outcast, rebel. *Jesse James was a famous outlaw of the old West.* –*vb.* **2.** abolish, forbid, prohibit, exclude, ban, bar, banish. *Someone should outlaw singing in the shower.* **Ant. 2.** legalize, allow, permit.

outlet *n.* passage, channel, route, opening, vent, exit. *This lake's outlet is a stream that flows into the ocean.*

outline *n.* **1.** silhouette, shape, contour, frame, tracing, border, edge. *All they could see was the outline of the mountains in the early dawn.* **2.** sketch, summary, draft, plan, brief, scenario. *He provided the publisher with an outline of his novel.* –*vb.* **3.** summarize, brief, sketch, draft, trace. *Would you outline your planned activities for the week ahead?* **Ant. 2.** specific, particular.

outlook *n.* **1.** viewpoint, attitude, perspective, stance, angle, standpoint. *We would all benefit if we adopted a more positive outlook.* **2.** prospect, future, opportunity, chance, forecast, expectation, promise. *The outlook for her investment seems excellent.* **3.** view, overlook, vista, panorama, scene, lookout. *The outlook from the rock was worth the climb.*

output *n.* production, yield, product, run, turnout. *The toy factory increased its output during the holiday season.*

outrage *n.* **1.** insult, affront, offense, slander, contempt. *Your remarks about the president are an outrage.* **2.** atrocity, evil, barbarism, brutality, cruelty. *The terrorist attack was an outrage.* –*vb.* **3.** insult, anger, enrage, offend, shock, infuriate, affront. *The minister was outraged by the attacks on his character.* **Ant. 1.** compliment, praise, flattery. **2.** help, good, blessing. **3.** please, soothe, calm.

outrageous *adj.* **1.** atrocious, brutal, vicious, evil, fiendish, monstrous, inhumane. *Outrageous crimes were committed by the Nazis in World War II.* **2.** shocking, disgraceful, shameful, offensive, horrible, awful. *Such outrageous behavior will not be permitted at this school.* **3.** excessive, unreasonable, enormous, extreme, immense. *The cost of housing is getting outrageous.* **Ant. 1.** humane, beneficial, kind. **2.** decent, acceptable, proper. **3.** reasonable, fair.

outside *adj.* **1.** outer, exterior, outward, external, outdoor. *Please open the outside door.* **2.** foreign, alien, outlying, unfamiliar, strange. *The astronauts discovered that an outside force was controlling their ship.* **3.** small, limited, improbable, slight, marginal. *There's an outside chance that my horse will win the race.* –*n.* **4.** exterior, surface, face, front. *The outside of the barn needs painting.* **Ant. 1.** inside, interior, indoor. **2.** known, familiar. **3.** excellent, likely, probable. **4.** inside, interior, center.

outspoken *adj.* candid, plain, blunt, frank, direct, honest. *It's refreshing to listen to such an outspoken individual.* **Ant.** reserved, tactful, guarded, timid.

outstanding *adj.* **1.** remarkable, exceptional, excellent, prominent, foremost. *His school record is outstanding.* **2.** unpaid, overdue, unsettled, due, owed, uncollected. *She took out a loan* *in order to pay her outstanding bills.* **Ant. 1.** ordinary, common, average. **2.** paid, settled, collected.

overall *adj.* total, complete, general, sweeping, entire, extensive, expansive. *The mechanic made an overall inspection of the car.* **Ant.** partial, incomplete, fragmentary.

overbearing *adj.* domineering, oppressive, overpowering, overwhelming. *The coach's overbearing attitude took the fun out of our game.* **Ant.** casual, subdued, timid.

overcast *adj.* cloudy, hazy, dark, murky, foggy, misty, gloomy. *How am I going to get a tan on an overcast day?* **Ant.** sunny, bright, clear.

overcome *vb.* conquer, defeat, beat, surmount, prevail, overwhelm. *The poor farmboy overcame great odds to become a millionaire.* **Ant.** surrender, submit, yield.

overdue *adj.* late, tardy, belated, delayed, behind. *The stagecoach was ten hours overdue.* **Ant.** punctual, early, premature.

overflow *vb.* **1.** spill, flood, swamp, gush, overrun. *Excess water overflowed into the street.* *-n.* **2.** spillage, flooding, deluge, excess, surplus. *A dam was built to catch the overflow from the water-treatment plant.*

overlook *vb.* neglect, ignore, omit, forget, skip, miss. *I will overlook your past mistakes.* **Ant.** notice, remember.

overrate *vb.* exaggerate, overpraise, overvalue, overestimate. *She overrated the quality of that movie.* **Ant.** underrate, minimize, undervalue.

overrule *vb.* repeal, cancel, reject, veto, revoke, rescind, disallow, overturn. *The Supreme Court overruled the original decision.* **Ant.** sustain, allow, accept, permit.

oversee *vb.* supervise, administer, manage, handle, direct, regulate, run. *The captain will oversee the loading of his ship.*

oversight *n.* **1.** error, omission, slip, blunder, mistake, neglect. *Her name was left off the list due to an oversight.* **2.** control, management, direction, supervision, directorship. *The city council was given oversight of the summer festival.*

overstate *vb.* exaggerate, embellish, overdo, magnify, inflate. *You overstated the extent of damage done to your car.* **Ant.** understate, minimize, underplay.

overthrow *vb.* **1.** conquer, overpower, destroy, vanquish, defeat, overturn, upset. *Rebels conspired to overthrow the government.* *-n.* **2.** toppling, takeover, coup, revolution, rebellion, collapse, fall. *The overthrow of the dictator was supported by the army.* **Ant. 1.** restore, support, uphold. **2.** preservation, protection.

overwhelm *vb.* overpower, overcome, devastate, shatter, defeat, beat, crush. *The baseball team was overwhelmed by their opponents.*

own *adj.* **1.** private, individual, personal, particular. *Bring your own pen for the test.* *-vb.* **2.** possess, have, hold, keep, retain, maintain. *Do you own the house on the corner?* **3.** admit, confess, declare, acknowledge, profess, grant, allow. *The child owned up to breaking the vase.* **Ant. 3.** deny, disclaim, refute, disavow.

owner *n.* possessor, holder, keeper, bearer, custodian. *Can you prove that you are the owner of this bicycle?*

pace *n.* **1.** step, stride, gait. *The goalposts were 30 paces apart.* **2.** rate, speed, velocity, tempo, quickness. *He reads at a slower pace than his classmates.* *-vb.* **3.** walk, tread, amble, stroll, stride, traipse. *The caged lion restlessly paced back and forth.*

pacify *vb.* quiet, calm, appease, soothe, allay, placate, tranquilize, lull, soothe. *The officer attempted to pacify the angry crowd.* **Ant.** anger, enrage, agitate, excite, aggravate.

pack *n.* **1.** package, parcel, knapsack, bundle, load, packet. *The traveler picked up his pack of belongings.* **2.** group, bunch, crowd, gang, band, mob, herd. *The pack of wild dogs searched for food in the hills.* *-vb.* **3.** load, fill, cram, store, fill, compress, stuff. *She told the movers to pack the books into two boxes.* **Ant. 3.** unload, empty, unpack.

pact *n.* contract, agreement, treaty, alliance, compact, arrangement, settlement. *The opposing leaders agreed to a pact on peace terms.*

pad *n.* **1.** cushion, padding, mattress, stuffing. *You will sit more comfortably if you place a pad on the wooden bench.* **2.** tablet, notebook, notepad, writing pad. *He wrote the message on a pad by the telephone.* *-vb.* **3.** stuff, fill, cushion, expand. *The bed should be padded for extra comfort.*

paddle *n.* **1.** oar, scull, pole. *Anyone who wants to row must have her own paddle.* *-vb.* **2.** row, oar. *She paddled the boat across the lake.*

page *n.* **1.** paper, sheet, leaf. *I have to read 30 pages in my textbook before tomorrow's class.* **2.** messenger, attendant, servant. *The senator asked his page to deliver a message.* *-vb.* **3.** call, summon. *Would you page the bellboy?*

pageant *n.* spectacle, show, display, extravaganza, parade. *Every year the villagers held a pageant honoring their founding fathers.*

pail *n.* bucket, canister, container, vessel. *The pail was filled with water.*

pain *n.* **1.** ache, hurt, discomfort, pang, agony, soreness. *My father has a pain in his back whenever he bends over.* **2.** suffering, misery, grief, sorrow, torment, anguish, torment, distress. *The children's insults caused the boy much pain.* *-vb.* **3.** hurt, ache, torment, agonize. *Does your shoulder pain you when I touch it?* **Ant. 1.** comfort, relief. **2.** delight, joy, pleasure. **3.** relieve, comfort, ease.

painful *adj.* **1.** aching, sore, agonizing, hurting, hurtful, racking, throbbing, inflamed. *She woke up with a painful headache.* **2.** distressing, difficult, unpleasant, disagreeable, grievous. *Visiting her sick friend in the hospital was a very painful experience.* **Ant. 1.** painless, soothing. **2.** pleasurable, enjoyable, easy.

painstaking *adj.* exacting, careful, meticulous, thorough, diligent. *The vaccine for polio was discovered through painstaking research.* **Ant.** careless, haphazard, slipshod.

paint *vb.* **1.** color, draw, sketch, coat. *The artist painted the canvas with a dark shade of blue.* *-n.* **2.** color, pigment, enamel, stain. *The house will need two coats of paint.*

painting *n.* **1.** picture, portrait, sketch, canvas. *The painting on the wall is by Picasso.* *-vb.* **2.** coloring, drawing, sketching. *He is painting a picture.*

pair *n.* **1.** couple, two, duo, doubles, twosome. *A pair of lovebirds were perched on the highest branch of the tree.* *-vb.* **2.** match, join, mate, couple, unite, combine. *The fighters were paired off and assigned times for the boxing competition.*

palace *n.* mansion, castle, chateau, royal residence. *Her house was as beautiful as a king's palace.* **Ant.** hovel, shack.

palatable *adj.* tasteful, delicious, enjoyable, agreeable, savory, pleasant, appetizing. *Horses find sugar cubes to be very palatable.* **Ant.** distasteful, repugnant, disagreeable.

pale *adj.* colorless, ashen, pallid, sickly, anemic. *The beautiful green pasture turned a pale gray under the moonlight.* **Ant.** bright, vivid.

pall *n.* **1.** cover, shroud, darkness, veil, shadow. *The dark clouds cast a pall over the school picnic.* *–vb.* **2.** bore, fade, weary, weaken, displease, depress. *The routine of driving the same road every day has started to pall.* **Ant. 1.** lightness, brightness. **2.** excite, interest, delight, please.

palpitate *vb.* pulsate, throb, flutter, tremble, pulse, beat. *His heart palpitates whenever he has to talk in front of an audience.*

paltry *adj.* small, insignificant, trivial, trifling, meager, petty, worthless. *She would not accept a job that paid such a paltry wage.* **Ant.** important, significant, major, worthy.

pamper *vb.* spoil, favor, indulge, coddle, cater to. *She pampers her cat like a child.* **Ant.** neglect, ignore, mistreat.

pamphlet *n.* booklet, leaflet, brochure, handbill, folder. *This pamphlet explains the purpose of our organization.*

pan *n.* **1.** skillet, pot, utensil, saucepan. *The bacon is sizzling in the pan.* *–vb.* **2.** criticize, condemn, attack, denounce. *The author's latest book was severely panned by the critics.* **Ant. 2.** praise, encourage, recommend.

panel *n.* **1.** committee, jury, group, assembly, board. *The site for the new library will be decided by a panel of community members.* **2.** partition, board, section, divider. *We will need six wall panels to finish the entire room.*

pang *n.* pain, hurt, twinge, throb, ache, stab. *A sudden pang occurred when he bumped the table with his elbow.*

panic *n.* **1.** terror, fear, alarm, fright, hysteria, dread, frenzy. *The bad financial news caused a panic in the stock market.* *–vb.* **2.** terrorize, alarm, scare, frighten, stampede, terrify. *The first rule in an earthquake is not to panic.* **Ant. 1.** calm, composure. **2.** calm, soothe.

panorama *n.* view, overview, perspective, scenic view, vista, scope. *The south rim of the Grand Canyon offers many breathtaking panoramas.*

pant *vb.* gasp, puff, wheeze, huff, blow. *The pace of the hike was tough enough to make her pant.*

pants *n.* trousers, jeans, slacks, breeches, shorts, dungarees. *She bought two pairs of pants and a shirt.*

paper *n.* **1.** notepaper, writing paper, stationery. *Bring plenty of paper for the essay test.* **2.** essay, article, report, composition, dissertation, manuscript, study. *The doctor submitted her paper on childhood illnesses to the medical institute.* **3.** newspaper, journal, publication, tabloid, periodical. *The Grumpville Gazette is our town paper.* **4.** document, certificate, deed. *This paper proves that you are the owner of the car.*

parable *n.* fable, allegory, lesson, moral tale. *Aesop's fables are excellent examples of parables.*

parade *n.* **1.** procession, display, pageant, show, march, review. *The circus began with a parade through town.* *–vb.* **2.** march, strut, walk, step, file. *The soldiers paraded down the field.*

paradise *n.* heaven, utopia, Eden, bliss, nirvana, ecstasy, euphoria. *Many fishermen think paradise is a fishing pole and a rushing stream.* **Ant.** hell, purgatory, misery.

paradox *n.* inconsistency, contradiction, enigma, mystery. *How he can eat so much and remain thin is a paradox to me.*

parallel *adj.* **1.** side by side, alongside, abreast. *Draw two lines parallel to each other.* **2.** alike, similar, resembling, like, corresponding. *There are two parallel thoughts on that issue.* *–n.* **3.** comparison, similarity, likeness, correspondence, resemblance. *The teacher discussed the parallels between the governments of Canada and Australia.* *–vb.* **4.** follow, run aside, run along to, run abreast of. *The cars paralleled each other through most of the race.* **5.** match, duplicate, resemble, equal, correspond. *The subject of her report parallels mine.* **Ant. 1.** nonparallel. **2.** unlike, divergent, different. **3.** difference, diversity. **5.** diverge, differ.

paralyze *vb.* stun, freeze, immobilize, cripple, deaden, disable. *The suddenness of the action left him paralyzed with indecision.*

parcel *n.* **1.** package, bundle, packet. *The parcel is to be delivered by Friday.* *–vb.* **2.** divide, allocate, assign, allot, distribute. *All assignments have been parceled out to the workers.* **Ant. 2.** collect, combine.

parched *adj.* dry, thirsty, dehydrated, scorched. *He was parched from hiking through the desert without water.* **Ant.** wet, moist, watered.

pardon *vb.* **1.** forgive, excuse, absolve, overlook, release. *The president has the power to pardon criminals.* *–n.* **2.** forgiveness, release, amnesty, excuse. *The convict received a pardon.* **Ant. 1.** condemn, sentence. **2.** condemnation, sentencing.

pare *vb.* **1.** peel, skin, clip, trim, cut. *He pared the apple before eating it.* **2.** reduce, cut, diminish, lessen, decrease, cut back. *She will have to get a higher-paying job or pare her living expenses.* **Ant. 2.** increase, boost, raise, inflate.

park *vb.* **1.** place, leave, deposit, put. *Park the car in the garage.* *–n.* **2.** garden, grounds, green, sanctuary, reserve, parkland, preserve. *Some of the activities you can do in the park include strolling, birdwatching, and picnicking.*

parody *n.* **1.** satire, take-off, imitation, burlesque, travesty. *That comedian does a very funny parody of the president.* *–vb.* **2.** satirize, spoof, lampoon, mock, ridicule, imitate, mimic. *The play parodied many aspects of our society.*

part *n.* **1.** piece, portion, section, segment, fraction, element, division, item. *Part of the jigsaw puzzle is missing.* **2.** share, role, participation, interest, function, task. *We should all take a part in protecting our natural resources.* *–vb.* **3.** divide, separate, open, split, detach. *He parted his hair down the middle.* **4.** leave, depart, exit, go. *The band parted company after the concert.* **Ant. 1.** whole, entirety, all, totality. **3.** unite, combine, attach, join. **4.** stay, remain, linger.

partake *vb.* participate, engage, enjoy, share, take. *All are welcome to partake in the festival.* **Ant.** exclude, abstain, refrain.

partial *adj.* **1.** incomplete, part, limited, unfinished, fragmentary, fractional. *A partial schedule of activities will be available.* **2.** biased, prejudiced, one-sided, partisan, unfair, unjust, unbalanced. *We lost the game because the referee was partial to the opposing team.* **3.** fond, favoring. *She's quite partial to ice cream.* **Ant. 1.** all, whole, complete. **2.** fair, impartial, balanced, just.

participate *vb.* take part, partake, join in, engage in, cooperate. *The game will be more enjoyable if everybody participates.* **Ant.** refrain, abstain.

particle *n.* piece, bit, trace, speck, shred, iota, fragment, scrap. *The dog left a particle of food in his dish.*

particular *adj.* **1.** special, distinctive, specific, notable, singular, exact. *She likes to wear a particular style of clothing.* **2.** detailed, fussy, demanding, precise, careful, finicky, picky, specific. *His roommate is very particular about cleaning the apartment.* *–n.* **3.** facts, detail, specific. *The officers knew the particulars about the accident on Main Street.* **Ant. 1.** general, vague, unspecified. **2.** careless, uncritical, undemanding, indifferent.

partition *n.* **1.** divider, wall, barrier, screen. *A partition was placed in the room in order to make two separate meeting areas.* **2.** division, separation, detachment, split-up, distribution. *The partition of the courts resulted in a civil and criminal branch.* *–vb.* **3.** divide, separate, break up, apportion, split, distribute. *The real-estate company partitioned the land into one-acre lots.* **Ant. 2.** unification, joining.

partly *adj.* partially, somewhat, relatively, slightly. *The information was only partly correct.* **Ant.** completely, totally.

partner *n.* associate, mate, colleague, accomplice, collaborator, friend, ally. *They decided to be partners on the project.*

partnership *n.* association, alliance, corporation, connection. *The two businesses formed a partnership.*

party *n.* **1.** celebration, festivity, get-together. *You are invited to my birthday party.* **2.** group, alliance, assembly, organization, coalition, association. *The disagreement split the union into two* *separate parties.* **3.** person, participant, individual, being, human. *She was the party responsible for the disturbance.*

pass *vb.* **1.** move, go, travel, proceed, progress. *The train will pass by Santa Fe in an hour.* **2.** cease, end, die, lapse, elapse, expire, depart, terminate. *All things must pass.* **3.** give, hand over, deliver, convey. *Please pass the salt.* **4.** approve, enact, authorize, ratify, establish, okay, confirm. *The law was passed by Congress.* **5.** complete, satisfy, accomplish, qualify, achieve. *He must study if he wants to pass this course.* **6.** exceed, surpass, excel, transcend, outshine. *She passed everyone's expectations.* **7.** ignore, disregard, overlook, neglect. *Due to a lack of time, the committee passed over the housing problem.* **8.** spend, expend, occupy, use, fill, while. *She passed the time reading.* *–n.* **9.** passageway, gap, route, course, way, pathway, passage. *Is there a pass through these mountains?* **10.** permit, permission, ticket, authorization. *You must have a pass to enter this building.* **11.** throw, toss, cast, pitch. *The pass to the wide receiver was incomplete.* **Ant. 1.**stop, cease. **2.** begin, start, continue. **3.** keep, retain, hold. **4.** disapprove, reject, deny, defeat. **5.** fail, flunk. **6.** falter, fall behind. **7.** consider, notice. **8.** waste, squander.

passable *adj.* **1.** acceptable, allowable, adequate, tolerable, fair, satisfactory. *His work is not very good, but it is passable.* **2.** clear, navigable, unobstructed. *The road will not be passable until a maintenance crew removes the fallen tree.* **Ant. 1.** unacceptable, inadequate, unsatisfactory. **2.** impassable, obstructed, closed.

passage *n.* **1.** movement, passing, progression, course, motion, transition, flow. *The situation improved with the passage of time.* **2.** voyage, journey, travel, expedition, trip. *The passages of the early explorers were filled with dangers.* **3.** passageway, course, route, corridor, path, channel. *There must be a passage out of this cave.* **4.** paragraph, sentence, section, portion, selection. *Please read a passage from "Moby Dick."*

passenger *n.* rider, commuter, traveler, tourist. *This ferry can transport both cars and passengers.*

passion *n.* **1.** love, desire, affection, fondness, liking, devotion. *The passion he felt for her was overwhelming.* **2.** emotion, fervor, feeling, intensity, zeal, zest. *She wrote about her adven-*

tures with deep passion. **Ant. 2.** indifference, apathy.

passionate *adj.* **1.** emotional, ardent, impassioned, intense, excitable, fervid, excited. *When people talk about their hobbies, they tend to become quite passionate.* **2.** erotic, amorous, desirous, loving. *She often has passionate thoughts about her boyfriend.* **Ant. 1.**apathetic, cold, cool, indifferent.

passive *adj.* inactive, quiet, submissive, apathetic, resigned, nonresistant, unresisting. *He is often too passive and submits to other people's desires too readily.* **Ant.** active, assertive, aggressive.

past *adj.* **1.** finished, done, gone, ended, over, expired, elapsed. *People worry too much about their past problems.* **2.** previous, preceding, former, prior, recent. *She has been looking for a job in the past week.* *–n.* **3.** yesteryear, yesterday, ancient times, olden times. *The days of the horse and carriage are in the past.* *–adv.* **4.** by, beyond. *The runners raced past the halfway point.* **Ant. 1.** ahead, coming. **2–3.** present, future.

paste *n.* **1.** glue, adhesive, binder, bond. *He attached the poster to the wall with a little paste.* *–vb.* **2.** stick, glue, fasten, attach, cement. *She pasted the photograph onto the page of her scrapbook.*

pastime *n.* entertainment, amusement, recreation, enjoyment, diversion, sport, hobby. *Bird-watching is a popular pastime.*

pastor *n.* minister, clergyman, priest, parson. *He is the pastor of our church.*

pasture *n.* meadow, field, meadowland, grassland. *The cows grazed in a green pasture.*

pat *vb.* **1.** tap, hit, strike, rap. *She patted him on the shoulder to get his attention.* **2.** stroke, fondle, caress, pet. *Puppies like to be patted on the head.* *–n.* **3.** tap, hit, strike, rap. *A gentle pat on the head reminded the child to behave.*

patch *vb.* **1.** repair, mend, fix, sew up, restore. *A tailor patched my suit.* *–n.* **2.** spot, lot, space, area, tract, clearing. *This patch of ground will be used as a garden.*

path *n.* walk, way, lane, route, pathway, road, trail, course, lane. *The path to the waterfall is very steep.*

pathetic *adj.* pitiful, sad, touching, pitiable. *The hungry cat meowed in a pathetic way.* **Ant.** laughable, amusing.

patience *n.* **1.** endurance, persistence, diligence, perseverance, tenacity. *It takes patience to learn to play a musical instrument.* **2.** calmness, tolerance, composure, serenity, self-control. *She has the patience of a saint.* **Ant. 1.** impatience, hastiness. **2.** impatience, intolerance.

patient *adj.* **1.** persistent, enduring, persevering, tenacious, determined. *It takes a patient person to wait in a long line.* **2.** calm, serene, uncomplaining, resigned. *Please be patient because he is a slow learner.* –*n.* **3.** invalid, shut-in, case, inmate. *The hospital currently has two hundred patients.* **Ant. 1.** impatient, restless. **2.** impatient, excitable.

patriotic *adj.* loyal, nationalistic, public-spirited, devoted. *It was her patriotic duty to serve her country.* **Ant.** treasonable, subversive, traitorous.

patrol *vb.* guard, watch, defend, protect. *Volunteers are needed to patrol the neighborhood.*

patronize *vb.* **1.** support, endorse, frequent, deal with. *You should patronize the local stores.* **2.** condescend, disrespect, disdain, humor. *That professor tends to patronize his students.* **Ant. 1.** boycott, spurn. **2.** flatter, respect.

pattern *n.* **1.** design, motif, decoration, figure. *He wore a shirt with a floral pattern.* **2.** model, example, prototype, guide, ideal. *The Beatles' musical style became the pattern for many bands.* –*vb.* **3.** fashion, imitate, model, follow, emulate, copy. *The architect patterned her house after a Spanish castle.*

pause *vb.* **1.** cease, stop, wait, break, hesitate, rest, delay. *She paused in the middle of her aerobics.* –*n.* **2.** halt, hesitation, stop, rest, wait, interlude, break, interruption. *His bitter remark caused a pause in the conversation.* **Ant. 1.** continue, proceed, perpetuate. **2.** continuation, progression.

pave *vb.* surface, cover, tar, asphalt. *A maintenance crew paved the street in front of our house.*

pawn *vb.* **1.** pledge, deposit, hock, secure. *The musician pawned his trumpet for twenty dollars.* –*n.* **2.** puppet, instrument, tool, stooge, toy, agent. *She wanted to make her own decisions and not be just another of her employer's pawns.*

peace *n.* **1.** harmony, accord, amity, friendship. *All nations should work to achieve world peace.* **2.** quiet, tranquillity, calm, serenity, peacefulness. *He deserves a little peace after a hard day's work.* **Ant. 1.** war, discord, conflict. **2.** turmoil, chaos, disorder.

peaceful *adj.* **1.** nonviolent, peaceable, nonaggressive, pacifistic, agreeable. *The two countries entered into peaceful negotiations.* **2.** calm, serene, quiet, tranquil, restful, composed, peaceable. *The house seemed very peaceful after her guests departed.* **Ant. 1.** hostile, warlike, violent. **2.** noisy, disturbed, restless.

peak *n.* **1.** top, summit, tip, pinnacle, crest, point, apex. *The climbers reached the highest peak.* **2.** climax, limit, maximum, top, zenith, apex. *The peak of her career was winning the Nobel Prize.* **Ant. 1.** bottom, base, foot. **2.** minimum, nadir, bottom.

peasant *n.* serf, farmer, peon, countryman, worker. *Peasants tended the king's fields.*

peculiar *adj.* odd, unusual, strange, distinctive, abnormal, queer, unique. *The platypus is a peculiar animal.* **Ant.** common, usual, ordinary, general.

peculiarity *n.* feature, particularity, trait, oddity, uniqueness, characteristic. *Singing in the shower is one of his peculiarities.*

peddle *vb.* sell, vend, hawk, market, barter. *The salesman peddled his goods at the fair.*

pedestrian *n.* **1.** walker, hiker, stroller. *The pedestrian walked across the street.* –*adj.* **2.** dull, slow, uninteresting, commonplace, ordinary, unimaginative, mundane. *She did not like the author's pedestrian style.* **Ant. 2.** interesting, exciting, compelling.

peek *vb.* **1.** glimpse, glance, look, peep. *The boy peeked around the corner.* –*n.* **2.** glimpse, glance, look, peep. *Let's take a peek through the telescope.*

peer *vb.* **1.** examine, stare, gaze, look, pry. *She peered at the sky, wondering if it were going to rain.* –*n.* **2.** equal, counterpart, match, colleague. *The young lawyer gained the respect of his peers.*

pelt *n.* **1.** hide, skin, fur, coat. *The trapper brought his beaver pelts to the market.* *–vb.* **2.** hit, strike, beat, batter, pummel, bombard. *Stop pelting that person with snowballs.*

pen *n.* **1.** ballpoint, quill, fountain pen. *All applications must be completed with a pen.* **2.** corral, coop, cage, compound, enclosure, stockade. *Herd the cattle into the pen.* *–vb.* **3.** write, compose, draft, inscribe. *He penned a letter to the editor.* **4.** confine, cage, restrain, coop. *The horses have been penned up too long.*

penalize *vb.* punish, discipline, chastise, chasten, castigate. *They should not penalize her for stating her opinion.* **Ant.** award, reward, praise.

penetrate *vb.* **1.** pierce, enter, puncture, bore, impale. *I can't get the nail to penetrate the wall.* **2.** permeate, infiltrate, saturate, invade, fill. *Outside sounds penetrated the conference room.*

pennant *n.* flag, streamer, banner, colors, pendant, standard. *She waved the team pennant every time they scored.*

pension *n.* allowance, grant, allotment, annuity, benefit. *He receives a pension from the government.*

pensive *adj.* reflective, meditative, absorbed, thoughtful, dreamy, melancholy. *Viewing the old photographs left her in a pensive mood.* **Ant.** happy, carefree, frivolous.

perceive *vb.* **1.** understand, realize, comprehend, grasp, know, apprehend, recognize. *He was beginning to perceive the basis for their misunderstanding.* **2.** notice, see, observe, discover, discern, distinguish, note, recognize. *Look closely and you will perceive a light stain on the fabric.* **Ant. 1.** misunderstand, misconceive. **2.** overlook, miss, ignore.

percentage *n.* part, proportion, fraction, share, piece. *A small percentage of the profits will be given to charity.*

perfect *adj.* **1.** exact, precise, complete, accurate, right. *The house was drawn in perfect detail.* **2.** flawless, faultless, ideal, unblemished, excellent. *The dancer's performance was perfect.* *–vb.* **3.** accomplish, complete, achieve, develop, attain. *Scientists are trying to perfect nuclear fusion.* **Ant. 1.** incorrect, incomplete, unfinished. **2.** flawed, faulty.

perform *vb.* **1.** act, play, portray, enact, present. *He will perform the role of Hamlet.* **2.** do, achieve, accomplish, execute, effect, complete, fulfill. *The gymnast will perform a triple somersault.*

perhaps *adv.* maybe, possibly, conceivably, perchance. *Perhaps we shall meet again.*

peril *n.* danger, risk, hazard, jeopardy, threat, pitfall. *The explorers faced many perils in the jungle.* **Ant.** safety, security.

period *n.* time, span, interval, term, duration. *She engages in a short period of meditation every day.*

perish *vb.* die, expire, cease, end, decease, vanish. *Many animals perished in the forest fire.* **Ant.** thrive, endure, appear.

permanent *adj.* lasting, stable, enduring, constant, perpetual. *She was relieved to find a more permanent place to live.* **Ant.** temporary, transient, fleeting, momentary.

permit *vb.* **1.** allow, authorize, let, tolerate, consent, approve, condone. *The teacher will not permit anyone to leave the classroom.* *–n.* **2.** license, permission, authorization, pass, sanction, warrant. *Do you have a permit to camp in this park?* **Ant. 1.** forbid, refuse, disallow, prohibit.

perpetual *adj.* everlasting, permanent, eternal, continuing, endless, continual, constant, ceaseless. *He was lulled to sleep by the perpetual motion of the ocean waves.* **Ant.** temporary, inconstant, brief, transitory.

perplex *vb.* confuse, puzzle, bewilder, confound, baffle, mystify. *The new computer program totally perplexed her.* **Ant.** enlighten, assure.

persecute *vb.* harass, oppress, torment, abuse, maltreat, hound, victimize, badger, bully. *It is wrong to persecute someone because of his or her religious beliefs.* **Ant.** support, uphold, favor, accommodate.

persevere *vb.* persist, continue, strive, endure, pursue. *The marathon runner persevered* *despite the pain in her leg.* **Ant.** stop, falter, discontinue.

persist *vb.* continue, persevere, insist, remain, endure. *The accused man persisted in claiming his innocence.* **Ant.** waver, cease, vacillate.

persistent *adj.* determined, constant, stubborn, relentless, tireless, unceasing. *His persistent complaining is starting to annoy me.* **Ant.** inconstant, wavering, changeable.

personal *adj.* private, individual, own, particular, intimate. *Keep out of my personal belongings.* **Ant.** public, common, general.

personality *n.* character, disposition, individuality, nature, temperament. *The leader of the group must have a strong personality.*

perspective *n.* **1.** view, vista, aspect, angle, viewpoint, scene, overview. *She had a different perspective of the city from the airplane.* **2.** judgment, understanding, viewpoint, outlook, appreciation, comprehension. *Read this and you will have a new perspective on reality.*

perspire *vb.* sweat, swelter, drip, moisten. *The laborers perspired under the hot sun.*

persuade *vb.* convince, induce, urge, influence, coax, prompt, sway, entice. *They persuaded her to go to the party.* **Ant.** discourage, dissuade.

persuasive *adj.* convincing, compelling, alluring, logical, inducing, effective, forceful. *The salesperson was very persuasive.* **Ant.** unconvincing, dubious, inconclusive.

pertain *vb.* concern, apply, belong, relate, befit. *The following message pertains to you.*

perturb *vb.* disturb, worry, trouble, upset, disquiet, fluster, unsettle. *She was perturbed by his bizarre behavior.* **Ant.** calm, quiet, soothe, compose.

peruse *vb.* examine, read, review, scrutinize, study, scan, observe. *The children perused the old magazines.*

perverse *adj.* contrary, stubborn, obstinate, unreasonable, headstrong. *He gets a perverse pleasure from being obnoxious.* **Ant.** agreeable, reasonable, proper.

perverted *adj.* distorted, corrupt, warped, depraved, sick, immoral, deviant, impaired. *He has a perverted sense of humor.* **Ant.** normal, balanced, sound, healthy.

pessimist *n.* defeatist, cynic, skeptic. *A pessimist never sees the bright side of life.* **Ant.** optimist, utopian.

pessimistic *adj.* gloomy, cynical, hopeless, doubtful, despairing. *The baseball team is pessimistic about winning the game.* **Ant.** optimistic, hopeful.

pest *n.* nuisance, annoyance, irritation, bother, irritant, pain. *Her little brother can be a big pest when he won't leave her alone.*

pester *vb.* bother, annoy, harass, irritate, torment, disturb, badger, trouble. *Don't pester me while I'm working.*

pestilence *n.* plague, pest, epidemic, scourge, disease, curse. *The virus was a pestilence in the confined spaces of the city.*

pet *vb.* **1.** stroke, fondle, caress, pat. *The child petted her kitten.* –*n.* **2.** favorite, darling, beloved, love. *He is considered the teacher's pet.* –*adj.* **3.** favorite, cherished, precious, loved, beloved. *Her pet charity is the Heart Association.* **Ant. 3.** disliked, unloved, despised.

petite *adj.* small, little, dainty, diminutive, trim, tiny, wee. *The petite poodle fitted perfectly in the child's lap.* **Ant.** big, large, ample.

petition *vb.* **1.** ask, appeal, request, entreat, plead, seek, solicit. *The lawyer petitioned the court to declare a mistrial.* –*n.* **2.** proposal, request, appeal, application, plea, entreaty, suit. *Please sign this petition to hire more teachers.*

petrify *vb.* **1.** stun, paralyze, daze, numb, transfix, immobilize, shock. *A charging elephant petrified the hunters.* **2.** fossilize, solidify, harden, mineralize, calcify. *Under the right conditions, wood will petrify into stone.* **Ant. 2.** soften, liquefy.

petty *adj.* **1.** small, trivial, little, unimportant, insignificant, minor, trifling, paltry. *She pays too much attention to petty details.* **2.** mean, spiteful, ornery, miserly, stingy. *The store manager is petty when it comes to refunding money.* **Ant. 1.** major, important, vital. **2.** generous, tolerant, bighearted.

phantom *n.* **1.** ghost, spirit, specter, apparition. *A phantom floated over the staircase.* *-adj.* **2.** unreal, illusory, spectral, hallucinatory, imaginary. *It is only that phantom marathon runner they are claiming to see.*

phase *n.* stage, aspect, feature, state, condition, level. *We are ready for the final phase of the experiment.*

phenomenal *adj.* extraordinary, miraculous, remarkable, amazing, fantastic. *The outfielder made a phenomenal catch.* **Ant.** ordinary, routine, unexceptional.

phobia *n.* fear, aversion, dread, terror, repulsion, dislike. *She has a phobia of cats.* **Ant.** attraction, like, fondness.

phony *adj.* **1.** fake, unreal, counterfeit, false, bogus, forged, fraudulent. *The art dealer was burdened with a phony Picasso painting.* *-n.* **2.** fake, counterfeit, imitation, hoax, forgery. *The old phony claimed to be Abraham Lincoln's grandson.* **Ant. 1.** real, true, genuine, authentic.

photograph *n.* **1.** picture, film, print, shot, snapshot. *Would you please take a photograph of our family?* *-vb.* **2.** shoot, take, film, snap. *He photographed couples at the senior prom.*

phrase *n.* **1.** expression, clause, catchword, idiom, saying, sentence. *Have you heard the phrase "A stitch in time saves nine"?* *-vb.* **2.** express, state, voice, put, describe. *Perhaps you can phrase it in a different way.*

physical *adj.* **1.** material, substantive, real, objective, actual, existing, substantial. *Geology and geography study the physical nature of Earth.* **2.** bodily, corporeal, fleshly, carnal, mortal. *The physical concerns of the human body should not negate spiritual matters.* **Ant. 1.** nonmaterial, intangible. **2.** spiritual, mental.

physician *n.* doctor, healer, medic, practitioner, surgeon. *If your pain continues, we will have to call a physician.*

physique *n.* build, form, shade, body, frame, appearance, anatomy, structure. *Look at the physique on that bodybuilder.*

pick *vb.* **1.** select, choose, elect. *Who do you pick as your team captain?* **2.** gather, pluck, collect, take, detach, get. *They picked grapes during harvest season.* *-n.* **3.** choice, best, prize, cream. *That flower arrangement is the pick of their selection.* **Ant. 1.** reject, refuse, ignore. **3.** worse, reject, least.

picket *vb.* **1.** demonstrate, protest, boycott, blockade. *The workers are picketing for better working conditions.* *-n.* **2.** fence, post, stake, peg. *The pickets were set in the ground to form a barrier.* **3.** guard, patrol, lookout, sentinel, sentry, watch. *The picket sounded his bugle when the reinforcements arrived.*

picture *n.* **1.** painting, drawing, photograph, illustration, depiction. *This is a picture of the Statue of Liberty.* **2.** movie, film, motion, picture, cinema. *"Citizen Kane" is my favorite picture.* **3.** image, likeness, description, representation. *The real-estate agent made the property sound like a picture of serenity.* *-vb.* **4.** imagine, conceive, envision, fancy. *Picture yourself on a beach in Tahiti.*

piece *n.* **1.** portion, part, amount, unit, section, segment. *Would you like a piece of pie?* *-vb.* **2.** fix, patch, repair, restore. *Let's try to piece this old jalopy back together.* **Ant. 1.** all, total, entirety. **2.** break, tear, crack.

pier *n.* dock, wharf, breakwater. *The boat was docked at the pier.*

pierce *vb.* **1.** puncture, enter, stab, penetrate, prick, impale, stick. *The needle pierced his skin.* **2.** wound, affect, sting, hurt, pain, move. *The sight of the starving children pierced her heart.* **Ant. 2.** calm, soothe, please.

pile *n.* **1.** heap, mass, stack, accumulation, collection, mound. *Rake all the leaves into one pile.* *-vb.* **2.** stack, amass, mass, accumulate, collect, assemble. *The boxes were piled in an orderly fashion.* **Ant. 2.** scatter, disperse, strew.

pilfer *vb.* steal, rob, plunder, thieve, swipe, lift, take, snatch. *She pilfered a magazine as soon as the attendant turned his back.*

pilgrimage *n.* journey, trip, voyage, tour, excursion, mission, expedition. *He went on a pilgrimage to his native country.*

pillage *vb.* **1.** rob, sack, plunder, loot, ransack, ravage, waste. *Many villages were pillaged during the war.* *-n.* **2.** theft, plundering, destruction, devastation, robbery. *The pillage continued throughout the night.*

pillar *n.* post, prop, column, support. *A series of pillars held up the ceiling of the cathedral.*

pillow *n.* cushion, headrest, pad, support, bolster. *She rested her head on a pillow.*

pilot *n.* **1.** aviator, helmsman, steersman, navigator, guide. *The pilot directed his ship through the icebergs.* –*vb.* **2.** steer, direct, guide, conduct, lead. *She piloted the plane to its destination.*

pin *vb.* **1.** fasten, fix, secure, staple, rivet, stick. *Please pin this announcement to the bulletin board.* **2.** hold, restrain, immobilize, pinion. *The wrestler pinned his opponent to the mat.* –*n.* **3.** brooch, clasp, stickpin, clip, ornament, tiepin. *She wore an emerald pin on her evening gown.*

pinch *vb.* **1.** tweak, nip, squeeze, compress, cramp. *He pinched his friend to keep him from falling asleep.* –*n.* **2.** tweak, nip, squeeze. *That was a painful pinch you gave me.* **3.** emergency, crisis, hardship, difficulty, predicament. *This flimsy tent is unreliable, but it will do in a pinch.* **4.** bit, speck, trace, little, iota. *A pinch of paprika will add flavor to the soup.* **Ant. 4.** lot, bunch, bundle.

pinnacle *n.* **1.** top, summit, apex, peak, zenith, crest, climax. *The author's third book was the pinnacle of his creative period.* **2.** spire, minaret, steeple, tower. *The pinnacle on the church was the highest structure in the city.* **Ant. 1.** bottom, low, nadir, depth.

pioneer *n.* **1.** settler, explorer, pathfinder, colonist, frontiersman. *Early pioneers opened the American West for further development.* **2.** originator, innovator, founder, developer, forerunner. *D. W. Griffith was a pioneer in the movie industry.* –*vb.* **3.** lead, start, initiate, develop, establish, originate. *The first satellites pioneered a massive development in space technology.* **Ant. 1.** descendant, successor. **2.** follower, disciple. **3.** follow, continue, succeed.

pious *adj.* devout, religious, holy, reverent, righteous, saintly. *The priest was a pious man.* **Ant.** impious, unholy, profane.

pirate *n.* **1.** buccaneer, privateer, plunderer, marauder. *Beware of pirates on the high seas.* –*vb.* **2.** steal, rob, appropriate, plagiarize. *Songs are sometimes pirated by corrupt people in the recording industry.*

pistol *n.* gun, revolver, firearm, handgun, automatic, weapon. *The gunfighter pulled out his pistol and fired.*

pit *n.* **1.** hole, cavity, crater, well, shaft. *The pit was so deep that they could not see the bottom.* **2.** seed, kernel, nut, stone. *An avocado pit is very large.* –*vb.* **3.** match, set, oppose. *The winners of the semifinals will be pitted against each other.*

pitch *vb.* **1.** toss, throw, hurl, cast, heave, fling. *She pitched a rock over the cliff.* **2.** erect, raise, set up, place, establish. *Let's pitch the tent by the lake.* **3.** rock, toss, lurch, plunge, drop, reel, roll. *The waves pitched the small boat back and forth.* –*n.* **4.** toss, throw, delivery, hurl. *The batter could not hit the pitch.* **5.** slant, slope, angle, incline, grade. *The pitch of the roof was too steep to walk on.* **6.** talk, spiel, speech. *He is vulnerable to a good sales pitch.* **7.** level, point, degree, peak, height. *When the audience had reached the right pitch of excitement, the band entered the auditorium.*

piteous *adj.* sad, pitiful, sorrowful, touching, heartbreaking, distressing, pathetic, poignant. *A hungry kitten is a piteous sight.* **Ant.** heartwarming, cheerful, delightful.

pitiless *adj.* cruel, heartless, ruthless, merciless, mean, unfeeling, hardhearted, uncaring. *The dictator was pitiless toward his enemies.* **Ant.** kind, merciful, gentle, compassionate.

pity *n.* **1.** sympathy, mercy, compassion, charity, kindness, condolence. *Have pity for the starving children.* –*vb.* **2.** sympathize, lament, commiserate. *I pity that old beggar on the street corner.* **Ant. 1.** cruelty, apathy, pitilessness.

pivot *vb.* turn, depend, hang, revolve, rely, hinge. *The entire drama pivoted on the opening scene.*

placate *vb.* calm, soothe, appease, pacify, quiet, satisfy. *Sometimes it is better to placate people than to argue with them.* **Ant.** anger, displease, dissatisfy.

place *n.* **1.** spot, area, location, site, region, section, point, locality. *There's a great place for camping across the river.* **2.** residence, home, dwelling, house, abode. *Come over to my place after the show.* **3.** position, post, situation, rank, station, standing. *He has a minor place in the business.* –*vb.* **4.** put, set, lay, arrange, deposit, situate. *Place the flower pot on the table.* **5.** hire, employ, assign, appoint, engage. *She was placed on the board of directors.* **6.** identify, remember, connect, recognize. *She could not place the face with the name.* **Ant. 4.** remove, detach, take away.

placid *adj.* calm, serene, tranquil, peaceful, quiet, untroubled. *The lake is placid now that the storm is over.* **Ant.** agitated, temperamental, turbulent.

plague *n.* **1.** epidemic, disease, illness, pestilence. *The entire population was wiped out by a deadly plague.* **2.** affliction, trouble, hardship, scourge, annoyance. *A plague of locusts destroyed the entire crop.* *–vb.* **3.** afflict, trouble, torment, worry, pester, annoy, burden. *This house is plagued by bad plumbing.* **Ant. 2.** boon, blessing, godsend. **3.** bless, comfort, placate.

plain *adj.* **1.** simple, ordinary, undecorated, common, unassuming, unadorned, modest. *This sofa comes in either a flowery design or plain white.* **2.** clear, simple, obvious, understandable, apparent, certain, unmistakable. *It was very plain that he did not enjoy their company.* **3.** honest, straightforward, frank, candid, sincere, open, blunt. *It was good to hear some plain facts instead of lies.* **4.** homely, unattractive, ugly. *He has a plain face but a great personality.* *–n.* **5.** prairie, plateau, grassland, savanna. *Large herds of buffalo once roamed the Plains.* **Ant. 1.** ornate, fancy, decorated. **2.** unclear, indistinct, vague. **3.** dishonest, indirect, deceptive. **4.** pretty, beautiful, attractive.

plan *n.* **1.** scheme, program, system, design, method, scenario, strategy. *We need to make an evacuation plan for our office.* *–vb.* **2.** arrange, intend, propose, devise, design, contrive, aim. *The senior class plans to hold a graduation party.*

plane *n.* **1.** airplane, aircraft, airliner, jet. *The plane left the airport at noon.* **2.** level, grade, stage, degree, elevation. *He seems to think on a different plane than I do.* *–adj.* **3.** level, even, flat, smooth, horizontal. *He sanded the board to a plane surface.*

plant *n.* **1.** vegetation, flora, greenery. *The plants in the garden are beginning to bloom.* **2.** factory, shop, workshop, works, mill, facility. *His father works at the auto plant.* *–vb.* **3.** sow, seed, scatter, transplant. *The farmer was ready to plant the corn.* **4.** put, implant, establish, place, deposit, instill. *Her testimony planted a grain of doubt in the jury.*

plausible *adj.* believable, likely, credible, reasonable, feasible, possible, probable. *He had a plausible reason for being late.* **Ant.** unbelievable, unlikely, implausible.

play *vb.* **1.** frolic, revel, romp, sport, cavort. *The children played until sunset.* **2.** compete, participate, contend, game. *Would you like to play a nice game of chess?* **3.** perform, act, present, enact, impersonate. *The actress played her role well.* *–n.* **4.** drama, performance, show, theatrical. *The summer theater will present a play by Shakespeare.* **5.** recreation, amusement, entertainment, diversion, pleasure, fun. *There will be time for play in the afternoon.* **Ant. 1.** work, labor, toil. **5.** work, drudgery, labor.

playful *adj.* lively, amusing, prankish, joking, frisky. *The puppy bounced around in a playful manner.* **Ant.** serious, somber, solemn, sedate.

plea *n.* **1.** appeal, request, petition, prayer. *Will anybody answer his plea for help?* **2.** defense, excuse, explanation, alibi, claim. *Her plea of not guilty surprised the judge.*

plead *vb.* **1.** ask, beg, appeal, request, beseech, implore. *The writer pleaded for an extension on her deadline.* **2.** declare, answer, argue, dispute, reason, express. *When asked why he had failed the test, he pleaded ignorance.*

pleasant *adj.* nice, agreeable, enjoyable, pleasurable, good, pleasing, delightful. *Did you have a pleasant trip?* **Ant.** unpleasant, disagreeable, bad, awful.

please *vb.* **1.** like, choose, want, wish, prefer, desire. *He does what he pleases.* **2.** satisfy, delight, gratify, pleasure, amuse. *The newspaper reviews pleased the playwright.* **Ant. 2.** displease, offend, annoy.

pleasure *n.* happiness, enjoyment, delight, gladness, joy, cheer. *The walks in the park brought her much pleasure.* **Ant.** unhappiness, distress, sadness.

pledge *vb.* **1.** promise, vow, agree, guarantee, swear, affirm. *She pledged her loyalty to the group.* *–n.* **2.** oath, vow, promise, agreement, word, commitment. *We expect you to honor your pledge.*

plenty *n.* abundance, enough, lots, much, fullness, sufficiency. *There will be plenty to eat at the banquet.* **Ant.** scarcity, shortage, need.

plight *n.* condition, state, circumstance, predicament, dilemma, difficulty, trouble. *The plight of starving children should be the concern of all.*

plod *vb.* **1.**tramp, drag, trudge, lumber, tread, walk. *The hikers plodded wearily up the hill.* **2.** toil, drudge, grind, labor, sweat. *She slowly plodded through her homework.*

plot *vb.* **1.** plan, scheme, conspire, concoct, contrive. *They were accused of plotting to overthrow the government.* *-n.* **2.** plan, conspiracy, scheme, design, intrigue. *He was unaware of the plot to steal his money.* **3.** story, theme, outline, narrative, scenario. *I can't read a book if the plot is dull.* **4.** area, space, tract, lot, clearing, section. *She was planning to buy a small plot of land in the country.*

plow *vb.* plough, till, cultivate, furrow, break, turn, prepare. *Spring is a good time to plow the fields.*

plug *n.* **1.** stopper, cork, bung. *The plug prevented leaking.* *-vb.* **2.** stop, stuff, block, obstruct, seal. *The little Dutch boy plugged the leaking dike with his finger.* **Ant. 2.** open, uncork, unplug.

plump *adj.* fat, chubby, round, portly, pudgy, stout, fleshy. *Overeating has made him quite plump.* **Ant.** thin, skinny, slender, slim.

plunder *vb.* **1.**rob, loot, pillage, ransack, raid, ravage, steal. *The pirates plundered several coastal villages.* *-n.* **2.** spoils, loot, booty, takings, prize. *All plunder from the raid was divided among the pirates.*

plunge *vb.* **1.**immerse, dip, submerge, dunk, sink, douse. *The thirsty hiker plunged his cup into the stream.* **2.** dive, jump, splash, fall, plummet, descend. *She took a deep breath and plunged into the icy water.* *-n.* **3.** fall, dive, jump, drop, leap, descent. *Let's take a plunge into the lake.*

plush *adj.* luxurious, lush, elegant, fancy, lavish, opulent. *She lived in a plush apartment in Beverly Hills.* **Ant.** simple, bare, poor, stark.

pocket *n.* **1.** pouch, receptacle, compartment. *My wallet is in my left pocket.* *-vb.* **2.** steal, take, lift, pilfer, swipe. *The shoplifter tried to pocket a diamond bracelet.*

poetic *adj.* lyric, imaginative, lyrical, romantic, creative. *The author's poetic style differs from today's realistic writing.* **Ant.** realistic, prosaic, literal.

point *n.* **1.** tip, end, spike, prong, apex. *The spear had a sharp point.* **2.** cape, headland, promontory. *The ship sailed around the point and into the harbor.* **3.** purpose, idea, aim, reason, objective, end, intent, meaning. *Is there a point to this discussion?* **4.** moment, period, instant, time, juncture. *At that point, the losing football team made a last attempt to score.* **5.** location, position, spot, place, locality, site. *There are many points of interest in this city.* **6.** detail, item, particular, part, section. *The lawyers went over every point in the contract.* *-vb.* **7.** show, indicate, designate, signify. *The gardener pointed out the best places to plant roses.* **8.** aim, direct, guide, turn, focus, train. *Don't point your finger at me.*

pointed *adj.* **1.** sharp, spiked, peaked, pointy. *Be careful of the pointed end of that knife.* **2.** pertinent, incisive, telling, piercing, penetrating. *He made a rather pointed remark about the condition of the apartment.* **Ant. 1.** dull, blunt, rounded. **2.** vague, aimless, pointless.

poise *n.* **1.**confidence, assurance, presence, composure, self-control. *The young dancers showed a lot of poise for their age.* *-vb.* **2.** balance, hover, suspend, hang. *The acrobat poised on the high wire.* **Ant. 1.** awkwardness, clumsiness.

poisonous *adj.* toxic, venomous, deadly, lethal, fatal. *The bite of a cobra is extremely poisonous.* **Ant.** beneficial, harmless, healthful.

poke *vb.* **1.** prod, jab, push, hit, shove, nudge, stab. *She playfully poked her boyfriend in the ribs.* *-n.* **2.** punch, jab, thrust, hit. *Do you want a poke in the nose?*

police *n.* **1.** authorities, law enforcement, cops, troopers, officers, guards. *The police arrived at the scene of the crime.* *-vb.* **2.** protect, guard, regulate, patrol, control. *We hired more guards to police the fair.* **3.** clean, tidy, straighten, spruce up, clean up. *The janitors policed up the playground.* **Ant. 3.** mess, dirty, neglect.

policy *n.* practice, program, procedure, system, approach, rule, custom, course, method, habit. *It is their policy to refer all complaints to the store manager.*

polish *vb.* **1.** shine, brighten, buff, burnish, wax, varnish, rub. *Please polish the furniture by Friday.* **2.** perfect, improve, refine, enhance. *The comedian needs to polish his routine.* *–n.* **3.** luster, shine, brightness, gloss, sheen, glaze, varnish. *Your silver has a beautiful polish.* **4.** refinement, grace, elegance, culture, cultivation, class, finish. *The princess exhibited the charm and polish expected of royalty.* **Ant. 1.** dull, tarnish, dim. **2.** cheapen, worsen, coarsen. **3.** dullness, flatness. **4.** boorishness, crudeness, coarseness.

polite *adj.* courteous, civil, respectful, gracious, well-mannered, considerate, cordial. *He was very polite to the judge.* **Ant.** rude, discourteous, insolent, impolite.

poll *n.* **1.** survey, census, sampling, canvass. *The latest poll shows that ninety percent of the population likes pizza.* *–vb.* **2.** interview, survey, question, canvass, inquire, sample. *One hundred students were polled about their political views.*

pollute *vb.* contaminate, foul, poison, infect, dirty, taint, befoul. *An oil spill severely polluted the harbor.* **Ant.** clean, purify, cleanse.

pompous *adj.* boastful, pretentious, arrogant, self-important, grandiose, vain, overbearing. *The chairperson of the board acts too pompous to be effective.* **Ant.** humble, modest, unassuming.

ponder *vb.* consider, study, think, examine, reflect, deliberate, contemplate. *Let's ponder the problem and not act hastily.*

poor *adj.* **1.** needy, impoverished, destitute, penniless, indigent, poverty-stricken, broke. *The old woman was too poor to buy a decent meal.* **2.** bad, inferior, inadequate, worthless, substandard, lacking, deficient. *It is difficult to grow corn in poor soil.* **3.** unlucky, unfortunate, pitiable, wretched, miserable, pitiful. *The poor man has been ill for six weeks.* **Ant. 1.** rich, wealthy, affluent. **2.** good, worthy, excellent. **3.** fortunate, lucky, enviable.

popular *adj.* **1.** favorite, accepted, approved, well-liked, celebrated, famous. *She is the most popular girl in school.* **2.** general, conventional, prevailing, common, current, familiar, widespread. *The erroneous opinion that most athletes are stupid is a popular belief.* **Ant. 1.** unpopular, disliked, unaccepted. **2.** unpopular, uncommon.

popularity *n.* favor, acceptance, acclaim, fame, celebrity, renown. *Popularity may fade, but talent will endure.* **Ant.** unpopularity, disregard, disfavor.

populated *adj.* inhabited, peopled, occupied, settled. *Southern California is one of the most heavily populated areas in America.*

population *n.* people, inhabitants, residents, populace, citizenry. *The population of the Earth is increasing at a dangerous rate.*

populous *adj.* crowded, teeming, dense, swarming, concentrated. *They moved from populous New York to uncrowded New Mexico.* **Ant.** sparse, scattered, underpopulated.

portable *adj.* movable, transportable, compact, transferable, light, lightweight. *A portable radio is essential at a beach party.* **Ant.** immovable, fixed, stationary.

portion *n.* **1.** part, piece, section, segment, share, fraction. *Each lottery winner received a portion of the prize money.* *–vb.* **2.** distribute, divide, allocate, disperse. *The inheritance was portioned out to his relatives.* **Ant. 1.** whole, all, entirety.

portray *vb.* depict, represent, describe, picture, characterize. *He was portrayed as a wicked old man.*

pose *vb.* **1.** sit, posture, model, stand. *I can't get the baby to pose for the camera.* **2.** impersonate, pretend, feign, act. *The secret agent entered the military base by posing as a general.* **3.** state, assert, submit, propose, present, suggest. *The current plan poses difficulties for some people.* *–n.* **4.** posture, position, stance, attitude. *I cannot hold this pose for long.*

position *n.* **1.** place, location, spot, point, site, station. *The position of the sun left no shade for our picnic.* **2.** view, attitude, belief, opinion, viewpoint, stand, conviction. *The president stated his position on the pending trade bill.* **3.**

state, situation, place, condition, predicament. *Your stubbornness has placed me in an awkward position.* **4.** job, employment, status, place, post, rank, duty. *The clerk was promoted to a supervisory position.* –*vb.* **5.** situate, place, put, arrange, set, pose. *She positioned the furniture in a more orderly fashion.*

positive *adj.* **1.** sure, confident, definite, undoubting, convinced, certain, emphatic. *He was positive that they had been here before.* **2.** practical, beneficial, pragmatic, real, effective, useful, good. *We need some positive suggestions on running our business.* **3.** optimistic, good, affirmative, hopeful. *She believes in the power of positive thinking.* **Ant. 1.** unclear, uncertain, dubious. **2.** impractical, useless, destructive, bad. **3.** negative, pessimistic.

possess *vb.* have, own, hold, enjoy, control. *Superman possesses the ability to leap tall buildings in a single bound.*

possessed *adj.* serene, controlled, collected, composed, poised, tranquil. *After a good sleep she was calm and possessed.*

possession *n.* **1.** ownership, custody, control, title. *Both parties claimed possession of the automobile.* **2.** property, belonging, resource, asset, effect. *He does not have very many possessions.*

possibility *n.* **1.** chance, likelihood, probability, prospect, odds. *What are the possibilities of getting tickets for the show?* **2.** potentiality, promise, potential. *The possibilities for advancement in that career are endless.*

possible *adj.* likely, feasible, practical, conceivable, imaginable, workable. *There are many possible answers to the question.* **Ant.** impossible, unlikely, unreasonable.

post *vb.* **1.** place, attach, install, put, fix. *Please post this notice on the bulletin board.* **2.** station, assign, position, situate, place. *The pilots were posted at an Alaskan air base.* **3.** inform, notify, report, advise, brief, enlighten. *Keep me posted on the situation.* –*n.* **4.** pole, stake, pillar, column. *Do we have enough fence posts for the job?* **5.** position, job, duty, station, function, role, assignment. *The treasurer is considered an important post in this organization.*

postpone *vb.* delay, defer, put off, suspend, shelve, hold. *The game will be postponed due to rain.* **Ant.** expedite, advance.

posture *n.* stance, shape, carriage, pose. *He has terrible posture.*

potent *adj.* strong, powerful, effective, mighty, forceful. *Self-confidence is a potent ingredient for success.*

potential *adj.* **1.** possible, latent, likely, conceivable. *The potential hazards of cave exploring are overshadowed by its rewards.* –*n.* **2.** possibility, ability, capability, potentiality, capacity. *Her potential as a concert pianist is excellent.* **Ant. 1.** inconceivable, actual.

pounce *vb.* jump, attack, leap, spring, strike. *The lion pounced on an unsuspecting gazelle.*

pound *vb.* hammer, hit, beat, strike, drum, pommel. *She pounded on the door till someone finally heard.*

poverty *n.* need, destitution, want, lack, neediness. *There is much poverty in India.*

power *n.* **1.** energy, strength, force, might, potency. *He's an incredible tennis player because there's so much power in his swing.* **2.** ability, capability, talent, skill, faculty. *This magic ring gives special powers to its wearer.* **3.** authority, control, rule, command, mastery, domination. *The royalty of ancient Egypt held great power over their subjects.* –*vb.* **4.** energize, operate, activate. *Nuclear energy powers most submarines.* **Ant. 1.** weakness, feebleness. **2.** inability, incapacity.

practical *adj.* efficient, workable, achievable, sound, sensible. *A practical method of filing is alphabetically.* **Ant.** impractical, unworkable, unsound.

practice *vb.* **1.** train, rehearse, drill, exercise, discipline, study. *A great musician must always practice his skill.* **2.** do, perform, observe, follow, pursue. *Good manners should be practiced daily.* –*n.* **3.** training, discipline, repetition, preparation, rehearsal. *All football players must show up for team practice.* **4.** custom, habit, tradition, rule, routine, way, fashion. *It is our practice to have coffee in the morning.* **5.** operation, application, execution, use, usage, action. *The new regulations go into practice next week.*

praise *n.* **1.** approval, compliment, commendation, acclaim, applause. *She received high praise from her peers.* –*vb.* **2.** approve, compliment, commend, admire, applaud, laud, honor, celebrate. *They praised the lifeguard for rescuing the drowning child.* **Ant. 1.** disapproval, criticism, ridicule. **2.** disapprove, belittle.

pray *vb.* appeal, beg, invoke, beseech, ask, request, plead, implore. *The condemned man prayed for mercy.*

preach *vb.* **1.** sermonize, lecture, evangelize, moralize, proclaim, teach. *The evangelist preached on the street corner.* **2.** urge, advocate, counsel, advise. *The wise guru preached humility and moderation to his disciples.*

precarious *adj.* hazardous, risky, perilous, treacherous, uncertain, unstable, unreliable, insecure. *Walking on the icy slope was a precarious undertaking.* **Ant.** safe, steady, dependable, certain.

precaution *n.* care, wariness, prudence, caution, safeguard, foresight, forethought. *The auto racer took every precaution to prevent mechanical breakdowns.* **Ant.** carelessness, neglect.

precede *vb.* lead, preface, go before, predate, introduce. *An overture usually precedes the singing in an opera.* **Ant.** follow, succeed, ensue.

precious *adj.* **1.** valuable, expensive, costly, priceless, invaluable, rare. *The museum displayed many precious works of art.* **2.** beloved, darling, cherished, dear, favorite. *He still considers his wife precious after thirty years of marriage.* **Ant. 1.** worthless, cheap, common. **2.** hated, disliked, despised.

precise *adj.* **1.** exact, specific, definite, explicit, correct, accurate. *The researchers insisted on precise measurements.* **2.** inflexible, rigid, strict, unbending. *The health department has precise regulations concerning the serving of food in restaurants.* **Ant. 1.** approximate, vague, ambiguous. **2.** informal, casual.

precision *n.* accuracy, exactness, correctness, care, attention. *The draftsman drew his plans with great precision.* **Ant.** carelessness, inaccuracy, vagueness.

preclude *vb.* prevent, stop, hinder, forestall, thwart, foil. *A rain shower will preclude plans for a picnic.* **Ant.** help, enable, allow, permit.

predicament *n.* dilemma, fix, mess, crisis, difficulty, condition. *If I had kept my mouth shut, I wouldn't be in this predicament.*

predict *vb.* prophesy, forecast, foresee, foretell, anticipate. *Can you predict my future?*

predominant *adj.* dominant, important, prevailing, primary, supreme, major, main. *Food, clothing, and shelter are some of the predominate concerns of human existence.* **Ant.** secondary, minor, lesser, subordinate.

preface *n.* **1.** foreword, prologue, introduction, preamble, prelude. *A book's preface will often give you helpful information.* –*vb.* **2.** begin, introduce, start, precede, open, initiate. *Television shows are usually prefaced by commercials.* **Ant. 1.** epilogue, postscript, appendix. **2.** end, conclude, finish.

prefer *vb.* favor, choose, fancy, elect, select, like. *She prefers to listen to classical music.* **Ant.** dislike, reject, hate.

preference *n.* **1.** liking, partiality, leaning, bias, prejudice, fancy. *Do you have a preference for either movie?* **2.** advantage, priority, precedence, supremacy. *Emergencies are to get preference over routine medical services.* **Ant. 1.** disliking, aversion. **2.** impartiality, equal treatment.

pregnant *adj.* **1.** expecting, expectant, gestational. *She took a leave of absence because she was pregnant.* **2.** meaningful, important, significant, expressive, weighty. *After a pregnant pause, he continued with his statement.* **3.** fertile, fruitful, rich, full, teeming, productive. *The jungle is pregnant with animal life.* **Ant. 2.** trivial, meaningless, empty. **3.** barren, sterile, poor.

prejudice *n.* **1.** bias, intolerance, partiality, unfairness, preconception, prejudgment, bigotry. *The judge's prejudices interfered with her ability to try the case.* –*vb.* **2.** sway, bias, influence, predispose, warp. *His unruly behavior prejudiced the teacher against him.* **Ant. 1.** objectivity, open-mindedness.

preliminary *adj.* opening, introductory, beginning, preparatory, starting. *Each lawyer was* allowed to make a preliminary statement. **Ant.** final, concluding, ending.

premature *adj.* early, hasty, unexpected, untimely, ill-timed. *The marathon runner's departure from the pack was premature.* **Ant.** late, overdue, timely.

premeditated *adj.* planned, intended, prearranged, plotted, prepared. *The demonstration may look spontaneous, but it was premeditated.* **Ant.** spontaneous, unplanned, accidental.

premium *n.* **1.** value, stock, appreciation, worth, price. *There's a high premium placed on honesty in these times.* **2.** reward, prize, compensation, bonus, gift. *When you buy three items, the store will give you an extra premium.*

preoccupied *adj.* engrossed, absorbed, engaged, involved, obsessed. *He seemed preoccupied with his job.*

prepare *vb.* arrange, ready, anticipate, adapt, plan. *Prepare yourself for a shock.*

preposterous *adj.* silly, ridiculous, unreasonable, outrageous, absurd, foolish, crazy. *Take that preposterous hat off your head.*

presence *n.* **1.** existence, appearance, attendance, occurrence, being. *The presence of smoke may indicate fire.* **2.** bearing, personality, appearance, feature, demeanor, air, manner, image. *His bulk and height gave him a towering presence.* **3.** company, vicinity, midst, neighborhood, proximity. *The murderer may be in our presence.*

present *vb.* **1.** give, grant, bestow, hand, provide, offer, confer. *The mayor presented her with the keys to the city.* **2.** introduce, acquaint. *May I present my mother?* **3.** show, exhibit, display, furnish, produce. *He presented his passport to the custom officer.* –*n.* **4.** gift, donation, offerings, gratuity. *Did you get any wedding presents?* **5.** now, today, moment. *Live for the present, not the past.* –*adj.* **6.** current, existing, existent, recent, immediate, latest. *The present situation appears to be out of control.* **7.** here, attending, near, nearby. *All clubs officers are present.* **Ant.** **1.** take, remove, reclaim. **5.** past, future. **6.** past, former, future, coming. **7.** absent, missing, away, gone.

preserve *vb.* **1.** save, protect, conserve, maintain, guard, keep, safeguard. *Help preserve our natural resources.* –*n.* **2.** jam, jelly, marmalade. *I like strawberry preserves on toast.* **3.** sanctuary, refuge, reserve, reservation, haven. *Endangered animals are often protected on wildlife preserves.*

preside *vb.* head, lead, officiate, administrate, govern, rule. *The judge presided over his court.*

press *vb.* **1.** push, depress, compress, squeeze, poke, crush. *She pressed down on the overstuffed suitcase.* **2.** hug, embrace, squeeze, clasp, snuggle. *He pressed the Teddy bear closely to him.* **3.** iron, smooth, steam, flatten. *Please press these pants.* **4.** urge, insist, beg, entreat, demand, plead. *The child pressed her father for an answer to her question.* **5.** push, shove, crowd, surge, swarm, jam, cram. *The fans pressed against the rock star.* –*n.* **6.** reporters, journalists, newspapers, media. *The Bill of Rights protects the freedom of the press.*

pressing *adj.* urgent, vital, critical, compelling, crucial, essential, necessary, important. *We have pressing business that must be taken care of immediately.* **Ant.** unnecessary, unimportant, trivial.

pressure *n.* **1.** compression, density, force, power, gravity, weight. *The bridge collapsed under the pressure of the trucks.* **2.** stress, strain, duress, tension, distress, anxiety. *The pressure of the job was too much for him.* –*vb.* **3.** compel, coerce, push, force, persuade. *She was pressured into working on Sundays.*

prestige *n.* importance, distinction, influence, status, authority, reputation. *His father has much prestige in the community.* **Ant.** insignificance, obscurity.

presume *vb.* assume, suppose, believe, surmise, guess, imagine, think. *Don't presume the results till you have all the facts.*

pretend *vb.* **1.** imagine, make believe, act, play, fantasize. *The children were pretending to be circus clowns.* **2.** fake, feign, falsify, bluff, effect. *He pretended to be ill in order to miss school.*

pretense *n.* deceit, deception, fabrication, sham, fake, fraud, falsification, lie. *The uninvited guest got into the party by pretense.* **Ant.** truthfulness, honesty, candor.

pretentious *adj.* pompous, self-important, showy, gaudy, affected, smug. *The meal was good, but our waiter was very pretentious.* **Ant.** modest, unassuming, simple.

pretext *n.* excuse, pretense, device, guise, reason, basis, alibi. *He needed a pretext to be in the gym during lunchtime.*

pretty *adj.* **1.** beautiful, attractive, lovely, comely, fair, good-looking, cute. *Your girlfriend is very pretty.* *–adv.* **2.** moderately, fairly, reasonably, somewhat, rather. *It's a pretty long drive to San Francisco.* **Ant. 1.** ugly, plain, homely, unattractive.

prevalent *adj.* common, prevailing, widespread, extensive, numerous, commonplace. *Trout are prevalent in mountain streams.* **Ant.** limited, rare, scarce.

prevent *vb.* stop, halt, obstruct, slow, thwart, defer, avoid, hinder, check. *Only you can prevent forest fires.* **Ant.** permit, allow, encourage.

previous *adj.* preceding, earlier, former, prior, foregoing, foregone. *The surfing was better in previous summers.* **Ant.** following, later, subsequent.

prey *n.* **1.** victim, quarry, target, catch, chase, game. *The lion stalked her prey.* *–vb.* **2.** victimize, seize, attack, hunt, exploit. *A gullible traveler may be preyed on by criminals.*

price *n.* **1.** cost, value, expense, worth, charge, amount, assessment. *What is the price of that diamond ring?* *–vb.* **2.** assess, value, rate, evaluate, appraise. *We priced the ring at $1,000.*

priceless *adj.* **1.** invaluable, irreplaceable, valuable, costly. *The Hope Diamond is a priceless gem.* **2.** fabulous, extraordinary, splendid, fantastic, unique, rare. *She has a priceless sense of humor.* **Ant. 1.** worthless, cheap. **2.** ordinary, common, dull, forgettable.

pride *n.* **1.** satisfaction, delight, fulfillment, happiness, enjoyment. *That artist takes great pride in her sculptures.* **2.** self-esteem, self-respect, dignity, self-worth, self-regard. *A person with pride does not beg.* **3.** arrogance, self-importance, conceit, vanity, egotism, snobbery, disdain. *Pride goes before a fall.* **Ant. 1.**

dissatisfaction, shame, embarrassment. **2.** self-hatred, guilt. **3.** humility, modesty, humbleness.

primary *adj.* **1.** main, principal, dominant, chief, leading, fundamental, basic, key. *The defense of our nation is the primary duty of the military.* **2.** first, original, initial, prime, beginning, earliest. *Her little sister is still in primary school.* **Ant. 1.** lesser, minor, secondary. **2.** last, later, next, following.

primitive *adj.* **1.** crude, undeveloped, simple, unrefined, rough. *His woodcarvings are primitive but beautiful.* **2.** prehistoric, ancient, primeval, aboriginal, savage, uncivilized. *Primitive people survived primarily by hunting.* **Ant. 1.** refined, complex, sophisticated. **2.** modern, civilized.

principal *n.* **1.** head, headmaster, dean, director, superior, chief, leader. *The principal of our school is a likable person.* *–adj.* **2.** primary, main, leading, dominant, essential, foremost, first. *The principal ingredient in apple pie is apples.* **Ant. 2.** secondary, minor, incidental.

principle *n.* **1.** rule, standard, law, fact, precept, fundamental, tenet, assumption. *A major principle in physics is "for every action there is a reaction."* **2.** virtue, standards, ethics, morality, honor, integrity, honesty. *Martin Luther King was a man of principles.* **Ant. 2.** dishonor, immorality, dishonesty.

print *vb.* **1.** engrave, imprint, stamp, mark, indent. *The address of the chapel was neatly printed on the wedding invitation.* **2.** publish, issue, reissue, reprint. *The second edition of his novel has been printed.* *–n.* **3.** printing, letters, type, writing. *She would rather read books with large print.* **4.** etching, engraving, lithograph, reproduction. *Currier and Ives created prints showing early American scenes.* **5.** mark, stamp, imprint, impression. *Someone left a print in the wet cement.*

prior *adj.* earlier, former, preceding, previous, past. *We already studied that in a prior semester.* **Ant.** later, following, subsequent.

prison *n.* jail, jailhouse, penitentiary, stockade, pen, dungeon, cell. *The convict spent twenty years in prison.*

private *adj.* **1.** personal, own, individual, exclusive, peculiar, particular. *Do not trespass on* *that person's private property.* **2.** secret, hidden, confidential, covert, classified, concealed. *Several businessmen held a private meeting to discuss the merger.* **Ant. 1.** public, common, general. **2.** known, open, publicized.

privilege *n.* benefit, freedom, advantage, permission, liberty, entitlement, license. *The right to vote is a privilege.*

prize *n.* **1.** award, reward, premium, winnings, bounty, honor, purse. *The prize for first place was a week in Hawaii.* *-vb.* **2.** value, esteem, cherish, treasure, admire, appreciate. *The millionaire prized her art collection.* *-adj.* **3.** award-winning, valued, outstanding, champion, acclaimed. *His prize pig won a blue ribbon at the fair.* **Ant. 2.** disregard, undervalue, dislike. **3.** ordinary, mediocre.

probable *adj.* likely, believable, credible, presumable, feasible, reasonable, expected, promising, presumed. *It's probable that the mountains will have snow by Saturday.* **Ant.** unlikely, improbable, unreasonable.

probe *vb.* **1.** investigate, examine, scrutinize, explore, search, research, study, inspect. *Astronomers are probing the mysteries of the universe.* *-n.* **2.** examination, research, investigation, exploration. *A shipwreck was discovered during the probe of the ocean floor.*

problem *n.* **1.** dilemma, difficulty, predicament, issue, quandary. *Her tardiness is getting to be a problem.* **2.** puzzle, question, riddle, mystery. *Did you solve the geometry problem?* *-adj.* **3.** difficult, unruly, unmanageable, uncontrollable, stubborn. *This is a special class for problem students.* **Ant. 2.** solution, answer. **3.** manageable, model, perfect.

procedure *n.* course, way, method, process, operation, action, policy, routine, strategy. *Each office follows a different procedure.*

proceed *vb.* continue, progress, advance, carry on, go. *Proceed to the next corner and turn right.* **Ant.** stop, retreat, halt, recede.

process *vb.* **1.** treat, prepare, handle, deal with, ready. *We will process your job application as soon as there is a vacancy.* *-n.* **2.** procedure, system, method, operation, way, conduct. *He is learning the process for baking bread.*

procession *n.* parade, march, file, caravan, line, cavalcade, train. *The funeral procession continued to the cemetery.*

proclaim *vb.* announce, declare, voice, state, herald, advertise. *The inventor proclaimed that he had developed an antigravity machine.*

procrastinate *vb.* delay, stall, postpone, put off, hesitate, defer, dally. *She tends to procrastinate until the very last moment.* **Ant.** expedite, hasten, hurry.

procure *vb.* get, obtain, acquire, secure, gain, win. *She is trying to procure tickets to the concert.*

prod *vb.* **1.** jab, poke, stab, nudge, push, goad. *He prodded the cattle into a pen.* **2.** excite, stir, prompt, encourage, push, spur, motivate. *The dance instructor prodded her students to practice daily.* **Ant. 2.** discourage, dissuade, restrain.

produce *vb.* **1.** bear, yield, bring forth, supply, furnish, give. *This farmland produces many tons of corn yearly.* **2.** create, make, generate, originate, form, formulate. *The local factory produces microwave ovens.* **3.** show, present, exhibit, display, bring, demonstrate. *Why do you accuse her when you can't produce any proof?* *-n.* **4.** harvest, crop, resource, product. *Rice is China's major produce.* **Ant. 3.** conceal, hide.

product *n.* **1.** result, outcome, output, effect, consequence, turnout, end. *Good health is a product of daily exercise and proper nutrition.* **2.** goods, merchandise, produce, stock, commodity. *Many products are imported from foreign countries.*

profane *adj.* **1.** wicked, sinful, obscene, blasphemous, worldly, secular. *He shocked the audience with his profane remarks.* *-vb.* **2.** debase, desecrate, abuse, offend, revile, violate, blaspheme. *Her behavior profaned the sanctity of the temple.* **Ant. 1.** proper, reverent, pious. **2.** revere, respect, honor.

profess *vb.* declare, claim, state, admit, avow, affirm, announce, proclaim, confirm. *The accused woman professed her innocence.*

profession *n.* **1.** career, occupation, vocation, employment, job, calling, field, business, work, discipline. *The profession of koala ranching* *is not in great demand.* **2.** declaration, avowal, announcement, statement, pledge, affirmation. *Their marriage ceremony was a profession of their love for each other.* **Ant. 1.** hobby, pastime, avocation. **2.** denial, negation, withholding.

professor *n.* teacher, instructor, scholar, educator, tutor. *She is a professor at Harvard University.*

proficient *adj.* skilled, competent, capable, qualified, talented. *It takes a proficient administrator to handle this department.* **Ant.** unskilled, incompetent, bad, inept.

profile *n.* **1.** outline, contour, side view, silhouette. *The artist wishes to draw your profile.* **2.** biography, character sketch, portrait. *There's a profile of the author on the back page of his book.* *–vb.* **3.** feature, highlight, write about, mention. *Our school yearbook profiled the homecoming queen.*

profit *n.* **1.** earnings, return, gain, income, pay, revenue, proceeds. *He made a respectable profit from the sale of his car.* **2.** benefit, improvement, advantage, advancement, good, value. *The time you spend studying will be of profit in the future.* *–vb.* **3.** gain, improve, advance, benefit, reap. *She learned to profit from her mistakes.* **Ant. 1.** loss, debit, debt. **2.** harm, damage. **3.** lose, worsen.

profitable *adj.* **1.** lucrative, gainful, paying, moneymaking. *Computer programming can be a profitable profession.* **2.** rewarding, worthwhile, favorable, beneficial, productive, fruitful, valuable. *His volunteer work in the hospital was a profitable experience.* **Ant. 1.** unprofitable, losing. **2.** harmful, damaging, useless, vain.

profound *adj.* **1.** deep, penetrating, thoughtful, wise, intellectual, insightful, learned, serious. *The professor offered some profound advice.* **2.** thorough, severe, deep, total, exhaustive, intense. *Pollution may have a profound effect on the earth's atmosphere.* **Ant. 1.** shallow, stupid, meaningless, silly. **2.** slight, superficial.

program *n.* **1.** agenda, schedule, plan, list, slate, docket. *The program for the festival includes both folk dancing and a juggling act.* *–vb.* **2.** schedule, arrange, slate, book, plan, engage, organize. *We programmed a wide range of activities for summer camp.*

progress *vb.* **1.** advance, improve, proceed, develop, grow, flourish. *The new research continued to progress at a steady pace.* *–n.* **2.** improvement, advancement, development, progression, growth. *The weightlifter measured her progress after each training session.* **Ant. 1.** regress, retreat, decay. **2.** regression, decline, loss.

prohibit *vb.* stop, forbid, ban, disallow, hinder, deny, restrict, impede, prevent. *Camping is prohibited in most city parks.* **Ant.** allow, permit, let, legalize.

prohibitive *adj.* restrictive, forbidding, suppressive, repressive, restraining, obstructive. *The teacher's prohibitive demands made his students uneasy.* **Ant.** permissive, accepting, open, tolerant.

project *vb.* **1.** extend, bulge, protrude, jut, overhang. *The diving board projected out from the swimming pool.* **2.** plan, outline, design, calculate, estimate, determine. *The library is projected to be the most expensive aspect of the new university.* **3.** throw, cast, send, shoot, propel, discharge, launch. *A catapult projected the jet into the air.* *–n.* **4.** plan, design, proposal, scheme, undertaking, task, venture. *His latest project is to build a yacht.*

projection *n.* **1.** ledge, protrusion, overhang, bulge, extension, shelf. *A projection gave the mountain climbers a place to rest.* **2.** estimate, guess, prediction, forecast, evaluation. *We need a projection of the costs for building a new gymnasium.*

prolific *adj.* productive, fertile, fruitful, creative. *That prolific author has written more than 100 books.* **Ant.** unproductive, unfruitful.

prolong *vb.* extend, lengthen, stretch, continue, delay, draw out. *The snowstorm prolonged their stay for two more days.* **Ant.** abbreviate, shorten, limit, curtail.

prominent *adj.* **1.** obvious, noticeable, conspicuous, evident, pronounced, visible. *The rock outcrop was quite prominent on the hillside.* **2.** important, famous, noted, notable, eminent, distinguished, celebrated, renowned. *That geologist is very prominent in her field.* **Ant. 1.** inconspicuous, hidden, indistinct. **2.** unimportant, unknown.

promise *vb.* **1.** pledge, swear, assure, vow, guarantee, agree. *Do you promise to come back tomorrow?* –*n.* **2.** assurance, oath, vow, pledge, commitment, word. *He is expected to keep his promise.* **3.** ability, talent, capacity, prospect. *That pianist shows a lot of promise.*

promising *adj.* encouraging, favorable, optimistic, hopeful, reassuring. *His opening remarks got the lecture off to a promising start.* **Ant.** discouraging, unfavorable, bleak.

promote *vb.* **1.** help, aid, assist, support, encourage, advance. *Her nonviolent actions promoted a belief in her sincerity.* **2.** advertise, publicize, sell, boost, plug, push. *He promoted his book on local television shows.* **3.** elevate, raise, advance, exalt, upgrade. *The company promoted the clerk to a supervisory position.* **Ant. 1.** impede, hinder, discourage, obstruct. **3.** demote, downgrade.

prompt *adj.* **1.** immediate, instant, quick, ready, punctual, quick, rapid, swift, efficient. *The firefighters took prompt action to extinguish the flames.* –*vb.* **2.** suggest, hint, assist, remind, cue, help, nudge. *The actor needed to be prompted on his lines.* **3.** stimulate, arouse, impel, motivate, cause, inspire, convince. *The accusations prompted the senator to defend herself.* **Ant. 1.** lax, slow, late, overdue. **3.** discourage, deter, dissuade.

prone *adj.* **1.** inclined, likely, tending, apt, disposed, predisposed, subject. *He is prone to be upset over the outcome of football games.* **2.** flat, horizontal, face down, reclining, prostrate. *Lie in a prone position if you still feel dizzy.* **Ant. 1.** unlikely, averse, reluctant. **2.** standing, upright, erect.

pronounce *vb.* **1.** proclaim, announce, state, declare, decree. *I now pronounce you husband and wife.* **2.** speak, say, voice, utter, articulate, enunciate, sound. *Her last name is hard to pronounce.*

pronounced *adj.* distinct, clear, definite, unmistakable, obvious, evident. *The difference between a horse and a donkey is pronounced.* **Ant.** subtle, unnoticeable, minor.

proof *n.* evidence, verification, documentation, confirmation, certification, testimony. *Do you have proof that the watch is yours?*

propel *vb.* move, push, drive, start, thrust, launch, shoot, eject, impel. *That toy boat is propelled by a rubber band.*

proper *adj.* right, correct, suitable, fitting, appropriate, conventional. *There is a proper technique for using chopsticks.* **Ant.** incorrect, wrong, unsuitable.

property *n.* **1.** belongings, possessions, assets, goods, effects, resources. *You can pick up your stolen property at the police station.* **2.** real estate, realty, land, acreage, acre, grounds, tract. *She bought a piece of property near the ski resort.*

prophecy *n.* prediction, forecast, divination, revelation, foretelling. *The gypsy's prophecy did not come true.*

prophesy *vb.* predict, forecast, foretell, divine, forewarn, soothsay. *The fortuneteller prophesied that he will meet a tall blond woman with a wart on her nose.*

prophet *n.* fortuneteller, predictor, soothsayer, oracle, seer, clairvoyant, diviner. *It is getting difficult to tell the true prophets from the false ones.*

proportion *n.* **1.** part, share, section, percentage, piece, amount, division, fraction. *The board of directors distributed a proportion of the profits to each shareholder.* **2.** balance, relation, comparison, symmetry, perspective, correspondence. *Make sure that the deck is in correct proportion to the size of the house.* –*vb.* **3.** balance, adjust, arrange, adapt, shape, form, fit, conform. *The architect proportioned the rooms so they would complement each other.* **Ant. 1.** whole, all, entirety. **2.** imbalance, unevenness, disparity.

proposal *n.* **1.** offer, suggestion, intent, bid, motion, invitation, proposition. *She accepted his proposal of marriage.* **2.** plan, program, scheme, project, design, conception, draft, idea. *He submitted his proposal for a new civic center to the city council.*

prosecute *vb.* indict, charge, try, sue, accuse. *The district attorney plans to prosecute her for burglary.*

prospect *n.* **1.** chance, expectation, hope, anticipation, likelihood, outlook, probability. *Her prospects for employment seemed excellent.* –*vb.*

2. seek, search, explore, delve, dig, mine, sift. *He prospected for gold in Alaska.*

prospective *adj.* future, proposed, coming, expected, impending, eventual, anticipated, planned. *They are auditioning for the prospective soap opera.*

prosper *vb.* thrive, succeed, flourish, advance, gain, boom, increase. *Her health has prospered since she started exercising.* **Ant.** decrease, fall, decline, fail.

prosperity *n.* success, wealth, fortune, affluence, riches, abundance. *The banker liked to brag about his prosperity.*

protect *vb.* guard, defend, shelter, safeguard, save, shield. *She tried to protect her children from the troubles of the world.* **Ant.** abandon, endanger, forsake, attack.

protection *n.* security, safety, safeguard, defense, shield, guard, assurance. *A burglar alarm offers some protection against robberies.* **Ant.** exposure, peril, danger.

protest *n.* **1.** objection, disagreement, complaint, opposition, disapproval. *She filed an official protest at city hall.* **2.** demonstration, picketing, boycott, strike. *The students held a protest in front of the administration building.* –*vb.* **3.** object, complain, dissent, oppose, disagree, resist. *The citizens protested the proposal for higher taxes.* **Ant. 1.** agreement, endorsement, approval. **3.** approve, endorse.

protrude *vb.* project, jut, extend, bulge, swell, stick out, overhang. *Pinocchio's nose protruded whenever he told a lie.*

proud *adj.* **1.** noble, dignified, honorable, grand, lofty, stately, revered. *Thanksgiving is a proud tradition in America.* **2.** self-important, arrogant, vain, haughty, boastful, disdainful, conceited, pompous, egotistical. *He is too proud to be seen with us.* **3.** honored, pleased, delighted, happy, glad, gratified. *I am proud of your actions.* **4.** splendid, glorious, magnificent, superb, enriching. *It was a proud moment when Armstrong walked on the Moon.* **Ant. 1.** shameful, undignified, lowly. **2.** modest, humble, unassuming. **3.** ashamed, displeased, embarrassed, saddened. **4.** painful, humiliating, upsetting, regrettable.

prove *vb.* show, verify, confirm, establish, justify, affirm, certify, authenticate. *You must prove your citizenship in order to vote.* **Ant.** disprove, dispute, contradict, invalidate.

proverb *n.* saying, moral, platitude, maxim, truism. *There is a wise proverb that says "the early bird gets the worm."*

provide *vb.* give, produce, offer, present, supply, bestow, deliver. *The librarian will provide the books you need for your research.* **Ant.** deprive, withhold, refuse.

providing *conj.* if, supposing, provided, given, assuming. *I will pay for dinner, providing you pay for the movie tickets.*

province *n.* **1.** area, field, concern, limits, domain, extent. *The subject was not within the province of his knowledge.* **2.** territory, state, division, region, district. *Alberta is a province of Canada.*

provision *n.* **1.** arrangement, preparation, readiness, prearrangement, precaution, plan. *She made provisions in case she could not catch her plane.* **2.** condition, term, requirement, qualification, stipulation, restriction. *There was a provision in the will stating that she could not sell the house.*

provoke *vb.* **1.** annoy, irritate, bother, irk, enrage, anger, aggravate, vex. *He provoked her with his endless complaining.* **2.** cause, prompt, incite, kindle, arouse, produce, awaken. *The decision of the court provoked anger in the community.* **Ant. 1.** calm, soothe, relax, ease. **2.** appease, prevent, quell, stop.

prowess *n.* strength, skill, courage, bravery, heroism, valor, might, power. *Conan the Barbarian was a man of great prowess.* **Ant.** weakness, cowardice, fear, incompetence.

prowl *vb.* sneak, slink, lurk, stalk, creep, roam, steal. *Why are you prowling around in my yard?*

prudent *adj.* **1.** cautious, discreet, careful, sensible, levelheaded, thoughtful, wise, cool. *A prudent person is less likely to leap to wrong conclusions.* **2.** frugal, thrifty, economical, sparing, saving. *With prudent spending, we should be able to stay within our budget.* **Ant. 1.** reckless, rash, careless, foolish. **2.** wasteful, extravagant.

prudish *adj.* prim, prissy, formal, puritanical, repressed, stuffy. *He was a prudish man, insisting that all guests follow exact customs.* **Ant.** casual, tolerant, natural, free.

pry *vb.* **1.** snoop, meddle, interfere, intrude, nose, peep, peer, poke. *Don't pry into my business.* **2.** lever, force, raise, lift, move, work, break. *The burglars attempted to pry open the safe.*

publish *vb.* release, issue, print, circulate, distribute. *A list of the crash victims will be published in the paper.*

pull *vb.* **1.** tow, tug, draw, drag, lug, haul. *The child pulled a toy wagon.* **2.** remove, extract, withdraw, yank, pluck, detach, take out. *She pulled the photograph out of the scrapbook.* **3.** divide, separate, rip, tear, shred, split. *The wrestler pulled the phone book apart with his bare hands.* **4.** move, go, drive, steer, maneuver. *A police officer signaled the driver to pull over.* **5.** wrench, strain, twist, dislocate, sprain. *She pulled a muscle in her neck.* –*n.* **6.** influence, power, leverage, weight, clout. *You must have a great deal of pull with the mayor.* **Ant. 1.** push, shove, thrust. **2.** insert, return, place, plant.

pulse *n.* **1.** rhythm, throbbing, beat, cadence, vibration, drumming. *Electrical current has a steady pulse.* –*vb.* **2.** beat, throb, pulsate, palpitate, pound, drum, vibrate. *Her heart pulsed faster as she ran.*

pulverize *vb.* grind, demolish, atomize, shatter, crumble, crush. *The champion boxer pulverized his opponent.*

pun *n.* wordplay, quip, malaprop, spoonerism, double entendre. *People who make puns should be "pun-ished."*

punch *vb.* **1.** hit, strike, box, knock, poke, whack, jab. *She punched him in the jaw.* –*n.* **2.** hit, thrust, blow, jab, poke, wallop, whack. *He deserves a punch in the face.*

punctual *adj.* timely, prompt, on time, exact, precise, dependable, reliable. *Please be punctual in arriving for the dinner party.* **Ant.** late, tardy, irregular.

puncture *n.* **1.** hole, rupture, opening, wound, cut, break, damage. *He has a puncture in his rear tire.* –*vb.* **2.** pierce, stick, prick, cut, punch, penetrate. *The balloon was punctured by the needle.*

pungent *adj.* **1.** sharp-tasting, spicy, strong, flavorful, peppery, seasoned, zesty. *Creole food has a very pungent taste.* **2.** biting, sharp, caustic, piercing, pointed, sarcastic, cutting. *Her sense of humor is too pungent for me.* **Ant. 1.** bland, mild, tasteless. **2.** dull, inane, banal, flat.

punish *vb.* penalize, chastise, discipline, chasten, admonish, sentence. *The thief was punished for his crime.* **Ant.** reward, excuse, praise, pardon.

punishment *n.* penalty, discipline, correction, payment, chastisement, sentence, penance, retribution. *The punishment should fit the crime.*

pupil *n.* student, learner, schoolmate, apprentice, trainee, scholar. *She is a pupil at Bullwinkle High School.*

puppet *n.* **1.** marionette, hand puppet, dummy. *The children were busy playing with puppets.* **2.** pawn, tool, slave, servant, instrument, stooge, dupe, flunky. *He is just a puppet of the government.*

purchase *vb.* **1.** buy, get, obtain, acquire, procure. *The farmer purchased a new tractor.* –*n.* **2.** buy, acquisition, investment, possession. *Your recent purchase was a bargain at any price.*

pure *adj.* **1.** clear, clean, unpolluted, untainted, uncontaminated, pristine, healthful. *She breathed the fresh, pure air of the wilderness.* **2.** genuine, unmixed, simple, real, undiluted, plain. *The necklace is made of pure gold.* **3.** innocent, virtuous, chaste, good, unworldly, unspoiled, uncorrupted. *The minister led a pure life.* **4.** total, absolute, complete, utter, thorough, sheer. *Pure skill and determination got the skier down the hill.* **Ant. 1.** polluted, dirty, contaminated. **2.** imperfect, flawed. **3.** corrupt, immoral, immodest, debauched. **4.** qualified, mixed.

purify *vb.* cleanse, clean, sanitize, decontaminate, clarify, filter, sterilize. *Stream water should always be purified before drinking.* **Ant.** pollute, dirty, infect, contaminate.

purpose *n.* **1.** aim, intent, meaning, end, objective, intention, goal, ambition, mission. *My little brother's purpose in life is to drive me crazy.*

2. use, application, function, reason, object, sense. *This item has no practical purpose.*

pursue *vb.* **1.** follow, hunt, chase, track, trail. *The police pursued the escaped convict.* **2.** continue, advance, cultivate, seek, undertake, follow. *The actress pursued her dream of stardom.*

push *vb.* **1.** shove, force, thrust, press, nudge, impel. *The boys pushed a wagon up the hill.* **2.** prod, encourage, inspire, prompt, coerce, pressure. *She had to be pushed into going to the party.* **3.** promote, advertise, sell, endorse, boost, tout, plug. *The store will be pushing their new toys till Christmas.* –n. **4.** nudge, shove, prod, thrust, jolt. *Give the door a push.* **5.** energy, ambition, drive, vitality, vigor, enterprise, initiative, pep. *A little push is needed to get this party going.* **Ant.**

1. pull, drag, tow, draw. **2.** discourage, dissuade. **4.** pull, yank, jerk. **5.** apathy, laziness, inertia.

put *vb.* **1.** place, set, lay, settle, deposit, situate, position. *Put the sofa in the corner of the room.* **2.** express, say, state, word, phrase. *No matter how she put it, her friend couldn't understand.* **Ant. 1.** take, remove, displace, dislodge.

putrid *adj.* rotten, spoiled, decayed, decomposed, moldy, rancid, bad, foul, rank. *Meat that is left out too long will become putrid.* **Ant.** fresh, healthy, unspoiled.

puzzle *n.* **1.** mystery, problem, dilemma, riddle, enigma, paradox. *It is a puzzle how he could pass that course without studying.* –vb. **2.** confuse, confound, bewilder, perplex, baffle, mystify, bemuse. *She was puzzled by his suspicious reaction to the question.*

quail *vb.* cower, cringe, flinch, tremble, shudder, shake. *The rabbit quailed in fear when it was cornered by a dog.*

quaint *adj.* old-fashioned, charming, unusual, uncommon, curious, odd. *That mountain village is known for its quaint shops and boutiques.* **Ant.** modern, new, everyday.

quake *vb.* **1.** tremble, shudder, quiver, shake, shiver. *The children quaked with fear during the thunderstorm.* –*n.* **2.** earthquake, tremor, temblor. *The quake was felt thirty miles away.*

qualification *n.* **1.** prerequisite, requirement, capability, skill, talent. *You're wasting your time applying for that job, because you lack the proper qualifications.* **2.** limitation, restriction, reservation, condition. *I can say without qualification that she is the nicest person I've ever met.*

qualify *vb.* **1.** fit, suit, train, prepare, enable, entitle. *Her experience qualifies her for a promotion.* **2.** limit, restrict, modify, moderate, mitigate, change. *He qualified his statement by changing "always" to "usually."* **Ant. 1.** disqualify, invalidate.

quality *n.* **1.** attribute, characteristic, trait, feature, property. *She has all the qualities necessary to make a good president.* **2.** value, worth, excellence, grade, status. *The inexpensive stereo turned out to be of poor quality.* –*adj.* **3.** excellent, fine, good, superior. *He got a quality education at Harvard.* **Ant. 2.** mediocrity. **3.** poor, inferior.

qualm *n.* misgiving, uncertainty, regret, doubt, reservation. *She had no qualms about cheating on the test.*

quantity *n.* amount, number, measure, volume, mass. *She consumes soft drinks in large quantities.*

quarantine *n.* **1.** isolation, segregation, seclusion, detention. *The returning astronauts were placed in medical quarantine.* –*vb.* **2.** isolate, confine, segregate, seclude, detain. *Doctors quarantined the smallpox victims to stop the disease from spreading.*

quarrel *n.* **1.** argument, dispute, altercation, fight, disagreement. *The children got into a quarrel over whose turn it was to use the bike.* –*vb.* **2.** argue, dispute, fight, bicker, altercate. *They quarreled over who should pay the bills.* **Ant. 1.** agreement, peacefulness. **2.** agree, concur, cooperate.

quarry *n.* victim, prey, target, object, goal. *The con artist used the elderly as his quarry.*

quarter *n.* **1.** fourth, fourth part, one-fourth. *She ate a quarter of the pizza.* **2.** section, district, region, area, zone. *He grew up in the city's poorer quarter.* **3.** mercy, clemency, compassion, pity, leniency. *The gladiator gave no quarter to his opponent.* –*vb.* **4.** lodge, house, accommodate, station, post. *The troops were quartered in old-fashioned barracks.* **Ant. 3.** cruelty, brutality, harshness.

quarters *n.* residence, dwelling, lodgings, housing, accommodations. *She's looking for new living quarters.*

quaver *vb.* tremble, shake, quiver, shiver, shudder. *The singer's voice quavered when he got to the high notes.*

queasy *adj.* nauseous, nauseated, sick, squeamish, uneasy. *The sight of blood makes me queasy.*

queer *adj.* strange, uncommon, odd, unusual, peculiar, weird. *Her behavior was so queer* *everyone wondered what was wrong.* **Ant.** normal, conventional, usual.

quell *vb.* suppress, extinguish, silence, subdue, stifle. *She quelled his fears with her reassurances.* **Ant.** incite, arouse, encourage.

quench *vb.* slake, allay, sate, satisfy, extinguish, suppress. *It takes more than a soda to quench my thirst on hot days.*

query *n.* 1.question, inquiry, request, interrogation. *Queries about repairs should be sent to the maintenance department.* –*vb.* 2. ask, question, inquire, quiz, interrogate. *His parents queried him about his late night out.*

quest *n.* search, hunt, pursuit, pilgrimage, journey. *King Arthur sent his knights on a quest for the Holy Grail.*

question *n.* 1. query, inquiry, interrogation, problem. *How many questions will there be on the test?* 2. matter, issue, point, topic, subject. *The article dealt with the question of life on Mars.* 3. doubt, uncertainty, confusion, controversy. *There is no question about her honesty.* –*vb.* 4. ask, inquire, query, interrogate, quiz. *The teacher questioned me about my tardiness.* 5. doubt, suspect, disbelieve, challenge, dispute. *She questioned his ability to take six classes and simultaneously hold a full-time job.* **Ant.** 1. answer, reply, response. 3. certainty, conviction. 4. answer, reply, respond. 5. agree, confirm.

questionable *adj.* 1. doubtful, debatable, suspect, unsure, uncertain. *It's still questionable as to whether or not I'll have the report done on time.* 2. dubious, improper, unseemly, disreputable, suspicious. *Going to the movies every day is a questionable way to spend your entire life.* **Ant.** 1. certain, definite, proven. 2. proper, legitimate.

quick *adj.* 1. fast, swift, hasty, rapid, speedy. *She had so much work to do she only had time for a quick lunch.* 2. nimble, agile, alert, keen, sharp. *He has a quick mind.* **Ant.** 1. slow, unhurried, leisurely. 2. dull, dense, sluggish.

quicken *vb.* accelerate, hasten, hurry, speed up. *You'd better quicken your pace, or we'll be late.* **Ant.** slacken, retard, hinder.

quiet *adj.* 1. silent, soundless, noiseless, hushed, still. *Please be quiet during the movie.* 2. calm, peaceful, tranquil, restful, undisturbed. *She was looking forward to a quiet evening at home.* –*n.* 3. silence, stillness, soundlessness, calm, tranquillity. *I can't think unless I have peace and quiet.* –*vb.* 4. quieten, silence, hush, shut up, still. *The boisterous children were reluctant to quiet down.* **Ant.** 1. noisy, loud. 2. restless, disturbed, fitful. 3. disturbance, noise, tumult.

quirk *n.* idiosyncrasy, peculiarity, mannerism, trait. *Putting peanut butter on ice cream is just one of his quirks.*

quit *vb.* 1. stop, cease, discontinue, terminate, end. *Would you please quit making so much noise?* 2. abandon, leave, resign, depart, renounce. *He quit his job to go back to school.* **Ant.** 1. start, begin, continue. 2. stay, remain, maintain.

quite *adv.* 1. completely, entirely, wholly, totally, thoroughly. *It was quite obvious that she was angry with me.* 2. really, actually, truly, indeed, rather. *Getting a master's degree in one year is quite an accomplishment.* **Ant.** 1. barely, hardly, scarcely.

quiver *vb.* shake, tremble, shiver, quake, vibrate. *The dog quivered with fear when strangers came to the house.*

quiz *n.* 1. test, examination, exam, puzzle. *She has an English quiz tomorrow.* –*vb.* 2. ask, question, interrogate, query, inquire. *Stop quizzing me about how I spent my money.* **Ant.** 2. answer, reply, respond.

quota *n.* portion, share, allotment, ration, part. *The relief supplies were divided such that each person received a fair quota.*

quotation *n.* quote, excerpt, extract, passage, selection. *Her report included numerous quotations from Shakespeare.*

quote *n.* 1. quotation, excerpt, extract, passage, selection. *You have too many quotes in your book report.* –*vb.* 2. cite, mention, repeat, excerpt, extract. *The minister started his sermon by quoting from the Bible.*

rabble *n.* mob, crowd, masses, riffraff, horde. *The rabble of the city surrounded the king's carriage, demanding more food.* **Ant.** elite, nobility, aristocracy.

race *n.* **1.** contest, competition, campaign, run, sprint, relay, marathon. *Runners compete in races during the Olympics.* **2.** lineage, descent, breed, species, color. *The United States is a country made up of people from many races.* *–vb.* **3.** hurry, run, rush, dash, sprint, scramble. *She raced to class when the bell rang.* **Ant. 3.** crawl, creep.

racism *n.* discrimination, prejudice, intolerance, bigotry. *Martin Luther King Jr. fought against racism because he believed all people should live together in equality.*

rack *n.* **1.** frame, stand, holder, shelf. *He kept his wine bottles in a cellar rack.* *–vb.* **2.** convulse, agonize, toss, torment. *Her body was racked with fever.* **3.** comb, search, scour, scan, strain. *They racked their minds for an answer to the teacher's difficult question.*

racket *n.* **1.** noise, uproar, commotion, clatter, clamor, shouting, yelling. *The racket from the party could be heard three blocks away.* **2.** illicit business, swindle, fraud, extortion. *The police found out about the mobster's racket.* **Ant. 1.** quiet, silence, peacefulness.

radiant *adj.* **1.** bright, shining, brilliant, gleaming, glowing. *The campers woke up to a radiant morning perfect for hiking.* **2.** joyful, happy, merry, delighted, blissful, beaming. *A radiant smile lit the face of the young girl when she opened her present.* **Ant. 1.** dull, gloomy, dreary. **2.** unhappy, sad, heartbroken.

radical *adj.* **1.** extreme, drastic, severe, revolutionary, sweeping. *It was a radical decision for him to leave home and join the army.* *–n.* **2.** revolutionary, leftist, anarchist, extremist, communist, fascist, rightist. *A group of radicals held*

a march protesting against constitutional government. **Ant. 1.** irrelevant, trivial. **2.** conservative, moderate.

rag *n.* tatter, scrap, shred, remnant. *The homeless woman was dressed in rags.*

rage *n.* **1.** tantrum, fury, frenzy, rampage, uproar. *The tennis player flew into a rage when they called the ball out.* **2.** fashion, craze, style, fad. *Large weddings are all the rage.* *–vb.* **3.** rave, rant, rampage, yell, scream, seethe. *The manager raged when she found the mess.* **4.** flare, burn, blaze. *The fire raged for weeks.* **Ant. 1.** calm, peacefulness, quietness. **3.** remain calm, be satisfied, be delighted.

ragged *adj.* shabby, shaggy, seedy, patched, unkempt, tattered, shoddy. *The poor children were dressed in ragged clothes.* **Ant.** new, neat, clean, fine.

raging *adj.* **1.** angry, enraged, furious, raving, irate, mad. *The raging bull charged the matador.* **2.** violent, stormy, howling, wild, windy, roaring. *Raging waters washed the sailor overboard.* **Ant. 1.** calm, peaceful, contented, composed. **2.** calm, still, quiet.

raid *n.* **1.** invasion, assault, onslaught, intrusion, sacking, foray. *The bandits made a raid on the village, looking for gold and loot.* *–vb.* **2.** attack, invade, assault, sack, ransack, pillage. *Vikings raided early English villages.*

raider *n.* attacker, invader, pillager, looter, bandit, pirate. *The raiders burned and destroyed the surrounding countryside.*

raise *vb.* **1.** lift, uplift, elevate, lever, heave, boost. *The knights ordered them to raise the drawbridge.* **2.** erect, construct, build. *The construction crew raised the tallest skyscraper in the city.* **3.** nourish, grow, foster, cultivate, rear, nurture. *Many farmers raise chickens.* **4.** gather, collect, mass, accumulate. *The telethon for the earthquake victims raised more money than ex-*

198

pected. **5.** increase, better, advance, improve, upgrade. *The president hopes to raise the standard of living.* **6.** ask, propose. *He raised several important points during our talk.* **7.** excite, energize, arouse, kindle. *The television producers hoped to raise viewers' interest.* **Ant. 1.** drop, lower. **2.** demolish, wreck, destroy. **5.** decrease, reduce, lower. **6.** suppress, check, squelch. **7.** extinguish, lessen.

rake *n.* **1.** hoe, spade, trowel. *The rusty old rake did a poor job of sweeping up the leaves.* **2.** playboy, rascal, womanizer, seducer, rogue. *That rake has chased after every attractive women he's met.* –*vb.* **3.** gather, clear, collect, catch. *They hope to rake together enough people to form a team.* **4.** scour, comb, search, ransack. *The police raked the neighborhood for the escaped prisoner.* **5.** machine-gun, shoot. *The gangsters raked the bank with bullets.*

rally *n.* **1.** assembly, meeting, conference, gathering, convention. *The students were called to a rally in the auditorium.* **2.** recovery, comeback, revival, improvement. *The team made a rally in the ninth inning to win the game.* –*vb.* **3.** gather, assemble, regroup. *The commander rallied his troops around him.* **4.** improve, recover, revive. *Her friends were relieved when she rallied from her illness.* **Ant. 2.** failure, setback, deterioration. **3.** scatter, disband, separate. **4.** worsen, collapse, fail.

ramble *vb.* **1.** babble, blather, digress, chatter. *The instructor always rambles on about things unrelated to the class subject.* **2.** roam, wander, meander, drift. *They rambled around Europe last summer.* –*n.* **3.** stroll, walk, jaunt, saunter. *We went for a ramble in the forest.*

rampage *n.* **1.** frenzy, spree. *The madman went on a rampage, destroying everything in his way.* –*vb.* **2.** rage, rant, rave, storm. *Rioters rampaged through the city.*

rampant *adj.* widespread, epidemic, uncontrolled, unrestrained, raging, unchecked. *Lawlessness was rampant in the Old West.* **Ant.** controlled, contained.

random *adj.* unplanned, undesigned, chance, haphazard, accidental. *Contest winners will be chosen in a random drawing.* **Ant.** planned, ordered, predetermined.

range *n.* **1.** reach, stretch, bounds, limit, span. *She felt the job was well within her range of talents.* **2.** line, variety, selection, series, scope. *The range of colors to choose from is overwhelming.* **3.** pasture, grasslands, plains. *The cattle grazed on the range.* **4.** ridge, chain, band, tier, series. *The Sierra Nevada is a large mountain range.*

rank *n.* **1.** position, status, class, grade, level, degree, seniority. *His rank of general impressed the public.* **2.** row, column, line, series, tier. *Ranks of bookshelves lined the library walls.* –*vb.* **3.** rate, count, stand, judge. *Getting my car fixed ranks high on my agenda.* **4.** arrange, array, align. *Please rank them according to height.* –*adj.* **5.** lush, tropical, overgrown, dense. *The explorers walked through miles of rank plant life.* **6.** smelly, foul, stinky, rotten, putrid. *A rank odor rose up from his old sneakers.* **Ant. 5.** sparse, spotty, scanty. **6.** sweet, pleasant, fresh, fragrant.

ransack *vb.* **1.** rummage, scour, comb. *She ransacked her closet, looking for something to wear.* **2.** plunder, rob, pillage, loot, sack. *Their apartment was ransacked by burglars.* **Ant. 2.** return, repair, restore.

rapid *adj.* fast, swift, quick, speedy, brisk, hurried, accelerated, express. *The space shuttle's rapid climb into the sky was seen by millions of viewers.* **Ant.** slow, sluggish, gradual, crawling.

rapidly *adv.* quickly, swiftly, speedily, briskly, hurriedly, fast. *The snow rapidly turned to slush when the sun rose.* **Ant.** gradually, slowly, sluggishly.

rapture *n.* delight, ecstasy, joy, elation, enchantment, devotion. *The worshiper looked with rapture upon the religious artifact.* **Ant.** sorrow, distress, misery.

rare *adj.* unusual, scarce, uncommon, infrequent, limited, unique. *Finding the last rare stamp for our collection was difficult.* **Ant.** plentiful, frequent, ordinary, common.

rarely *adv.* seldom, infrequently, hardly, irregularly, occasionally. *Her car is covered with dust because she rarely washes it.* **Ant.** frequently, regularly, often.

rash *adj.* **1.** hasty, brash, thoughtless, sudden, careless, foolhardy. *In her anger, she made* *a rash decision and quit her job.* –n. **2.** outbreak, eruption, torrent, explosion, tumult. *The authorities were stumped by a rash of burglaries in the neighborhood.* **Ant. 1.** thoughtful, careful, calm, cautious.

rate *n.* **1.** speed, velocity, pace, gait. *At that rate you will never finish the puzzle.* **2.** fee, fare, rent, price, dues, cost. *The ski rental had daily and weekly rates posted inside the store.* –vb. **3.** grade, rank, evaluate, judge, consider. *I rate this food among the worst I've ever eaten.*

ratify *vb.* confirm, certify, verify, uphold, authorize, sanction, validate. *Both leaders must sign the treaty to ratify it.* **Ant.** invalidate, veto, oppose.

ratio *n.* proportion, fraction, distribution. *The ratio of high-school teachers to students is about 1 to 30.*

ration *n.* **1.** quota, allotment, share, provision. *Their ration of gasoline was ten gallons.* **2.** stores, supplies, provisions, stocks. *The travelers bought rations in the nearest town.* –vb. **3.** distribute, assign, allocate, disperse. *Many countries had to ration scarce products during World War II.*

rational *adj.* logical, sensible, reasonable, wise, analytical, intelligent, well-grounded. *Vulcans act in a very rational manner.* **Ant.** irrational, crazy, unreasonable, rash.

rattle *vb.* **1.** shake, clatter, clank, jingle, clink, clang. *The small baby rattled its toy.* **2.** upset, confuse, shake, fluster, muddle. *The performer became rattled when someone yelled out.* **3.** chatter, babble, blather, blab, jabber. *My friend rattled on about her vacation.* –n. **4.** knocking, clatter, clank, clanging, clang. *We heard the rattle of the windows as the truck passed our house.*

ravage *vb.* **1.** destroy, ruin, devastate, waste, demolish, rape, violate. *The city was ravaged by the bombing.* –n. **2.** destruction, devastation, violation, rape, burning, razing. *The ravage caused by the bombs was still visible many years later.* **Ant. 1.** build, repair, improve. **2.** repair, improvement.

ravenous *adj.* **1.** starving, hungry, famished. *The travelers were ravenous after being lost in the desert with no food.* **2.** plundering,

predatory, greedy, piratical, insatiable. *The company's ravenous methods gained it huge profits but bad publicity.* **Ant. 1.** satiated. **2.** charitable.

ravishing *adj.* captivating, enchanting, bewitching, fascinating, beautiful, seductive. *The actress wore a ravishing gown.* **Ant.** repulsive, revolting, disgusting.

raw *adj.* **1.** unprepared, uncooked, unrefined, natural, unprocessed. *They feed the lions slabs of raw meat.* **2.** unschooled, untrained, immature, undisciplined, unsophisticated. *The raw power of the young man was impressive as he fought the trained boxer.* **3.** direct, candid, outspoken, blunt, frank. *His raw comments were received in silence by the offended audience.* **4.** harsh, wet, cold, numbing, biting, chilly. *The raw weather kept us inside.* **Ant. 1.** prepared, cooked, refined. **2.** trained, experienced, disciplined. **3.** indirect, flowery. **4.** warm, pleasant, mild.

raze *vb.* destroy, demolish, topple, crush, smash, ruin, wreck, annihilate. *The violent hurricane razed much of the coastal city.* **Ant.** build, repair, restore.

reach *vb.* **1.** make, attain, achieve, arrive at. *Our horse will not reach the finish line in time.* **2.** grasp, seize, stretch, clutch, grab. *She spilled her soda when she reached for the ketchup.* **3.** span, extend, stretch, spread, approach. *The cost of the new stadium will reach into the millions.* **4.** find, contact, get. *If he needs to reach me, have him telephone the hotel.* –n. **5.** span, length, expanse, stretch. *The basketball player's reach was impressive.*

react *vb.* respond, answer, reply, act. *Paramedics react as quickly as possible to emergencies.*

reaction *n.* response, answer, reply, reflex, backlash. *The biologist recorded the dolphin's reaction to underwater sounds.*

ready *adj.* **1.** prepared, set, equipped, willing, fit, eager. *Are you ready to leave?* **2.** quick, swift, prompt, immediate, instant. *She had a ready answer to his question.* –vb. **3.** prepare, equip, set, arrange. *The pilot was told to ready the engines for takeoff.* **Ant. 1.** unprepared, unready, unfit. **2.** slow, delayed, late.

real *adj.* **1.** genuine, actual, authentic. *That was a real diamond, not an imitation.* **2.** factual, true, truthful, undeniable, valid, unquestionable. *She doesn't believe ghosts are real.* **3.** sincere, heartfelt, honest, genuine. *Please give them a real round of applause.* **Ant. 1.** fake, imitation, unreal. **2.** imaginary, mythological, unreal. **3.** insincere, false.

realism *n.* **1.** authenticity, naturalism, reality, naturalness. *The artist's use of lifelike colors added a strong sense of realism to his painting.* **2.** reasonableness, straightforwardness. *She approached her problems with a realism that was admirable.* **Ant. 1.** unnaturalness, unreality, fantasy. **2.** unreasonableness.

reality *n.* actuality, truth, existence, realness, fact. *The insane man had a warped sense of reality.* **Ant.** fantasy, unreality.

realize *vb.* **1.** understand, comprehend, recognize, perceive, gather, appreciate. *My friend's kindness yesterday made me realize how much I really like him.* **2.** complete, perfect, achieve, accomplish. *Their final goal was never fully realized.*

realm *n.* domain, kingdom, sphere, region, province. *The queen's realm extended to the sea.*

reap *vb.* harvest, cut, gather, obtain, acquire. *He hoped to reap the profits of his investments.* **Ant.** lose, miss.

rear *n.* **1.** tail, back, end, posterior, rump. *The two tired runners fell to the rear.* *–adj.* **2.** back, posterior, aft. *The rear window of our station wagon fogs up in cold weather.* *–vb.* **3.** rise, tower, soar. *The bear reared up to defend its cubs.* **4.** raise, develop, train, nurture, foster. *She rears thoroughbreds on her ranch.* **Ant. 1.** front, anterior, forepart. **2.** front, leading. **3.** drop, descend, sink.

reason *n.* **1.** explanation, cause, justification, incentive, basis, excuse. *The reason he did not come was that his car broke down.* **2.** logic, sensibility, wisdom, rationality. *Will you listen to reason and take someone with you?* *–vb.* **3.** figure, understand, solve. *She was able to reason out the math problem.* **4.** argue, discuss, debate. *She won't listen to me, so will you reason with her?* **Ant. 2.** irrationality, stupidity.

reasonable *adj.* **1.** sensible, practical, logical, wise, intelligent, fair. *Your suggestion to split the cost between us seems reasonable.* **2.** fair, just, moderate, honest. *He bought the jacket at a reasonable price.* **Ant. 1.** unreasonable, impractical, unintelligent. **2.** unfair, unjust.

rebel *n.* **1.** agitator, malcontent, revolutionary, revolter, guerrilla. *The rebels launched an attack against government forces.* *–vb.* **2.** resist, defy, mutiny, revolt, strike, secede. *The students rebelled against the unreasonable school regulations.* **Ant. 2.** comply, obey, submit.

rebellion *n.* uprising, revolt, resistance, revolution, upheaval, insubordination. *The American Revolution was a rebellion against British control.*

rebuff *n.* **1.** rejection, denial, refusal. *The manager's strong rebuff of my suggestion was upsetting.* *–vb.* **2.** reject, deny, refuse, decline, spurn. *If you always rebuff people's attempts to make friends, they will stop trying.* **Ant. 1.** acceptance, approval, agreement. **2.** accept, welcome.

rebuke *vb.* **1.** reprimand, scold, reproach, censure, chide. *He was strongly rebuked for arriving home late.* *–n.* **2.** reprimand, scolding, reproach, chiding. *What did I do to deserve your rebuke?* **Ant. 1.** praise, approve. **2.** praise, encouragement.

recall *vb.* **1.** remember, recollect, recognize. *Do you recall the time we were in the amusement park and you got lost?* **2.** retract, revoke, withdraw, cancel. *They had to recall the automobiles because of faulty brakes.* *–n.* **3.** memory, recollection, remembrance. *His recall of the accident is hazy.* **Ant. 1.** forget. **3.** forgetfulness.

recede *vb.* retreat, dwindle, diminish, regress, leave, subside. *We watched the harbor recede from view as our ship headed out to sea.* **Ant.** emerge, advance, increase.

receive *vb.* accept, assume, gather, get, hold, obtain, embrace, welcome. *The astronauts will receive awards at tonight's celebration.* **Ant.** refuse, reject, discard.

recent *adj.* latest, new, modern, novel, fresh. *The two freshmen were recent additions to our soccer team.* **Ant.** old, dated.

reception *n.* **1.** acceptance, welcome, admission. *What type of reception did the new songs receive?* **2.** party, tea, gathering, affair, hearing. *She went to the wedding reception.*

receptive *adj.* acceptant, open, sympathetic, open-minded, willing. *Do you think my parents will be receptive to my plan?* **Ant.** unreceptive, unsympathetic, close-minded.

recess *n.* **1.** intermission, break, pause, halt, rest. *We have our recess after English class.* **2.** hole, break, dent, nook, hollow, gap. *The injured sea gull hid itself in a recess of the cliff wall.* **Ant. 1.** continuation.

recession *n.* **1.** decline, inflation, slump, slowdown, crisis. *Jobs are scarce during recessions.* **2.** indentation, hollow, nook. *The treasure was hidden in a recession in the cave floor.* **Ant. 1.** improvement, recovery, upturn.

recite *vb.* repeat, quote, recount, narrate, speak. *The class recited the Pledge of Allegiance.*

reckless *adj.* wild, rash, thoughtless, careless, unthinking, irresponsible. *Her reckless behavior almost cost us our lives.* **Ant.** thoughtful, careful, responsible.

recline *vb.* lounge, loll, repose, rest. *The sunbathers reclined on their lawn chairs.*

recluse *n.* hermit, monk, ascetic, loner. *The woman living up in the cave was a recluse.*

recognize *vb.* **1.** identify, place, detect, know, spot. *I'm sure I would recognize you in that disguise.* **2.** honor, reward, appreciate. *The scientist was recognized by the president for her outstanding achievements.* **3.** acknowledge, accept, sanction, endorse. *The United States decided to recognize the People's Republic of China in 1979.* **Ant. 2.** ignore, neglect. **3.** ignore, overlook.

recollect *vb.* recall, remember, place, reminisce. *I seem to recollect that you borrowed my skis last winter.* **Ant.** forget, overlook.

recommend *vb.* suggest, promote, endorse, commend, advocate. *He will recommend me for the job.* **Ant.** denounce, censure.

recommendation *n.* **1.** guidance, advice, suggestion, counsel. *I asked for the doctor's recommendation on my treatment.* **2.** endorsement, referral, approval, testimonial. *She needs a letter of recommendation to the program.* **Ant. 2.** criticism, condemnation.

reconcile *vb.* **1.** resign, adjust, adapt, submit. *He reconciled himself to doing his homework.* **2.** settle, heal, mend, resolve. *The two countries must reconcile their differences before a treaty can be signed.* **3.** reunite, conciliate, harmonize. *Someone should try to reconcile the two feuding coaches.*

record *n.* **1.** log, account, journal, report, chronicle, diary, transcript, history. *My parents keep a record of how much money I owe them.* **2.** unbeaten mark, ultimate time. *The athlete hoped to break the world record.* –*vb.* **3.** chronicle, register, document, note, log, tape. *The alien traveler wanted to record human behavior on Earth.* –*adj.* **4.** best, unbeaten, fastest, top. *The marathon runner crossed the finish line in record time.* **Ant. 3.** disregard, ignore, erase. **4.** slowest.

recover *vb.* **1.** heal, improve, rally, revive, recuperate. *My brother needs time to recover from his cold.* **2.** retrieve, reclaim, regain, salvage. *I hope we can recover the things taken by the thieves.* **Ant. 1.** worsen, relapse, die. **2.** lose.

recovery *n.* **1.** recuperation, comeback, rehabilitation, regeneration. *His recovery after the climbing accident was miraculous.* **2.** retrieval, reclamation, repossession. *The sunken treasure's recovery was difficult.* **Ant. 1.** death, setback. **2.** loss.

recreation *n.* pastime, hobby, relaxation, sport, amusement. *Softball was their favorite form of recreation.* **Ant.** job, work.

recruit *vb.* **1.** enlist, enroll, induct, draft, obtain. *Please recruit people who can help us at the bake sale.* –*n.* **2.** enlistee, volunteer, selectee, draftee, soldier, private. *The new recruits were lined up outside the army barracks.*

rectify *vb.* correct, fix, mend, right, amend. *She hoped to rectify the problem by apologizing.*

recur *vb.* reappear, return, repeat, continue. *We hope the computer malfunction does not recur.*

redeem *vb.* **1.** retrieve, recover, regain, rescue, ransom. *The minister sought to redeem his followers' souls.* **2.** exchange, cash. *Can I redeem this coupon at the counter?* **3.** deliver, free, liberate, absolve, acquit. *He hopes to redeem himself of his past failures.* **Ant. 1.** lose, abandon.

reduce *vb.* **1.** lessen, cut, diminish, decrease, shorten, weaken, subtract, restrict. *Our football team must reduce the number of mistakes it makes.* **2.** humble, degrade, lower, demote. *The man was reduced to scavenging in the garbage when he lost his job.* **Ant. 1.** increase, strengthen, lengthen, extend. **2.** raise, boost.

redundant *adj.* repetitive, unnecessary, wordy. *Those two paragraphs are so much alike that it is redundant to include both of them.* **Ant.** necessary, vital.

reel *n.* **1.** spindle, bobbin, wheel. *The movie reel broke during the screening.* *–vb.* **2.** sway, stagger, roll, totter, rock, stumble. *The cowboy in the movie reeled from the punch.*

refer *vb.* **1.** direct, send, suggest, point. *May I refer you to another doctor?* **2.** mention, cite, quote, allude. *The author of the magazine article refers to several experts.* **3.** apply, pertain, touch, involve. *Her comments were meant to refer to only one person in class.* **4.** consult, address, turn, go. *Why don't you refer to your handbook for the answer?*

referee *n.* **1.** umpire, judge, moderator, arbitrator. *The referee was very fair in his calls during the game.* *–vb.* **2.** umpire, judge, moderate, arbitrate. *My mother refereed our soccer game.*

refine *vb.* **1.** improve, perfect, polish, cultivate, better. *The sculptor will be more successful when she refines her technique.* **2.** purify, filter, strain, process, distill. *The metal was refined in the factory.* **Ant. 1.** worsen, coarsen. **2.** pollute, dirty, contaminate, defile.

reflect *vb.* **1.** mirror, flash, echo, reproduce. *Sunlight often reflects off our car window.* **2.** ponder, meditate, study, deliberate, contemplate. *I need some time alone to reflect on what just happened.* **3.** display, show, manifest, demonstrate, illustrate. *His positive outlook was reflected in the quality of his life.* **Ant. 1.** absorb. **3.** mask, obscure, veil.

reform *n.* **1.** improvement, correction, revision, change, betterment. *Social reforms led to the abolition of slavery.* *–vb.* **2.** improve, correct, change, rehabilitate, refashion. *The camp tried to reform criminals.*

refrain *vb.* **1.** restrain, stop, resist, abstain, desist. *My brother could not refrain from yelling out during the movie.* *–n.* **2.** theme, melody. *The chorus sang the refrain in the production.* **Ant. 1.** persist, pursue.

refresh *vb.* freshen, revive, reinvigorate, renew, rejuvenate, stimulate. *She took a shower to refresh herself.* **Ant.** tire, drain, exhaust.

refreshing *adj.* reviving, regenerating, rousing, strengthening, invigorating, stimulating. *That cold soda was very refreshing.* **Ant.** tiring, weakening, depleting.

refreshment *n.* food, snacks, nourishment. *We bought refreshments after the game.*

refuge *n.* shelter, sanctuary, asylum, haven, retreat, protection. *The wildlife refuge was protected from poachers.*

refugee *n.* exile, fugitive, evacuee, emigrant. *Thousands of refugees left their wartorn country.*

refund *vb.* **1.** repay, reimburse, return, restore. *The store will refund the money for the dress.* *–n.* **2.** rebate, repayment, reimbursement, return. *I returned the shirt and received a refund.* **Ant. 1.** keep, withhold.

refusal *n.* unwillingness, dissent, rejection, denial, opposition. *The dog's refusal to go farther forced his owner to carry him home.* **Ant.** acceptance, agreement, approval.

refuse *vb.* **1.** forbid, disallow, reject, veto, prohibit. *Did your mother refuse to let you go out Monday night?* *–n.* **2.** garbage, trash, rubbish, waste, litter. *Refuse piled up when the sanitation workers went on strike.* **Ant. 1.** allow, agree, accept, approve.

refute *vb.* disprove, counter, challenge, deny, rebut. *The executive tried to refute the statements written about him.* **Ant.** confirm, prove, establish.

regal *adj.* royal, majestic, stately, noble, splendid, imperial, grand. *The entire house was decorated in regal furnishings.* **Ant.** tawdry, cheap.

regard *vb.* **1.** consider, judge, view, think, rate. *I regard her as my best friend.* **2.** admire, value, honor, appreciate, respect. *I have always highly regarded this author's work.* **3.** watch, observe, scan, view. *The teacher silently regarded* *her class as they took the test.* —n. **4.** attention, notice, care, consideration. *Please give some regard to what I tell you.* **5.** respect, admiration, appreciation, honor. *We have enormous regard for the surgeons who saved his life.* **6.** matter, aspect, subject, respect. *In that regard, there can be no going back.* **Ant. 1.** reject, disregard. **2.** disregard, dislike, detest, dishonor. **3.** ignore, overlook. **4.** disregard, indifference. **5.** disregard, dislike, hatred, loathing. **6.** disregard.

regardless *adv.* despite, nonetheless, notwithstanding. *I will attend the concert regardless of what you say.*

region *n.* **1.** area, district, section, territory, zone. *The train finally reached the country's forested region.* **2.** scope, field, sphere. *Her region of expertise is business law.*

regional *adj.* geographical, territorial, provincial, sectional. *The two widely separated villages have regional differences.*

register *vb.* **1.** check in, sign up. *Did you register to vote yet?* **2.** display, express, portray, exhibit, record. *The surprise they felt was registered on their faces.* —n. **3.** log, logbook, journal, diary, record. *The museum has a register for visitors to sign.* **Ant. 2.** hide, conceal, mask.

regret *vb.* **1.** grieve, mourn, lament, repent. *We regret that we left before the banquet was over.* —n. **2.** remorse, concern, sorrow, disappointment, self-reproach, grief. *Try not to have too much regret over your lost necklace.* **Ant. 1.** celebrate, rejoice. **2.** satisfaction, comfort.

regretful *adj.* remorseful, sorrowful, sorry, repentant, apologetic. *I felt very regretful about the argument we had.* **Ant.** unremorseful, pleased, happy.

regular *adj.* **1.** normal, usual, common, standard, habitual, customary, frequent, established. *The bus will arrive at the regular time today.* **2.** uniform, flat, smooth, even. *The jeep moved across a regular and barren landscape.* —n. **3.** patron, client, starter. *Our store sends Christmas cards to customers who are regulars.* **Ant. 1.** unusual, uncommon, atypical, irregular, infrequent. **2.** irregular, uneven.

regulate *vb.* **1.** govern, supervise, control, direct. *Laws regulate the amount of money politicians receive.* **2.** arrange, adjust, set. *The new*

equipment in his fish tank will regulate the temperature. **Ant. 1.** ignore, neglect. **2.** disrupt, jumble.

rehearse *vb.* prepare, review, practice, drill. *She will rehearse her speech before class.*

reign *n.* **1.** rule, sway, sovereignty, regency, regime, power. *The queen's reign lasted many years.* —vb. **2.** command, rule, govern, lead, manage. *The king reigned during the medieval ages.*

reinforce *vb.* strengthen, toughen, support, fortify, uphold, supplement. *The added logs will reinforce our dam.* **Ant.** weaken, lessen, cripple.

reject *vb.* **1.** refuse, shun, decline, rebuff, discard, veto. *Don't reject his solution until you've tried it.* —n. **2.** discard, castoff, leftover, dregs. *The assembly-line rejects were thrown away.* **Ant. 1.** accept, choose, select, approve. **2.** chosen, selected.

rejection *n.* turndown, veto, refusal, dismissal, spurning, rebuff. *Their rejection of me for the school play was upsetting.* **Ant.** acceptance, selection, choice, approval.

rejoice *vb.* celebrate, exult, revel, glory. *The heroes in the comic book rejoiced over their defeat of the evil invaders.* **Ant.** mourn, grieve.

relapse *vb.* **1.** backslide, reverse, lapse, revert, decline, deteriorate. *After being neat for a week, she relapsed into her messy habits.* —n. **2.** return, recurrence, reappearance. *The man had a relapse of his former illness.* **3.** backslide, decline, setback, reverse, deterioration. *The recovering patient suffered a relapse.* **Ant. 2.–3.** recovery, cure.

relate *vb.* **1.** repeat, describe, recount, tell, communicate, narrate. *Please relate the events of your year in Africa.* **2.** link, refer, pertain, apply. *His essay did not relate to the subject we've been studying.* **3.** identify, respond, empathize, understand. *I can really relate to the book's main character.* **Ant. 1.** conceal, hide. **2.** detach, disconnect, separate.

relation *n.* **1.** association, connection, link, bond, relationship. *Relations were friendly between the two countries.* **2.** kin, relative. *She is a relation of mine.* **3.** relevance, connection, bearing, correlation. *His comments have no relation to* our discussion. **4.** narration, recitation, account, recital, report. *My sister's relation of the story was slightly exaggerated.* **Ant. 1.** disassociation, disconnection.

relax *vb.* **1.** rest, loaf, lounge, unbend, unwind. *They relax after school by playing video games.* **2.** calm, ease, quiet, soothe, loosen. *I think this music will relax you.* **Ant. 1.** work, labor, toil. **2.** tighten, tense, excite.

relaxation *n.* resting, unbending, unwinding, lounging, leisure. *Sitting in a sauna is a great method of relaxation.* **Ant.** tightening, laboring, working.

release *vb.* **1.** free, unfasten, unchain, unhook, detach, disconnect. *It took me a while to release the gate's latch.* **2.** free, loose, discharge, liberate. *The rangers will release the eagle after its wing heals.* **3.** unveil, distribute, exhibit, publish. *The company decided to release the movie during the summer.* –*n.* **4.** freedom, discharge, liberation. *The prisoner looked forward to his release.* **5.** distribution, circulation, publication. *The movie's release was awaited eagerly by fans.* **Ant. 1.** fasten, chain, hook. **2.** cage, imprison, hold. **3.** conceal, withhold. **4.** imprisonment, detention. **5.** withdrawal.

relent *vb.* bend, yield, soften, capitulate, relax. *My parents would not relent in their refusal to let me attend the party.*

relentless *adj.* harsh, ruthless, unyielding, unmerciful, hard. *Our leader set a relentless pace as we marched through the desert.* **Ant.** yielding, gentle, considerate, merciful.

relevant *adj.* connected, significant, related, associated, pertinent. *The detective discovered several relevant facts.* **Ant.** irrelevant, insignificant, unrelated.

reliable *adj.* trustworthy, dependable, honest, conscientious, responsible. *Reliable people can be trusted to do their jobs.* **Ant.** unreliable, untrustworthy, undependable.

reliance *n.* confidence, trust, conviction, belief, dependence. *He placed great reliance on the article's accuracy.* **Ant.** distrust, disbelief, independence.

relic *n.* artifact, remain, antique, remembrance, memento. *The old ship is a relic from World War II.*

relief *n.* **1.** release, respite, refreshment, comfort. *It was a relief to get out of the sun.* **2.** aid, help, comfort, rescue. *The Red Cross sent relief to the famine victims.* **3.** replacement, substitute, backup. *The team sent its reliefs into the game.* **Ant. 1.** suffering, discomfort, irritation, burden. **2.** neglect, harm.

relieve *vb.* **1.** lighten, reduce, release, remove. *The medicine helped to relieve the pain.* **2.** free, deliver, ease, release, discharge. *His forgiveness relieved me of my guilt.* **Ant. 1.** increase, maintain. **2.** burden, load.

religion *n.* belief, faith, spirituality, devotion, worship. *Freedom of religion is an important human right.* **Ant.** atheism, nihilism, unbelief.

religious *adj.* **1.** spiritual, theological, devotional, devout, divine. *The religious painting hung in the church's entrance.* **2.** rigid, loyal, devoted, conscientious, unfailing. *He was religious about his daily exercising.* **Ant. 1.** irreligious, secular. **2.** unfaithful, unreliable.

relinquish *vb.* surrender, abandon, renounce, discard, release, forsake. *The small girl would not relinquish her doll.* **Ant.** keep, maintain, retain.

reluctant *adj.* unwilling, resistant, opposed, hesitant, slow. *He was very reluctant to show his parents his report card.* **Ant.** willing, enthusiastic, eager.

rely *vb.* depend, trust, count, lean. *If you're in trouble, you can rely on your friends.*

remain *vb.* stay, wait, linger, continue, persist, last. *Part of the group decided to remain behind.* **Ant.** leave, disappear, depart.

remainder *n.* excess, remains, leftovers, surplus, residual. *Put the remainder of the meal in the refrigerator.*

remark *vb.* **1.** comment, observe, state, express, mention. *The librarian remarked on how much I resemble my sister.* –*n.* **2.** comment, observation, statement, assertion, expression. *His cruel remark really angered me.*

remarkable *adj.* impressive, surprising, noteworthy, unbelievable, astonishing. *It was remarkable how quickly she rowed across the lake.* **Ant.** unremarkable, unimpressive, insignificant.

remedy *n.* **1.** treatment, cure, antidote, corrective, therapy. *The medicine was a remedy for her fever.* –*vb.* **2.** cure, relieve, mend, heal, correct, rectify. *I think this should remedy the problem.* **Ant. 1.** poison. **2.** worsen, intensify.

remember *vb.* recall, recollect, recognize, relive, reminisce. *There are many facts to remember for the test.* **Ant.** forget, neglect.

remembrance *n.* **1.** memory, recall, recollection. *Her remembrance of that day is rather hazy.* **2.** memorial, memento, keepsake, reminder. *They left flowers at the grave as a remembrance of their grandfather.* **Ant. 1.** forgetfulness.

remind *vb.* caution, warn, prompt, admonish, notify. *Remind him that he should clear away the dishes.*

reminder *n.* memo, notice, prompting, warning, cue, suggestion. *My mother put a note on my door as a reminder that I have baseball practice today.*

remiss *adj.* forgetful, negligent, neglectful, slack, thoughtless, lazy. *She has been very remiss in doing her homework.* **Ant.** thorough, hard-working, earnest, careful.

remnant *n.* remainder, trace, remains, record, residue, leftover. *The explorers found the remnants of an ancient civilization.*

remorse *n.* shame, guilt, self-reproach, regret, embarrassment, sorrow. *Doesn't the drunk driver have any remorse over the accident?* **Ant.** contentment, fulfillment, pride.

remote *adj.* **1.** faraway, distant, isolated, solitary, secluded. *The park ranger's cabin was in a remote forest area.* **2.** slim, faint, unlikely, improbable. *There is a remote chance we will get out early today.* **3.** withdrawn, detached, distant, disinterested. *He seemed very remote because he has a lot on his mind.* **Ant. 1.** close, nearby. **2.** likely, probable. **3.** interested, involved, animated.

removal *n.* **1.** erasure, transfer, extraction, evacuation, withdrawal. *The exterminators prom-*ised complete removal of the termites. **2.** expulsion, discharge, ejection, dismissal. *They wanted his removal from office.* **Ant. 1.** replacement, introduction. **2.** confirmation, establishment.

remove *vb.* **1.** shed, unload, dislodge, move, shift, transplant, extract. *Please remove your books from the table.* **2.** erase, eliminate, delete, cancel. *See if you can remove the smudge on my cheek.* **3.** dismiss, discharge, unseat, discard. *The voters removed the judge from office.* **Ant. 1.** deposit, replace, keep. **2.** add, set, plant. **3.** install, instate, confirm.

rendezvous *n.* **1.** date, meeting, encounter, appointment. *The couple arranged a midnight rendezvous by the fountain.* **2.** meeting place, haunt. *The fountain was their rendezvous.* –*vb.* **3.** meet, collect, assemble, gather. *They rendezvoused at the fountain.*

renegade *n.* **1.** fugitive, outlaw, deserter, traitor, rebel. *The man committed a crime and is now a renegade from the law.* –*adj.* **2.** traitorous, disloyal, mutinous, treacherous, unfaithful. *Renegade soldiers kidnaped the queen.* **Ant. 1.** loyalist, follower. **2.** loyal, faithful.

renew *vb.* refresh, regenerate, reestablish, revive, rejuvenate. *I need to renew my driver's license.* **Ant.** cancel, discontinue, abolish.

renewal *n.* continuation, resumption, restoration, recommencement, revival. *Did you get your library-card renewal yet?* **Ant.** cancellation, discontinuation.

renounce *vb.* relinquish, abandon, forgo, cease, discard. *The preacher said she must renounce her evil ways.* **Ant.** maintain, keep, continue.

renovate *vb.* renew, remodel, repair, revive, regenerate. *A contractor has been hired to renovate the old house.* **Ant.** destroy, ruin.

rent *vb.* **1.** lease, hire, charter, contract, sublet. *She will rent a sailboat for this afternoon.* –*n.* **2.** due, fee, payment, price, tariff. *My father pays the apartment rent.* **3.** tear, rip, gash, split, break. *The opposing quarterback dashed through a rent in our defensive line.*

repair *vb.* **1.** fix, mend, patch, restore, rebuild. *He repaired the hole yesterday.* –*n.* **2.** fixing, patching, reconstruction, mending, overhaul. *My car is in the shop for repairs.* **Ant. 1.** wreck, smash. **2.** destruction, damaging.

repeal *vb.* **1.** cancel, void, revoke, annul. *The unfair law was finally repealed by the voters.* *–n.* **2.** cancellation, annulment, withdrawal. *They voted for a repeal of the unpopular tax law.* **Ant. 1.** install, confirm. **2.** confirmation, validation.

repeat *vb.* **1.** restate, recount, recite. *Can you please repeat what you just told me?* **2.** redo, remake, replay, duplicate. *I hope she can repeat her excellent performance in tomorrow's game.* *–n.* **3.** rerun, replay, duplication, rebroadcast. *The television show was a repeat of a previously shown episode.*

repel *vb.* **1.** disgust, sicken, revolt, offend. *The sewer's smell really repels me.* **2.** repulse, resist, deflect, frustrate. *The army must repel the invaders.* **Ant. 1.** attract, delight, please. **2.** attract, invite.

repent *vb.* regret, lament, bewail, lament, deplore. *I hope the criminal repents her crime.* **Ant.** rejoice, celebrate.

replenish *vb.* refill, restock, restore, replace. *He went to the store to replenish our food supply.* **Ant.** empty, drain.

replica *n.* model, reproduction, imitation, duplicate. *The museum has a replica of a covered wagon.*

reply *vb.* **1.** answer, respond, retort, react. *You must reply to the invitation by the 12th of December.* *–n.* **2.** answer, response, reaction, acknowledgment. *We are waiting for a reply to our letter.* **Ant. 1.** question, ask. **2.** question, inquiry.

report *n.* **1.** description, account, narrative, article, summary. *His book report was due today.* **2.** bang, crack, backfire, detonation. *The loud report of the rifle could be heard throughout the forest.* *–vb.* **3.** narrate, account, relate, describe, summarize, state, disclose, reveal. *The scout reported that it was safe to continue.* **4.** arrive, appear. *You must report to the general in one hour.* **Ant. 1.** concealment, deletion. **2.** silence, quiet. **3.** conceal, hide.

reprisal *n.* revenge, vengeance, retaliation. *They feared the escaped prisoner's reprisal.*

represent *vb.* **1.** stand for, act for, serve. *A lawyer will represent the defendant in court.* **2.** symbolize, characterize, illustrate, signify, exemplify. *This monument represents the millions who died during the war.*

representation *n.* **1.** description, depiction, portrayal, portrait, illustration. *The picture's abstract representation was confusing.* **2.** representatives, delegates. *Those two men are New York's representation in the Senate.*

representative *n.* **1.** delegate, emissary, spokesperson, envoy, ambassador. *Our school sent a representative to the competition.* **2.** legislator, congressman, congresswoman, assemblywoman, assemblyman. *The House of Representatives is formed from officials chosen in district elections.* *–adj.* **3.** typical, characteristic, descriptive, illustrative. *I hope his behavior is not representative of other students' behavior.* **4.** elected, democratic. *The U.S. has a representative government.*

repress *vb.* check, curb, restrain, suppress, quiet, crush. *You must repress your tendency to get into fights.* **Ant.** release, encourage, express.

reproach *vb.* **1.** reprimand, scold, criticize, condemn. *Don't reproach me for something I did not do.* *–n.* **2.** reprimand, scolding, criticism, condemnation. *She deserved your reproach for stealing money.* **Ant. 1.** praise, compliment. **2.** praise, compliment.

repulsive *adj.* sickening, disgusting, revolting, offensive, disagreeable. *That monster costume is repulsive.* **Ant.** pleasing, attractive, agreeable.

reputable *adj.* trustworthy, respected, honored, dependable. *They went to a reputable doctor.* **Ant.** disreputable, untrustworthy.

request *vb.* **1.** ask for, call for, beg for, petition. *I requested a bicycle for my birthday.* *–n.* **2.** appeal, call, plea, summons, application. *Her request for more help was denied.* **Ant. 1.** refuse, reject. **2.** refusal, rejection.

require *vb.* necessitate, direct, need, compel, command, demand. *The law requires you to be eighteen before you can vote.*

requisition *n.* **1.** request, call, summons, command, demand. *He sent in a requisition for* *more supplies.* –*vb.* **2.** request, demand, command. *The army requisitioned more equipment.* **Ant. 1.** refusal. **2.** refuse, reject.

rescue *vb.* **1.** save, deliver, recover, free, retrieve. *The lifeguard rescued the drowning man.* –*n.* **2.** saving, recovery, deliverance, retrieval. *We watched the rescue of the people caught in the fire.* **Ant. 1.** lose, abandon, relinquish, imprison. **2.** loss, abandonment.

research *n.* **1.** investigation, experimentation, exploration, analysis, study. *Much of the chemist's research was done in the laboratory.* –*vb.* **2.** investigate, study, explore, examine. *My friend and I will research our papers at the library.*

resemblance *n.* likeness, similarity, sameness. *He bears a remarkable resemblance to his father.* **Ant.** difference, dissimilarity, distinction.

resemble *vb.* look like, take after, appear like, be similar to. *She resembles the famous television actress.* **Ant.** differ from, contrast with.

resent *vb.* be jealous of, be offended by, be annoyed by, dislike. *You should not resent your brother's success.* **Ant.** like, respect, admire, approve.

resentment *n.* bitterness, jealousy, displeasure, soreness, malice, anger, envy. *She felt resentment toward the winner.* **Ant.** pleasure, cheerfulness, friendliness.

reservation *n.* **1.** uncertainty, doubt, reluctance, hesitancy. *I have reservations about skiing down the steep slope.* **2.** booking, engagement. *I have a reservation at the restaurant.* **3.** preserve, territory, tract. *The U.S. took most of the Indians' land and resettled them on reservations.*

reserve *vb.* **1.** hold, retain, keep, preserve, save. *I reserve the right to change my mind.* **2.** book, schedule, retain, prearrange. *She reserved two tickets for next week's show.* –*n.* **3.** stock, supply, stockpile, store, savings. *She has an emergency food reserve.* **4.** coolness, restraint, remoteness, aloofness. *His reserve kept me from attempting to be friends.* –*adj.* **5.** unused, extra, backup, spare. *The reserve forces were called into battle.* **Ant. 1.** give, relinquish, discard. **4.** friendliness, warmth.

reside *vb.* live, dwell, inhabit, abide, stay. *Our family resides in New York.*

residence *n.* home, household, habitation, dwelling, address. *The president's residence is the White House.*

resident *n.* citizen, dweller, inhabitant, householder, native. *My grandmother is a resident of a small town.*

residue *n.* remainder, remains, surplus, leavings, waste. *There is soap residue in the bathtub.*

resign *vb.* **1.** leave, quit, renounce. *Richard Nixon was forced to resign his position as president.* **2.** submit, surrender, abandon. *Resign yourself to several more hours of waiting.* **Ant. 1.** keep, maintain.

resist *vb.* refuse, reject, oppose, withstand. *I was on a diet but could not resist eating the ice cream.* **Ant.** enjoy, accept.

resistance *n.* struggle, opposition, rebellion, defiance. *Our attempt at bathing the cat was met with resistance..*

resolute *adj.* determined, unbending, stubborn, unyielding, firm. *He was resolute in his decision to climb Mt. Everest.* **Ant.** irresolute, undecided, wavering.

resolution *n.* **1.** plan, goal, determination, objective, aim. *Her New Year's resolution is to stop smoking.* **2.** solution, answer, end. *The problem's resolution took a while.* **3.** proposal, recommendation, declaration. *The committee finally passed the resolution.*

resolve *vb.* **1.** settle, answer, fix, solve. *We must resolve the current crisis.* **2.** plan, propose, mean. *I resolve never to tell a lie again.* –*n.* **3.** determination, goal, intention. *Our resolve to build the fastest car has not weakened.*

resort *vb.* **1.** turn, go, refer, employ, use. *Why did he resort to violence?* –*n.* **2.** retreat, hotel, hideaway. *The wealthy singer took a vacation at a Caribbean resort.* **3.** hope, choice, opportunity, option. *As a last resort, she will sell her house.*

resource *n.* **1.** asset, strength, wealth, capital, possession. *Oil is an important resource in the Middle East.* **2.** source, storehouse, reserve. *The library is a good resource for foreign-language tapes.*

resourceful *adj.* inventive, creative, clever, imaginative. *My friend is very resourceful in finding ways to skip her chores.* **Ant.** unresourceful, uninventive, unimaginative.

respect *n.* **1.** admiration, honor, praise, approval. *I have an enormous amount of respect for the famous astronomer.* –*vb.* **2.** honor, admire, praise, adore, revere, obey, follow, acknowledge. *The rabbi was respected by the community.* **3.** reference, matter, regard, aspect. *In that respect, I must disagree with you.* **Ant. 1.** disrespect, scorn, contempt. **2.** disrespect, scorn, mock.

respectful *adj.* polite, considerate, courteous, mannerly, attentive. *We maintained a respectful silence at the funeral.* **Ant.** unrespectful, rude, impolite.

respite *n.* break, pause, recess, intermission, relaxation. *They took a respite from their work.* **Ant.** continuation.

respond *vb.* answer, reply, react, return, acknowledge. *I will respond to my pen pal's letter tomorrow.*

response *n.* reaction, feedback, reply, answer, acknowledgement. *The crowd's response was incredible.*

responsibility *n.* **1.** trust, charge, answerability, obligation. *It's my responsibility to take out the trash.* **2.** trustworthiness, reliability. *He is a person of responsibility.* **Ant. 2.** untrustworthiness, unreliability.

responsible *adj.* **1.** answerable, accountable, obligated, chargeable. *You should not feel responsible for your friend's accident.* **2.** reliable, trustworthy, dependable, capable. *The leader must be a responsible person.* **Ant. 1.** excusable, unaccountable. **2.** irresponsible, unreliable.

responsive *adj.* receptive, open, sensitive, awake, alive. *The politician was responsive to problems in her community.* **Ant.** unresponsive, indifferent, impassive.

rest *n.* **1.** sleep, relaxation, quiet, calm, peacefulness. *I need some rest after that exhausting race.* **2.** pause, break, recess, halt. *She took a rest from studying.* **3.** support, base, stand, platform. *The statue was set on a marble rest.* **4.** remainder, balance, residue. *The rest of you may go back to class.* –*vb.* **5.** sleep, relax, nap, pause, halt. *We will rest an hour before continuing our walk.* **6.** depend, hang, hinge, lie. *The game's outcome rests on this final toss.* **7.** lean, lay, set, prop. *Rest your umbrella against the wall.* **Ant. 1.** unrest, work, excitement, disturbance., **5.** work, toil.

restful *adj.* **1.** peaceful, relaxing, calming, quieting. *The sound of the ocean waves was very restful.* **2.** peaceful, calm, quiet, untroubled. *The lake's surface was restful.* **Ant. 1.** irritating, annoying, disturbing. **2.** agitated, troubled.

restless *adj.* jumpy, fidgety, anxious, uneasy, sleepless. *The restless woman paced back and forth.* **Ant.** restful, calm, peaceful, relaxed.

restore *vb.* revive, renew, reclaim, refresh, reinstate, rebuild. *The artists will restore the old painting.*

restoration *n.* repair, reconstruction, revival, recovery. *The historic building is undergoing a restoration.*

restrain *vb.* check, stop, curb, hold, constrain, bind. *The cowboy restrained the bucking horse.* **Ant.** release, free.

restraint *n.* **1.** bonds, handcuffs, gag, ties. *The kidnaped man struggled against his restraints.* **2.** self-control, moderation, reserve, poise. *He acted with restraint, although he was very angry.*

restrict *vb.* limit, check, curb, constrain, constrict, restrain. *This movie's rating restricts it to people seventeen or older.*

restriction *n.* limitation, curb, regulation, constraint. *The contest restriction says you can only enter once.*

result *vb.* **1.** arise, issue, happen, flow, follow. *Arguments often result from misunderstandings.* **2.** conclude, end, terminate. *Her poor study habits will result in bad grades.* –*n.* **3.** outcome, product, consequence, aftermath. *The parrot's death was the result of poor care.* **Ant. 3.** source, cause.

resume *vb.* continue, restart, proceed, reestablish. *After a refueling stop, the plane will resume its flight.* **Ant.** discontinue, halt, stop.

retain *vb.* keep, hold, remember, grasp, preserve. *My friend retains facts much better than I do.* **Ant.** lose, dismiss.

retard *vb.* check, curb, block, slow, halt. *Hopefully this chemical will retard the fire's spread.* **Ant.** advance, encourage.

reticence *n.* quietness, shyness, reserve, restraint. *My friend's reticence was sometimes mistaken as conceit.* **Ant.** loudness, sociability.

reticent *adj.* quiet, silent, withdrawn, subdued, unsociable. *Some students are very reticent during final exams.* **Ant.** noisy, talkative, sociable.

retire *vb.* withdraw, depart, retreat, leave, resign. *He will retire from his teaching position at the end of this semester.*

retract *vb.* **1.** withdraw, recant, recall. *Please retract your false accusation.* **2.** withdraw, retreat, recoil. *We saw the turtle's head retract into its shell.* **Ant. 1.** confirm, endorse, uphold. **2.** advance, protrude.

retrieve *vb.* recover, reclaim, regain, rescue, fetch. *Watch my dog retrieve the ball.*

return *vb.* **1.** restore, replace, reinstall, repay, reestablish. *He will return the pen when he's finished.* **2.** reappear, reoccur, recur, revisit. *We will return from our vacation in August.* –*n.* **3.** restoration, replacement, reestablishment. *The quick return of our money was surprising.* **4.** reappearance, recurrence, returning. *The ghost's return frightened him.* **5.** profit, gain, earnings, yield. *She achieved huge returns on her investments.* **Ant. 1.** keep, hold. **2.** depart, disappear. **3.** removal, withdrawal. **4.** departure, disappearance.

reveal *vb.* display, uncover, expose, disclose, divulge. *Lifting up the leaf revealed a spider beneath it.* **Ant.** conceal, hide, mask.

revel *vb.* delight, enjoy, rejoice, luxuriate. *We will revel in the weekend's celebrations.*

revelation *n.* discovery, announcement, confession, disclosure. *The facts about his past were a shocking revelation.* **Ant.** coverup, concealment.

revenge *vb.* **1.** avenge, punish, vindicate, reciprocate. *The team will try to revenge its loss in tomorrow's game.* –*n.* **2.** vengeance, retaliation, retribution, repayment, satisfaction. *He wanted revenge against the person who had dishonored him.* **Ant. 1.** forgive, forget, ignore. **2.** forgiveness, pardon.

revere *vb.* honor, adore, worship, admire, respect. *The pope is revered by virtually all Catholics.* **Ant.** dislike, scorn, hate, despise.

reverse *adj.* **1.** opposite, contrasting, counter, inverse, back. *On the photograph's reverse side is a short message.* –*n.* **2.** opposite, converse, contrary. *She did the reverse of what she had originally planned.* –*vb.* **3.** invert, shift, upset, override, recall, repeal. *I will reverse my decision when I see evidence against it.* **Ant. 3.** keep, uphold, maintain.

revert *vb.* return, backslide, reverse, relapse. *We hope our dog does not revert to its old habits while we're gone.*

review *n.* **1.** evaluation, criticism, critique, commentary, editorial. *We read the movie review before we saw the movie.* **2.** reexamination, reevaluation, rundown, survey, study. *My review of the test material took less time than expected.* –*vb.* **3.** reexamine, reevaluate, restate, retrace, study. *Please review the steps with me once again.* **4.** criticize, critique, evaluate, examine. *A magazine writer reviewed the new novel.*

revise *vb.* change, alter, rewrite, redo, modify, rework. *The screenwriter must revise his script.*

revive *vb.* reawaken, renew, freshen, resuscitate, recharge. *Doctors were able to revive the comatose woman.*

revoke *vb.* withdraw, cancel, void, repeal, nullify. *The judge will revoke the drunk driver's license.* **Ant.** restore, award, preserve.

revolt *vb.* **1.** rebel, mutiny, protest, riot. *The slaves revolted against their owners.* **2.** sicken, disgust, shock, offend, horrify. *Will the gory movie revolt us?* –*n.* **3.** rebellion, uprising, revolution. *A peasant led the revolt against wealthy landowners.* **Ant. 1.** obey, follow. **2.** please, attract, delight.

revolution *n.* **1.** upheaval, uprising, overthrow, rebellion, revolt. *American patriots fought in a revolution against the British.* **2.** rotation, circle, cycle, spin. *The wheel made a complete revolution.* **Ant. 1.** counterrevolution, restoration.

revolve *vb.* rotate, circle, orbit, spin, reel. *The nine planets revolve around the Sun.*

reward *n.* **1.** prize, payment, compensation. *We will give a reward to the person who finds our lost puppy.* –*vb.* **2.** repay, compensate, award, acknowledge. *The king will reward the brave knight with gold.* **Ant. 1.** penalty, punishment. **2.** confiscate, punish.

rhythm *n.* pulsation, movement, throb, beat, meter. *They danced to the music's rhythm.*

rich *adj.* **1.** wealthy, prosperous, affluent. *England's royal family is very rich.* **2.** splendid, lavish, vivid, luxurious. *The painting's rich colors were breathtaking.* **3.** fertile, fruitful, bountiful. *The rich farmland produced an abundance of food.* **4.** fattening, sweet, creamy, flavorful. *This chocolate cake is too rich.* **Ant. 1.** poor, poverty-stricken, impoverished. **2.** plain, cheap. **3.** unfertile, depleted, barren. **4.** bland, unappetizing.

rid *vb.* free, cleanse, clear, purge, purify. *The queen's soldiers will rid the forest of bandits.*

riddle *n.* **1.** puzzle, mystery, problem, enigma. *He gave us a riddle to solve.* –*vb.* **2.** pierce, penetrate, honeycomb. *The old tree trunk was riddled with beetle holes.*

ridicule *n.* **1.** sarcasm, mockery, teasing, scorn, sneering. *I was very upset over the ridicule my idea received.* –*vb.* **2.** mock, insult, taunt, belittle. *He never ridicules his students.* **Ant. 1.** praise, approval. **2.** praise, commend, applaud.

ridiculous *adj.* foolish, idiotic, silly, comical, laughable. *That clown looks ridiculous.*

right *adj.* **1.** proper, good, honorable, fair, just. *That was the right thing to do.* **2.** correct, accurate, perfect, true, factual, faultless, proper. *His answer was right.* **3.** rational, sane, sensible. *She may act crazy, but she's in her right mind.* –*n.* **4.** permission, liberty, freedom, authorization. *Do I have the right to park here?* **5.** goodness, justice, honor, fairness, virtue. *The criminal's sense of right and wrong is distorted.* –*adv.* **6.** directly, quickly, instantly, promptly. *Don't worry; I'll be right over.* **6.** directly, quickly, instantly, promptly. *Don't worry; I'll be right over.* **7.** exactly, correctly, perfectly, properly. *The clothes do not fit right.* –*vb.* **8.** correct, fix, mend, repair. *We must right the injustice done to this woman.* **Ant. 1.** wrong, improper, dishonorable.

2. wrong, incorrect, imperfect, faulted. **3.** irrational, insane. **5.** wrong, badness, injustice, sinfulness. **6.** indirectly, slowly. **7.** wrong, improperly, poorly.

rigid *adj.* stiff, immovable, unbending, firm, set, inflexible. *The frozen fish were very rigid.* **Ant.** soft, bending, flexible, limp.

rigorous *adj.* tough, stern, demanding, challenging, severe. *She had a rigorous aerobic session.* **Ant.** easy, undemanding.

rim *n.* edge, lip, border, brim, fringe, ledge. *The rim of my coffee cup is chipped.* **Ant.** inside, center.

ring *n.* **1.** hoop, loop, circle, coil. *The couple exchanged wedding rings.* **2.** gang, mob, band, club, clique. *The police broke up the gambling ring.* **3.** chime, dong, knell, peal, clang, sound. *The telephone's ring was very loud.* –*vb.* **4.** sound, chime, toll, jingle, knoll. *The church rings its bell on Christmas.* **5.** circle, encircle, surround, enclose, loop. *Please ring the fire pit with stones.*

riot *n.* **1.** lawlessness, disorder, violence, uproar, protest, outbreak. *Many cars were burned during the riot.* –*vb.* **2.** rampage, protest, revolt, rage, rebel. *Angry workers rioted over the increase in food prices.*

rip *vb.* **1.** tear, strip, split, shred. *Why did you rip apart the letter?* –*n.* **2.** tear, split, slit, rent, rupture. *I will sew the rip in my pants.*

ripe *adj.* mature, ready, developed, seasonable, timely. *That green banana is not ripe.* **Ant.** unripe, unready, unfit, raw.

ripen *vb.* age, mature, season, develop. *She left the green tomatoes on her counter to ripen.*

rise *vb.* **1.** climb, ascend, soar, lift, rocket, surge, arise. *The sun rises in the east.* **2.** increase, grow, swell, upswing, intensify, strengthen. *The temperature usually rises during the day.* –*n.* **3.** climb, soaring, ascent, mounting, uplift. *We watched the rise of the sun from our porch.* **4.** increase, strengthening, upsurge, expansion. *There was a rise in crime during the holiday season.* **Ant. 1.** fall, descend, drop. **2.** fall, descend, decrease. **3.** fall, descent. **4.** fall, decrease, weakening.

risk *n.* **1.** gamble, uncertainty, hazard, danger. *Parachuting from that plane was a big risk.* –*vb.* **2.** gamble, dare, endanger, venture. *The gambler risked all his money on one last spin.* **Ant. 1.** certainty, safety, security.

ritual *n.* ceremony, rite, custom, habit, routine. *Brushing my teeth is part of my morning ritual.* **Ant.** departure, deviation.

rival *n.* **1.** opponent, challenger, enemy, foe. *My rival in the competition was well-prepared.* –*adj.* **2.** opposing, competing, contending. *The rival team scored the first goal.* –*vb.* **3.** match, meet, approach, equal. *He rivals you in speed if not in strength.* **Ant. 1.** ally, friend, assistant, co-worker. **2.** allied, cooperating.

rivalry *n.* contest, struggle, opposition, competition. *There was a friendly rivalry between our two schools.* **Ant.** cooperation, alliance, teamwork.

road *n.* street, path, lane, route, highway. *The winding road went up to the mountaintop.*

roam *vb.* wander, drift, stray, ramble, rove, range. *The hobo roamed around America.*

rob *vb.* burglarize, steal, thieve, pilfer, cheat. *The burglars robbed a bank.*

robust *adj.* strong, healthy, sturdy, brawny, husky. *Santa Claus is a jolly and robust man.* **Ant.** scrawny, weak, sickly.

rock *n.* **1.** stone, boulder, pebble. *My sister enjoys skipping rocks in the lake.* **2.** sway, roll, pitch, bob, swing. *The rock of the boat made it difficult to stand.* –*vb.* **3.** shake, pitch, roll, sway, jar. *The earthquake rocked our house.*

role *n.* part, character, portrayal, place. *She was given the role of Dorothy in "The Wizard of Oz."*

roll *vb.* **1.** tumble, throw, toss, rotate, revolve, pitch. *Please roll the dice.* **2.** wrap, wind, whirl, twist, ball. *We must roll up our sleeping bags.* **3.** rumble, roar, thunder, boom. *The thunder rolled loudly.* –*n.* **4.** bun, biscuit, pastry, bread. *She ate cinnamon rolls for breakfast.* **5.** attendance, roster, register, list. *The teacher called the roll to see who was absent.* **6.** boom, thunder, clap, rumble. *The storm's loud roll startled me.*

romance *n.* love, love affair, courtship, flirtation. *He carried on a romance with the girl next door.*

romantic *adj.* **1.** passionate, emotional, sentimental, loving. *I have a romantic girlfriend who always sends me flowers.* –*n.* **2.** dreamer, idealist, visionary. *The poet was a romantic.* **Ant. 1.** unromantic, unemotional, unsentimental.

room *n.* **1.** chamber, cubicle, compartment, lodgings, apartment. *My mother gets angry when my room is messy.* **2.** space, clearing, expanse. *Please give him more room to do his stunt.* –*vb.* **3.** live, dwell, stay, lodge. *The student rooms at the dormitory.*

root *n.* **1.** substructure, base, bottom, foundation. *The tree's roots were sticking up through the ground.* **2.** lineage, ancestry, heritage, bloodline. *I traced my family roots back to Africa.* –*vb.* **3.** cheer, applaud, clap, support. *We rooted for our soccer team.* **4.** fix, fasten, set, embed. *Fear rooted him to the ground.*

rot *vb.* **1.** decay, spoil, mold, poison, corrupt. *These fruits will rot if you don't refrigerate them.* –*n.* **2.** decay, mold, corruption. *Dry rot weakened the cabin's timbers.*

rotate *vb.* revolve, spin, turn, whirl, circle. *Please rotate the observatory dome so we may view a different section of the sky.*

rough *adj.* **1.** coarse, scaly, rocky, jagged, uneven, scratchy. *The sandpaper felt very rough.* **2.** difficult, hard, tough, harsh, brutal. *That was a rough test.* **3.** unfinished, incomplete, crude. *This is a rough draft of my final paper.* –*vb.* **4.** beat, thrash, pound, batter. *The thugs roughed up the frightened man.* **Ant. 1.** smooth, soft. **2.** easy, mild. **3.** final, finished, complete.

round *adj.* **1.** circular, globular, oval, spherical, elliptical. *The Halloween pumpkin was round.* **2.** arched, curved, bowed. *The paper was rounded at the corners.* –*n.* **3.** series, circle, sequence, cycle. *A round of toasts was given before the meal.* **4.** watch, tour, route, circuit. *The doctor completed her rounds.* –*vb.* **5.** circle, orbit, skirt, go around. *The racing car rounded the turn.* **6.** close, terminate, end, finish, conclude. *We will round off the celebration with a final song.* **Ant. 1.** square, rectangular. **2.** straight. **6.** start, open.

rouse *vb.* awaken, call, summon, animate, stir, arouse. *My father rouses me in the morning.* **Ant.** hush, soothe, quiet, still.

rout *n.* **1.** defeat, conquest, beating, upset, licking. *The team's loss by a hundred points was a complete rout.* *-vb.* **2.** overwhelm, defeat, conquer, vanquish, smash. *The attacking army routed the ill-prepared defenders.* **Ant. 1.** success, victory. **2.** succeed, triumph.

route *n.* **1.** path, course, way, track, road, lane. *The plane flies a direct route to London.* *-vb.* **2.** direct, detour, send, dispatch. *The construction workers routed us onto a side road.*

routine *n.* **1.** procedure, habit, pattern, custom, performance. *The gymnast practiced his routine before the competition.* *-adj.* **2.** regular, usual, normal, customary. *Every six months I visit the dentist for a routine checkup.* **Ant. 2.** unusual, uncustomary, irregular.

rove *vb.* wander, drift, ramble, range, roam. *The photographer roved the country looking for great photo opportunities.*

row *n.* **1.** line, column, string, chain, sequence. *Our car was parked at the row's end.* **2.** quarrel, fight, argument, altercation, spat. *There was a row in the apartment below us.* *-vb.* **3.** paddle, oar, scull, pull. *We rowed a boat across the lake.*

royal *adj.* **1.** imperial, monarchical, noble, highborn. *Britain's royal family lives in a palace.* **2.** magnificent, majestic, grand, splendid. *They gave us a royal welcome.* **Ant. 1.** common, plebeian. **2.** plain, modest, lowly.

rub *vb.* **1.** massage, knead, scrub, stroke, scour. *Please rub my sore back.* *-n.* **2.** massage, rubdown, kneading, stroking. *A good back rub relaxes me.*

rubbish *n.* **1.** trash, garbage, waste, refuse. *The rubbish was unloaded into the dump.* **2.** nonsense, babble, gibberish. *That story you told is rubbish.*

rude *adj.* **1.** impolite, insulting, discourteous, surly, inconsiderate, disrespectful. *The rude man ignored her when she spoke to him.* **2.** primitive, rough, crude, rustic, unpolished. *There was a rude shelter on the island.* **Ant. 1.** polite, courteous, considerate, courtly. **2.** finished, elegant, polished.

rudimentary *adj.* **1.** basic, elementary, elemental, fundamental. *The alphabet is rudimentary knowledge for students.* **2.** incomplete, imperfect, simple, crude. *She had only a rudimentary understanding of what had happened.* **Ant. 1.** advanced. **2.** complete, finished, perfect.

rue *vb.* regret, repent, mourn, grieve. *You will rue the day you made that promise.*

ruffle *vb.* **1.** disturb, upset, disorder, jumble, stir. *The wind ruffled the bird's feathers.* *-n.* **2.** frill, edging, flounce. *Ruffles covered the shirt's front.* **Ant. 1.** settle, smooth, calm.

rugged *adj.* harsh, stern, severe, rough, tough, solid, sturdy. *The mountains presented a rugged landscape to the hikers.* **Ant.** soft, frail, cultivated.

ruin *n.* **1.** destruction, downfall, collapse, decay, misfortune, disrepair. *Bad investments left him in financial ruin.* **2.** relics, remains, remnants, wreckage. *We visited the ruins of an ancient Roman coliseum.* *-vb.* **3.** destroy, spoil, wreck, shatter, smash. *The rain ruined my painting.* **Ant. 1.** creation, success, improvement. **3.** improve, create.

rule *n.* **1.** law, regulation, order, guideline, principle, maxim. *The school's rule says you need your parent's signature.* **2.** control, command, government, administration. *They suffered under the king's cruel rule.* *-vb.* **3.** control, command, lead, administer, govern. *The queen tried to rule her people with justice.* **4.** judge, decide, determine, resolve, settle. *The judge ruled that neither person should get the winnings.*

rumble *vb.* **1.** thunder, roar, boom, resound. *His voice rumbled from the next room.* *-n.* **2.** thunder, roar, booming, roll, growl. *The avalanche's rumble was heard down in the valley.*

rumor *n.* **1.** gossip, hearsay, report, story, whisper. *The rumor that I am leaving is incorrect.* *-vb.* **2.** gossip, tattle, whisper, circulate. *It was rumored that the principal was being fired.*

rummage *vb.* hunt, search, explore, ransack, probe. *He had to rummage through the attic to find the old painting.*

run *vb.* **1.** rush, hurry, race, dash, flee, gush, surge. *After hitting the ball, you must run to first base.* **2.** operate, work, function. *The car runs on gasoline.* **3.** campaign, compete. *The politician will run for office.* **4.** vary, stretch, extend. *Their ages run from five to eighteen.* **5.** unravel, separate, snag. *I hope the socks do not run.* **6.** publish, print, show, display. *The article was run in today's paper.* *-n.* **7.** race, dash, jog, sprint, marathon. *His crosscountry run took 60 days.* **8.** stretch, series, streak. *She had a run of good test scores.* **9.** freedom, control, liberty. *They have the run of the house while their parents are gone.* **10.** snag, tear, pull. *She had a run in her stocking.* **Ant. 1.** walk, stroll, crawl. **2.** stop, pause, quit, halt. **7.** walk, stroll, crawl.

rupture *n.* **1.** break, split, crack, fissure, rent. *The rupture in the tire was fixed.* *-vb.* **2.** burst, split, crack, break, divide. *We must fix the dam before it ruptures.* **Ant. 1.** repair, mend. **2.** repair, mend, heal, unite.

rural *adj.* country, agricultural, pastoral, rustic, farm. *They live in a rural area.* **Ant.** urban, cosmopolitan.

ruse *n.* trick, deception, dodge, hoax, ploy. *The thief's ruse misled the police.*

rush *vb.* **1.** race, run, hurry, dash, hustle. *We must rush to the store before it closes.* *-n.* **2.** sprint, dash, race, run. *There was a rush to the ticket booth when it opened.* **Ant. 1–2.** walk, crawl, stroll.

rustic *adj.* **1.** country, rural, backwoods, farm, unsophisticated. *Our cabin was in a rustic setting.* *-n.* **2.** farmer, provincial, peasant. *The hillbilly was a rustic.* **Ant. 1.** urban, city, sophisticated. **2.** sophisticate.

ruthless *adj.* unmerciful, heartless, cold, relentless, brutal, unfeeling. *She was ruthless toward her opponents.* **Ant.** merciful, compassionate, kind.

sack *n.* **1.** bag, pouch, pack. *I take my lunch to school in a sack.* **2.** destruction, burning, plunder, devastation, pillage. *The sack of Rome by the Vandals occurred in 455.* –*vb.* **3.** bag, pack. *Clerks sack groceries at the market.* **4.** level, destroy, demolish, waste, pillage, plunder. *Vikings sacked a series of coastal villages.*

sacred *adj.* holy, revered, hallowed, religious, blessed. *Mecca is a sacred Islamic city.* **Ant.** profane, secular.

sacrifice *n.* **1.** offering, gift, homage. *The Aztecs of Mexico made sacrifices to their gods.* **2.** loss, surrender, relinquishment. *I sold my coin collection at a sacrifice.* –*vb.* **3.** offer, surrender, give, forfeit, cede, relinquish. *She sacrificed her free time to tutor her younger brother.* **Ant. 2.** profit, return, gain.

sad *adj.* unhappy, gloomy, depressed, mournful, melancholy, joyless. *The end of summer vacation was a sad event.* **Ant.** happy, joyful, glad, cheerful.

saddle *n.* **1.** seat, pad, perch. *She kept slipping off the horse's saddle.* –*vb.* **2.** equip, outfit, prepare. *The rider saddled his horse.* **3.** burden, weight, overwhelm, load, tax, strain. *We were saddled with extra paperwork.* **Ant. 3.** relieve, unburden.

safe *adj.* **1.** protected, secure, defended, guarded. *You must escape to a safe place.* **2.** harmless, sound, reliable. *Talking to strangers is not always safe.* **3.** unhurt, uninjured, undamaged, unbroken, intact. *Don't worry; your friend is safe.* –*n.* **4.** strongbox, vault, chest. *Robbers blew open the bank's safe.* **Ant. 1.** unsafe, unprotected. **2.** unsafe, harmful. **3.** hurt, injured.

safeguard *n.* **1.** protection, defense, armor, guard, shield. *Seatbelts are a safeguard against serious injuries.* –*vb.* **2.** armor, protect, guard, fortify, shield, screen. *High walls safeguard cas-*

tles from attackers. **Ant. 1.** threat, danger. **2.** risk, endanger.

sag *vb.* **1.** droop, drop, sink, slump, flop. *His bag sagged with Halloween candy.* –*n.* **2.** droop, sinking, slump, dip, hollow. *We fixed the roof's sag.* **Ant. 1.** rise, soar. **2.** rise, upturn.

saga *n.* tale, history, narrative, chronicle, epic. *The Civil War saga will be a television miniseries.*

sagacious *adj.* clever, wise, shrewd, cunning, knowing, smart. *She asked the sagacious wizard for guidance.* **Ant.** stupid, dumb, ignorant.

sail *n.* **1.** canvas, mainsail. *The boat's sail flapped in the wind.* **2.** cruise, outing, voyage, excursion. *They took an afternoon sail across the lake.* –*vb.* **3.** navigate, pilot, captain. *She sailed her boat in the harbor.* **4.** boat, cruise, yacht, skim, float. *He will sail down the river.* **5.** glide, slide, fly, flow, dart, shoot. *I sailed through the exam.* **Ant. 5.** plod, trudge.

salary *n.* wage, earnings, payment, fee, stipend. *The store's owner raised her employee's salary.*

sale *n.* **1.** closeout, markdown, discount, bargain, special. *We rushed to the holiday sale.* **2.** exchange, transfer, selling, buying, purchasing. *The house was up for sale.*

salvage *n.* **1.** recovery, reclamation, rescue, saving, retrieval. *The shipwreck's salvage was carried out by professional divers.* –*vb.* **2.** save, reclaim, redeem, rescue, recover. *Do you think we can salvage this old coat?* **Ant. 1.** loss. **2.** discard, lose, waste.

salve *n.* **1.** remedy, ointment, balm, lotion. *This cream is a salve for skin rashes.* –*vb.* **2.** ease, heal, relieve, pacify, reduce. *An apology would salve her wounded pride.* **Ant. 2.** annoy, irritate, inflame.

same *adj.* identical, exact, matching, duplicate, equal, similar. *My sister and I have the same last name.* **Ant.** different, unlike, unequal.

sample *n.* **1.** specimen, example, illustration, instance, taste. *He showed us samples of his poetry.* –*adj.* **2.** illustrative, representative, test, trial. *This is a sample sentence.* –*vb.* **3.** try, test, experience, taste, sip. *She asked if she could sample the different ice cream flavors.*

sanction *n.* **1.** permission, consent, leave, approval, authorization. *Unless you have your parents' sanction, you cannot go.* **2.** penalty, pressure, punishment. *Sanctions were leveled against the terrorists' country.* –*vb.* **3.** authorize, confirm, certify, legalize, allow. *Their marriage was sanctioned by the priest.* **Ant. 1.** refusal, disapproval. **2.** reward. **3.** reject, ban, block.

sanctuary *n.* hideout, refuge, shelter, protection, preserve. *The beautiful garden was her sanctuary from the world.*

sand *n.* **1.** grit, gravel, silt. *Sand got in her eye.* –*vb.* **2.** grind, file, scour, smooth. *Please sand the wood's rough edges.*

sane *adj.* rational, sound, reasonable, sensible, balanced. *Why would a sane man pretend he was crazy?* **Ant.** insane, irrational, mad, foolish.

sanitary *adj.* clean, healthy, sterile, disinfected, wholesome. *The park's rest room was not sanitary.* **Ant.** dirty, unhealthy, grimy, unclean.

sanity *n.* reason, rationality, saneness, sensibleness, normality. *People questioned Van Gogh's sanity after he cut off his ear.* **Ant.** insanity, madness, irrationality.

sap *n.* **1.** juice, milk, fluid, lifeblood. *The tree's sap stuck to her hands.* –*vb.* **2.** drain, exhaust, reduce, weaken, deplete. *Fasting quickly sapped his strength.* **Ant. 2.** replace, restore.

sarcastic *adj.* insulting, mocking, sneering, scornful, bitter. *Why were you so sarcastic to your father?* **Ant.** pleasant, flattering, agreeable.

satisfaction *n.* fulfillment, pleasure, gratification, comfort, delight, happiness. *Her high test scores gave her a great deal of satisfaction.* **Ant.** dissatisfaction, displeasure, unhappiness.

satisfactory *adj.* acceptable, adequate, sufficient, enough, passable. *The finished work was satisfactory.* **Ant.** unsatisfactory, unacceptable.

satisfy *vb.* **1.** gratify, please, comfort, pacify, content. *This drink will satisfy your thirst.* **2.** convince, persuade, assure, reassure. *Her explanation satisfied my doubts.* **Ant.** dissatisfy, displease.

satisfying *adj.* pleasing, gratifying, comforting, refreshing. *The meal was very satisfying.* **Ant.** dissatisfying, displeasing.

saturate *vb.* soak, drench, cover, waterlog, glut. *She saturates her vegetables with butter.*

saunter *vb.* **1.** stroll, promenade, amble, wander, straggle. *Even though she was quite late, she just sauntered into class.* –*n.* **2.** stroll, amble, ramble, jaunt. *He took a saunter in the park.* **Ant. 1–2.** run, race, dash.

savage *adj.* **1.** fierce, vicious, brutal, merciless, ruthless, cruel. *The hunter tried to fend off the tiger's savage attack.* –*n.* **2.** barbarian, brute, primitive, ruffian. *I get embarrassed when he acts like a savage.* **Ant. 1.** gentle, timid, tender.

save *vb.* **1.** rescue, deliver, free, protect, help, safeguard. *Several people tried to save the beached whale.* **2.** keep, maintain, reserve, store. *You should save your work before you turn off the computer.* **Ant. 1.** risk, endanger. **2.** lose, spend, waste.

savior *n.* lifesaver, messiah, deliverer, champion. *After killing the evil dragon, the knight was honored as the village's savior.*

savor *n.* **1.** taste, tang, flavor, nature, character. *The barbecued steaks had the savor of hickory smoke.* –*vb.* **2.** relish, enjoy, like, appreciate. *She savored the last bite of chocolate.*

say *vb.* **1.** speak, state, utter, declare, recite, tell. *Can you say the names of the first three presidents?* –*n.* **2.** statement, expression, declaration. *I want a say in what we decide to do.*

saying *n.* proverb, expression, maxim, motto. *There is a saying that "two heads are better than one."*

scald *vb.* burn, char, sear, scorch, blister, heat. *The hot water scalded her hand.*

scamper *vb.* **1.** scurry, run, dash, race, scramble. *Mice scampered across the floor.* *-n.* **2.** scurry, dash, frolic, frisk, romp. *He heard the scamper of small children in the next room.*

scan *vb.* search, inspect, examine, explore, study, check. *The spaceship scanned the planet for signs of life.*

scandal *n.* disgrace, embarrassment, shame, dishonor. *The president had to resign because of the scandal.* **Ant.** honor, praise, flattery.

scanty *adj.* meager, skimpy, insufficient, sparse, inadequate. *The newspaper gave only scanty information on the plane crash.* **Ant.** abundant, sufficient.

scar *n.* **1.** blemish, mark, injury, disfigurement. *A childhood fall left a scar on her cheek.* *-vb.* **2.** mark, blemish, damage, disfigure, injure. *Fire scarred the inside of the building.*

scarce *adj.* rare, unusual, uncommon, infrequent. *Hunting has made grizzly bears scarce in the United States.* **Ant.** common, usual, frequent.

scarcely *adv.* barely, hardly, slightly, only, just. *She had scarcely enough time to finish the test.*

scarcity *n.* rarity, want, need, shortage, insufficiency. *There is a scarcity of water in the desert.*

scare *vb.* **1.** frighten, shock, alarm, startle, terrify. *Horror movies really scare me.* *-n.* **2.** fright, shock, alarm, start. *The accident gave him quite a scare.* **Ant.** 1–2. calm, comfort.

scatter *vb.* spread, disperse, sprinkle, strew, separate. *Wind scattered leaves over the sidewalk.* **Ant.** collect, group, unite.

scene *n.* **1.** landscape, location, locale, place, spot, region. *The artist painted an ocean scene.* **2.** episode, act, segment, event, part. *The movie's opening scene was violent.* **3.** disturbance, commotion, outburst, exhibition, display. *The angry man made a scene when they denied his request.*

scenic *adj.* beautiful, pretty, picturesque, unspoiled, spectacular. *He drove through a scenic part of the Rocky Mountains.* **Ant.** ugly, unattractive, ordinary.

scent *n.* **1.** smell, aroma, fragrance, odor. *Roses have a nice scent.* *-vb.* **2.** smell, sniff, detect, perceive, sense. *Our dog ran off when she scented the rabbit.* **3.** perfume, deodorize, aromatize. *We scented the room with incense.*

schedule *n.* **1.** program, timetable, calendar, agenda. *The college sent him its class schedule.* *-vb.* **2.** plan, arrange, slate, book, time. *The plane was scheduled to leave at one o'clock.*

scheme *n.* **1.** plan, design, idea, program, system, procedure. *The thief's scheme was foiled by the police.* *-vb.* **2.** plot, plan, intrigue, conspire. *Bandits schemed for a way to kidnap the prince.*

scholar *n.* **1.** intellectual, academic, authority, specialist, sage. *An important scholar is speaking at our campus.* **2.** student, pupil, learner, disciple. *The professor is a scholar of Russian history.*

school *n.* **1.** kindergarten, elementary school, high school, college, university. *My school has many students.* **2.** group, faction, set, doctrine, theory. *My father adheres to the school of thought that believes "children should be seen and not heard."* *-vb.* **3.** teach, instruct, educate, coach, train. *A judo instructor schooled her in the mysteries of the martial arts.*

scold *vb.* **1.** rebuke, reproach, reprimand, upbraid, criticize, berate. *Please don't scold him for being late.* *-n.* **2.** complainer, nag, faultfinder. *I try not to be a scold.* **Ant.** 1. praise, compliment.

scope *n.* range, spread, reach, sphere, extension. *The scope of the destruction was enormous.*

scorch *vb.* toast, singe, burn, char, bake, sear. *The hills were scorched by the fire.*

score *n.* **1.** count, tally, record, points. *The game's score is four to one.* **2.** groove, cut, scratch, nick, mark, notch. *The old table had scores along its surface.* *-vb.* **3.** earn, make, win, achieve. *We must score two goals to win the game.* **4.** nick, gash, scratch, mark, gouge. *Meteorites scored the starship's hull.* **5.** grade, judge, evaluate, rate, rank. *The judges will score our performances.*

scoundrel *n.* rogue, villain, knave, rascal, swindler. *That scoundrel drove off in my car.*

scour *vb.* **1.** scrub, rub, cleanse, wash, polish. *He scoured the pots after dinner.* **2.** comb, search, rake, scan. *They scoured the mountains for the lost hikers.*

scout *n.* **1.** guide, outrider, lookout, escort. *A scout was sent ahead to find the trail.* *–vb.* **2.** survey, inspect, examine, reconnoiter. *She scouted the area for a good camping place.*

scramble *vb.* **1.** race, rush, scurry, hurry, clamber, struggle. *She scrambled up the rocks.* **2.** mix, disorder, jumble, shuffle. *His father scrambled the eggs.* *–n.* **3.** rush, race, struggle, run, tumble. *There was a scramble for the exit when the fire broke out.* **Ant. 2.** order, arrange.

scrap *n.* **1.** bit, fragment, part, piece, portion, crumb. *I used a scrap of cloth for the patch.* *–vb.* **2.** junk, discard, abandon, throw away, reject. *He plans to scrap his old beat-up car.* **Ant. 2.** repair, fix, keep.

scrape *vb.* **1.** skin, peel, grind, graze, scour. *She scraped gum off the bottom of her shoe.* **2.** abrade, rub, scratch, skin, bruise. *He scraped his knees when he fell.* **3.** collect, gather, acquire, obtain, assemble. *He was barely able to scrape together enough money to buy a house.* *–n.* **4.** graze, abrasion, scuff, scratch, bruise, rub. *The fall left a scrape on his arm.* **5.** screech, grate, rasp. *The scrape of fingernails across a chalkboard is quite nerve-wracking.* **6.** dilemma, predicament, muddle, trouble, difficulty. *I hope she can get out of this scrape.*

scratch *vb.* **1.** scrape, rub, abrade, claw, graze. *Can you scratch my itchy back?* **2.** cancel, erase, eliminate, remove, delete, withdraw. *He was scratched from the team.* *–n.* **3.** scrape, gash, abrasion, mark, score. *The cat left a scratch on her hand.* **Ant. 2.** add, include.

scream *vb.* **1.** shriek, screech, howl, yell. *People often scream during scary movies.* *–n.* **2.** shriek, yell, cry, shout, screech. *We heard his screams for help.* **Ant. 1–2.** whisper, mumble, mutter.

screech *vb.* **1.** shriek, scream, squawk, squeal, cry. *The owl screeched all night long.* *–n.* **2.** shriek, scream, squeal, cry. *I was startled by the screech of the car's brakes.*

screen *n.* **1.** curtain, shade, mesh, netting, divider. *A screen in our doorway keeps out insects.* **2.** cover, veil, cloak, mask, disguise, shield. *The fog served as a screen for the attacking army.* *–vb.* **3.** filter, sift, sort, rate, grade, evaluate. *Television talk shows screen their phone callers.* **4.** shelter, veil, shield, protect, cloak. *Smoke screened our getaway.* **Ant. 4.** reveal, disclose, show.

screw *n.* **1.** bolt, pin, fastener. *The desk was fastened to the floor with screws.* *–vb.* **2.** twist, twirl, whirl, turn, attach, fasten. *Please screw the lid back onto the jar.*

script *n.* **1.** handwriting, cursive, calligraphy. *The invitation's letters were written in script.* **2.** screenplay, playbook, manuscript. *The actress read from the movie's script.*

scrub *vb.* **1.** scour, rub, brush, polish, wash, cleanse. *Please scrub the floor until it shines.* *–n.* **2.** rub, brush, polish, cleansing, washing. *That dirty shirt needs a good scrub.* **3.** brush, brushwood, bushes. *We walked through low scrub.*

scrutinize *vb.* study, examine, observe, inspect, investigate. *He thoroughly scrutinized the car before buying it.*

scrutiny *n.* observation, inspection, watching, examination, investigation. *The teacher's scrutiny during the test prevented cheating.*

sculpture *n.* statue, figure, carving, bust. *Michelangelo is famous for his sculptures and paintings.*

scuttle *vb.* **1.** hurry, scamper, scurry, scramble, scoot. *The crab scuttled into the cave.* **2.** ditch, abandon, sink, wreck, destroy. *The sailors were forced to scuttle their old leaky boat.*

seal *n.* **1.** badge, stamp, emblem, sign, mark, insignia. *The state's seal must be on all official documents.* **2.** closure, fastening, seam, tape. *Don't use a jar if its seal is broken.* *–vb.* **3.** close, shut, bind, secure, fasten, plug. *Please seal the bottle so no water spills out.* **Ant. 3.** open, unseal, unbind.

sear *vb.* burn, scorch, singe, char, roast, blister. *The hot driveway seared his bare feet.*

search *vb.* **1.** seek, scour, explore, investigate, probe. *The librarian helped us search for the book.* *–n.* **2.** hunt, quest, pursuit, scouting, investigation. *Her search led her to the lost city.*

season *n.* **1.** era, time, term, span, period, quarter. *Christmas comes during the winter season.* *–vb.* **2.** spice, flavor, accent, enhance, embellish. *The cook seasons her food with herbs.*

secluded *adj.* hidden, isolated, remote, unvisited, lonely. *The hermit's cave was in a secluded place.* **Ant.** public, open, visited.

secret *adj.* **1.** private, hidden, concealed, unrevealed, masked. *Our club has a secret password.* *–n.* **2.** confidence, mystery, intrigue. *She wrote secrets in her diary.* **3.** formula, recipe, cause, explanation, key, answer. *What's the secret of her success?* **Ant. 1.** open, unconcealed, disclosed. **2.** disclosure, revelation.

secrete *vb.* hide, conceal, cache, stash, store, horde. *He secreted his money in a place where it could never be found by thieves.*

section *n.* **1.** part, piece, portion, slice, segment. *She reads the business section of the newspaper.* *–vb.* **2.** cut, divide, separate, split, slice. *Please section the cake into 12 pieces.* **Ant. 1.** whole, entirety. **2.** join, unite.

secure *adj.* **1.** safe, protected, defended, unthreatened, sheltered. *Burglar alarms make him feel secure.* **2.** certain, sure, guaranteed, assured, confident. *He has a secure position at the university.* *–vb.* **3.** get, gain, win, obtain, acquire, procure. *She secured a place in line for us.* **4.** tie, bind, attach, chain, fasten. *The sailors secured the boxes with rope.* **5.** protect, shield, guard, safeguard, shelter. *The police secured the area where the robbery occurred.* **Ant. 1.** insecure, unprotected, unsafe. **2.** insecure, uncertain. **3.** lose, forfeit. **4.** loose, unbind, untie. **5.** expose, endanger.

sedate *adj.* calm, quiet, still, unexcited, composed, serious. *Being at the library requires sedate behavior.* **Ant.** agitated, excited, loud.

sedative *adj.* **1.** calming, soothing, relaxing, numbing, narcotic. *Sleeping pills have a sedative effect.* *–n.* **2.** drug, tranquilizer, narcotic. *The doctor prescribed a sedative for her pain.* **Ant. 1.** arousing, stimulating. **2.** stimulant.

seduce *vb.* tempt, snare, lure, trap, attract. *Don't be seduced by a criminal's fancy lifestyle.* **Ant.** repel, repulse, disgust.

see *vb.* **1.** observe, view, notice, behold, detect. *Did he see the new movie yet?* **2.** discover, learn, determine, ascertain. *Please see if you can fix it.* **3.** understand, comprehend, perceive, grasp, realize. *Try to see my side of the argument.* **4.** imagine, visualize, envision, picture. *I can't see a way out of this crisis.* **5.** date, court, meet. *They started to see each other about a month ago.* **Ant. 1.** overlook, miss, ignore. **3.** misunderstand, disregard, ignore.

seek *vb.* pursue, search for, look for, chase, solicit. *She will seek a job with her father's company.*

seem *vb.* appear, look, resemble, suggest. *It may not be a lot of money, but it seems like a fortune to me.*

seep *vb.* ooze, dribble, leak, drip, trickle. *Honey seeped out of the broken jar.* **Ant.** gush, surge, stream, rush.

segment *n.* **1.** part, portion, piece, section, slice. *The final segment of the show will be on tomorrow.* *–vb.* **2.** divide, split, section, separate, slice. *He segmented the candy bar into four pieces.* **Ant. 1.** whole, all, totality. **2.** join, combine.

seize *vb.* grab, grasp, capture, snatch, clutch. *Police seized the smuggler at the airport.* **Ant.** lose, drop.

seldom *adv.* rarely, infrequently, uncommonly, scarcely, hardly. *Busy students seldom have time to play.* **Ant.** frequently, commonly, always.

select *vb.* **1.** pick, choose, elect, draw, decide on. *Which movie video did you select?* *–adj.* **2.** first-rate, special, outstanding, elite, exclusive. *The soldier was part of a select army unit.* **Ant. 2.** ordinary, common.

selection *n.* **1.** choosing, picking, election, determination, nomination. *The judge waited for the selection of the jury.* **2.** variety, range, pick, choice, option. *The restaurant's dessert selection was rather limited.*

self-conscious *adj.* unsure, shy, modest, bashful, embarrassed. *She was self-conscious about her new haircut.* **Ant.** confident, bold, open, unreserved.

selfish *adj.* self-centered, stingy, uncharitable, ungenerous, greedy. *Scrooge was a very selfish man.* **Ant.** unselfish, charitable, generous.

sell *vb.* market, vend, peddle, trade, retail. *The store sells shoes at a cheap price.* **Ant.** buy, purchase.

send *vb.* transmit, transfer, disseminate, launch, mail. *He sends Christmas cards to all his relatives.* **Ant.** get, receive.

senior *adj.* **1.** older, elder, elderly. *My grandfather is a senior citizen.* **2.** ranking, superior, top, chief. *She's a senior officer at her bank.* –*n.* **3.** elder, superior, better, chief, head. *He is my senior at the office.* **Ant. 1.** junior, younger. **2.** inferior, lower. **3.** junior, inferior.

sensational *adj.* spectacular, extraordinary, exciting, amazing, thrilling. *He performed a sensational dive.* **Ant.** ordinary, boring, dull.

sense *n.* **1.** faculty, capacity, capability, function, sensation. *The dog's sense of smell was well-developed.* **2.** understanding, knowledge, awareness, perception. *I admired her strong sense of honor.* **3.** meaning, message, significance, content. *What he said had no sense to it.* –*vb.* **4.** perceive, feel, detect, recognize, discern. *He could sense someone hiding in his closet.* **Ant. 3.** nonsense, gibberish. **4.** overlook, miss.

senseless *adj.* **1.** stupid, dumb, ridiculous, foolish, illogical. *Bringing snowshoes to the beach was rather senseless.* **2.** insensible, unconscious, unaware. *The boxer was knocked senseless.* **Ant. 1.** sensible, smart, wise. **2.** conscious.

sensible *adj.* intelligent, thoughtful, wise, logical, reasonable. *Wearing heavy clothing is sensible in cold weather.* **Ant.** senseless, stupid, foolish.

sensitive *adj.* **1.** receptive, perceptive, sympathetic, responsive, understanding. *She is sensitive to her friends' problems.* **2.** tender, painful, sore, aching, delicate. *His bruise is still very sensitive.* **3.** accurate, precise, exact, subtle, responsive. *A seismograph is a sensitive measuring device.* **Ant. 1.** insensitive, unfeeling, indifferent. **2.** insensitive, numb. **3.** inaccurate, approximate.

sentimental *adj.* nostalgic, emotional, dreamy, romantic. *Her old boyfriend's letters made her feel sentimental.* **Ant.** unsentimental, unemotional.

separate *vb.* **1.** part, split, divide, detach, sever. *Our teacher separates students who talk to each other.* –*adj.* **2.** different, individual, disconnected, distinct, isolated. *The zoo's lions and giraffes are kept in separate cages.* **Ant. 1.** join, unite. **2.** joined, connected.

separation *n.* **1.** division, partition, boundary, gap, space. *The Berlin Wall was a separation between East and West Berlin.* **2.** breakup, divorce, split, break, parting. *His parents' separation made him feel sad.* **Ant. 1.** union, junction. **2.** marriage, joining.

sequence *n.* series, string, chain, line, cycle, progression, arrangement. *The safe's combination is a sequence of numbers.*

serene *adj.* calm, quiet, peaceful, restful, unexcited. *After the noisy city, the forest seemed very serene.* **Ant.** excited, agitated, stormy.

serenity *n.* peacefulness, calmness, restfulness, tranquillity. *The beautiful garden gave him a feeling of serenity.* **Ant.** excitement, anxiety, agitation.

series *n.* sequence, run, succession, progression, cycle, row. *She endured a series of misfortunes.*

serious *adj.* **1.** grave, grim, reflective, solemn, sober, pensive. *My serious friend never laughs at jokes.* **2.** sincere, decided, earnest, definite, resolute. *Is she really serious about selling her car?* **3.** significant, important, crucial, consequential, momentous. *Deciding what college to attend is a serious decision.* **4.** dangerous, bad, alarming, grave, critical. *The patient's condition was serious.* **Ant. 1.** silly, jolly. **2.** insincere, undecided, joking. **3.** minor, unimportant, meaningless. **4.** mild, superficial.

seriously *adv.* gravely, solemnly, thoughtfully, earnestly. *He takes everything I say so seriously.* **Ant.** lightly, jokingly.

sermon *n.* lesson, lecture, speech, discourse, homily. *We heard the preacher's sermon.*

serpent *n.* snake, viper, reptile. *A monstrous serpent attacked the brave warrior.*

serve *vb.* **1.** give, pass, offer, deliver, supply. *The waiter served us our meal.* **2.** work, perform, labor, complete, spend. *He served two years in the Peace Corps.* **3.** help, aid, assist, attend, support. *I will serve you to my fullest ability.* **Ant. 3.** ignore, neglect.

service *n.* **1.** help, aid, assistance, support, attendance. *Please call room service.* **2.** army, navy, air force, marines, military. *His brother joined the service for four years.* **3.** agency, department, bureau, facility, utility. *She joined the Forest Service.* **4.** ceremony, ritual, rite, observance. *Church services were held on Sunday.* –*vb.* **5.** repair, fix, restore, maintain, adjust. *Our car was serviced by trained mechanics.*

servitude *n.* slavery, bondage, serfdom, vassalage. *Peasants are usually in a landlord's servitude.*

set *vb.* **1.** put, place, lay, rest, install. *Please set your things on the counter.* **2.** arrange, order, adjust, fix, prepare. *She set the table for dinner.* **3.** drop, sink, settle, descend, lower. *The sun sets in the west.* **4.** harden, solidify, stiffen, thicken. *The concrete must set before we can walk on it.* **5.** start, begin, depart, embark. *They set off on their trip.* –*n.* **6.** receiver, machine, apparatus. *Her television set is broken.* **7.** packet, group, bunch, assortment, collection. *He bought a set of new dishes.* **8.** stage, setting, scene. *We watched the actor on the movie set.* **9.** bearing, posture, position, carriage. *Anger showed in the set of his shoulders.* **10.** clique, crowd, clan, society, club. *Those of the jet set often drive fancy cars.* –*adj.* **11.** fixed, regular, customary, habitual, definite. *She has a set way of doing things.* **12.** decided, prepared, determined, arranged. *The time of our departure has already been set.* **Ant. 1.** remove, lift. **2.** disarrange, disorder. **3.** rise, ascend. **4.** soften, liquefy. **5.** finish, conclude. **11.** flexible, impromptu.

settle *vb.* **1.** decide, agree, set, fix, choose. *She finally settled on the blue sweater.* **2.** locate, live, dwell, reside, inhabit, colonize. *The emigrants decided to settle in Oregon.* **3.** sink, drop, descend, subside, lower. *He settled into the soft chair.* **4.** quiet, calm, soothe, pacify, tranquilize. *The medicine settled her upset stomach.* **5.** heal, resolve, mend, close, terminate. *Please try to settle your argument.* **Ant. 1.** waver, hesitate. **3.** ascend, rise. **4.** upset, disturb.

sever *vb.* **1.** separate, detach, dismember, part, amputate. *The dog's tail was severed in the accident.* **2.** end, stop, discontinue, cease, dissolve. *The two warring nations severed all diplomatic ties.* **Ant. 1.** join, attach, unite. **2.** continue, maintain.

several *adj.* some, a few, sundry, various, certain, divers. *He had several goldfish.* **Ant.** many, lots.

severe *adj.* **1.** harsh, cruel, ruthless, fierce, violent. *School was canceled due to a severe snowstorm.* **2.** serious, grim, stern, strict, grave. *The teacher gave the tardy student a severe look.* **Ant. 1.** mild, gentle, moderate. **2.** gentle, tender, cheerful.

severity *n.* harshness, seriousness, roughness, gravity. *The storm's severity kept people inside their homes.* **Ant.** mildness, gentleness, triviality.

shabby *adj.* **1.** worn, ragged, tattered, scruffy. *The homeless woman wore a shabby coat.* **2.** low, mean, dishonorable, unfair. *Calling people names is a shabby thing to do.* **Ant. 1.** fine, new, neat. **2.** honorable, nice, kind, considerate.

shack *n.* hut, shanty, hovel, shed. *The old miner lives in a shack.* **Ant.** mansion, palace.

shackle *n.* **1.** chain, manacle, bond, handcuff, cuff. *Slaves were often kept in shackles.* –*vb.* **2.** chain, bind, restrain, cramp. *Why did you shackle me with more work?* **Ant. 2.** free, unchain, aid.

shadow *n.* **1.** silhouette, outline, trace, image, shade. *The sun made a shadow behind him.* **2.** hint, bit, touch, tinge, trace. *There's not a shadow of doubt concerning her honesty.* –*vb.* **3.** follow, trail, track, stalk, pursue. *The detective shadowed his suspect.*

shadowy *adj.* **1.** shaded, protected, sheltered, dark, murky. *The forest was cold and shadowy.* **2.** vague, unclear, obscure, indistinct, ghostly. *Shadowy figures were at the back of the alley.* **Ant. 1.** sunny, open, unshaded. **2.** clear, distinct.

shake *vb.* **1.** vibrate, rattle, jiggle, tremble, jar. *An earthquake shook our house last night.* **2.** weaken, undermine, disturb, drain, diminish. *Nothing you say will shake my confidence in her.*

–n. **3.** vibration, rattle, jiggling, trembling, quaking. *He gave the bottle a shake to mix its contents.* **Ant. 1.** settle, calm, quiet. **2.** increase, augment.

shallow *adj.* superficial, simple, empty, frivolous, trivial. *The movie star was very shallow.* **Ant.** deep, complex, complicated.

shame *n.* **1.** remorse, regret, dishonor, disgrace, humiliation, embarrassment. *She felt shame over her arrest.* **2.** disappointment, misfortune, disgrace. *It was a shame that you couldn't attend the party.* –vb. **3.** dishonor, disgrace, humiliate, embarrass. *He was shamed by the terrible way his friend acted.* **Ant. 1.** honor, pleasure, pride. **3.** honor, please.

shameful *adj.* dishonorable, disgraceful, humiliating, degrading. *Cheating on the test was a shameful thing to do.* **Ant.** honorable, admirable, noble.

shape *n.* **1.** figure, form, outline, contour, pattern. *The Earth has a circular shape.* **2.** condition, health, trim, state, order. *The overweight man was in bad shape.* –vb. **3.** form, mold, fashion, model, design. *The sculptor shaped the clay.*

share *n.* **1.** part, piece, portion, segment, division. *They each got a share of the winnings.* –vb. **2.** divide, split, partition, apportion. *He shared his sandwich with his friend.*

sharp *adj.* **1.** cutting, edged, keen, pointed, thorny. *A shark has very sharp teeth.* **2.** sudden, abrupt, rapid, steep. *There was a sharp drop to the valley below.* **3.** aware, intelligent, clever, shrewd, quick. *She is a sharp student.* **4.** harsh, cutting, bitter, stinging. *He had sharp words for the young thief.* –adv. **5.** suddenly, abruptly, rapidly, unexpectedly. *The driver stopped sharp when he saw the crack in the road.* **6.** exactly, promptly, precisely, punctually. *Please be there at one o'clock sharp.* **Ant. 1.** dull, blunt. **2.** gradual, gentle, slow. **3.** dull, unaware. **4.** gentle, soft, pleasant. **5.** slowly, gradually.

sharpen *vb.* point, hone, grind, edge, file. *Will you please sharpen the knife?* **Ant.** dull, blunt.

shatter *vb.* **1.** break, burst, smash, fragment, splinter. *The glass shattered when I dropped it.* **2.** devastate, crush, dumbfound,

overwhelm, destroy. *News of his death shattered her.* **Ant. 2.** uplift, reinforce.

shear *vb.* **1.** shave, cut, fleece, clip, trim. *The rancher sheared his sheep.* –n. **2.** scissors, pruners, clippers. *Please trim the bushes with these shears.*

shed *n.* **1.** shack, shanty, hut, barn, garage. *She keeps her tools in the shed.* –vb. **2.** discard, drop, remove, cast off. *Snakes shed their old skins.* **3.** cast, spread, shine, give, emit. *Her report should shed some light on the problem.* **Ant. 2.** keep, retain. **3.** withhold, repress.

sheepish *adj.* shy, self-conscious, embarrassed, bashful, uncomfortable. *They were both rather sheepish on their first date.* **Ant.** confident, immodest, aggressive.

sheer *adj.* **1.** fine, thin, transparent, translucent, gauzy, clear. *She bought a pair of sheer panty hose.* **2.** absolute, total, complete, unrestrained, pure. *The movie was sheer entertainment.* **3.** abrupt, vertical, perpendicular, precipitous, steep. *The rock climbers went up a sheer cliff.* **Ant. 1.** thick, coarse. **2.** partial, incomplete. **3.** sloping, gradual.

shelter *n.* **1.** safety, protection, refuge, cover. *We ran for shelter when it began to rain.* **2.** accommodation, home, dwelling, habitation, quarters. *The city built a shelter for homeless people.* –vb. **3.** protect, guard, safeguard, defend, shield, cover. *The church sheltered the poor refugees.* **Ant. 1.** exposure, danger. **3.** uncover, expose.

shield *n.* **1.** protection, guard, defense, screen, cover. *The spacecraft raised its shields against enemy fire.* –vb. **2.** protect, guard, shelter, cover, screen. *Her umbrella shielded her from the sun.* **Ant. 1.** danger, risk. **2.** endanger, uncover, expose.

shift *vb.* **1.** transport, transfer, relocate, move, carry. *The movers shifted the furniture to their truck.* **2.** change, switch, adjust, alter, vary. *The driver shifted into second gear.* –n. **3.** change, switch, move, alteration, turning. *We were surprised by the president's policy shift.* **4.** assignment, stint, period, duty. *She is working the late shift tonight.*

shimmer *vb.* **1.** twinkle, glimmer, sparkle, glisten, ripple. *The lake shimmered in the summer* sun. -n. **2.** sparkle, glimmer, twinkling, glittering, luster, glow. *The shimmer of his sequined costume caught our attention.*

shine vb. **1.** gleam, glow, beam, radiate, flash. *The doctor shined a light into my eyes.* **2.** polish, buff, burnish, wax. *Please shine the silverware for tonight.* **3.** excel, exceed, dominate, stand out. *Music is an area in which he shines.* -n. **4.** glow, gleam, brightness, sparkle, flash. *The new car has a nice shine.* **Ant. 2.** blacken, darken, dull. **3.** fail. **4.** darkness, dullness.

ship n. **1.** boat, steamer, liner, freighter, yacht. *He crossed the ocean in a large ship.* -vb. **2.** embark, leave, depart, move. *The soldiers will ship out tomorrow.* **3.** send, transport, dispatch, transmit, forward. *She shipped the package to South America.*

shirk vb. avoid, dodge, escape, evade, ignore. *He often tries to shirk his responsibilities.* **Ant.** fulfill, accomplish, do.

shiver vb. **1.** tremble, shake, quiver, shudder, quake. *She shivered in the cold air.* -n. **2.** quiver, quake, shudder, tremble. *Scary movies send shivers down my spine.*

shock n. **1.** blow, jolt, jar, start, upset. *His bad report card gave him quite a shock.* **2.** paralysis, trauma, distress, collapse, stupor. *The accident victim was in a state of shock.* -vb. **3.** stagger, stun, upset, disturb, offend. *Her bad behavior really shocked us.*

shoot vb. **1.** wound, hit, plug, nick, kill. *The soldier was shot in the leg.* **2.** fire, propel, discharge, project, eject. *He shoots arrows with an old Indian bow.* **3.** spring, leap, dash, rush, explode. *The runners shot out of the starting blocks.* -n. **4.** sprout, bud, sprig, twig. *The deer chewed on green shoots.*

shop n. **1.** store, market, boutique, outlet. *He bought her gift at a nearby shop.* -vb. **2.** buy, purchase, browse, look. *We went to shop at the mall.*

shore n. **1.** beach, coast, seaside, waterfront, riverbank. *She found seashells on the shore.* -vb. **2.** hold, support, brace, buttress, reinforce, prop. *Workers tried to shore up the crumbling dam.* **Ant. 2.** weaken, destroy, overwhelm.

short adj. **1.** small, little, low, tiny, stunted, squat. *Horse jockeys are usually short.* **2.** brief, concise, momentary, fleeting. *He's only been waiting a short time.* **3.** abrupt, sharp, curt, rude, snappish. *The angry woman was very short with us.* -adv. **4.** suddenly, abruptly, quickly, forthwith. *The driver stopped short when she saw the injured animal.* -n. **5.** bermudas, cutoffs, trunks. *She wears shorts in the summer.* **6.** brief, summary, conclusion. *In short, there is no turning back.* **Ant. 1.** tall, long, rangy. **2.** long, extended. **3.** patient, wordy. **4.** slowly, gradually. **5.** pants, trousers. **6.** full, complete.

shortage n. scarcity, lack, shortfall, deficit, drought. *During gas shortages, people should drive as little as possible.* **Ant.** overabundance, surplus, excess.

shortcoming n. failing, flaw, fault, drawback, defect. *I like her despite her shortcomings.* **Ant.** strength, virtue.

shorten vb. reduce, decrease, trim, cut, condense. *The sleeves were too long, so we shortened them.* **Ant.** lengthen, increase, extend.

shoulder n. **1.** rim, edge, ledge, bank, shelf. *His car hit the shoulder of the road.* -vb. **2.** push, shove, jostle, elbow, crowd. *She shouldered her way into the crowded room.* **3.** accept, carry, bear, assume, take. *I need you to shoulder more of the work.*

shout vb. **1.** yell, scream, shriek, howl, roar. *The angry tennis players shouted at each other.* -n. **2.** yell, scream, cry, call, roar, howl. *We couldn't hear the announcer over the shouts of the crowd.* **Ant. 1–2.** whisper, mumble.

shove vb. **1.** push, move, thrust, jostle, shoulder. *He shoved the dog off the chair.* -n. **2.** push, nudge, boost, jostle, thrust, prod. *The toy began rolling when she gave it a shove.*

show vb. **1.** display, exhibit, uncover, reveal, demonstrate. *Will you show your science project to the class?* **2.** lead, conduct, escort, steer. *Please show her to the door.* -n. **3.** performance, program, production, entertainment. *The theater's late show begins at midnight.* **4.** display, presentation, demonstration, exhibition. *Let's see a show of hands.* **Ant. 1.** hide, conceal, cover. **4.** hiding, concealment.

shred *n.* **1.** bit, scrap, piece, fragment, trace. *The criminal didn't leave a shred of evidence.* –*vb.* **2.** rip, tear, snip, slice, fragment. *The student shredded newspaper for his papier-mache project.*

shrewd *adj.* clever, sharp, keen, intelligent, cunning, artful. *She made some shrewd business investments.* **Ant.** stupid, unwise, naive.

shriek *n.* **1.** scream, cry, squeal, screech, yell. *I let out a shriek when I saw the ghost.* –*vb.* **2.** scream, squeal, screech, yell, roar. *The people riding the roller coaster shrieked in delight.*

shrink *vb.* **1.** retreat, retire, withdraw, cringe, cower. *He shrank from the horrible monster.* **2.** reduce, constrict, shrivel, shorten, decrease. *Jeans left too long in the dryer will shrink.* **Ant. 1.** confront, face. **2.** increase, expand, lengthen.

shrivel *vb.* wither, wilt, shrink, fade, contract. *Plants shriveled during the drought.* **Ant.** grow, expand.

shudder *vb.* **1.** shiver, tremble, shake, quake, convulse. *Just thinking about spinach makes him shudder.* –*n.* **2.** convulsion, shiver, tremble, quiver, twitch. *The dying porpoise gave one last shudder, then sank from view.*

shuffle *vb.* **1.** drag, hobble, scrape, limp, shamble. *A homeless man shuffled down the sidewalk.* **2.** mix, intermix, jumble, rearrange, disorder, *The gambler shuffled the card deck.* –*n.* **3.** limp, hobble, dragging, shambling. *She walks with an odd shuffle.* **Ant. 2.** order, arrange.

shun *vb.* avoid, reject, spurn, refuse, forgo. *Lepers were often shunned by other people.* **Ant.** welcome, accept, embrace.

shut *vb.* **1.** close, seal, secure, latch, block. *Please shut the door when you leave.* **2.** confine, cage, pen, enclose, lock. *The farmer shut the animals in the barn.* –*adj.* **3.** closed, sealed, blocked, unopened. *The road was shut for repairs.* **Ant. 1.** open, unseal. **2.** free, release. **3.** open, opened, unsealed.

shutter *n.* blind, shade, curtain, screen. *Shutters on our windows keep the sunshine out.*

shy *adj.* **1.** bashful, modest, timid, sheepish, cautious. *The shy girl was afraid of speaking in front of her class.* **2.** short, under, deficient, lacking, scant. *The ball was several yards shy of a field goal.* –*vb.* **3.** flinch, jerk, quail, cringe, start. *The horse shied away from the crowd.* **Ant. 1.** immodest, bold, brash. **2.** over, above.

sick *adj.* **1.** ill, unwell, nauseated, queasy, troubled. *Roller coaster rides make him sick.* **2.** repulsive, offensive, disgusting, shocking. *That was a sick joke.* **3.** tired, weary, bored, fed up. *She was sick of doing homework.* **Ant. 1.** well, healthy. **2.** tasteful, pleasant. **3.** eager, fresh.

sift *vb.* rummage, filter, sort, search, probe. *The archaeologist sifted through the dirt for ancient pottery shards.*

sight *n.* **1.** vision, eyesight, seeing. *The old dog's sight was poor.* **2.** appearance, view, vision, glance, glimpse. *The sight of so much food made her mouth water.* **3.** wonder, marvel, scene, view, spectacle. *The Grand Canyon is quite a sight.* –*vb.* **4.** see, view, discern, glimpse, observe. *They sighted a plane flying overhead.* **Ant. 1.** blindness.

sign *n.* **1.** symbol, token, representation, indication, warning. *Geese flying south are a sign that winter has arrived.* **2.** gesture, signal, motion, wave, nod. *The coach gave a sign for the batter to bunt.* **3.** billboard, signpost, guidepost, bulletin. *The bus stopped at the stop sign.* –*vb.* **4.** endorse, initial, inscribe, autograph. *Your parents must sign your report card.* **5.** gesture, signal, flag, motion, wave. *The police officer signed for our car to pass.*

significance *n.* importance, consequence, influence, weight, meaning. *The American Revolution has great significance in the history of the United States.*

significant *adj.* **1.** large, sizable, considerable, substantial, major. *I noticed a significant improvement in his dancing after he took lessons.* **2.** important, noteworthy, crucial, vital, valuable. *She felt that the last chapter was the only significant part of the entire book.* **Ant. 1.** insignificant, small, minor, trivial. **2.** insignificant, unimportant, meaningless, invaluable.

silence *n.* **1.** quiet, hush, stillness, noiselessness, speechlessness, muteness. *Mourners stood in silence beside the grave.* –*vb.* **2.** quiet, still, extinguish, subdue, calm, muffle. *The librarian silenced our loud talking.* **Ant. 1.** loudness, noise, talkativeness. **2.** encourage, inflame.

silent *adj.* **1.** quiet, soundless, mute, speechless, noiseless. *We remained silent during the principal's speech.* **2.** unspoken, unstated, undeclared, implicit, tacit. *We had a silent agreement.* **Ant. 1.** noisy, talkative, loud. **2.** spoken, declared.

silly *adj.* foolish, ridiculous, comical, idiotic, stupid. *The circus clown was very silly.* **Ant.** serious, intelligent, sensible.

similar *adj.* close, comparable, like, related, parallel. *My friend's taste in music is similar to mine.* **Ant.** dissimilar, different, contrary.

similarity *n.* resemblance, likeness, sameness, closeness, equivalence. *People commented on the similarity between the two brothers.* **Ant.** dissimilarity, difference, unlikeness.

simmer *vb.* stew, bubble, cook, boil, sizzle. *He let the soup simmer on the stove.*

simple *adj.* **1.** easy, uncomplicated, elementary, understandable, basic. *She answered the simple problems first.* **2.** uneducated, unsophisticated, unassuming, naive, unworldly. *The peasant was a simple man.* **3.** plain, unadorned, bare, natural, naked. *All we wanted was the simple truth.* **Ant. 1.** complicated, difficult, advanced. **2.** complicated, sophisticated, worldly. **3.** pretended, varnished.

simplicity *n.* easiness, directness, plainness, straightforwardness, openness. *She was surprised by the problem's simplicity.* **Ant.** complexity, difficulty, sophistication.

simplify *vb.* summarize, shorten, streamline, clarify, unravel. *He tried to simplify the long and complicated explanation.* **Ant.** elaborate, embellish.

sin *n.* **1.** wrong, violation, wickedness, offense, misdeed. *She confessed her sins to the priest.* *–vb.* **2.** err, stray, transgress, offend, trespass. *The minister said the thief had sinned.* **Ant. 1.** sinlessness, goodness.

sincere *adj.* real, genuine, earnest, honest, heartfelt. *Do you think his apology was sincere?* **Ant.** insincere, fake, pretended.

sincerity *n.* genuineness, earnestness, frankness, honesty. *Hopefully, most donations to charities are given with sincerity.* **Ant.** insincerity, artificiality, emptiness.

sing *vb.* vocalize, intone, melodize, croon, chant. *He plans to sing several new songs at the concert.*

singe *vb.* sear, scorch, char, blacken, blister. *The fire singed the edge of his hair.*

sinister *adj.* dangerous, wicked, threatening, evil, frightening. *In the movie, the two stars were stalked by a sinister figure.* **Ant.** harmless, safe.

sink *vb.* **1.** descend, fall, plunge, flounder, dip, slump, decline. *The ship began to sink after hitting the reef.* **2.** invest, risk, venture, drop. *Are you going to sink more money into the business?* **3.** bore, drill, dig, plant, lay. *Workers sank an oil well outside the city.* *–n.* **4.** basin, washbowl, washbasin. *Dirty dishes were piled in the sink.* **Ant. 1.** rise, lift, climb. **2.** remove, withdraw.

site *n.* place, location, position, spot, area. *The king found the perfect site for his new castle.*

situate *vb.* place, set, put, position, stand, station. *We must decide how to situate the new furniture in this room.* **Ant.** move, shift, remove.

situation *n.* predicament, circumstances, condition, state, case. *The situation at the accident was critical.*

size *n.* measurement, dimension, area, volume, expanse. *The salesman asked him for his shoe size.*

sketch *n.* **1.** drawing, diagram, chart, graph. *The artist drew a pencil sketch of my friend.* **2.** skit, scene, vignette. *The drama students acted out a sketch.* *–vb.* **3.** draw, pencil, outline, picture, graph. *The architect sketched her plans for the new building.*

sketchy *adj.* incomplete, vague, fuzzy, unfinished, crude. *She gave a sketchy explanation of where she had been.* **Ant.** complete, detailed, finished.

skill *n.* ability, talent, technique, trade, craft. *Painting is a skill that takes considerable practice to master.* **Ant.** inability, awkwardness, incompetency.

skillful *adj.* gifted, talented, capable, experienced, masterful. *We hired a skillful carpenter to build our new home.* **Ant.** unskillful, untalented, incapable, clumsy.

skimp *vb.* conserve, economize, pinch, scrimp, withhold. *The cook skimped on the sugar to save money.* **Ant.** waste, squander.

skimpy *adj.* scanty, small, puny, meager, inadequate. *Some people wore skimpy bathing suits at the beach.* **Ant.** large, enormous, extensive, lavish.

skinny *adj.* lean, scrawny, thin, gaunt, shrunken. *After dieting for several months, she became quite skinny.* **Ant.** fat, plump, bulky, fleshy.

skip *vb.* **1.** spring, bounce, jump, hop, leap. *She skipped from rock to rock.* **2.** miss, omit, neglect, dodge, avoid. *He got into trouble after he skipped class.* *-n.* **3.** spring, jump, hop, leap. *He took a skip over the crack in the sidewalk.* **Ant. 1.** shuffle, drag. **2.** include, attend, cover.

skirmish *n.* **1.** battle, fight, clash, engagement, conflict. *A skirmish took place between two platoons.* *-vb.* **2.** battle, fight, struggle, clash, collide. *Soldiers skirmished for control of the hill.*

skirt *n.* **1.** dress, gown, frock, miniskirt, maxiskirt. *She wore her skirt just above the knees.* *-vb.* **2.** avoid, bypass, dodge, circle, sidestep. *They skirted the valley where the evil wizard lived.* **Ant. 2.** confront, enter, meet.

slack *adj.* **1.** loose, limp, relaxed, lax. *Keep the sail slack until the wind increases.* **2.** lazy, idle, negligent, sloppy. *The manager criticized them for being slack at their jobs.* *-adv.* **3.** loosely, limply, easily, relaxed. *The rope hung slack in her hands.* *-n.* **4.** decrease, decline, slowing, cutback. *Bad weather caused a slack in the store's business.* **Ant. 1.** tight, rigid, tense. **2.** competent, careful, attentive. **3.** tightly, rigidly, stiffly. **4.** increase, upswing.

slam *vb.* **1.** bang, smack, smash, dash, hurl. *The basketball player slammed the ball into the basket.* *-n.* **2.** banging, crashing, smack, smash. *We knew he was angry when we heard the slam of his door.*

slander *n.* **1.** falsehood, untruth, defamation, libel, distortion. *The actress sued the magazine for slander.* *-vb.* **2.** defame, smear, malign, slur, defile. *Her enemy slandered her good name.*

slant *vb.* **1.** tilt, slope, pitch, cant, list. *The floor slanted where the ground had sunk.* **2.** bias, twist, distort, weight, prejudice. *He slants his speeches toward a liberal viewpoint.* *-n.* **3.** tilt, slope, pitch, leaning, list. *The tree grew with a slant because of strong northerly winds.* **4.** bias, distortion, viewpoint, prejudice, emphasis. *The newspaper is written with a conservative slant.*

slap *n.* **1.** smack, clap, blow, whack, bang. *The slap of waves hitting the beach lulled us to sleep.* *-vb.* **2.** smack, hit, whack, strike. *The loose sail slapped her in the face.* **3.** dash, fling, cast, toss, hurl. *Workers slapped paint on the house.*

slash *vb.* **1.** cut, slice, hack, gash, lacerate. *He accidentally slashed his hand on some broken glass.* **2.** cut, drop, trim, pare, reduce. *The editor slashed several pages from the manuscript.* *-n.* **3.** cut, gash, slit, slice, rent, tear. *Cereal fell through a slash in the box.* **4.** reduction, cut, drop, markdown. *The store advertised its price slash.* **Ant. 2.** add, keep, maintain. **4.** increase, markup.

slaughter *n.* **1.** massacre, killing, murder, bloodshed, butchering. *The slaughter on the battlefield sickened him.* *-vb.* **2.** massacre, annihilate, kill, butcher, exterminate. *Hunters slaughtered much of the deer herd.*

slavery *n.* bondage, enslavement, servitude, serfdom, enthrallment. *The captives were sold into slavery.* **Ant.** freedom, liberty, emancipation.

slay *vb.* kill, murder, annihilate, assassinate, slaughter. *The knight rode out to slay the dragon.*

sleek *adj.* silky, shiny, glossy, smooth, glistening. *The tiger's fur was sleek from the rain.* **Ant.** dull, rough, coarse.

sleep *vb.* **1.** slumber, rest, repose, doze, nap. *My sister and I sleep in a bunk bed.* *-n.* **2.** slumber, rest, repose, snooze, nap. *The tired child needs a good night's sleep.* **Ant. 1.** arouse, awaken. **2.** wakefulness.

slender *adj.* slim, thin, lean, slight, narrow, reedy. *The slender trees bent with the wind.* **Ant.** thick, solid, fat.

slice *n.* **1.** piece, wedge, chunk, cut, portion. *Please give me a slice of pizza.* *-vb.* **2.** carve, segment, cut, divide, separate. *She sliced a tomato for her salad.*

slick *adj.* **1.** slippery, treacherous, sleek, glossy, shiny. *The road was slick from the gas spill.* **2.** smooth, suave, glib, sharp, cunning. *They distrusted the slick saleswoman.* –*n.* **3.** film, coating, scum, spill. *An oil slick washed up on the beach.* **Ant. 1.** rough, textured, coarse. **2.** amateurish, clumsy.

slide *vb.* **1.** glide, slip, skim, skate, coast. *The softball player tried to slide into second base.* –*n.* **2.** chute, tube, trough, slope. *She went down the pool's slide.*

slight *adj.* **1.** small, slender, light, frail, delicate. *The boy seemed very slight on the large stage.* **2.** minor, unimportant, insignificant, modest. *There's a slight chance of snow today.* –*vb.* **3.** insult, snub, affront, rebuff, spurn. *He slighted her with his inattention.* –*n.* **4.** snub, insult, slur, affront. *Ignoring him was a slight.* **Ant. 1.** large, strong, solid. **2.** great, considerable.

slim *adj.* **1.** slender, thin, lean, slight, small. *The slim athlete was constantly exercising.* –*vb.* **2.** slenderize, reduce. *We joined a sports club to slim our waistlines.* **Ant. 1.** large, fat, thick.

sling *n.* **1.** brace, support, band, strap, bandage. *Her broken arm is in a sling.* –*vb.* **2.** fling, cast, jerk, pitch, heave. *The cook slung raw hamburger onto the grill.*

slip *vb.* **1.** glide, skim, slide, flow, slither. *She slipped between the bed covers.* **2.** skid, fall, trip, tumble. *He slipped on the ice.* **3.** decline, decrease, fall, lapse, sink. *The temperature slipped into the low twenties.* –*n.* **4.** blunder, error, mistake, oversight. *He made a slip in telling me about my gift.* **5.** fall, drop, downturn, decline. *A slip in the patient's condition worried the doctor.* **6.** stub, paper, note, certificate, coupon. *You should always save the sales slip.* **7.** undergarment, petticoat, chemise. *She wore a slip under her summer dress.* **Ant. 3.** increase, rise, improve. **4.** improvement, upturn, increase.

slit *vb.* **1.** cut, split, rip, slash, slice. *She slit the envelope open.* –*n.* **2.** opening, groove, fissure, cut, slash. *He peered through a slit in the curtains.*

slope *vb.* **1.** slant, lean, bank, angle, incline. *The trail slopes uphill for the next mile.* –*n.* **2.** bank, ramp, angle, incline, descent. *Only experienced skiers should go down the steep slopes.* **Ant. 1.** flatten. **2.** horizontal, plane.

sloppy *adj.* messy, slovenly, disorderly, untidy, careless. *The sloppy diner spilled mustard on her shirt.* **Ant.** neat, orderly, tidy.

slovenly *adj.* messy, sloppy, unclean, slack, careless. *I am disgusted by his slovenly habits.* **Ant.** neat, clean, careful.

slow *adj.* **1.** unhurried, plodding, sluggish, crawling, gradual, delayed. *The slow dripping of the water annoyed him.* **2.** dumb, dull, dense, obtuse, stupid. *The dog was too slow to learn new tricks.* –*vb.* **3.** delay, decelerate, moderate, slacken, break. *The car slowed in the heavy traffic.* **Ant. 1.** fast, hurried. **2.** smart, clever, bright. **3.** accelerate.

sluggish *adj.* slow, crawling, listless, unhurried, plodding. *Cars are often sluggish in cold weather.* **Ant.** lively, quick, frisky.

slumber *vb.* **1.** sleep, doze, nap, snooze. *The baby looks peaceful when she slumbers.* –*n.* **2.** sleep, nap, rest, repose, siesta. *Our slumber was disturbed by a loud noise.*

sly *adj.* cunning, foxy, crafty, wily, crooked. *The sly politician gave out false information about his opponent.* **Ant.** open, honorable, straightforward.

smack *n.* **1.** hit, slap, whack, spank, blow. *She gave the dog a smack for biting the neighbor.* –*vb.* **2.** hit, whack, strike, slap, slam. *He smacked his head against the low doorway.* **3.** taste, smell, suggest, resemble. *That tale smacks of falsehood.*

small *adj.* **1.** little, tiny, petite, puny, miniature. *Only five people could fit in the small theater.* **2.** scant, meager, limited, piddling. *She has a small number of projects to finish.* **3.** minor, insignificant, unimportant, secondary, trivial. *We will deal with the small matters last.* **Ant. 1.** big, large, gigantic. **2.** great, enormous. **3.** major.

smart *adj.* **1.** intelligent, bright, clever, brainy, sharp. *Marie Curie, winner of a Nobel Prize, was a very smart scientist.* –*vb.* **2.** sting, burn, hurt, throb, itch. *His scraped knee still smarts.* **Ant. 1.** dumb, stupid, unintelligent.

smash *vb.* **1.** crush, shatter, pulverize, demolish, break. *The troll smashed the rocks blocking his path.* –*n.* **2.** blow, shattering, crash, bang. *Our car got quite a smash when it hit the tree.* **3.** hit, triumph, success, winner. *The new movie was a smash.* **Ant. 3.** failure, flop.

smear *vb.* **1.** spread, coat, cover, layer, dab. *She smeared suntan lotion across her arms.* **2.** smudge, blur, streak, stain, soil. *The rain smeared the actor's makeup.* –*n.* **3.** smudge, blotch, streak, stain, spot. *The ink smear blotted out several words.*

smell *vb.* **1.** scent, sniff, detect, sense, perceive. *I could smell the cookies baking in the oven.* **2.** stink, reek. *The bus fumes really smelled.* –*n.* **3.** scent, odor, aroma, fragrance, stink. *The garbage gave off a horrible smell.*

smile *vb.* **1.** grin, beam, smirk. *We smiled for the photographer.* –*n.* **2.** grin, beam, smirk. *The happy boy gave us a big smile.* **Ant. 1–2.** frown.

smite *vb.* hit, strike, smack, blast, demolish. *Lightning sometimes smites the tallest trees.*

smooth *adj.* **1.** even, polished, glassy, silky, unwrinkled. *A bowling ball is smooth to the touch.* **2.** easy, orderly, uneventful, untroubled. *The doctor hoped for a smooth operation.* **3.** suave, sophisticated, glib, slick, urbane. *The smooth politician expertly fended off questions of a personal nature.* –*vb.* **4.** flatten, even, sand, polish, press. *He smoothed out the crumpled letter.* **Ant. 1.** rough, uneven, coarse, bumpy. **2.** uneven, difficult, troubled. **3.** unsophisticated. **4.** wrinkle, crumple, roughen.

smother *vb.* suffocate, strangle, choke, extinguish, snuff. *The forest rangers smothered the fire with dirt.*

smolder *vb.* fume, smoke, simmer, sizzle, fester. *His anger smoldered for days.*

smudge *n.* **1.** smear, blotch, stain, blot. *She wiped the smudge off her windshield.* –*vb.* **2.** stain, smear, spot, soil, dirty. *The baby smudged his face with mud.* **Ant. 2.** clean, cleanse.

snag *n.* **1.** hitch, catch, obstacle, complication, difficulty. *Losing the plane tickets was a snag in our plans.* –*vb.* **2.** catch, pull, tear, rip. *He snagged his sweater on the fence.*

snake *n.* serpent, viper, rattlesnake, cobra, ophidian. *The zoo keeps its snakes in the reptile section.*

snap *vb.* **1.** click, crack, crackle, pop. *The audience snapped its fingers to the melody.* **2.** break, crack, fracture, separate. *She snapped the branch into two pieces.* **3.** clasp, join, catch, secure. *Please snap your jacket together in this cold weather.* **4.** nip, bite, chop. *The lizard snapped at the fly.* **5.** growl, grumble, snarl, bark. *She snapped at him when he asked a question.* –*n.* **6.** pop, crack, crackle, click. *I heard the snap of tree branches breaking.* **7.** catch, fastener, clasp. *The snap broke on his jeans.* **8.** nip, bite, chomp, snatch. *A crocodile's snap can be dangerous.* –*adj.* **9.** quick, sudden, hasty, abrupt. *Don't make a snap decision.* **Ant. 9.** thoughtful, careful, cautious.

snare *n.* **1.** trap, lure, decoy, net, noose. *A snare was set out to catch the injured racoon.* –*vb.* **2.** trap, capture, hook, catch, seize. *The police snared the thief before he could get away.*

snatch *vb.* **1.** seize, grab, take, pluck, steal. *A mugger snatched the woman's purse.* –*n.* **2.** piece, part, fragment, portion, bit. *I overheard snatches of their conversation.*

sneak *vb.* **1.** slip, slink, creep, crawl, slither. *Let's sneak into the old haunted house tonight.* **2.** steal, smuggle, spirit, slip. *She tried to sneak a bowl of ice cream.* –*n.* **3.** scoundrel, rascal, knave, coward. *Only a sneak would leave without telling his friend.* –*adj.* **4.** covert, surprise, secret, underhand, unexpected. *The castle was captured in a sneak attack.*

snub *vb.* **1.** insult, slight, offend, spurn, shun. *The king snubbed his guest by refusing to shake his hand.* –*n.* **2.** insult, slight, rejection, discourtesy. *Not inviting him to your party was a snub.*

snug *adj.* **1.** cozy, safe, secure, comfortable, sheltered. *She felt snug in her warm bed.* **2.** tight, close-fitting, compact, close. *The shirt was a bit snug.* **Ant. 1.** unprotected, threatened. **2.** large, loose.

snuggle *vb.* cuddle, hug, nuzzle, embrace, nestle. *The girl snuggled with her puppy.*

soak *vb.* **1.** drench, flood, saturate, permeate, wet. *Rain soaked the dirt racing track.* **2.** mop, sop, dry, absorb. *She used a paper towel to soak up the spilled milk.*

soar *vb.* **1.** fly, glide, sail, float, wing, coast. *The falcon soared high in the sky.* **2.** rise, climb, mount, escalate, tower. *Temperatures soared during the summer.* **Ant. 2.** descend, fall.

sob *vb.* **1.** cry, weep, bawl, wail, snivel. *I sobbed when I heard the bad news.* –*n.* **2.** cry, wail, whimper, lamentation. *A sob escaped the unhappy man.* **Ant. 1–2.** laugh, giggle.

sober *adj.* **1.** serious, grim, grave, subdued, mellow. *The team's bad loss was a sober awakening.* **2.** dry, abstinent, temperate. *The sober man drove his drunken friend home.* **Ant. 1.** merry, joyful, silly. **2.** drunk, intoxicated.

sociable *adj.* friendly, outgoing, hospitable, neighborly, cordial. *Ignoring your doorbell is not very sociable.* **Ant.** unsociable, unfriendly, withdrawn.

social *adj.* **1.** outgoing, sociable, friendly, amiable, extroverted. *Social people often like large parties.* **2.** community, communal, civic, common, public. *He's majoring in social studies.* **Ant. 1.** antisocial, introverted, solitary.

society *n.* **1.** humanity, humankind, civilization, public, population. *Criminals are a danger to society.* **2.** group, association, organization, club, union. *She joined a bird-watching society.*

sock *n.* **1.** stocking, hose, hosiery, anklet. *Her sock showed through the hole in her shoe.* **2.** punch, blow, smack, hit, strike. *The man was knocked out by a hard sock.* –*vb.* **3.** punch, hit, box, pound, smack. *The boxer socked his opponent.*

soft *adj.* **1.** downy, silky, furry, smooth. *He fell asleep on the soft pillow.* **2.** mushy, squashy, spongy, doughy. *Please mash the potatoes until they become soft.* **3.** mellow, low, subdued, gentle, mild. *She likes listening to soft music.* **Ant. 1.** hard, stiff, rough. **2.** hard, solid, solidified. **3.** harsh, loud, strong, violent.

soggy *adj.* soaked, saturated, drenched, pasty, mushy. *The sandwich was soggy after she dropped it in the pond.* **Ant.** dry, hard.

soil *n.* **1.** earth, dirt, ground, humus, loam. *Farmers need fertile soil for their crops.* –*vb.* **2.** dirty, stain, muddy, smudge, foul. *The baby soiled her diapers.*

solace *n.* **1.** comfort, support, cheer, encouragement. *The priest's presence was a solace to the dying man.* –*vb.* **2.** comfort, cheer, console, hearten. *Her kind words solaced her heartbroken friend.* **Ant. 1.** upset, pain, agony. **2.** upset, distress, sadden.

sole *adj.* only, single, exclusive, lone, solitary. *He was the sole survivor of the terrible airplane crash.* **Ant.** multiple, shared.

solemn *adj.* grave, grim, unsmiling, somber, serious. *People were solemn during the funeral service.* **Ant.** frivolous, smiling, jolly.

solicit *vb.* request, seek, plead, beseech, beg. *That charity solicits money from people.*

solid *adj.* **1.** dense, hard, condensed, firm, compacted. *Ice is a solid form of water.* **2.** reliable, sound, steady, stable, worthy. *The actor gave a solid performance.* **3.** unbroken, continuous, uninterrupted. *She wore a solid yellow sweatshirt.* **Ant. 1.** liquid, gaseous. **2.** shaky, unsteady. **3.** discontinuous.

solidify *vb.* harden, thicken, set, fix, compress. *Molten lava eventually solidifies into rock.* **Ant.** dissolve, liquefy.

solitary *adj.* isolated, secluded, reclusive, individual, single. *The mountain man lived a solitary lifestyle.*

solution *n.* **1.** answer, key, explanation, clarification, unraveling. *She figured out the solution to the math problem.* **2.** liquid, fluid, mixture, emulsion, solvent. *He heated the chemical solution.* **Ant. 1.** problem, question, dilemma.

solve *vb.* answer, resolve, untangle, unravel, explain. *It took several hours to solve the crossword puzzle.*

somber *adj.* grim, serious, gloomy, solemn, mournful. *We listened to her somber retelling of the story.* **Ant.** joyful, happy, gleeful.

song *n.* melody, tune, verse, hymn, refrain, ballad. *They danced to their favorite songs.*

soon *adv.* quickly, rapidly, directly, shortly, promptly. *The starving child needs food as soon as possible.*

soothe *vb.* relieve, ease, calm, relax, quiet. *A massage soothed his sore muscles.* **Ant.** irritate, upset, agitate.

sordid *adj.* vulgar, corrupt, unclean, dirty, foul. *The actor's sordid affair gained national attention.* **Ant.** clean, upstanding, moral.

sore *adj.* **1.** painful, tender, sensitive, bruised. *His cut is still very sore.* **2.** angry, annoyed, upset, irritated, resentful. *Are you still sore about yesterday's argument?* *–n.* **3.** injury, cut, gash, bruise, hurt, wound. *I bandaged the large sore on his leg.* **Ant. 2.** pleased, glad.

sorrow *n.* **1.** sadness, grief, anguish, unhappiness, distress. *We felt sorrow for the crash victims' families.* **2.** misfortune, disaster, loss, hardship, affliction. *His mother's death was a hard sorrow for him to bear.* *–vb.* **3.** mourn, grieve, despair, agonize, lament. *She sorrowed over the seal pup's death at the hands of hunters.* **Ant. 1.** gladness, happiness. **2.** joy, pleasure. **3.** celebrate.

sorrowful *adj.* sad, unhappy, gloomy, depressed, heartbroken. *The novel had a sorrowful ending.* **Ant.** happy, joyous, merry.

sorry *adj.* **1.** remorseful, apologetic, regretful, ashamed. *She said she was sorry for being rude.* **2.** sad, unhappy, downcast, depressed. *We are sorry you missed the party.* **3.** miserable, wretched, pitiful, sad. *My mother said my room was in a sorry state.* **Ant. 1.** happy, unremorseful. **2.** pleased, joyful. **3.** fine, decent.

sort *n.* **1.** kind, type, manner, variety, brand. *She's not the sort of person who tells lies.* *–vb.* **2.** sift, search, comb, rummage, probe. *She sorted through the trash for her lost letter.* **3.** arrange, organize, categorize, classify, index. *Please sort the papers by subject matter.*

sound *n.* **1.** noise, clamor, racket, blare, ring, creak. *He heard the sound of music coming from the auditorium.* *–vb.* **2.** ring, toll, reverberate, peal, rumble. *The alarm sounded throughout the city.* **3.** seem, appear, look. *Your trip sounds interesting.* **4.** pronounce, voice, express, articulate. *Please sound out the long words.* *–adj.* **5.** strong, sturdy, solid, undamaged, firm. *The inspector said the old house is still sound.* **Ant. 5.** unsound, unstable, shaky, damaged.

sour *adj.* **1.** tart, vinegary, tangy, bitter, acidic. *Lemons have a sour taste.* **2.** spoiled, curdled, fermented, bad. *I think the old milk is sour.* *–vb.* **3.** spoil, curdle, ferment, turn. *The milk soured after several weeks.* **Ant. 1.** mild, pleasant, sweet. **2.** fresh, good.

source *n.* **1.** origin, head, beginning, start. *The river's source is high in the mountains.* **2.** informant, advisor, reference, authority. *He used several magazine sources for his term paper.* **Ant. 1.** end, termination, outcome.

souvenir *n.* keepsake, memento, reminder, remembrance. *Tourists often bring back souvenirs.*

sovereign *n.* **1.** monarch, emperor, ruler, lord, queen, king. *The peasants bowed before their sovereign.* *–adj.* **2.** monarchical, imperial, absolute, supreme. *The peasants resented the ruler's sovereign power.* **3.** independent, self-ruling, self-governing. *The United States is a sovereign nation.*

space *n.* **1.** separation, gap, opening, break, span, interval. *Please leave a space between your first and last names.* **2.** area, expanse, room, distance, spread. *She needs her own personal space.* *–vb.* **3.** place, separate, order, arrange, distance. *He spaced his trophies a foot apart.*

spacious *adj.* roomy, sizable, large, uncrowded, vast. *The mansion was quite spacious.* **Ant.** crowded, small, tiny, narrow.

span *vb.* **1.** cover, cross, bridge, join, link. *A bridge spanned the river.* *–n.* **2.** length, range, stretch, duration, period. *A Sequoia tree's life span can be several thousand years.*

spare *vb.* **1.** save, rescue, exempt, withhold, pardon. *The pig was spared from the slaughterhouse.* **2.** sacrifice, afford, lend, give, relinquish. *Can you spare a dollar?* *–adj.* **3.** extra, unused, substitute, reserve. *She used her spare tire to replace the one that had gone flat.* **4.** lanky, lean, skinny, thin, gaunt. *My aunt is strong despite her spare build.* **Ant. 1.** condemn, doom, expose. **4.** large, stocky.

sparkle *vb.* **1.** glitter, twinkle, flash, shimmer, glimmer. *The gems sparkled in the treasure chest.* *–n.* **2.** spark, gleam, glitter, twinkle, dazzle. *There is a sparkle in his eyes when he laughs.*

sparse *adj.* scarce, scattered, scanty, thin, meager. *The Sahara Desert has sparse vegetation.* **Ant.** abundant, dense, lush, rank.

spasm *n.* seizure, contraction, convulsion, fit, cramp. *She had a painful spasm in her lower back.*

speak *vb.* talk, communicate, vocalize, converse, discuss, lecture. *She can speak in both English and Japanese.*

spear *n.* **1.** lance, harpoon, javelin, spike. *Early American Indians used spears to hunt buffalo.* –*vb.* **2.** pierce, lance, impale, spit. *The warrior speared the buffalo.*

special *adj.* **1.** distinctive, unique, individual, particular, exceptional, extraordinary. *She gave her boyfriend a special gift.* –*n.* **2.** specialty, highlight, feature, selection. *The restaurant's Thursday special is roast beef.*

specialty *n.* focus, specialization, competence, strength, distinction. *The scientist's specialty is Greek archaeology.*

species *n.* classification, category, type, breed, kind. *Dogs belong to the canine species.*

specific *adj.* detailed, precise, exact, definite, particular. *Please give more specific directions to your house.* **Ant.** general, vague, inexact, ambiguous.

specify *vb.* state, indicate, define, stipulate, detail, clarify. *When placing an order, please specify your shirt size.*

specimen *n.* sample, example, representative, piece, cutting. *The geologist brought back several rock specimens.*

speck *n.* fleck, particle, spot, drop, dot. *He wiped a speck of lint off his glasses.*

spectacle *n.* presentation, performance, pageant, extravaganza, sight. *We watched the fireworks spectacle.*

spectacular *adj.* sensational, impressive, remarkable, dramatic, magnificent. *The volcano erupted with a spectacular explosion.* **Ant.** unimpressive, ordinary, tame.

speculate *vb.* **1.** guess, ponder, contemplate, conjecture, hypothesize. *We can only speculate about her chances of success.* **2.** trade, gamble, venture. *The investment firm speculates in real estate.*

speech *n.* **1.** talk, oration, discussion, conversation, lecture. *The president's speech was televised nationally.* **2.** speaking, talking, dialect, language. *People's speech differs throughout the country.*

speed *n.* **1.** quickness, swiftness, haste, velocity, rapidity, promptness. *He solved the problem with amazing speed.* –*vb.* **2.** advance, further, promote, stimulate, assist. *Heat will speed the drying process.* **3.** race, whiz, shoot, rush, fly, zoom. *We watched cars speed around the racetrack.* **Ant. 1.** slowness, sluggishness. **2.** slow, halt. **3.** walk, crawl.

speedy *adj.* rapid, swift, quick, fast, fleet. *The pizza parlor promises a speedy delivery.* **Ant.** slow, late, unhurried, leisurely.

spell *n.* **1.** stretch, span, period, interval, bout. *We had a spell of bad weather.* **2.** enchantment, charm, bewitchment, incantation. *The sorceress cast an invisibility spell to cloak our escape.*

spend *vb.* **1.** pay, expend, invest, disburse, waste. *People often spend large sums of money on holiday gifts.* **2.** pass, occupy, fill. *She is going to spend the weekend at the beach.* **Ant. 1.** conserve, keep, maintain, save.

sphere *n.* **1.** globe, ball, oval, orb, spheroid. *A bowling ball has the shape of a sphere.* **2.** field, domain, realm, area, scope. *That subject is not within his sphere of knowledge.*

spice *n.* **1.** seasoning, herb, flavoring, relish. *The chef added spices to the soup.* **2.** relish, charm, appeal, zest. *Variety is the spice of life.* –*vb.* **3.** season, flavor, accent, enliven. *She spiced her muffins with nutmeg and cinnamon.*

spike *n.* **1.** peg, nail, stud, prong, point, barb. *Soccer shoes have spikes on their bottoms.* –*vb.* **2.** pierce, prick, spear, stick, impale. *I spiked the marshmallows with a skewer.*

spill *vb.* **1.** slosh, splash, empty, drop, pour. *Juice spilled out of the overturned glass.* –*n.* **2.** seepage, leakage, leak, outflowing. *It took many months to clean up the oil spill.* **3.** tumble, fall, plunge, roll, accident. *He took a bad spill on his bike.*

spin *vb.* **1.** turn, whirl, twirl, revolve, rotate. *The contestants will spin a giant wheel.* **2.** narrate, relate, tell, concoct, invent. *The old sailor liked to spin tall tales.* *–n.* **3.** turn, twirl, rotation, revolution. *She gave the wheel a spin.* **4.** ride, drive, jaunt, run. *We took a spin in the new car.*

spirit *n.* **1.** soul, essence, psyche, heart, life force. *Religious people believe their spirits will survive after death.* **2.** ghost, phantom, shade, wraith, ghoul. *She was afraid of evil spirits in the haunted house.* **3.** enthusiasm, energy, eagerness, zeal, bravery. *She lives life with a great deal of spirit.* **4.** mood, emotions, morale, resolve, feelings. *Our spirits were low after the team's loss.* **5.** alcohol, liquor, whiskey. *The liquor store sold several types of spirits.* *–vb.* **6.** abduct, kidnap, seize, snatch. *A kidnaper spirited away the two children.* **Ant. 1.** body, flesh. **3.** lifelessness, fearfulness, timidity.

spiritual *adj.* **1.** bodiless, nonmaterial, psychic, ghostly, supernatural. *The cemetery was haunted by spiritual creatures.* **2.** pious, devout, religious, holy, righteous. *The nuns led a spiritual life.* **Ant. 1.** physical, material. **2.** nonspiritual, secular, worldly.

spite *n.* **1.** resentment, malice, hatred, revengefulness. *That cruel remark was said out of spite.* *–vb.* **2.** annoy, irritate, provoke, needle, nettle. *He missed the party just to spite you.* **Ant. 1.** love, kindness, forgiveness. **2.** please, delight, humor.

splendid *adj.* magnificent, brilliant, remarkable, excellent, beautiful. *We were pleased by her splendid musical performance.* **Ant.** poor, unremarkable, dreadful, awful.

splendor *n.* magnificence, brilliance, beauty, nobility, glory. *The splendor of the palace is awe-inspiring.* **Ant.** dullness, drabness, plainness.

splice *vb.* join, connect, bind, graft, link, unite. *The editor spliced two pieces of film together.* **Ant.** cut, break, disconnect.

split *vb.* **1.** divide, separate, break, allocate, allot. *The friends plan to split the prize money between them.* **2.** burst, break, splinter, snap, rip. *The man's bulging suitcase split open.* *–n.* **3.** break, rift, separation, tear, rent. *These pants have a split in the seam.* *–adj.* **4.** mixed, divided, separated, ruptured, broken. *The judges said it was a split decision.* **Ant. 1.** join, unite, merge. **3.** merger, connection, closure. **4.** unbroken, whole, unanimous.

spoil *vb.* **1.** ruin, wreck, destroy, damage, impair. *The rain spoiled our plans for a picnic.* **2.** rot, decay, mold, sour, curdle. *Meat left out of the refrigerator will spoil.* **3.** pamper, baby, indulge, overindulge, coddle. *His wealthy parents have spoiled him.* *–n.* **4.** loot, plunder, booty, takings. *The pirates gloated over the spoils.* **Ant. 1.** improve, better. **2.** keep, preserve. **3.** discipline, toughen.

sponsor *n.* **1.** supporter, endorser, promoter, advisor, patron. *Her sponsor in the drug recovery program is very supportive.* *–vb.* **2.** finance, support, endorse, back, promote. *A local business has agreed to sponsor our softball team.*

spontaneous *adj.* impulsive, unplanned, unhesitating, automatic, natural. *Small children's actions are often quite spontaneous.* **Ant.** planned, deliberate, calculated.

sport *n.* **1.** game, athletics, competition, contest, recreation. *Her favorite sport is volleyball.* *–vb.* **2.** trifle, toy, play, frolic, romp. *The cat sported with an injured mouse.* **3.** display, exhibit, bear, wear, show off. *The car sported a sunroof.* **Ant. 1.** work, job. **2.** work, toil.

spot *n.* **1.** place, location, site, position, point. *The campers found a good spot for their tent.* **2.** dot, blot, mark, speck, dab. *The paint left a spot on her shirt.* *–vb.* **3.** sprinkle, speck, mark, dot, stain. *Spilled ink spotted the table.* **4.** detect, spy, see, observe, discover, perceive. *A detective spotted the suspicious man as he entered the airport.*

spout *vb.* **1.** spurt, squirt, gush, spew, erupt, discharge. *Water spouted from the broken pipe.* *–n.* **2.** vent, nozzle, nose, outlet. *Water shot out of the whale's spout.* **3.** jet, spray, fountain, flow, spurt. *A spout of water and steam emerged from the geyser.* **Ant. 1–3.** drip, dribble, trickle.

sprawl *vb.* flop, loll, slump, slouch, lie. *The tired track runner sprawled on the field.*

spray *n.* **1.** drizzle, droplets, shower, mist, foam, splatter. *Ocean spray soaked the front of the ship.* *–vb.* **2.** shower, drizzle, splatter, spatter. *The gardener sprayed water on his flowers.*

spread *vb.* **1.** stretch, extend, unfold, widen, increase. *The soldiers spread out to search the area.* **2.** cover, coat, smear, smooth, blanket. *She spread jam on her toast.* **3.** circulate, broadcast, distribute, radiate, scatter. *Please spread the word about the changes we've made.* –*n.* **4.** expansion, growth, increase, advance. *The fire's spread was aided by fierce winds.* **5.** range, expanse, sweep, stretch. *The rancher's spread is enormous.* **6.** cover, quilt, blanket, mantle. *The spread fell off my bed during the night.* **Ant. 1.** collect, compress. **3.** confine, suppress. **4.** shrinkage.

spring *vb.* **1.** jump, leap, bound, lunge, bounce. *A bobcat sprang from behind the bushes.* **2.** release, trigger, discharge, free. *The mouse sprang the trap when it ate the cheese.* **3.** emerge, arise, sprout, appear, spurt. *Flowers sprang up all over the hillside.* –*n.* **4.** hop, bounce, jump, leap, buoyancy. *There was a spring in the joyful woman's walk.* **5.** coil, spiral. *The mattress spring broke when I jumped on the bed.* **6.** pool, water hole, well, fountain. *The moose drank from a mountain spring.* **Ant. 1.** crawl, slither, creep, drop.

sprinkle *vb.* **1.** spray, shower, powder, splatter, spread. *We sprinkled the cookies with tiny candies.* **2.** drizzle, dribble, rain, shower, mist. *It may sprinkle during the night.* –*n.* **3.** scattering, smattering, dash, touch, trace. *There was a sprinkle of gray in his hair.* **4.** drizzle, shower, mist, dribble, rain. *Do we need an umbrella in this light sprinkle?*

sprout *vb.* **1.** develop, grow, blossom, bud, bloom, flower. *New buds sprouted on the tree.* –*n.* **2.** seedling, shoot, offshoot, stem. *She enjoys bean sprouts in her salad.*

spur *n.* **1.** incentive, stimulus, goad, encouragement, motive. *The extra money was a spur to the artist's progress.* –*vb.* **2.** goad, prod, encourage, hasten, stimulate. *The will to succeed spurred her on to great accomplishments.* **Ant. 1.** discouragement, curb, obstacle. **2.** restrain, discourage.

spurn *vb.* reject, dismiss, rebuff, scorn, disregard. *He spurned her offer of help.* **Ant.** accept, welcome.

spy *n.* **1.** agent, secret agent, mole, operative, saboteur. *The spy was caught stealing secret information.* –*vb.* **2.** snoop, scout, peep, pry, eavesdrop. *He was accused of having spied for the enemy.* **3.** glimpse, see, detect, observe, notice. *She spied the famous singer entering through the back door.*

squad *n.* unit, group, outfit, platoon, company, troop. *A special police squad was called in to dismantle the bomb.*

squalid *adj.* filthy, miserable, shabby, dingy, impoverished. *The poor family lived in squalid conditions.* **Ant.** royal, fine, attractive.

squall *n.* storm, gale, gust, flurry, tempest. *A sudden squall dropped ten inches of rain.*

squander *vb.* waste, misspend, misuse, blow, lavish. *She squandered her money on fancy cars.* **Ant.** save, hoard.

square *n.* **1.** quadrangle, quad, rectangle, block, box. *My room is shaped like a square.* **2.** plaza, park, marketplace, commons. *A band was playing in the town square.* –*vb.* **3.** agree, match, fit, conform, correspond. *His story squares with all the news reports.* **Ant. 1.** circle, triangle. **3.** disagree, differ.

squash *vb.* **1.** crush, smash, squeeze, mash, flatten. *The closing door squashed her hand.* **2.** suppress, strangle, smother, crush. *The dictator squashed all public demonstrations.* **Ant. 2.** encourage, support, back.

squat *vb.* **1.** crouch, stoop, hunker, hunch, kneel. *The camper squatted down by the fire.* **2.** settle, encamp, inhabit, live, dwell. *A homeless family squatted in the abandoned building.* –*adj.* **3.** thickset, chunky, short, stocky, pudgy. *The squat man was unable to reach the top shelf.* **Ant. 1.** stand. **3.** lean, lanky, slim.

squeal *vb.* **1.** shriek, yelp, screech, wail. *The pigs squealed in delight when the farmer fed them.* **2.** inform, tell, betray, incriminate. *My brother squealed on me.* –*n.* **3.** shriek, yelp, screech, scream. *The small child let out a squeal when he saw the snake.*

squeamish *adj.* queasy, nauseous, sick, upset, shaky. *Do you become squeamish when you dissect frogs?*

squeeze *vb.* **1.** stuff, crowd, jam, pack, compress. *Ten people squeezed themselves into the tiny car.* **2.** wring, crush, twist, force, press. *She* *squeezed juice from the orange.* –n. **3.** embrace, hug, crushing, pinching, pressing. *Please give your beach towel a good squeeze to remove any excess water.*

squelch *vb.* hush, quiet, quell, crush, squash. *The harsh government squelched all forms of protest.* **Ant.** encourage, provoke, arouse.

squirm *vb.* wiggle, wriggle, twist, jerk, shift. *A worm squirmed in the bird's beak.*

squirt *vb.* **1.** splash, spray, spurt, splatter, jet. *Juice squirted from the ripe tomato.* –n. **2.** spurt, spray, fountain, jet, stream. *My brother hit me with a squirt from his water pistol.*

stable *adj.* **1.** steady, fixed, firm, immovable, sound, enduring, lasting. *My parents have stable incomes that our family depends on.* –vb. **2.** pen, corral, house, quarter. *She stabled her horse in the nearest stall.* –n. **3.** barn, stall, corral, pen. *The donkeys were kept in a stable.* **Ant. 1.** unstable, unsteady, shaky, momentary.

stack *n.* **1.** heap, pile, mound, batch, bundle. *He poured syrup on his pancake stack.* **2.** smokestack, chimney, funnel, flue. *Smoke billowed from the factory's stack.* –vb. **3.** heap, pile, lump, load, assemble. *The clerk stacked bottles on the shelf.* **Ant. 3.** scatter, spread.

staff *n.* **1.** cane, stick, rod, pole, wand. *The sorceress used her staff to destroy the monster.* **2.** crew, force, team, employees, personnel. *The famous restaurant has a talented staff.* –vb. **3.** manage, tend, service, work. *Local residents staff the village inn.*

stage *n.* **1.** phase, step, level, leg, period. *Our movie is in the first stage of production.* **2.** platform, podium, dais, stand. *Curtains concealed the theater's stage.* **3.** theater, arena, location, setting, place. *The South was the stage for many Civil War battles.* –vb. **4.** perform, act, present, produce, dramatize. *The drama students staged a Shakespearean play.*

stagger *vb.* **1.** stumble, reel, lurch, sway, totter. *The injured woman staggered into the hospital.* **2.** stun, shock, startle, astound, jolt. *He was staggered by the news of his friend's death.* **3.** alternate, fluctuate, zigzag, overlap. *The theater staggered its seats.*

stagnant *adj.* motionless, stationary, inactive, stale, polluted. *Frogs often live in stagnant ponds.* **Ant.** moving, running, fresh, unpolluted.

stagnate *vb.* stop, pause, idle, decline, fester, rot. *The rate of unemployment rose when the nation's economy stagnated.* **Ant.** grow, flow, flourish, expand.

stain *n.* **1.** blot, blemish, mark, discoloration, smear. *She tried to remove the grass stains on her shoes.* –vb. **2.** blemish, dirty, blotch, smear, discolor. *The vicious rumor stained his good name.*

stake *n.* **1.** peg, spike, pin, picket, post. *A vampire can be killed by a stake through the heart.* **2.** jackpot, spoils, winnings, wager, bet. *The stakes were high in the horse race.* –vb. **3.** mark, outline, reserve, delimit. *The gold miner staked out a claim.* **4.** peg, spike, fasten, secure, lash. *The campers staked their tent to the ground.* **5.** bet, wager, gamble, invest, venture, risk. *I won't stake any money on his chances of winning.*

stale *adj.* hardened, moldy, dry, tasteless, bland. *These old doughnuts are rather stale.* **Ant.** fresh, tasty.

stalemate *n.* deadlock, draw, standstill, standoff, checkmate. *The driver and mechanic reached a stalemate concerning repair costs.* **Ant.** decision, resolution.

stalk *vb.* **1.** hunt, pursue, shadow, track, trail. *Leopards often stalk antelope.* **2.** stamp, march, stride, tramp, strut. *The angry woman stalked out of the room.* –n. **3.** stem, shaft. *He enjoys eating raw celery stalks.*

stall *n.* **1.** booth, stand, kiosk, store. *The farmer sold vegetables from a roadside stall.* **2.** stable, shed, pen, corral. *He put hay in the horse's stall.* –vb. **3.** stop, halt, interrupt, delay, linger. *The elevator stalled on the first floor.* **Ant. 3.** start, advance, continue.

stamina *n.* endurance, energy, fitness, ruggedness, hardiness. *It takes stamina to be a triathlete.*

stammer *vb.* **1.** stutter, falter, stumble, sputter. *People often stammer when giving speeches.* –n. **2.** stammering, stutter, stuttering. *Her stammer becomes noticeable when she is frightened.*

stamp *vb.* **1.** squash, mash, trample, crush, stomp. *Please make sure you stamp out your campfire.* **2.** label, mark, imprint, print, impress. *The postal clerk stamped "airmail" on the package.* –*n.* **3.** seal, mark, label, symbol, emblem. *Meat is required to have a USDA inspection stamp.*

stampede *n.* **1.** rush, flight, rout, scattering. *The rock band was overwhelmed by a stampede of fans.* **2.** flee, bolt, run, scatter, dash, panic. *The hunter's scent caused the elephants to stampede.*

stand *vb.* **1.** be upright, be vertical, be erect, rise. *Strong winds made it difficult to stand.* **2.** erect, place, set, put. *Please stand your skis in the corner.* **3.** last, remain, persist, exist, continue. *Egypt's pyramids have stood in the desert for thousands of years.* **4.** withstand, endure, bear, handle, undergo. *She didn't think she could stand the pain.* **5.** support, promote, argue, favor. *You should stand up for what you believe.* –*n.* **6.** resistance, defense, opposition, front. *The Indian tribe made a stand against the invading army.* **7.** viewpoint, opinion, position, policy. *What is your stand on this issue?* **8.** rest, support, platform. *We set the figurine on a wooden stand.* **9.** booth, stall, counter, table. *She bought refreshments at a food stand.* **10.** grove, copse, woodland, thicket. *We walked through a stand of redwood trees.* **11.** bleachers, grandstand. *He watched the ballgame from the stands.* **Ant. 1.** sit, lie, recline. **6.** withdrawal, retreat.

standard *n.* **1.** model, pattern, guidelines, principle, specification. *His family has strict standards of behavior.* **2.** flag, banner, pennant. *The castle's standard was placed on the highest tower.* –*adj.* **3.** usual, normal, regular, accepted, customary. *Driving on a road's left side is standard practice in Great Britain.* **Ant. 3.** unusual, abnormal, atypical.

staple *n.* **1.** resource, necessity, feature, essential. *Corn was a staple of many American Indian diets.* –*adj.* **2.** primary, basic, essential, fundamental, chief. *The staple food of several Asian countries is rice.* **Ant. 1.** extra, accessory. **2.** secondary, minor.

star *n.* **1.** sun, heavenly body, celestial body, red giant, white dwarf, quasar, pulsar. *Astronomers study distant stars.* **2.** celebrity, lead, principal, headliner, dignitary. *The talented actress was the star of the film.* –*vb.* **3.** feature, present, showcase, headline. *The movie will star my favorite actor.*

stare *vb.* **1.** gape, goggle, gaze, gawk, glare. *It's not polite to stare at people.* –*n.* **2.** gaping, goggling, ogling, scrutiny, regard. *I shut the door on the man's bold stare.*

start *vb.* **1.** begin, commence, activate, initiate. *My school starts on the eighth of September.* **2.** embark, leave, depart, set out. *They wish to start for the mountains later today.* **3.** establish, create, found, pioneer, launch. *My father started a new travel business.* **4.** jerk, twitch, flinch, jump, spring. *I started when the car honked its horn.* –*n.* **5.** beginning, onset, origin, inception, birth. *Runners lined up at the start of the race.* **6.** jerk, jar, jolt, twitch, spasm. *The loud noise gave him a start.* **Ant. 1.** finish, end, stop. **2.** delay, dawdle. **5.** finish, ending.

startle *vb.* surprise, scare, frighten, jolt, jar, shock. *The thunder's loud boom startled her.* **Ant.** calm, quiet, comfort, soothe.

starve *vb.* hunger, famish, wither, perish, die. *Many deer starved during the long and harsh winter.*

starvation *n.* famine, hunger, deprivation, malnutrition. *Many villagers died of starvation after drought destroyed their crops.* **Ant.** plenty, abundance.

state *n.* **1.** condition, stage, shape, form, situation. *Ice is a solid state of water.* **2.** republic, nation, country, dominion. *The state of Israel was founded in 1948.* –*adj.* **3.** governmental, federal, official, ceremonial. *The president attended the state dinner.* –*vb.* **4.** announce, declare, speak, proclaim, express. *Please clearly state your name and age.*

statement *n.* announcement, proclamation, declaration, explanation, comment. *The spokeswoman read the president's prepared statement.*

static *adj.* **1.** changeless, stationary, unvarying, stagnant, fixed. *He was bored by his static life.* –*n.* **2.** interference, crackling, humming. *Static often makes phone conversations difficult.* **Ant. 1.** changing, moving, dynamic. **2.** silence, quiet.

station *n.* **1.** terminal, depot, stop. *We picked up my grandparents at the train station.* **2.** position, post, assignment, placement, place. *The security guard was criticized for leaving his station.* **3.** headquarters, station house, office, center. *Our class was given a tour of the fire station.* –*vb.* **4.** post, place, assign, position. *The soldiers will be stationed in Europe.*

stationary *adj.* motionless, fixed, unmoving, steady, changeless. *The clouds appeared stationary in the windless sky.* **Ant.** moving, running, changing, varying.

stationery *n.* notepaper, paper, letterhead. *The secretary wrote a memo on the company's stationery.*

statue *n.* figure, likeness, image, sculpture, bust. *There is a huge statue of Abraham Lincoln in Washington, D.C..*

stature *n.* **1.** height, size, tallness. *That basketball player is a man of large stature.* **2.** status, rank, standing, importance, position. *The university's high stature was beyond question.* **Ant. 2.** inferiority, insignificance, lowliness.

status *n.* **1.** rank, standing, grade, position, significance. *Fancy cars are a symbol of high status to some people.* **2.** state, shape, condition, situation. *We questioned the park attendant on the status of the new ride.*

staunch *adj.* **1.** dedicated, loyal, devoted, firm, steadfast, solid. *The forest ranger was a staunch environmentalist.* –*vb.* **2.** stop, dam, check, halt, block. *She tried to staunch the flow of blood.* **Ant. 1.** unfaithful, shaky, hesitant, uncommitted. **2.** encourage, aid.

stay *vb.* **1.** remain, continue, dwell, persist, wait. *Let's stay at home since it's snowing.* **2.** check, curb, restrain, arrest, hinder. *The reinforced riverbank stayed the rising water.* –*n.* **3.** delay, suspension, postponement, deferment, break. *The lawyer requested a stay of sentencing.* **4.** vacation, visit, holiday, sojourn, stopover. *She enjoyed a one-week stay at camp.* **Ant. 1.** leave, go, depart. **2.** release, free. **3.** extension.

steady *adj.* **1.** stable, constant, regular, fixed, continuous. *The unemployed woman hoped to find a steady job.* –*vb.* **2.** balance, stabilize, brace, secure, support. *The tightrope walker steadied himself with a long pole.* **Ant. 1.**

unsteady, unstable, unreliable, shaky. **2.** unbalance, shake.

steal *vb.* **1.** rob, filch, snatch, pilfer, thieve. *The thief stole a diamond necklace.* **2.** sneak, creep, slink, slip. *The prisoner stole past the sleeping guards.* **Ant. 1.** give, replace.

stealthy *adj.* sneaky, sly, devious, shady, shifty. *A stealthy robber crept into the house.* **Ant.** obvious, conspicuous.

steam *n.* **1.** vapor, condensation, mist, moisture. *Steam rose from the kettle's spout.* –*vb.* **2.** heat, boil, cook, simmer, stew. *The chef will steam our vegetables.* **3.** sail, cruise, ply, run. *The boat steamed into port.*

steep *adj.* **1.** sheer, sharp, abrupt, sudden, vertical. *The train chugged up the steep mountainside.* –*vb.* **2.** soak, immerse, submerge, saturate. *The anthropologist steeped herself in the local culture.* **Ant. 1.** gentle, gradual, horizontal.

steer *vb.* guide, drive, pilot, conduct, navigate. *The driver steered his car down the winding road.*

step *n.* **1.** footstep, footfall, tread, walk, stride, pace. *The cave echoed with the sound of our steps.* **2.** act, measure, move, action, deed, stage. *Writing an outline should be your first step.* **3.** rung, stair, foothold. *How many steps does your ladder have?* –*vb.* **4.** move, stride, walk, pace, tread. *I stepped closer to read the poster's small print.*

sterilize *vb.* disinfect, clean, cleanse, purify. *A nurse sterilized my cut with alcohol.* **Ant.** infect, dirty.

stern *adj.* **1.** strict, sharp, severe, harsh, hard. *The police officer gave the motorist a stern warning.* –*n.* **2.** rear, back, end, tail. *The cargo was moved to the ship's stern.* **Ant. 1.** soft, gentle, kind. **2.** front, head.

stew *vb.* **1.** simmer, boil, cook, heat, seethe. *She let the meat and vegetables stew for several hours.* –*n.* **2.** mixture, mishmash, chowder. *His beef stew is quite good.*

stick *n.* **1.** branch, stem, switch, limb, twig. *We roasted the hot dogs on a stick.* –*vb.* **2.** puncture, pierce, prick, spear. *The nurse stuck a needle in my arm.* **3.** place, position, set, locate. *My boss stuck me in the back room.* **4.** fasten, glue, attach, paste, tape, pin. *Please stick this to the bulletin board.* **5.** hold, cling, adhere, stay. *Stick to the job you were assigned.* **Ant. 3.** remove, dislodge. **4.** unfasten, detach. **5.** break, separate.

sticky *adj.* **1.** gummy, clinging, gluey, adhesive. *Honey is very sticky.* **2.** humid, moist, wet, clammy, muggy. *His shirt clung to his back in the sticky weather.* **Ant. 1.** slippery. **2.** dry, arid.

stiff *adj.* **1.** rigid, taut, inflexible, inelastic, hard. *The handkerchief was stiff with dried paint.* **2.** strong, forceful, powerful, keen, intense. *Our plane was flying into a stiff wind.* **3.** difficult, hard, tough, laborious. *There is a stiff climb to the top.* **4.** harsh, severe, stern, strict, unsparing. *The criminal was given a stiff sentence.* **Ant. 1.** bendable, flexible, supple. **2.** weak, faltering. **3.** gentle, easy. **4.** soft, gentle, mild.

stifle *vb.* smother, choke, strangle, suppress, restrain. *The writer felt stifled by the government's harsh rules.* **Ant.** encourage, free, release.

stigma *n.* disgrace, shame, dishonor, blemish, taint. *The exconvict spent the rest of his life with the stigma of being a murderer.* **Ant.** honor, glory, acclaim.

still *adj.* **1.** motionless, calm, unmoving, peaceful, stationary. *A single ripple broke the pond's still waters.* **2.** silent, quiet, noiseless, hushed. *Late at night our house becomes very still.* –*n.* **3.** silence, quiet, hush, peacefulness, tranquillity. *The still of the night was broken by a loud crash.* –*adv.* **4.** yet, currently, nevertheless, nonetheless. *Are you still coming to the party?* –*vb.* **5.** silence, quiet, hush, calm, lull. *A lullaby stilled the crying baby.* **Ant. 1.** moving, turbulent, agitated. **2.** noisy, loud, boisterous. **3.** noise, commotion. **5.** disturb, upset, agitate.

stimulate *vb.* arouse, excite, awaken, quicken, spur. *A tour of the hospital stimulated my desire to become a doctor.* **Ant.** deaden, kill, dull.

stimulating *adj.* arousing, exciting, enlivening, exhilarating. *It was an evening of stimulating conversation.* **Ant.** dreary, boring, dull.

sting *vb.* **1.** prick, stab, bite. *The bee stung her face.* **2.** burn, irritate, chafe, smart. *Salt water stung my eyes.* **3.** pain, wound, insult, offend, anger. *I was stung by his cruel remark.* –*n.* **4.** prick, bite, nip, puncture, stab. *A bee sting may hurt for some time.* **5.** pain, hurt, distress, anguish. *The sting of her criticism stayed with him for days.* **Ant. 2.** soothe, caress. **3.** soothe, please. **5.** pleasure, caress.

stingy *adj.* **1.** miserly, cheap, ungenerous, sparing, tight. *My stingy friend never pays for dinner.* **2.** meager, slight, scanty, skimpy, lean. *The captives were given stingy amounts of food.* **Ant. 1.** generous, lavish. **2.** abundant, profuse.

stink *vb.* **1.** smell, reek. *This pile of unwashed clothes stinks.* –*n.* **2.** stench, reek, odor, fume, smelliness. *The stink of the frightened skunk filled the cage.* **Ant. 2.** perfume, fragrance.

stir *vb.* **1.** whip, beat, churn, mix, agitate. *Please stir the soup before it burns.* **2.** awaken, rouse, revive. *The bear stirred from its long hibernation.* **3.** whip, incite, excite, encourage, enflame. *He stirred up trouble in the schoolyard.* –*n.* **4.** movement, motion, rustle, flutter. *There was a stir in the audience when the popular singer entered.* **5.** upheaval, commotion, excitement, uproar, disturbance. *The scandal caused quite a stir in the small town.* **Ant. 3.** calm, deaden. **4.** stillness, silence. **5.** dullness, boredom.

stitch *n.* **1.** suture, loop, tack, tuck. *His deep wound required twelve stitches.* **2.** garment, article, piece, scrap. *I don't have a stitch to wear.* **3.** pain, ache, twinge, spasm, pang. *The runner got a stitch in her side.* –*vb.* **4.** mend, repair, sew, suture, connect. *I stitched the tear in my shirt.*

stock *n.* **1.** supply, store, inventory, hoard, reserve. *The store is running low on its stock of potato chips.* **2.** shares, capital, investments. *I own stock in my mother's company.* **3.** livestock, cattle, animals, herd. *The farmer rounded up his stock.* **4.** parentage, lineage, ancestry, line, breed. *My dog comes from pedigree stock.* –*adj.* **5.** regular, standard, basic, customary, staple. *Bread is a stock item at the supermarket.* –*vb.* **6.** supply, furnish, equip, outfit. *She stocked her cabinets with canned goods.* **Ant. 5.** irregular, unusual, extra. **6.** drain, empty.

stocky *adj.* thick, sturdy, burly, stout, solid. *The wrestler has a stocky build.* **Ant.** skinny, slender, delicate.

stomach *n.* **1.** belly, abdomen, gut, intestinal cavity. *His stomach hurt after eating so much* *candy.* **2.** liking, fondness, appetite, taste, desire. *She has no stomach for raw fish.* –*vb.* **3.** stand, endure, bear, abide, suffer. *She could not stomach the killing of animals for their furs.* **Ant. 2.** dislike, distaste. **3.** condemn, reject.

stone *n.* **1.** rock, pebble, cobble, boulder. *The old wall was built from stones.* **2.** gem, gemstone, jewel, diamond. *The jeweler polished the ring's stones.* –*vb.* **3.** pelt, bombard, batter. *In ancient times, criminals were sometimes stoned to death.*

stoop *vb.* **1.** bend, crouch, duck, squat, bow. *The tall woman stooped to enter the low doorway.* **2.** sink, resort, fall, succumb. *Why did he stoop to such petty thievery?* –*n.* **3.** slump, slouch, bend, droop, dip. *The elderly man stands with a stoop.*

stop *vb.* **1.** halt, pause, discontinue, tarry, rest. *We stopped at a gas station.* **2.** block, check, restrain, bar, prevent, intercept. *He stopped the small child from running into the street.* **3.** quit, discontinue, cease, desist, suspend, terminate. *Please stop grinding your teeth.* –*n.* **4.** end, halt, delay, finish, discontinuation. *The rain forced the coaches to call a stop to the game.* **5.** layover, break, rest, stay. *The plane makes a stop in Chicago.* **6.** station, terminal, depot. *A bus stop is on the corner of Broadway and First.* **Ant. 1.** continue, proceed. **2.** assist, encourage, speed. **3.** start, begin. **4.** start, continuation, resumption.

store *n.* **1.** market, supermarket, mart, shop, outlet. *He went to the store to buy groceries.* **2.** supply, stock, reserve, accumulation, hoard, lot. *Our store of toilet paper is almost gone.* –*vb.* **3.** save, keep, hoard, stash, stockpile, collect. *She stores extra vegetables in her basement.*

storm *n.* **1.** tempest, blizzard, hurricane, gale, downpour. *The ship sank in a heavy storm.* **2.** outbreak, outburst, outcry, rush, blast. *The mayor's announcement provoked a storm of protest.* –*vb.* **3.** pour, howl, rain, snow. *It stormed for seven nights.* **4.** rage, rave, rush, thunder, stomp. *The angry woman stormed into the store, demanding a refund.* **5.** attack, assault, charge, assail, raid. *Peasants stormed their wicked landlord's castle.*

story *n.* **1.** tale, fable, legend, narrative, anecdote. *My favorite story is "Pinocchio."* **2.** report, account, tidings, description, version. *I don't know whether I believe his story.* **3.** floor, level, terrace, deck. *Her apartment is on the building's seventh story.*

stout *adj.* **1.** thickset, husky, brawny, stocky. *The humans and elves were accompanied by five stout dwarves.* **2.** bold, fearless, loyal, brave, determined. *The warrior was known to be of stout heart.* **Ant. 1.** thin, lean, spare. **2.** fearful, weak, cowardly.

straggle *vb.* lag, stray, ramble, drift, tarry. *I was so tired that I straggled behind everyone else.*

straight *adj.* **1.** unbent, unswerving, perpendicular, plumb, even. *Please stand in a straight line.* **2.** true, truthful, honest, reliable, accurate. *I want a straight answer this time.* **3.** orderly, tidy, arranged, neat. *Is your room straight?* **4.** continuous, unbroken, uninterrupted, consecutive. *There's been five straight days of bad weather.* –*adv.* **5.** directly, immediately, instantly, now. *Please go straight to bed.* **6.** straightly, upright, erectly, evenly. *The photographer asked us to stand up straight.* **Ant. 1.** crooked, curved, bent. **2.** false, untruthful, unreliable. **3.** messy, disarranged. **4.** broken, interrupted. **5.** indirectly, eventually. **6.** crookedly, unevenly.

strain *vb.* **1.** labor, struggle, strive, stretch, extend, fatigue, tax. *The runner strained to keep up with the group.* **2.** sprain, wrench, pull, twist. *He strained his back lifting the heavy box.* **3.** filter, sieve, drain, sift. *Please strain the peas.* –*n.* **4.** drain, drag, burden, stress, tension, pressure. *The unexpected medical expenses were a strain on our budget.* **5.** breed, family, variety, type, stock. *Where did you find this strain of wheat?* **6.** melody, tune, theme. *I recognize that strain of music.* **7.** streak, trace, grain, trait. *There is a strong strain of rebellion in her.* **Ant. 1.** relax, loosen, yield.

strand *vb.* **1.** ground, wreck, maroon, abandon. *The shipwreck stranded them on a desert island.* –*n.* **2.** shore, beach, coast, seashore. *He walked along a strand of white sand.* **3.** filament, fiber, thread, string. *There is a strand of hair in my soup.*

strange *adj.* weird, unusual, peculiar, odd, unfamiliar, exotic. *The science-fiction movie had some really strange creatures.* **Ant.** normal, usual, familiar.

stranger *n.* newcomer, outsider, foreigner, alien, immigrant. *She was a stranger to our town.* **Ant.** resident, friend, acquaintance.

strangle *vb.* choke, throttle, suffocate, smother, stifle. *The boa constrictor strangled the small animal.*

strap *n.* **1.** tie, fastening, thong, lash, belt. *His backpack strap broke.* –*vb.* **2.** lash, tie, fasten, bind, attach. *She strapped her boots into the snowshoe bindings.* **Ant. 2.** unfasten, untie, remove.

strategy *n.* tactic, plan, arrangement, method, blueprint. *The coach revealed a new strategy for tomorrow's game.*

stray *vb.* **1.** wander, roam, rove, ramble, range, drift. *A little lamb strayed from the herd.* –*n.* **2.** lost animal, waif, vagabond. *Several strays showed up on her doorstep.* –*adj.* **3.** lost, wandering, homeless, abandoned, unclaimed. *He fed the stray cat.*

streak *n.* **1.** band, stripe, line, bar, bolt. *There were streaks of gold in her sun-bleached hair.* **2.** period, interval, bout, spell, touch. *The gambler had a streak of bad luck.* –*vb.* **3.** mark, stripe, striate, band, stain. *His face was streaked with dirt and sweat.* **4.** flash, dash, race, sprint, fly, zoom. *Several bicyclists streaked across the finish line.* **Ant. 4.** crawl, limp.

stream *n.* **1.** river, creek, brook, rivulet, tributary. *She went fishing in the small mountain stream.* **2.** flow, jet, current, gush. *The kite soared on a stream of wind.* –*vb.* **3.** flow, rush, surge, cascade, spill. *A herd of caribou streamed past our cabin.*

street *n.* road, avenue, boulevard, highway, freeway, lane. *We crossed the street at a light.*

strength *n.* **1.** power, might, muscularity, brawn, vigor, force. *The elephant is an animal of great strength.* **2.** intensity, seriousness, firmness, resolution. *No one could question the strength of his convictions.* **3.** mainstay, forte, greatness, competence. *Debating is one of her strengths.* **Ant. 1–2.** weakness, feebleness. **3.** frailty, shortcoming.

strengthen *vb.* reinforce, renew, fortify, enhance, buttress. *The army was strengthened with two new battalions.* **Ant.** weaken, undermine.

strenuous *adj.* vigorous, energetic, laborious, active, tiring. *The doctor told the sick woman to avoid strenuous exercise.* **Ant.** relaxed, lazy, easy.

stress *n.* **1.** distress, strain, tension, anxiety, worry. *During exams, students often experience stress.* **2.** emphasis, weight, significance, importance, urgency. *There is a lot of stress placed on achieving good grades.* –*vb.* **3.** emphasize, underscore, accent, highlight. *Her parents stressed the importance of a good education.* **Ant. 1.** peacefulness, calm, serenity. **2.** unimportance, insignificance. **3.** deemphasize, ignore.

stretch *vb.* **1.** extend, expand, widen, lengthen, spread. *The desert stretched on for miles.* –*n.* **2.** spell, expanse, spread, distance, sweep. *The truck hit a stretch of rough road.* **3.** elasticity, give, spring, flexibility. *Rubber is a material with a lot of stretch.* **Ant. 1.** shrink, contract, retract, narrow.

strict *adj.* unyielding, stern, inflexible, rigid, exact. *His parents were strict about his curfew.* **Ant.** lax, flexible, permissive.

strife *n.* conflict, fighting, hatred, unrest, discord. *Several Middle Eastern countries have experienced years of strife.* **Ant.** peace, quiet, calm.

strike *vb.* **1.** hit, smack, knock, punch, pound. *Her snowball struck me on the arm.* **2.** attack, charge, assault, raid. *A group of evil trolls struck the village just before midnight.* **3.** impress, affect, reach, please, seem. *Her idea struck me as a workable plan.* **4.** eliminate, cancel, remove, erase, delete. *A two-night stay in Paris was struck from the tour agenda.* **5.** ring, toll, sound. *The clock struck twelve.* **6.** picket, protest, walk out, boycott. *The workers will strike for better wages.* –*n.* **7.** blow, smack, knock, pounding. *We heard the strike of the blacksmith's hammer.* **8.** attack, assault, raid, charge. *The general launched a strike against the enemy.* **9.** walkout, protest, boycott. *The workers called a strike after negotiations broke down.* **Ant. 1.** caress, pat, stroke. **4.** add.

strip *vb.* **1.** peel, skin, scrape, remove, clear. *We plan to strip the old paint off our wall.* **2.** undress, disrobe, uncover. *He stripped before entering the bathtub.* –*n.* **3.** band, ribbon, belt, slat, stripe. *We pulled our boat up on a strip of beach.* **Ant. 1.** replace, add, restore. **2.** dress, cover.

stripe *n.* band, bar, streak, line, striation, score. *The tiger had stripes on her coat.*

stroke *n.* **1.** hit, blow, smack, clip, knock. *The ball entered the hole on the golfer's second stroke.* **2.** seizure, attack, collapse. *My grandmother suffered a stroke yesterday.* **3.** sounding, peal, knell, toll. *The New Year begins at the stroke of midnight.* **4.** flourish, movement, dash. *She marked the incorrect answers with a stroke of her pen.* **5.** happening, event, occurrence, accomplishment, achievement. *Finding you here was a stroke of good fortune.* *–vb.* **6.** caress, fondle, pet, rub, pat. *He stroked the kitten's head.*

stroll *vb.* **1.** walk, amble, meander, wander, ramble. *She strolled down the shaded avenue.* *–n.* **2.** walk, ramble, saunter, excursion. *We took a stroll along the beach.* **Ant. 1.** race, run, dash. **2.** run, dash.

strong *adj.* **1.** powerful, mighty, brawny, muscular, sturdy. *Weightlifters are quite strong.* **2.** firm, unbending, deep, dedicated. *The monks had very strong religious beliefs.* **3.** intense, potent, concentrated, sharp, bitter. *The cough medicine has a strong taste.* **4.** distinct, notable, pronounced. *The sound of the waves was quite strong from where we stood.* **5.** clear, sharp, quick, competent, keen. *He has a strong grasp of the essentials.* **Ant. 1.** weak, feeble, frail. **2.** weak, shallow, shaky. **3.** weak, bland, tasteless. **4.** weak, inconclusive. **5.** weak, slight, slim.

structure *n.* **1.** building, construction, erection. *The parking structure has five levels.* **2.** arrangement, form, pattern, construction, configuration. *The structure of the mineral was quite complex.* *–vb.* **3.** build, form, construct, design, arrange. *This class will be structured around outside field trips.*

struggle *vb.* **1.** fight, battle, wrestle, scuffle, labor. *The lion struggled to get out of its cage.* *–n.* **2.** fight, battle, labor, striving, push. *Civil-rights activists wage a constant struggle against discrimination.* **Ant. 1.** surrender, yield.

stubborn *adj.* unmovable, unbending, headstrong, dogged, relentless. *The stubborn explorers refused to turn back.* **Ant.** wavering, hesitant, indecisive.

student *n.* pupil, scholar, learner, trainee. *There are 500 students at my school.* **Ant.** teacher, professor.

study *vb.* **1.** read, learn, research, meditate, cram. *He usually studies at the library.* *–n.* **2.** learning, examination, reading, research, exploration. *She finds the study of computer languages interesting.* **3.** office, library, workroom, room. *My parents do their work in the study.*

stuff *n.* **1.** goods, things, articles, material. *What sort of stuff did you buy at the store?* *–vb.* **2.** pack, fill, cram, jam, load. *The pillow was stuffed with feathers.* **Ant. 2.** empty, drain, unpack.

stuffy *adj.* **1.** suffocating, sweltering, airless, close, muggy. *He began to sweat in the stuffy room.* **2.** congested, clogged, filled. *People with colds often suffer from stuffy noses.* **3.** reserved, pompous, smug, dull, cold. *He is so stuffy at formal dinners.* **Ant. 1.** airy, ventilated. **2.** open, unblocked. **3.** friendly, natural.

stumble *vb.* trip, fall, stagger, blunder, tumble. *I stumbled over an exposed tree root.*

stump *vb.* perplex, puzzle, baffle, bewilder, mystify. *She was stumped by the difficult puzzle.*

stun *vb.* shock, surprise, astonish, jar, overwhelm. *News of his arrest stunned us.*

stunning *adj.* dazzling, electrifying, astonishing, striking, brilliant. *The football player made a stunning catch.* **Ant.** dull, unimpressive, unremarkable, mild.

stunt *vb.* **1.** dwarf, slow, curb, check, arrest. *Too much darkness will stunt a plant's growth.* *–n.* **2.** feat, exploit, trick, number, act, performance. *The motorcyclist's favorite stunt was riding through a burning hoop.* **Ant. 1.** speed, stimulate.

stupefy *vb.* stun, daze, dumbfound, astonish, confuse. *We were stupefied by his decision to join the Foreign Legion.*

stupid *adj.* dumb, unintelligent, dense, mindless, foolish. *A stupid dog stood in the middle of the busy street.* **Ant.** intelligent, bright, clever.

stupor *n.* coma, daze, numbness, insensibility, lethargy. *The man was in a drunken stupor.*

sturdy *adj.* rugged, strong, tough, durable, solid. *She bought a sturdy backpack for her difficult journey.* **Ant.** fragile, frail.

stutter *vb.* **1.** stammer, sputter, falter, hesitate. *He often stutters when telling a lie.* *-n.* **2.** stammer, stammering, stuttering. *The speaker had a pronounced stutter.*

style *n.* **1.** fashion, design, form, pattern, shape, arrangement. *She wears a short hairstyle.* *-vb.* **2.** fashion, design, form, shape, arrange. *He styled his hair with a blow dryer.*

stylish *adj.* fashionable, elegant, chic, dapper, modish. *My stylish friend is always shopping for new clothes.* **Ant.** unstylish, unfashionable, outmoded.

subdue *vb.* pacify, check, overwhelm, restrain, silence. *Bystanders tried to subdue the violent woman.* **Ant.** inflame, arouse, excite.

subdued *adj.* unresponsive, unemotional, quiet, hushed, solemn. *The subdued audience did not react to his emotional speech.* **Ant.** excited, emotional, loud.

subject *n.* **1.** theme, topic, substance, matter, question. *The subject of my report is solar energy.* **2.** course, discipline, study, topic. *His favorite school subject is geography.* *-vb.* **3.** expose, bare, submit, give, treat. *She subjected me to hours of worry by not calling.*

subjective *adj.* personal, individual, biased, nonobjective. *Musical taste is subjective.* **Ant.** objective, impersonal, unbiased.

submerge *vb.* **1.** sink, plunge, dip, immerse. *The submarine submerged.* **2.** drown, flood, engulf, deluge, immerse. *Flood waters submerged the low field.* **Ant. 1.** surface, emerge. **2.** uncover, bare.

submit *vb.* **1.** present, offer, proffer, propose. *The reporter submitted a story to his editor.* **2.** yield, surrender, accept, endure, tolerate. *The patient refused to submit to any more testing.*

subordinate *n.* **1.** assistant, aide, underling, junior, employee. *She gave the unpleasant jobs to her subordinates.* *-adj.* **2.** inferior, lower, junior, auxiliary, secondary. *A vice-president is subordinate to a president.* **Ant. 1.** superior, boss, chief. **2.** superior, senior.

subscribe *vb.* take, accept, support, buy, purchase. *The saleswoman wanted me to subscribe to several magazines.*

subsequent *adj.* next, following, ensuing, successive, succeeding. *Subsequent issues of the comic book will arrive each month.* **Ant.** previous, earlier.

subside *vb.* decrease, diminish, shrink, dwindle, lessen. *The waves subsided as the storm passed.* **Ant.** increase, rise, grow.

subsist *vb.* survive, live, last, remain, continue. *The lost explorers had to subsist on nuts and berries.* **Ant.** die, perish.

substance *n.* **1.** material, matter, ingredient, element. *The spaceship was made from a special substance.* **2.** reality, solidity, actuality, essence, meaning. *There is no substance to your accusations.* **3.** wealth, property, riches, means. *Only a person of substance could afford that expensive house.*

substantial *adj.* great, large, sizable, considerable, significant. *She won a substantial amount of money in the state lottery.* **Ant.** small, tiny, insignificant.

substitute *n.* **1.** replacement, backup, alternative, relief, reserve. *Our class was taught by a substitute today.* *-vb.* **2.** replace, change, exchange, swap, switch. *I usually substitute margarine for butter.* *-adj.* **3.** alternative, temporary, secondary, replacement. *The substitute teacher was harassed by several students.* **Ant. 2.** keep, maintain. **3.** original, primary.

subtle *adj.* inobvious, delicate, elegant, understated, refined. *Your plea for money was not very subtle.* **Ant.** obvious, blunt.

subtract *vb.* remove, deduct, withdraw, diminish. *Five subtracted from twelve is seven.* **Ant.** add.

succeed *vb.* prosper, flourish, thrive, triumph. *She wanted to succeed at her new job.* **Ant.** fail, falter, flounder.

success *n.* accomplishment, achievement, triumph, prosperity. *The wealthy man had great success with his investments.* **Ant.** failure, downfall, disaster.

successful *adj.* **1.** effective, victorious, fruitful, triumphant. *I was successful in convincing my friend to come with me.* **2.** rich, prosperous, wealthy, renowned. *She was a successful businesswoman.* **Ant. 1.** unsuccessful, ineffective. **2.** unsuccessful, unprosperous.

successive *adj.* consecutive, succeeding, following, adjacent, subsequent. *The earthquake was followed by two successive tremors.*

succumb *vb.* yield, surrender, submit, capitulate. *The tired woman succumbed to sleep.* **Ant.** resist, fight.

sudden *adj.* unexpected, unannounced, unforeseen, abrupt, instant. *The driver was forced to make a sudden stop.* **Ant.** expected, gradual, foreseen.

sue *vb.* beg, plead, petition, appeal, ask, entreat. *The losing army sued for peace.*

suffer *vb.* **1.** hurt, ache, agonize. *The boy suffered from the pain in his leg.* **2.** sustain, experience, tolerate, endure, withstand, bear. *Do what I say, or suffer the consequences.*

sufficient *adj.* enough, adequate, abundant, satisfactory. *I think I have sufficient funds for only two more weeks.* **Ant.** insufficient, inadequate, unsatisfactory.

suffocate *vb.* smother, gag, choke, strangle. *The firefighter almost suffocated in the smoke-filled room.*

suggest *vb.* propose, offer, recommend, urge, advise. *I suggested that she take an aspirin for her headache.*

suggestion *n.* advice, counsel, recommendation, proposal. *I followed his suggestion and bought the less expensive car.*

suggestive *adj.* **1.** remindful, reminiscent, expressive, indicative. *The color was suggestive of a red wine.* **2.** indecent, improper, shameless, tasteless. *He posed in a very suggestive manner.* **Ant. 2.** decent, tasteful, modest.

suit *n.* **1.** outfit, costume, attire, clothing, tuxedo. *He wears business suits to formal meetings.* **2.** appeal, petition, case, request, plea. *Her suit for leniency was denied.* –*vb.* **3.** satisfy, please, content, delight, fit. *My small car suits me just fine.* **4.** clothe, dress, equip, furnish. *The astro-*naut suited up for her space walk. **Ant. 3.** dissatisfy, displease.

suitable *adj.* right, appropriate, proper, qualified, fit. *Do you think he is suitable for the job?* **Ant.** unsuitable, inappropriate, unfit.

sulk *vb.* **1.** pout, mope, grouch, grouse, brood. *She sulked when we said she couldn't come.* –*n.* **2.** pout, snit, sulkiness, grumpiness. *Why did he go off in a sulk?*

sullen *adj.* resentful, sulky, bitter, angry, glowering. *She gave us a sullen look for punishing her.* **Ant.** pleasant, cheerful, happy.

sum *n.* **1.** total, amount, value, result. *The sum of five plus six is eleven.* –*vb.* **2.** add, total, calculate, compute. *The student summed up his total points.* **3.** summarize, review, outline, close, conclude. *Please sum up your report in a few words.* **Ant. 2.** subtract.

summary *n.* **1.** review, digest, outline, breakdown, analysis. *The teacher asked us to write a summary of the book we read.* –*adj.* **2.** brief, condensed, compact, shortened, abridged. *He provided her with a summary report.* **Ant. 2.** complete, lengthy, detailed, unabridged.

summit *n.* peak, tip, pinnacle, top, crest. *The climbers rested after reaching the mountain's summit.* **Ant.** bottom, base.

summon *vb.* **1.** call, order, ask, command. *She was summoned to the principal's office for misbehaving.* –*n.* **2.** order, directive, call, notification. *The soldier received his summons to active duty.*

sunken *adj.* submerged, submersed, immersed, drowned. *The sailors spoke of a sunken treasure lying off the coast.* **Ant.** floating, surface.

sunny *adj.* **1.** sunlit, cloudless, clear, radiant, bright. *It's fun to have a picnic on a sunny day.* **2.** cheerful, smiling, happy, joyful, jolly. *She has a very sunny outlook on life.* **Ant. 1.** cloudy, overcast, dark. **2.** gloomy, unhappy, unsmiling.

sunrise *n.* dawn, daybreak, sunup, daylight. *She woke early, to see the sunrise.* **Ant.** sunset, dusk, twilight.

sunset *n.* dusk, twilight, nightfall, sundown. *We must try to get back before sunset.* **Ant.** sunrise, dawn, daybreak.

superb *adj.* excellent, admirable, praiseworthy, magnificent, fine. *The students did a superb job on this year's musical.* **Ant.** poor, bad, terrible, awful.

superficial *adj.* shallow, surface, skin-deep, external. *He suffered only superficial cuts.* **Ant.** deep, internal.

superior *adj.* **1.** exceptional, unrivaled, first-rate, lofty, admirable. *She feels that Cadillacs are superior cars.* –*n.* **2.** supervisor, manager, boss. *All final decisions are made by my superior.* **Ant.** **1.** inferior, poor, average. **2.** inferior, employee, subordinate.

supernatural *adj.* mystical, spectral, occult, spiritual, otherworldly. *Do you believe in supernatural things like ghosts?* **Ant.** natural, worldly.

supervise *vb.* oversee, administer, manage, direct, govern. *Please supervise your younger sister while I go to the store.* **Ant.** neglect, ignore.

supervisor *n.* manager, boss, administrator, chief, commander. *The supervisor made sure the employees were doing their jobs.* **Ant.** underling, subordinate.

supplement *n.* **1.** addition, complement, attachment, extra, continuation. *A vitamin supplement was recommended by the doctor.* –*vb.* **2.** increase, extend, enlarge, augment, fortify. *She supplements her allowance with money from baby-sitting.*

supply *vb.* **1.** provide, equip, furnish, outfit. *The company supplies nearby hospitals with medicine.* –*n.* **2.** store, stock, reserve, hoard. *The hikers ate their entire supply of chocolate.*

support *vb.* **1.** brace, prop, uphold, sustain. *Thick concrete columns supported the bridge.* **2.** back, champion, favor, aid, assist. *Her friends supported her in the class election.* –*n.* **3.** brace, post, pillar, buttress. *The bridge collapsed when its supports gave way.* **4.** help, aid, assistance, backing, encouragement. *He received financial support from his parents while he was away at college.*

suppose *vb.* guess, imagine, think, assume, believe. *Do you suppose we will get out of class early?*

suppress *vb.* stop, restrain, curb, smother, squelch. *They tried to suppress their laughter during the movie.* **Ant.** unleash, express, encourage.

supreme *adj.* **1.** highest, top, chief, head, primary. *The general is the supreme commander in Europe.* **2.** outstanding, prime, unequaled, superlative, matchless. *The restaurant's hamburgers are supreme.* **Ant.** **1.** lowest, secondary. **2.** poor, mediocre.

sure *adj.* **1.** certain, positive, definite, confident, convinced. *She was sure she saw something move behind the bushes.* **2.** firm, solid, steady, reliable. *The surgeon had a sure hand.* **Ant.** **1.** unsure, uncertain, doubtful. **2.** unsure, shaky, unsteady.

surely *adv.* doubtlessly, definitely, certainly, assuredly. *Surely you don't believe in Big Foot?*

surface *n b.* **1.** top, crust, exterior, outside, skin. *The road's surface was cracked.* –*adj.* **2.** exterior, outer, outward, superficial. *The quick washing only removed the surface dirt.* –*vb.* **3.** rise, ascend, emerge, appear, materialize. *Dolphins surface to breathe.* **4.** cover, overlay, pave, blanket. *A maintenance crew surfaced the street with fresh asphalt.* **Ant.** **1.** interior, insides, depths. **2.** interior, internal, inside. **3.** submerge, descend, sink. **4.** uncover, expose.

surmise *vb.* **1.** guess, imagine, conjecture, assume, conclude. *I can only surmise why she left without telling anyone.* –*n.* **2.** guess, assumption, conjecture, idea, opinion. *My surmise is that he quit because of the low pay.*

surmount *vb.* overcome, conquer, top, climb, master. *The student surmounted his reading difficulties.*

surpass *vb.* exceed, outdo, outperform, outshine, transcend. *The new spaceship surpasses all others in speed.*

surplus *n.* **1.** excess, oversupply, glut, overload. *A food surplus was kept in the warehouse.* –*adj.* **2.** extra, excess, unused, remaining, spare. *The store sold surplus army equipment.*

surprise *vb.* **1.** astonish, amaze, startle, shock, stun. *The movie's ending surprised me.* –*n.* **2.** wonder, amazement, astonishment, marvel, shock. *It was a surprise to see him after so many years.* **Ant. 1.** bore, weary.

surprising *adj.* astonishing, amazing, startling, unusual, unexpected. *There was a surprising snowstorm last summer.* **Ant.** expected, routine, predictable.

surrender *vb.* **1.** yield, release, relinquish, submit. *The defenders surrendered their castle to the victorious attackers.* *–n.* **2.** yielding, submission, resignation, relinquishment. *The losing army announced its surrender.*

surround *vb.* circle, ring, enclose, envelop, bound. *A moat surrounds the castle.*

survey *vb.* **1.** review, scan, observe, inspect, assess. *A critic surveyed the painting.* *–n.* **2.** poll, investigation, review, study, examination, assessment. *The survey said that half the town's residents were employed locally.*

survival *n.* living, continuation, continuance. *A nuclear war would threaten the survival of the entire planet.* **Ant.** death, ending.

survive *vb.* live, persist, endure, exist, withstand. *They hoped the injured horse would survive.* **Ant.** die, perish, succumb.

susceptible *adj.* vulnerable, defenseless, receptive, open, sensitive. *Malnutrition leaves people susceptible to disease.* **Ant.** unsusceptible, invulnerable, unreceptive.

suspect *vb.* **1.** mistrust, distrust, question, doubt. *I suspect his intentions.* **2.** guess, imagine, think, suppose, surmise. *I suspect it will rain tomorrow.* *-adj.* **3.** questionable, suspicious, doubtful, dubious, debatable. *The dishonest woman's story was suspect.* *-n.* **4.** accused, defendant, culprit. *The police said they had no suspects in the case.* **Ant. 1.** trust, believe. **2.** know. **3.** trustworthy, reliable.

suspend *vb.* **1.** hang, dangle, sling. *She suspended the bird feeder from her porch.* **2.** postpone, withhold, delay, defer. *Mother suspended my allowance because I told a lie.* **3.** expel, dismiss, eject, evict. *He was suspended from school for fighting.*

suspense *n.* uncertainty, tension, anticipation, apprehension, edginess. *Horror movies are filled with suspense.*

suspension *n.* stay, interruption, postponement, halt, pause. *The boy's suspension from school will last one week.* **Ant.** continuation, restoration.

suspicion *n.* **1.** mistrust, distrust, doubt. *He was under suspicion for last night's burglary.* **2.** idea, feeling, guess, hunch, notion. *I had a suspicion that she was the one who did it.* **Ant. 1.** trust, confidence.

sustain *vb.* **1.** bear, carry, endure, tolerate, continue. *The runner could not sustain the rapid pace.* **2.** nourish, nurture, feed, maintain. *The lost hiker had only candy bars to sustain himself.*

swallow *vb.* **1.** gulp, guzzle, imbibe, swill, bolt. *The boy swallowed his aspirin with a glass of water.* *–n.* **2.** gulp, drink, sip, mouthful. *She took a swallow from the canteen.*

swamp *n.* **1.** marsh, bog, morass, quagmire, everglade. *Alligators live in Florida's coastal swamps.* *–vb.* **2.** flood, deluge, submerge, saturate, overwhelm. *The singer was swamped with fan letters.*

swap *vb.* trade, exchange, switch, barter, substitute. *My friend and I swap comic books.*

swarm *n.* **1.** horde, host, cloud, multitude, throng. *A swarm of locusts darkened the sky.* *–vb.* **2.** crowd, flock, mass, throng, congregate. *People swarmed around the popular singer.* **Ant. 2.** scatter, separate, disperse.

swat *vb.* **1.** hit, whack, slap, knock, smack. *She tried to swat the fly with her magazine.* *–n.* **2.** hit, slap, whack, smack. *He gave the tennis ball a good swat.*

swear *vb.* **1.** promise, pledge, vow, affirm, assert. *She swore she would tell the truth.* **2.** curse, cuss. *Please do not swear when you're angry.*

sweep *vb.* **1.** brush, whisk, wipe, push, clear, dust. *Will you sweep the leaves off the patio?* *–n.* **2.** swoop, push, drive, thrust, stroke. *The police sweep resulted in the arrest of several suspected drug dealers.* **3.** stretch, span, spread, range, measure, reach. *A sweep of white beach extended down the coast.*

sweet *adj.* **1.** sugary, candied, rich, honeyed. *Candy is much too sweet for me to eat.* **2.** kind, nice, gracious, affectionate, friendly. *It was really* *sweet of her to send flowers.* **Ant. 1.** sour, bitter. **2.** selfish, inconsiderate.

swell *vb.* **1.** rise, increase, inflate, bulge, puff. *His sprained ankle swelled to twice its normal size.* –*n.* **2.** wave, breaker, comber, rise, hill. *The raft rose up on an ocean swell.* **Ant. 1.** descend, shrink, lower. **2.** dip, depression.

swelling *n.* lump, inflammation, bulge, protuberance. *The boxer had a swelling under his bruised eye.* **Ant.** depression, indentation.

swelter *vb.* sweat, broil, cook, bake, roast, wilt. *We sweltered in the desert heat.*

swerve *vb.* twist, turn, veer, shift, move. *The driver swerved to miss a cat.*

swift *adj.* fast, rapid, quick, fleet, brisk, nimble. *The cheetah is a swift runner.* **Ant.** slow, sluggish.

swindle *vb.* **1.** cheat, trick, con, bilk, deceive, defraud. *She swindled me out of several hundred dollars.* –*n.* **2.** fraud, trick, deception, hoax, racket. *He was arrested for cheating people in a stock swindle.*

swing *vb.* **1.** sway, seesaw, lurch, hurl, rock. *An ape swung through the trees.* **2.** curve, veer, twist, turn, swerve. *The road swings to the left.* –*n.* **3.** swaying, rocking, rolling, motion, vibration. *The swing of the rope bridge made it difficult to get across.* **4.** stroke, sweep, swat. *The batter took a swing at the ball.*

swirl *vb.* **1.** whirl, spin, twist, twirl, swish. *Water swirled down the drain.* –*n.* **2.** whirl, twist, twirl. *I would like a swirl of chocolate on my sundae.*

switch *vb.* **1.** exchange, swap, trade, change, shift. *Will you switch seats with me?* –*n.* **2.** change, alteration, shift, swap, trade. *I made a switch in my vacation plans.* **3.** branch, twig, stick, rod, whip. *The shepherd used a switch to drive the lambs forward.*

sword *n.* blade, saber, cutlass, rapier, foil. *The king's jeweled sword hung at his side.*

symbol *n.* figure, sign, emblem, image, representation. *The bald eagle is a symbol for America.*

symmetrical *adj.* balanced, proportional, even, regular, parallel. *Individual snowflakes are symmetrical, but no two are alike.* **Ant.** asymmetrical, unbalanced, uneven.

sympathize *vb.* empathize, relate, agree, appreciate, understand. *I can really sympathize with your fear of speaking in front of crowds.* **Ant.** disagree, belittle.

sympathy *n.* understanding, empathy, concern, compassion, support. *I expressed my sympathy to the owner of the dog killed in the accident.* **Ant.** indifference, aloofness, insensitivity, disinterest.

symptom *n.* sign, signal, indication, trait, feature. *His headache is only one symptom of his illness.*

synthetic *adj.* artificial, manufactured, unnatural, imitation. *Polyester is a synthetic material.* **Ant.** natural, organic, genuine.

system *n.* **1.** setup, structure, layout, arrangement. *What type of computer system does she have?* **2.** method, methodology, plan, practice, procedure. *Do you understand our billing system?*

table *n.* **1.** stand, counter, bench, bar. *Please set the table for dinner.* **2.** index, list, chart, tabulation, schedule, catalog, itemization. *This science book has many useful photographs, drawings, and tables.* *-vb.* **3.** delay, postpone, defer, shelve, put aside. *The city council tabled discussion of the controversial new ordinance.* **Ant. 3.** resume, continue, proceed, begin, start, initiate.

tablet *n.* **1.** pad, writing pad, notebook, sketchbook. *The university bookstore stocks a large supply of writing tablets.* **2.** pill, capsule, lozenge, drop. *Medicinal tablets come in a large variety of sizes and shapes.*

taboo *adj.* **1.** prohibited, banned, forbidden, outlawed, illicit, unacceptable. *During the Middle Ages, many scientific theories were taboo subjects.* *-n.* **2.** prohibition, ban, restriction, limitation. *Many religions have taboos against eating certain types of meat.* **Ant. 1.** permissible, acceptable, approved, allowed, permitted. **2.** acceptance, approval, endorsement, sanction.

tacit *adj.* implied, understood, assumed, acknowledged, unspoken, unstated. *The roommates had a tacit agreement to keep their apartment neat and clean.*

tack *vb.* **1.** fasten, attach, affix, pin, nail. *Tack this notice up where everyone can see it.* *-n.* **2.** strategy, course, plan, policy, approach, method. *The new chairwoman hoped to start her department off on a fresh tack.* **Ant. 1.** remove, detach, take down, take off.

tackle *vb.* **1.** undertake, take on, attack, attempt, accept, assume, embrace, begin, start. *Don't tackle a project you can't finish.* **2.** capture, catch, intercept, seize, grab, stop. *The quarterback was tackled before he could pass the ball.* *-n.* **3.** gear, equipment, apparatus, paraphernalia, materials, tools. *Since fishing was out of season, she left her tackle at home.* **4.** ropes, roping, rigging, cordage. *He used a block and tackle to extract the car's engine.* **Ant. 1.** avoid, evade, reject, forgo, hesitate, delay, postpone.

tact *n.* discretion, diplomacy, delicacy, judgment, finesse, consideration, courtesy. *Embarrassing situations sometimes require lots of tact to avoid hurting a person's feelings.* **Ant.** tactlessness, insensitivity, indiscretion, crudeness.

tactful *adj.* considerate, sensitive, thoughtful, delicate, diplomatic, discrete, polite. *A considerate manager tries to be tactful when dealing with an employee's mistake.* **Ant.** tactless, untactful, blunt, indiscrete, indelicate, clumsy, thoughtless, insensitive.

tactic *n.* plan, strategy, policy, scheme, course, approach, method, system. *The millionaire employed questionable tactics in the pursuit of her fortune.*

tactless *adj.* impolite, inconsiderate, insensitive, thoughtless, rude, untactful, tasteless, undiplomatic. *His tactless remarks offended everyone at the party.* **Ant.** tactful, considerate, thoughtful, diplomatic, polite.

tag *n.* **1.** label, marker, ticket, tab, slip, sticker. *Check the price tag to see how much it costs.* *-vb.* **2.** mark, label, identify, classify, ticket. *Please tag these for immediate delivery.* **3.** follow, tail, trail, accompany, shadow. *Her dog tags along wherever she goes.*

tail *n.* **1.** appendage, extension, attachment, back, rear. *He could see the comet's tail through his telescope.* *-vb.* **2.** follow, trail, shadow, pursue. *The detective tailed two suspects.* *-adj.* **3.** rearmost, hindmost, final, last, concluding. *A marching band brought up the tail end of the parade.* **Ant. 1.** front, head. **3.** beginning, foremost, front, start.

taint *n.* **1.** stain, blot, blemish, impurity, imperfection, defilement, contamination. *The one incident made a permanent taint on his reputation.* *-vb.* **2.** spoil, rot, putrefy, decay, contaminate, ruin. *Refrigerate this meat or it will taint.* **3.** tarnish, blemish, blight, besmear, soil, stain. *Her remarks were tainted with prejudice.* **Ant. 2.** purify, disinfect, clean. **3.** boost, enhance, elevate.

take *vb.* **1.** obtain, acquire, seize, get, gain, have. *Take a number and wait your turn.* **2.** carry, bring, move, transport, transfer, haul, fetch. *Many students take their books home every day.* **3.** escort, guide, conduct, chaperon, usher. *Take your little brother to the movies with you.* **4.** remove, appropriate, confiscate, steal, rob, misappropriate. *Who took my car?* **5.** swallow, consume, ingest, eat, drink. *Take two aspirin and get some rest.* **6.** tolerate, endure, suffer, undergo, accept, abide, go through. *Her parents couldn't take any more of her loud music.* **7.** subtract, deduct, remove, eliminate, withdraw. *Take 30 from 40 to get 10.* **8.** understand, interpret, comprehend, grasp, perceive, infer. *I take your silence to mean you're unhappy with me.* **9.** accept, heed, follow, observe, obey. *Take my word for it.* **10.** demand, require, necessitate, need, entail. *This report will take three days to prepare.* **11.** cheat, defraud, swindle, trick, bilk. *The con artist took me for a hundred dollars.* **12.** attract, fascinate, enchant, charm, bewitch. *He seems to be taken with you.* **Ant. 1.** release, relinquish, surrender, return, let go. **4.** return, restore, surrender. **7.** add, annex, affix, attach. **9.** reject, spurn, renounce, repudiate. **12.** repel, repulse, disgust.

tale *n.* **1.** story, narrative, anecdote, yarn, report, account. *The traveler had many fascinating tales to share.* **2.** lie, fib, fabrication, falsehood, fiction. *Mark Twain was a literary master of the tall tale.*

talent *n.* skill, ability, gift, aptitude, capability, capacity, expertise. *She has a talent for playing the piano.*

talented *adj.* gifted, brilliant, expert, skilled, proficient. *She is a talented artist.* **Ant.** untalented, unskilled, mediocre.

talk *n.* **1.** conversation, chat, discussion, conference, dialogue, consultation. *The parents wanted to have a talk with their son about the late hours he'd been keeping.* **2.** lecture, speech, address, discourse, oration. *A local celebrity gave a talk to our class.* **3.** gossip, rumor, hearsay, tales, stories, comments. *There's been some talk going around about the actress and her new boyfriend.*

–vb. **4.** speak, converse, discuss, chat, communicate, confer, consult. *We need to talk about your new proposal.*

talkative *adj.* garrulous, loquacious, long-winded, windy, verbose. *The talkative man was continuously interrupting everyone else.* **Ant.** silent, mute, quiet, taciturn.

tall *adj.* towering, high, lofty, long, lengthy, soaring. *She gets dizzy looking up at tall buildings.* **Ant.** short, squat, low.

tame *adj.* **1.** domesticated, broken, subdued, submissive, docile, timid, mild, obedient. *The animal trainer liked to pet his tame lion.* **2.** unexciting, bland, boring, uninteresting, dull, commonplace, tedious. *Life ashore seemed pretty tame to the veteran sailor.* *–vb.* **3.** domesticate, break, train, discipline, soften, subdue, moderate. *She likes to tame wild animals.* **Ant. 1.** untamed, undomesticated, wild, feral, savage, fierce. **2.** exciting, stimulating, thrilling, interesting.

tamper *vb.* interfere, intrude, meddle, change, alter, mess, fool. *The writer hoped his publisher would not tamper with his manuscript.*

tang *n.* flavor, taste, quality, aroma, trace, hint, suggestion. *This spaghetti sauce has a tang of garlic.*

tangible *adj.* substantial, solid, obvious, concrete, real, physical, material. *She presented tangible proof of her innocence.* **Ant.** intangible, vague, imaginary.

tangle *vb.* **1.** twist, snarl, knot, muddle, mess, ravel, dishevel. *A strong breeze tangled the wind chime.* *–n.* **2.** snarl, knot, mess, maze, morass, muddle. *The cat turned the ball of yarn into a hopeless tangle.* **Ant. 1.** untangle, disentangle, unravel, untwist.

tantrum *n.* outburst, fit, scene, snit, storm, rampage. *The spoiled child went into a tantrum whenever he didn't get what he wanted.*

tap *n.* **1.** rap, pat, knock, light blow, strike, touch. *Who wouldn't be startled by a tap at the window on a dark and stormy night?* **2.** faucet, spigot, spout, valve. *The outside tap froze last night.* *–vb.* **3.** rap, pat, drum, strike, knock. *She tapped her feet in time to the music.* **4.** use, utilize, draw on, exploit, manipulate. *The runner tapped all her reserves to finish the marathon.*

tape *n.* **1.** strip, ribbon, band, roll, reel, spool. *This measuring tape is 50 feet long.* –*vb.* **2.** wrap, bind, tie, seal, secure, fasten. *Tape the package securely before mailing it.* **3.** record. *He taped his favorite TV show.* **Ant. 2.** unwrap, untie, unfasten. **3.** delete.

taper *vb.* decrease, lessen, abate, diminish, dwindle, slacken, weaken. *The storm tapered off at sunset.* **Ant.** increase, strengthen, intensify.

target *n.* goal, objective, object, end, aim, mark. *Their target is to complete the project by next summer.*

tarnish *n.* **1.** discoloration, stain, blemish, spot. *The unused silver bowl had accumulated a solid coat of tarnish.* –*vb.* **2.** dim, dull, darken, oxidize, discolor, corrode, stain. *The silverware has tarnished.* **3.** taint, besmear, defile, disgrace, darken, blemish, soil. *His public image was tarnished by the scandal.* **Ant. 2.** brighten, shine, sparkle, gleam. **3.** enhance, heighten, improve, strengthen.

tarry *vb.* linger, loiter, dawdle, dally, delay, procrastinate, remain, wait, stay. *Don't tarry or we'll miss the movie.* **Ant.** hurry, hasten, rush.

tart *adj.* **1.** sour, acid, sharp, tangy, bitter. *These strawberries are too tart.* **2.** biting, cutting, caustic, acerbic, sharp. *The radio announcer was known for her tart commentaries.* **Ant. 1.** sweet, sugary, honeyed, mild, flat. **2.** pleasant, gentle, kind, polite, friendly.

task *n.* assignment, obligation, responsibility, job, chore, duty, work. *His task is to wash the dishes.*

taste *n.* **1.** flavor, savor, savoriness, essence, tang. *I'll never forget the taste of fresh strawberries.* **2.** judgment, discernment, propriety, discrimination, decorum. *Racist jokes are in very poor taste.* **3.** preference, inclination, penchant, fondness, liking. *She has a taste for good literature.* –*vb.* **4.** savor, sample, experience, partake of, encounter, test. *Have you ever tasted anything so good?* **Ant. 3.** distaste, dislike, objection, aversion. **4.** miss, elude.

tasteful *adj.* elegant, aesthetic, beautiful, artistic, becoming, discriminating. *The socialite always dressed in a tasteful way.* **Ant.** tasteless, unbecoming, vulgar, inelegant, ugly.

tasteless *adj.* **1.** tactless, gauche, unrefined, rude, crude, crass, coarse, vulgar, offensive, improper. *His tasteless remark offended all his co-workers.* **2.** flavorless, bland, savorless, insipid, dull, boring. *The school cafeteria is known for its tasteless food.* **Ant. 1.** tasteful, elegant, refined. **2.** tasteful, tasty, flavorful.

tattered *adj.* ragged, frazzled, frayed, torn, shabby, shoddy. *The accident-prone lion trainer has a tattered appearance.*

taunt *n.* **1.** jeer, gibe, scoff, insult, slur, provocation, ridicule. *The short boy dreaded the cruel taunts of his classmates.* –*vb.* **2.** deride, ridicule, insult, provoke, torment, harass. *Why is it some people taunt anyone less fortunate than themselves?* **Ant. 1.** praise, compliment. **2.** commend, flatter, praise.

taut *adj.* tight, tense, drawn, extended, firm, rigid, stiff, stretched, strained. *Please hold this string taut.* **Ant.** slack, loose, flexible.

tavern *n.* bar, barroom, saloon, pub, inn, alehouse, roadhouse. *Jim Hawkins met Long John Silver in a tavern.*

tax *n.* **1.** tariff, levy, excise, assessment, duty. *Americans have to pay their income taxes on April 15th.* **2.** burden, strain, imposition, responsibility, duty, chore. *Putting three children through college was a severe tax on her financial resources.* –*vb.* **3.** assess, levy. *The government taxes everything we make.* **4.** burden, strain, encumber, load, saddle, exhaust, weaken. *The hyperactive child taxed his parents' patience.*

teach *vb.* educate, instruct, lecture, inform, enlighten, tutor, train. *Will you teach me Spanish?* **Ant.** learn, study.

team *n.* **1.** group, unit, company, crew, band, squad. *She tried out for the basketball team.* –*vb.* **2.** pair, couple, unite, join, combine, mate. *Let's team up to get this project done faster.* **Ant. 2.** unjoin, uncouple, separate.

tear *n.* **1.** teardrop, drop. *The child was no longer crying, but there were still tears in his eyes.* –*vb.* **2.** water, swim, mist. *Peeling an onion made her eyes tear.*

tear *n.* **1.** rip, split, rent, gap, break, damage, injury. *There's a tear in your jeans.* *–vb.* **2.** rip, rend, split, pull, apart, shred, divide. *Tear up this old sheet to get the rags you need.* **3.** rush, dash, bolt, race, charge, hustle, scramble. *The cat tore out of the yard with a dog in hot pursuit.* **Ant. 2.** patch, mend, repair, sew. **3.** saunter, amble, stroll.

tease *vb.* taunt, ridicule, provoke, heckle, torment, pester, annoy, harass, bother. *Try not to tease your little sister.* **Ant.** commend, flatter, praise, compliment.

technique *n.* procedure, method, system, approach, skill, form, style. *The golfer spent considerable time perfecting her technique.*

tedious *adj.* dreary, irksome, weary, tiresome, boring, monotonous, uninteresting, routine. *Memorizing multiplication tables is a tedious task.* **Ant.** interesting, exciting, challenging, stimulating.

teeming *adj.* overflowing, overrun, swarming, bristling, dense, thick. *The forest was teeming with mosquitoes.* **Ant.** empty, unoccupied, vacant.

teeter *vb.* wobble, sway, stagger, lurch, weave. *His heart pounded as he teetered on the brink of the precipice.*

tell *vb.* **1.** narrate, describe, relate, recite, speak, utter, voice, express, impart, convey, communicate. *The children love to have their grandfather tell stories.* **2.** order, direct, command, bid, require. *You'd better do what you're told.* **3.** distinguish, discern, determine, discover, perceive, ascertain. *Can you tell good apples from bad ones?* **4.** reveal, divulge, disclose, apprise, inform. *Could you tell me what time it is?* **Ant. 3.** confuse, mix up.

temper *n.* **1.** rage, anger, fury, ire, wrath, outburst, irritation, passion. *She yelled at him in a fit of temper.* **2.** mood, disposition, composure, self-control. *He loses his temper easily.* *–vb.* **3.** moderate, soften, soothe, pacify, quiet. *It is wise to temper justice with mercy.* **4.** toughen, harden, strengthen, fortify, anneal. *Her resolve was tempered by the many injustices she had endured.* **Ant. 1.** calmness, composure. **3.** intensify, increase, arouse. **4.** soften, weaken.

temperamental *adj.* moody, irritable, excitable, capricious, volatile, passionate, emotional. *Artists, poets, and musicians are among the most temperamental people I know.* **Ant.** serene, steady, calm, stable, unexcitable.

temperate *adj.* **1.** mild, pleasant, agreeable, clement, mellow, balmy. *Miami is blessed with a temperate climate.* **2.** moderate, restrained, controlled, self-controlled, composed, collected, rational, reasonable. *Temperate eating habits are rare on Thanksgiving Day.* **Ant. 1.** intemperate, inclement. **2.** excessive, extreme, unrestrained.

tempest *n.* storm, gale, commotion, turmoil, uproar, clamor, tumult. *When the teacher assigned two new books, the class erupted in a tempest of protest.* **Ant.** peace, quiet, calm, serenity.

tempo *n.* pace, rate, speed, velocity, measure, beat, rhythm. *She's leading her life at too fast a tempo.*

temporary *adj.* momentary, passing, transient, fleeting, short, brief, short-lived. *She's holding a temporary job while searching for a career position.* **Ant.** permanent, lasting, long-lived, enduring.

tempt *vb.* attract, entice, induce, invite, lure, lead on, seduce, tantalize. *He was having so much fun that he was tempted to extend his vacation.* **Ant.** discourage, dissuade, repel, repulse.

temptation *n.* attraction, enticement, lure, allurement, pull, draw. *A chocolate sundae is a temptation that's hard to resist.*

tempting *adj.* attractive, alluring, enticing, inviting, provocative, appetizing, tantalizing. *That pizza sure looks tempting.* **Ant.** unattractive, uninviting, repulsive.

tenacious *adj.* determined, stubborn, obstinate, persistent, strong, firm, clinging, set, unyielding. *The dog had a tenacious grip on his master's slipper.* **Ant.** lax, slack, loose, yielding.

tenant *n.* occupant, resident, inhabitant, dweller, renter, lodger, leaseholder. *Have you met the new tenants next door?*

tend *vb.* **1.** lean, incline, verge, be disposed. *She tends to spend too much time playing computer games.* **2.** protect, watch, guard, attend, look after, care for, supervise. *Will you tend my plants while I'm on vacation?* **Ant. 2.** neglect, ignore, disregard.

tendency *n.* inclination, leaning, disposition, trend, bias, bent, propensity, penchant, habit. *He has a tendency to sleep late.* **Ant.** disinclination, aversion.

tender *adj.* **1.** soft, gentle, caring, compassionate, kindhearted, warm, warmhearted, affectionate, fond, loving. *The lioness was very tender with her cubs.* **2.** delicate, frail, fragile, weak, soft, vulnerable. *Because of her dental problems, she could only eat tender foods.* **3.** sore, uncomfortable, painful, sensitive, aching, troublesome. *His sprained ankle is still tender.* *–vb.* **4.** offer, bid, present, propose, submit, advance, suggest, give. *The unhappy employee tendered her resignation.* **Ant. 1.** callous, harsh, unfeeling, heartless, insensitive. **2.** tough, strong, sturdy. **3.** painless, insensitive. **4.** retract, withdraw.

tense *adj.* **1.** stretched, strained, taut, tight, drawn, stiff. *His arms were tense from doing too many push-ups.* **2.** nervous, anxious, apprehensive, fearful, excited, uneasy, uptight, jittery. *She was very tense just before her math final.* **Ant. 1.** slack, loose, limp, relaxed. **2.** relaxed, calm, cool.

tentative *adj.* conditional, unconfirmed, contingent, provisional, indefinite, temporary. *The new employee has been given a tentative work schedule.* **Ant.** confirmed, definite, settled, final.

tenuous *adj.* weak, thin, small, feeble, insubstantial, shallow, uncertain. *He has only a tenuous grip on reality.* **Ant.** strong, firm, sound, solid, substantial.

term *n.* **1.** word, name, expression, phrase, appellation. *This dictionary has an extensive listing of computer terms.* **2.** period, time, interval, duration, session, season. *She was elected for a term of two years.* **3.** condition, stipulation, provision, detail, item, limit. *What are the terms of your agreement with your parents?*

terminal *adj.* **1.** concluding, final, end, last, fatal, lethal, mortal. *His cancer was in its terminal stage.* *–n.* **2.** station, terminus, end, depot. *You'll find her at the computer terminal.* **Ant. 1.** initial, beginning, first, nonlethal.

terminate *vb.* finish, end, conclude, stop, cease, discontinue, expire, halt. *Her temporary job terminates next week.* **Ant.** begin, start, commence, inaugurate.

terrible *adj.* horrible, horrid, horrifying, awful, dreadful, fearful, frightful, alarming. *A terrible earthquake devastated Mexico City.* **Ant.** pleasant, mild, harmless.

terrific *adj.* **1.** great, superb, magnificent, wonderful, marvelous, extraordinary, splendid. *It was a terrific movie.* **2.** terrible, horrible, awful, dreadful, severe, intense, huge. *The storm did terrific damage.* **Ant. 1.** mediocre, poor, bad, unpleasant. **2.** minor, moderate, slight.

terrify *vb.* frighten, scare, alarm, terrorize, horrify, petrify, appall, dismay. *The thought of a major earthquake terrifies many Southern Californians.* **Ant.** reassure, comfort, soothe, calm.

territory *n.* domain, region, area, terrain, locale, realm, district. *A grizzly bear roams over a territory of about 100 square miles.*

terror *n.* fear, dread, horror, panic, alarm, apprehension, anxiety. *The child was filled with terror at the approach of a thunderstorm.*

terse *adj.* brief, concise, short, curt, succinct, crisp. *Her terse comments indicated she was displeased.* **Ant.** lengthy, long, wordy, verbose, rambling.

test *n.* **1.** examination, exam, quiz, analysis, investigation, trial. *You have to take a test to get a driver's license.* *–vb.* **2.** examine, question, quiz, analyze, investigate, assess, check. *The manufacturer thoroughly tested the new product before releasing it.*

testify *vb.* affirm, declare, swear, attest, state, confirm, substantiate. *Will there be anyone to testify on your behalf?*

testimony *n.* declaration, statement, oath, evidence, proof, affirmation. *The victim's testimony led to a conviction.*

text *n.* **1.** textbook, schoolbook, book, manual, tome. *The class is using the same text as last semester.* **2.** words, wording, contents, subject, topic, theme. *The local newspaper printed the full text of the mayor's speech.*

textile *n.* woven fabric, knitted fabric, cloth, material, fiber. *Cotton is the most commonly used textile in the garment industry.*

texture *n.* structure, composition, consistency, character, quality, nature, touch, feel. *Frozen yogurt has a pleasingly smooth texture.*

thankful *adj.* grateful, appreciative, obliged, gratified, pleased. *He was very thankful for the pay raise.* **Ant.** thankless, ungrateful, unappreciative.

thankless *adj.* unappreciated, unacknowledged, unheeded, unrewarded. *Cleaning up after a party is a thankless chore.*

thaw *vb.* **1.** defrost, soften, warm, melt, dissolve. *Frozen hamburger should be thawed before frying.* –*n.* **2.** melting, warming, thawing. *Many animals come out of hibernation during spring's first thaw.* **Ant. 1.** freeze, solidify, stiffen, harden. **2.** freeze, frost.

theater *n.* **1.** playhouse, cinema, stage, auditorium, hall. *When you said you were going to the theater, I didn't know if you meant a movie or a play.* **2.** site, field, setting, scene, sector, zone. *The army was prepared to cope with a widespread theater of operations.*

theft *n.* robbery, stealing, larceny, burglary, pilfering, looting. *She was heartbroken by the theft of her wedding ring.*

theme *n.* **1.** topic, subject, point, thesis, premise, argument. *Do you understand the theme of this novel?* **2.** essay, article, composition, paper, report. *He has to write a theme for his English class.*

theory *n.* hypothesis, assumption, conjecture, speculation, guess, deduction, proposition, idea, explanation. *Everyone had a theory about who had committed the crime.* **Ant.** proof, certainty, knowledge.

therefore *adv.* consequently, accordingly, hence, thus, then, ergo. *She has a cold and therefore could not go to school.* **Ant.** but, however, nevertheless.

thick *adj.* **1.** broad, deep, hefty, bulky, thickset, massive, large. *He improvised a bookshelf from concrete blocks and thick boards.* **2.** viscous, syrupy, condensed, concentrated, heavy, solid. *She likes thick and chunky spaghetti sauce.* **3.** crowded, dense, tight, swarming, teeming, crammed. *The forest was thick with hunters.* **Ant. 1.** slim, slender, thin, narrow, small. **2.** diluted, watery, runny, liquid. **3.** bare, barren, empty, void.

thief *n.* burglar, robber, bandit, pilferer, criminal, crook, racketeer, swindler, defrauder. *A thief stole my new watch.*

thin *adj.* **1.** slim, lean, slender, skinny, gaunt, narrow, flimsy, slight. *Pencil lead is very thin.* **2.** watery, diluted, weak, runny, diffused, scant, sparse, spare. *This soup is too thin for my tastes.* –*vb.* **3.** diminish, reduce, decrease, weaken, dilute, water down. *His hair has begun to thin on top.* **Ant. 1.** thick, fat, stout, wide, bulky. **2.** heavy, thick, dense, concentrated. **3.** thicken, increase, concentrate.

thing *n.* **1.** object, entity, article, being, item. *Anyone know what this thing is?* **2.** matter, circumstance, condition, factor, quality, attribute, feature. *There's not a thing wrong with me.* **3.** statement, utterance, thought, expression, point. *I haven't heard a single thing you've said.* **4.** possession, belonging, personal effect, clothing, apparel, attire. *Will all your things fit in this closet?* **5.** act, action, deed, feat, accomplishment. *A good artist can do incredible things with a blank canvas.*

think *vb.* **1.** reason, reflect, ponder, meditate, contemplate, speculate, deliberate, rationalize. *Let's think about it before making a decision.* **2.** believe, presume, suppose, propose, guess, assume, imagine, conclude. *Do you think it'll rain today?*

thinking *adj.* **1.** thoughtful, contemplative, pensive, meditative, intelligent, smart. *Chess is a thinking person's game.* –*n.* **2.** thought, reasoning, reflection, calculation, judgment. *He acted without thinking.* **Ant. 1.** unthinking, thoughtless.

thirst *n.* **1.** longing, craving, yearning, desire, hunger, yen, appetite. *She has a nearly insatiable thirst for knowledge.* –*vb.* **2.** crave, covet, desire, want, long, ache, yearn. *The art collector thirsted for an original Van Gogh.* **Ant. 1.** aversion, distaste, revulsion, dislike.

thorough *adj.* total, complete, entire, full, perfect, absolute, exhaustive. *The doctor gave his* *patient a thorough physical.* **Ant.** incomplete, partial, imperfect, inadequate, careless.

thought *n.* **1.** thinking, reasoning, reflection, idea, concept, notion, judgment, opinion, belief. *Do you have any thoughts on the subject being discussed?* **2.** intent, intention, plan, design, purpose, aim, goal, objective. *It's his thought to take a vacation next summer.*

thoughtful *adj.* **1.** kind, kindhearted, considerate, attentive, caring, concerned, courteous. *Visiting her in the hospital was a thoughtful thing for you to do.* **2.** contemplative, meditative, reflecting, reflective, thinking. *She's in a thoughtful mood.* **Ant. 1.** unkind, inconsiderate, mean. **2.** thoughtless, unreflective.

thoughtless *adj.* **1.** careless, heedless, regardless, neglectful, inattentive, stupid, dumb. *This report reflects thoughtless and hasty writing.* **2.** rude, discourteous, impolite, inconsiderate, insensitive, unkind. *Your comment about the weight he's gained was very thoughtless.* **Ant. 1.** thoughtful, careful, intelligent. **2.** thoughtful, polite.

thrash *vb.* flog, whip, beat, trounce, punish, defeat, conquer, vanquish. *She thrashed her opponent on the tennis court.*

threat *n.* warning, intimidation, omen, menace, danger, risk, peril, hazard. *This year's drought poses a threat to our crops.* **Ant.** protection, reassurance.

threaten *vb.* **1.** intimidate, menace, warn, imperil, terrorize, bully. *His teacher threatened to fail him if he didn't start trying harder.* **2.** portend, forebode, augur, loom, impend, indicate. *The approaching cold front threatens snow.* **Ant. 1.** protect, defend, reassure.

threshold *n.* **1.** entrance, entranceway, doorsill, doorway, gateway. *Many visitors have tripped on our raised threshold.* **2.** verge, beginning, outset, start, edge, brink, opening, dawn. *Humanity is on the threshold of conquering outer space.* **Ant. 2.** end, close, conclusion, finish, twilight.

thrifty *adj.* economical, economizing, saving, frugal, sparing, conserving, careful. *The thrifty shopper is constantly on the lookout for sales.* **Ant.** wasteful, extravagant, uneconomical, prodigal.

thrill *n.* **1.** excitement, joy, pleasure, stimulation, sensation, adventure. *She gets her thrills riding roller coasters.* –*vb.* **2.** excite, delight, stimulate, move, arouse, please. *The parents were thrilled when their daughter was accepted into law school.* **Ant. 1.** boredom, tedium. **2.** bore, tranquilize, annoy.

thrilling *adj.* exciting, stirring, moving, fascinating, sensational. *Winning a gold medal was the most thrilling moment of his life.* **Ant.** boring, dull, unexciting, uninteresting.

thrive *vb.* prosper, flourish, bloom, advance, progress, succeed, increase, grow. *She thrives on adversity.* **Ant.** stagnate, shrivel, languish, wither, wane, fail, die.

thriving *adj.* flourishing, blooming, prospering, prosperous, successful, succeeding. *His new hamburger stand is already thriving.* **Ant.** failing, dying, withering.

throb *vb.* **1.** pound, thump, beat, pulsate, vibrate, tremble. *Her heart throbbed with excitement.* –*n.* **2.** beat, pulse, tremor, spasm, vibration, stab. *He felt a quick throb of pain the moment he sprained his ankle.*

throng *n.* **1.** horde, host, crowd, multitude, swarm, mass, flock, herd. *A throng of mosquitoes hovered about us.* –*vb.* **2.** crowd, jam, swarm, teem, press, push, gather, assemble. *The rock star was thronged by a horde of admirers.*

through *adj.* **1.** direct, straight, uninterrupted. *She was able to get a through flight to New York.* **2.** finished, completed, ended, done, over. *Are you through with the book I loaned you?* **Ant. 1.** interrupted, indirect. **2.** begun, started, commenced.

throw *vb.* **1.** pitch, toss, fling, cast, hurl, hurtle, sling, lob, heave, propel. *He threw a penny into the wishing well.* –*n.* **2.** toss, pitch, cast, fling, lob. *Her first throw missed the dart board.*

thrust *vb.* **1.** push, shove, force, butt, ram, drive. *The chairman thrust all objections aside.* –*n.* **2.** push, shove, drive, lunge, plunge, advance. *He made a threatening thrust with his knife.*

thus *adv.* therefore, accordingly, consequently, hence, ergo. *It's raining; thus I'll take my umbrella.* **Ant.** but, however, nevertheless.

thwart *vb.* frustrate, obstruct, oppose, hinder, foil, prevent, bar, stop, defeat. *The city council thwarted the developer's plan to build a new shopping mall.* **Ant.** assist, support, help, encourage, abet.

ticket *n.* **1.** voucher, permit, coupon, passport, pass. *We have tickets for the six o'clock performance.* **2.** label, tag, tab, sticker, marker. *Check the sales ticket to see how much it costs.* **3.** ballot, roster, slate, list, register. *She supports the Democratic ticket.* *–vb.* **4.** label, mark, identify, characterize. *This is ticketed as a sale item.*

tickle *vb.* **1.** please, delight, amuse, excite, interest, fascinate, cheer. *It tickles me to hear you say that.* **2.** caress, stroke, brush, tingle, twitch. *Most people laugh when you tickle them.* **Ant. 1.** irritate, annoy, bother.

ticklish *adj.* delicate, difficult, intricate, awkward, sensitive, tough, complicated. *Marriage is a ticklish subject to discuss with a newly divorced person.* **Ant.** easy, simple, uncomplicated.

tide *n.* stream, flow, current, drift, flux, tendency, drift, direction. *The tide of battle turned against Napoleon at Waterloo.*

tidy *adj.* **1.** orderly, neat, organized, trim, well-kept, regular. *It's a rare child who keeps his or her room tidy.* **2.** large, vast, substantial, considerable, ample, respectable. *He won a tidy sum in the state lottery.* *–vb.* **3.** neaten, organize, clean, straighten, arrange. *She had to tidy up her accounts before the auditor arrived.* **Ant. 1.** untidy, disheveled, messy, unorganized. **2.** small, tiny, insignificant. **3.** disarrange, disorder, mess up.

tie *vb.* **1.** bind, attach, fasten, secure, join, connect, tether, unite, hold. *The mountaineers tied two ropes together for a long rappel.* **2.** draw, deadlock, stalemate, match. *She tied him for first place in the chess tournament.* *–n.* **3.** bond, link, connection, attachment, affiliation. *The secretary of defense should not have strong ties with the defense industry.* **4.** cord, rope, string, line, fastener, fastening. *Do you have a tie for this garbage bag?* **5.** draw, deadlock, stalemate, check. *It's rare for a football game to end in a tie.* **Ant. 1.** untie, unfasten, separate, disconnect, detach.

tier *n.* layer, level, story, stratum, step, row, rank. *Their wedding cake had three tiers.*

tight *adj.* **1.** secure, firm, fixed, set, fast, strong, immovable. *She couldn't undo the tight knot.* **2.** taut, tense, stretched, strained, drawn, rigid, stiff. *The clothesline is too tight.* **3.** snug, small, constricted, narrow, little. *She likes to wear tight jeans.* **4.** full, crammed, packed, crowded, overloaded, busy, demanding. *My schedule is too tight to meet you for lunch.* **Ant. 1.** insecure, loose, flexible, movable. **2.** slack, lax, pliant, loose. **3.** large, roomy, ample. **4.** empty, vacant, void, easy, light.

tighten *vb.* fasten, fix, secure, tauten, cinch, contract, constrict. *Tighten your belt before your pants fall down.* **Ant.** loosen, slacken, release.

till *prep.* **1.** until, before, prior to, up to. *He'll be at the office till nine o'clock.* *–vb.* **2.** cultivate, plow, harrow, hoe, turn. *In the springtime, farmers till their fields in preparation for planting.* *–n.* **3.** cash register, cashbox, coffer, safe, vault. *He was caught with his hand in the till.*

tilt *n.* **1.** incline, slope, slant, list, lean, cant, pitch. *The Leaning Tower of Pisa has so much tilt it looks as if it should fall.* *–vb.* **2.** tip, pitch, slope, slant, incline. *Sometimes it's hard to resist the urge to tilt a pinball machine.*

time *n.* **1.** interval, term, period, spell, span, space, stretch, while. *When the school year starts, it seems like a long time until Christmas break.* **2.** age, epoch, era, period, eon. *Life was difficult during the time of the caveman.* **3.** beat, meter, rhythm, tempo, measure, pace. *Play this song in three-four time.* *–vb.* **4.** measure, regulate, adjust, pace, gauge. *The socialite timed her appearance for maximum effect.*

timely *adj.* convenient, fitting, opportune, favorable, suitable, prompt, punctual, early. *The timely arrival of reinforcements saved the army from defeat.* **Ant.** untimely, inconvenient, inopportune, late.

timid *adj.* shy, bashful, diffident, unassertive, hesitant, cautious, unassuming, afraid, apprehensive, fearful. *He is too timid to ask her for a date.* **Ant.** bold, assertive, confident, forward, fearless.

tinge *n.* **1.** color, tint, trace, hint, touch, shade, suggestion, streak. *There was a tinge of* *anger in her voice.* –*vb.* **2.** color, tint, touch, season. *The document was tinged yellow with age.*

tinker *vb.* putter, fiddle, doodle, fuss, mend, fix, repair. *She tinkered with the lawn mower until she got it running again.*

tint *n.* **1.** tinge, color, hint, trace, shade, suggestion. *The wallpaper has a slight pinkish tint.* **2.** dye, stain, coloring. *The local supermarket carries tints for both hair and fabrics.* –*vb.* **3.** tinge, color, tone, dye, stain. *She tinted her hair to keep the gray from showing.*

tiny *adj.* small, little, minute, miniature, dwarfish, midget, petite. *The tiny kitten could fit in the palm of her hand.* **Ant.** huge, enormous, colossal, immense, large, big.

tip *n.* **1.** top, point, peak, head, apex, extremity, end. *This pencil has a dull tip.* **2.** advice, suggestion, information, clue, hint, warning. *Do you have any good tips on how I should invest my savings?* **3.** gratuity, bonus, gift, reward. *Let's give the waitress a good tip.* –*vb.* **4.** tilt, upset, overturn, overthrow, topple. *The lamp tipped over and fell to the floor.* **5.** pay, reward, recompense, remunerate. *We should probably tip both the bellboy and the maid.* **Ant. 1.** bottom, base, foot.

tirade *n.* outburst, outpouring, harangue, diatribe, scolding, rant. *The manager delivered a tirade to the late employee.*

tire *vb.* **1.** weaken, fatigue, exhaust, weary, enervate, wear out, drain. *She was tired from playing three games of tennis.* **2.** bore, irk, bother, disgust, exasperate, annoy. *She quickly tired of her dog's continuous barking.* **Ant. 1.** refresh, revive, invigorate. **2.** delight, please, excite.

tired *adj.* exhausted, weary, fatigued, enervated, worn, spent, drained. *The runner was too tired to finish the marathon.* **Ant.** rested, refreshed, energetic, fresh, tireless.

tireless *adj.* untiring, inexhaustible, energetic, enduring, unceasing, determined, steady. *The senator's tireless campaign against drunk drivers resulted in a tough new law.* **Ant.** tired, unenergetic, inactive, listless.

title *n.* **1.** name, designation, heading, caption, legend. *What's the title of the new movie everyone's talking about?* **2.** deed, claim, right, ownership. *The mortgage bank still holds the title to my house.* **3.** crown, championship, honors. *The unknown boxer has dreams of wresting the title from the current champion.* –*vb.* **4.** name, call, designate, term, entitle. *What will you title your new play?*

together *adv.* jointly, collectively, mutually, simultaneously. *Let's go to the party together.* **Ant.** separately, individually, singly, alone.

toil *n.* **1.** work, labor, exertion, effort, struggle, drudgery, hardship. *He was ready to retire after thirty years of toil.* –*vb.* **2.** labor, slave, sweat, work, struggle, strain, strive. *She toiled night and day to get her law degree.* **Ant. 1.** leisure, relaxation, rest. **2.** relax, rest, loll.

token *n.* **1.** symbol, sign, mark, evidence, expression, indication, souvenir, memento, keepsake. *The rose was a token of her love for him.* –*adj.* **2.** superficial, perfunctory, symbolic, pretended. *The hiring of only one minority employee was merely token compliance with equal opportunity laws.* **Ant. 2.** genuine, real, actual.

tolerable *adj.* acceptable, adequate, bearable, endurable, allowable, supportable. *Tumultuous behavior is not tolerable in the classroom.* **Ant.** intolerable, unbearable, unacceptable.

tolerant *adj.* indulgent, lenient, permissive, patient, accepting, understanding, forbearing, liberal. *The parents were overly tolerant of their child's mischievousness.* **Ant.** intolerant, uncompromising, strict, harsh, rigid.

tolerate *vb.* **1.** bear, endure, suffer, take, abide. *I can't tolerate much more of this cold weather.* **2.** condone, allow, permit, approve, authorize, accept. *Most restaurants have sections where smoking is not tolerated.* **Ant. 2.** prohibit, forbid, ban, discourage.

toll *n.* **1.** expense, cost, price, tax, charge, tariff, fee. *You have to pay a toll to use that bridge.* –*vb.* **2.** ring, chime, peal, knell, strike. *The bells are tolling in honor of the new pope.*

tomb *n.* grave, crypt, vault, burial place, mausoleum, sepulcher. *Abraham Lincoln's tomb is a national shrine.*

tone *n.* **1.** sound, pitch, note, noise. *Only a dog can hear the tone of this whistle.* **2.** attitude, mood, temper, spirit, manner. *Although she tried* *to be cheerful, the tone of her letter seemed to indicate that she was unhappy.* **3.** color, tint, tinge, hue, shade. *He dyed his shirt three tones of blue.* **4.** vigor, health, strength. *She used aerobics to maintain good muscle tone.*

tongue *n.* language, dialect, speech, idiom, vocabulary, jargon. *His native tongue is German.*

too *adv.* **1.** also, additionally, besides, likewise, moreover, furthermore. *Let's take in dinner and a movie too.* **2.** very, excessively, extremely, overly, unduly. *This house is too small for the three of us.*

tool *n.* **1.** implement, utensil, instrument, device, apparatus, gadget. *A hammer, saw, and screwdriver are useful tools for household repairs.* **2.** pawn, puppet, agent, figurehead, hireling. *The dictator was only a tool of his country's army.*

top *n.* **1.** summit, peak, pinnacle, tip, apex, head, zenith, crest. *The view from the top was worth the difficulties of climbing the mountain.* **2.** lid, cover, cap, stopper. *Put the top back on the jar when you're through with it.* *–adj.* **3.** highest, topmost, leading, main, uppermost, foremost, chief, principal. *All the top rock stars performed at the benefit concert.* *–vb.* **4.** excel, surpass, exceed, transcend, beat, better, best. *Her new novel tops anything she's written before.* **Ant. 1.** bottom, base, foot, nadir. **3.** lowest, worst, least.

topic *n.* subject, theme, thesis, point, question, issue, matter, text. *He has to write a report on a topic related to ecology.*

topple *vb.* overturn, overthrow, upset, fall, drop, collapse. *His dream of an early retirement was toppled by the stock-market crash.*

torch *n.* **1.** light, burning brand, flame, flare, lamp, flashlight, spotlight. *Angry villagers chased after Frankenstein with burning torches.* *–vb.* **2.** burn, set afire, ignite, kindle, inflame. *An angry mob torched the desperado's hideout.*

torment *n.* **1.** suffering, pain, anguish, agony, misery, torture, distress, despair. *Her migraine headaches were a continuous source of torment.* *–vb.* **2.** agonize, pain, distress, torture, plague, annoy, provoke. *He was tormented with remorse for his past indiscretions.* **Ant. 1.** pleasure, joy, comfort. **2.** soothe, ease, relieve.

torrent *n.* deluge, flood, downpour, inundation, rain, stream, outburst, outpouring. *The manager faced a torrent of protests when she tried to eliminate coffee breaks.*

torture *n.* **1.** torment, brutality, cruelty, punishment, ordeal, suffering, agony, pain, anguish. *Going to a party can be sheer torture for a shy person.* *–vb.* **2.** torment, agonize, afflict, maim, mutilate, mistreat, abuse. *The soldiers tortured their prisoners to exact information.* **Ant. 1.** pleasure, joy, comfort. **2.** soothe, ease, comfort.

torturous *adj.* excruciating, agonizing, tormenting, torturing, painful, anguished, distressful. *The lost hiker experienced a torturous night alone in the woods.* **Ant.** painless, pleasant, comforting.

toss *vb.* **1.** throw, pitch, cast, hurl, fling, heave. *The bachelor's apartment had dirty clothes tossed everywhere.* **2.** turn, stir, sway, tumble, writhe, wriggle. *The insomniac spent yet another night tossing around in bed.* **3.** discuss, debate, argue, deliberate, consider. *The committee tossed around the new proposal.* *–n.* **4.** throw, pitch, cast, fling. *The decision was made by a toss of a coin.*

total *n.* **1.** sum, whole, entirety, totality, aggregate. *The cost of my new computer and programs came to a total of $2,000.* *–adj.* **2.** entire, whole, complete, full, inclusive, absolute, outright. *She unhappily acknowledged that the evening had been far from a total success.* *–vb.* **3.** add, compute, calculate, reckon, sum up. *When he totaled his bills, he realized he didn't have enough to pay them all.* **Ant. 2.** partial, limited, qualified, incomplete.

totally *adv.* completely, utterly, wholly, entirely, thoroughly, absolutely, perfectly. *She isn't being totally honest with you.* **Ant.** partially, incompletely.

totter *vb.* reel, falter, stagger, wobble, sway, falter, shake, flounder. *A loose rock tottered on the brink of the precipice.*

touch *n.* **1.** contact, feeling, touching, handling, brush, stroke. *His injury was so sensitive that even the slightest touch was painful.* **2.** feel, texture, quality, nature, character. *This blanket has a soft touch.* **3.** trace, hint, shade, tinge, dash, suggestion. *This paint needs just a touch more blue to match the original color.* –vb. **4.** finger, feel, handle, probe, stroke, manipulate. *Do not touch the wet paint.* **5.** affect, move, stir, impress, influence, sway, arouse. *The old recluse was touched by a child's kindness.* **6.** border, abut, meet, contact, join, converge. *During the dry season, their dock didn't even touch the water.* **7.** mention, discuss, allude to, refer to, note. *The report was full of trivialities, and it didn't even touch the real issue.* **Ant. 6.** diverge, part, separate. **7.** ignore, disregard, omit.

touchy *adj.* sensitive, delicate, controversial, divisive, ticklish, risky. *Offshore drilling is a touchy issue to discuss with an environmentalist.* **Ant.** safe, uncontroversial, easy.

tough *adj.* **1.** strong, hard, hardy, sturdy, durable, resilient. *Denim is a tough fabric.* **2.** difficult, laborious, arduous, demanding, strenuous, rigorous. *Chinese is a tough language to learn.* **Ant. 1.** delicate, fragile, soft, weak. **2.** easy, simple.

tour *n.* **1.** visit, journey, excursion, trip, outing, expedition. *She took a tour of the pyramids.* **2.** term, period, shift, time, turn, assignment. *He served a three-year tour in the army.* –vb. **3.** travel, visit, journey, roam, sightsee, see, explore. *She will be touring England next year.*

tourist *n.* traveler, sightseer, visitor, tourer. *Disneyland attracts tourists from all over the world.*

tournament *n.* contest, match, competition, game, meet. *Who's favored to win this year's bowling tournament?*

tow *vb.* **1.** drag, draw, pull, haul, tug. *There was so much snow in his driveway, he had to have his car towed out.* –n. **2.** towing, drag, draw, pull, haul. *Can you give my car a tow?*

tower *n.* **1.** spire, steeple, turret, minaret, column. *The church has a picturesque bell tower.* –vb. **2.** ascend, soar, loom, dominate, overlook. *The basketball player towers above all his friends.*

town *n.* municipality, community, settlement, village, metropolis, city. *Life in small towns is less hectic than in big cities.*

toxic *adj.* poisonous, noxious, harmful, injurious, unhealthy, deadly. *No one likes to live next to a toxic-waste dump.* **Ant.** nontoxic, nonpoisonous, harmless, healthy.

toy *n.* **1.** plaything, pastime, trifle, trinket, bauble. *His computer is just another toy to him.* –vb. **2.** play, trifle, tease, fiddle, sport. *Don't toy with my emotions.*

trace *n.* **1.** vestige, remains, mark, sign, track, trail, evidence, proof. *The search-and-rescue team could find no trace of the lost hiker.* **2.** hint, suggestion, touch, tinge, tint, streak. *There's just a trace of smog today.* –vb. **3.** track, trail, follow, hunt, pursue, search, seek. *The police traced the stolen car and found the thief.* **4.** copy, draw, sketch, outline, diagram. *The student's report included several drawings traced from a science textbook.*

track *n.* **1.** trail, spoor, footprint, mark, sign, trace. *Last winter I found bear tracks near my mountain cabin.* **2.** course, path, pathway, route, road, trail, way. *The new president hoped to get his administration started on the right track.* –vb. **3.** trail, follow, hunt, pursue, search, seek, trace. *The sheriff tracked the fugitive to his hideout.* **4.** carry, drag, bring, bear. *The child tracked snow into the house.*

tract *n.* region, area, district, territory, expanse, parcel, space. *The new national park contains a vast tract of tundra.*

traction *n.* grip, hold, friction, clutch, clasp, pull, drag. *Her new tires give good traction on icy roads.*

trade *n.* **1.** commerce, business, industry, traffic, transactions, dealings. *Japan's economy is dependent upon foreign trade.* **2.** art, craft, occupation, profession, job, employment. *He hopes to learn the plumber's trade.* **3.** exchange, barter, swap. *A classmate gave her two cookies in trade for her candy bar.* –vb. **4.** exchange, barter, swap, bargain. *Let's trade sandwiches.*

tradition *n.* custom, convention, ritual, standard, habit, practice. *She has a tradition of making popcorn balls for Halloween.*

traditional *adj.* customary, usual, ritual, habitual, normal, routine. *It's traditional to have turkey for Thanksgiving dinner.* **Ant.** unusual, uncommon, rare.

traffic *n.* **1.** trade, sale, commerce, exchange, business, marketing. *Control of the drug traffic is a national priority.* **2.** travel, movement, transit, transport. *The freeway is congested with rush-hour traffic.* *–vb.* **3.** smuggle, bootleg, trade, barter, buy, sell. *He was arrested for trafficking in stolen art objects.*

tragedy *n.* disaster, catastrophe, calamity, misfortune, accident, adversity, unhappiness. *The tragedy could have been avoided had they not attempted to fly in bad weather.* **Ant.** fortune, happiness, success.

tragic *adj.* unfortunate, dreadful, deplorable, unhappy, sad, mournful, grievous, awful, bad. *She was killed in a tragic accident.* **Ant.** happy, fortunate, bright, cheerful.

trail *vb.* **1.** track, hunt, trace, follow, pursue, stalk. *A team of detectives trailed the suspect night and day.* **2.** follow, come after, tail, lag. *His team trailed by seven points at halftime.* **3.** draw, pull, drag, tow, troll, trawl. *The girl trailed a string of tin cans behind her bike.* *–n.* **4.** path, footpath, track, way, route, course. *This trail leads to Yosemite Falls.* **5.** track, scent, spoor, sign, mark, trace. *Hyenas found the injured animal by following its trail.* **Ant. 2.** lead, head, go before.

train *n.* **1.** chain, succession, series, sequence, line, string. *He had trouble following her train of thought.* **2.** staff, followers, retinue, entourage, suite, attendants. *The princess was accompanied by a large train.* **3.** caravan, procession, column, line, string. *Supplies had to be brought in by mule train.* *–vb.* **4.** teach, educate, instruct, drill, tutor, prepare. *How long will it take to train your new employee?*

trait *n.* characteristic, attribute, feature, quality, property. *Self-discipline is a trait necessary for success as a writer.*

traitor *n.* betrayer, turncoat, renegade, spy, deserter, defector, deceiver, mutineer. *A traitor told the enemy our plans.* **Ant.** supporter, defender.

tramp *n.* **1.** vagabond, hobo, vagrant, derelict, bum. *Tramps can frequently be found near railroad yards.* **2.** hike, stroll, walk, ramble, saunter, excursion. *She's out on a tramp through the forest.* *–vb.* **3.** trek, trudge, plod, slog, hike, walk, stroll, ramble. *The mountaineers spent several days merely tramping up a glacier.* **4.** stamp, stomp, tromp, trample. *The spoiled child tramped out of the room in a fit of anger.*

trample *vb.* crush, squash, flatten, stamp, stomp, tromp, tramp. *Neighborhood children trampled his new lawn.*

trance *n.* daze, daydream, reverie, spell, muse, coma, stupor. *The hypnotist put her into a deep trance.*

tranquil *adj.* quiet, peaceful, calm, serene, restful, still, unperturbed. *The arrival of unannounced visitors shattered his hopes for a tranquil weekend.* **Ant.** agitated, disturbed, tumultuous.

tranquillity *n.* peacefulness, serenity, calmness, stillness, peace, quiet, restfulness, repose. *After a hectic day at the office, she longed for the tranquillity of home.* **Ant.** commotion, disturbance, disorder.

transaction *n.* negotiation, deal, agreement, arrangement, settlement, business. *Both parties agreed to the terms of the loan transaction.*

transfer *vb.* **1.** move, transport, carry, shift, convey, relocate, send, ship, consign, assign, relegate. *She transferred all her files from her old computer to the new one.* *–n.* **2.** change, move, shift, transferal, assignment, relocation. *The soldier stationed overseas eagerly awaited his transfer back to the United States.*

transform *vb.* change, convert, alter, turn, modify, refashion, remake, transmute. *Cinderella's fairy godmother transformed a pumpkin into a carriage.*

transformation *n.* alteration, modification, conversion, change, shift, make-over. *Taking a bath created a complete transformation in the child's appearance.*

transient *adj.* temporary, brief, passing, fleeting, momentary, short-lived, ephemeral. *The actor hoped his new fame would not be a transient phenomenon.* **Ant.** permanent, enduring, lasting, perpetual.

transition *n.* change, alteration, modification, transformation, shift. *New graduates sometimes have trouble coping with the transition from student to worker.*

translate *vb.* change, transform, convert, modify, alter, render. *Her job was to translate Japanese technical manuals into English.*

transmission *n.* **1.** conveyance, transfer, transference, transmittal, passage, delivery, sending. *Mosquitoes cause the transmission of malaria.* **2.** broadcast, signal, report, message, communication. *Because their radio batteries were weak, we were barely able to receive their transmission.*

transmit *vb.* send, convey, forward, dispatch, relay, conduct, transfer, deliver, disperse, broadcast. *Many companies use FAX machines to transmit documents instantaneously.*

transparent *adj.* **1.** obvious, evident, plain, visible, apparent, unmistakable, blatant. *The defendant's testimony was full of transparent lies.* **2.** clear, lucid, translucent, see-through. *He covered his notebook with transparent plastic.* **Ant. 1.** hidden, invisible, concealed. **2.** opaque.

transport *vb.* **1.** transfer, convey, conduct, carry, move, shift, ferry. *Coal is typically transported by railroad cars.* *–n.* **2.** transportation, conveyance, shipment, transfer, transference, shipping, carrying. *Many people don't like to see their local roads used for the transport of toxic wastes.*

transportation *n.* transport, transfer, transference, conveyance, movement, transit. *Many forms of transportation are available to anyone wishing to tour Europe.*

trap *n.* **1.** snare, pitfall, pit, net, deception, ploy, ruse, trick, morass, quagmire. *The sheepherder set out traps to protect his flock from coyotes.* *–vb.* **2.** catch, capture, entrap, ensnare, net. *In the 19th century, mountain men trapped beaver for their pelts.* **Ant. 2.** release, free, liberate.

trash *n.* **1.** garbage, junk, waste, rubbish, refuse, litter, debris. *Whose turn is it to take the trash to the dump?* **2.** nonsense, drivel, inanity, malarkey, gibberish. *This magazine is pure trash.* **Ant. 1.** treasure, valuables. **2.** sense, substance.

travel *n.* **1.** tour, trek, journey, trip, touring, traveling, journeying. *Tell me about your latest travels.* *–vb.* **2.** tour, wander, roam, trek, journey, visit, sightsee. *Let's travel through Europe next summer.* **3.** move, proceed, advance, progress, go. *Sound waves cannot travel through a vacuum.* **Ant. 2.** stay, remain, linger.

treacherous *adj.* **1.** dangerous, unsafe, hazardous, precarious, perilous, risky, undependable. *Snow and ice make for treacherous driving conditions.* **2.** traitorous, disloyal, treasonous, unfaithful, deceitful. *A treacherous guard let assassins into the palace.* **Ant. 1.** safe, reliable, sound. **2.** loyal, faithful, dependable.

tread *vb.* **1.** walk, step, tramp, stamp, stomp, trample. *Don't tread on the new grass.* *–n.* **2.** footstep, step, football, walk, plod. *She heard the tread of someone approaching.*

treason *n.* disloyalty, betrayal, treachery, subversion, sedition, conspiracy. *The patriot thought that treason against his country was the worst possible crime.* **Ant.** loyalty, allegiance, patriotism.

treasure *n.* **1.** riches, hoard, trove, fortune, wealth, jewels, gems, gold. *Many children dream of finding a pirate's buried treasure.* *–vb.* **2.** cherish, value, prize, esteem, love, adore, revere. *She treasures her family more than anything else.*

treat *n.* **1.** pleasure, enjoyment, joy, delight, comfort, delicacy, morsel. *Ice-cream cones are a treat most people enjoy.* *–vb.* **2.** handle, manage, consider, regard, respect, use, utilize. *She is tired of being treated like a child.* **3.** doctor, medicate, remedy, relieve, cure, heal. *You'd better go to the hospital to get that burn treated properly.*

treatment *n.* handling, management, dealing, usage, application. *The new manager is known for her fair treatment of all employees.*

treaty *n.* agreement, accord, pact, compact, arrangement, understanding. *The negotiations eventually led to the signing of an arms-control treaty.*

tremble *vb.* shake, quake, quiver, shiver, shudder, throb, pulsate. *The cornered deer trembled with fright.*

tremendous *adj.* **1.** huge, gigantic, enormous, immense, vast, great, mammoth, large. *Writing a book is a tremendous amount of work.* **2.** wonderful, marvelous, exceptional, remarkable, extraordinary, fabulous, excellent. *This new program does a tremendous job of organizing* *computer files.* **Ant. 1.** small, tiny, little. **2.** ordinary, average, mediocre.

tremor *n.* shake, shaking, quiver, quivering, tremble, trembling, flutter. *The nervous speaker had a slight tremor in her voice.*

trench *n.* ditch, furrow, trough, excavation, channel, gully. *We need to dig a trench for the new water pipe.*

trend *n.* direction, inclination, tendency, course, drift, style, fashion, vogue. *During the oil crisis, there was a trend toward the purchase of more fuel-efficient cars.*

trespass *vb.* enter, penetrate, intrude, encroach, infringe, invade. *He was arrested when he trespassed on private property.*

trial *n.* **1.** test, tryout, check, examination, analysis, try, attempt. *She took the new car out for a trial before purchasing it.* **2.** lawsuit, suit, hearing, litigation, case. *Due to a backlog in the courts, his trial won't start for another month.* **3.** ordeal, trouble, misfortune, hardship, difficulty, torment, worry. *Since adopting five rowdy children, her life has been one trial after another.*

tribe *n.* clan, race, group, family, stock, kindred, sect. *The museum had trouble finding a volunteer to live with the tribe of cannibals.*

tribute *n.* **1.** praise, compliment, acclaim, acknowledgment, recognition. *The actress gave tribute to her director when she accepted her Oscar.* **2.** tax, levy, payment, duty, assessment, bribe. *The defeated country was forced to pay tribute to the victor.* **Ant. 1.** condemnation, disrespect, dishonor.

trick *n.* **1.** deception, fraud, deceit, ruse, ploy, scheme, wile, trickery, stratagem. *Resetting the car's mileage was just one of the tricks employed by the unscrupulous dealer.* **2.** feat, stunt, accomplishment. *Rolling over is just one of the dog's many tricks.* **3.** joke, jest, prank, gag, antic, mischief. *Soaping someone's window is a Halloween trick that the victim isn't likely to find funny.* *–vb.* **4.** cheat, dupe, deceive, delude, defraud, fool, swindle. *The con artist tricked me out of $100.* **Ant. 1.** truth, sincerity, honesty.

trickle *n.* **1.** dribble, drop, droplet, drip, seepage. *The old pump provided the barest trickle of water.* *–vb.* **2.** seep, leak, ooze, drop, drip,

dribble. *Blood trickled from the small wound.* **Ant. 1.** gush, flood, stream. **2.** pour, spurt, gush, stream.

trifle *n.* **1.** bauble, triviality, trinket, plaything, toy, nothing. *She likes costume jewelry and similar trifles.* **2.** little, bit, trace, touch, tinge. *My scratch hurts just a trifle.* *–vb.* **3.** fool, fiddle, play, toy. *The flirtatious man enjoyed trifling with the emotions of his female acquaintances.*

trifling *adj.* trivial, petty, unimportant, insignificant, inconsequential, slight, negligible, small. *Since both brands are virtually identical, the choice between them is a trifling matter.* **Ant.** important, significant, considerable, large.

trigger *vb.* begin, start, set off, touch off, cause, produce. *Heavy snowfall triggered a major avalanche.* **Ant.** prevent, stop, block.

trim *vb.* **1.** prune, clip, cut, crop, shorten, neaten. *He needs to have his beard trimmed.* **2.** decorate, adorn, ornament, embellish, furbish. *She trimmed her house by painting the doors and window frames a lighter color.* *–n.* **3.** order, condition, repair, shape, state, fitness. *His yacht is in fine trim.* **4.** decoration, adornment, embellishment, border. *This lace will make a nice trim for your blouse.* **5.** pruning, clipping, cutting, cropping, shortening. *Your hair could use a trim.* *–adj.* **6.** neat, tidy, compact, lean, slim, slender. *She's looking fit and trim from doing aerobics.* **Ant. 6.** messy, sloppy, disordered.

trip *n.* **1.** journey, excursion, tour, jaunt, outing, voyage, cruise. *Let's take a trip to Europe next summer.* *–vb.* **2.** stagger, stumble, slip, tumble, fall. *He tripped over the dog and fell to the ground.*

trite *adj.* ordinary, routine, common, everyday, stale, dull, banal, overused. *The teacher was tired of hearing the same trite excuses.* **Ant.** fresh, original, new, unique.

triumph *n.* **1.** victory, success, conquest, win, mastery. *The boxer savored his triumph in the ring.* *–vb.* **2.** succeed, win, prevail, conquer, vanquish, defeat, outdo. *In most movies, the good guys triumph over the bad guys.* **Ant. 1.** defeat, failure. **2.** lose, fail, succumb.

triumphant *adj.* victorious, winning, conquering, triumphal, joyful, exultant. *Napoleon made a triumphant entry into Moscow.* **Ant.** defeated, unsuccessful, humbled.

trivial *adj.* unimportant, insignificant, petty, slight, trifling, meaningless, worthless. *The new textbook is quite good, though it does contain a few trivial errors.* **Ant.** significant, important, serious, substantial.

troop *n.* **1.** group, unit, band, squad, company. *A troop of cavalry rode by.* –*vb.* **2.** march, file, step, stride, proceed, advance, parade. *A long line of inmates trooped across the prison courtyard.*

trophy *n.* prize, award, medal, citation, laurels, crown, cup. *She won a trophy for placing first in the chess contest.*

trouble *vb.* **1.** distress, bother, pester, annoy, vex, disturb, inconvenience, worry, upset, pain. *Her worried look indicated something was troubling her.* –*n.* **2.** difficulty, predicament, dilemma, problem, quandary. *Most of his troubles stem from his laziness.* **3.** inconvenience, exertion, effort, pains, care, bother, work. *He went to a lot of trouble to make this wallet for you.* **Ant. 1.** soothe, please, appease.

troublesome *adj.* annoying, irritating, disturbing, upsetting, exasperating, bothersome, worrisome. *Her toothache was so troublesome that she finally agreed to see a dentist.* **Ant.** calming, soothing, innocuous.

truce *n.* cease-fire, armistice, peace, cessation, stop, halt, respite, lull, intermission. *The bickering couple agreed to a temporary truce until their visitors left.*

trudge *vb.* tramp, plod, slog, shamble, shuffle, limp, trek, hike. *He trudged through the deep snow.*

true *adj.* **1.** valid, accurate, correct, real, factual, exact, right. *She gave the jury a true account of the accident.* **2.** genuine, authentic, legitimate, actual, absolute. *The child who saved his brother from drowning is a true hero.* **3.** faithful, loyal, trustworthy, dependable, reliable, steady. *You are a true friend.* **4.** just, rightful, lawful, legitimate, legal, official. *The jury tried to determine who was the true heir to the millionaire's estate.* **Ant. 1.** false, invalid, incorrect. **2.** phony, artificial, imitation. **3.** faithless, disloyal. **4.** illegal, illicit, unauthorized.

truly *adv.* really, actually, honestly, truthfully, sincerely, genuinely, absolutely. *I'm truly sorry for the problems I've caused.* **Ant.** insincerely, untruthfully, uncertainly.

trust *n.* **1.** confidence, faith, reliance, belief, conviction, hope, expectation. *Rock climbers need to have trust not only in their equipment but also in themselves.* **2.** care, keeping, protection, custody, guardianship. *The orphan was placed in the trust of foster parents.* –*vb.* **3.** believe in, rely on, depend on, swear by. *You can't always trust what a salesman tells you.* **4.** presume, suppose, assume, expect, anticipate. *I trust you won't be late again.* **Ant. 1.** mistrust, suspicion, doubt. **3.** mistrust, question.

trustworthy *adj.* reliable, dependable, responsible, faithful, loyal, proven. *Every manager hopes for trustworthy employees.* **Ant.** untrustworthy, unreliable, undependable, irresponsible.

truth *n.* truthfulness, facts, reality, veracity, trueness, honesty, authenticity. *The truth of the matter is that I don't like him.* **Ant.** falsehood, untruth, falseness.

try *vb.* **1.** attempt, endeavor, strive, aim, struggle, aspire, undertake. *Please try to be nice tonight.* **2.** test, prove, check, examine, inspect, experiment, investigate. *The new medicine was tried on animals before being released.* **3.** judge, deliberate, adjudicate, consider. *The superior court tried three cases last week.* –*n.* **4.** trial, test, experiment, attempt, endeavor, effort. *Let's give the car one more try before we call a tow truck.*

trying *adj.* difficult, hard, tough, arduous, troublesome, bothersome, distressing. *Everyone had a trying time during the Depression.* **Ant.** easy, comforting, simple.

tug *vb.* **1.** pull, jerk, yank, heave, haul, drag, draw. *A fish tugged on his line.* –*n.* **2.** pull, jerk, yank, heave. *Give his beard a tug and see what happens.*

tumble *vb.* **1.** topple, fall, sprawl, slip, drop, plunge, stumble, trip. *She tumbled off her horse.* **2.** roll, somersault, toss, bounce, pitch, reel. *We could see our clothes tumbling in the dryer.* –*n.* **3.** fall, spill, sprawl, plunge, drop. *He took a tumble when he tripped on the rug.*

tumult *n.* commotion, disturbance, uproar, furor, clamor, ferment, turmoil, confusion. *The* *classroom was in a state of tumult when the snake got out of its cage.* **Ant.** peace, quiet, serenity, tranquillity.

tune *n.* **1.** refrain, melody, song, strain, air, theme. *What's the name of that lovely tune you're singing?* **2.** pitch, harmony, agreement, conformity, concord, accord. *Someone's guitar is badly out of tune.* –*vb.* **3.** adjust, adapt, reconcile, conform, fix. *When was the last time you had your piano tuned?* **Ant. 2.** discord, discordance, dissonance.

tunnel *n.* **1.** passage, passageway, corridor, tube, shaft. *An underground tunnel connects the two buildings.* –*vb.* **2.** burrow, dig, excavate, quarry, mine. *The prisoners tunneled under the walls.*

turbulent *adj.* tumultuous, disturbed, agitated, wild, raging, stormy. *We didn't go sailing because the lake was too turbulent.* **Ant.** calm, quiet, placid, orderly.

turmoil *n.* tumult, pandemonium, chaos, uproar, commotion, ferment. *Rapidly rising interest rates threw the housing market into turmoil.* **Ant. 1.** order, peace, quiet, tranquillity.

turn *n.* **1.** occasion, stint, shift, spell, chance, opportunity, attempt. *It's your turn to do the dishes.* **2.** rotation, revolution, spin, twist, twirl, whirl, cycle. *She gave the steering wheel a quick turn in order to avoid hitting the dog.* **3.** change, shift, deviation, alteration, turning. *Her condition has taken a turn for the better.* **4.** curve, twist, zigzag, bend, angle, corner. *This road makes a hairpin turn just ahead.* –*vb.* **5.** revolve, rotate, spin, twirl, whirl, circle. *You have to turn that handle to the left.* **6.** divert, deflect, redirect, swerve, shift. *The road turns west to follow the river.* **7.** transform, alter, change, become, reform, reshape. *The rain turned to snow when the temperature dropped.* **8.** sprain, twist, wrench. *He turned his ankle playing basketball.* **9.** sour, spoil, curdle, ferment, clabber. *Put the cream back in the refrigerator before it turns.*

tutor *n.* **1.** teacher, instructor, educator, coach, trainer. *His parents hired a private tutor to help him prepare for the entrance examination.* –*vb.* **2.** teach, instruct, educate, inform, train, prepare. *She tutors math for a living.*

twilight *n.* **1.** sundown, sunset, dusk, evening, nightfall. *Nocturnal animals become active at twilight.* **2.** finale, decline, ebb, end, close. *Her career is in its twilight, and she'll be retiring soon.* **Ant. 1.** dawn, sunrise, daybreak. **2.** start, beginning, peak.

twinkle *vb.* glitter, sparkle, shine, glimmer, glow, blink, wink, flutter. *He could see a faint light twinkling in the distance.*

twirl *vb.* whirl, turn, rotate, spin, revolve, wheel. *The cowgirl twirled her rope overhead as she prepared to lasso the calf.*

twist *n.* **1.** curve, bend, turn, zigzag, angle. *This rope is so stiff I can't get the twists out.* **2.** variation, novelty, change, development, treatment, notion, idea. *This movie has a new twist to an old plot.* –*vb.* **3.** wind, twine, encircle, entwine, coil, curl, roll, wrap. *Garbage bags have ties that you twist to close.* **4.** distort, contort, deform, distort, warp. *The wrecked car was twisted beyond recognition.* **5.** squirm, writhe, wrest, yank, pull. *The child twisted out of his mother's grasp.* **6.** sprain, wrench, turn. *She twisted her ankle when she fell off the horse.* **Ant. 3.** untwist, unwind, uncoil, unroll.

type *n.* kind, sort, class, group, variety, category, brand. *What type of music do you like?*

typical *adj.* representative, characteristic, standard, normal, average. *The magazine ran a series on the typical American family.* **Ant.** atypical, unusual, odd, unique.

tyranny *n.* despotism, dictatorship, oppression, repression, severity, cruelty. *A popular rebellion ended the government's tyranny.* **Ant.** benevolence, humanity, kindness.

tyrant *n.* dictator, despot, autocrat, totalitarian, oppressor. *The cruel tyrant used his secret police to suppress opposition.*

ubiquitous *adj.* everywhere, omnipresent, widespread, universal, pervasive. *Errors were ubiquitous in his hastily typed manuscript.*

ugly *adj.* **1.** unsightly, unattractive, repulsive, hideous, repugnant. *That purple and green tie certainly is ugly.* **2.** unpleasant, vicious, vile, nasty, mean, foul. *Because she was upset, she made some ugly comments she later regretted.* **Ant. 1.** beautiful, lovely, pretty. **2.** pleasant, agreeable, nice.

ulterior *adj.* hidden, concealed, covert, unexpressed, undeclared, selfish. *He had ulterior motives for dating the wealthy girl.* **Ant.** obvious, open, plain, unselfish.

ultimate *adj.* **1.** final, last, concluding, end, highest, supreme, greatest, maximum. *The ultimate award for an athlete is an Olympic gold medal.* *–n.* **2.** summit, apex, height, peak, extreme, culmination. *He personifies the ultimate in selfishness.* **Ant. 1.** first, beginning, lowest, least.

ultimately *adv.* finally, eventually, at last, in due time. *She ultimately decided against going to graduate school.*

umpire *n.* **1.** referee, judge, arbitrator, mediator, moderator. *We need an umpire for Saturday's baseball game.* *–vb.* **2.** referee, judge, arbitrate, mediate, moderate. *Will you umpire our softball game?*

unable *adj.* incapable, ineffective, powerless, incompetent, helpless, inept. *He's unable to do his homework without help.* **Ant.** able, capable, competent.

unabridged *adj.* uncut, complete, full, entire. *It took her two weeks to read the unabridged version of "War and Peace."* **Ant.** abridged, cut, shortened, condensed.

unanimity *n.* accord, agreement, unity, conformity, consent. *There was complete una-nimity amongst the striking employees.* **Ant.** disagreement, discord.

unanimous *adj.* united, undivided, unified, agreed, agreeing, harmonious. *The council members were unanimous in their support of the new ordinance.* **Ant.** divided, disagreed, disagreeing, differing.

unassuming *adj.* modest, humble, reserved, retiring, unpretentious, simple, plain. *When I met the successful actor at a party, I was surprised to find him so unassuming.* **Ant.** vain, arrogant, pretentious.

unauthorized *adj.* unapproved, unsanctioned, unofficial, illegitimate, illegal. *Since the writer did not have her subject's permission, the resulting book is an unauthorized biography.* **Ant.** authorized, approved, sanctioned, official.

unavoidable *adj.* inevitable, inescapable, unpreventable, compulsory, certain, sure. *It was an unavoidable mistake.* **Ant.** avoidable, preventable.

unaware *adj.* heedless, oblivious, ignorant, unfamiliar, uninformed. *She was unaware of how much homework the course required.* **Ant.** aware, conscious, informed.

unawares *adv.* unexpectedly, abruptly, suddenly, without warning. *The rain shower caught her unawares.* **Ant.** prepared, forewarned.

unbelievable *adj.* incredible, improbable, preposterous, questionable, farfetched, absurd. *He told an unbelievable story about being abducted by Martians.* **Ant.** believable, credible, convincing.

unbiased *adj.* impartial, unprejudiced, disinterested, fair, just, neutral. *Since my job is at stake, I definitely do not have an unbiased attitude toward the new proposal.* **Ant.** biased, prejudiced, slanted.

uncanny *adj.* remarkable, amazing, extraordinary, fantastic, strange, mysterious, curious. *Though the two women are not related, they bear an uncanny resemblance to each other.* **Ant.** common, ordinary, average.

uncertain *adj.* indefinite, undecided, unpredictable, unclear, unsure, obscure, doubtful, dubious. *Uncertain weather forced us to change our vacation plans.* **Ant.** definite, predictable, certain.

uncivilized *adj.* **1.** savage, barbaric, barbarous, primitive, wild. *Those cannibals certainly are uncivilized.* **2.** uncouth, coarse, uncivil, rude, vulgar. *His racist comment was uncivilized.* **Ant. 1.** civilized. **2.** civil, refined, cultured.

uncomfortable *adj.* **1.** painful, causing discomfort. *The sofa bed was lumpy and uncomfortable.* **2.** uneasy, embarrassed, awkward, troubled, distressing, nervous. *She was uncomfortable the first time she met her future mother-in-law.* **Ant. 1.** painless. **2.** comfortable, relaxed, untroubled.

uncommon *adj.* unusual, unique, rare, strange, remarkable, exceptional. *He seeded his lawn with an uncommon variety of grass.* **Ant.** common, familiar, ordinary.

unconcerned *adj.* indifferent, uninterested, uninvolved, apathetic, unperturbed, oblivious. *The failing student seemed unconcerned about her low grades.* **Ant.** concerned, interested, involved.

unconditional *adj.* absolute, unqualified, unlimited, total, full, complete. *Only an unconditional surrender was acceptable to the victorious army.* **Ant.** qualified, limited, incomplete.

unconscious *adj.* **1.** insensible, senseless, comatose. *He was unconscious for several hours after the accident.* **2.** unknowing, unaware, ignorant, unmindful. *She was unconscious of the effect her story was having on her listeners.* **3.** accidental, inadvertent, unintentional. *Unconscious mistakes are sometimes called "Freudian slips."* **Ant. 1.** conscious, alert, aware. **2.** conscious, familiar, knowing. **3.** deliberate, intentional.

unconventional *adj.* odd, eccentric, peculiar, strange, unusual, bizarre. *His unconventional behavior worried his parents.* **Ant.** conventional, ordinary, routine.

uncouth *adj.* rude, impolite, discourteous, crude, coarse, crass, vulgar. *He offended everyone with his uncouth remarks.* **Ant.** polite, courteous, refined.

uncover *vb.* reveal, disclose, expose, discover, open, show. *A private detective uncovered the truth about the woman's past.* **Ant.** conceal, hide, disguise, cover.

undaunted *adj.* undismayed, unfazed, unfaltering, courageous, brave, fearless, valorous. *The climber was undaunted by the steep cliff.* **Ant.** daunted, dismayed, fazed, meek, fearful.

undecided *adj.* undetermined, uncertain, unsure, unresolved, wavering, hesitant. *She's still undecided about which college to attend.* **Ant.** decided, determined, certain, resolved.

under *prep.* **1.** beneath, below, underneath. *You'll find your shoes under the bed.* **2.** subject to, according to, following. *That move is not permissible under international chess rules.* –*adv.* **3.** beneath, below, underneath, lower. *The captain watched as his ship went under.* –*adj.* **4.** subordinate, inferior, lower, lesser, junior. *He is the under secretary for international affairs.* **Ant. 1–3.** above, over. **4.** superior, higher.

undercover *adj.* secret, covert, clandestine, concealed, hidden, disguised. *Her brother is an undercover police detective.* **Ant.** open, undisguised, unconcealed.

undergo *vb.* experience, encounter, endure, bear, suffer, withstand. *She underwent considerable hardships while in the army.* **Ant.** miss, avoid, forgo.

underneath *prep.* **1.** below, under, beneath. *She found a worm underneath the rock.* –*adv.* **2.** below, under, beneath, lower. *When she moved the rock, she didn't know what she would find underneath.* **Ant. 1–2.** above, over.

understand *vb.* comprehend, perceive, realize, recognize, discern. *I can't understand why anyone would pay that much for a new car.* **Ant.** misunderstand, misinterpret, confuse.

understanding *n.* **1.** agreement, pact, bargain, arrangement, accord, compromise. *Management and labor have reached an* *understanding that should end the strike.* **2.** knowledge, comprehension, perception, grasp, appreciation. *Though he can use a computer, he has no understanding of its inner workings.* – *adj.* **3.** sympathetic, compassionate, sensitive, kind, tender. *The troubled child was fortunate to have an understanding teacher.* **Ant. 1.** misunderstanding. **2.** ignorance, incomprehension. **3.** unsympathetic, uncompassionate, insensitive.

undertake *vb.* try, attempt, venture, endeavor, assume, accept, begin, start. *Cleaning the bathroom was a chore no one wanted to undertake.* **Ant.** avoid, refuse, abstain, stop.

undertaking *n.* project, task, job, enterprise, endeavor, venture. *Climbing Mt. Everest is a serious undertaking.*

undesirable *adj.* distasteful, objectionable, offensive, unacceptable, unwelcome, unwanted. *She didn't quit her job because the alternatives were undesirable.* **Ant.** desirable, inviting, attractive, welcome.

undivided *adj.* complete, entire, whole, total, exclusive. *You have my undivided attention.* **Ant.** partial, incomplete.

undo *vb.* **1.** free, open, loosen, unfasten, disentangle, unravel, untie. *The child couldn't undo the lacings on her dress.* **2.** reverse, cancel, annul, offset, neutralize, rectify. *It will take months to undo the damage caused by the disgruntled employee.* **Ant. 1.** fasten, tie, close. **2.** do, accomplish, uphold.

undoing *n.* downfall, ruin, destruction, disgrace, fall, defeat, upset. *Bad investments proved to be the undoing of his plans for an early retirement.* **Ant.** success, victory, triumph.

unduly *adv.* excessively, extremely, overly, inordinately, unnecessarily, unusually. *The parents were unduly concerned with their daughter's shyness.* **Ant.** properly, appropriately, reasonably.

undying *adj.* eternal, immortal, endless, unceasing, perpetual, permanent. *He assured her of his undying love.* **Ant.** temporary, fleeting, brief, momentary.

uneasy *adj.* **1.** worried, troubled, nervous, apprehensive, disturbed, anxious. *She felt uneasy about taking on more responsibilities.* **2.**

uncomfortable, disturbing, unpleasant, strained, embarrassed. *They experienced an uneasy pause in their conversation.* **Ant. 1.** easy, calm, unworried. **2.** easy, comfortable, pleasant.

unemployed *adj.* jobless, out of work, unoccupied, inactive, idle. *Approximately one out of every fifteen workers is unemployed.* **Ant.** employed, working, busy.

unending *adj.* endless, ceaseless, everlasting, eternal, immortal, perpetual, constant. *Books can be an unending source of pleasure.* **Ant.** brief, fleeting, momentary.

unequal *adj.* uneven, disparate, disproportionate, different, unlike, dissimilar, biased. *The champion won the unequal match with a knockout in the first round.* **Ant.** equal, even, like, similar.

uneven *adj.* **1.** irregular, rough, jagged, lopsided, unbalanced, coarse, unlevel. *Bush pilots frequently have to use uneven dirt or gravel landing strips.* **2.** unequal, disparate, different, unlike, dissimilar. *The uneven chess match had a novice playing a master.* **Ant. 1.** smooth, level, straight. **2.** even, equal, balanced.

unexpected *adj.* unforeseen, unanticipated, unpredicted, sudden, abrupt. *She was delighted when she received an unexpected promotion.* **Ant.** expected, anticipated, planned.

unfair *adj.* unjust, biased, discriminatory, partial, prejudiced. *The fired employee felt he had received unfair treatment.* **Ant.** fair, just, impartial, honest.

unfaithful *adj.* treacherous, disloyal, deceitful, faithless, false, untrue. *She was betrayed by an unfaithful friend.* **Ant.** faithful, loyal, true.

unfamiliar *adj.* **1.** strange, new, unknown, different, unusual, exotic, foreign, novel. *She couldn't understand the unfamiliar dialect.* **2.** unacquainted, inexperienced, unaware, uninformed. *He is unfamiliar with the latest computer technology.* **Ant. 1.** familiar, accustomed, common. **2.** familiar, acquainted.

unfavorable *adj.* adverse, detrimental, negative, unsuitable, inconvenient, poor, bad. *Since he has just lost his job, it is an unfavorable time to ask him for a loan.* **Ant.** favorable, positive, good.

unfinished *adj.* incomplete, uncompleted, undone, undeveloped, partial. *An unfinished manuscript was found after the author's death.* **Ant.** finished, complete, whole.

unfit *adj.* **1.** unsuitable, inappropriate, inadequate, unqualified, unprepared. *The shy man is unfit for a career in politics.* **2.** unhealthy, weak, debilitated, infirm. *The long illness has left her physically unfit.* **Ant. 1.** suitable, qualified, competent. **2.** fit, healthy, robust.

unforeseen *adj.* unexpected, unanticipated, unpredicted, sudden, surprise, abrupt. *Unforeseen events made him miss his deadline.* **Ant.** foreseen, expected, anticipated.

unforgettable *adj.* memorable, notable, significant, remarkable, outstanding, exceptional. *Her first view of the ocean was an unforgettable experience.* **Ant.** ordinary, common, routine.

unfortunate *adj.* unlucky, luckless, untimely, unhappy, regrettable. *An unfortunate injury ended his athletic career.* **Ant.** fortunate, lucky, timely.

unfriendly *adj.* **1.** unsociable, aloof, haughty, snobbish, cool, distant, remote. *Her unfriendly behavior is the main reason she's not popular.* **2.** hostile, malevolent, antagonistic, warlike. *The Cold War is abetted by unfriendly actions between nations.* **Ant. 1.** friendly, sociable, warm. **2.** friendly, peaceful.

ungainly *adj.* awkward, clumsy, bungling, ungraceful, inelegant. *The shy young man was ungainly on the dance floor.* **Ant.** graceful, elegant.

ungrateful *adj.* unappreciative, thankless, unthankful, selfish, heedless. *The ungrateful boy refused to acknowledge how much his friends had done for him.* **Ant.** grateful, thankful, appreciative.

unhappy *adj.* sad, depressed, sorrowful, dejected, wretched, miserable, downcast. *She's unhappy because she can't get what she wants.* **Ant.** happy, cheerful, gay, joyful.

unhealthy *adj.* **1.** ill, unwell, sick, sickly, infirm, frail, weak. *Because of his heart condition, he's going to be unhealthy the rest of his life.* **2.** unhealthful, harmful, poisonous, virulent, noxious. *Many people fear it's unhealthy to live next to a toxic-waste dump.* **Ant. 1.** healthy, well, robust. **2.** healthy, beneficial.

unheeded *adj.* unnoticed, disregarded, unobserved, unused. *Advice that isn't asked for usually goes unheeded.* **Ant.** heeded, noticed, used.

unification *n.* consolidation, merger, union, alliance. *The new law resulted in the unification of all the city's school districts.* **Ant.** disunification, separation, division.

uniform *n.* **1.** outfit, attire, costume, regalia, dress. *You can tell a police officer by his or her uniform.* *–adj.* **2.** identical, alike, equal, similar. *Most paperback books are of uniform size.* **3.** even, constant, unvarying, unchanging, undeviating. *The old furnace is not capable of providing uniform heating.* **Ant. 2.** unalike, unequal, dissimilar. **3.** uneven, variable.

unify *vb.* unite, combine, consolidate, bind, connect, link, join, merge. *The American colonies were unified in their struggle against British domination.* **Ant.** separate, divide, disunite.

unimportant *adj.* inconsequential, trivial, petty, insignificant, minor, paltry, trifling. *My boss does not like to bother with unimportant details.* **Ant.** important, significant, major.

uninhabited *adj.* unoccupied, vacant, empty, deserted, abandoned. *Neighborhood kids thought the old uninhabited house was haunted.* **Ant.** inhabited, occupied.

uninhibited *adj.* uncontrolled, unrepressed, unrestrained, free, open, liberated. *Her uninhibited behavior shocked many of her friends.* **Ant.** inhibited, controlled, suppressed.

union *n.* **1.** combination, consolidation, incorporation, mixture, joining, merger. *Bronze is formed by the union of copper and tin.* **2.** association, alliance, partnership, league, order, society. *His sister joined a labor union.* **Ant. 1.** separation, division.

unique *adj.* distinctive, singular, unrivaled, incomparable, exceptional, extraordinary. *She has the unique ability to do her homework while talking on the phone.* **Ant.** common, ordinary, routine.

unite *vb.* unify, combine, join, connect, link, associate, merge. *The two companies united to form a big corporation.* **Ant.** disunite, divide, separate, part.

universal *adj.* boundless, unlimited, widespread, general, total, entire. *This classic children's book has universal appeal.* **Ant.** limited, local, restricted, individual.

unjust *adj.* wrongful, wrong, unfair, undeserved, biased, prejudiced. *Her reputation was hurt by an unjust accusation.* **Ant.** just, fair, right, impartial.

unkempt *adj.* slovenly, disheveled, sloppy, careless, neglected. *He has an unkempt appearance.* **Ant.** neat, tidy, well-groomed.

unkind *adj.* unfeeling, unsympathetic, inconsiderate, thoughtless, harsh, cruel, mean. *It was unkind of you to comment so bluntly on the weight he's gained.* **Ant.** kind, sympathetic, considerate, thoughtful.

unknown *adj.* unidentified, anonymous, unrecognized, nameless, mysterious, obscure. *Despite having written several books, her name is still unknown to the average reader.* **Ant.** known, recognized, identified, familiar.

unlike *adj.* different, dissimilar, unrelated, opposite. *She is completely unlike her sister.* **Ant.** like, similar, identical.

unlikely *adj.* improbable, doubtful, questionable, implausible. *It's unlikely to snow today.* **Ant.** likely, probable, certain.

unmistakable *adj.* clear, obvious, evident, distinct, plain, apparent, conspicuous. *He bears an unmistakable resemblance to his father.* **Ant.** vague, unclear, uncertain, obscure.

unnecessary *adj.* unneeded, needless, useless, superfluous, pointless. *The soldiers were cautioned not to take unnecessary risks.* **Ant.** necessary, essential, useful.

unnoticed *adj.* unobserved, unseen, undiscovered, unheeded. *He hoped that his mismatched socks would go unnoticed.* **Ant.** noticed, observed, discovered.

unoccupied *adj.* uninhabited, vacant, empty, deserted, idle, open. *You may stay in our unoccupied guest room.* **Ant.** inhabited, occupied, full.

unpleasant *adj.* disagreeable, objectionable, displeasing, offensive, repulsive. *The room had an unpleasant odor.* **Ant.** pleasant, agreeable, pleasing.

unpopular *adj.* disliked, unloved, unwanted, friendless, unwelcome, undesirable. *Eliminating summer vacation is an idea that is unpopular with most schoolchildren.* **Ant.** liked, loved, wanted, desired.

unqualified *adj.* **1.** incompetent, incapable, inexperienced, unprepared, unsuited, unfit. *He is completely unqualified to be an astronaut.* **2.** absolute, total, complete, utter, unconditional. *Her response to the marriage proposal was an unqualified yes.* **Ant. 1.** qualified, competent, capable. **2.** conditional, limited.

unreal *adj.* imaginary, imagined, pretended, dreamlike, fictitious, false, imitation. *Though the movie was delightful, the world it portrayed is unreal.* **Ant.** real, realistic, factual, true.

unreasonable *adj.* **1.** absurd, irrational, senseless, illogical, foolish. *It's unreasonable to expect all the world's problems will be solved overnight.* **2.** excessive, extreme, exorbitant, unfair, impossible. *Don't place unreasonable demands on your friends.* **Ant. 1.** reasonable, logical, sensible. **2.** moderate, fair.

unreliable *adj.* undependable, untrustworthy, irresponsible, uncertain, questionable. *His information comes from an unreliable source.* **Ant.** reliable, dependable, responsible.

unrest *n.* turmoil, turbulence, disturbance, trouble, agitation, disorder, dissatisfaction. *There is much unrest in the world today.* **Ant.** peace, quiet, calm.

unrivaled *adj.* incomparable, unequaled, peerless, matchless, greatest, finest. *He is the unrivaled chess champion of our school.*

unruly *adj.* ungovernable, uncontrollable, unmanageable, disobedient, disorderly, wild. *Police tried to control the unruly mob.* **Ant.** controllable, manageable, obedient, docile.

unsafe *adj.* hazardous, dangerous, risky, perilous, insecure, precarious, unreliable, vulnerable. *Heavy flooding undermined the bridge* *and made it unsafe to cross.* **Ant.** safe, secure, harmless, reliable.

unsatisfactory *adj.* unacceptable, inadequate, insufficient, poor, deficient, unsuitable. *The new employee's output is unsatisfactory.* **Ant.** satisfactory, adequate, appropriate.

unselfish *adj.* altruistic, selfless, generous, considerate, magnanimous. *Her unselfish behavior earned everyone's respect.* **Ant.** selfish, greedy, egotistical.

unskilled *adj.* inexperienced, untrained, untalented, inexpert. *Since he's an unskilled worker, he is having trouble finding a job.* **Ant.** skilled, trained, experienced.

unsophisticated *adj.* naive, inexperienced, unassuming, simple, natural, plain. *A child's view of the world is usually unsophisticated.* **Ant.** sophisticated, experienced, complex.

unstable *adj.* **1.** unsteady, insecure, unsafe, precarious, shaky, infirm. *Your ladder is pretty unstable the way you've got it positioned.* **2.** fluctuating, changing, changeable, vacillating, volatile. *That chemical compound is unstable at room temperature.* **Ant. 1.** stable, steady, safe. **2.** stable, unchanging, constant.

unsuccessful *adj.* failed, abortive, fruitless, unproductive, futile, vain, unprosperous. *He was unsuccessful in his attempt to make the basketball team.* **Ant.** successful, productive, winning.

unsuitable *adj.* inappropriate, unfitting, unsatisfactory, improper, unacceptable. *He was unsuitable for the job because he had no relevant experience.* **Ant.** appropriate, satisfactory, fitting.

unthinkable *adj.* inconceivable, unimaginable, incomprehensible, incredible, absurd, ridiculous, preposterous. *For dedicated students, cutting class is unthinkable.* **Ant.** conceivable, believable.

unused *adj.* **1.** new, fresh, pristine, untouched, untried, original. *Here's an unused toothbrush for you.* **2.** unutilized, unemployed, vacant, idle. *You can stay in our unused guest room.* **3.** unaccustomed, unfamiliar with, unacquainted with. *The bachelor was unused to the commotion caused by his friend's children.* **Ant.**

1. used, old, secondhand. **2.** used, utilized. **3.** accustomed.

unusual *adj.* exceptional, extraordinary, uncommon, rare, unique, strange. *It's unusual for him to turn down a second piece of cake.* **Ant.** usual, common, ordinary, typical.

unwary *adj.* incautious, careless, reckless, imprudent, unsuspecting, rash. *The accident was caused by an unwary driver.* **Ant.** wary, cautious.

unwell *adj.* sick, ill, ailing, unhealthy, indisposed, poorly, weak, frail. *Since she's feeling unwell, she decided to stay home.* **Ant.** well, healthy, fit, vigorous.

unwilling *adj.* reluctant, disinclined, opposed, loath, averse. *The bank was unwilling to lend more money to the bankrupt company.* **Ant.** willing, amenable, inclined.

unwitting *adj.* unknowing, unaware, unconscious, inadvertent, accidental, involuntary. *By telling a friend about her bank's procedures, she became an unwitting accomplice to a robbery.* **Ant.** knowing, voluntary, intentional.

unyielding *adj.* inflexible, resolute, persistent, obstinate, stubborn, firm, rigid. *The negotiations are stalled because both sides have taken unyielding stands.* **Ant.** yielding, flexible, adaptable.

up *adv.* **1.** upward, aloft, higher, above, overhead. *She looked up and saw the airplane.* *–vb.* **2.** increase, raise, lift, boost, hike. *They upped their prices.* *–adj.* **3.** awake, alert, ready, prepared, set. *He's up for tomorrow's midterm.* **Ant. 1.** down, below. **2.** lower, reduce, decrease. **3.** unprepared.

upcoming *adj.* forthcoming, approaching, coming, nearing, imminent, momentary. *She's getting nervous about her upcoming wedding.* **Ant.** distant, remote.

update *vb.* revise, modernize, renew, refresh, renovate. *She updated her resume to show her most recent work experience.*

uphold *vb.* support, maintain, sustain, defend, preserve, protect. *Police officers are sworn to uphold the law.*

upkeep *n.* maintenance, repair, support, overhead, backing, provision. *More money needs to be allocated for the upkeep of our roads.*

upper *adj.* higher, superior, greater, top, topmost, eminent, important. *She wants to become a member of the upper class.* **Ant.** lower, inferior.

upright *adj.* **1.** vertical, perpendicular, erect, raised. *The arrow missed the target and landed in an upright position.* **2.** honest, just, virtuous, honorable, moral, trustworthy. *Since we had thought he was upright, we were surprised when he lied to us.* **Ant. 1.** horizontal, prone. **2.** dishonest, corrupt, unethical.

uprising *n.* revolt, rebellion, revolution, insurrection, mutiny, outbreak, upheaval. *The American War of Independence was a popular uprising against British rule.*

uproar *n.* commotion, turmoil, tumult, clamor, furor, stir, noise, disturbance. *People were in an uproar over the new taxes.* **Ant.** serenity, tranquillity, peace, calm.

upset *vb.* **1.** overturn, upend, topple, invert, capsize. *The inexperienced sailors upset their boat on a calm day.* **2.** disturb, distress, agitate, perturb, dismay, bother, annoy. *The news of her friend's accident upset her.* **3.** disorganize, disorder, confuse, jumble, change, cancel. *The unexpected rain upset our plans for a softball game.* **4.** sicken, turn, afflict, indispose. *Eating all that cake will upset your stomach.* *–adj.* **5.** overturned, upended, upturned, toppled, capsized. *All lanes of the freeway were blocked by an upset truck.* **6.** perturbed, distressed, disturbed, troubled, bothered, annoyed. *She was upset by my tactless remark.* **7.** sickened, turned, afflicted, indisposed. *She has an upset stomach.* **Ant. 2.** soothe, calm, pacify. **3.** organize, order, stabilize. **5.** upright, standing, erect. **6.** unperturbed, calm, quiet.

urban *adj.* city, metropolitan, municipal, civic, cosmopolitan. *The small-town boy had trouble adjusting to urban living.* **Ant.** rural, rustic, pastoral.

urbane *adj.* suave, sophisticated, elegant, refined, cultivated, polished, courteous, polite. *The young man was impressed by the socialite's urbane mannerisms.* **Ant.** crude, unrefined, inelegant, tactless.

urge *vb.* **1.** plead, beg, implore, beseech, entreat, advise. *They urged me to join their club.* **2.** force, drive, push, press, prod, impel. *She urged her horse over the jump.* *–n.* **3.** impulse, yearning, longing, desire, wish. *He has an urge for a pineapple pizza.* **Ant. 1.** discourage, dissuade, caution. **2.** restrain, prevent. **3.** distaste, repugnance, aversion.

urgent *adj.* pressing, compelling, crucial, essential, critical, important, immediate. *She was called out of town on urgent business.* **Ant.** unimportant, insignificant, unnecessary.

usage *n.* use, treatment, employment, application, handling. *His skis are still in good shape despite years of hard usage.*

use *vb.* **1.** utilize, employ, operate, work, manipulate, apply. *Do you know how to use a computer?* **2.** consume, expend, spend, exhaust, deplete. *That old air-conditioner uses too much electricity.* *–n.* **3.** service, application, employment, utilization, usage, work. *She's gotten a lot of use out of that old car.* **4.** benefit, utility, advantage, significance, value. *There's no use talking to him because he won't listen.* **Ant. 2.** save, conserve. **3.** disuse, unemployment. **4.** disadvantage.

useful *adj.* helpful, beneficial, advantageous, valuable, practical. *A microwave oven is useful if you don't have much time for cooking.* **Ant.** useless, worthless, unhelpful.

useless *adj.* valueless, worthless, ineffectual, unserviceable, futile, unavailing. *This old saw is so dull it's now useless.* **Ant.** useful, practical, worthwhile.

usual *adj.* normal, customary, habitual, regular, accustomed, typical, ordinary. *She took her usual seat at the table.* **Ant.** uncommon, unusual, rare, unique.

usurp *vb.* seize, steal, grab, preempt, appropriate, assume. *I feel like he's trying to usurp my authority.* **Ant.** surrender, yield, relinquish.

utensil *n.* implement, instrument, tool, device, apparatus, gadget. *Please lay out the eating utensils.*

utilize *vb.* use, employ, exploit, handle, apply. *What kind of fuel does your camp stove utilize?*

utmost *adj.* **1.** maximum, extreme, greatest, largest, highest, most. *I have the utmost respect for his accomplishments.* –*n.* **2.** ultimate, best, maximum, peak. *She did her utmost to help him.* **Ant. 1–2.** least, minimum.

utter *adj.* **1.** complete, total, entire, absolute, extreme, thorough, unqualified. *His room is an utter mess.* –*vb.* **2.** speak, say, articulate, express, pronounce, talk. *She didn't utter a single word.* **Ant. 1.** incomplete, partial, limited.

utterly *adv.* completely, thoroughly, entirely, totally, wholly, fully. *Dinner was utterly enjoyable.* **Ant.** partially, incompletely.

vacant *adj.* unoccupied, empty, uninhabited, unfilled, void, open, clear. *The apartment next to ours is vacant.* **Ant.** occupied, full, filled.

vacate *vb.* leave, clear, empty, relinquish, give up. *Since our house has been sold, we have to vacate it in two weeks.* **Ant.** occupy, fill, possess.

vacation *n.* holiday, break, rest, leave, furlough. *She's going to Mexico on her vacation.*

vacuum *n.* **1.** emptiness, void, nothingness, empty space. *Sound cannot travel through the vacuum of outer space.* –*vb.* **2.** clean, sweep. *Please vacuum the rug.*

vague *adj.* indefinite, uncertain, intangible, confusing, indistinct, fuzzy, hazy. *The suspect gave only a vague response when questioned about his activities.* **Ant.** definite, certain, clear, specific.

vain *adj.* **1.** conceited, arrogant, proud, smug, egotistical, haughty. *The actor was so vain he assumed everyone admired him.* **2.** useless, futile, worthless, unsuccessful, ineffective. *She made a vain attempt to save the crippled bird.* **Ant. 1.** humble, modest, unassuming. **2.** successful, effective.

valiant *adj.* courageous, valorous, brave, heroic, fearless, gallant, bold. *Valiant men and women are needed to lead the struggle against drug and alcohol abuse.* **Ant.** cowardly, timid, fearful.

valid *adj.* **1.** sound, logical, acceptable, suitable, justifiable. *The child could not offer a valid explanation for missing school.* **2.** authentic, genuine, legitimate, real, legal, lawful. *You need a valid passport to enter that country.* **Ant. 1.** unacceptable, unconvincing. **2.** invalid, fake, illegal.

valley *n.* basin, vale, dale, dell, glen. *Her dream is to have a cabin in a remote mountain valley.*

valor *n.* courage, bravery, heroism, fearlessness, gallantry. *The firefighter was decorated for valor after he saved three people from a burning home.* **Ant.** cowardice, fear.

valuable *adj.* **1.** important, worthy, worthwhile, valued, invaluable. *Though he's not getting paid much, he's gaining valuable experience.* **2.** costly, expensive, high-priced, precious. *She has a valuable collection of first-edition books.* **Ant. 1.** unimportant, worthless. **2.** inexpensive, cheap, valueless.

value *n.* **1.** importance, merit, worth, significance, use, usefulness. *Having a knowledge of computers can be of great value when looking for a job.* **2.** cost, price, expense, amount, charge. *The value of gold changes from day to day.* –*vb.* **3.** price, appraise, assess, evaluate, estimate. *My art collection has been valued at $20,000.* **4.** treasure, appreciate, prize, cherish, revere, esteem. *I truly value your friendship.* **Ant. 1.** unimportance, insignificance. **4.** disdain, disregard.

vandal *n.* destroyer, wrecker, despoiler, plunderer, hoodlum. *Vandals did extensive damage to several of the school's classrooms.*

vandalism *n.* destruction, defacement, mutilation, sabotage, mischief. *He was charged with vandalism for tipping over tombstones.*

vanish *vb.* disappear, fade, evaporate, dissolve, dematerialize. *The sorceress vanished into thin air.* **Ant.** appear, materialize.

vanity *n.* pride, conceit, arrogance, egotism, smugness. *She liked to flirt because the responses she got appealed to her vanity.* **Ant.** humility, humbleness, modesty.

vanquish *vb.* overcome, conquer, defeat, subdue, beat, eliminate, master. *The shy boy was able to vanquish his fear of meeting girls.* **Ant.** lose, surrender, yield, submit.

vapor *n.* mist, fog, haze, smoke, steam, moisture. *In old horror movies, the monsters frequently appear amidst clouds of vapor.*

variable *adj.* **1.** changing, changeable, shifting, fluctuating, unsteady, unstable. *In the spring, weather conditions are highly variable.* –*n.* **2.** uncertainty, contingency, possibility. *It's hard to predict the weather because there are so many variables.* **Ant. 1.** invariable, unchanging, constant. **2.** certainty, constant.

variety *n.* **1.** diversity, diverseness, variation, change, difference. *For the sake of variety, let's go camping on our next vacation.* **2.** collection, assortment, mixture, conglomeration, hodgepodge. *The mountaineer carried a large variety of climbing hardware.* **3.** type, sort, class, kind, brand, species, classification. *The local supermarket stocks apples of many different varieties.* **Ant. 1.** uniformity, similarity, monotony.

various *adj.* different, diverse, varied, varying, assorted, numerous, many. *There are various ways to deal with this problem.* **Ant.** identical, uniform, few.

vary *vb.* deviate, change, differ, alter, diversify, fluctuate, shift. *The price of gasoline varies almost continuously.*

vast *adj.* immense, enormous, colossal, huge, limitless, infinite. *The starship Enterprise explores the vast reaches of outer space.* **Ant.** minute, small, tiny, limited.

vault *n.* **1.** tomb, crypt, sepulcher, mausoleum, grave. *The pyramid's vault contained the mummified remains of an Egyptian pharaoh.* **2.** safe, strongroom, depository, repository. *The bank's vault is sealed with a time clock.* –*vb.* **3.** leap, spring, jump, bound, hurdle, hop. *The deer vaulted gracefully over a fallen tree.*

veer *vb.* swerve, pivot, turn, shift, curve, drift. *The driver had to veer sharply to avoid a head-on collision.*

vegetation *n.* flora, plant life, plants, shrubbery, foliage, growth. *Jungle travel is difficult because of the thick vegetation.*

vehement *adj.* passionate, enthusiastic, ardent, fervent, zealous, forceful, eager. *She's a vehement advocate of animal rights.* **Ant.** indifferent, unconcerned, apathetic.

vehicle *n.* **1.** conveyance, transportation, transport. *Bicycles and automobiles are two examples of commonly used vehicles.* **2.** means, medium, agency, instrument, channel, tool. *The actress hoped her small role would be a vehicle to greater recognition.*

veil *n.* **1.** cover, covering, screen, mask, curtain. *The mountaintop was hidden behind a veil of clouds.* –*vb.* **2.** hide, cover, screen, conceal, mask. *The bandit veiled his face with a bright red scarf.* **Ant. 2.** reveal, expose, show.

vein *n.* **1.** seam, streak, course, line, stratum, layer. *The prospector was overjoyed when he found a large vein of gold.* **2.** manner, style, mood, character, tone, bent. *Mark Twain typically wrote in a humorous vein.*

velocity *n.* speed, pace, rate, swiftness, quickness. *Sound waves travel at a velocity of approximately 740 miles per hour.*

vendor *n.* peddler, seller, purveyor, merchandiser, supplier. *She has a part-time job as an ice-cream vendor.* **Ant.** buyer, purchaser, customer.

venerable *adj.* honored, revered, respected, respectable, dignified, worthy. *The venerable old man took his customary place at the head of the table.* **Ant.** dishonorable, undeserving, unworthy.

vengeance *n.* revenge, retaliation, reprisal, retribution, avenging. *The honorable hero of "Les Miserables" did not seek vengeance against those who had wronged him.*

venom *n.* **1.** poison, toxin. *A rattlesnake can control the amount of venom it injects.* **2.** hate, hatred, bitterness, malice, spite, spitefulness. *The disillusioned critic wrote reviews that were always full of venom.* **Ant. 2.** kindness, love, charity.

vent *n.* **1.** outlet, opening, aperture, hole, passage. *She opened the vent to let fresh air into her car.* **2.** expression, exposure, voice, utterance. *The child gave vent to her anger by kicking the door.* –*vb.* **3.** discharge, release, emit, express, air. *He vented his frustrations on his hapless employees.* **Ant. 3.** suppress, repress, restrain.

ventilate *vb.* **1.** air, aerate, refresh. *This room needs to be ventilated.* **2.** expose, divulge, examine, discuss, publicize, circulate. *The open-door policy was designed to give employees an opportunity to ventilate their grievances.* **Ant. 2.** conceal, repress, suppress.

venture *n.* **1.** risk, chance, hazard, gamble, endeavor, undertaking. *The daredevil's ventures were well publicized.* –*vb.* **2.** risk, chance, gamble, hazard, speculate. *She was unwilling to venture her money on the stock market.* **3.** journey, travel, go, advance. *A firefighter ventured into the burning building.* **Ant. 2.** save, preserve, protect.

verbal *adj.* spoken, oral, voiced, unwritten. *The witness gave police a verbal description of the suspect.* **Ant.** written, documented.

verdict *n.* decision, judgment, finding, ruling, conclusion. *The jury took five days to reach a verdict.*

verge *n.* **1.** edge, rim, margin, brink, threshold. *The boy was on the verge of tears when his parents scolded him.* –*vb.* **2.** approach, approximate, border, touch. *Her remark verges on heresy.*

verify *vb.* attest, confirm, affirm, authenticate, corroborate, prove, substantiate. *Her testimony verified that the suspect could not have been at the scene of the crime.* **Ant.** refute, deny, disprove.

versatile *adj.* **1.** multifaceted, many-sided, all-around, adaptable, talented, gifted. *The versatile ballplayer was as good in the infield as he was in the outfield.* **2.** all-purpose, practical, useful, handy, convenient. *A Swiss army knife is a versatile tool.* **Ant. 1.** specialized, limited. **2.** impractical, useless.

version *n.* **1.** account, rendition, story, report, description. *Each driver had his own version of how the accident occurred.* **2.** rendering, adaptation, portrayal, translation. *She makes her living writing modern versions of old fairy tales.*

vertical *adj.* perpendicular, upright, erect, plumb, standing. *She easily scaled the vertical rock face.* **Ant.** horizontal, flat, level.

very *adv.* **1.** extremely, especially, immensely, enormously, remarkably, exceedingly. *He's a very good tennis player.* –*adj.* **2.** exact, precise, specific, perfect, genuine, real. *This is the very thing you need to cure your cold.* **3.** mere, bare, sheer, simple. *The very idea of climbing a mountain makes most people uneasy.* **Ant. 1.** scarcely, hardly, barely. **2.** inappropriate, wrong, useless.

vessel *n.* **1.** boat, ship, craft. *The port was crowded with many types of sailing vessels.* **2.** container, receptacle, utensil, pot, jar. *This acid must be stored in a glass vessel.*

vestige *n.* **1.** trace, hint, suggestion, remnant, remains, evidence. *A few stone implements were the only vestiges of the lost tribe.*

veteran *n.* **1.** old-timer, master, expert, professional, pro. *The golf veteran had played in numerous previous tournaments.* –*adj.* **2.** experienced, practiced, seasoned, skilled, proficient, expert. *The veteran Congressman was elected to a sixth term.* **Ant. 1.** novice, beginner, recruit. **2.** inexperienced, unpracticed.

veto *vb.* **1.** refuse, reject, deny, forbid, kill, void. *The president vetoed the new tax bill.* –*n.* **2.** denial, refusal, disapproval, rejection, ban. *The mayor's veto was overturned by the city council.* **Ant. 1.** approve, endorse, ratify. **2.** approval, endorsement.

vex *vb.* annoy, bother, irritate, trouble, distress, provoke, worry. *She is frequently vexed by her friend's constant complaining.*

vibrate *vb.* shake, tremble, quiver, quaver, quake. *Our windows vibrate whenever a plane passes overhead.*

vibration *n.* trembling, shaking, quivering, throbbing, tremor. *We could feel the vibrations caused by a big truck driving by outside.*

vice *n.* **1.** immorality, depravity, corruption, evil, ill, sin. *The local newspaper ran a series on vice in the city.* **2.** weakness, shortcoming, frailty, fault, flaw, bad point. *Her only vice is a constant craving for sweets.* **Ant. 1.** virtue, morality. **2.** good point, strong point.

vicinity *n.* proximity, neighborhood, environs, region. *We live in the vicinity of the airport.*

vicious *adj.* **1.** savage, dangerous, ferocious, fierce, violent. *Pit bulls have a reputation for being vicious dogs.* **2.** depraved, wicked, evil, vile, terrible. *Kidnaping is a vicious crime.* **3.** spiteful, malicious, hateful, hurtful, cruel, mean. *He told a vicious lie about his sister.* **Ant. 1.** tamed, gentle, friendly. **2.** moral, decent, virtuous. **3.** kind, good-natured, complimentary.

victim *n.* **1.** casualty, injured, fatality. *There were five victims in yesterday's accident.* **2.** dupe, loser, target, prey, scapegoat, sufferer. *The con artist swindled his victims out of all their savings.*

victor *n.* winner, champion, conqueror, vanquisher. *The United States and its allies were the victors of World War II.* **Ant.** loser, defeated, vanquished.

victorious *adj.* winning, triumphant, successful, conquering, champion. *The victorious team advanced to the state finals.* **Ant.** losing, defeated, beaten.

victory *n.* triumph, success, conquest, supremacy, primacy, win. *The candidate claimed victory before the polls closed.* **Ant.** defeat, loss, failure.

view *n.* **1.** vista, panorama, scene, outlook, sight, vision. *We have a lovely view of the surrounding hills from our front porch.* **2.** look, sight, glimpse, glance, peek. *As we turned up the driveway, we got our first view of our new home.* **3.** opinion, thought, conviction, sentiment, notion, judgment. *What are your views on nuclear energy?* –*vb.* **4.** see, watch, behold, witness, observe. *People come from all over the world to view the splendors of Yosemite.*

vigilant *adj.* observant, watchful, attentive, heedful, alert, wary. *A vigilant guard foiled the attempted robbery.* **Ant.** negligent, careless, heedless.

vigor *n.* energy, vitality, animation, fervor, strength, force, might. *She presented her idea with great vigor.* **Ant.** indifference, apathy, weakness.

vigorous *adj.* energetic, active, robust, dynamic, strong, forceful, lively. *He was very tired after playing a vigorous set of tennis.* **Ant.** lethargic, unenergetic, feeble, weak.

vile *adj.* **1.** offensive, disgusting, objectionable, nauseating, revolting, repugnant. *Rotten eggs have a vile odor.* **2.** evil, wicked, corrupt, immoral, vicious, sinful. *Terrorism is widely considered to be one of the most vile crimes imagin-*

able. **Ant. 1.** agreeable, pleasant, appealing. **2.** righteous, moral.

village *n.* hamlet, settlement, municipality, small town, community. *The Swiss village was nestled among the Alps.* **Ant.** city, metropolis.

villain *n.* scoundrel, rascal, rogue, knave, brute, devil, wretch. *The audience cheered when the movie's villain was defeated.* **Ant.** hero, heroine, champion.

vindictive *adj.* spiteful, revengeful, vengeful, malicious, bitter. *The fired employee spread vindictive rumors about his ex-boss.* **Ant.** forgiving, charitable.

violate *vb.* breach, break, infringe, disobey, disregard, defy. *By staying out late, she violated her parents' trust.* **Ant.** respect, uphold, obey.

violation *n.* breach, infraction, infringement, dishonoring. *He will lose his driver's license if he gets another moving violation.* **Ant.** observance, obedience, compliance.

violence *n.* **1.** force, brutality, savagery, ferociousness, roughness. *Many people think there is too much violence on television.* **2.** intensity, severity, might, power, magnitude. *We were not prepared for a storm of such violence.* **Ant. 1.** nonviolence, peacefulness. **2.** mildness, weakness.

violent *adj.* **1.** powerful, strong, forceful, intense, severe. *The sailboat was capsized by a violent wind.* **2.** brutal, cruel, destructive, murderous, savage, ferocious. *There is too much violent crime in our city.* **3.** fiery, passionate, uncontrollable, ungovernable. *He has a violent temper.* **Ant. 1.** mild, weak. **2.** nonviolent, peaceful. **3.** composed, collected.

virgin *adj.* unused, untouched, unspoiled, pristine, pure, new. *There is not much virgin wilderness left in the world today.* **Ant.** used, spoiled, contaminated.

virtue *n.* **1.** morality, integrity, goodness, righteousness, honor, honesty. *Her virtue is unquestioned.* **2.** strength, quality, merit, advantage, value, benefit. *The fact that this computer is easy to use is just one of its many virtues.* **Ant. 1.** immorality, sinfulness, vice. **2.** disadvantage, drawback.

virtuous *adj.* moral, good, righteous, honorable, ethical, principled. *He seems so virtuous, it's hard to believe he could tell a lie.* **Ant.** immoral, bad, sinful.

visible *adj.* **1.** observable, seeable, viewable, noticeable, perceptible. *Our house is not visible from the road.* **2.** apparent, evident, obvious, clear, plain. *She has made no visible progress toward her college degree.* **Ant. 1.** invisible, hidden, concealed. **2.** imperceptible, unapparent.

vision *n.* **1.** sight, eyesight, seeing. *Her vision was correctable to 20/20 with eyeglasses.* **2.** foresight, imagination, perception, intuition, wisdom. *The company's success is largely due to the vision of its founder.* **3.** dream, fantasy, fancy, idea, notion. *The young actor has visions of becoming a famous star.*

visit *vb.* **1.** call on, see, attend, go to, drop by. *Let's visit Grandmother next weekend.* *–n.* **2.** call, stop, visitation, stopover, stay, sojourn. *Our neighbor came over for a short visit.*

visitor *n.* **1.** guest, caller, company. *I can't go out tonight because I'm expecting visitors.* **2.** tourist, traveler, vacationer, sightseer. *We're visitors in your country.*

visual *adj.* visible, observable, perceptible, discernible, seeable. *The air-traffic controller does not yet have visual contact with the approaching plane.*

vital *adj.* **1.** essential, crucial, critical, important, imperative, necessary. *Her contributions were vital to the project's success.* **2.** energetic, dynamic, spirited, lively, animated, active. *Despite his age, he still has a vital personality.* **Ant. 1.** unimportant, insignificant. **2.** lethargic, listless.

vitality *n.* strength, vigor, energy, life, liveliness, spirit. *Grandmother's vitality continuously amazes me.* **Ant.** weakness, lifelessness.

vivid *adj.* **1.** keen, sharp, intense, strong, acute, clear. *He has vivid recollections of his childhood.* **2.** bright, brilliant, loud, colorful, shiny. *She painted her bike a vivid green.* **Ant. 1.** average, routine. **2.** dull, drab, colorless.

vocal *adj.* **1.** said, spoken, oral, uttered, voiced, vocalized. *The parrot made many vocal sounds, but it couldn't really speak.* **2.** outspo-ken, blunt, frank, free, candid, direct. *You shouldn't be so vocal in your criticism of others.* **Ant. 1.** unspoken, unvoiced. **2.** silent, quiet, reserved.

vocation *n.* occupation, profession, career, business, employment. *What vocation are you preparing for?*

vogue *n.* fashion, style, fad, rage, custom, practice. *Skinny ties have not been in vogue for years.*

voice *n.* **1.** speech, speaking, vocalization, verbalization, articulation, utterance. *She has temporarily lost her voice due to laryngitis.* **2.** opinion, choice, option, vote, say, role, part. *Local residents should have a voice in running their town government.* *–vb.* **3.** say, state, speak, utter, verbalize, express, proclaim. *If you have any complaints, please voice them now.*

void *adj.* **1.** empty, vacant, barren, devoid, destitute. *The movie was completely void of any redeeming qualities.* **2.** invalid, meaningless, worthless, useless, canceled. *This contest is void wherever prohibited by law.* *–n.* **3.** vacuum, emptiness, nothingness, hollow. *After he lost his job, his life seemed to be a meaningless void.* *–vb.* **4.** cancel, nullify, invalidate, revoke, annul. *Since the salesman had lied to her, she wanted to void her purchase contract.* **Ant. 1.** full, complete, occupied. **2.** valid, binding, useful. **4.** validate, enforce, uphold.

volume *n.* **1.** book, publication, tract, treatise. *She has written several volumes of poetry.* **2.** capacity, size, bulk, dimensions. *The jar has a volume of three liters.* **3.** amount, quantity, mass, measure, extent. *The new video store did a large volume of business on its opening day.* **4.** sound, power, intensity, loudness. *Do you mind if I turn up the volume on the TV?*

voluntary *adj.* optional, free, willing, unforced, volunteered. *Only voluntary confessions are admissible in a court of law.* **Ant.** involuntary, forced, coerced, compelled.

volunteer *adj.* **1.** voluntary, willing, unforced, unpaid, nonprofessional. *The Revolutionary War was won by volunteer soldiers.* *–n.* **2.** unforced person, voluntary person, unpaid person. *The Senator asked for volunteers to staff his reelection committee.* *–vb.* **3.** offer, give, provide, donate, contribute. *She volunteered her time to* *serve on the fund-raising committee.* **Ant. 1.** involuntary, forced, paid. **3.** withhold, refuse.

vote *n.* **1.** ballot, ticket, selection, choice, preference. *Who did you cast your vote for? –vb.* **2.** cast a ballot, elect, select, choose. *Don't forget to vote in this year's elections.*

vouch *vb.* guarantee, affirm, assure, confirm, verify, certify. *I can vouch for her honesty.* **Ant.** deny, refute, repudiate.

vow *n.* **1.** pledge, promise, oath, assurance, guarantee. *He made a vow to stop drinking. –vb.* **2.** pledge, promise, swear, resolve, declare. *She vowed to stop smoking by next week..*

voyage *n.* **1.** cruise, sail, crossing, passage, journey, excursion. *She took her new sailboat on a long voyage. –vb.* **2.** cruise, sail, navigate, boat, journey. *People will someday be able to voyage between the stars.*

vulgar *adj.* coarse, crude, rude, impolite, unrefined, tasteless, indecent. *Vulgar language has no place in school.* **Ant.** polite, refined, tasteful.

vulnerable *adj.* defenseless, susceptible, unguarded, unprotected, exposed. *His weakened condition left him vulnerable to disease.* **Ant.** protected, guarded, invincible.

wad *n.* batch, lump, mass, chunk, plug, pack. *She chewed on a huge wad of gum.*

wage *n.* **1.** salary, pay, payment, fee, compensation, earnings. *His new job pays only minimum wage.* *-vb.* **2.** conduct, pursue, undertake, make, carry on. *She is waging a personal war against drunk drivers.*

wager *n.* **1.** bet, gamble, speculation, chance. *They made a wager on the outcome of the bowling tournament.* *-vb.* **2.** bet, gamble, venture, speculate, risk. *He wagered five dollars at the race track.*

wail *n.* **1.** moan, cry, whine, lamentation, howl. *The siren's wail could be heard throughout town.* *-vb.* **2.** moan, weep, cry, whine, howl, roar. *The wind wailed all night long.*

wait *vb.* **1.** linger, tarry, dally, remain, delay, stay. *Let's wait till next week to wash the car.* *-n.* **2.** delay, pause, holdup, postponement, lull. *We have a two-hour wait before the next bus leaves.* **Ant. 1.** begin, start, commence.

waive *vb.* relinquish, renounce, drop, forgo, resign, yield. *She signed an agreement that waived her right to sue.* **Ant.** demand, require, claim.

wake *vb.* **1.** arouse, rouse, stir, awaken, waken. *Please wake me at seven o'clock.* *-n.* **2.** aftermath, track, trail, course, path. *There was great damage in the wake of the hurricane.* **Ant. 1.** sleep, doze, slumber.

walk *vb.* **1.** stroll, saunter, amble, hike, march. *Let's walk to school today.* *-n.* **2.** stroll, hike, saunter, ramble, trek. *Grandfather likes to take a walk after dinner.* **3.** sidewalk, pathway, path, lane, passage. *It's your turn to shovel the front walk.* **4.** field, sphere, dominion, domain, area. *The new TV show appeals to people from all walks of life.*

wall *n.* barrier, partition, divider, barricade, fence. *The castle's walls were crumbling with age.*

wallow *vb.* **1.** roll, slosh, grovel, tumble, nestle. *On hot days, pigs keep cool by wallowing in mud.* **2.** flounder, stumble, reel, stagger, blunder. *The hunters wallowed through miles of swampland.* **3.** indulge, revel, bask, luxuriate, delight. *Since winning the lottery, she's been wallowing in luxury.* **Ant. 3.** abstain, refrain, forbear.

wander *vb.* **1.** rove, roam, ramble, range, drift, amble, stroll. *She wandered through the store, looking for an unusual gift.* **2.** stray, deviate, swerve, veer, digress. *His attention wandered as he watched the boring movie.* **Ant. 1.** stay, remain. **2.** conform, follow.

want *vb.* **1.** desire, wish, yearn, crave, covet, need, require. *She wants a computer for her birthday.* *-n.* **2.** need, requirement, necessity, desire, yearning, craving. *Since inheriting his father's fortune, he has no more material wants.* **Ant. 1.** loathe, hate, reject. **2.** abundance, sufficiency.

war *n.* **1.** warfare, combat, battle, conflict, struggle, fight, strife. *The war against drugs is an international effort.* *-vb.* **2.** fight, battle, attack, struggle, combat. *The two factions have been warring against each other for years.* **Ant. 1.** peace, harmony, alliance.

ward *n.* **1.** district, precinct, borough, zone. *The city is divided into seven administrative wards.* **2.** room, section, annex, department. *She has been admitted to the hospital's intensive-care ward.* **3.** charge, dependent, client. *The juvenile delinquent has become a ward of the court.* *-vb.* **4.** avert, avoid, evade, deter, block, repel. *This repellent will ward off mosquitoes.* **Ant. 4.** permit, accept, allow.

warden *n.* custodian, guardian, keeper, superintendent, supervisor. *He has retired from his position as warden of the state prison.*

wares *n.* merchandise, goods, products, stock, supplies. *The travelling merchant sold his wares at various swap meets.*

warlike *adj.* hostile, belligerent, bellicose, combative, militant. *A naval blockade is a warlike act.* **Ant.** peaceful, friendly, conciliatory.

warm *adj.* **1.** heated, lukewarm, tepid. *He enjoys warm spring days.* **2.** sunny, sunshiny, summery, mild. *She likes to dress in warm colors.* **3.** loving, affectionate, tender, friendly, kind. *She gave him a warm smile.* **4.** enthusiastic, lively, ardent, eager, sympathetic. *He was not particularly warm to the suggestion that he retire early.* –*vb.* **5.** heat, thaw, cook, simmer. *He warmed his hands over the campfire.* **6.** cheer, please, comfort, gladden, delight. *The sight of children playing warmed the old man's heart.* **Ant. 1.** cool, cold, chilly. **2.** dull, drab. **3.** unfriendly, uncaring. **4.** indifferent, apathetic. **5.** cool, chill. **6.** depress, sadden.

warn *vb.* forewarn, alert, caution, advise, admonish, inform. *She warned me not to eat the second pizza.*

warning *n.* notice, notification, signal, sign, omen, hint. *The police officer let me off with only a warning.*

warranty *n.* guarantee, assurance, pledge, security. *Her new car has a five-year warranty against defects.*

warrior *n.* fighter, soldier, combatant, military person. *Barbarian warriors swept down on the defenseless village.*

wary *adj.* cautious, suspicious, careful, watchful, guarded. *After losing her investment, she's wary of buying any more stocks.* **Ant.** unwary, unsuspecting, incautious.

wash *vb.* **1.** clean, cleanse, scrub, launder, bathe. *Please wash your hands before dinner.* **2.** drift, float, ride, slide, bob. *Debris from the sunken ship washed up on the beach.* **3.** carry away, remove, destroy, sweep. *Flood water washed out the local bridge.* –*n.* **4.** washing, cleaning, cleansing, laundering, bath. *Your car is in bad need of a wash.* **5.** laundry, clothes washing. *Since I have no clean clothes left, I'd better do the wash today.*

waste *vb.* **1.** squander, misuse, dissipate, throw away, deplete. *Don't waste your money buying clothes you don't need.* **2.** devastate, despoil, ravage, destroy, ruin. *The tornado wasted everything in its path.* **3.** decline, weaken, diminish, decrease, fade. *His strength wasted away during his long illness.* –*n.* **4.** garbage, rubbish, trash, debris, litter. *Toxic waste should be properly decontaminated before disposal.* **5.** extravagance, squandering, misuse, misapplication. *It's a waste of time and money trying to fix that old car.* **Ant. 1.** save, conserve, economize. **3.** strengthen, improve, increase. **5.** saving, conservation, economy.

wasteful *adj.* extravagant, squandering, uneconomical, nonproductive. *It's wasteful to throw away plastic containers that can be recycled.* **Ant.** economical, thrifty, productive.

watch *vb.* **1.** look, observe, see, view, notice, eye. *He thought no one was watching when he ate the last cookie.* **2.** guard, protect, attend, tend, supervise, oversee. *She asked her neighbor to watch her dogs while she was on vacation.* –*n.* **3.** observation, attention, surveillance, notice, heed. *The lifeguard kept a close watch over the children in the pool.* **4.** guard, sentry, sentinel, vigil, patrol, shift. *The night watch comes on duty in two hours.* **5.** timepiece, wristwatch, pocket watch, clock. *Don't forget to set your watch to daylight savings time.*

watchful *adj.* attentive, alert, vigilant, aware, wary. *The bank guard kept a watchful eye on the suspicious-looking man.* **Ant.** inattentive, unobservant, unaware.

water *vb.* moisten, wet, sprinkle, irrigate, soak. *Please water the plants while I'm on vacation.* **Ant.** parch, dehydrate, dry.

wave *n.* **1.** swell, breaker, surf, roller, comber. *Most surfers prefer big waves.* **2.** curl, twist, curve, spiral, coil. *A wave of hair kept blowing into her eyes.* **3.** pulse, pulsation, vibration, undulation. *Sound travels in waves.* **4.** surge, upsurge, flood, deluge, rush. *His announcement was greeted with a wave of protest.* **5.** gesture, hand, signal, sign, motion. *The police officer signaled us to stop with a wave of his hand.* –*vb.* **6.** sway, ripple, flutter, shake, waver. *The trees waved in the wind.* **7.** gesture, signal, motion. *She waved good-bye to her friends as they drove away.*

wax *vb.* **1.** polish, shine, buff, gloss. *It's time to wax the car.* –*n.* **2.** polish, resin, silicon. *Use this wax on the furniture.*

way *n.* **1.** method, style, manner, approach, technique. *What's the best way to solve this puzzle?* **2.** direction, route, course, path, trail. *The lost hiker couldn't find her way out of the forest.* **3.** distance, span, space, stretch. *The stranded motorist had to walk a long way to find a gas station.* **4.** wish, desire, will, fancy, choice. *That spoiled child throws a fit if he can't have his way.*

weak *adj.* **1.** feeble, frail, fragile, infirm, delicate, powerless. *After her long illness, she's too weak to walk.* **2.** thin, diluted, watery, cut, tasteless. *This tea is too weak.* **Ant. 1.** strong, powerful, sturdy. **2.** thick, concentrated.

weaken *vb.* soften, lower, lessen, fade, fail, thin, exhaust. *Her enthusiasm for the project is beginning to weaken.* **Ant.** strengthen, increase, improve.

weakness *n.* **1.** frailty, feebleness, infirmity, debility. *His weakness is the result of not exercising properly.* **2.** shortcoming, flaw, fault, defect, blemish. *Her biggest weakness is that she doesn't like to follow directions.* **3.** fondness, passion, liking, inclination, bias. *She has a weakness for frozen yogurt.* **Ant. 1.** strength, vitality. **2.** effectiveness. **3.** dislike, aversion.

wealth *n.* **1.** fortune, money, assets, capital, riches. *The heiress is a woman of great wealth.* **2.** abundance, profusion, store, fund, bounty. *He has discovered a wealth of information on that subject.* **Ant. 1.** poverty, destitution. **2.** scarcity, lack, shortage.

wealthy *adj.* rich, affluent, prosperous, well-off. *The wealthy woman buys a new sports car every year.* **Ant.** poor, needy, destitute.

wear *vb.* **1.** have on, dress in, don, bear. *She wore blue jeans to the party.* **2.** use up, exhaust, consume, abrade, fray. *He's had that shirt so long it's totally worn out.* **3.** tire, fatigue, strain, drain, exhaust. *She was worn out from working seven days a week.* n. **4.** apparel, clothes, clothing, garments. *Does this store sell men's wear?* **5.** use, service, utilization, employment. *She's gotten a lot of wear out of that jacket.* **Ant. 2.** save, conserve. **3.** refresh, revitalize.

weary *adj.* **1.** tired, exhausted, fatigued, drained, spent. *She was very weary after the long hike.* **2.** tiring, tiresome, fatiguing, tedious, boring, dull. *Most people consider writing a dictionary to be a weary task.* –*vb.* **3.** tire, fatigue, exhaust, wear out. *The long lecture wearied the entire audience.* **Ant. 1.** refreshed, revived, energetic. **2.** refreshing, interesting, exciting. **3.** refresh, revive.

weather *n.* **1.** climate, elements, conditions, temperature. *What's the weather like in California?* –*vb.* **2.** season, dry, bleach, age, wrinkle. *His face is weathered from the long years he has worked outside.* **3.** survive, endure, withstand, come through. *Her large yacht easily weathered the storm.* **Ant. 3.** succumb, yield, fail.

weave *vb.* **1.** knit, braid, plait, lace, spin. *A loom is used to weave cloth.* **2.** zigzag, wind, careen, wobble, stagger. *She had to weave her way through a large crowd to find an exit.*

web *n.* maze, tangle, net, network, snare, trap. *The spy was caught in the web of intrigue he had helped create.*

wed *vb.* marry, unite, bind, join, link, devote, dedicate. *He is wedded to his old-fashioned ways.* **Ant.** divorce, separate, divide.

weep *vb.* cry, sob, lament, mourn, grieve. *The sad movie made me weep.*

weight *n.* **1.** mass, poundage, heaviness. *The wrestler had to get his weight down to qualify for the tournament.* **2.** burden, strain, pressure, load, anxiety. *She's strong enough to carry the weight of her responsibilities.* **3.** importance, significance, influence, impact, authority. *Her opinion carries a lot of weight with me.* **Ant. 1.** weightlessness. **3.** unimportance, insignificance.

weird *adj.* odd, bizarre, strange, peculiar, queer, unnatural, eerie. *My car is making weird noises.* **Ant.** normal, usual, natural, ordinary.

welcome *vb.* **1.** receive, greet, hail, meet, accept. *She was sad because no one was there to welcome her home.* –*n.* **2.** greeting, reception, welcoming, acceptance. *He always gives his guests a warm welcome.* –*adj.* **3.** agreeable, pleasant, pleasing, delightful, enjoyable. *Hearing about your new job was welcome news.* **Ant. 1–2.** snub, rebuff. **3.** unwelcome, unwanted.

weld *vb.* braze, solder, connect, join, unite, combine. *The boy heated the piece of plastic to weld it into place.* **Ant.** detach, separate, sever.

welfare *n.* well-being, happiness, fortune, good, prosperity. *This law has been enacted for the welfare of the people.*

well *n.* **1.** hole, shaft, pit, spring, fountain. *We get our water from a well.* –*adj.* **2.** healthy, sound, robust, hale, hearty. *Though she has been sick, she's now feeling well.* –*adv.* **3.** satisfactorily, adequately, favorably, agreeably, nicely. *She hasn't slept well for the past several days.* **4.** fully, thoroughly, considerably, substantially, amply. *His new car is worth well over $20,000.* **Ant. 2.** sick, ill, infirm. **3.** badly, poorly. **4.** somewhat, scarcely.

wet *adj.* **1.** moist, damp, soaked, soaking, drenched, soggy. *Take off those wet clothes.* **2.** rainy, stormy, showery. *The last wet spell lasted for three weeks.* –*vb.* **3.** moisten, dampen, water, soak, saturate, drench. *The directions say you should wet your hair before applying this shampoo.* **Ant. 1.** dry, waterless. **2.** arid, parched. **3.** dry, dehydrate.

wharf *n.* dock, pier, jetty, berth, landing, mooring. *This wharf is used for the unloading of cargo ships.*

wheedle *vb.* coax, cajole, persuade, charm, flatter. *He wheedled his sister into taking him to the movies.*

wheel *vb.* **1.** turn, rotate, revolve, pivot, spin, twirl. *She wheeled around when she heard someone approaching from behind.* **2.** roll, push, maneuver, shove, propel. *They used a dolly to wheel the stove out to the moving van.*

whet *vb.* sharpen, excite, stimulate, arouse, entice. *Her brief story whet my curiosity to hear more about her travels.* **Ant.** satisfy, stifle, deaden.

whim *n.* impulse, inclination, caprice, notion, whimsy, fancy. *He bought that dreadful suit on a whim.*

whine *vb.* cry, sob, whimper, moan, complain. *The spoiled child whined to get what he wanted.*

whip *vb.* **1.** beat, strike, lash, flog, flail. *The stern schoolmaster whipped any student who misbehaved.* **2.** whisk, flick, jerk, snatch, sweep. *He whipped his sword out of its scabbard.* **3.** defeat, vanquish, overcome, trounce, beat. *Our women's softball team whipped their opponents.* –*n.* **4.** switch, lash, strap, crop. *The animal trainer used a whip to keep the lion at a safe distance.*

whirl *vb.* **1.** twist, spin, rotate, reel, revolve, turn. *The windmill's blades whirled in the breeze.* –*n.* **2.** turn, spin, revolution, rotation, twirl. *The dancers executed a graceful whirl.* **3.** bustle, rush, flurry, tumult, uproar. *There was a whirl of last-minute activity as we prepared the house for guests.*

whisk *vb.* **1.** brush, flick, sweep, swish, swipe. *She used her beach towel to whisk the sand off her legs.* **2.** hurry, speed, rush, hasten, zip. *The jogger was startled when a car whisked by.* **Ant. 2.** crawl, creep, drag.

whisper *vb.* **1.** speak softly, mumble, mutter, murmur. *It's impolite to whisper during the minister's sermon.* **2.** rustle, drone, sigh, buzz. *She enjoys listening to the wind whisper through the trees.* –*n.* **3.** murmur, mumble, mutter, undertone. *Though she spoke in a whisper, everyone heard what she said to her friend.* **Ant. 1–3.** shout, scream, bellow.

white *adj.* **1.** colorless, pallid, pale, blanched, bleached. *He turned white with fear.* **2.** snowy, pearly, milky, silvery, snow-white. *The bride wore a beautiful white gown.* **3.** harmless, innocent, innocuous, inoffensive. *He told a white lie when he said he liked your present.* **Ant. 1.** flushed, florid. **2.** black, ebony. **3.** harmful, hurtful.

whole *adj.* **1.** entire, complete, undivided, full, total. *He ate the whole cake by himself.* –*n.* **2.** entirety, totality, aggregate, sum, all. *She spent the whole of her vacation in England.* **Ant. 1.** incomplete, partial, divided. **2.** part, piece.

wholesome *adj.* **1.** healthy, healthful, nutritious, nourishing. *A wholesome diet is essential for good health.* **2.** moral, virtuous, decent, pure, clean. *She writes wholesome children's books.* **Ant. 1.** unwholesome, unhealthy, harmful. **2.** immoral, sinful.

wholly *adv.* completely, entirely, totally, fully, thoroughly. *He was wholly responsible for the accident.* **Ant.** incompletely, partially, partly.

wicked *adj.* immoral, bad, sinful, evil, vile, foul. *You should be ashamed of yourself for saying such a wicked thing about your friend.* **Ant.** moral, good, noble.

wide *adj.* **1.** broad, large, vast, extensive, spacious. *They can park two cars side by side on their wide driveway.* **2.** far, distant, off, remote, away. *His free-throw attempt was wide of the basket.* *-adv.* **3.** fully, completely, totally, entirely. *She had to hold her mouth wide open while the doctor examined her tonsils.* **Ant. 1.** narrow, thin, small. **2.** close, near, nearby. **3.** partially, incompletely, narrowly.

width *n.* breadth, broadness, girth, reach, range. *What is the width of your new garage?*

wield *vb.* command, exercise, manage, handle, exert, use. *The boxer's agent wields total control over his career.*

wild *adj.* **1.** untamed, undomesticated, uncivilized, primitive, savage. *She thinks wild animals shouldn't be caged in zoos.* **2.** unruly, undisciplined, uncontrolled, unrestrained. *A group of wild kids vandalized the school.* **3.** crazy, fantastic, foolish, silly, reckless. *That's just another of his wild schemes to get rich quick.* **4.** violent, ferocious, turbulent, raging, stormy. *A wild wind blew down the tree in our front yard.* **Ant. 1.** tamed, domesticated, civilized. **2.** disciplined, controlled. **3.** thoughtful, practical, realistic. **4.** calm, mild, gentle.

will *n.* **1.** resolution, determination, purpose, conviction, volition. *You'll have a hard time getting her to do anything against her will.* **2.** legacy, testament, bequest. *Were you mentioned in your late uncle's will?* *-vb.* **3.** resolve, determine, wish, desire, want. *You can do whatever you will with your life.* **4.** bequeath, endow, bestow, confer. *She willed her book collection to the local library.*

willing *adj.* consenting, agreeing, ready, inclined, disposed. *He was a willing accomplice to the robbery.* **Ant.** unwilling, reluctant, disinclined.

wilt *vb.* droop, sag, wither, languish, fade, weaken, die. *This hot weather has wilted my house plants.* **Ant.** thrive, flourish, bloom.

win *vb.* **1.** triumph, conquer, vanquish, defeat, beat, succeed. *She usually wins when we play tennis.* **2.** attain, achieve, obtain, gain, acquire. *He won a television set in last year's contest.* *-n.* **3.** victory, triumph, conquest, success. *Our team needs three wins out of the next four games.* **Ant. 1.** lose, fail, fall. **2.** lose, miss. **3.** defeat, loss, failure.

wind *n.* **1.** breeze, gust, draft, blow, gale. *The wind blew strongly just before the storm hit.* **2.** breath, air. *The football player had the wind knocked out of him.* **3.** hint, clue, suggestion, scent, smell. *If he catches wind of our plans, all our work will be lost.*

wind *vb.* **1.** coil, wrap, twist, entwine, screw. *Please wind this string into a ball.* **2.** turn, wander, meander, weave, twist. *The trail winds its way up the mountain.*

wing *n.* **1.** appendage, annex, addition, extension, branch, section. *The construction of a new wing doubled the hospital's size.* *-vb.* **2.** fly, soar, drift, glide, sail, speed. *In the fall, migratory birds wing their way south.*

winner *n.* victor, champion, vanquisher, conqueror. *She's the winner of our school's poetry contest.* **Ant.** loser.

wipe *vb.* **1.** rub, mop, scrub, cleanse, polish, dry. *Please wipe off the countertop.* **2.** erase, eradicate, eliminate, extinguish. *The hurricane wiped out an entire village.*

wire *n.* **1.** cable, filament, strand, cord. *I need a piece of wire to fix my pack.* **2.** telegraph, telegram, cable, cablegram. *News of the disaster arrived by wire.* *-vb.* **3.** fasten, tie, bind, lash, secure. *He wired the broken parts together.* **4.** telegraph, cable. *The traveling student wired home for more money.* **Ant. 3.** loosen, unfasten, untie.

wiry *adj.* sinewy, stringy, lean, tough, strong, athletic. *His wiry build is a result of all the running he does.* **Ant.** stout, fat, weak.

wisdom *n.* judgment, discernment, understanding, sense, sagacity. *People typically gain wisdom as they grow older and more experienced.* **Ant.** stupidity, foolishness, folly.

wise *adj.* bright, smart, intelligent, knowledgeable, educated. *She made a wise decision when she bought that business.* **Ant.** unwise, foolish, dumb, ignorant.

wish *n.* **1.** desire, want, hope, longing, yen, yearning. *His wish is to become a successful author.* *–vb.* **2.** desire, want, crave, covet, long for. *Everyone wishes to be healthy, wealthy, and wise.*

wit *n.* **1.** wittiness, witticism, humor, cleverness, fun. *I enjoy her books because they're full of wit.* **2.** intelligence, understanding, cleverness, reason, judgment. *He had sufficient wit to know he couldn't finish the job by himself.* **3.** comedian, comic, humorist, jester, joker. *She was known as the office wit.* **4.** mind, sanity, reason, senses. *He was frightened out of his wits.* **Ant. 1.** dullness, solemnity. **2.** stupidity, foolishness.

witch *n.* sorceress, enchantress, enchanter, magician. *In the "Wizard of Oz," Dorothy dissolved the Wicked Witch of the West.*

withdraw *vb.* **1.** remove, extract, subtract, deduct, retract. *She withdrew her name from consideration.* **2.** retire, retreat, depart, leave, quit. *The defeated army withdrew from the battlefield.* **Ant. 1.** submit, introduce. **2.** arrive, stand, maintain.

wither *vb.* shrivel, dry, wilt, droop, fade, fail. *His plants withered because he forgot to water them.* **Ant.** flourish, thrive, prosper.

withhold *vb.* hold, keep, retain, repress, suppress. *The teacher asked her students to withhold their questions till the end of class.* **Ant.** give, provide, reveal.

withstand *vb.* oppose, resist, defy, endure, confront, brave. *The champion boxer withstood all contenders for his title.* **Ant.** yield, capitulate, surrender to.

witness *n.* **1.** eyewitness, spectator, viewer, observer, onlooker. *Were there any witnesses to the crime?* *–vb.* **2.** see, observe, view, watch, notice. *Did you witness the accident?*

witty *adj.* humorous, funny, amusing, clever, entertaining. *Everyone enjoyed her witty comments.* **Ant.** dull, witless, humorless.

wizard *n.* **1.** mage, magician, sorcerer, conjuror. *A wizard set out to slay the dragon.* **2.** expert, genius, prodigy, master, pro. *She is known for being a computer wizard.* **Ant. 2.** duffer, amateur, imbecile.

wobble *vb.* sway, stagger, totter, shake, quake. *This chair wobbles when you sit in it.*

woe *n.* grief, distress, unhappiness, sorrow, anguish, misery. *He endured poverty, illness, and other woes.* **Ant.** joy, happiness, delight, pleasure.

wonder *n.* **1.** astonishment, surprise, amazement, awe, fascination. *We watched in wonder as she scaled the steep cliff.* **2.** curiosity, spectacle, marvel, sensation. *Can you name the seven wonders of the ancient world?* *–vb.* **3.** speculate, conjecture, question, meditate, query. *She wondered what the world will be like in the next century.* **Ant. 1.** apathy, indifference. **2.** triviality, banality.

wonderful *adj.* amazing, marvelous, fantastic, astonishing, magnificent, excellent. *She is a wonderful dancer.* **Ant.** ordinary, routine, unremarkable.

wood *n.* **1.** lumber, timber, logs, planks, boards. *He needs some more wood to finish the deck he's building.* **2.** forest, grove, trees, timberland, woodland. *Her dog loves to romp through the woods.*

word *n.* **1.** term, expression, name, designation. *What's the word that describes someone who's afraid to go outside?* **2.** chat, conversation, talk, discussion. *I'd like to have a word with you.* **3.** promise, pledge, assurance, vow. *She gave me her word that she would return the money in two weeks.* **4.** message, news, tidings, report, communication. *He received word that his mother was in the hospital.* *–vb.* **5.** term, express, phrase, formulate. *She worded the memo carefully in order to assure that no one misunderstood it.*

wordy *adj.* verbose, rambling, long-winded, windy, redundant. *His books are so wordy that few people enjoy reading them.* **Ant.** concise, succinct, brief.

work *n.* **1.** labor, toil, effort, exertion, trouble. *He didn't want to clear the weeds from his yard because it would take too much work.* **2.** employment, profession, business, occupation. *What line of work do you plan to go into?* **3.** task, chore, assignment, job, project. *The soldier checked the duty roster to see what his work would be for the day.* **4.** creation, achievement, accomplishment, product. *That author has written numerous works.* –vb. **5.** labor, toil, strive, strain, endeavor. *She worked hard to finish college in just three years.* **6.** perform, function, operate, run. *My microwave does not work properly.* **Ant. 1.** effortlessness, rest. **2.** unemployment. **3.** recreation, play, leisure. **5.** rest, play. **6.** stop, fail.

world *n.* **1.** Earth, planet, globe, orb. *Overpopulation is a problem that affects everyone in the world.* **2.** humanity, humankind, the human race, everyone. *The world watched when trouble broke out in the Middle East.* **3.** group, class, system, kingdom, realm. *The blue whale is the largest mammal in the animal world.* **4.** multitude, large amount, mass, pile, lots. *Taking some time off work did her a world of good.*

worry *vb.* **1.** fret, agonize, chafe, grieve, dread. *It's useless to worry about the weather.* **2.** disturb, perturb, upset, distress, annoy. *His son's erratic behavior is beginning to worry him.* –n. **3.** anxiety, concern, apprehension, dread, trouble. *She doesn't have a worry in the world.* **Ant. 2.** soothe, relieve, comfort. **3.** relief, contentment, serenity.

worsen *vb.* deteriorate, degenerate, decline, fail, sink. *He hasn't been taking care of himself, and his health continues to worsen.* **Ant.** improve, better, recover.

worship *vb.* **1.** revere, venerate, exalt, extol, glorify. *Do you worship God?* **2.** adore, idolize, admire, love. *She worships her grandfather.* –n. **3.** adoration, reverence, homage, devotion. *Churches, synagogues, and mosques are all places of worship.* **Ant. 1.** blaspheme, dishonor. **2.** scorn, hate, detest.

worth *n.* **1.** value, usefulness, merit, importance, significance. *Her new invention may prove to be of little worth.* **2.** wealth, riches, assets, estate, holdings. *His personal worth has been estimated at several million dollars.* **Ant. 1.** worthlessness, uselessness.

worthless *adj.* valueless, useless, unimportant, insignificant. *The stocks he bought turned out to be worthless.* **Ant.** worthwhile, worthy, valuable.

worthwhile *adj.* important, useful, beneficial, valuable, helpful. *Instead of wasting your time, you ought to do something worthwhile.* **Ant.** worthless, useless, unimportant.

worthy *adj.* worthwhile, deserving, fitting, excellent, good. *She willed her entire fortune to a worthy cause.* **Ant.** worthless, undeserving, useless.

wound *n.* **1.** injury, hurt, harm, sore, damage. *His old wound still bothers him.* –vb. **2.** injure, hurt, harm, damage, traumatize. *Her pride was wounded by her friend's careless remark.*

wrap *vb.* enclose, cover, envelop, sheathe, enfold. *Have you had a chance to wrap your Christmas presents yet?* **Ant.** unwrap, uncover, open.

wrath *n.* anger, rage, fury, ire, vexation. *I aroused my boss's wrath when I was late three days in a row.* **Ant.** serenity, forbearance, calm.

wreak *vb.* inflict, unleash, commit, exercise, work. *Godzilla wreaked havoc on the city of Tokyo.*

wreck *vb.* **1.** ruin, damage, destroy, shatter, demolish, break. *If you don't drive more carefully, you'll wreck the car.* –n. **2.** ruins, remains, destruction, devastation, mess. *This old jalopy is a total wreck.* **Ant. 1.** save, protect, preserve.

wrench *vb.* **1.** strain, sprain, twist, pull, tear. *The jogger wrenched her ankle when she stumbled on a rock.* **2.** jerk, tug, wring, wrest, pull. *A young hoodlum wrenched the purse out of the woman's hands.*

wrestle *vb.* **1.** grapple, tussle, scuffle, fight. *We're not allowed to wrestle inside the house.* **2.** struggle, strive, labor, strain, toil. *She's been wrestling with her smoking problem for years.*

wretch *n.* villain, scoundrel, knave, rogue, rascal. *The movie's heroine was abducted by a heartless wretch.*

wretched *adj.* **1.** distressed, miserable, forlorn, depressed, unhappy. *She's been feeling wretched ever since she lost her puppy.* **2.** despicable, contemptible, dreadful, horrid, terrible. *He has a wretched sense of humor.* **Ant. 1.** happy, cheerful, gay. **2.** admirable, wonderful.

wring *vb.* force, twist, squeeze, extract, wrench. *She wrung the water out of the washcloth when she was through using it.*

wrinkle *n.* **1.** crease, furrow, ridge, line, groove. *Wrinkles at the corner of the mouth are* sometimes called "smile lines." –vb. **2.** crease, crumple, rumple, groove, furrow. *He wouldn't sit down because he didn't want to wrinkle his new suit.* **Ant. 2.** smooth, straighten, iron.

write *vb.* **1.** inscribe, scribe, record, mark, note. *Please use the answer sheet provided and don't write on the test.* **2.** author, pen, compose, create, produce. *He writes mystery novels.*

writhe *vb.* squirm, twist, wriggle, wiggle, weave. *The snake writhed through the grass.*

wrong *adj.* **1.** incorrect, inaccurate, false, erroneous, untrue. *The game-show contestant missed winning a new car when she gave a wrong answer.* **2.** immoral, sinful, bad, wicked, unethical. *It was wrong of him to lie.* **3.** improper, unsuitable, inappropriate, unfit, unacceptable. *A bathing suit is the wrong thing to wear to a formal dinner party.* **4.** faulty, amiss, awry, out of order. *The mechanic figured out what was wrong with my car.* –adv. **5.** incorrectly, inaccurately, falsely, erroneously. *If you thought I stole the money, you thought wrong.* –n. **6.** sin, evil, wickedness, crime, vice. *Do you know the difference between right and wrong?* –vb. **7.** injure, hurt, harm, mistreat, abuse, victimize. *She felt she had been wronged when I didn't tell her everything.* **Ant. 1.** right, true, correct. **2.** moral, good, ethical. **3.** proper, suitable, appropriate. **4.** all right. **5.** rightly, correctly, accurately. **6.** morality, goodness.

wrongful *adj.* criminal, unlawful, illegal, illicit, dishonest, immoral. *Wrongful conduct is punishable by law.* **Ant.** rightful, legal, proper.

wry *adj.* **1.** twisted, crooked, slanted, contorted, distorted. *Her wry smile means she's not happy with you.* **2.** dry, ironic, sarcastic, cynical, bitter. *She didn't appreciate his wry joke.* **Ant. 1.** straight, direct, normal.

xerox (tradename) *n.* **1.** photocopy, copy, duplicate, reproduction, facsimile. *Though he lost his original manuscript, fortunately he still has his xeroxes.* *–vb.* **2.** reproduce, copy, photocopy, duplicate. *Please xerox this report for me.*

x-ray *n.* **1.** diagnostic picture, medical photograph, radiograph, radiogram. *Medical technicians took x-rays of the suspected fracture.* *–vb.* **2.** photograph. *Hospital personnel x-rayed the broken ankle before the doctor set it.*

yacht *n.* boat, ship, pleasure craft, sloop, ketch. *The millionaire's yacht was her pride and joy.*

yank *vb.* **1.** wrench, jerk, pull, tug, snatch, extract. *The police officer yanked a gun from the suspect's hand.* –*n.* **2.** jerk, pull, tug, wrench, joggle. *That window needs a hearty yank to get it open.* **Ant. 1.** push, shove, replace, return. **2.** push, shove.

yard *n.* grounds, lawn, court, compound, enclosure, confine. *Our school yard has a decent playground.*

yarn *n.* **1.** fiber, thread, flax, wool. *This red yarn will make an attractive sweater.* **2.** story, tale, anecdote, account, narrative, reminiscence. *The old man has many entertaining yarns to tell.*

yawn *vb.* **1.** gape, open, open wide. *A deep crevasse yawned in front of the startled mountaineers.* **2.** doze, drowse, nap, snooze. *Tired students have been known to yawn off during boring lectures.*

yearn *vb.* crave, desire, want, covet, ache, hunger, thirst. *The new immigrant yearned to meet someone from her native country.* **Ant.** dread, fear, abhor, hate, loathe, despise.

yearning *n.* craving, desire, longing, wish, inclination, hunger, thirst. *Though he was a vegetarian, he still experienced an occasional yearning for a pepperoni pizza.*

yell *vb.* **1.** shout, scream, holler, bellow, howl, shriek, cry. *Don't yell at me.* –*n.* **2.** call, shout, cry, holler. *Give a yell if you need anything.*

yellow *adj.* **1.** lemon, canary, mustard, gold, ocher. *The golfer was dressed in a bright yellow jacket.* **2.** cowardly, fearful, afraid, apprehensive, craven. *Conscientious objectors don't refuse to fight because they're yellow but because it's against their beliefs.* **Ant. 2.** brave, bold, daring, courageous, fearless.

yen *vb.* **1.** yearn, crave, desire, long, pine, hunger. *The hapless dieter yenned for a banana split.* –*n.* **2.** craving, desire, longing, appetite, yearning, hunger. *Anyone have a yen for popcorn?* **Ant. 1.** abhor, disdain, scorn. **2.** revulsion, abhorrence, aversion.

yield *vb.* **1.** produce, bear, supply, generate, furnish, return. *This grapefruit tree yields fruit all year long.* **2.** surrender, submit, succumb, relinquish, acquiesce, capitulate. *Sometimes it's difficult not to yield to temptation.* **3.** fail, buckle, collapse, break, give way. *The old bridge yielded under the weight of the heavy truck.* –*n.* **4.** harvest, crop, produce, return, product, output. *The farmer hoped for a bountiful yield.* **5.** interest, earnings, proceeds, gain. *Bankers are always concerned with the yields of their investments.* **Ant. 2.** resist, oppose, thwart, stop. **3.** endure, sustain, withstand.

yoke *n.* **1.** load, strain, weight, burden, oppression, servitude, enslavement. *The yoke of poverty keeps many people from fulfilling their dreams.* **2.** pair, brace, couple, span, team. *The heavy plow was pulled by a yoke of oxen.* **3.** bond, link, attachment, collar, harness, connector. *A computer yoke connects two or more magnetic reading heads.* –*vb.* **4.** join, link, attach, combine, couple, hitch, harness. *The driver yoked his horses to the stagecoach.* **Ant. 1.** freedom, independence, liberty. **4.** separate, unhitch.

yonder *adj.* distant, remote, farther, far-off. *The grass is greener in yonder valley.* **Ant.** close, near, nearby.

young *adj.* **1.** youthful, juvenile, adolescent, underage, immature, undeveloped, inexperienced. *He was too young to understand what was happening.* –*n.* **2.** offspring, descendants, child, baby. *It's best not to approach a mother bear when she's with her young.* **Ant. 1.** old, mature, full-grown, experienced. **2.** parent.

youngster *n.* child, youth, juvenile, minor, adolescent, boy, girl. *The youngsters are in bed.* **Ant.** oldster, adult, grownup.

youth *n.* **1.** child, juvenile, minor, adolescent, boy, girl, youngster. *He was still a youth when he immigrated to this country.* **2.** infancy, beginning, start, onset. *The computer age is still in its youth.* **3.** childhood, adolescence, boyhood, girlhood. *In her youth, she wanted to be an explorer.* **Ant. 1.** adult, grownup, oldster. **2–3.** adulthood, maturity.

youthful *adj.* **1.** young, juvenile, adolescent, boyish, girlish, immature, inexperienced. *He has a youthful appearance.* **2.** fresh, energetic, optimistic, robust, lighthearted, vigorous, dynamic. *She has a youthful outlook on life.* **Ant. 1.** old, mature, grown-up, experienced. **2.** tired, weary.

zany *adj.* **1.** ludicrous, clownish, foolish, absurd, funny, comical, silly. *He has a zany sense of humor.* –*n.* **2.** jester, joker, clown, fool, comic, buffoon. *Every party seems to have its drunken zany.*

zeal *n.* enthusiasm, eagerness, zest, fervor, ardor, passion, devotion. *Her zeal for work might mean she's hoping for a promotion.* **Ant.** indifference, apathy, unconcern, disinterest.

zealot *n.* enthusiast, fanatic, fan, devotee, addict, disciple, follower. *Some religious zealots do not try to understand other people's beliefs.*

zealous *adj.* enthusiastic, ardent, fervent, eager, obsessed, fanatic, devoted. *The businesswoman was a zealous collector of Oriental art.* **Ant.** apathetic, uninterested, unenthusiastic, passionless.

zenith *n.* peak, top, high point, crest, climax, culmination, maximum. *Winning an Olympic medal was the zenith of her athletic career.* **Ant.** low point, bottom, nadir, depths.

zero *adj.* **1.** nonexistent, nothing, insignificant, nil, naught. *His chances of making the team are zero.* –*vb.* **2.** aim, direct, point, level, train. *The basketball player zeroed in on the hoop from a distance of twenty feet.*

zest *n.* gusto, ardor, fervor, passion, zeal, delight, enthusiasm, eagerness, thrill, pleasure. *The salesman's zest for his product is so great that he set a new sales record.* **Ant.** distaste, dislike, aversion, apathy.

zestful *adj.* exciting, thrilling, delightful, stimulating, enjoyable. *Grandmother's baking fills the house with zestful aromas.* **Ant.** boring, dull, unexciting, unenjoyable.

zone *n.* **1.** region, territory, area, sector, district, precinct, province, locality. *The "zone" of television's classic series "The Twilight Zone" refers to a region where one's imagination runs free.* –*vb.* **2.** divide, sector, separate, allocate. *This neighborhood is zoned for residential use only.*

zoo *n.* menagerie, vivarium, animal farm. *Many people do not like to see animals caged in zoos.* **2.** madhouse, insane asylum, crush, press, throng, horde. *The shopping mall is a zoo at Christmastime.*

zoom *vb.* **1.** race, flash, streak, fly, whiz, zip, speed. *She zoomed through the book in no time at all.* **2.** climb, soar, rise, ascend, escalate, advance. *Real-estate values zoomed after the new factory came to town.* **Ant. 2.** plummet, drop, fall, decrease.